Jonathan Wilson is a columnist for the *Guardian* and *World Soccer* and the founder and editor of the *Blizzard*. He co-hosts the football history podcast *It Was What It Was*, and is one of the seven voices of *Libero* podcast. He is the author of fourteen books, including *Inverting the Pyramid: The History of Football Tactics*, *Behind the Curtain: Football in Eastern Europe*, *Angels with Dirty Faces: The Footballing History of Argentina*, *The Barcelona Legacy*, *The Names Heard Long Ago* and *Two Brothers*.

Praise for *The Power and the Glory*:

'An outstanding book by a truly outstanding writer. Jonathan Wilson understands not only the long history of the game, and the characters who gloriously shaped it, but also the essentials of the game itself. Once you've finished reading *The Power and the Glory*, you'll want the next World Cup finals to kick off tomorrow' Duncan Hamilton

'Meticulously researched and well-organised – an informative account of how the World Cup became the global event it is today' Jamie Carragher

'Essential . . . rich in political and cultural content' David Goldblatt, *New Statesman*

'A history of the World Cup that is also a four yearly temperature check on the history of the entire world. Epic in scope, awesomely rich in detail, and compulsively entertaining' Tom Holland

'Jonathan Wilson is a master at telling football's greatest ever stories . . . Breathtaking. Wilson's eye for detail and his elegant writing brings the World Cup to life like no other book on the topic I have ever read' Elis James

'Unfailingly lucid and objective, as well as packed with fascinating characters and anecdotes, Jonathan Wilson's *The Power and the Glory* is the authoritative history we have long needed about football's ultimate tournament' David Kynaston

'For the biggest show in sport, that has almost everything, this was the book the World Cup long needed. The definitive history, told through the elevation of the tournament's compelling storylines, as well as brilliant new details' Miguel Delaney

Also by Jonathan Wilson

Behind The Curtain: Travels in Eastern European Football

Sunderland: A Club Transformed

Inverting the Pyramid: The History of Football Tactics

The Anatomy of England

Brian Clough: Nobody Ever Says Thank You

The Outsider: A History of the Goalkeeper

The Anatomy of Liverpool

Angels With Dirty Faces: The Footballing History of Argentina

The Anatomy of Manchester United

The Barcelona Legacy: Guardiola, Mourinho and the Fight for Football's Soul

The Names Heard Long Ago: How the Golden Age of Hungarian Football Shaped the Modern Game

Streltsov: A Novel

Two Brothers: The Life and Times of Bobby and Jackie Charlton

Jonathan Wilson

THE POWER AND THE GLORY

A New History of the World Cup

abacus
books

ABACUS

First published in Great Britain in 2025 by Abacus
This paperback edition published in 2026 by Abacus

3 5 7 9 10 8 6 4 2

A CIP catalogue record for this book is available from the British Library.

ISBN 978-0-349-14573-0

Typeset in Sabon by M Rules
Printed and bound in India by Manipal Technologies Limited

Papers used by Abacus are from well-managed forests and other responsible sources.

Abacus
An imprint of
Little, Brown Book Group
Carmelite House
50 Victoria Embankment
London EC4Y 0DZ

The authorised representative
in the EEA is
Hachette Ireland
8 Castlecourt Centre
Dublin 15, D15 XTP3, Ireland
(email: info@hbgi.ie)

An Hachette UK Company
www.hachette.co.uk

www.littlebrown.co.uk

For Nicola

CONTENTS

PROLOGUE

The final whistle blows, and Uruguay are the first world champions. Two pale-shirted figures embrace and topple to the mud. A player skips in delight, arms flapping above his head. The stands ripple with flags as cheering fans brandish their hats in the air. Men in suits hasten onto the pitch and hug players. Backs are slapped. The captain, José Nasazzi, is carried on the shoulders of two men, one of them a police officer in uniform jacket and cap. As the squad undertakes a celebratory lap of the pitch, clutching the trophy – a 14-inch-high representation of Nike, the goddess of victory – and a bouquet of flowers, they are joined by boys in shorts.

Soldiers hold aloft their sabres to create a guard of honour; as the players pass through it, the band strikes up 'La Marseillaise'. Perhaps it's a tribute to Jules Rimet, the French Fifa president whose idea the World Cup was, but until a couple of years earlier, it had been the official anthem of the *Colorados*, the party of the president of the republic, Juan Campisteguy. Who are the band celebrating? Football, Fifa, the victors or the politicians who made it happen and whose image was bolstered by it? It's an ambiguity that was there at the start and that has never really gone away.

Within four years, Mussolini had hijacked the tournament to promote his ideal of a muscular, successful Italy. The

Argentinian junta may have inherited the 1978 World Cup, and it may have been a terrible financial burden to them, but they exploited it just as ruthlessly as Mussolini had. Long before the term 'sportswashing' had entered the general consciousness, long before Russia and Qatar had shown that you didn't have to win the tournament to gain a propaganda success, that hosting it was enough, the World Cup was being exploited. Every host has tried to use the tournament as an expression of self-confidence or modernity, or just to prove that they are relevant, a central part of a broader global community.

But it's not just about hosting. Successes allow leaders to strut and pontificate, to make grand speeches about the symbolic ramifications of victory. Football has, at least if claims made in the moment of glory are to be believed, put Uruguay on the map, reintegrated post-war West Germany into the global community and ended racism in France. It's almost entirely nonsense, of course, but that doesn't mean that the assertions are not revealing. And football does matter, does offer insights, often unconscious, into the desires and doubts of a culture, never more so than in the quadrennial snapshot offered by the World Cup. At the very least, it provides collective memories that pervade more broadly and deeply than almost anything else. For the English, does any line from the sixties resonate more than 'They think it's all over ...'? Maradona's Hand of God shapes feelings about Argentina just as much as the Falklands War. There is no image more evocative of the shift from hard-nosed Thatcherism to the more sentimental nineties (however conditioned they remained by neoliberalism) than Gazza's tears. Every country has its equivalents, from Herbert Zimmermann's West German commentary at the end of the 1954 World Cup final to Papa Bouba Diop's dance after scoring for Senegal against France in 2002, from Pelé's volley in 1958 to Saeed al-Owairan's remarkable goal against Belgium in 1994, from

France's sweat-sodden defeat in Seville in 1982 to North Korea's improbable victory in Middlesbrough in 1966.

What Rimet began in 1930 has developed into a vast global spectacle, the final the most watched sporting event in the world. The Champions League may represent the highest level of football, but it is the World Cup that has the attention, that stirs the passions of nations, that confers lasting glory. But as was apparent even from that first iteration, an awkward coming together of thirteen teams in Montevideo, what is popular is powerful and what is powerful will always attract politics and politicians, interests beyond the game.

This is a book about the World Cup, about great players and great goals and great matches, but it is also about football as a tool for self-projection and for influence-peddling, about the role it has played in nation building and about the role it increasingly plays as countries negotiate their positions in a globalised world.

From its inception, the World Cup has been a vehicle for far more than football.

1930

THE DREAMERS

The *Conte Verde*, an ocean liner named after Amadeus VI, count of Savoy, was built in Dalmuir near Glasgow in 1923, and sunk for the final time in 1945, by which time she was in the service of the Japanese navy and known as *Kotobuki Maru*. The twenty years in between had been extremely eventful. She carried the Chinese Olympic team to Berlin in 1936 and a year later ran aground in a typhoon at the eastern end of Hong Kong. She helped 17,000 Jewish refugees flee Nazi persecution for Shanghai and was used in a mass exchange of interned diplomats and other citizens between Japan and the US in 1942. And in 1930, she took the national teams of France, Belgium and Romania, four referees (one of them was the Romania coach Costel Rădulescu), and the Fifa president Jules Rimet across the Atlantic for the inaugural World Cup.

'It was like a holiday camp,' said the France forward Lucien Laurent, who would go on to score the first goal in World Cup history. 'Not until years later did we appreciate our place in history. It was just adventure. We were young men having fun.'[1] His brother Jean was also in the squad. For them, going to Uruguay to play in the World Cup was a tremendous lark, an almost incomprehensible opportunity to break the monotony of everyday life at the Peugeot factory in Sochaux, for whose works team they and their international team-mates André Maschinot and Étienne Mattler played.

The voyage took just over a fortnight. 'There was no talk of tactics or anything like that, no coaching,' said Laurent. 'It was just running about the boat on the deck . . . Down below we would do exercises – stretching, jumping, running up stairs, lifting weights. There was also a swimming pool there, which we all used until the weather got cooler. We would be entertained by a comedy act or a string quartet.' They would train early in the morning so as not to disturb other passengers.[2]

The Romania forward Constantin Stanciu spoke of how the French seemed obsessed by fitness, something that troubled his team-mates enough that they began to join in. Although a lot of players suffered from seasickness, there was, he said, 'excellent camaraderie' on board. He found Rimet 'very charismatic' but knew he was 'disappointed' that so few European teams had travelled. 'He believed the football World Cup could only be a force for the better,' said Stanciu.[3]

That belief might have been challenged had Rimet spent much time with France's captain, the elegant Algeria-born centre-half, Alexandre Villaplane. Amid the innocence and the excitement, there was evil. Villaplane changed clubs regularly, drawn by offers of greater and greater benefits at a time when French football was theoretically amateur, and was later sanctioned after his Antibes side was found to have fixed its championship play-off against Lille in 1932–33, the first season of professionalism in France. Villaplane didn't play for France after the World Cup, as the French federation had realised that, for all his ability, he was an extremely troublesome figure. Even in the twenties he had been an habitué of the demi-monde, blowing his wages in cabarets and casinos and at the racetrack. He was jailed for fixing horse races in 1935, and was in and out of prison for a variety of offences before being convicted of racketeering and blackmail shortly after the Nazi occupation of France in 1940.

It was then that he got his big break, being recruited as a driver for the notorious Henri Lafont, who was put in charge of the French Gestapo after destroying the Belgian resistance.[4] He rose through the ranks and was set to eradicating the *Maquis* in the south. He went about his task with cynical efficiency, promising his victims safety if they paid him off, only to let loose his thugs anyway.[5] He was captured by French forces later that year and executed alongside Lafont on 26 December, a day after his thirty-ninth birthday.[6]

Whatever Rimet thought of the young Villaplane, he seemed to have fun on board, attending humorous talk-ins with the Belgian referee John Langenus and his quieter colleague Henri Christophe,[7] and winning a dancing competition after making a cardboard hat for his partner with a blue star on a red background so it resembled the funnel of the ship.

When he got to Uruguay, he was invited to an *asado* with President Campisteguy; the political role of the tournament was apparent right from the start. The World Cup has always been a vessel for far more than football.

Fifa was an organisation rooted in expediency. Perhaps there was some idealism when it was founded by football federations from Belgium, Denmark, France, the Netherlands, Spain, Sweden and Switzerland in 1904 but there was a reason its formation was driven through by the Frenchman Robert Guérin. He was a representative of the *Union des sociétés françaises de sports athlétiques*, one of the three bodies that sought to organise football in France at the time. Being France's representative at Fifa gave them legitimacy; the first of Fifa's articles of association is that members should mutually recognise each other 'as being the only associations governing the sport of Association Football in their countries'.[8]

By 1920, Fifa was organising the football tournament at the Olympics. By then, in the aftermath of the First World War, sport's role in the world had begun to be questioned.[9] It had taken on a nationalistic aspect, perhaps inevitably so given the overt sense, in the English public schools, German *Turnen* clubs and beyond, that it was a useful preparation for war, or at least the rigours of overseas service.[10]

From 1921, though, Fifa had a president who was determined to challenge that: Jules Rimet. Born in 1873, Rimet was a devout Catholic and had been profoundly influenced by Pope Leo XIII's 1891 encyclical on capital and labour, *De rerum novarum*,[11] which sought to address and alleviate 'the misery and wretchedness pressing so unjustly on the majority of the working class'.[12] Rimet saw sport as a key weapon in that battle and in 1897 founded Red Star in Paris. At his new club, unusually, class distinctions were ignored and political discussion banned. He organised poetry readings to help educate and develop the players and argued against amateurism as a barrier to working-class involvement in football, calling it 'the antisocial pretension of a privileged oligarchy'.[13]

He 'believed that sport could unite the world'[14] and saw Fifa as a sort of footballing League of Nations. The British associations remained predictably sceptical: England having the same voting rights as Uruguay or Paraguay, Brazil or Egypt, Bolivia or Pan-Russia, the league official Charles Sutcliffe told an FA meeting in 1919 after a squabble at Fifa over the post-war readmission of Germany, was 'a case of magnifying the midget'.[15]

Nor, in truth, at the 1920 Olympics, did the football suggest an activity the power of which could be harnessed to avert conflict. Czechoslovakia walked off during the final against Belgium in protest at the 39th-minute dismissal of

Karel Steiner, resulting in their ejection from the competition and leading to a complicated play-off for the silver and bronze medals. But football was, nonetheless, the biggest draw of any sport at the Games.

By 1924, when non-European sides competed for the first time at the Olympics, football made even more headlines, thanks largely to the excellence of Uruguay. The myth, propagated by Eduardo Galeano – who, whatever his qualities as a writer and political theorist, was never over-troubled by facts – is that the team that travelled to France comprised meat-packers, ice salesmen, marble-cutters and grocers, but it is not true. They may not have been openly professional – the Uruguayan league was officially amateur until 1932 – but neither were they working full-time in other trades. One of the reasons Argentina didn't send a side was a concern over whether their players would be considered amateur, and it's not clear Uruguay's would have passed the test but for the intervention of Rimet after an appeal from their football federation.[16] When the Fifa vice-president Gabriel Bonnet praised Switzerland, the side Uruguay beat in the final, as 'true amateurs', the implication was obvious.[17]

Whatever the qualms about their status, though, Uruguay were brilliant.

Uruguay had been established as a buffer state between Argentina and Brazil with the help of Britain, formally declaring independence in 1830. The remainder of the nineteenth century was bloody as those of European descent first massacred the indigenous peoples and then fell to a series of civil wars between the *Blancos*, the conservatives championing the rights of landowners, and the *Colorados*, the liberals based largely in Montevideo. Although the *Colorados* won every election held between 1865 and 1958, it took a long time for that to equate to stability. By 1900, Uruguay had suffered around fifty coups and uprisings.[18]

Football had been introduced by the British, with the first official match in Uruguay taking place in June 1881 as Montevideo Cricket Club took on Montevideo Rowing in a match refereed by the British consul-general, Edmund Monson. Central to the spread of the game was William Leslie Poole, a Kent-born Anglo-Scot, who arrived in Montevideo in 1885 at the age of eighteen and became a schoolteacher at the English High School, which served the sons of both British residents and the local elites. Regarding football as essential for instilling physical resilience, teamwork and the capacity to handle victory and defeat with equanimity, he would take his pupils by horse-drawn tram to the fields of Punta Carretas, where the Rio de la Plata meets the Atlantic, to learn and play the game.[19]

Poole became a leading player for Albion, the first football-specific club established in Uruguay, and later served as president of both the Uruguayan Football Association (AUF) and the league. He is widely recognised as the father of the Uruguayan game, carrying the spirit of Muscular Christianity he had experienced at school and at Cambridge University[20] and finding it married easily with the Comtean positivism* that shaped education in Montevideo.[21] Sport took on an even more central role after the expulsion of Spain from Cuba in 1898, which led to widespread fears that Latins would yield inevitably before an Anglo-Saxon takeover. 'Our education,' said Pablo De María, the rector of the

---

* Comtean positivism, with its emphasis on learning as a social good and insistence on rationality as a basis for decision-making, underpinned most educational theory in South America in the late nineteenth century. It underlies the '*Ordem e Progresso*' motto on Brazil's flag, and was explicitly regarded by Domingo Faustino Sarmiento, the second president of the Argentinian republic, as a means of tackling 'frontier backwardness'. Uruguay was no less enthusiastic.

University of the Republic, 'is not virile like that of the people of northern Europe and north America.'[22]

Football took on a curious role: diversion, stiffener of sinews and symbol of fraternity, something that could be appreciated by both sides as civil war continued to simmer. On Easter Sunday 1897, for instance, the day after the battle of Cerro Colorado, a record crowd of 1,500 turned out to watch Albion, one of the leading clubs, take on a combined British Navy XI.[23] Punta Carretas, the newspaper *El Dia* proclaimed, became a 'true public space, a meeting place of society', football an ecumenical sphere in which men and women, black and white, rich and poor, young and old, British and *criollo*, *Blanco* and *Colorado* could mix[24] – off the pitch at least; on it, players were universally male and white.

The death of the *blanco* leader Aparicio Saravia in 1904 brought an end to a further episode of civil war, and José Batlle y Ordóñez's second term as president finally brought peace and stability. There was investment in sanitation works and the electrification of the tram network, an overhaul of labour rights, the introduction of universal suffrage and, as exports of beef boomed, high-school education was made free to all while sport was promoted through the National Commission of Physical Education.[25] Under Batlle's government, there were also the beginnings – slow and extremely tentative – of a recognition of Uruguay's black population,[26] leading to the eventual selection of the half-back Juan Delgado and the forward Isabelino Gradín for the national side. Both were key members of the squad that won the inaugural Campeonato Sudamericano* in 1916.

But the politics of football remained complex, with the two most popular clubs, Peñarol and Nacional, constantly

* The forerunner of the Copa América.

in dispute. In 1922, Peñarol were expelled from the AUF for playing a friendly against the Argentinian club Racing, who had disaffiliated from the Argentinian Football Association. Peñarol then established their own federation (FUF), so that in 1923 two rival Uruguayan championships were staged. The AUF's decision to affiliate to Fifa that year was largely conditioned by a desire to resolve the schism by making themselves the officially sanctioned authority. The foreign minister Pedro Manini Rios, one of the founders of Nacional and a leader of the AUF, wired the minister plenipotentiary of Uruguay in Switzerland, Enrique Buero, and asked him to attend the Fifa Congress in Geneva to secure Uruguay's accession. While there, Buero took the unilateral decision that Uruguay should enter the following year's Olympics.[27]

There were two major issues. First, given the schism, it was unclear which players would be available for the tournament. And second, nobody knew how the AUF was going to afford it. But what was significant was the involvement of Manini Rios, which suggested Uruguay's participation in the Olympics was sanctioned, perhaps even encouraged, at the highest political level.

No players from either Peñarol or Central, both members of the rebel FUF, were selected, while Uruguay's passage across the Atlantic was paid for in part by Atilio Narancio, the president of the AUF, who put his house up as collateral for a loan. Although the later perception was of great camaraderie, the players left to general disinterest. There were no great crowds to wave them off, food on board was poor and there was limited space to train.

To generate revenue, Uruguay played nine friendlies in Spain, winning them all, playing a style of football that combined individual flair with organisation and structure. A report in the Spanish newspaper *El Eco* described them as 'full of method ... a true collective ... rarely lifting the ball from the ground. Fast ... very open, great movement. But the truly captivating aspect ... is the quality of the pass.'[28]

In Paris, Uruguay stayed near the Stade De Colombes in Argenteuil, a north-western suburb, in a villa that had been used as an occasional headquarters by the German General Staff following the occupation of Paris in the Franco-Prussian War. They continued the form they had shown in Spain, hammering the Kingdom of Serbs, Croats and Slovenes,* the USA and France by a combined score of 15–1. After a 5–1 victory over the hosts in the quarter final, *Le Figaro* was moved to write of Uruguay's 'precision, speed and good combinations ... supported by the marvellous defence of [Pedro] Arispe and [José] Nasazzi'.[29] The essayist and novelist Henry de Montherlant compared Uruguay's play to the writing of the seventeenth-century fabulist Jean de la Fontaine: 'great art,' he said, 'is always simple.'[30] An indication of their style is given by the Catalonian writer Enrique Guardiola Cardellach, who described a move in that game of 'seventeen or eighteen short passes in a row without the ball having been stopped for a single moment' that involved every outfield player and ended with Héctor Scarone hitting both posts.[31]

Uruguayan football has always prided itself on its '*garra*' – literally 'claw', although the term encompasses toughness, resilience and streetwiseness and has often been used to justify the worst excesses of the Uruguayan game – but, as the poet and essayist Aldo Mazzucchelli argues, there is little to suggest the team of the 1920s was unusually reliant on the characteristic, appealing as the concept of *garra* may be to explain how such a small country could lead the world.[32]

The Dutch were beaten 2–1 in the semi-final, despite a remarkable performance from their goalkeeper Gejus van der

* It would not be renamed Yugoslavia until 1929.

Meulen* who kept a toy rabbit in his net and made so many saves that Scarone began to believe it held magical powers.[33] By then, Uruguay were big news.[34] As journalists flocked to Argenteuil to uncover the secrets of the Uruguayans, the players amused themselves by pretending their dribbling ability came from chasing chickens at a young age, a claim that was dutifully repeated by a surprising number of newspapers.[35]

The captain and full-back José Nasazzi, who played always in a homemade knitted white hat, and the inside-forward Héctor Scarone were players of great ability, while the centre-forward Pedro Patrone, with his immaculately brilliantined hair, was rapid and a fine finisher, but the Uruguayan who attracted most attention was the midfielder José Leandro Andrade, commonly described at the time as football's first global superstar.[36] Beyond his obvious ability as a free-ranging centre-half, and the fact he was one of four players to play in both Uruguay's Olympic triumphs and the World Cup success, Andrade now seems more myth than man, his life a collection of implausible stories. He was also black.

Andrade was born in Salto in 1901 to an Argentinian mother. His father's identity is unknown, although it was said to be José Ignacio Andrade, supposedly a ninety-eight-year-old African-born expert in magic who had escaped slavery in Brazil and whose name appeared on the centre-half's birth certificate as a witness.[37] At an early age, Andrade moved to Montevideo to live with an aunt. He earned money shining shoes and selling newspapers on street corners but also found work as a musician and was gifted enough to lead the drum corps for a carnival *comparso*.[38]

---

* Van der Meulen was a qualified paediatrician and when his playing career came to an end, he opened a clinic in Haarlem. After joining the National Socialist Movement in the Netherlands, he became an outspoken supporter of Hitler's compulsory sterilisation laws. He joined the SS after the German invasion, served on the eastern front and was subsequently jailed by the Dutch for collaboration.

Football, though, was his great skill. He was quick and athletic, at least early in his career, but dominated games more through his understanding of space and angles than by physically imposing himself. He was reputed to be an extremely clean tackler and to have developed a technique called *la tijera* (the scissors) in which he would go to ground with left leg extended and play the ball with his right. But it wasn't just his talent that made him stand out in Paris. Before 1924, there had never been a black footballer at the Olympics and, to French fans and European journalists, that gave him an air of the exotic. Add his charisma and good looks, and the result was a potent celebrity.

The writer Colette, later best known for her novella *Gigi* but at the time notorious for an on-stage lesbian kiss at the Moulin Rouge, was sent by *Le Matin* to report on a party at Uruguay's villa in Argenteuil to celebrate the second-round win over the USA.* To the backing of an Argentinian orchestra, in Paris to perform at a musical, Andrade and his team-mate Alfredo Zibechi dressed in elaborate costumes and demonstrated a range of dances. 'Uruguayans,' Colette wrote, 'are a strange combination of civilisation and barbarism.† Dancing the tango they are wonderful, sublime, better than the best gigolo. But they also dance African cannibal dances that make you shiver.'[39]

It's striking how much of the coverage focused on Andrade's race. When a photograph of him appeared on the cover of

* The editor who commissioned her, Henry de Jouvenel, was her former husband, their marriage having ended in part because she seduced his sixteen-year-old son, her stepson, arguing that it was time he became a man.

† This is surely a reference to the use of the phrase by the Unitarian Party during the Argentinian Civil War (1814–53) setting 'civilisation' – liberal European ideals – against 'barbarism' – their rejection. It was classically expressed by Sarmiento, in his 1845 work *Facundo: Civilización y Barbarie* or, perhaps more relevantly for a French audience, by Alexandre Dumas (*père*) in his 1850 novel *Montevideo, ou une nouvelle Troie* which references Sarmiento while dealing explicitly with the Uruguayan Civil War.

*L'Auto** in June 1924, for instance, the accompanying text described him as 'the marvellous and black half-back'.[40] It's clear as well the extent to which descriptions of Andrade were shaped by primitive modernism,[41] the popularity of which, expressed through the work of painters from Picasso to Chagall, the writing of Apollinaire and the music of Stravinsky, was at its height in Paris at the time.[42] Nothing better embodied the belief that 'black' or 'African' culture was simultaneously primitive and modern than jazz and so there was a certain inevitability about the meeting of Andrade with a singer who had also attracted the nickname 'the Black Pearl', Josephine Baker. Two years later, she would draw global fame for her *danse sauvage*, performed in nothing more than a skirt comprising sixteen bananas and some strategically arranged necklaces. That Andrade and Baker danced a tango together is well-attested; whether their relationship went further is unclear.

There certainly were liaisons with wealthy and fashionable French women, even if the suspicion must be that many stories were exaggerated and embellished. Andrade often left the villa at night and, when concerned officials sent his team-mate Angelo Romano to track him down one evening, he found Andrade 'in a luxury apartment in one of the most exclusive areas of the city, surrounded by beautiful women, like a sultan in his harem'.[43] By the time Andrade returned to Montevideo, he was dressing as a dandy, wearing leather boots, yellow gloves, a silk cravat and a top hat.

Andrade continued to enjoy the high life and regularly missed training sessions with Nacional. On a tour of Europe in 1925 he fell ill and, visiting a doctor in Brussels, was diagnosed with syphilis. He fled to Paris to recuperate and by the time he returned to Montevideo had lost weight and much of his sparkle. At first he decided he didn't want to travel to

* The newspaper which invented the Tour de France.

Amsterdam for the 1928 Olympics, but had a change of heart when he saw his team-mates boarding their steamer to cross the Atlantic. Again he played a key role, despite an incident in the semi-final in which he ran into a goal-post. Some say it was as a consequence of that that he later lost the sight in one eye; others that it was the syphilis.

The 1930 World Cup final was the last game Andrade played for his country. After it, he left Nacional for their great rivals Peñarol. As his playing career came to an end, he struggled. He was unreliable, drank too much. He couldn't hold down a job and slipped into poverty. He was a guest of honour at the 1950 World Cup, where his nephew Victor Rodríguez Andrade – who insisted on using the maternal as well as the paternal surname as a mark of respect for his uncle – had a vital role in Uruguay's victory. Six years later, the German journalist Fritz Hack tracked Andrade down in Montevideo. He was living in desperate conditions, unable to follow Hack's questions. A few months later, penniless and alcoholic, he moved into an asylum. He died soon after, at the age of fifty-six. Even the basic arc of his story, from poverty to glory and back to poverty again feels mythic. Paris was the zenith of his career.

Demand to watch the final in Paris was vast. Officially, just over 40,000 were admitted, although the true figure may have been higher, while around 10,000 were locked out. Those who did get in saw Uruguay cruise to a 3–0 win over Switzerland. While many in Europe revelled in the accomplishment of the champions, of the possibilities that they had demonstrated for the game – the great journalist Gabriel Hanot, a former France international, famously dismissed suggestions that Britain might still be the world leader by saying 'it is like comparing Arab thoroughbreds to farm horses'[44] – what mattered to Uruguayans was that Uruguay was being talked about at all. 'You are now the motherland, boys ...' wrote Lorenzo Batlle Berres in *El Día*, 'the symbol of that little dot, nearly invisible on the map ... which has been getting larger, larger, larger.'[45]

But this was more than simply a newspaper celebrating its country's victory. *El Día* was the newspaper of the *Colorados*. Moreover, Batlle Berres was the nephew of the former president José Batlle y Ordóñez. The sense was that Uruguay's victory was a victory for *battlismo* and the values of modernity, liberalism, rationality and Uruguayan exceptionalism it represented. 'In South American diplomatic circles,' *El Día* reported, 'it is said that the performance of the Uruguay team ... has done more for the fame of Uruguay than thousands of dollars spent on propaganda.'[46]

When the Uruguay squad returned home, a national holiday was declared for state workers and half-price train tickets to the capital arranged so the whole country could join the party. For days the streets of Montevideo heaved in celebration. The post office, emphasising that this was a victory for the national project, produced a stamp to salute the Olympic champions. The illustrated magazine *Mundo Uruguayo*, meanwhile, claimed that Uruguay would no longer be ignored or confused with its larger neighbours; the football team had proved it was a 'civilised nation' that could export culture as well as meat.[47]

There was a sense that Uruguay had not merely overcome the anxiety of European influence but reversed it, returning the European game to the metropole in more sophisticated form. If there was not quite the same Oedipal frisson as would be suffered by, say, Spanish literature in the face of Latin American modernism,[48] it was only because the game's true parents in Britain had absented themselves from the Olympics and the possibility of defeat. It would eventually arrive in the form of the rivalry between England and Argentina.

*

The praise for Uruguay was deeply annoying for Argentina. If only they had sent a team to Paris, ran their logic, surely they'd have beaten their little neighbour – even though at that point Argentina had won one Campeonato Sudamericano to Uruguay's four and had beaten them in only five of their previous twenty-four meetings. A home-and-away tie was arranged to determine, in the Argentinian mind at least, who the real champions were.

The game in Montevideo ended 1–1; the second leg, in Buenos Aires, was chaos. Overcrowding at the Estadio Sportivo Barracas led to a postponement of four days. For the rearranged game, fences had been erected at the front of the stands but the outcome was still disorder. Argentina went 2–1 up – their first goal having been scored direct from a corner by Cesáreo Onzari, the origin of the term '*gol olímpico*'* – but as the game became increasingly violent, their defender Adolfo Celli suffered a broken leg. Fans responded by hurling stones at the Uruguayans, particularly targeting Andrade. Uruguay's players returned fire and, as police intervened, Scarone was arrested for kicking an officer. Uruguay walked off, and Argentina declared themselves the victors. Hostilities continued the following day on the dockside as Uruguay set off for home with their players and an angry crowd hurling coal at each other. It had all been deeply unsavoury.

In 1928, Argentina had the chance to win an Olympic medal for real as they sent a team to Amsterdam. They surged to the final, beating USA 11–2, Belgium 6–3 and Egypt 6–0, with Domingo Tarasconi scoring at least a hat-trick in each game.

* The term perhaps suggests the significance Argentinians attached to the game: the original 'Olympic goal' was not a goal scored at the Olympics but against the Olympic champions in what Argentina were pretending was a *de facto* Olympic decider. In fact, had the goal been scored at the 1924 Olympics, it would not have counted.

This time, with Peñarol players reintegrated, Uruguay had been seen off from the docks in Montevideo by adoring crowds, and were greeted in Le Havre and then Amsterdam by fans who were almost as enthusiastic. Enrique Buero, who had moved from Bern to become ambassador for Belgium and the Netherlands and who was, by this point, fully on board with the idea that football was part of his remit, booked an old country house for the squad about forty-five minutes outside Amsterdam. This, though, was not Paris. Uruguay were not a curiosity to be marvelled over; they were the best football team in the world and were there to be beaten.

Prince Consort Henry of Mecklenburg-Schwerin, the husband of Queen Wilhelmina, made the draw and, after pairing the hosts with Uruguay, immediately apologised and asked, presumably jokingly, if he could have another go. Van der Meulen and his rabbit proved stubborn again, but Uruguay won 2–0. The quarter-final against Germany was an ugly, violent game in which Nasazzi and two Germans were sent off as Uruguay won 4–1. Italy, having beaten France and Spain, could reasonably claim to be the best side in Europe, and took the lead in the semi-final, but Uruguay fought back to win 3–2. In the absence of Great Britain, which had refused to send a team after 1920 because of a dispute over definitions of amateurism, and with the mass exodus of players and coaches from Hungary prompted by the various political and economic crises,[49] few doubted that *rioplatense* football was the peak of the world game and a meeting of Uruguay and Argentina in the final a true clash of the best sides in the competition.

Throughout the tournament, huge crowds had gathered outside newspaper offices in Montevideo and Buenos Aires to listen to updates of games. Correspondents at the stadium would send fifteen-word telegrams back to their offices – *La Nación* claimed the fastest arrived in just 52 seconds[50] – which would then be relayed to those waiting outside via loudspeaker.

Interest was hardly less keen in Europe. There were around 250,000 requests for tickets to watch the final, at a stadium that held an eighth of that. Football, indisputably, had become a mass phenomenon across the globe.

'Argentina,' wrote the Italian journalist Gianni Brera, 'play football with a lot of fantasy and elegance but the technical superiority cannot compensate for the abandonment of tactics.'[51] This, it should be said, is a characterisation rejected by Aldo Mazzucchelli, who argues there is an element of back projection from later in the century, by which time Uruguay had become a team that relied far more on stubbornness and organisation.[52] In *100 años de fútbol*, a collection of magazines published in the build-up to the 1970 World Cup, the Uruguayan writer Julio Bayce suggests Uruguay were a largely counter-attacking team,[53] but Mazzucchelli rejects that as well, suggesting he had been influenced by the radio commentaries of Esteban Elena, who would essentially invent action to fill the gaps left between cables he was receiving from the ground. The truth is that where video evidence is lacking, it is very hard to tell, particularly given the slipperiness of terminology, especially when shifting between languages, and the variability of expectation. All that can be said is that the footage that does exist from the 1930 World Cup makes Uruguay look a very technically accomplished short-passing team.[54]

After an injury to Héctor Castro, who had lost his right hand in a buzzsaw accident when he was thirteen, Uruguay played much of the game with only ten men. They drew 1–1, then took the lead in the replay, a goal that was greeted in Montevideo by the sounding of sirens. It was a wet day – photos show the majority of the crowds outside the newspaper offices clutching umbrellas – but they stayed on as Argentina equalised before Scarone got the winner with 17 minutes remaining.

He was probably the greatest player of that generation, short and quick, noted for his choppy stride and the spring that made him surprisingly good in the air for somebody who measured just 5ft 6in. He was regarded as high-maintenance, but it's a measure of his importance to Uruguay that Scarone started every international for which he was fit between 1917 and 1930.

For Uruguay, those Olympic successes are as good as World Cups – which is why they wear four stars on their shirts; two for their World Cup wins, but two also for the Olympic golds. 'They were in fact real world championships,' Rimet agreed.[55] The quality and variety of teams in Paris in 1924 and in Amsterdam in 1928 was little different to the intra-war World Cups, and that Uruguay won them in Europe arguably makes them a greater achievement than the World Cup they would win at home in 1930.

Fifa had been aware for a while that it needed its own tournament. English football had been professional since 1885 and, by the mid-1920s, Austria, Hungary, Italy and the USA were paying players, making them ineligible for the Olympics. Uruguay and Argentina weren't the only countries that operated in a grey zone somewhere between amateurism and full professionalism. It was clear that, as the Fifa secretary Henri Delaunay put it, 'football no longer fits entirely within the framework of the Olympic status and that many countries could no longer have their best footballers represented at the Games tournament'.[56] The Olympics anyway struggled to accommodate football, staging the competition in 1928 between 27 May and 13 June, when the main part of the Games did not begin until 28 July – an issue caused by the difficulties of juggling various league seasons and a shortage of accommodation.[57] In May 1928, at the seventeenth Fifa Congress, in Amsterdam, it was agreed that a tournament should be staged in 1930.

Senior Uruguayan political figures soon decided that they should bid to host it; it was, after all, a pleasing coincidence that 1930 would mark the centenary of Uruguay's independence. Fifa had hoped that Germany might volunteer as host, but it had taken a firm stand against professionalism. Hungary, Italy, the Netherlands, Spain and Sweden had all expressed an interest, which led at the 1929 Congress in Barcelona to the sort of self-interested politicking for which Fifa would later become notorious.[58] Buero was an excellent negotiator[59] but although he secured the votes of the central European bloc, led by Italy, he suspected they thought Uruguay a useful backwater for Fifa's tournament while they pursued their own tournaments for national and club sides, the Central European International Cup* and the Mitropa Cup. In truth, Italy might have travelled but for an unfortunately timed power vacuum at the Italian Olympic committee after its leader, Augusto Turati, was forced to resign following revelations he frequented a sadomasochistic brothel.[60]

Uruguay, having promised to subsidise travel for all competing sides, won the vote, but that was only half the battle. There was much bitterness in the country about the reluctance of European sides to travel, and dark talk of boycotts, but most European federations, like Argentina in 1924, lacked the resources or organisational will to undertake a lengthy voyage. Getting European sides to commit remained difficult, even after it was agreed that the first round would be played on a group system so nobody would have to make the trip for a single fixture. Rimet could guarantee France would travel, although their coach Gaston Barreau and their leading centre-forward Manuel Anatol stayed at home. The Belgian

* A round-robin tournament, occasionally known after the men who at various points provided the trophy: Antonín Švehla, the prime minister of Czechoslovakia, and then, after the Second World War, Dr Josef Gerö, a director of the ÖFB.

Fifa vice-president Rudolf Seeldrayers, and a media campaign orchestrated by Buero, persuaded his national team to go, although they were weakened because their great star, the forward Raymond Braine, had opened a café in breach of their football federation's definition of amateurism – and football in Belgium was still an amateur sport. Romania sent a team only because the newly crowned King Carol II insisted upon it, selecting the squad himself and guaranteeing the players three months' paid leave. Only Yugoslavia seem to have travelled with anything approaching enthusiasm.

The two Asian invitees, Japan and Siam, both withdrew – Japan would have been represented by the Imperial University's team – while Egypt, Africa's sole representatives, who had achieved notable results at the Olympics, beating Hungary in 1924 and reaching the semi-final in 1928, were held up by a storm in the Mediterranean and so missed their connection in Marseille; they should have travelled with Yugoslavia on the pleasure steamer *Florida*. As a result, the first World Cup went ahead with thirteen participants.

In 1930, before the full impact of the Wall Street Crash had been felt, Montevideo was a thriving, culturally vibrant city. Le Corbusier had visited in 1927 and approved of the modernist capital. The poster for the tournament was produced by the painter Guillermo Laborde, one of the founders of planism, the characteristic austere geometric lines of which are evident in the image of a goalkeeper stretching to save a shot heading for the top corner.

Juan Antonio Scasso, an architect, director of public works in Montevideo and later a president of Peñarol, was appointed to design a stadium that would not merely be the centrepiece of the World Cup but would also celebrate the centenary of Uruguay's independence. He produced the world's first stadium in reinforced concrete, the four double-tiered stands supposedly opening like a flower to represent the blooming of Uruguay. What made it instantly identifiable, though, was a tower, its nine storeys reflecting the nine stripes of the Uruguayan flag, thrusting up from the main stand to a height of more than 100m above the sunken pitch.

There were only two problems. The 1929 Crash had squeezed the budget, so the proposed capacity of 90,000 was reduced to 69,000, while heavy rain delayed construction – establishing what was to become a very familiar World Cup theme as local organisers raced to complete infrastructure – meaning, after early-morning snow, that the inaugural World Cup fixtures were played simultaneously at the 20,000-capacity Estadio Parque Central and the 10,000-capacity Estadio Pocitos.

It was the smaller stadium that had the honour of seeing the first World Cup goal in the game between France and Mexico as the goalkeeper Alex Thépot, of Rimet's Red Star, played the ball long for Augustin Chantrel; he helped it on to Ernest Libérati, who cut it back for Laurent to score – on Bastille Day – with a controlled volley after 19 minutes. Chantrel, a right-half, had to play the final hour in goal after a head injury to Thépot but France still won 4–1. *El Día* was not impressed, saying the game 'completely disappointed the public'.[61]

At the Parque Central, the USA beat Belgium 3–0. *El Diario* dismissed the counter-attacking US style as 'monotonous and sometimes childish'.[62] There was a clear sense among Uruguayan observers of what football should look like, and what they had seen on the opening day of the World Cup was not it.

An eccentric schedule forced France into action against Argentina forty-eight hours after their opener. Despite being effectively reduced to nine men by injuries they held out until the 81st minute when the Argentina captain Luis Monti drilled in a free-kick. But France's Marcel Langiller was reputedly clean through when the Brazilian referee Almeida Rêgo blew for full-time – with six minutes still to play. As gleeful Argentinian fans invaded the pitch, the French players protested and the game was, eventually, restarted. Argentina held out to the disgust of Uruguayans in the crowd, whose reaction was so hostile that Argentina threatened to withdraw from the tournament before being placated by a personal guarantee of safety from Campisteguy.

There was an element of farce about much of that first World Cup. Fifa may have turned its back on amateurism, but football remained endearingly amateurish. Penalty spots were marked in the wrong place, police encroached on the pitch, much refereeing was suspect and the identity of certain goalscorers remains unclear. Argentina's captain and centre-forward Nolo Ferreira, meanwhile, returned to Buenos Aires to take his law exams after that first game, and was replaced for the second match, against Mexico, by the 5ft 6in centre-forward Guillermo Stábile, who scored five times in the group games against Mexico and Chile.

Yugoslavia took control of their group by beating a shambolic Brazil who seemed to relish neither the cold wind nor the mudbath the Parque Central had become as overnight snow melted. It was Brazil's first full international for five years and an internal power struggle meant only players based in Rio de Janeiro took part, the Santos forward Araken Patusca getting round the Paulista boycott by registering before the tournament for the Rio side Flamengo, for whom he never played a game. A 4–0 win over Bolivia followed and ensured Yugoslavia's place in the last four.

The first player to be sent off in World Cup history was Plácido Galindo of Peru, dismissed by Alberto Warnken of Chile after breaking the leg of Romania's Adalbert Steiner. Only 300 were there to see it, though, still the lowest ever World Cup crowd. There were rather more in attendance for

Peru's second game, as they faced Uruguay in the hosts' opener, delayed until 18 July so they could begin their World Cup campaign 100 years to the day after the signing of the Uruguayan constitution. Around 57,000 were admitted to the Centenario, capacity having been cut because of safety concerns at the not quite completed stadium.

For eight weeks before the tournament, Uruguay had been sequestered in the Prado hotel in a park in Montevideo to prepare. The players seem to have found seclusion stifling and the goalkeeper Andrés Mazzali, who had married earlier in the year, was caught, shoes in hand, trying to sneak back into his room having broken curfew to meet his mistress. He had won two Olympic gold medals but was kicked out of the squad, his place in the team taken by Enrique Ballestrero. Nacional players threatened to withdraw from the squad in solidarity before Mazzali himself persuaded them to stay on.

They beat Peru only 1–0, Castro's shot half-saved and dribbling apologetically over the line. Had the soft pitch affected them? Had they been overwhelmed by the occasion? Or had their coach Alberto Suppici overdone it with his fitness drills?

Romania had beaten Peru 3–1 but as Uruguay clicked in the final group game, shifted to 21 July to coincide with a general strike, a 4–0 defeat meant they missed out on the semi-final. On the boat home, the midfielder Alfred Eisenbeisser (also known as Fredi Fieraru) fell in love with a seventeen-year-old Brazilian girl who was heading to Paris with her tutor. 'She finished me,' he wrote in a journal belonging to his captain Rudy Wetzer. 'She is more beautiful than Pola Negri.'* Determined no one else should dance with her, he forced himself to keep going despite sweating profusely and experiencing stabbing pains in his back.[63]

* A Polish actress and singer, a lover of Charlie Chaplin and Rudolph Valentino.

Eisenbeisser was examined by a doctor who diagnosed double pneumonia. He had a fever, was coughing up blood and lost weight rapidly. A priest, called to administer the last rites, asked him to confess his sins. 'Something,' he said, 'told me that if I could make fun of the gravedigger in front of me, everything would be all right . . . "Father, it's true, I made a big mistake against Peru when I thought the ball would go out of play. [José María] Lavalle crossed the ball and that cross led to a goal . . ."'[64]

When the ship docked in Genoa, Eisenbeisser remained behind in a sanatorium, whereupon reports began to circulate that he had died. His grief-stricken mother arranged a funeral and was at the wake when, the story goes, Eisenbeisser strolled in, having made the journey by land. Not only was he not dead, he recovered sufficiently to win three league titles with Venus Bucharest and to come thirteenth in the pairs figure-skating at the 1936 Winter Olympics in Garmisch-Partenkirchen.

Argentina thrashed the USA 6–1 in the first semi-final, a game that was perhaps not quite so one-sided as the scoreline might suggest. Ralph Tracey missed a couple of chances for the US before Monti put Argentina ahead but was forced off at half-time with a wrenched knee. The goalkeeper Jim Douglas then hurt his leg in the second half and matters were further complicated as the midfielder Andy Auld was apparently temporarily blinded when their physio Jack Coll dropped a bottle of chloroform while giving him treatment for a split lip.[65]

Uruguay ended up winning their semi-final against Yugoslavia comfortably enough, but it was not without controversy. It too finished 6–1 but Yugoslavia felt a clear sense of grievance.

That meant the final everybody had expected and perhaps hoped for, a rematch of Amsterdam 1928, the 111th *rioplatense* derby, the biggest football match that had ever been played. There was a huge demand for tickets on both sides of the estuary. An estimated 15,000 Argentinians poured onto steamers and the transatlantic liners that docked in Montevideo on their way to Europe. Thousands more saw them off at the port, chanting '*Argentinos, sí! Uruguayos, no!*' Fog, though, meant that very few from Argentina made it across the River Plate in time for the game. Offices closed, although many workers stayed behind to listen to the radio together; General Motors shut down its production line, and the Chamber of Deputies abandoned its afternoon sitting; while an estimated 50,000 gathered outside newspaper offices to hear updates relayed by telex.

The official attendance was 68,346, although some estimates suggest perhaps as many as 25,000 more squeezed in, with huge crowds packing the streets around the stadium. Fans were searched for weapons on their way in, while the Belgian referee John Langenus was so concerned for his own safety that he had an escape route planned to a ship moored in the harbour. Even before the game, he had to settle a dispute, with Argentina protesting about the ball Uruguay wanted to use: the first half, Langenus decided, would be played with a ball favoured by the Argentinians (made in Scotland) and the second half with one favoured by the Uruguay (made in England).* That wasn't the only inconsistency that looks bizarre to eyes familiar with the hyper-regulated branding of the modern game: Juan Evaristo, Argentina's right-half, played in a beret and Nasazzi in his trademark white hat, while Andrade, rather than wearing black shorts like the rest of his team, played in a white pair. Langenus himself, a huge man who towered over both captains, wore a

* Or at least that is the commonly told story. There seems, though, to be no contemporary reference to it, nor does Langenus, having described the toss for choice of ball, mention it in his autobiography. The ball preferred by Argentina was preserved and is housed in the National Football Museum in Manchester. If a different ball was used in the second half, it has vanished.

blazer, plus fours and a striped yellow tie.

Two days before the game, Monti received a death threat that he took so seriously that he initially refused to play. For Argentina that was an enormous problem, not only because their captain was such a fine player, tough and skilful, but because the obvious candidate to replace him, the experienced half-back Adolfo Zumelzú, was injured. Eventually, on the morning of the game, Monti decided he would play. Preparation and morale, though, had been affected.

Even eight decades later Pancho Varallo, Argentina's inside-right, had not forgiven him. 'The Uruguayans beat us because they were sly,' he said. 'They took advantage of being the hosts. Luis Monti was a great player but that day he was totally pale.'[66] Varallo was the last survivor of the 1930 final, which gave him the advantage of being able to shape the narrative long after those who might have contradicted him had passed on. His recollection of Monti's performance, though, is corroborated by the report in *El Gráfico*, which described Argentina's captain 'standing, literally soulless, without being the great playmaker that in normal circumstances he would have been'.[67]

Varallo played despite a knee injury, having passed a fitness test that involved taking shots in a henhouse near the hotel on the morning of the game. Varallo's father was one of the few Argentinians in the stadium but even he ended up wrapping himself in a Uruguayan flag to ensure he could leave safely.

Uruguay took an early lead, as the one-handed Castro, selected only after Anselmo suggested that, being more of a fighter, he was better suited for the centre-forward role against Argentina, reacted first to a blocked Scarone shot, and rolled the ball to his right for Pablo Dorado to smash home. But going behind seemed to settle Argentina and Ferreira, back from his law exams to slot in at inside-left, released the winger Carlos Peucelle to level before Stábile put Argentina in front before half-time. It was Stábile's eighth goal of the tournament, making him its top scorer; remarkably, the four games he played at the World Cup were his only appearances for Argentina.

'We were winning comfortably,' said Varallo. 'We were making them dance.'[68] Argentina had chances to make it 3–1, first through Stábile and then through Varallo. 'I got the ball on a counter-attack,' he said, 'took a shot and it went past the keeper, directly towards the top corner ... The stadium was silent. It hit the angle of crossbar and post and then it went out. The worst part is that the shot was so fierce that I injured my knee properly. I kept playing crippled. That goal would have changed everything.'

Within a few minutes, Uruguay were level, Pedro Cea nudging in Scarone's clever hooked pass. Then Ernesto Mascheroni dispossessed Varallo, advanced and played in Santos Iriarte, whose low shot was past the Argentina keeper Juan Botasso before he had dived. 'We lost it because we lacked guts,' Varallo said. 'Some of our players really felt the intimidation and became chickens.'[69] A looping header from Castro in the final minute sealed Uruguay's 4–2 victory.

Rimet presented the trophy to Raúl Jude, the president of the Uruguayan federation, Langenus made it safely to his ship and Uruguay revelled in an investment that had paid off. They did not know, could not have known, what the World Cup would become, but they were the inaugural champions, their status as the world's greatest football team, established by the Olympic successes, emphatically confirmed. This was a triumph for Scarone, Nasazzi, Andrade and Cea, the four players who played in all three finals, but it was also a triumph for the *batllista* vision of Uruguay.

Whatever feeling of positivity was generated, though, could not endure the economic consequences of the Crash. Campisteguy was succeeded in 1931 by Gabriel Terra who, with the financial picture worsening, split from *batllista* leaders in November 1932 and led a coup on the night of 31 March 1933, ruling as dictator until elections in 1934 when he won a mandate for his presidential reforms.

Meanwhile, in the immediate aftermath of the World Cup final, the mood in Buenos Aires turned ugly. The Uruguayan embassy was attacked and a woman on a balcony who waved a Uruguayan flag as disappointed Argentinian fans paraded past was pelted with stones. An editorial in *La Prensa* blamed 'men who fall at the first blow, who are in danger of fainting at the first onslaught even if they are clever in their footwork'. 'These "lady-players",' it said, 'should be eliminated.'[70]

Others looked outside as they sought reasons for their defeat. 'Langenus let the Uruguayans go unpunished with violent challenges,' wrote Alfredo Rossi in *El Gráfico*. 'I also complain about the off-pitch behaviour of the Uruguayans, threatening players with anonymous calls and letters.'[71] *Critica* declared Argentina the 'moral champions', setting a template that would be pursued repeatedly in the decades that followed. How justified the protests were is almost impossible to know. As Mazzucchelli points out, it wasn't until two days after the final that the first complaints began to be heard from Argentinians, mostly from the dandyish head of their delegation, Augusto Rouquette.[72]

Rimet had envisaged the World Cup not only as a tournament for professionals but as a way of fostering a spirit of brotherhood between nations. It didn't take long for those ideals to be subverted. 'The World Cup is over,' read the editorial in *El Gráfico*. 'Triumphantly for Uruguay and happily for everybody because, it must be said, the development of this competition brought not only an unpleasant atmosphere, but also an ungrateful one.' Were international tournaments, *El Gráfico* asked, worth the hassle at all? 'Football has been again ... a vehicle for great shows of a lack of culture, for violent behaviour, passion and insults . . . It looked as though in these twenty-two men trying to kick the ball in the opposition goal lay the future of a nation.'[73]

The pattern was set.

1934

THE TRIUMPH OF FASCISM

In August 1933, the Austrian chancellor Engelbert Dollfuß flew to the Italian beach resort of Riccione for crisis talks with Benito Mussolini. German radio stations were broadcasting anti-Dollfuß propaganda and, given the growing possibility of a Hitler-inspired coup in Austria, Dollfuß needed to know that he had Mussolini's support. When he got to Riccione, though, he found that Mussolini was swimming in the sea, showing little inclination to return to shore. Deciding it was undignified to wait, Dollfuß hired a skiff and rowed out to Mussolini who swam a few strokes alongside him and then clambered aboard. As they arrived back on the beach, holiday-makers cheered.[1]

As they walked together up the sands, Mussolini's purpose was clear. Wearing just his trunks, he towered over the 4ft 11in Dollfuß, who was formally dressed. Through the appearance of their leaders a clear message was conveyed: Italy was powerful, athletic and modern; Austria was fussy, weak and old-fashioned.

Later that day, talks continued at the Grand Hotel. Dollfuß agreed to Mussolini's plans for a trading bloc joining Italy,

Austria and Hungary and in return Mussolini guaranteed Austrian independence. Five months earlier, Dollfuß had suspended parliament to a run a Catholic corporatist regime that owed a lot to the example of Mussolini.

Six months before that, Italy had been named as host of the 1934 World Cup. For Mussolini, it represented a tremendous opportunity. The idea of Italy as a vigorous, muscular nation lay at the heart of his conception of fascism and he was often pictured skiing or riding a horse bare-chested.

Sporting success was a necessary part of the projection of that image.[2] 'When you compete abroad,' Mussolini told Italian athletes, 'the honour and sporting prestige of the nation is entrusted to your muscles and above all your spirit.'[3] At the 1920 Olympics in Antwerp, the Italy squad had been a dishevelled bunch who had sung 'The Red Flag'; by 1932 in Los Angeles they marched into the opening ceremony wearing black shirts and singing '*Giovinezza*', the official hymn of the Italian Fascist party, and went on to finish second in the medals table.

Mussolini was no great football fan,[4] but he recognised its power both in terms of projecting an image of strength and in bringing the country together (it had been politically united only in 1861). Accordingly, at the end of 1925–26, journalists and senior figures from Italian football met in the Tuscan resort of Viareggio to discuss the future of the game. Southern teams were admitted to the league, paving the way for the coming of professionalism and the advent of Serie A, a truly national competition, in 1929–30. Foreign players were banned from the 1927–28 season to try to raise the level of Italian football and stimulate the growth of an Italian football culture, although foreign coaches remained and clubs soon began to evade the ban by signing South Americans of Italian descent – the *oriundi*, as they became known, the 'returners'.

The Viareggio conference wasn't the state's only involvement in football. Vast sums were invested in stadium infrastructure, while municipalities often insisted on the merger of local clubs to create one entity that could represent the city in the national league. To an extent it worked. Having lost to Switzerland in the quarter-final of the 1924 Olympics, Italy claimed bronze in 1928. Although they didn't travel to Uruguay for the inaugural World Cup, Bologna showed what progress had been made with victories in the Mitropa Cup in 1932 and 1934. The meaning of such successes was clear; as early as 1928, the Fascist newspaper *Il Littorale* insisted that victories overseas were 'clear signs of racial superiority that are destined to reflect in many fields outside of sport'.[5]

Bombast and intent, though, could only carry a country so far. Mussolini was desperate that Italy should offer an affirmation of the greatness of his regime by winning the World Cup. With Uruguay declining to travel, their likeliest rivals for that title were Austria. Mussolini could dominate Dollfuß; getting the better of Hugo Meisl and the *Wunderteam* was rather less straightforward. The point had been underlined as Austria beat Italy 2–1 in Vienna in the Central European International Cup in March 1932, both their goals coming from their slight, cerebral centre-forward Matthias Sindelar, a player whose very lack of physical robustness seemed a refutation of Mussolini's vision of sport and the world.

The footballing leaders of Italy and Austria had met for the first time in Stockholm in June 1912. Italian football was still in its infancy, their appearance at the Olympic Games their first at an international tournament. Their coach was Vittorio Pozzo, a twenty-six-year-old enthusiast who had become obsessed by the game in England, and their first match was against Finland. The referee was Meisl, five years Pozzo's senior, but a man from a similar middle-class background with similar

Anglophile instincts. Meisl could speak Italian; Pozzo could speak German. They would become good friends, despite fighting on opposite sides on the Isonzo front during the First World War.

Italy lost the game 3–2 after extra time, casting them into the consolation tournament. Meisl, as well as being president of the Austrian football association (ÖFB), was the senior member of their selection committee. In the consolation semi-final, his side met Italy, the first direct match-up of the two great coaches. Austria won 5–1 but Meisl recognised in Pozzo the same zeal and passion for football that he felt. Managing a national team, the Austrian told the Italian, was a difficult and thankless task. Pozzo replied that he had no intention of doing it in the future, to which Meisl responded with a knowing smile.

Twenty-two years later, they would meet again in a far more consequential semi-final.

It was while working in Bradford that Vittorio Pozzo had fallen in love with football. He had been a gifted 400m runner, taking gold at the Piedmont Student Games, and had played a little football as a student but had had no notion it might be anything other than an occasional recreation. He had been a fan, though, and aged twelve he and some schoolfriends had sold their Latin textbooks to travel from Turin to watch Internazionale de Torino play Genoa in the final of the inaugural Italian championship. He studied at the International School of Commerce in Zurich, where he learned English, French and German, then moved to London before his father's influence secured a position in West Yorkshire for him to study the manufacture of wool. Pozzo threw himself into the English way of life. Although a Catholic, he would attend the local Anglican church on a Sunday, work for five days, and then go to watch football on a Saturday. In the routine, he found a sense of purpose and was so inspired that when his parents called him home to work at his brother's engineering firm, he refused to go. His father cut off his allowance, so he made ends meet by offering language lessons.

His favourite team was Manchester United, with its fabled half-back line of Dick Duckworth, Charlie Roberts and Alec Bell. After games he would hang around by the players' entrance, eventually becoming good friends with Roberts. Pozzo also befriended Herbert Chapman, who responded to the 1925 change in the offside law by developing the W-M formation, withdrawing a midfielder into the defensive line and then pulling back two forwards to compensate, effectively transforming the old 2-3-5 to a 3-2-2-3.[6] While the Arsenal manager made the centre-half into an 'overcoat' to sit on the shoulders of the opposing centre-forward, Pozzo wanted him still to resemble the elegant, playmaking Roberts. And so, when he finally became a coach, Pozzo developed what he termed the *metodo*, a refinement of the W-M formation (*sistema* as he termed it) that was effectively a W-W in which the centre-half, although dropping deeper than in the classic 2-3-5, retained a creative function.

Pozzo went back to Italy for his sister's wedding in 1911, after which his family prevented him returning to England. He started writing about football for various newspapers, then found work at the Italian football federation (FIGC) and was asked to lead the national side as *comisario tecnico* at the 1912 Olympics in Stockholm.

He served just three games, resigning after the defeat to Austria. He worked for Pirelli, continued his journalism and took a job with Torino, leading them on a tour of South America. They left shortly after the assassination of Franz Ferdinand in Sarajevo. By the time they returned, Europe was at war. As their steamer neared Gibraltar, it was stopped by a British cruiser looking for German reservists returning to fight. They found two, and thought they had found a third when Pozzo, not realising the seriousness of the situation, jokingly spoke to them in German. Only a rapid switch into English and a discussion of Manchester United persuaded a Royal Navy officer to allow him to continue.[7] The following May, Italy entered the war on the side of the Allies, hoping to seize Austro-Hungarian territory around the north edge of the Adriatic to complete, as they saw it, the process of Risorgimento. In August, Pozzo was drafted as an officer and served in the Alps until, the following March, he was recalled to Genoa and, because of his facility with languages, given a role checking foreign mail for the military censor.

When his wife Caterina died a few months after he had led Italy to the quarter-final of the 1924 Olympics, Pozzo resigned. Moving to Milan, he worked for Pirelli and spent his spare time walking his dog in the mountains. When he was dismissed by AC Milan in 1926, he resolved never to work in football again.

After Italy took bronze under Augusto Rangone at the 1928 Olympics, Leandro Arpinati, a leading Fascist who was president of the FIGC and *podestà* of Bologna, told Mussolini that the national team needed Pozzo back. By then, Pozzo was an executive of Pirelli and a regular writer for *La Stampa*, and had little interest in returning to the stress of football management. Rangone had effectively ensured he would be dismissed by publicly complaining that he had not been allowed to call up Julio Libonatti, an Argentina-born centre-forward who had joined Torino in 1926 as the first of the *oriundi*. Although Libonatti had already played for both Argentina and Italy before the Olympics, and although he was officially left out for fears he might breach rules on professionalism, there was a clear implication that he had been omitted for not being sufficiently Italian for Mussolini's project.

With Rangone gone and Pozzo refusing to take the job, Arpinati turned to the Alessandria coach Carlo Carcano, who retained his club job while leading the national side. Carcano is one of the great mysteries of Italian football. He joined Juventus in 1930, led them to four successive league titles and looked set for a fifth when he was dismissed without explanation in December 1934. Although there is no definitive proof, it now seems widely accepted that he was gay* and that his abrupt departure was occasioned by a suppressed scandal.[8]

Quite how much control Carcano had over the national side is unclear and it may be that Rangone was still running things in the background. But after defeats to Austria and Germany in April 1929, Carcano was removed and Arpinati stepped up his campaign to appoint Pozzo. Finally, in November, Pozzo agreed to take the job, although he refused a salary and retained his positions at Pirelli and *La Stampa*.

The first competitive game of Pozzo's third stint as national coach came away to Hungary in May 1930, in what was effectively a play-off for the Central European International Cup. On the way to Budapest, Pozzo took his players to the First World War battlefields of Oslavia and Gorizia, where Italy had fought Austria-Hungary, and stopped at the monumental cemetery at Redipuglia. Fired with patriotism, Italy won 5–0, with Giuseppe Meazza scoring a hat-trick. Given Italy had never previously beaten Hungary away and had imported Hungarians by the dozen through the twenties to learn the game from them,[9] that was a major vindication for Pozzo.

On the journey home, the train braked suddenly, sending

* The Penal Code of 1930 – commonly known as the Rocco Code – initially proposed making homosexuality a crime, punishable by imprisonment. A ministerial commission, though, struck it out, asserting that 'much to the fortune and pride of Italy, the abominable vice ... is not so widespread as to justify the legislator's intervention ... Against habitual and professional perpetrators of the vice, who in truth are very rare and all of exclusively foreign extraction, the police shall take steps as of now through the immediate enforcement of measures of security and imprisonment.' Nevertheless, the subtext was clear: there was no place for homosexuality in Mussolini's bristlingly virile republic.

players stumbling and falling. Pozzo watched in horror as the trophy, the Švehla Cup, fashioned of cut glass, fell from the shelf and crashed onto the floor. Miraculously it survived, apart from a chip taken off the stopper. Pozzo took the splinter and put in his pocket as a good-luck charm.

Hugo Meisl had been born to a Jewish family in Bohemia, before moving to Vienna as a child. He became involved in football early, joining the Vienna Cricket & Football Club as a fourteen-year-old, and was one of three Austrians in the side that challenged Wiener AC for the first Austrian Challenge Cup.

He studied in Vienna, Trieste and Paris and showed great aptitude for languages, speaking eight with a degree of fluency. As a player he was nicknamed the '*Hirnfußballer*' – the player with a brain – but he became frustrated by his relative lack of ability and trained as a referee, taking charge of his first international in 1907. Like Pozzo, he found journalism a useful sideline, working as a columnist for the *Neue Wiener Sportblatt*, although his main job was with Länderbank. He was made secretary of the ÖFB, writing a manual explaining the game and, at twenty-three, became the federation's first secretary general. Given he was also secretary of the Cricket & Football Club, which became Wiener Amateure and then Austria Vienna, Meisl effectively *was* Austrian football by the time of the 1912 Olympics.

In the First World War, Meisl was posted first to Serbia and then to Krn in Slovenia; like Rimet, he had a vision of football as a force that could encourage brotherhood among nations and, like Rimet, he recognised amateurism was an impediment to the involvement of people of all classes, which was a major reason the Austrian league turned professional in 1924.[10]

Although Austria were one of the leading European powers

in the twenties (the issue of professionalism kept them out of the Olympics from 1924), it wasn't until 1931 that the *Wunderteam* came into being. Meisl preferred a powerful striker and was sceptical of the claims of Sindelar, the darling of the coffee-houses, a clever centre-forward with a tendency to drop deep whose slightness earned him the nickname '*Der Papierene*' – the Paper Man. Meisl had dropped Sindelar after a 5–0 defeat to Germany in 1929 when, on a soaking pitch, Sindelar disagreed with his coach's plan to adopt a more direct approach, but he had started to be selected regularly following a performance of undeniable brilliance in a 5–0 defeat of Scotland in 1931. The *Wunderteam* was born, and Sindelar was its brain.

Beating Hungary was one thing but even more vital for Pozzo was a first ever win for Italy over Austria and Meisl. It came in the first game of the second edition of the Central European International Cup in February 1931, three months before Austria's demolition of Scotland in front of a rapturous crowd of 45,000 in Milan. Pozzo had argued vehemently that he should be allowed to call up *oriundi* – how could it be, he asked, that they were eligible for national service but not for the national football team? – and reaped the benefit as the winner was scored by Raimundo Orsi, a rapid left-winger who had been born in Argentina but had joined Juventus in 1928. This was a victory for discipline and organisation and, most of all, for Pozzo, whose position had become essentially unchallengeable.

Perhaps that emboldened him. The following month, the Roma midfielder Attilio Ferraris scrapped with Orsi during a league game, then reacted violently to a hard challenge from the Juve midfielder Renato Cesarini. Ferraris and Cesarini were both sent off, as was the Juve left-back Umberto Caligaris for striking the Roma forward Rodolfo Volk. That left Pozzo with a problem. His national side met up ten days later for a game against Switzerland and he was determined there should be no lingering bad blood or cliques in his squad. So he told Ferraris and Cesarini they were rooming together, but that they should leave their door open so he could hear if either attacked the other. He then gave each a piece of caramel 'to sweeten their mouths',[11] at which Meazza and Eraldo Monzeglio, who had been listening nearby, insisted they had just had a blazing row and asked if they could have a piece of caramel as well. The crisis passed and Italy drew 1–1 with Cesarini scoring a late equaliser.

Italy finished behind Austria, leading Pozzo to conclude his side was missing two elements: a top-class centre-half and a combative centre-forward. At centre-half, he had tended to use either the rugged Ferraris, who lacked creativity, or the more elegant Fulvio Bernardini, an economics graduate who was less than reliable defensively. What he needed was somebody who combined their attributes. It turned out that in summer 1931, the ideal solution had landed in Genoa.

After the 1930 World Cup final, Luis Monti's career had collapsed. He had been released by his club, San Lorenzo, and decided to quit football to run a shop selling pasta. It evidently became a passion: by the time he turned thirty in May 1931, Monti was around 15kg overweight. But Juventus decided to take a gamble on him. It took time, and winter training on a farm amid snow and mud, for him to recover his fitness, but he played a key role as Juve retained the title. He was tough, defensively aware and a fine passer of a ball; he was just what Pozzo needed. He made his Italy debut in a 4–2 friendly win over Hungary on 27 November 1932.

At inside-forward, Pozzo had Meazza, a graceful and inventive player who loved champagne, cigarettes and the cabaret. He had scored thirteen goals in his first fifteen internationals and had been top scorer in Serie A in 1929–30, but he did not offer an aerial threat. Pozzo, perhaps influenced by his fascination with the English game, wanted somebody who could hold the ball up, and reasoned that Meazza might be more dangerous coming from deep, from one of the inside-forward positions. The ideal candidate was Angelo Schiavio of Bologna, but he had repeatedly turned down international call-ups because of commitments to his family's clothing store.

That presented another problem. In 1929, Bologna had toured South America and Schiavio had clashed with Monti. The former Argentina captain was not the sort of man to forget. When Juventus met Bologna in 1932, he clattered Schiavio, badly damaging his knee. So Pozzo pursued his familiar tactic, called both into his squad and made them share a room. It would be an exaggeration to say they became friends, but they could at least be team-mates.

Pozzo's other major issue was political. From December 1931, Achille Starace, the national secretary of the Party, began to campaign against Arpinati, presenting Mussolini with seventeen allegations against the head of the FIGC, including friendship with anti-Fascists, overly liberal ideas and anti-regime activities. Mussolini stripped Arpinati of all offices.

'But Starace's an idiot,' Arpinati supposedly protested.

'Yes,' said Mussolini. 'But he's an obedient idiot.'[12]

Arpinati was replaced as president of the FIGC by Giorgio Vaccaro, a former fencer and cyclist who had been president of Lazio, where he had gained notoriety for kicking the Roma full-back Mario De Micheli during a derby in May 1931. Vaccaro was a powerful figure but Pozzo, his position strengthened by the fact he was still working for free, insisted he must have complete autonomy. The only challenge to that came when Starace demanded he should pick only Party members. There were only three non-members he really wanted to select – the full-backs Luigi Allemandi and Eraldo Monzeglio, and the midfielder Attilio Ferraris – but Pozzo held firm.

There was a fragility about the *Wunderteam* that meant they seemed always to be considered not quite as good as they once had been, always on the brink of collapse. A 4–3 defeat to England at Stamford Bridge in December 1932, in which many considered they had been the better side, undone only by some indecisive finishing, was regarded as proof they were one of the best sides in the world, yet just four months later, after thrashings of Belgium and France, a 2–1 defeat to Czechoslovakia had *Sport-Tagblatt* lamenting that 'once there used to be a *Wunderteam*'.[13] Meisl seemed despondent. 'I feel compelled,' he said, 'to inject new red cells into the blood of our old anaemic *Wunderteam*. Time passes for everyone, and Sindelar is obviously no exception.'[14] He wasn't quite thirty.

The sense of the national team in decline was perhaps a reflection of broader concerns that Austria itself and the carefree, artistic values of old Vienna were in retreat. Under pressure from Nazis in Germany and Communists at home, Dollfuß decided the real enemy was the Social Democrats. In February 1934, Dollfuß declared a nationwide crackdown and, as the Social Democrats resisted, Austria endured sixteen days of civil war. Notoriously, Dollfuß deployed artillery against the Karl-Marx-Hof, a social housing project where the last remaining leftists had holed up, despite the risk to residents uninvolved in the conflict.

That same month, Meisl's side ended a run of uncertain performances with a 4–2 victory away to Italy. When, forty days before the opening game of the World Cup, they beat Hungary 5–2 at home, Meisl decided to go with a forward pairing of Sindelar and the twenty-year-old Pepi Bican, who would become the most prolific goalscorer in history before Cristiano Ronaldo.

The World Cup wasn't just about whether Italy played well; it was also about whether Italy hosted well. The president of the FIGC, General Giorgio Vaccaro, described it as an opportunity to demonstrate 'the organisational efficiency of fascist sport in general and football in particular, highlighting, in times of so-called "crisis" our infinite national resources'.[15] The FIGC subsidised the trips of foreign fans, internal travel between host cities was discounted and match commentary was broadcast by radio to twelve of the competing nations. An unprecedented range of merchandise was created, all of it made to the highest specifications to show off Italian craftsmanship. Even match tickets were printed on high-quality paper to encourage fans to keep them as souvenirs. And of course everything bore the image of the *fasces*, the bundle of rods that had been a signifier of power in Italy from Roman times.

The Futurist artist Filippo Marinetti was commissioned to design a poster that focused on a powerful, thrusting figure in Italian kit with the *fasces* in one corner. But the greatest symbol of Mussolini's takeover of the World Cup was his introduction of the Coppa del Duce as a supplementary prize for the winner. Sculpted in bronze, it depicted footballers playing in front of *fasces* and stood six times taller than the Jules Rimet trophy.

The total of thirty-six entrants demanded qualifying tournaments and suggested not only the popularity of the World Cup, but also the fact that it was easier to persuade more countries to get involved when the tournament was staged in Europe. Uruguay refused to travel, supposedly in retaliation for the reluctance of European sides to cross the Atlantic in 1930, although economic issues after the Wall Street Crash, the aftermath of the 1933 coup and the fact that the golden age of their football had passed clearly played a part. The withdrawals of Chile and Peru meant that Brazil and Argentina were awarded the two of the three berths open to the Americas without having to qualify, although a schism in the federation following the introduction of professionalism meant Argentina sent an amateur side, which lost its only game, to Sweden.

The USA entered late, but were permitted a play-off in Rome against Mexico for the remaining American slot. The USA won 4–2, all their goals being scored by Aldo 'Buff' Donelli. He scored again in the first round proper, his only other international, but the USA were hammered 7–1 by Italy. Brazil, whose black players had been banned from mixing with other passengers on their twelve-day voyage across the Atlantic, also went out in the first round, losing 3–1 to Spain. The four sides from the Americas had travelled a long way to play just four games between them.

The only other non-European side in Italy was Egypt who, after Turkey's withdrawal, beat Mandatory Palestine 11–2 in a two-legged qualifying play-off. They had a decent record in the Olympics, and had famously beaten Hungary 3–0 at the 1924 Games, but this time the Hungarians won 4–2.

The British nations had not rejoined Fifa but Italy, determined to invest their World Cup with as much credibility as possible, invited England and offered to pay their expenses. The FA secretary Frederick Wall, though, had unhappy memories of watching England draw 1–1 in Rome in 1933, when a fevered crowd had chanted for Mussolini. 'I have no desire again to be a guest of the Italian football federation,' he said.[16]

The Roma wing-half Attilio Ferraris had always enjoyed an active social life. As he approached his thirtieth birthday, he was drinking increasingly heavily. His body was in decline. He would spend his evenings smoking and playing billiards, and then turn up late to training, which led to him being kicked out of the club in 1933.

Pozzo still wanted Ferraris in his squad, even though he had not played for the national team in two years. He went to visit him in his bar and told him Italy needed him. Ferraris was, eventually, convinced. He gave up alcohol, slashed his intake of cigarettes from forty a day to two and began training like a demon. By June, he was ready.

Pozzo trusted experience. Seven of his twenty-two-man squad for the 1934 World Cup were aged thirty or over. The goalkeeper Gianpiero Combi was thirty-one and would have retired to run a bar, as he did immediately after the World Cup, had not Pozzo persuaded him to stay on. He was supposed to be back-up for Carlo Ceresoli, but the Inter goalkeeper damaged his elbow in training two weeks before the tournament began and Combi was thrust into action.

Mussolini, wearing a yachting cap, was among the 25,000 in the crowd at the Stadio Nazionale del PNF (National Fascist Party), having supposedly bought his own ticket and those of his family himself – freeloading, apparently, was most unfascist – to watch Italy's opening demolition of the USA.

To get his players used to the heat, Meisl scheduled training sessions for noon and to stimulate competition he would put up fountain pens as a prize for races, only for Bican, who was ferociously competitive, to win every time. An injury to the left-half Walter Nausch hampered preparations while both Sindelar and the defender Karl Sesta arrived in Italy with toothache. Austria were unconvincing in beating France in the first round, and then struggled to see off Hungary 2–1 in the quarter-final, despite their opponents being reduced to nine by an injury to Géza Toldi and the dismissal of Imre Markos.

Spain in the quarter-final proved the sternest test for Italy. Injury meant the captain Virginio Rosetta was replaced at full-back by Monzeglio, with Combi taking the armband. Lest anybody forget what they were representing, the game was played at the Stadio Giovanni Berta, named after a Fascist thrown off a bridge by left-wingers in 1921. Combi and his revered counterpart Ricardo Zamora both made a number of saves, a Luis Regueiro volley gave Spain the lead on the half-hour and Giovanni Ferrari levelled just before half-time with Zamora protesting vehemently he had been fouled as a free-kick was played into the box.

It finished 1–1, which meant a replay the following day. Zamora was ruled out with a swollen knee and a black eye, and Spain were forced into six other changes. Pozzo had to make four replacements, including bringing in Ferraris to create a formidable half line alongside Bertolini and Monti, who was given greater licence to push forward. That meant all three of the non-Party members Pozzo had insisted upon were in the team. It was another brutal game but Italy won 1–0 thanks to Meazza's 11th-minute header from an Orsi corner, as Spain once again protested about a foul on the goalkeeper.

The climactic meeting of Pozzo's Italy and Meisl's Austria came at San Siro for the semi-final, forty-eight hours after Italy's replay against Spain. Ferrari and Schiavio had recovered sufficiently to return. Rosetta was also fit again but Pozzo preferred to stick with Monzeglio at right-back; Rosetta stormed out, packed his bag and took a train back to Turin. He never played for Italy again.

Mussolini, again in his yachting cap, again having ostentatiously paid for his own ticket, sat in the stand, watching in focused silence, with Rimet perched in obvious discomfort next to him. A clutch of Italian royals surrounded them. A heavy thunderstorm shortly before kick-off soaked the pitch, the mud making it harder for Austria and their close-passing game.

And it was already hard enough. There are plenty of rumours about Ivan Eklind, the Swedish referee, the youngest official at the tournament, and it perhaps says something about his performance that he was promptly installed to take charge of the final – certainly, it's hard to imagine that happening had he been perceived as too strict on Italy. That he was selected as the Swedish representative at all was controversial. Most had expected the more experienced Otto Ohlsson to be chosen but Anton Johanson, the Swedish football association's representative at Fifa, picked Eklind, who was seemingly a friend, although it may be that being less experienced he was perceived as more suggestible. Johanson, a noted political climber, had already initiated warm relations with Italy by withdrawing Sweden's bid to host the tournament. He returned from the World Cup boasting of the lucrative friendly Sweden would soon play against the world champions, although it never actually materialised.[17]

That said, there is no concrete evidence that Eklind was paid off or in any other way corrupted. Indeed, he was revered when he returned to Sweden, attracting the nickname the 'Count of Rome' – which seems to have been bestowed without irony – and overseeing two Swedish Cup finals and five all-Sweden bandy finals,* as well as officiating at both the 1938 and 1950 World Cups.

---

* A winter sport, popular in Scandinavia, Russia and Kazakhstan, bandy resembles ice hockey played outdoors on a larger pitch but with a ball rather than a puck.

Eklind was proud of his record of never having sent a player off, but later admitted that he possibly should have done in that final. 'There was a roaring lion by the name of Monti,' he said, 'who at one stage made me stop the game to rebuke him and stop the cataclysm of bad language.'[18]

In the semi-final, Monti had been able to impose himself physically on Sindelar to the extent that the forward had to go to an orthopaedic clinic after the game; Pozzo subsequently wrote him a letter to apologise.[19] The only goal came after 19 minutes, Guaita poking in after Platzer had saved from Schiavio. Had there been a foul on the keeper? Austria thought so, Italy didn't and neither, crucially, did Eklind. 'It was impossible to beat Italy in such a context,' said Meisl. 'You have to give up and grant the title to the Azzurri but this does not mean that their football is better and that the title is deservedly achieved.'[20]

Germany had overcome its reservations about playing against professionals, but the debate over style remained acute. The most successful side of the Nazi era were Schalke 04, who won six championships between 1934 and 1942 playing an Austrian-influenced game of intermovement and close passing known as the *Kreisel*, the spinning-top. Germany's coach Otto Nerz, though, favoured the W-M formation and a direct approach that made him sceptical of Schalke and their two great stars of the era, the forwards Ernst Kuzorra and his brother-in-law Fritz Szepan with their 'fiddling and dribbling around'.[21] An early member of the Nazi party who became a member of the SA in 1933, rising to the rank of *Obersturmbannführer* by the end of the war, Nerz had no qualms about the announcement on 2 June 1933 that Jews were to be expelled from sports clubs.

Although Germany were widely disdained by the Italian

media, they had won seven and drawn two of the nine games they'd played in the fifteen months before the tournament. In Italy, they had beaten Belgium 5–2 with a hat-trick from Edmund Conen before overcoming Sweden 2–1 in the quarter-final.

Szepan, although an inside-forward at club level, had been deployed as the centre-half; the use of a ball-player at the heart of the defence would become a familiar German trope. But with the inside-right Karl Hohmann, scorer of both goals against the Swedes in the quarter-final, picking up an injury that kept him out of the semi, it was widely assumed that Szepan would move to the forward line with a centre-half called up to replace him. Sure enough, the Aachen defender Reinhold Münzenberg was told to postpone his wedding and make his way to Italy. But the president of the German football federation (DFB), Felix Linnemann, who was closely aligned to the Nazi government, insisted that there should be as little disruption to the line-up as possible and so, for the semi-final against Czechoslovakia, Rudolf Noack replaced Hohmann with Szepan remaining at centre-half.

Czechoslovakia played their own variant of the Danubian style and were blessed with an extremely gifted forward line, of whom the stand-out was the inside-left Oldřich Nejedlý. Having scored against Romania in the first round and Switzerland in the quarter-final, he was decisive against Germany, scoring a hat-trick in a 3–1 win, two of his goals stemming from errors by the goalkeeper Willi Kreß.

Third-place games are rarely of much consequence but this one was, partly because it pitted Germany against Austria, confirmed rivals on the pitch as well as having a fraught political relationship, and partly because that game marked the beginning of Germany's development as a major power. Rudi Gramlich, the right-half, had gone back to Frankfurt after the quarter-final because the Jewish leather traders for whom he worked needed help* – possibly evidence of the impact of Nazi restrictions on Jewish businesses – and Nerz had, mystifyingly, sent the full-back Siggi Haringer home in disgrace after the semi-final, apparently for the crime of eating an orange on a station platform. Other changes, though, seemed to be made with an eye to the future. Münzenberg played at centre-half, releasing Szepan to the forward line. Hans Jakob replaced Kreß in goal while Otto Siffling came in at centre-forward.

It was not, it should be said, a full-strength Austria side, but equally it would be misleading to suggest they did not take the game seriously – as was proved by the silliness at kick-off, as both teams refused to change out of their white shirts. Only after Ernst Lehner had given Germany a fourth-minute lead did the Italian referee Albino Carraro force the Germans to change into red.[22] Germany went on to win 3–2 and, for the historian Karl-Heinz Huba, that was the origin of the side that, three years later, would pass into legend as *die Breslau-Elf*.[23]

For Italy, Czechoslovakia were not just any opponents; memories of Juventus's Mitropa Cup semi-final against Slavia Prague remained vivid. Slavia won the first leg 4–0 but Juve scored two early goals in the return in Turin. Slavia responded by time-wasting, incensing the home fans to the extent they hurled stones at the Slavia players. When Slavia's goalkeeper František Plánička, who was also the national captain, was struck on the head, Slavia refused to play on. That further enraged fans who besieged the Czechs' dressing-room for

* Gramlich was, though, a committed Nazi, joining the SS in 1936. From 1942 he was stationed in Krakow where he became head of the football section of the *Totenkopfverbände*, one of the 'death's head units' that administered the concentration and extermination camps. Although arrested in 1947 on suspicion of war crimes, he was never charged and between 1955 and 1970 served as chairman of Eintracht Frankfurt. In 2020 the club stripped him of his honorary titles because of concerns over his involvement with the Nazis.

hours until around 1,500 soldiers and police formed enough of a cordon for them to escape. The Mitropa Cup committee disqualified both sides, leaving Bologna, who had beaten First Vienna in their semi-final, as champions. The national teams met later that year in the Central European International Cup, explicitly talking of reconciliation and, despite anxiety on both sides, the game passed off largely without note, Czechoslovakia winning 2–1. But that did not mean the bad blood had disappeared.

The day of the final was extremely hot. Pozzo, though, superstitious as ever, insisted on keeping on the jacket he had worn throughout the tournament, the sliver of the Švehla Cup still in his pocket. When Antonín Puč was released by Jiří Sobotka after 71 minutes, escaped Ferraris and put Czechoslovakia ahead with a precise shot, it seemed Pozzo's luck may have run out. But František Svoboda then hit the post and, with nine minutes remaining, Orsi picked up a loose ball, beat two men and swept an equaliser past Plánička. Pozzo, as he had in the first game against Spain, switched Schiavio and Guaita and, on this occasion, it worked, Schiavio coming in from wide to score the winner five minutes into extra time.

Rimet presented the World Cup, Mussolini handed over the Coppa del Duce and, as Pozzo rushed to the hotel lobby to phone through his copy to *La Stampa*, Italy celebrated glorious vindication.

Not everybody was so enamoured. 'In the majority of countries,' said the Belgian referee John Langenus, 'the World Cup was called a sporting fiasco, because beside the desire to win, all other sporting considerations were non-existent, and because, moreover, a certain spirit brooded over the whole championship.'[24]

Despite the quibbles, the World Cup clearly worked as a

propaganda event – even if there were predictable English reservations. Charles Sutcliffe, for instance, the member of the Football League Management Committee with responsibility for drawing up the fixture list, described the 1934 World Cup as 'a joke' and suggested that the Home Championship represented 'a far better World Championship than the one to be played in Rome'.[25] Others within the hierarchy of English football, though, were less blinkered. 'If anyone entertains the idea that this comprehensive title of world champions has been cheaply won by Italy,' said Wall, 'it were wise to discard that opinion.'[26]Would England have won had they entered? They would certainly have had a good chance. Although they'd lost to Spain in 1929, blaming the defeat on the intense heat, a hard pitch and an impassioned crowd,[27] and to Hungary and Czechoslovakia in May 1934, it wouldn't be until 1973 that they lost to Italy. Spain, meanwhile, who would push Italy closer than anybody else at the 1934 tournament, had prepared for the World Cup with three games against Sunderland, none of which they won.[28]

The Italian press delighted in reprinting enthusiastic endorsements of Italian hospitality from overseas. 'The spontaneous and heartfelt statements of our foreign colleagues,' wrote Bruno Rogli in *La Gazzetta dello Sport*, 'are more than sufficient to show Mussolini's Italy – that was once little Italy of all improvisations and apologies – has organised the festival of football with style, flexibility, precision, even the courtesy and the meticulousness that indicate an absolute maturity and preparedness.'[29]

There was little doubt about the broader significance of what had happened on the pitch. Victory, the Florentine weekly *Il Bargello* said, was 'the affirmation of an entire people, an indication of its virile and moral strength'.[30]

1938

THE LAST WALTZ

In late March 1938, around ten weeks before the World Cup was due to begin, the Austrian football federation sent a telegram to Fifa. 'Sorry to cancel World Cup enrolment,' it read. 'Austrian football federation is gone.'[1] It wasn't just the football federation.

On 25 July 1934, Dollfuß was assassinated by Austrian Nazis as part of a failed putsch. Unifying the two countries was a long-term goal for Hitler, who had been born in Braunau am Inn, just south of the border, and grown up in Linz and Vienna, but it became more pressing after April 1937 when Hermann Göring, who was in charge of the Four-Year Plan to get Germany ready for a European war by 1940, told senior ministers there was a need to annex Austria so Germany could take control of its steel production. Within a few months Hitler had accepted that Austria would have to be taken by force and at the beginning of 1938, he stepped up the propaganda campaign, calling ever more vociferously for a union.

At the same time, Austrian Nazis plotted a coup, plans for which were uncovered in a raid on their headquarters on 25 January. On 12 February, the Austrian Chancellor Kurt Schuschnigg met Hitler and agreed to appoint various Nazi figures to key posts in exchange for Hitler reaffirming Austrian sovereignty. Just eight days later, though, Hitler gave a speech to the Reichstag in which he insisted that 'the German Reich is no longer willing to tolerate the suppression of ten million Germans across its borders'.[2] Clearly aimed at Germans living in Austria and Czechoslovakia, it was broadcast by Austrian radio and further heightened tensions. Schuschnigg was concerned enough to do deals with both the Socialists and the Social Democrats, effectively ending the one-party system in return for their support in a plebiscite on Austrian independence which he announced would be held on 13 March.

Insisting the vote would be subject to fraud, Hitler said that Germany would not accept the result. On 11 March, he issued an ultimatum, threatening an invasion unless power were handed to Austrian Nazis. Schuschnigg resigned, accepted Hitler's terms to avoid the shedding of '*Bruderblut*' and, on 12 March, German troops marched into Austria. Not only did they face no opposition, but they were actively welcomed by enthusiastic crowds. On 15 March in the Heldenplatz in Vienna, Hitler announced the absorption of Austria into the German Reich.

Argentina, assuming the World Cup would alternate between Europe and South America, had thought it would host the 1938 tournament. With the continent in turmoil, though, there was even less appetite for transatlantic travel on the part of the European powers than there had been in 1930. When Argentina then withdrew from the tournament, there were riots outside the AFA offices in Buenos Aires.

That left just two candidates for Fifa to decide between at their Congress in Berlin: Germany and France. Recognising both the contribution of Rimet to the World Cup and the fact that France was unlikely to exploit the tournament as Italy had in 1934, the Congress voted nineteen to four in France's favour.

The Berlin Olympics, which began two days later, gave a clear indication of the spectacle they'd managed to avoid.

But the political tensions inevitably had an impact. Spain, embroiled in civil war, did not enter. Japan pulled out following its invasion of China, leaving the Dutch East Indies to take the sole Asian berth. There were other withdrawals. Six Central and North American sides scratched, leaving Cuba to qualify. Egypt, who were part of European qualifying, objected to being asked to play during Ramadan, giving Romania a walkover. The Romanians, to widespread shock, then lost in the first round to Cuba, who were hammered 8–0 in the quarter-final by Sweden. And the British nations, as ever, remained aloof, England rejecting a late offer to step in for Austria. So the World Cup went ahead with fifteen teams, twelve of them European.

Although French administrators had played a leading role in the foundation of Fifa and the establishment of the World Cup, there was no great football culture in France. The first clubs had been founded by British expats in the late nineteenth century and while there were French devotees, notably Rimet, it was only after troops were exposed to the game in the trenches in the First World War that football gained anything approaching a widespread following. Major work had to be done to bring the infrastructure to the required level.[3]

No World Cup has been less about the self-aggrandisement of the hosts and yet no World Cup has ever been so overtly political, as exiles from Germany and Italy took the opportunity to make very public their opposition to fascism. It was almost midnight when the world champions Italy arrived in Marseille, but between 3,000 and 4,000 protesters had gathered at the station to greet them with boos and jeers.

Mussolini's invasion of Abyssinia in 1935 and subsequent

need for military support from Germany pushed Italy into a closer alliance with Hitler which, in turn, led to the imposition of anti-Jewish legislation. Pozzo absented himself from the directorate of the federation when it voted unanimously to expel 'non-Aryan' members in November 1938, making the excuse that he had a pre-existing commitment to coach the regional team of Lombardy before a friendly against Alsace. Alongside his friendships with Hugo Meisl and the Inter and Bologna coach Árpád Weisz, who died at Auschwitz,[4] that can be taken as evidence that he disapproved of the prevailing antisemitic mood – but equally that he felt powerless to do anything about it beyond making sure he didn't offer any overt endorsement.

The political situation had other consequences with a number of *oriundi*, most notably Enrique Guaita, returning to South America for fear of being called up to fight in Abyssinia. Orsi had already gone back to Argentina to look after his sick mother, while Monti had retired. Italy's squad in 1934 had been extremely experienced; Pozzo knew that there would have to be a complete overhaul for 1938.

There were changes in his life too. In November 1934, Italy travelled to London to play England, a meeting of the world champions and the team that believed itself the best in the world. It was a violent, unsatisfactory affair: Monti broke a bone in his foot in the second minute and England scored three times in the quarter of an hour that followed but, after two England players had also suffered broken bones, Italy came back in the second half and lost only 3–2. Two days before the game, Pozzo had sat down in his room at the Metropole Hotel and written to his second wife, Concetta Longo, whom he had married in 1930 and with whom he had a child, to tell her that he no longer loved her. They separated the following year but there was no possibility of divorce.

The evolution of his side went well. Italy won the Central

European International Cup for a second time in 1935 and, with what was essentially a student team, claimed Olympic gold in 1936. Slowly his team began to take shape. Three players from his Olympic side became regulars: the Juventus full-backs Alfredo Foni and Pietro Rava, and the Inter left-half Ugo Locatelli. Aldo Olivieri, *il Gatto Magico* (the Magic Cat), who had survived a fractured skull that required drilling to save his life and left him with chronic headaches, became the first-choice goalkeeper. His agility had been sharpened, it was said, by the ballet lessons imposed by his coach at Lucchese, Ernő Erbstein – like Weisz, one of the many Hungarian Jews who shaped Italian football between the early 1920s and the imposition of the Nuremberg Laws in 1938. Gino Colaussi took Orsi's place on the left wing and the prolific and versatile Lazio forward Silvio Piola came in at centre-forward. Only two players played in both the 1934 and 1938 finals, the inside-forwards Giovanni Ferrari and the great Giuseppe Meazza.

The German distaste for professionalism meant that, with the exception of Fritz Szepan, who had lost his amateur status after being caught up in an expenses scandal with Schalke in 1930, they could field their strongest side in the 1936 Olympics. It started well as they beat Luxembourg 9–0, a performance impressive enough to persuade Hitler that he should attend his first ever football match and watch their quarter-final against Norway at the Poststadion. He was joined by a number of senior Nazis including Joseph Goebbels, Hermann Göring and Rudolf Hess.

The assistant coach Sepp Herberger was not there. He had instead gone to watch Italy play Japan, the winners of which Germany would play if they got through. After watching Pozzo's side stroll to an 8–0 victory, Herberger returned to the team camp to find it deserted. He settled down to eat dinner and was tucking in to knuckle of pork and sauerkraut when another coach, Georg Knöpfle, walked in. Herberger knew from his face the news was bad: Germany had dominated and been picked off on the break, losing 2–0. Herberger pushed his plate away and never ate knuckle of pork again.[5] Hitler never went to another football match.

A scapegoat had to be found. Nerz, it was noted, had arranged only one friendly in the two months before the tournament – against Everton – and it was suggested his rigorous approach had left players exhausted. But there was a strange reluctance in German football to sack managers, so it was merely suggested that he might like to spend more time lecturing at the Academy for Physical Education. Herberger was appointed as Nerz's replacement but for eighteen awkward months they effectively shared the job.

Herberger was a curious figure. Although he joined the Nazi Party early, he seems to have done so as a matter of expediency, caring little for politics or for anything other than football – although, it should be said, he stood by his family doctor who was ostracised for having married a Jew, and once intervened when he saw a Jew being beaten up in the street. He left 361 files of notes but they deal almost exclusively with football. If Nazism or the war are mentioned at all, it is for the impact they have on his coaching schedule: air-raid warnings, he observed, were bad for players' stamina. He was quite prepared to fight the authorities when it came to protecting his players from obligatory reservists' training, but only because that made his life as coach harder.[6]

Under Herberger, German football moved away from the English model to something, if not quite Viennese, then at least prepared to incorporate the Schalke style of shorter passing. His side reached its apotheosis in Breslau (now Wrocław in Poland) on 16 May 1937 when, with Otto Siffling as a deep-lying centre-forward and three Schalke players including

Szepan in the forward line, they demolished Denmark 8–0. Nerz had distrusted Siffling because of his love of a drink, but he scored five in a little over half an hour. They became known as the *Breslau-Elf* and their impact was enormous. 'The robot style people like to pin on Germany sank into legend,' wrote the journalist Gerd Krämer. 'Artistic football triumphed.'[7]

Three days later, Schalke won 6–2 against Brentford, who had finished sixth in the English league that season. The German game seemed in rude health and, as the national side went on to win each of their four remaining games in 1937, there seemed little reason why they shouldn't make a serious challenge for the 1938 World Cup.

And then the Anschluss happened.

In February 1937, Hugo Meisl arranged a meeting at the offices of the ÖFB with the promising young forward Richard Fischer to resolve some confusion over his exact age. During their conversation, Meisl suffered a heart attack. Fischer rushed to seek help, but by the time a doctor arrived, Meisl was dead. He was fifty-five. With him died the *Wunderteam* and the golden age of Viennese football.

Its peak had probably come in 1932 but Austria finished second behind Italy in the third edition of the Central European International Cup, in 1935, and in May 1936, a day after Italian troops had marched into Addis Ababa, there was at last a win over England, 2–1 in Vienna. At the same time, Austrian clubs dominated the Mitropa Cup, winning it on four occasions between 1930 and 1936. Just because it was not quite as good as it had been at its absolute peak, and just because a declinist melancholy rather suited the mood of Viennese football, does not mean Austria would not still have been a serious contender at the 1938 World Cup.

But the political climate was beginning to impinge on

football. In March 1937, as Italian militia fought on Franco's side in Spain, prompting anti-Fascist demonstrations in the stands, Austria's Central European International Cup match against Italy had to be abandoned because of on-pitch violence. Clashes between Italian and Austrian clubs in the Mitropa Cup became common, reaching a climax when Mussolini cancelled Genoa's home leg of a tie against Admira after a brawl in the first leg. It was only three years since Mussolini had acted to guarantee Austrian independence but his increasing reliance on German support amid the chaos of the Abyssinian campaign changed the atmosphere completely.

Even after the Anschluss, Herberger would have preferred both Germany and Austria to send teams to the World Cup but that was never plausible; the German authorities were keen to deny any hint that Austria was not an integral and undeniable part of the German nation. And so the teams had to be merged, an act marked symbolically by the '*Versöhnungsspiel*' – the 'reconciliation game' on 3 April 1938 between the teams that had been Germany and Austria.

It was a match fraught with complication: what, after all, were the Austrian team to be called? To use the term 'Österreich', the name for Austria from the end of the First World War to 1938, was to acknowledge their difference, so instead they went either under the name 'Ostmark' – which had been used for the region between the tenth and twelfth centuries when, as part of the Holy Roman Empire, it was a march (borderland) on the eastern frontier of Saxony or Bavaria – or '*Gaumannschaft*' – 'regional team'.

It became a match obscured by myth. The *Gaumannschaft* won 2–0, with goals from Matthias Sindelar and Karl Sesta, but, from 1945 onwards, the game began to be manipulated into evidence that Austria, or at least Viennese football, had been an unwilling partner in Nazism. Sindelar died the following year, almost certainly as the result of a gas leak at his girlfriend's flat, but the circumstances were suspicious enough that those who wanted to believe him a martyr could claim he had been murdered or had killed himself. To a romantic liberal mind, to the Viennese emigrés in Paris, what could better symbolise Austria at the point of the Anschluss than this athlete-artist, the darling of the coffee-houses, being gassed? 'Sindelar followed the city, whose child and pride he was, to its death,' the theatre critic Alfred Polgar wrote in his obituary. 'He was so inextricably entwined with it that he had to die when it did ... For to live and play football in the downtrodden, broken, tormented city meant deceiving Vienna with a repulsive spectre of itself ... But how can one play football like that? And live, when a life without football is nothing?'[8]

After the war, it was claimed that Sindelar had demanded the *Gaumannschaft* should play in Austria's national colours of red and white as a gesture of defiance. But red and white was Austria's second kit. They, like Germany, played in white shirts and black shorts. Given Germany couldn't in any way identify as an away team, what else would they have worn? It was also claimed that Sindelar deliberately, almost sarcastically, missed a number of chances in the first half, and then, when they did finally score, he celebrated wildly in front of the Nazi Party box.

The truth seems far more mundane. All twenty-two players gave the Nazi salute during the anthem. The crowd, most of whom were Nazi Party members or soldiers, applauded politely at good play from both sides.[9] Sindelar, returning after injury, was described as being nearly back to his best by the *Völkischer Beobachter*,[10] but the *Neue Wiener Tagblatt* thought he had been insufficiently involved.[11] Contemporary reports make no suggestion that either his performance or his celebration were anything out of the ordinary. A week later, meanwhile, on the day that Austria voted overwhelmingly in a referendum to be incorporated into the Reich, *Völkischer Beobachter* published a photograph of Sindelar with the caption, 'We players thank our Führer from the bottom of our hearts and we will vote YES! [to unification with Germany].'[12] How much agency he had over that is impossible to say, but Sindelar certainly wasn't seen as a rebel.

At half-time, two Austrian reserves, Rudolf Zöhrer and Otto Marischka, had paraded around the pitch with a banner that read, 'Sportsmen vote YES.' There were speeches from Hermann Neubacher, the mayor of Vienna, and the *Reichssportführer* Hans von Tschammer und Osten. 'The Viennese football school [is] unique in the world,' Von Tschammer und Osten said, 'and we would be fools to destroy it.' Yet destroy it they did.

A day after the annexation of Austria was completed, the Zionist club Hakoah, champions in 1925, was wound up. Just over a month later, on 22 April, the Nazi authorities, obsessed by ideals of sporting amateurism and convinced that professionalism was somehow inherently Jewish, announced that all contracts in Austrian football would be terminated on 30 June. Soon after, Sindelar announced his retirement, which meant he would not be going to the World Cup as part of Herberger's squad. To those who wished to paint him as an anti-Nazi martyr, this was further evidence: had he not refused to play for Germany in the World Cup? Did his Gestapo file, which came to light after the war, not describe him as 'a Social Democrat and Jews' friend'?[13]

But Sindelar then accepted a job from the *Sportgauführer* Thomas Kozich to look after the Praterstadion, having already bought a café from a Jew forced to sell by the Nuremberg laws. His apologists insist he offered a fair price to Leopold Simon Drill but recent research has shown that he paid RM20,000 for a business initially priced at RM54,000.[14] Drill himself died at Theresienstadt on 26 March 1943.

It's hard to believe that Sindelar's withdrawal from the

World Cup squad could have been prompted by anti-Nazi sentiment when he was at the same time quite prepared to take a job and buy a café from the Nazi authorities. More likely, at thirty-five and with professionalism coming to an end, he simply decided to retire and reasoned that being integrated into a squad representing greater Germany was more bother than it was worth.

Herberger himself was well aware of the problems. It was not just that he had to meld two separate groups of players with all the resentment that was likely to cause, but that Germany and Austria played very different styles of football. While the 8–0 win over Denmark had shown what was possible with a fusion of a more technical style with Germany's traditional physicality, eight of the *Breslau-Elf* had played in the *Versöhnungsspiel* and lost to the Austrians' more mannered approach.

The two groups of players did not get on. There were regular reports of clashes in training. On one occasion, Pepi Stroh juggled the ball in the dressing-room and received rapturous applause from his fellow Austrians. A challenge had been laid down and was taken up by Szepan, who mimicked Stroh's virtuosity and then volleyed the ball against the wall, just above the heads of a clutch of Austrians, muttering, 'You arseholes,' as he did so.[15] This was never a team that was going to work together.

To make Herberger's task even harder, Austria was beginning to shed players. Pepi Bican had returned to his father's homeland of Czechoslovakia, although too late to complete the residency requirement to play for them in the World Cup. The forwards Karl Zischek and Camillo Jerusalem went to France. And the great captain of the Wunderteam, Walter Nausch, who had been offered a coaching job if he divorced his Jewish wife, was making plans to flee to Switzerland.

The authorities had no thought, though, for team-building. Herberger was told by the DFB president Felix Linnemann that he had to integrate the two squads and, when it came to the World Cup, pick six from one and five from the other. Others suggested the stopper centre-half was an English aberration and should be abandoned.[16] Herberger's notes suggest that, had he persuaded Sindelar to play, he would have adopted an Austrian-style deep-lying centre-forward.

For Germany's first game after the referendum, a 1–1 friendly draw against Portugal, Herberger picked eleven Germans. Three weeks later, he did the same again as Germany lost 6–3 in Berlin to England. The following day, he selected eleven Austrians for a game against Aston Villa. Befuddled by the English side's offside trap, Germany lost 3–2. Before the Anschluss, Germany had been unbeaten in ten; they went into the World Cup without a win in four.

Herberger picked nine Austrians in his twenty-two-man squad, intending to field Austrian forwards and German defenders to meet Linnemann's quota. Sesta was not among them, dropped following a series of training-ground rows. Herberger's line-up to face Switzerland in the first round did indeed comprise six Germans and five Austrians, one of whom, Hans Pesser, was sent off in extra time as the game finished 1–1. 'Germans and Austrians prefer to play against each other even when they're on the same team,' noted the German journalist Christian Eichler.[17]

The quota was maintained in the replay as well with the only Austrian outfielder to play in both games, Willi Hahnemann, who had never played for Austria itself, putting Germany ahead. An own-goal doubled their advantage but as in the first game, the Swiss, inspired by André Abegglen and a French crowd that was vociferously anti-Fascist, came back, three goals in quarter of an hour securing a 4–2 win.

Germany were out, the remnants of the *Breslau-Elf* and the *Wunderteam* scattered to the winds.

*

Károly Dietz, short, round-faced and bespectacled, had had something of a career in league football before and during the First World War while serving as head of the State Police Department of Budapest and then had been appointed national chief of police. Jailed during Béla Kun's short-lived Communist regime, he had resumed his position afterwards before quitting to work as a bookkeeper and then, after taking a law degree, setting up his own legal firm. He had never worked as a football coach when he was – inexplicably given the coaching talent available – appointed to manage Hungary at the 1934 World Cup.

Hungary's experience of global tournaments up to that point had not been happy. Although they had been one of football's boom nations in the years after the First World War – their league had professionalised in 1926 and their tactical influence had been felt across Europe and the Americas[18] – they had been embarrassed by Egypt at the 1924 Olympics, a defeat that prompted a parliamentary inquiry, and hadn't gone to the World Cup in 1930. In 1934, although there was a cathartic win over Egypt, Hungary were eliminated in the quarter-final by Austria.

As a result, nobody quite knew what to expect from Hungary in France, even though their clubs had won three of eleven Mitropa Cups. Dietz, perhaps recognising his own lack of experience, in 1937 appointed as his assistant Alfréd Schaffer, a legendary goalscorer, womaniser and bon viveur, who had had some success in his own coaching career. The collaboration went well, and Hungary won four and drew one of six games in 1937–38 before thrashing Greece 11–1 in their sole World Cup qualifier.

Hungary did not have the most testing start. Nine of the Dutch East Indies side made their international debuts in that game, including their goalkeeper Mo Heng Tan, who gained notoriety for the large doll he would carry as a mascot; he was also the only player to represent both the Dutch East Indies and, after the war, Indonesia. The Dutch East Indies were captained by Achmad Nawir, a qualified doctor, who played in glasses. Hungary's captain, György Sárosi, meanwhile, was nicknamed 'Doctor' but, although he was a qualified lawyer, he did not have a doctorate. Hungary won 6–0.

Despite an earthquake in Lille that shook tiles from the rooftops and plaster from the ceilings, and persistent problems with mosquitoes – so bad the goalkeeper Antal Szabó played with a large iodine stain on his face where he had been bitten – Hungary beat Switzerland 2–0 in the quarter-final.

Italy began their campaign in Marseille against Norway. When the team gave the Fascist salute before kick-off they were greeted with a hail of abuse. Pozzo told his players that they represented the *Patria*, not any political system and told them to give the salute again, which may have been good for team unity but confirmed in the minds of spectators that they were a Fascist team. Pozzo was perhaps saying what he had to say, but he didn't help matters when he claimed that Fascism had inculcated a 'spirit of self-denial and courage' among Italians.[19] Italy won, 2–1.

France awaited in the quarter-final at Colombes and won the toss to wear blue. Italy's usual change kit was white, but orders came from Rome that they were to wear black. Although they had done so against France in 1935 and against Yugoslavia shortly before the World Cup, the symbolism was deliberately provocative, and Italy were booed throughout. Pozzo made three changes and was rewarded with a much-improved performance and a 3–1 win.

After unremarkable performances in 1930 and 1934, 1938 was the tournament at which Brazil first made an impression. On a waterlogged pitch in Strasbourg, they beat Poland 6–5 after extra time, their great centre-forward Leônidas da Silva getting a hat-trick as Ernst Wilimowski became the first player ever to score four in a World Cup match. So treacherous was the surface that at one point Leônidas tried to play barefoot, only for the referee, the Swede Ivan Eklind, to make him put his boots back on.

Their quarter-final against Czechoslovakia was a rather different affair, so brutal it drew the nickname the Battle of Bordeaux. Two Brazilians and one Czechoslovak were sent off; Nejedlý suffered a broken leg from which he never truly recovered; Plánička stayed on despite breaking his arm; and, with an array of other injuries on both sides, it finished 1–1 after extra time. The replay, for which Brazil made nine changes and Czechoslovakia five, was far tamer and was won 2–1 by Brazil.

Pozzo had sent Gianpiero Combi, his goalkeeper from 1934, to watch the quarter-final and he returned with the assessment that Brazil were skilful but tactically 'zero' and advised playing on the counter.[20] They made eight changes for the replay, including leaving out Leônidas, a decision that has fuelled countless conspiracy theories, although it seems he was carrying a calf injury. He would return in the third-place play-off, his two goals in a 4–2 win over Sweden making him the tournament's top scorer.

Italy frustrated Brazil then struck twice in five minutes, first through Colaussi and then from the penalty spot after Domingos da Guia, one of the stars of the tournament, made a rare misjudgment and fouled Piola. The elastic on Meazza's shorts snapped as he placed the ball on the spot but, unruffled, clutching the waistband in one hand, he converted. Romeu's 87th-minute strike was too late to make a difference.

In the other semi-final Hungary produced an exceptional performance in beating Sweden 5–1. The centre-forward Gyula

Zsengellér scored twice, but the strength of the team seemed his link up with the two inside-forwards, Sárosi and the abrasive Géza Toldi. Yet Toldi was replaced for the final by the Újpest forward Jenő Vincze while Gyula Polgár, who had not played for the national team for a year, came in at full-back for his Ferencváros team-mate Lajos Korányi and György Szűcs replaced József Turay at centre-half.

As Italy travelled to the stadium for the final, Pozzo caught sight of a familiar face in the crowd: Matthias Sindelar. He sent Monzeglio from the bus to go and get him and the great symbol of the old Vienna ended up watching the final with the Italy reserves – a detail that rather complicates Sindelar's status as an anti-Fascist hero. The truth is that, whatever people tried to make him, Sindelar was essentially a footballer trying to get by, the need to make a living and the bonds of old friendships outweighing any ideology. Pozzo, similarly, was for a long time after the war regarded as an awkward reminder of the Fascist past, but he helped provide food to partisans and helped Allied prisoners of war escape to Switzerland. 'They forced a patriot to hope the war would be lost,' he said.[21]

Before anything else, Pozzo was a football coach – although he had never formally qualified, something which had never been an issue until that final. A complaint had been raised and, given unqualified coaches were banned from passing on instruction, he had to sit between the president of the Belgian federation and a Uruguayan delegate, who were supposed to ensure he didn't offer any dangerously unsanctioned advice. Using a mixture of Piedmontese and Genovese dialect, though, he managed to get his message to his assistant, Luigi Burlando, who was qualified and so permitted to stand on the touchline.

With Michele Andreolo marking Sárosi, Italy proved far too quick for Hungary and two goals each for Colaussi and Piola sealed a 4–2 win. *Nemzeti Sport*'s response to the defeat was relatively measured, preferring to celebrate the achievement of reaching the final than probe too deeply into the reasons behind Hungary's defeat. 'We were a very serious opponent for the Italians,' their report said, 'but it cannot be disputed: the right side won. Our direct defence did everything but the game of our forward line could not succeed against the tough Italian rearguard.'[22]

But three days later, the newspaper did raise the mystery of Toldi's absence, printing a cartoon that showed Pozzo as a knight in a besieged castle gratefully throwing a bucket of boiling water over Dietz, as he sat on a donkey marked 'Vincze' armed with just a slingshot while a huge battering ram marked 'Toldi' stood unused behind him.

So what was going on? Turay had been struggling with an ankle injury, although he had played the previous three games without apparent problems, but there were no questions about Toldi's fitness. Gyula Zsengellér told his son Zsolt that Toldi was dropped following a half-hour meeting between Dietz and Pozzo and other Italian officials, seemingly because it was felt his aggressive style would not be in keeping with the 'continuing spirit of friendship between the two countries'. At that, Korányi and Turay supposedly pulled out in protest.[23] Toldi barely mentions the World Cup in his 1962 Danish-language memoir.[24]

In the paranoid, conspiracy-obsessed world of Communist Hungary, the theory that the game had been fixed began to circulate. Péter Szegedi, who co-wrote the definitive work on the tournament, is sceptical:

> The idea has come up that maybe the Hungarian coach got an order from Budapest to throw the match, so that the Hungarian political powers could be assured of Italy's good-will towards their desire to revise Trianon [the post-First World War treaty under which Hungary ceded vast tracts of its territory]. No proof of that has been presented and

> it is not likely that politics would have interfered in such a direct way. And we haven't even mentioned the question that rightfully arises: if the Italians had to be made to win the match, why didn't the coach leave out the best Hungarian forward, Sárosi, or Zsengellér, who had scored five goals in the tournament?[25, 26]

It's at least as likely, as Szegedi said, that Dietz 'wanted to offer evidence of his own genius with unexpected moves'.

The World Cup was the first of three great Italian sporting triumphs in Paris that June. The thoroughbred Nearco, ridden by Pietro Gubellini, won the Grand Prix de Paris and then the cyclist Gino Bartali won the Tour de France. For Fascists determined to view sport as an expression of Italian superiority, there seemed plenty of evidence.

The players celebrated with Pozzo in his room and then returned to Italy with a life-size bronze statue of a cockerel given them by Italian expats, not all of whom, apparently, were scandalised by their symbolic role as agents of the Fascist state. In 1934, when Mussolini had asked the players what they wanted as a reward for winning, Monzeglio had blurted out that he desired nothing more than a signed photograph of il Duce. This time the players thought about it in advance and asked for lifetime rail passes, which they were granted. Starace gave the players a signed photograph of himself as well.

Thankfully, other members of the Italian delegation were less self-absorbed. Ottorino Barassi undertook to look after the Jules Rimet trophy until the following World Cup and, when Germany invaded Italy to head off the Allied invasion in September 1943, smuggled the trophy out of the bank where it was being kept, took it home and hid it in a shoebox under his bed to keep it out of Nazi hands.

Barassi had helped organise the 1934 World Cup and when the Brazilian federation sought his help in 1950, he was able to hand it over. Despite all the turmoil and tragedy, the World Cup survived.

1950

HUBRIS AND THE SALAMI SALESMAN

'You players,' the mayor of Rio de Janeiro, Ângelo Mendes de Moraes, said before kick-off, 'will be hailed as champions by millions of compatriots in just a few hours! ... You, who I already salute as victors! I fulfilled my promise, building this stadium. Now, do your duty and win the World Cup!'[1]

Hubris was everywhere. Everybody thought Brazil would get at least the draw they needed against Uruguay to win the 1950 World Cup. After all, this was being played in the Maracanã, 'the biggest and most perfect stadium in the world,' as *A Noite* had it, 'dignifying the competence of its people'.[2] As various candidates in local elections cosied up to the Brazil squad, most spoke of them as inevitable winners. 'World football has a new master,' boasted the *Diário Carioca*. 'Brazil is the name of the new star.'[3]

On the day of the game, *O Mundo*'s early editions printed a photograph of the Brazil team with the headline, 'These are the world champions!' Legend has it that the Uruguay captain Obdulio Varela bought up every copy from the hotel newsstand and had his team-mates urinate on them. One of the Uruguayan football federation's delegates supposedly told players that their job was simply to maintain their dignity, losing by no more than four and not having anybody sent off.[4]

Only one person seemed to have any doubts, Brazil's coach Flávio Costa. 'I'm afraid,' he said, 'that my players will take the field on Sunday as though they already had the championship shield sewn on their jersey.'[5] But there was little evidence of complacency as the game kicked off. Varela had urged Uruguay's players to look at their opponents and not at the crowd, to remember that the game was about eleven against eleven, but the story has it that the winger Júlio Pérez wet himself in fear during the anthems.

At half-time it was still 0–0, but an incident had occurred that would later be imbued with great significance: Varela had punched – or slapped, or stuck his finger up the nose of, depending which version you prefer – the Brazil left-back Bigode. Some say he warned him he would take dire retribution if he kicked Uruguay's winger Alcides Ghiggia again.[6] Both players said it was barely more than a tap and played down its significance but in the mythology of Maracanazo, as that game became known, it was vital in resetting the psychological balance – and perhaps in making Bigode tentative when Ghiggia ran at him.

But none of that seemed to matter as Friaça put Brazil ahead two minutes after half-time. Varela, aware of the danger of being overwhelmed if the game kicked off again immediately, protested vehemently that the goal had been offside, demanding an interpreter to make his case. Seven minutes passed before Uruguay kicked off, and some of Brazil's momentum had gone. Still, so long as Brazil did not concede twice, they would be world champions.

The first blow came after 66 minutes. Varela released Ghiggia, who beat Bigode and crossed for Juan Schiaffino, who finished into the top right-hand corner. Anxiety fell across the stadium. Ghiggia darted down the right again and cut into the box. Brazil's goalkeeper Moacir Barbosa anticipated a cross and was wrongfooted as Ghiggia drove a shot in at the near post, chalk puffing up like gunsmoke as the ball scuffed the line. The Brazilian commentator Luiz Mendes couldn't believe it. Six times he said, '*Gol do Uruguay*,' in varying intonations, as though passing through phases of grief, from disbelief to fury to eventual gloomy acceptance. Brazil still had 11 minutes to score a goal that would have won the World Cup, but they were shattered, finished, and the stadium was silent.

The planned presentation was abandoned by common consent. There was no guard of honour, no anthems, just a disbelieving pitch invasion. Amid the chaos, Jules Rimet found Varela on the pitch, shook his hand, and gave him the trophy that now bore his name – tribute to his twenty-five years as president of Fifa. Uruguay's players had been warned not to go out that night for fear of reprisal but having demolished the hotel's supply of wine, they went drinking in Rio and found themselves largely ignored. A bust of the mayor was knocked over but by and large Brazil's fans were too stunned, too devastated to think of doing anything but wander around in despair.[7]

Immediately, it was recognised this was no ordinary defeat. 'It is a Waterloo of the tropics,' Paulo Perdigão wrote in his extraordinary meditation on the Maracanazo, *Anatomia de una derrota*, 'and its history our *Götterdämmerung*.'[8] Roberto Muylaert, in his biography of Barbosa, described the footage of Ghiggia advancing into the box as the equivalent of the Zapruder footage of the assassination of John F. Kennedy: the two clips, he said, shared 'the same movement, rhythm . . . the same inexorable trajectory'.[9]

'Everywhere has its irremediable national catastrophe, something like a Hiroshima,' wrote the playwright Nelson Rodrigues. 'Our catastrophe, our Hiroshima, was the defeat to Uruguay in 1950.'[10] The claim is obviously overstated, distasteful even, but just as the World Cup win in 1970, Brazil's third title, would be compared to the moon landings, a major politico-cultural event in the history of another nation, so there was an urge to compare the Maracanazo to huge events elsewhere, to a horror beyond comprehension.

There was a sense in which all Brazilian history had been building to that game at the Maracanã. The Portuguese court, fleeing Napoleon, had transplanted itself to Rio in 1808, ruling the Empire from there. Although a notional independence was secured in 1822 when Dom Pedro I returned to Portugal, his son, Dom Pedro II, stayed behind to run the Brazilian Empire. Only when he was deposed in 1889 and the Brazilian Republic declared was there a real break with Europe. That perhaps slowed the process of nation-building, which was never going to be straightforward in a country as vast and diverse as Brazil. Football was crucial to the creation of Brazil, reaching across class and, eventually, racial divides. And, critically, it was something of which Brazil could be proud.

The legend has it that football was introduced to Brazil in 1894 by Charles Miller, the son of a Scottish railway engineer based in Rio and a Brazilian mother of English descent. He was sent to public school near Southampton and supposedly stepped off the boat back clutching two balls and a copy of the laws of the game, announcing to his sceptical father he had graduated in football. In so doing, he established the sense of Brazilian football as impertinent and disdainful of authority.[11]

The first entity that could be considered a Brazil national team emerged in 1914 as a selection of players from Rio and São Paulo took on a touring Exeter City team, and Brazil then took part in the inaugural Campeonato Sudamericano in 1916, finishing third after two draws and a defeat to the champions Uruguay. They won the third iteration of the tournament on home soil in 1919 and again in 1922, when the championship was part of the Independence Centenary International Exposition, an attempt to raise the profile of the nation as a whole by transforming Rio.

Football was woven into Brazilian life. In his 1928 novel *Macunaíma*, Mário de Andrade identified football alongside the coffee bug and the cotton boll weevil as one of the three 'main pests' of Brazilian life.[12] Yet in truth, for a long time Brazil remained a minor power, some distance behind Uruguay and Argentina. They didn't win a third Campeonato Sudamericano until 1949, again as host, by which point the political landscape had changed radically.

Getúlio Vargas, the governor of Rio Grande do Sul, had seized power after contesting the result of the 1930 presidential election. He dissolved Congress, purged the army of regionalists and replaced all but one state governor in a programme of centralisation. Vargas ruled by emergency decree until a new constitution was drawn up in 1933. It gave women the vote and allowed Vargas to rule as president until 1937 when elections were supposed to be held. Vargas, though, staged a pre-emptive coup, surrounding Congress with troops and declaring the Estado Novo on radio.

Political parties were outlawed, civil rights curtailed and state flags burned by federal officials, their ashes being kept in an urn at the Museu Histórico. As a semi-corporatist model not unlike that of Italy under Mussolini was instituted, elected state governors and city mayors were deposed and replaced by *interventores* appointed by the central administration in Rio de Janeiro. A minimum wage was introduced in return for government control of trades unions, protectionist trade barriers were imposed and a wave of state-sponsored infrastructure projects launched. Vargas lacked the charisma for a cult of personality and so there was a conscious effort to invoke *brasilidade*, a spirit of Brazilianness. Portuguese was made compulsory in schools. Music, publishing and film production were placed under the control of state bodies, while the government not only controlled the output of radio, the medium that united the nation, but set up speakers in public places.

Nothing was better at projecting *brasilidade* than football, the universal cultural pursuit and nothing those speakers broadcast was more popular than football commentary, something that was very apparent during the 1938 World Cup as vast crowds gathered in squares to listen to updates being sent by telegram. They would then flock to cinemas a couple of days after each game to watch footage flown back from France.

Football, very obviously, was an important political tool. Luiz Aranha, who had backed Vargas in the coup in 1930 and whose brother Oswaldo was finance minister, became president of the Brazilian sports confederation (CBD). A third brother, Citro, became president of Vasco da Gama, whose São Januário stadium began to be used to stage civic events and vast cultural displays, which often culminated in football.

Yet for all the government support for football, what transformed Brazil into a major footballing power was the arrival in Rio in 1937 of the Hungarian Dori Kürschner, as he was appointed coach of Flamengo. Kürschner had been a gifted centre-half at MTK and later returned to the club as a coach, initially working under the great Jimmy Hogan before embarking on a successful career in Germany and Switzerland. By the mid-thirties he was highly respected, not only as a coach but as a trusted fixer, somebody who could help struggling clubs secure a loan or find jobs for out-of-work former players. Then, abruptly, he moved to Rio after being offered the Flamengo job by their ambitious president José Bastos Padilha. The circumstances in which he emigrated and his reasons for doing so remain opaque, although the money would have been exceptional and it's reasonable to speculate that, as a prominent Jew, he was uneasy about rising antisemitism in Europe.

Kürschner lasted little more than a year at Flamengo before

being sacked, but his influence was profound. His attempts to instil a central-European style W-M formation were resisted by players and fans who regarded it as overly defensive, while his assistant Flávio Costa, whom he had replaced as coach, regularly briefed against him in the press, taking advantage of Kürschner's lack of Portuguese. But Costa learned from him and when he took over again, he implemented what he insisted was a radically new way of playing, the *diagonal*. In reality, it was a minor modification of the W-M, just tilting the midfield square so one wing-half operated slightly deeper and one inside-forward slightly more advanced, a vital step in the transition from W-M to the 4-2-4 with which Brazil would, two decades later, conquer the world.[13]

After a brief stint at Botafogo, Kürschner contracted a virus and died in 1941. Flávio Costa went on to great success, winning five Carioca* titles with Flamengo and three with Vasco da Gama, becoming national coach in 1944.

As Uruguay and Argentina had recognised, there was another political aspect to football, the sense of the national team and the way it played as somehow representative of the nation. So how was Brazilian national character expressed through football? 'Our style of football,' the sociologist Gilberto Freyre wrote in *Correio da Manhã* the day before the 1938 semi-final, 'seems to contrast with the European style because of a set of characteristics such as surprise, craftiness, shrewdness, readiness . . . individual brilliance and spontaneity, all of which express our "mulattoism" . . .'[14] Where European football was Apollonian, Brazilian football was Dionysian, Freyre argued, coining the term '*futebol arte*' to describe what he regarded as a distinctively Brazilian preference for football that was aesthetically pleasing rather than necessarily bringing victory.

* That is to say, from the state of Rio de Janeiro.

In *Casa-Grande e Senzala* (*The Masters and the Slaves*), Freyre set out his theory of lusotropicalism, romanticising miscegenation and arguing that mulattoism was a positive force that should be celebrated as the defining characteristic of Brazil. His ideas may be widely disregarded today – they downplay the racism that has always permeated Brazilian society and tend to ignore the brutality of slavery[15] – but had a huge influence over Brazilian self-perception.

They were popularised in a football context by the journalist Mário Filho (after whom the Maracanã is officially named), both through his journalism and his 1947 book *O Negro no Futebol Brazileiro* in which he argued that 'mulattoism' lay at the heart of Brazilian football. For many, this became fused with the notion of the '*malandro*', a *carioca* archetype of a trickster, charismatic and clever, happy to sidestep societal norms. And that in turn has a specific relevance in capoeira, the acrobatic Afro-Brazilian martial art, in which *malandragem* – the capacity to understand and then deceive the opponent – is a key tenet, linked to Oxóssi, the Yoruba spirit of the hunt.* 'My older brother,' said the forward Domingos da Guia, one of the stars of the 1938 World Cup, 'used to tell me: a *malandro* is a cat that always lands on his feet. I used to be really good at dancing and that helped me on the field. I swerved a lot.'[17] He said that one way he had of dribbling consciously imitated the samba.

Picking through the overlapping and interlinked strands is complex, but the basic point is an optimistic belief that the commingling of races in Brazil had produced a unique and superior culture. Writing in the *Jornal dos Sports*, the novelist José Lins do Rego, for instance, wrote that he believed 'in

* 'Oxóssi' is the Portuguese rendering of Oshosi, an orisha (a divine spirit in the Yoruba religion of West Africa, and subsequently in related faiths of Latin America) linked with the hunt, the forest, animals and wealth and associated with astuteness and craftiness. In Rio de Janeiro, Oxóssi is syncretised with St Sebastian, the patron of the city.

Brazil, in the eugenic quality of our mestizos, in the energy and intelligence of the men that the Brazilian land forged with diverse bloods, giving them originality that one day will shock the world'.[18]

Vargas saw the hosting of the World Cup as the perfect way to promote *brasilidade* and an official bid to host the 1942 tournament was made in 1937. Germany had already declared its intention to bid and Argentina would subsequently do so. Given Brazil had been the only South American nation to travel to France for the 1938 tournament, it seems likely, the lobbying power of the Nazis notwithstanding, that Vargas's willingness to pour state resources into the project would have been decisive. War, though, meant two editions were missed and, with Fifa desperate to keep the tournament going despite the weariness of the international community, Brazil was unopposed as it bid to host in 1950.

Brazil maintained a position of official neutrality when the Second World War began in 1939 but, by 1942, economic pressure applied by the US and the UK had persuaded Vargas to side with the Allies. Fighting on the same side as the USSR meant the Communist Party had, at least briefly, to be recognised – one of its members was Oscar Niemeyer, the architect whose work designing the new capital of Brasilia would make him one of the most globally celebrated non-footballing Brazilians – and with Vargas's authoritarianism rendered incoherent by Brazil's new alliances, he was forced to step down in October 1945. He effectively anointed General Eurico Dutra as his successor and it was early in Dutra's reign that Brazil was confirmed as host for 1950. He would remain as president until the end of the year.

The 1950 World Cup was envisioned as a way for Brazil to announce its modernity and relevance to the world. Mário

Filho, whose brother Nelson Rodríguez would make the Hiroshima comparison, was aware of the impression made by the venues of previous finals and insisted Brazil had to build a vast new stadium in Rio for the World Cup. In *Jornal dos Sports* he argued that however important hospitals, schools and roads may be, government had also to consider posterity. 'This stadium,' he said, 'will be a gift from this generation to the next, strengthening the human wealth of Brazil.'[19] Work began on the Maracanã in August 1948. One of the first structures made of concrete in Brazil, with hidden steel cantilevers, it had an official capacity of 160,000 and was startlingly modern. Mário Filho spoke of Brazil acquiring a new soul.

Only thirty-one of Fifa's seventy-three members entered and there was a spate of withdrawals. Japan had been suspended in 1945 for a failure to pay its subscription while the German football federation had been disbanded at the end of the war. Neither would be readmitted until 1950 and it would be two further years before East Germany joined.

Uruguay, Bolivia, Chile and Paraguay qualified without playing a game, and India looked to have done the same when Burma, Indonesia and the Philippines scratched, only to then decide they couldn't afford the travel (the oft-repeated claim that they withdrew after being told they would not be allowed to play barefoot is a myth). Scotland qualified by finishing runners-up in the Home Championship, as the British nations finally decided to join in, but refused to take up their place because they hadn't won the competition. Turkey eliminated Syria and qualified when Austria withdrew, only themselves then to withdraw. France, Portugal and Ireland were invited to take up vacant slots; only France accepted, but pulled out when they realised how much travel would be involved even after getting to Brazil. All of which meant the tournament eventually went ahead with thirteen teams, arranged into four groups: two of four teams, one of three and, thanks to France's late withdrawal, one of two.

Brazil's confidence was understandable. Flávio Costa had led them to that third Campeonato Sudamericano title in 1949. Argentina weren't there but it was a crushing victory nonetheless as Brazil won six of their seven games in the group, scoring thirty-nine goals as they did so. A play-off against Paraguay for the title at the São Januário was won 7–0.

The World Cup opening ceremony was spectacular, although in hindsight it seems almost comically ill-omened. According to the English referee, Arthur Ellis, the twenty-one-gun salute showered him and the players in a fine plaster dust, while the message of peace symbolised by the release of 5,000 doves contrasted awkwardly with the simultaneous incursion of Communist forces across the 38th Parallel, precipitating the Korean War. Not that many Brazilians noticed as their side swept to a 4–0 victory over Mexico, Ademir scoring twice.

They played their second game in São Paulo, brought in three *paulista* players for diplomatic reasons and were held to a 2–2 draw by Switzerland. The Swedish embassy in Rio was attacked in response by enraged and confused locals. The draw meant jeopardy: only the top side progressed to the final group and Yugoslavia had won both of their opening games.

Back at the Maracanã, Costa returned to something much closer to his original line-up with nine *carioca* players. The corridor outside the dressing-rooms flooded, and players had to walk over a wooden plank to reach the tunnel. As he crossed on his way out for kick-off, Yugoslavia's captain Rajko Mitić banged his head on an exposed girder. The Welsh referee Mervyn Griffiths, who would become notorious as a linesman in the 1954 final, insisted the game should kick off as scheduled and, by the time Mitić had got onto the pitch after having the wound stitched, Ademir had given Brazil the lead. Yugoslavia put Brazil under severe pressure but Zizinho's goal midway through the second half made the game safe.

England, having finally deigned to turn up, were soon embarrassed. Although they beat Chile 2–0 in their opening game, they then lost 1–0 to a USA team of semi-professionals. Much has been made of the absence of Stanley Matthews, who had missed the opener because he was on an FA tour of Canada (which itself suggests England still regarded the World Cup with a degree of disdain), but England still had more than enough talent to at least pass comfortably through the first phase. Having arrived in Brazil only a couple of days before the tournament began, enough time to moan about the food but not to acclimatise, England were further unsettled by the tight, rutted pitch in Belo Horizonte. They hit the post twice, were repeatedly thwarted by the US keeper Frank Borghi, believed Jimmy Mullen had scored only for the referee to rule the ball had not crossed the line, and lost to a diving header from the Haiti-born Joe Gaetjens that diverted a Walter Bahr cross-shot past Bert Williams. Still England could have forced a play-off for qualification by beating Spain in their final game, but they lost 1–0.

A 3–2 win over an Italy side devastated by the Superga air crash[20] helped Sweden through their three-team group while Uruguay, who had qualified without playing a game, completed the final four by battering Bolivia 8–0 in their only group match.

In their first game in the final group, Brazil beat Sweden 7–1, with Ademir scoring four. Uruguay were trailing Spain 2–1 with 17 minutes to go when Varela got the equaliser. Brazil then thrashed Spain 6–1, while Uruguay were 2–1 down to Sweden with 13 minutes remaining when Óscar Miguez scored twice in eight minutes to ensure the final game would at least be a contest.

Even if Uruguay hadn't had to travel from São Paulo to Rio, it would have been hard to make a case for them. They hadn't played a qualifier, their only group game had been against a sub-par Bolivia and they'd then struggled against two sides Brazil had demolished. Only an itinerant Hungarian coach called Imre Hirschl seemed unconvinced by Brazil, describing them as 'a team of worn-out players' in the Uruguayan press,[21] although that was admittedly on the morning before Brazil hammered Sweden. But Hirschl would have a vital role to play.

Uruguay's road to the Maracanazo had begun six years earlier at a disciplinary hearing of the Argentinian football association that looked into an attempt to fix a game between Ferro Carril Oeste and Banfield. Nine men were convicted of 'sporting immorality' and given life bans from the Argentinian game; among them was Hirschl.

Hirschl had been born in Apostag, a Jewish community south of Budapest, in 1900. Aged sixteen, he'd lied about his age and signed up to fight alongside his elder brother in a Zionist regiment under British command in Palestine. He was shot in the wrist and suffered shrapnel wounds to the chest from a grenade attack. When he returned to Budapest, he worked as a salesman for his uncles' salami business.[22] In 1929, he emigrated to Brazil, landing at Santos, and was living in poverty when Hakoah New York passed through on tour. They were a team comprising mainly central European Jews who had been drawn to play in the American Soccer League and had embarked on a money-raising tour as economic conditions deteriorated in the wake of the Wall Street Crash.

Short of money and jobless, Hirschl approached the ageing centre-half Béla Guttmann, later a great coach who would lead Benfica to two European Cups, and asked for help. He gave Guttmann a massage and, on his recommendation, was taken on by Hakoah as a masseur. He accompanied the team south, through Uruguay to Argentina but, in Buenos Aires, with money tight, Hakoah were forced to release him. Hirschl, though, had been seen with the club and, exaggerating his role, managed to persuade the directors of Gimnasia y Esgrima La Plata to give him a job. According to Guttmann, Hirschl's plan was to get sacked and use his pay-off to bring his wife and son over from Budapest, so he picked players out of position – but they won. 'Hirschl was scratching his head, then in the second match he made an even bigger mess of the team,' said Guttmann. 'And they won again! ... People started to praise him. He was labelled a great coach.'[23]

It's a lovely story, and the idea of Hirschl as a sort of footballing version of Max Bialystock from *The Producers*, inadvertently successful as he desperately sought failure, an appealing one. But it's almost certainly untrue. What seems to have happened is that Hirschl implemented a more European approach and dropped a number of senior players in favour of youngsters more willing to accept his tactical instruction, leading to claims he was picking wilfully eccentric teams. But it worked. Gimnasia narrowly missed out on the title in 1933[24] but Hirschl had caught the eye and he was appointed manager of River Plate, winning a double with them in 1936: a remarkable rise for somebody who, three years earlier, had zero experience of coaching.

He loved Buenos Aires and the ban imposed in 1944 for having agreed to act as a go-between in the match-fixing case was a grievous blow. It was overturned by the General Inspection of Justice on 10 May that year, but the stigma was such that, if he was to continue to be involved in football, Hirschl had to leave Argentina. He went first to Brazil, pursuing an itinerant career, never staying anywhere long and then, in 1949, he was appointed manager of Peñarol in Montevideo, succeeding the Englishman Randolph Galloway, whose attempts to impose a man-marking W-M had led to the players going on strike.[25]

One of Hirschl's first acts was to promote the twenty-two-year-old Alcides Ghiggia, preferring him, to widespread surprise, over a pair of forwards who had played for Uruguay.[26] Ghiggia would prove a vital piece of the '*escuadrilla de la muerta*' (death squad) forward line that carried Peñarol to all three domestic titles in 1949. Hirschl, said Ghiggia, was 'a man of very precise and original ideas', who possessed an 'enormous discipline and a tactical and distinctly attacking football'.[27]

When Enrique Fernández resigned as national coach in March 1950, the football federation lined up Hirschl. But those of a Nacional persuasion could not accept somebody with such close ties to Peñarol. Although Hirschl was appointed in secret in April, the decision was never ratified and, on 23 May, five weeks before the World Cup began, Uruguay turned to Juan López.[28] But Varela remained the dominant presence in the dressing-room and, having initially been sceptical, he had been won over by Hirschl and remained in regular contact with him throughout the tournament, taking tactical advice.

Six of the players who started the final match against Brazil, including both goalscorers, were from Peñarol. Varela had the side adopt a more defensive line-up, seemingly dropping behind the defensive line to operate as something akin to a *libero* in a 1-3-3-3 as one wing-half fell in between the full-backs and the inside-forwards dropped deep alongside the other.[29] Nothing in the contemporary Uruguayan media coverage gave Hirschl much credit, but then why would they highlight the (unofficial) influence of a Hungarian who had spent much of his life in Argentina when the prevailing narrative was of the victory of 'Uruguayan players and Uruguayan tactics'?[30]

But Ghiggia had no doubt as to Hirschl's importance. 'He was a real expert,' he said. 'He understood the language of footballers, he was very prepared, he knew everything about football. He was an intelligent man and we loved him very much.'[31] And Flávio Costa always acknowledged that, while complacency had been a factor, Brazil fundamentally were tactically outthought.[32]

The sense of stupefaction did not last long. The mood in Rio on the night of the final may have been of stunned disbelief, but there was a need for scapegoats.

The newspaper *Correio de Manhã* decided Brazil's white shirts were unlucky and, with the backing of the CBD, launched a competition to design a new one using all four colours of the national flag. It was won by a nineteen-year-old illustrator for a local newspaper from a small town on the southern border with Uruguay, Aldyr Garcia Schlee, who had not even watched the final. He later became an award-wining novelist and, in his 1995 collection of short stories *Cuentos de Fútbol*, describes how, on the afternoon of the game, he had crossed the Mauá Bridge into Uruguay to go to the cinema. The film was interrupted for an announcement that Uruguay had become world champions, at which the audience stood up and sang the national anthem.[33] While he lived in Brazil, when it came to football Schlee was always a Uruguay fan and, although he won awards for journalism in Brazil, he was more popular as a writer in Uruguay.[34] Yet it was he who gave Brazil their iconic yellow shirts (originally with green collar and cuffs), blue shorts and white socks.

But others wanted players to blame. Barbosa may have been voted goalkeeper of the tournament, but had he not committed the cardinal sin of letting in a shot at his near post? Had Bigode not been intimidated by Varela, and then let Ghiggia get away from him? It happened Barbosa and Bigode were two of Brazil's three black players and Juvenal, the third, also found himself a target. No matter that Varela, the great leader of the side that had won, was black, the racist theory ran that black players were weak, a fatal flaw that would inevitably undermine the nation.[35]

It was Barbosa who had it worst. He told a documentary of going into a shop in 1970 and hearing a woman point him out to her son: 'He's the man who made all of Brazil cry.'[36] He continued to suffer up to his death in 2000. 'Under Brazilian law, the maximum sentence is thirty years,' he said, 'but I served fifty.'[37] In his biography of the goalkeeper, Roberto Muylaert describes an expiatory barbecue Barbosa held for friends in 1963 at which he burned the goalposts. Whether that actually happened – and there seems some scepticism – it didn't help. Barbosa was regarded as such an emblem of failure that when the BBC tried to take him to the Brazil camp before the 1994 World Cup, he was turned away in case his misfortune proved contagious. One goal and his life was ruined.

But why did the hurt run so deep? Why does the Maracanazo continue to resonate more than any of Brazil's footballing triumphs? 'It is perhaps the greatest tragedy in contemporary Brazilian history,' said the anthropologist Roberto DaMatta, 'because it happened collectively and brought a united vision of the loss of a historic opportunity. Because it happened at the beginning of a decade in which Brazil was looking to assert itself as a nation with a great future. The result was a tireless search for explication of, and blame for, the shameful defeat.'[38]

The 1950 World Cup was supposed to be Brazil's coming out as a nation, its announcement of itself to the post-war world as a modern, thriving country, but the defeat, or rather the reaction to it, exploded Freyre's racially harmonious ideal. What the Maracanazo made clear was that black players were still regarded as a potential liability; when things went wrong, it would still be them who took the blame. In defeat, Brazil's optimistic self-image was exposed as sham.

1954

'CALL ME CRAZY'

The anxious eleven-year-old narrator of Friedrich Christian Delius's 1994 novella *Der Sonntag, an dem ich Weltmeister wurde* (*The Sunday I Became World Champion*) is fearful of his father, of God and of pretty much everything else. He suffers from psoriasis and nosebleeds and has a stutter that makes him even shier than he would already have been. On the morning of Sunday, 4 July 1954, he sits through a church service led by his father, a pastor, and endures agonies of fevered anticipation, waiting for the moment when he can turn on the radio to listen to commentary of the World Cup final, asking himself constantly, 'Could the Hungarians be stopped?'

As West Germany come back from 2–0 down, the narrator is transported by a quasi-religious ecstasy. His stutter disappears so that when his father asks him the score, he is able to respond fluently, even though the repeated 'z' sound in '*zwei zu zwei*' is something with which he usually struggles.[1]

The metaphor is a little too obvious, knowingly so: West Germany, sick and full of self-doubt, wracked by guilt, afraid to express itself, finding in a wholly unexpected World Cup triumph a measure of self-respect that allows it to re-engage with the world. 'We've shown the world what we're worth, we're back, losers no more . . .' as Günter Grass wrote.[2] Or as the feeling was popularly expressed: '*Wir sind wieder wer!*' (We are somebody again!) But then the narrator goes outside and realises 'everything was as if nothing had changed with this World Cup.'[3]

The use of the World Cup win as a metaphor has itself become a cliché; what better way to express the *Wirtschaftswunder*, the economic miracle of West Germany's boom in the fifties, than through the tournament? How better to encapsulate rebirth of the nation than through the comeback against Hungary? Take for example Rainer Werner Fassbinder's 1979 film *Die Ehe der Maria Braun* (*The Marriage of Maria Braun*), in which the eponymous heroine, while continuing to love and insist she remains loyal to her imprisoned husband, has affairs with a US serviceman and then a rich factory owner, becoming wealthier but also increasingly unfeeling. The radio is regularly heard in the background: first appeals for missing German soldiers, then news reports about the chancellor Konrad Adenauer's rearmament negotiations before, in the climactic scene as Maria's financial future is secured, Herbert Zimmermann's famous commentary on the final: from being literally lost during the war to slow and awkward self-assertion to glorious stepping out as a nation again. But as the final whistle blows to confirm West Germany's victory, Maria's bourgeois house explodes, killing both her and her recently released husband. The implication is that the cost of recovery, or at least this form of recovery, is too great, leading to alienation and ultimately devastation.

Das Wunder von Bern (the miracle of Bern) has become a familiar part of the story of post-war Germany, the question less whether it was a significant step than exactly what that significance was. Hindsight, certainly, has added nuance, but even at the time there was an unease about the success with *Süddeutsche Zeitung*, as though worried that bellicose nationalism could at any moment be unleashed, urging restraint.

'Well now, celebrate the players,' it cautioned. 'But let's sober up again: the game is over, and it was just a game.'[4]

It was not a problem anybody anticipated before the tournament. For West Germany even to be in Switzerland was something of a triumph.

The story of Hungarian football is one of tragedy, of wasted potential and a vibrant culture destroyed by cruelty and political intransigence. Italy may have had the two World Cups but, in the years between the wars, Hungary was the most influential football nation in the world, turning out high-class players and innovative coaches in sufficient numbers to sustain an extremely high domestic standard while also shaping the game in Italy, Germany, Scandinavia, France, Yugoslavia and South America. The informal games on the *grunds*, the vacant lots of Budapest, provided the raw materials to be refined by the coffee-house theorists, the constant urge for improvement driven by a rivalry between MTK and Ferencváros that seemed to hit just the right pitch of ferocity: enough to encourage each side to perpetual effort, but never so intense it became destructive.[5]

By the early fifties, when Hungary produced its greatest side, the culture that produced it had already suffered two catastrophic blows. First there was the far-right government of Miklós Horthy which, as it drew closer to Nazi Germany in the late thirties, began to implement similar antisemitic legislation. MTK, the club of the assimilated Jewish middle classes, was forcibly disbanded in 1940. It was reconstituted after the war but too many of its members had been killed or had fled for it to continue in the vanguard of tactical development even if the environment had been conducive to radicalism and experimentation, which it was not.

The Communists took power in 1947 and nationalised

football clubs two years later. Ferencváros were immediately downgraded because of their nationalistic and largely ethnic German fanbase. And so the other great wellspring of Hungarian football culture was blocked.

In the short term, though, nationalisation was a boon for Hungarian football. Gusztáv Sebes, who was appointed national coach in 1949, realised how Italy had benefited in the thirties from having most of their players based at Juventus and so sought to replicate the model in Hungary. Kispest, home of two of Hungary's most promising young talents, Ferenc Puskás and József Bozsik, were selected as the favoured club. They were taken over by the army, which could effectively draft players from other sides, and changed their name to Honvéd, which literally means 'defender of the homeland', but had been used as a term for soldiers since the mid-nineteenth century.

Sebes was a committed Communist; there was nothing feigned about his regular homilies on the socialist system. Before becoming a footballer he had been a union organiser in Budapest and then at the Renault factory in Paris. He spent thirteen years as a player at MTK, his leadership abilities evident in the fact that when their coach Gyula Feldmann suffered a stroke, he was asked to take over. But his skill was as a project manager and a negotiator of the various Party committees. He needed a tactical brain to work alongside him and turned to his former MTK team-mate Gyula Mándi, who at the time was managing a lower division side while running a shop that sold shirts.

Mándi was Jewish and had survived the Holocaust thanks to the quick thinking of his (gentile) brother-in-law, György Szomolány. For two years, Szomolány had been able to protect him by securing papers so Mándi could work in his factory, which had been converted from a paper-mill to make the wooden stocks for rifles, but in 1944, Mándi had been picked up and packed onto a train bound for Ukraine.

By good fortune, he had in his pocket a postcard and a stub of pencil, which he used to scribble a note to Szomolány. By even better fortune, when he threw it from the train, the postcard was found and sent on, eventually arriving tattered and stained at its destination. Much of the message had been rendered illegible, but Szomolány could make out the word 'Ekelpuszta' and realised Mándi must have been taken to the transit camp there. He put on his First World War officer's uniform, strode into the camp and demanded five men for an essential task, spiriting Mándi and four others into hiding.[6]

Sebes and Mándi rapidly put together a remarkable team, the so-called *Aranycsapat*, the Golden Squad, winning the Olympics in 1952 and then, in November 1953, beating England 6–3, the first time a foreign side had ever won at Wembley, a victory of such comprehensiveness that it obliterated any lingering belief that English football might still be the best in the world. The symbolism seemed clear: vigorous, modern socialist Hungary had gone to the Empire Stadium, as Wembley was still known, the design of which explicitly evoked Lutyens's work in New Delhi, the jewel of empire, and had exposed the conservatism of lumbering old hidebound England.[7]

That, certainly, was how the defeat was taken in England, where it led, eventually, to a questioning of the old ways and a wave of innovation that culminated with the World Cup win in 1966. But in Hungary, even by 1953, it had become increasingly difficult to maintain the belief that Communism represented an optimistic vision for the future. The Stalinist Mátyás Rákosi, as general secretary of the Communist Party,[8] led a brutally repressive regime and, in 1950, launched a Five-Year Plan that implausibly sought to increase industrial production by 380 per cent. That would have been all but impossible even in favourable conditions but Hungary was exporting vast quantities of raw materials to the Soviet Union while paying 20 per cent of national income in war reparations. By 1949, disposable income had returned to 90 per cent of the levels of 1938 but, by 1952, it had fallen to around two-thirds.[9] And even if people did have money, there was very little to spend it on, with major shortages of bread, sugar, flour and meat.[10]

The death of Stalin on 5 March 1953 began to erode Rákosi's authority and in July the reformer Imre Nagy was appointed as chairman of the council of ministers, offering hope of greater openness and prosperity. In the meantime, the football team marched on. 'In those days of dictatorship, it was football that united people in Hungary with the 5 million Hungarians living outside the borders,' said the goalkeeper Gyula Grosics.[11] By the time the World Cup began, Hungary were unbeaten in over four years. In their final warm-up, they had hammered England 7–1 in Budapest. Hungary went to Switzerland as overwhelming favourites.

Switzerland had been named hosts for 1954 at the same 1946 Fifa Congress that gave the 1950 tournament to Brazil, its wartime neutrality making it pretty much the only European nation with the infrastructure to stage the tournament.

There were 37 entrants, the highest figure yet, although China, Peru and Poland all withdrew without playing a qualifier. Egypt, the only Africans, were, like Israel, lumped in with Europe, but lost out to Italy while South Korea beat Japan to become Asia's second World Cup participant after the Dutch East Indies in 1938. There were two major European fallers: Sweden, who had come third in Brazil four years earlier, but finished behind Belgium in their qualifying group; and Spain.

Spain's elimination was West Germany's first major stroke of luck. Fifa had announced the eight seeds before the qualifiers were complete. Although seven of them made it to Switzerland, Spain, who had finished fourth in 1950, did not. They beat Turkey 4–1 in Madrid, but lost 1–0 in Istanbul which, in the days before aggregate score was taken into account, meant a play-off in Rome. Shortly before kick-off, a man turned up claiming to be a Fifa executive and brandishing a letter that stated that the centre-forward László Kubala was ineligible to play for Spain.

Kubala had been born in Budapest to an ethnically Slovak family and had represented both Czechoslovakia and Hungary before escaping west disguised as a Russian soldier in 1949 and settling in Barcelona.[12] Although he had played in the game in Istanbul, Kubala was withdrawn, but the following day Fifa reacted with surprise: it had sent no official to Rome and had no problems with Kubala's eligibility. Who the man was has never been discovered.

After the play-off had finished 2–2, Luigi Franco Gemma, the fourteen-year-old son of a stadium employee, was blindfolded and asked to choose between two pieces of paper. He picked the one that said 'Turkey', and Spain were out, with Turkey taking their seeded place.

That made clear a flaw that should have been obvious in the tournament format. The two seeded sides in each group played the two unseeded sides (with games going to extra time if level at 90 minutes), teams level on points being separated by a play-off. But there was no seeding for the quarter-finals: the sides topping their groups had no guarantee of meeting a runner-up in the next round. That was West Germany's second stroke of luck: having faced Turkey, by far the weakest of the seeds, they then managed to avoid another group-winner until their rematch with Hungary in the final.

For a long time during the Second World War, German football had gone on as though nothing had changed. Sepp Herberger continued to make his notes and became adept at securing the release of players from their regiments. Only in February 1943 when, with Stalingrad lost and Rommel in retreat in North Africa, a state of 'total war' was declared, did Germany finally abandon international sport.

Given the difficulties all countries faced in putting teams together, it's very hard to know how much store to place by results in the years between the 1938 World Cup and that decision but there was one game, against Hungary in May 1942, that would have profound consequences. At half-time, Germany trailed 3–1 but, inspired by Fritz Walter, they came back to win 5–3, their first ever away victory over the Hungarians.

Walter had been born in Kaiserslautern, about forty miles west of Herberger's home town of Mannheim. His father had been a lorry driver until losing an eye in a traffic collision, after which he established a restaurant. Walter was a gifted inside-forward but he was also hard-working and modest, the ideal of a Herberger player. The war took him to France before he was recruited to the Rote Jäger, a crack team of footballers put together by the Luftwaffe officer Hermann Graf that was briefly coached by Herberger. Captured at the end of the war, Walter was on his way to Siberia when, after a bout of malaria led to him being hospitalised and separated from his regiment, he joined in a game at a transit camp on the Romania–Ukraine border. One of the other players, a guard, recognised him from the fixture in Budapest and arranged for Walter's name to be scratched off the list to be sent east.

Inevitably there were changes at the top of the DFB as both Nerz and Linnemann were imprisoned for their Nazi connections. Herberger was investigated but it soon became obvious that, although a member of the NSDAP since 1933, he was in no sense an ideological Nazi, leading to his categorisation as a *Mitlaüfer* – a fellow-traveller, but a term used specifically in the years after the war to denote somebody who had passively gone along with the Nazi system. Living in a tiny flat belonging to his wife's parents in Weinheim, he spent the first months after the war writing hundreds of letters to try to find out what had happened to his players and was soon reinstated by Peco Bauwens, the former referee who became the first post-war president of the DFB.

The initial plan when the war came to an end was for all clubs to be disbanded as part of a broader denazification. In practice, though, with the threat of mass starvation meaning leadership structures had to be put in place quickly, the full process was never completed. As early as November 1945, a league began in the US zone, which had by far the most liberal approach, although clubs spent much of their time travelling to villages in the countryside, playing exhibitions in exchange for food. Only in September 1947 did anything resembling nationwide football resume, but even that was only in the west.

That was a start, but readmission to global football was another issue. The Swiss, making appeals to the unifying mission of sport, organised 'city matches' with German sides to provide some international competition and lobbied enthusiastically but it was only in September 1950 that West Germany's application to join Fifa was accepted.

Initial results were mixed and there were suggestions that defeat to Spain in December 1952 would have led to Herberger being replaced. They drew, 2–2. When West Germany lost a qualifier for the 1954 World Cup away to the Saarland,* who were managed by their future manager Helmut Schön, *Kicker* described the result as 'a shrill SOS'.[13] There was discontent among the wider public as well. The thickset Helmut Rahn, who made no secret of his love of beer, began to be booed by fans. Five Kaiserslautern players – Fritz Walter and his brother Ottmar, Werner Kohlmeyer, Horst Eckel and Werner Liebrich – were regulars in Herberger's squad, something that irritated supporters of other clubs. When, three weeks before

* The Saarland remained distinct from West Germany until 1956 and had been granted Fifa membership in 1950.

the World Cup began, Kaiserslautern lost 5–1 to Hannover 96 in the championship final in Hamburg, the crowd mockingly chanted Herberger's name: these are your favourites, they seemed to be saying, and they are getting hammered.

For the tournament, Herberger billeted his players in a camp at Spiez on Lake Thun. The spirit that was kindled there has become legendary. That's true for almost all world champions as their preparations are examined to see what they did that might be replicated by future contenders, but there does seem to have been something special about West Germany's sense of camaraderie; or at least, that was what was focused on in the aftermath of victory, which may say less about the actuality than the political situation, the sense of a nation coming together after the humiliations of the immediate post-war years.

The format meant that after beating Turkey 4–1 in their opening game, West Germany knew that if defeated against Hungary in their second they would almost certainly face a play-off against Turkey for a place in the quarter final. Accordingly, Herberger rested eight players for the Hungary game; although an 8–3 defeat was mildly embarrassing, it fundamentally didn't matter,[14] not that that stopped certain elements of the German press from tearing into their manager. 'It seemed the time had come,' *Der Spiegel* said, 'to hang the treacherous coach Herberger from a sour apple tree*.'[15]

* There is a reason why the apple tree is specified. Martin Luther was widely believed to have said, 'If I knew the world would end tomorrow, I would plant an apple tree today,' although the theologian Martin Schloemann (1931–2022) has proved it derives not from Luther himself but from a nineteenth-century woodcut of Luther depicting him as a pious father tending the family garden. The image became a common symbol of reconstruction after the Second World War. Following the – startling – logic through, Herberger is thus depicted as a relict of the pre-war era who must be sacrificed on the tree of progress. (Although, as the Irish journalist Ken Early observed, the purpose of planting the apple tree was presumably not so that in the future people would have a readymade gallows.)

But two things happened in the game that did matter. Rahn played well and scored, a performance that led to his selection for the quarter-final. And Werner Liebrich caught Puskás late, causing a hairline fracture of the ankle. How intentional the foul was is impossible to say, although he had switched positions with the right-half Jupp Posipal 10 minutes before the foul. Sebes thought it a deliberate ploy but there is a big difference between a physical player being deployed against the opposition's best creator and a calculated plot to injure him.

In his autobiography, published the following year, Puskás described 'a vicious kick on the back of my ankle . . . when I was no longer playing the ball',[16] but he later backtracked and concluded it was the result of clumsiness rather than malice. Hidegkuti called it 'a correct challenge, and quite accepted in football . . . He was just trying to tackle Puskás, who strained his ankle.'[17]

Die Welt, though, was outraged. 'We did not behave well,' it said. 'The meanest act was committed by the rough Liebrich. He took revenge on that wonderful player only because Puskás was the better man.' It suggested Liebrich should never play for West Germany again and that fouls like that were more harmful than ten defeats. The sense was that it didn't pay for the new Germany to be too assertive, that rehabilitation would come not by winning but by playing the game well.[18]

West Germany won the play-off against Turkey straightforwardly enough, Max Morlock scoring a hat-trick in a 7–2 win to set up a quarter-final against Yugoslavia.

Scotland had again finished second in the Home Championship behind England, but this time they chose to take up the qualification that brought. Their first appearance at a World Cup, though, was a shambles. They were undermined by Rangers who, having queried the legality of the national federation taking away their employees, then arranged a tour of Canada to clash with the finals so none of their players could be called up. The Scottish Football Association (SFA) compounded the issues, taking a squad of only thirteen players to Switzerland, two of them goalkeepers, rather than the maximum permitted of twenty-two.

'Our forwards have been instructed to go all out for an early goal, knowing from experience that the continentals don't like to have to fight back,' said Tam Reid, the head of the SFA's selection committee with the blithe sense of superiority that characterised British football officials of the time. 'Special emphasis has been laid on the necessity of hard, but always fair, tackling. This should knock some of the funny notions out of the heads of the Austrians.'[19]

Scotland actually played well in losing 1–0 to Austria, after which the manager Andy Beattie, sick of SFA meddling and having fallen out with certain players, resigned, leaving the selection committee to take charge of the second game, against Uruguay – not, with only eleven outfield players available, that there was a huge amount of selection to be done. Scotland needed to beat the world champions to force a play-off but lost, 7–0, still their record defeat.

Even four decades later, the referee Arthur Ellis was appalled by the memory. 'They behaved like animals,' he said. 'It was a disgrace. It was a horrible match.'[20] The quarter-final between Hungary and Brazil, two sides at the forefront of tactical development, both on the cusp of moving from W-M to 4-2-4,[21] could have been a classic but it became notorious as the Battle of Bern.

József Tóth had already been forced off with a torn hamstring when, with Hungary leading 3–2, Bozsik was chopped down by Bauer. When he returned to the field following treatment, he was clearly spoiling for a fight and found one with Nílton Santos, who subsequently made allegations of racial abuse. Both were sent off after trading punches. Djalma Santos, spitting and gesticulating wildly, chased Czibor behind the referee's back. Hidegkuti stamped on Indio having shoved him to the ground and when Didi sought retribution, photographers spilled onto the pitch and were cleared only by the intervention of police. Eventually Humberto Tozzi became the third man sent off after a flying kick at Lóránt, Ellis unmoved as he fell to his knees and begged for forgiveness.

Kocsis eventually added a fourth to make the game safe, but as the players left the pitch a bottle thrown from the Hungarian bench struck Pinheiro. Fighting continued into the tunnel, photographers clashed with police and, after the lights had gone out, Brazilian players surged into the Hungary dressing-room. Sebes emerged with a cut above his eye that required four stitches. 'This was a battle; a brutal, savage match,' he said. 'A small war broke out in the corridor to the dressing rooms – everyone was having a go; fans, players and officials.'[22] The head of the Brazilian federation, João Lyra Filho, filed an official complaint with Fifa ludicrously accusing Ellis of being a Kremlin agent carrying out a Communist plot.[23] Ellis himself later condemned Fifa for turning a 'blind eye' to the violence. 'Too many committee members,' he said, 'were afraid of losing trips to nice places.'[24]

Brazil had been involved in the first World Cup 'battle', against Czechoslovakia in Bordeaux in 1938, but the violence of their exit in Bern probably had more to do with their defeat to Uruguay four years earlier and a reaction to the suggestion they had lacked toughness, moral fibre or a sufficiently passionate patriotism. But while the Brazilian popular press largely celebrated the fact that their players had been prepared to stand up physically to Europeans, the official CBD report continued to obsess over Brazil's racial make-up. 'The Brazilian players lacked what is lacking for the Brazilian people in general,' it read. 'The ills are deeper than the game's tactical system ... They go back to genetics itself.'[25]

Battered and bruised, Hungary went on to Lausanne for a semi-final against the defending champions Uruguay, who had swept aside England in the last eight. Hungary were without Tóth and Puskás but Uruguay were also depleted with their great captain Obdulio Varela, the winger Julio César Abbadíe and the centre-forward Omar Míguez all injured. What followed was a game widely considered the greatest in the history of the World Cup until Italy's victory over Brazil in 1982.[26]

Goals from Czibor and Hidegkuti early in each half had Hungary 2–0 up, but Juan Hohberg pulled one back on 76 minutes and then bundled in the equaliser with three minutes remaining, both goals set up by Schiaffino. He almost completed his hat-trick early in the second half of extra time but hit the post and, two minutes later, László Budai crossed for Kocsis to score with a characteristic header. He headed another with four minutes remaining, his thirteenth goal of the tournament, and Hungary were in the final. 'It was a battle of real men, a tough contest with some excellent football,' said the referee Mervyn Griffiths. 'The match had everything – brilliant individual runs, excellent combined moves and marvellous saves by both goalkeepers.'[27]

West Germany beat Yugoslavia 2–0 in the last eight, an own goal and a late strike from Rahn setting up a semi-final against Austria, who had beaten Switzerland 7–5 in an extraordinary quarter-final; played in intense heat in Lausanne, it was the highest scoring game in World Cup finals history. Posipal was brought in at right-back to replace his Hamburg team-mate Fritz Laband and West Germany outplayed their old rivals. With Kurt Schmied still suffering from the sunstroke that had afflicted him against the hosts, Walter Zeman returned in goal for Austria. He was an experienced and respected keeper who would go on playing regularly for the national side until 1960, but he had a dreadful afternoon. The West German success, though, was mostly down to their domination of midfield as the elegant Ernst Ocwirk, the last of the great creative centre-halves, was overrun. The fate that had long been predicted for the self-conscious artistry of the Austrian style finally came to pass – and Tam Reid perhaps felt some vindication.

In West Germany, for the first time, the public en masse began to pay attention to the World Cup.[28] *Der Spiegel* reported a spike in the sales of TV sets in the days leading up to the final:[29] there had been 11,655 in private hands in West Germany at the beginning of the year; by the end there were 84,278.[30] Yet the nature of the new Germany meant there could be no hint of triumphalism. Intellectuals remained disdainful of football,[31] while even Herbert Zimmermann began his commentary by noting, 'This is a proud day. Let's not be so presumptuous as to expect it has to end successfully.'

Or perhaps that was simply realism. Hungary, after all, were unbeaten in thirty-two games over four years.

The morning of 4 July dawned wet and got wetter. For Hungary, that was a concern; the better the pitch the more likely their passing style and intricate interchanges were to prevail, but by kick-off it had been raining for thirty-six hours. For one West German in particular, though, this was great news. Since contracting malaria during the war, Fritz Walter had struggled in hot weather, but when it rained he came alive. Even before the World Cup, Germany recognised the phenomenon of *Fritz-Walter-Wetter*. Afterwards, it would become an essential part of the national myth.

If there had been fatalism in Zimmermann's words, it soon

seemed justified. Puskás seized on the rebound after a Kocsis shot was half-blocked to put Hungary ahead and then Turek fumbled Kohlmeyer's back pass to allow Czibor to make it 2–0 after eight minutes. Walter thought back to the game in Budapest in May 1942, when Germany had come from two behind to beat the Hungarians. On that occasion, they'd cut the deficit almost immediately, and they did so again.

Max Morlock was the son of a factory foreman from Nuremberg. He was only 5ft 7in but he was ferociously determined. As a child he had caught pneumonia after bathing in an icy pond in an attempt to toughen himself up for a life in football. Fritz Walter described him as 'the greatest fighter I've ever known'.[32] At 2–0 down, he wasn't beaten. 'Now let's show them!' he shouted as West Germany kicked off again. Within two minutes, Rahn's low cross from the right deflected off Bozsik and Morlock adjusted his feet sharply, stretched out his right leg and, with the very end of his toe, diverted the ball past Grosics.

Herberger liked to say that success was the result of equal parts skill, togetherness and luck.[33] All three were present in Bern. They might have collapsed having gone 2–0 down, particularly having lost 8–3 to the same opponents two weeks earlier, but they had the collective resolve to keep going. In the minutes after Morlock's goal, they dominated, reaching such unexpected levels that Kohlmeyer backheeled a clearance and Walter moved the ball on with a needlessly flamboyant flick. Victory, of course, imbues such moments with significance but the sense was of West Germany demonstrating they had no fear of the Hungarians. As Grosics flapped and missed a corner, Rahn sidefooted an equaliser at the back post. There were still only 18 minutes played.

Then came the fortune as Hungary rallied. Turek made a string of fine saves, Hidegkuti and Kocsis both hit the bar, Kohlmeyer twice cleared off the line. And then, with six minutes to go, the unthinkable as Rahn gathered a Mihály Lantos clearance, cut onto his left foot and drilled his shot into the bottom corner. '*Rahn schiesst* ...' screamed Zimmermann. '*Tor! Tor! Tor! Tor!*' ('Rahn shoots ... Goal! Goal! Goal! Goal!') There followed eight seconds of ecstatic silence. '*Tor für Deutschland! Drei zu zwei führt Deutschland! Halten Sie mich für verrückt, halten Sie mich für übergeschnappt!*' ('Goal for Germany! Germany lead 3–2! Call me mad, call me crazy!') They are words that became as familiar to Germans as any piece of commentary ever has to any nation, the words that consecrated the new federal republic. After the initial joy, determining what that meant would prove far more complicated.

But there was still one vital moment to negotiate. With four minutes remaining, Mihály Tóth played in Puskás. He let the ball run across his body. Liebrich couldn't get back. Karl Mai was steaming across but wasn't going to get there. Puskás hit his shot hard and true with his left foot. Turek was beaten. The keeper lay face down in the mud, crushed. Mai followed the ball into the net waving his hands above his head. Liebrich pointed at Puskás, a desperate inquiry for offside rather than a real appeal.

Belatedly, Mervyn Griffiths raised his flag. No goal: the Hungarians, it turned out, *could* be stopped, even if Turek, Posipal and Liebrich ultimately needed the assistance of a fastidious schoolteacher from Newport. Puskás was outraged. 'I couldn't believe it,' he said. 'I could have murdered him. To lose the World Cup on such a decision just isn't right.'[34] Video evidence is inconclusive, although it's at least intriguing that Zimmermann, long before the flag went up, was assuring his audience that the goal would be ruled out.

Why had Hungary lost? After four years unbeaten, how had they lost the one that really mattered? Was it the rain and the mud, which hampered Hungary's passing game and for which West Germany were better equipped because Adidas had given them screw-in studs? Was it the accumulated fatigue of the games against Brazil and Uruguay? Was it the brass band practice that had disturbed Hungary's sleep the night before, or the policing error that meant the Hungary team bus stopped some distance from the stadium on the way to the game and players were forced to battle their way through the crowds? Was Puskás fully fit after his ankle injury? At the very least, his inclusion meant a rejig; the industrious Mihály Tóth had been brought in on the left wing to cover for Puskás's lack of mobility, while Czibor switched from left to right to replace László Budai, who had played well against Uruguay. Was it to do with the way Horst Eckel, performing a disciplined man-marking job, had reduced the impact of Hidegkuti? Was it just one of those things, fortune finally going against Hungary after thirty-two games?

But it could never just be luck. There always had to be an explanation. When Rahn, the Walter brothers, Morlock and Mai went down with jaundice two months after the final, it was seized on in Hungary as evidence of doping. Rahn wondered whether a syringe used to inject players with glucose and vitamins had been contaminated, although given that the Essen goalkeeper Fritz Herkenrath demonstrated similar symptoms, it's possible he and his clubmate Rahn had picked up an illness on a tour to South America.[35] A study by Humboldt University and the University of Munster, published in 2013, offered circumstantial evidence to suggest players had been injected with pervitin, a methamphetamine given to German troops during the Second World War.[36]

Puskás blamed complacency. 'It was our own fault,' he said. 'We thought we had the match won, then we gave away two stupid goals.'[37] There were suggestions that extended beyond the specific context of the game. At least two players and possibly as many as six broke curfew to meet their wives and girlfriends who had been permitted to travel to Bern for the final.

Why, others asked, had the MTK winger Karóly Sándor gone to Switzerland? He was a gifted player and there were those who would have selected him, but the sense was that Sebes found him self-indulgent – and he had once told Sándor that if his wife wanted to be a better Communist she should wear less make-up. But why take Sándor if he wasn't in the official squad? Was it really only because Puskás liked playing cards with him? And if that were true, what did that say about priorities?

The previous November, when the players had returned after victory at Wembley, they had been greeted at Keleti Station in Budapest by adoring crowds. This time, as people poured onto the street in fury, they had to divert to the northern mining town of Tata. 'The reaction in Hungary was terrible,' said Grosics. 'Hundreds of thousands of people poured into the streets in the hours after the match.'[38] As rumours spread that the game had been thrown for a fleet of Mercedes, the apartments of some players were attacked. There were transparently nonsensical claims that Mihály Tóth had been selected for the final only because he was Sebes's son-in-law – Sebes's only daughter was ten at the time.

The eruption was uncoordinated and soon died down but it made clear that if crowds were big enough they could not be controlled. 'On the pretext of football,' Grosics said, 'they openly demonstrated against the regime ... In those demonstrations ... lay the seeds of the 1956 Uprising.'[39]

As West Germany lost nine of the twelve games they played after the final, Hungary went unbeaten for a further eighteen games. Over a period of almost six years they lost only one of fifty-one matches: the World Cup final. But something fundamental was broken in Bern. The spirit of the side never recovered and neither did their reputation with the public. Puskás found himself barracked at Honvéd away games, Sebes's son was beaten up at school and Grosics, who had trained for the priesthood and had always been an outsider, was arrested, accused of 'conduct incompatible with the laws and morals of the Hungarian People's Republic'. He was placed under house arrest and taken off once a week for interrogation by the ÁVH, the secret police.

When the Uprising came in October 1956 in response to the government's swing back to authoritarianism, Grosics allowed his house to be used as an armoury by demonstrators. As the protest was crushed by Soviet tanks, Puskás, Kocsis, Czibor and the entire Under-21 squad defected. To lose so many players of such stature would have had a profound impact on the football of any country, but for Hungary it was devastating because MTK and Ferencváros, the two great fountainheads of the culture that had created the *Aranycsapat*, had been damaged beyond repair. When a generation of players was swept away, it turned out there was nothing to replace it. As such, Bern, which could have been its apotheosis, stands as the final doomed spasm of the golden age of Hungarian football.[40]

No World Cup win has ever been greeted by the winners with such ambivalence. Not even a decade had passed since the end of the Second World War. Quite apart from the complicated feelings of the east, for West Germany, only constituted in 1949, anything overtly nationalistic was to be avoided at all costs. Which was, of course, precisely why the World Cup meant so much: football was the only space in which it felt even vaguely acceptable to celebrate being German.[41] The question was how, and how much.

When the anthem was played after the final, Germans in the crowd ignored official advice to sing only the third stanza – '*Einigkeit und Recht und Freiheit* ...' ('Unity, justice and freedom ...') – and belted out the nationalistic first stanza that had been in regular use since 1922 – '*Deutschland über alles* ...' Both Swiss and East German radio were so appalled they cut coverage immediately.

But that was euphoric fans, perhaps acting instinctively, perhaps not even aware that the anthem had changed. And the joy was real enough. As the squad travelled home, hundreds of thousands lined the railway to celebrate, frequently spilling onto the tracks. More telling, perhaps, in terms of West Germany's initial tottering steps towards reconciliation was how uncomfortable many were with the public celebrations. The Bundespräsident Theodor Heuss had the flame lit at the Olympiastadion in Berlin, which inevitably called to mind the 1936 Olympics.[42] Then, at an official reception for the team in a Munich bierkeller, the head of the DFB, Peco Bauwens, perhaps forgetting himself amid the atmosphere of booze and jingoism, gave a speech of staggering insensitivity. Having praised the heart and spirit of the players, he invoked Wotan, the supreme Germanic deity whose spirit underpinned the more mystical aspects of Nazism, before speaking of the importance of *Führerprinzip*, the term used for Hitler's creation of a totalitarian state under his personal authority. Bavarian radio abandoned its coverage of the event and conveniently mislaid the tapes.

Bauwens was a classic example of the complications of the time. He had not merely never joined the NSDAP but his wife, who killed herself in 1940, had been Jewish; in that sense he had seemed the perfect candidate to lead the post-war DFB. But since 1927 he had been a chairman of the Kölner Sports Club, which had enthusiastically promoted nationalist (and often antisemitic) speakers who rejected the Treaty of Versailles, insisted the German army in the First World War had been defeated by internal enemies and spoke of a need for German rebirth. He had applied to join the NSDAP in 1933 but was rejected because his wife was Jewish. Why she killed herself is impossible to say, but their son blamed his father's habitual womanising, even suggesting that his father may have bought the sleeping draughts for her, may have goaded her into taking them, may even have mixed them into her wine himself.[43] Nobody was entirely without fault, but the flaws of Bauwens were more egregious than most.

So what could Germans celebrate? Herberger had regularly spoken during the tournament of the importance of '*Kameradschaft*',[44] the *Westdeutsche Allgemeine Zeitung* was typical of the newspapers in saluting 'a team of eleven comrades fighting unquestioningly',[45] and two days after the final the leader of Bavaria, Hans Ehard, described football as 'a game in which comradeship and mutual understanding often means more than the skilful art of ball control'.[46] Comradeship, perhaps, remained one of the very few aspects of the war that was remembered fondly and that was not irredeemably tainted by association with Nazism.[47]

When Herberger's squad visited Bonn, the interior minister Gerhard Schröder made explicit this sense of Bern as a triumph of comradeship.* 'We are not as rich as other nations in terms of national events and symbols which provide a strong collective experience,' he acknowledged. 'Thus we are all the more grateful for every event which mediates such a real sense of community to us.'[48]

Beyond the immediate sense of joy, that probably was the widespread feeling of the time: a sense that, with discipline, hard work and togetherness, hardships could be overcome. Perhaps on some level the victory eased the pressure on Chancellor Adenauer, and bought time for the *Wirtschaftswunder*, which

* This Gerhard Schröder, a Christian Democrat born in 1910, is an entirely different Gerhard Schröder to the Social Democrat born in 1944 who served as Chancellor between 1998 and 2005.

was by no means secure in July 1954, even if industrial output that year grew by 11 per cent and exports by 20 per cent.[49] It helped that there were certain similarities between Herberger and Adenauer, both wise old men whose avuncular charm disguised a ruthlessness and who delighted in a gnomic apophthegm. It was only much later, though, after reunification, that the success began widely to be described as 'a miracle', as though the mature democracy undergoing a great disruption came to need a foundation myth.[50]

Its status was confirmed on the fiftieth anniversary of the final, as the chancellor Gerhard Schröder described Bern as a national memorial to stand alongside Weimar and the Berlin Wall.[51]

1958

PRODIGY

In the village of Don Viçoso in the south of the Brazilian state of Minas Gerais, there lived a young widow called Maria Rosalina. She had had a son just before her husband died and she loved him dearly. He was a fine healthy boy but for one thing: he would not speak. By the age of two he had still not uttered a word, so Maria Rosalina called together the local *benzedeiras*, folk-medicine healers, who performed rituals on moonlit nights. They gathered around the boy's cot and intoned the traditional incantation: '*Bili-bilu-teteia*, *Bili-bilu-teteia*.'

But still the boy did not speak. So the women tried again, and again. And finally, after several weeks of chanting on numerous moonlit nights, the spells had their effect. The boy called out his first syllables, as though trying to copy the chant of the *benzedeiras*. '*Bilé*,' he called. '*Bilé*!' And so that became the nickname by which the boy, José Lino, was known.

Bilé grew up to be strong and athletic. He adored football and turned out in goal for Vasco da Gama in São Lourenço, a little over twenty miles to the north-east. A local man would take his young son, only three or four years old, to watch training sessions. That boy loved Bilé and loved football. Whenever he played in goal and made a save, he would call out his hero's name. Except that he mangled the sound, changing the B to a

P: 'Pilé! Pilé!' When he and his family then moved to Bauru in the state of São Paulo, his Minas Gerais accent meant his teammates misheard his shout. And so was born the most famous nickname in football: Pelé.

At least, that's one story. Unconvinced when he worked on his first autobiography in 1977, Pelé seemed to have accepted the explanation by the time of his second, thirty years later. Brazil is a land of myth, a place where objective fact struggles for traction, and few have been so mythologised as Pelé.

His father, Dondinho, was a footballer, a gifted centre-forward who was signed by Atlético Mineiro in 1940. In his first game, against São Cristóvão, he tore his knee ligaments. Almost before it had begun, Dondinho's top-level career was ended. He moved to the municipality of Três Corações, playing for the local side for next to nothing. After every game his knee would swell up painfully. It was there that Pelé was born. Dondinho and his family moved with his career and in 1946 he joined Lusitana in Bauru. He had been offered a public service job there to supplement his income but, shortly after he joined, the club was taken over and new directors quietly forgot the promise of employment.

Pelé grew up desperately poor. He was usually barefoot, and wore cast-off clothes. The roof of their small house leaked and dinner was often just bread and a banana. But on 16 July 1950, Dondinho held a party at his house. There were cakes, sweets, sandwiches and beer for around fifteen friends who came over to listen on the radio as Brazil played Uruguay at the Maracanã. The nine-year-old Pelé and his friends played football in the street, running in and out to keep up to date with the score. As Uruguay came back to win and lift the World Cup, Pelé was struck by the sight of his 'father and all his friends absolutely silent'. It was, he said, 'the first time I saw my father cry.'[1] Afterwards, Pelé knelt before the picture of Christ in his father's room and asked why Brazil had been allowed to lose.

He comforted his father by promising he would win him the World Cup himself.

Sweden ended up being the only bidder when the decision on who should host the 1958 World Cup was taken in 1950. Like Switzerland, they had benefited from wartime neutrality; five years after the war, no European combatant could have contemplated the sort of investment necessary.

For the first time, the Home Championship was not used for qualifying, and the result was that all four British nations made it to Sweden. Tommy Taylor scored eight times as England finished above Ireland and Denmark but he, Duncan Edwards and Roger Byrne were lost to the Munich air disaster. 'It affected the mood,' said Tom Finney.[2]

Scotland qualified ahead of Spain and Switzerland, but Munich robbed them of Matt Busby, who would have taken charge for the finals. As he recuperated, he was replaced by the physio Dawson Walker, who never managed a club side.

Busby's assistant Jimmy Murphy, meanwhile, had not gone to Belgrade because of his secondary role as manager of Wales. They had finished second in their qualifying group behind Czechoslovakia but were the beneficiaries of a new rule Fifa had instituted after South Korea's poor showing in 1954, saying that no side should qualify without playing at least one qualifier; they were drawn as the opposition for Israel, whom Turkey, Sudan, Egypt and Indonesia had all refused to play for the Asian/African berth. It was when Murphy got back to Old Trafford after Wales had won the second leg in Cardiff, clutching a crate of oranges given to him by the Israelis, that he was told about the crash in Munich earlier that afternoon.

Northern Ireland drew 2–2 with Italy in what should have been their final qualifier, a result that would have taken Italy through. But the Italians had insisted the game should have only friendly status after the Fifa-appointed referee was absent because of fog in London. Northern Ireland won a rearranged fixture 2–1 and Italy were eliminated – although they were almost reprieved as Northern Irish officials contemplated withdrawing when it became apparent they would have to play on a Sunday.[3]

Born three days before Christmas 1880 in Theux, the Belgian had been one of the students at the Collège Saint-Servais who had founded Standard de Liège in 1898. He moved on to the University of Liège where he graduated as a mining engineer. He taught at the University of Lima, but found the constant travel to Peru exhausting. When he was thirty-two he got his big break as he was offered a job as a representative for US Steel in Rio de Janeiro. One last term remained to be taught in Lima. He decided he would travel across the Atlantic in style and booked a ticket on board the *Titanic*. But he was late; he missed his train to Liège and by the time he got to Southampton, the liner had left. He was already aboard another ship when the *Titanic* went down.

On his return journey, the Belgian met Juliette Ludivine Calmeau, the daughter of an industrialist. They soon married and moved to Brazil, where he graduated from selling steel to dealing in arms. On 8 May 1916, the Belgian had a son: Jean-Marie Faustin Godefroid – João – de Havelange. Nobody has ever had such an influence over the politics of football.

Havelange was tall, imposing and physically fit. He played as a midfielder for Fluminense but his main sport was swimming. He competed in the 400m and 1500m freestyle for Brazil at the 1936 Berlin Olympics – where he had 'a wonderful time' and was impressed by the 'efficiency' of the transport.[4] Later that year he began work for the steel company his father was still attached to but, after graduating in law in 1940, he became legal advisor to a local bus company. He soon became a director. At the 1952 Olympics, Havelange competed in the water polo. By the 1956 games, he was the Brazilian Olympic squad's head of delegation and was elected vice-president of the CBD. He set up an insurance company in Rio de Janeiro, running it, rent-free, out of the offices of the CBD, and bought into Orwec, a São Paulo-based firm specialising in waste disposal and chemical manufacture, particularly explosives. His will to power was remarkable and it came at just the right time for Brazilian sport.

It wasn't just Pelé who was determined to put right the failure of 1950. Winning the World Cup for Brazil became a great state project for a government desperate to bolster itself with whatever legitimacy it could find. Juscelino Kubitschek won presidential elections in 1955 and continued the drive to make Brazil a more urban and industrial culture. He promised 'fifty years progress in five' and, riding the post-Korean War boom, oversaw rapid growth. He finally instituted plans that had existed since a new constitution was drawn up in 1891 for a new capital. Lúcio Costa was appointed as the main urban planner, while the majority of the public buildings were designed by Oscar Niemeyer. Between them they created a strikingly modern city, free of the memories of the Portuguese court that still haunted Rio de Janeiro. Based on a cross design that resembled an aeroplane and, theoretically, made for easier automobile access, the inspiration was clearly Le Corbusier and European modernism, but it retained an aesthetic not dissimilar to the sweeping concrete of the Maracanã. It was Bauhaus with a Latin American sensuousness; Freyre had similarly contrasted European angularity with the curves of Brazil.

The Kubitschek government, recognising the importance of football, also provided a grant to prepare the national team for

1958, and the squad raised further funds with a tour of Italy. Havelange had become president of the CBD in 1958, and Paulo Machado de Carvalho, head of the football department at São Paulo, was put in charge of the delegation for the World Cup in Sweden. 'Look, Doctor Paulo,' Havelange said to him. 'I need a squad that will make people forget about the 1950s, a victorious squad, a winning team. And because I need all of that, I want you as boss. Arm yourself with everything however you want it. You have carte blanche.'[5]

As coach, he turned to Vicente Feola, a clubbable *bon vivant* who had led São Paulo to the Paulista championship twice, although as those had come as long ago as 1948 and 1949, the main arguments in his favour were that he was a safe pair of hands and, perhaps most significantly, that he had spent the previous few months working as assistant to the great Hungarian Béla Guttmann and might therefore have picked up some European expertise.

Guttmann's influence could be seen in Feola's preference for a 4-2-4 formation. Flávio Costa's development of Dori Kürschner's W-M into the *diagonal* had been mirrored by Hungary's own evolution, but Brazil's use of 4-2-4 in 1958 was the first time the fully formed system had been seen on a global stage. The addition of a second centre-back had two major benefits. If an opposing winger attacked down one flank, the full-back on the other side could stay relatively tight to the winger he was marking rather than having to provide cover in the middle, denying that winger acceleration room if play were switched. In possession, meanwhile, the full-backs had licence to get forward, creating overloads and opening up new angles with players arriving from deep. Brazil's left-back in 1958, Nílton Santos, can be regarded as the first modern attacking full-back.[6]

At the time, though, what seemed most striking was less Brazil's tactical approach than the thoroughness of their preparation. Havelange always insisted the same principles applied to running a football team as to running a business and sought to apply a 'broad-based administrative concept', which meant bringing in as many experts as possible.[7]

Little was left to chance. Feola was provided with a vast backroom staff including a scout, a doctor, a dentist, a trainer, a treasurer and a psychologist. After initial examinations, the majority of the squad had to be treated for intestinal parasites, while one player was diagnosed with syphilis. The dentist, meanwhile, extracted a total of 470 teeth from the thirty-three players in the provisional squad.

The psychologist, Dr João Carvalhaes, was usually unshaven and would always wear a grey sweater, his presence an indication of the feeling that the failings of 1950 and 1954 had been mental rather than anything else: a loss of nerve at the Maracanã and a loss of discipline in Bern. Havelange told him that the players had to be persuaded 'to abandon their natural violence'.[8]

As part of his evaluation of the players, Carvalhaes had them each draw a picture of a man; the more sophisticated they were, he reasoned, the more detailed their drawing would be. When Garrincha drew just a circle with a line extending from the top and the bottom, saying it showed an overhead view of a cyclist wearing a big hat, Carvalhaes determined him insufficiently intelligent for a World Cup; on a subsequent IQ test he failed to achieve the minimum threshold necessary to be a bus driver in Rio. Pelé, meanwhile, Carvalhaes assessed as 'obviously infantile. He lacks the necessary fighting spirit.'[9] Feola paid little attention.

A delegation led by the doctor, Hilton Gosling, was sent to Sweden to select a training base; they looked at twenty-five sites before settling on a hotel in Hindas, a resort near Gothenburg. To reduce distractions, all twenty-eight female members of staff were replaced with men for the duration of the tournament, although requests that a local nudist colony should cover up fell on deaf ears.

This was the same technocratic spirit that underlay everything in Kubitschek's Brazil, from the construction of Brasilia to the Five-Year Plan. Havelange brought organisation, and there was modernity in the tactics and preparation, but beyond that there was also something more overtly and self-consciously artistic that gave Brazil the identity Freyre had claimed as characteristic.

Brazil began with a 3–0 win over Austria in which the nineteen-year-old centre-forward José Altafini* scored twice, but the sense was that they hadn't played especially well. Altafini and Vavá both hit the post in a goalless draw with England – the first 0–0 at a World Cup. Pelé had not played in either match because of injury, having hurt his knee in a pre-tournament friendly against Corinthians, while Garrincha was left out of the first game because a more defensive figure was needed to drop back to help match Austria in midfield, and omitted for the second because it was feared he might retaliate against the robust England left-back, Tommy Banks.

The third game was against the USSR, of whose 'scientific football' and supposed superhuman fitness Brazil had an almost pathological anxiety. There was a feeling they needed an unpredictable presence and an early lead to unsettle their opponents: who better to provide that than Garrincha? The inclusion of Pelé and Garrincha had an extraordinary impact. In the first three minutes both struck the woodwork and then Vavá scored. He added a second with thirteen minutes remaining and Brazil were through as group winners.

At that, Dr Carvalhaes insisted on another set of psychological assessments. When Gilmar, the goalkeeper, struggled

---

* At the time Altafini was known by his nickname 'Mazzola' after the great Italian forward Valentino Mazzola, but having joined AC Milan later in 1958 he reverted to his given name.

to draw a set of parallel lines, Carvalhaes decided he was too nervous to play. Asked to draw anything, Didi sketched a house. Asked what it was, he said it was the home he hoped to build with the money he made from winning the World Cup; Carvalhaes dismissed him as a mercenary. Garrincha drew a rough circle with spokes projecting from it, saying it represented his Botafogo team-mate Quarentinha. Carvalhaes wrote him off as mentally unfit. In total, he rejected nine of the eleven who would play in the quarter-final. Feola ignored him.[10]

Argentina went to Sweden not only as South American champions but convinced their football was the best in the world. They had not sent a serious team to the World Cup for twenty-eight years and had withdrawn from the Campeonato Sudamericano in both 1949 and 1953; while that fitted with the general isolationist stance of the president Juan Perón,[11] the absences were probably more to do with an ongoing dispute with the Brazilian federation and the players' strike of 1948–49.[12]

Argentina's return to international action at the Campeonato Sudamericano in 1955 seemed to offer confirmation of their assumption of their own pre-eminence; in the eleven Campeonatos in which they'd competed from 1925, Argentina had won eight and come second in three.

Although they came third in 1956, the 1957 tournament in Peru represented a glorious apotheosis. Argentina won their first four games by a combined score of 21–4, then sealed the trophy with a game to spare by beating Brazil 3–0. Two of the goals came in the last three minutes, but that should not be taken as evidence that the margin of victory was exaggerated; they had demolished their rivals. As the players celebrated on the pitch, a microphone was shoved into the hand of the River Plate defender Federico Vairo. 'It's . . .' he said uncertainly, '. . . it's all thanks to these *caras sucias*, to these five *sinvergüenzas* ...' At which he broke down in tears, but his point had been made.

The players he was referring to specifically were the forward line of Omar Corbatta, Humberto Maschio, Antonio Angelillo, Omar Sívori and Osvaldo Cruz, but Vairo was also invoking the spirit of Argentinian football, its self-image as a game played by *pibes* with their 'dirty faces', the urchins 'without shame' who had learned the game on the streets and brought to the professional game both technical excellence and a sense of mischief, the style known as '*la nuestra*'.[13]

But in the weeks after the tournament, Maschio, Angelillo and Sívori all moved to Serie A. Argentina refused to select players who played abroad and all three ended up playing for Italy. Then Rogelio Domínguez went to Real Madrid. Finally, the AFA did what the national coach Guillermo Stábile had been urging since the interest of European clubs became apparent during the tournament and prohibited transfers abroad. 'It was too late,' said Stábile. 'For a few million pesos we'd lost everything that had been achieved in Lima.'[14]

That was a convenient way of shifting the blame but the issue ran far deeper than the loss of four players. The Argentinian focus on individual technique had led to physical preparation being neglected, as the former England centre-half Neil Franklin discovered when he quit Stoke City to join Independiente of Santa Fé in the Colombian rebel league in 1950. 'They were very good ball players, very good exhibitionists,' he said, 'but they were incredibly lazy in the training sessions.'[15]

There was little sense that football demanded sacrifice. Life was to be enjoyed, on-field and off – and that was as true of Stábile as it was of the players. 'He used to take the girls off us,' said Maschio, whose interest in women was legendary. 'Sívori started dating the telephonist in the hotel [in Lima] and I was going out with one of her friends. And when the girls called, he said to us, "Give me the phone; I want to talk to her." He always tried to steal our conquests. He was really good-looking. We didn't have a chance.'[16]

Qualifying went well but European sides presented a different challenge. In Sweden, Argentina were overwhelmed by the pace and power of West Germany in the first game, at which Stábile recalled the 39-year-old Ángel Labruna for the meeting with Northern Ireland. The Irish midfielder Jimmy McIlroy described the Argentina team as 'a lot of little fat men with stomachs, smiling at us and pointing and waving at girls in the crowd'.[17] The Argentinians were fortunate to win 3–1.

But it was the following game against Czechoslovakia in Helsingborg that ended Argentina's golden age. Argentina couldn't keep up. Again and again, Czechoslovakia worked the ball to the byline, cut it back and scored. It finished 6–1, and it could have been a lot worse. The goalkeeper Amadeo Carrizo blamed disorganisation, pointing out that Brazil had chartered their own plane while Argentina had spent forty hours getting to Sweden on scheduled flights.

There was truth to that, but the problems were more fundamental. 'We were used to playing really slowly, and they were fast,' said the defender José Ramos Delgado. 'We hadn't played international football [that is, against non-South American opponents] for a long time, so when we went out there we thought we were really talented, but we found we hadn't followed the pace of the rest of the world. We'd been left behind. The European teams played simply. They were precise. Argentina were good on the ball, but we didn't go forwards.'[18]

It wasn't even that Czechoslovakia were a great side. They didn't make it out of the group, losing in a play-off for a quarter-final place to a Northern Ireland side who performed heroically given the number of injuries they had sustained.

The reaction at home was savage. The players were pelted with coins and fruit after arriving back at the airport at Ezeiza, and targeted for abuse in league games. Stábile was sacked. Within three weeks, the journalist Dante Panzeri was speaking of the 'collective psychosis' engendered by the defeat.[19]

As the complacent belief in Argentina's superiority was swept away, it was asked why players based overseas had been left out; nobody in the wake of Helsingborg could continue to believe that the Argentinian league had such a wealth of resources that players of the talent of Sívori, Maschio and Angelillo could be ignored.[20]

Yet the players who had left were a symptom as much as a cause. Part of the Perón government's populist approach had been to grant football clubs cheap loans, effectively a state subsidy, something ended by the military regime of Pedro Aramburu after the fall of Perón in 1955. At the same time, the expansion of the middle class, itself a result of Peronist economic policy, the increasing availability of televisions and the growing number of matches being broadcast reduced the number of people going to the stadium, something exacerbated by disillusionment following the disgrace of Helsingborg. That reduced the clubs' revenues and placed greater emphasis on victory at the expense of spectacle.

Perón had gone, and the debacle against Czechoslovakia dashed away another of life's apparent certainties. *La nuestra* was just another example of Argentinian utopianism that couldn't quite survive reality. And as with so many other dreams, it was cast aside absolutely; the cycle of idealism and cynicism feels characteristically Argentinian.[21] As V.S. Naipaul observed, because colonisers and immigrants regarded Argentina as a *tabula rasa*, the tendency was always for grand idealistic visions; even Eva Perón, a 'saint' of the utopian faith, was a myth, reinvented in life as she changed her age and her appearance; and again in death as she underwent a secular beatification.[22]

For Europeans, Argentina has always been a land of reinvention. 'It's a society that builds up dreams,' the essayist and economist Enrico Udenio wrote in *La hipocresía argentina*, 'and, when they aren't realised, it looks outside itself for explanations and to apportion blame.' The tendency to oscillate between the two extremes 'helps raise some of the[ir] representatives to the level of gods, with the same speed and facility it can convert them to demons'.[23]

Brazil's success might have been seen as an endorsement of *la nuestra*, particularly given memories of the victory in Lima in 1957, but instead its aesthetic principles were rejected, its technocratic methods venerated. The shame of the defeat outweighed all else. 'The national team had to be modified,' said Ramos Delgado. 'Football became less of an art after that.'[24]

The lessons Argentina drew from Sweden were that their football had to be tougher, faster and stronger, that discipline and cynicism had to replace skill and romance. The Argentina team that went to Chile four years later would be very different from the one that had gone to Sweden.

France, having seen off Belgium and Iceland in qualifying, were playing in their fifth World Cup – only Brazil had played in more – and, at last, they made an impression, going a stage further than they had as hosts in 1938 and reaching the semi-final.

The war had, inevitably, meant major upheavals in how the game was run. The former tennis star Jean Borotra, one of the 'Four Musketeers' who had dominated the game in the twenties and early thirties, was appointed Commissioner of Education and Sport in the Vichy government. Under him, professional sport was abolished, women's football banned and men's matches reduced to 80 minutes. He fell from favour in 1942* and was replaced as Commissioner by Colonel Joseph Pascot, a former rugby player. Matches were restored to 90 minutes but he too was suspicious of professionalism. Rimet resigned early as president of the French football federation, an act that allowed him to return after the war without taint of collaboration.

French football recovered remarkably quickly after the war, but after missing out on 1950 they were eliminated in the group stage in 1954 despite being seeded. There was progress at club level, though. Reims, led by the visionary Albert Batteux, who was also national manager, had reached the first European Cup final, in 1956, and would get there again in 1959. Six of the France squad played for Reims, while Raymond Kopa had left them to join Real Madrid after that first European Cup final.

A lot of top players remained amateur. For many, it simply didn't make financial sense to give up a reasonably well-paid job in a factory or on a farm for the paltry salary and insecure life of a footballer. It was immigrants who saw football as a career, a worthwhile alternative to a life in the pit.[25] Kopa was the son of Polish immigrants (he had been born Kopaszewski), his Reims team-mate Just Fontaine had been born in Marrakech to a Spanish mother and Roger Piantoni, also of Reims, was of Italian descent. After the 1958 tournament, the pre-eminent

---

* Later that year Borotra was arrested by the SS for 'patriotic fervour' and sent to the camp at Sachsenhausen. He was then moved to Itter Castle in Tirol, Austria, where he was held for two years with other prominent French detainees, including De Gaulle's sister, Marie-Agnès Cailliau, and the former prime ministers Édouard Daladier and Paul Reynaud. The castle was taken by a small detachment of US troops and anti-Hitler Wehrmacht five days after Hitler's suicide in 1945. The Waffen-SS launched a counter-attack, though, and the defenders were running out of ammunition when Borotra vaulted a wall and, disguised as a peasant, sprinted 40 yards across open country in range of the SS guns to reach the cover of a wood. After being recognised by a Canadian journalist (René Lévesque, subsequently the premier of Quebec), he was able to summon help, his bravery a major reason why he was not charged with collaboration by French authorities after the war.

French football writer of the age, Jacques Ferran, himself the grandson of a Neapolitan goldsmith, described French football as '*une salade Russe* ... a hotch-potch of doctrines'.[26] Forty years later, the diversity of France's first World Cup winners was celebrated, but French football has always been diverse;[27] in 1986, *l'Équipe* estimated that a third of all France internationals were of 'foreign' descent. But in 1958 that diversity was regarded as a far more ambiguous.[28]

Ferran was writing in the context of a wider debate of what French football should be. He wasn't opposed to the 'jumble'; rather he was reflecting on the difficulty of identifying a characteristic French style. Before the tournament, Gabriel Hanot had spoken of the 'individualism' and 'inconstancy' of the France national team, which he said was characteristic of France more generally.[29] This too was part of a wider debate. Hanot, like most writers for *l'Equipe* and *France Football*, was a proponent of 'the new France' of greater efficiency and mechanisation, as represented by the return of De Gaulle. After the collapse of the Fourth Republic as a result of the Algerian crisis, he had been installed as head of the government on 1 June 1958 to oversee the transition to the Fifth Republic, a week before France began their World Cup campaign against Paraguay.[30]

From a football point of view, Hanot said, the new France meant more 'triers' and fewer 'stars'. That seemed a fairly obvious attack on Kopa whom he would describe on the eve of the World Cup as 'overly celebrated as a Messiah'.[31] Despite scoring France's late winner against Mexico from the penalty spot, Kopa had been abused in the aftermath of 1954 with fans chanting, 'Kopa, go back to the mine.'[32] After 1958, though, he became emblematic of the 'good immigrant', a symbol of the value of 'hard work'.[33]

The France squad in 1958 was largely isolated from the chaos back home. Based in an idyllic training camp at Kopparberg, they played cards and *petanque*, went fishing and paid very little attention to the news.[34] They could not, though, be said to be unaware of the war in Algeria. Ten players based in France, including the internationals Rachid Mekhloufi and Mustapha Zitouni, had quit their professional careers to join the team set up by the National Liberation Front (FNL), which for four years toured the world raising funds for and awareness of the Algerian cause.

Victories over Paraguay and Scotland took France through top of the group. Fontaine might not have started but for an injury to René Bliard. He then tore his boots and had to borrow a pair from his reserve Stéphane Bruey. He nonetheless ended the tournament with thirteen goals, which remains a record for a single tournament.

The USSR had won Olympic gold in 1956 and should have been serious challengers in Sweden. A defeat to Poland in qualifying necessitated a play-off against the Poles in Leipzig and, although the Soviets won 2–0, the fixture brought the first indications of problems ahead. The Soviet coach Gavriil Kachalin's preferred strike pairing was the Torpedo duo of Valentin Ivanov and Eduard Streltsov. Ivanov was twenty-three, and would go on to score twice in the semi-final as the Soviets won the inaugural European Championship in 1960 and to be joint top scorer at the 1962 World Cup.* But it was Streltsov who really excited people. He was twenty, charismatic, good-looking and enormously talented. He was, his international team-mate Nikita Simonyan said, 'very big, muscular, he could do everything with the ball, had great understanding on the game. He had a great connection with Ivanov.'[35]

---

* His son, also called Valentin, born in 1961, became an international referee, taking charge of the notorious 'Battle of Nuremberg' between Portugal and the Netherlands at the 2006 World Cup when he showed a then-record sixteen yellow cards and four reds.

Streltsov had confirmed his status in the 1956 Olympic semi-final against Bulgaria when, effectively down to nine men because of injury, the Soviets came from behind to win 2–1, Streltsov scoring one and setting up the other. Kachalin, though, liked his strike pairing to play together at club level and so, when Ivanov failed to recover for the final, Streltsov was left out as well. In those days, only the eleven who had started the final were awarded gold medals so, after the USSR had beaten Yugoslavia 1–0, Simonyan, who had replaced him, offered his to Streltsov. 'Don't worry, Nikita,' he replied. 'I will win plenty of medals.'[36]

Streltsov, shuttled around official reception after official reception to celebrate the Olympic win, began to drink increasingly heavily, and his behaviour became increasingly erratic.[37] At an official banquet at the Kremlin, he may have said something unwise to the culture minister Yekaterina Furtseva, whose teenage daughter was seemingly fixated on him.[38] He began to attract official criticism: the timing of his wedding was said to have disrupted preparations for the season and, when he was sent off against Spartak Minsk, *Sovetsky Sport* called him a 'hooligan'[39] and published letters supposedly from members of the public denouncing him as an example of the 'evils of western imperialism'.[40]

But the situation became far more serious that November before the qualifying play-off against Poland. The squad was booked on the night train from Moscow to Berlin but Ivanov and Streltsov, both at least slightly drunk, arrived late at the station. They were bundled into a taxi and caught up the train when it made an unscheduled stop for them at Mozhaisk. Streltsov had missed several league games with a leg injury and aggravated the problem early in the game. Realising the only way to avoid further condemnation was a starring performance, though, he persuaded the physio to patch him up to carry on. As he tended to in those days, Streltsov turned it on when he needed to, scoring one and setting up the other in a 2–0 win.

It was not enough. The Soviet machine had turned against him. After his dismissal against Spartak Minsk, Streltsov had been banned for three games, an unusually harsh sanction.[41] In February 1958, *Pravda* published a lengthy condemnation written by the infamous feuilletonist Semyon Narignani that attacked every aspect of his character: Streltsov was portrayed as selfish, alcoholic, arrogant and stupid, a victim of what the headline termed 'star disease'.[42]

If anything, though, Streltsov's form reached new heights in the first half of 1958. He kept drinking, he kept womanising, he kept getting into scrapes and he kept scoring goals. He couldn't be omitted from the squad for the World Cup. And then on the final day of the pre-tournament training camp at Tarasovka, just outside Moscow, after the players had their tournament suits fitted, Streltsov went for a picnic with two other players, an air force officer recently returned from the east called Eduard Karakhonov and some young women. They drank heavily and ended up spending the night at Karakhonov's dacha. The following morning, one of the women, Marina Lebedeva, accused Streltsov of rape. He was arrested, convicted and sentenced to eleven years in the gulag, of which he served six.

His guilt has been a matter of intense speculation ever since. There has been a campaign to clear his name convinced that Streltsov took the blame for Karakhonov, or that the whole thing was a set-up designed to bring him down, whether because he was seen as too much of an individual, because he was considered a defection risk or because Furtseva had it in for him. But photographs in the KGB archive show Streltsov with scratches down his cheek and Lebedeva with a pair of black eyes, while forensic evidence proves she had sex that night with somebody of Streltsov's blood group. 'It's a mysterious thing,' said Simonyan. 'He wrote to his mother that he was taking the blame for someone else. I don't know for sure if he committed rape, but he and the girl spent the night together.'[43]

With Streltsov awaiting trial and the captain Igor Netto missing the first two games through injury, the Soviets were far from their best when they arrived at the World Cup, but they were good enough to win a play-off against England for a place in the quarter-final, in which they were beaten 2–0 by Sweden. 'We'd played five games in eleven days,' said Simonyan. 'They had had rest and we had not, and because of fog the plane was delayed so we didn't get to bed on the day of the game until 3 a.m. Our legs were heavy, and that's why we lost.'[44]

For a long time in Sweden, it felt as though Wales's biggest opponents were their own directors. To save money, Wales took a squad of only eighteen to Sweden when twenty-two were permitted, yet funds were found to take sixteen Football Association of Wales directors. When the squad gathered in London, their tracksuits hadn't arrived and their pitch booking fell through, so they ended up training in Hyde Park wearing borrowed kit.

Wales's great star was John Charles, but it wasn't clear until four days before the first game whether Juventus would release him. The Swedish press was baffled by the delay: their federation had sent delegates to petition the Italian clubs to make sure their players were available and ready in good time; the Welsh had relied on a single letter. This was the first World Cup at which Sweden considered professionals playing outside the country for the national team: their reward for securing the services of Nils Liedholm, Kurt Hamrin, Arne Selmosson, Lennart Skoglund and Bengt Gustavsson was to reach the final.

When Charles's plane from Turin was then delayed, nobody bothered to wait for him at the airport so, after taking ninety minutes to find out where Wales were staying, he was eventually given a lift to the hotel by Dewi Lewis of the *Western Mail*, walking in at breakfast three days before facing Hungary.[45]

The Hungarians, devastated by defections, were nothing like the side they had been in 1954. Only six players from the 1954 squad were also included in 1958, only three of those were selected against Wales and of them, the captain Nándor Hidegkuti, was well past his best. One of the other veterans of 1954, József Bozsik, put Hungary in front after five minutes, but John Charles equalised from a corner and, although Jack Kelsey made a couple of good saves, Wales held out comfortably enough for a draw.

Wales were poor in drawing 1–1 with Mexico and dour in a 0–0 against Sweden that secured a play-off against Hungary. The day before that game, Imre Nagy, the reformist prime minister, was hanged, having been convicted of treason in a secret trial in Budapest. MTI, the Hungarian news agency, reported his death on the morning of the match,[46] which may explain in part the distracted nature of Hungary's performance in a 2–1 defeat. Ferenc Sipos was sent off late on but from Wales's point of view the damage had already been done; with the scores level, a kick from Sipos had left John Charles with an injured buttock ligament.

That Wales had no back-up centre-forward was the fault of nobody but the FAW's directors. Trevor Ford had been a world-record signing when he'd joined Sunderland from Aston Villa in 1950 and even at thirty-four he was still playing at a high standard. He was doing so, though, for PSV Eindhoven, having been banned from English league football for three years after admitting in his 1956 autobiography that he'd taken under-the-counter payments.[47] He was still eligible for Wales, but the committee wouldn't touch him. Arsenal's Derek Tapscott, meanwhile, had effectively ruled himself out by refusing to join Cardiff City when the FAW director Fred Dewey, who was on the club's board, suggested a move would help his World Cup prospects.[48]

Non-footballing issues had also cost Wales the centre-half Ray Daniel, who could conceivably have come in to release Mel Charles to move to centre-forward. After the qualifying defeat to Czechoslovakia, he tried to lighten the mood on the bus by belting out a series of songs from *Guys and Dolls*, which appalled the chapel-going FAW secretary Herbert Powell.

In the end, Wales turned to the Manchester United inside-forward Colin Webster, who had not been on the flight that crashed at Munich because of flu. He was already on the FAW blacklist after an incident in a Stockholm club in which he'd headbutted a waiter[49] but necessity spared him for one final game for his country. Twice in the opening 20 minutes he narrowly failed to convert crosses that John Charles, almost six inches taller, might have put away.

Finally, with 17 minutes remaining, Pelé seized on a Didi header, flicked the ball on the turn past Mel Charles and jabbed a volley into the bottom corner. It was the first of twelve goals Pelé would score at World Cups, and it ended Wales's involvement in World Cup finals tournaments for sixty-four years.

France were comfortable 4–0 winners over a depleted Northern Ireland in the last eight, Fontaine scoring twice. They probably wouldn't have beaten Brazil in the semi-final anyway, but their task was made far harder ten minutes before half-time when the experienced Reims centre-half Robert Jonquet was injured by a bad foul from Vavá with the score at 1–1. Didi had Brazil ahead within four minutes and a second-half hat-trick from Pelé completed a 5–2 win.

Garrincha, supposedly, was surprised to find the next game was the final, saying the World Cup couldn't matter very much if it could be over in six games; in the Paulista championship, you had to play everybody twice. It's a nice story that reflects both his unworldliness and his capacity to live in the moment, but it's almost certainly untrue. Almost all the anecdotes that paint him as some sort of *idiot savant* – selling a radio he had bought in Sweden because he didn't speak the language, for instance – were made up by the journalist Sandro Moreyra and faithfully repeated by Mário Filho in his book on the 1962 World Cup.[50]

After all the fuss about shirts and the replacement of the white kit of 1950, Brazil ended up not wearing the famous yellow as they won the World Cup for the first time. So outraged were they that Sweden did not automatically grant them the right to wear their preferred colours that they refused to turn up for the drawing of lots to decide the issue. Sweden won and so the Brazilian delegation, having thought of everything else, had to dispatch a functionary to a Stockholm sports shop to find a set of blue shirts. Other issues were taken care of more efficiently: Havelange managed to have the cheerleaders who had inspired Sweden to semi-final victory over West Germany banned, while the head of the Brazil delegation Mozart di Giorgio approached the French referee Maurice Guigue who had been allocated the final and offered him an all-expenses paid trip to Rio. Although he supposedly refused the offer, a year later Guigue and his family did take a holiday in Rio.[51] Brazil were much the stronger side and Guigue made no obviously outrageous decisions but, in the technocratic world of Brazilian football, nothing was left to chance.

As he lined up in unfamiliar colours for the final, Pelé remembered his promise. 'As the anthems played,' he said, 'I had a sudden vision of Dondinho at home, my father hunched over the radio, at once nervous and proud.'[52]

The Sweden coach George Raynor, not unreasonably given

what had happened at the previous two World Cups, had said he expected Brazil to crack mentally if they fell behind, which they did as Nils Liedholm wandered through two challenges at the edge of the box after four minutes. But this Brazil turned out to be rather more resilient than their predecessors. Pelé spoke of feeling 'a strange calmness ... a strange feeling of invincibility'[53] and within five minutes Vavá had levelled from close range. He put Brazil ahead before half-time.

Then, ten minutes into the second half, a ball was slung in from the left. Pelé got to it before Sigge Parling and, as Bengt Gustavsson approached, lifted it over his head before volleying low past the keeper. To modern eyes it appears nothing particularly special; in fact because the ball drops slightly too close to Pelé and he has to dig it out, it looks almost clumsy, lacking the grace of, say, Paul Gascoigne's similar goal against Scotland at Euro 96. But, as Pelé said, 'no one had scored a goal like that before.'[54] It was skilful, it was innovative and it propelled the seventeen-year-old to a new level of stardom. *Paris Match* ran a feature on him referring to him as 'King Pelé'. It was as though he had bypassed a whole stage of development, leaping straight from teenage potential to global celebrity.

Mário Zagallo added a fourth and, after Tore Simonsson had pulled one back, Pelé completed a 5–2 win with a great leap and header. At the final whistle, weeping with the emotion of it all, his promise to his father fulfilled far earlier than anybody could have reasonably expected, he was lifted onto the shoulders of a handful of team-mates, while others performed a lap of honour with the flag.

The day after the final, the initial phase of the construction of Brasilia was completed. The symbolic resonance was profound: this was a key moment in Brazil's emergence as a post-colonial nation. For Nelson Rodrigues, it was the casting off of what he called the 'mongrel complex', which he defined as 'the inferiority in which Brazilians put themselves, voluntarily, in comparison to the rest of the world'[55] as a result of their racially mixed origins; in the context of the scapegoating of three black players after the Maracanazo it seemed significant that the side that won in Stockholm featured three black players and two of mixed race.[56] As intoxicated by the success as he had been crushed by the failure of eight years previously, Rodrigues claimed the effect was physical, claiming that the day after the final he saw 'a small black woman' from the slums transformed into Joan of Arc while black men, 'attractive, brilliant, luxurious', became 'like fabulous Ethiopian princes'.[57]

For Gilberto Freyre, miscegenation had been Brazil's superpower; for Rodrigues it was the source of an insecurity that needed to be overcome. But Brazilian football has always been paradoxical. Its reputation, its self-mythology, is of off-the cuff improvisation that makes a distinction between art and results and prioritises the former. But packed with brilliantly skilful individuals as that 1958 side was, their victory was also the result of the thoroughness of their preparation and the tactical advantage given them by their development of 4-2-4.

'In football,' as Roberto DaMatta wrote, 'there is art, dignity, genius, bad luck, gods and demons, freedom and fate, flags, hymns and tears, and above all the discovery that although Brazil is bad at a lot of things, it is good with the ball.'[58]

And for Havelange, this was his route to real power, not only in Brazil but beyond.

1962

A PIG, A DOG AND A MYNAH BIRD

Antonio Ghirelli and Corrado Pizzinelli were well-known Italian journalists, working respectively for the *Corriere della Sera* in Milan and *La Nazione* in Florence. They had gone to Santiago for the draw, five months before the World Cup began, and weren't impressed. The pieces they wrote reflected a mixture of realistic concerns about infrastructure, the understandable frustrations of journalists, but also something rather darker and less explicable; in Pizzinelli's case there is overt racism.

Pizzinelli wrote of Santiago as 'a sad symbol of one of the underdeveloped countries of the world, afflicted by all possible evils: malnutrition, prostitution, illiteracy, alcoholism, misery'.[1] Ghirelli, meanwhile, described 'a World Cup 13,000km away' as 'madness' and went on, 'Chile is a small, poor and proud country ... The capital city has 700 hotel beds. The phones don't work. Taxis are as rare as faithful husbands. A cable to Europe costs an arm and a leg. A letter takes at least five days by airmail.'[2]

The tone of the articles is unsympathetic, particularly in light of the earthquake Chile had suffered in 1960, but the underlying point about the country's suitability as hosts was not entirely without validity – even if their perspective was obviously Eurocentric; after all, everywhere is 13,000km from somewhere. But they also prepared the ground for one of the most notorious games the World Cup has known. There have been four 'Battles of . . .' in World Cup history, but it is the Battle of Santiago that stands out. It was, as the BBC presenter David Coleman described it in his introduction to the highlights, 'the most stupid, appalling, disgusting and disgraceful exhibition of football in the history of the game'.[3]

When Chile's ambassador in Italy was alerted to the articles, he sent them to the Chilean national *El Mercurio*, sparking outrage. Or that's one theory. The Italy defender Mario David wondered if something else was going on, whether West Germany, who had been drawn in the same group, had used their news agencies deliberately to stir things up.[4]

Either way, when Chile met Italy in their second game in the group, tensions were high. 'The Italian players were not to blame for what was published in their country,' said Chile's left-winger Leonel Sánchez, 'but we had this anger inside us.'[5] Italy, trying to placate the ferocious 65,000 crowd at the Estadio Nacional, walked out with white flowers before kick-off but when they tried to distribute them to fans, the bouquets were flung back at them.

David kicked Sánchez early and when he then clattered the midfielder Jorge Toro, angry players surrounded the English referee Ken Aston. As photographers spilled onto the pitch, the Italy midfielder Humberto Maschio punched Sánchez in the face, knocking him to the ground. A couple of minutes after play resumed, Italy's Giorgio Ferrini kicked Honorino Landa from behind. Aston sent him off. He refused to leave the pitch – perhaps not unreasonably wondering why his offence, of all the many that had already taken place, was the one being penalised, and as journalists flooded the pitch it took ten minutes for Ferrini to depart, escorted by police. There were still only eight minutes of actual football gone.

Sánchez, the son of a boxer, took his revenge on Maschio with a savage punch, and towards the end of the half landed a right hook on David's jaw. David kicked him repeatedly, in front of the linesman Leo Goldstein,* but Aston took no action beyond awarding a free-kick. Just before half-time, David took his own revenge with a flying kick to Sánchez's head, for which he was sent off.

Maschio had been born in Argentina and, as one of four *oriundi* in the Italy side, found himself targeted. 'They broke my nose in the first 20 minutes and then they kicked my ankle,' he said. 'Chileans shouted at me, "Traitor, you should be at Rancagua [where Argentina were based]."'[6]

The second half was rather calmer as, eventually, Chile made their two-man advantage count, winning 2–0 to secure their place in the quarter-final. 'It did cross my mind to abandon the match,' said Aston, 'but I couldn't be responsible for the safety of the Italian players if I did.' Making sure he was near the tunnel, he blew the whistle exactly on 90 minutes, then ran for the dressing-rooms as fights broke out behind him. Ghirelli and Pizzinelli, fearing for their safety, had not returned to Santiago after the draw.[7]

But the Battle of Santiago did not happen in isolation. It was not just about tensions between Chile and Italy. Football had changed. In 1954, there had been an average of 5.38 goals per game; by 1962 that average was down to 2.78. Football had become more defensive, more cynical and more violent. And that represented an existential threat. 'If the World Cup is

* Goldstein was himself a remarkable figure. A Polish Jew, he was pulled out of the line to the gas chambers at Auschwitz by a guard, apparently a league player, who recognised him as a referee and had him officiate games between camp guards. Having survived the war, he took Israeli citizenship before emigrating to New York where he worked as a referee and taxi driver.

going to survive in its present form,' Coleman said, 'something has got to be done about teams that play like this.'[8]

Chile was not an uncontroversial choice as host; even their own press acknowledged they were a long way from Europe, and even from much of the Americas.[9] West Germany and Argentina had also declared their intention to bid, but the Germans complied with Fifa's request to withdraw to avoid the prospect of three successive World Cups being hosted in Europe.

Knowledge of the horrors that followed the 1973 coup in which Augusto Pinochet seized power from the democratically elected Marxist Salvador Allende means that the entirety of its post-war politics up to that point can feel like prologue. The Radicals, who opposed the power of the great landowners but were essentially centrist, emerged from the 1946 elections as the largest party and were supported by the Communists. When the far left opposed a wage freeze imposed to try to reduce inflation, though, the three Communist ministers were dismissed from the cabinet and the Communist Party was effectively outlawed. Pablo Neruda, a Communist senator, was forced to go on the run, escaping across the Andes into Argentina. It was there that he composed *Canto general*, in which he identified socialist revolution as necessary for genuine national independence in South America.

The bid to host the World Cup was the brainchild of Ernesto Alvear, a director of the Chilean football federation who attended the Fifa Congress in Helsinki in 1952. The event coincided with the Olympic Games in Finland and, impressed, he reasoned that if a small country in the far north could host a major sporting event, why couldn't his country in the far south?[10] The economic outlook, though, was not good. The end of the Korean War had led to a fall in the price of copper that harmed Chile's balance of payments, driving up inflation. The president Carlos Ibáñez applied to the International Monetary Fund for a bailout, which it granted in return for austerity, leading to conflict with the left – who tended to see the issue as proving Neruda's point.

Argentina was a clear favourite to get the tournament. Some in the Chilean press called for Chile to withdraw rather than face embarrassment.[11] The head of the Chilean delegation, Carlos Dittborn, though, proved a tireless campaigner and a persuasive public speaker. The decision was taken at the Fifa Congress in Lisbon in 1956. 'We can start the World Cup tomorrow,' said Raúl Colombo, the president of the Argentinian football association (AFA). 'We have everything.' To which Dittborn replied, 'Because we have nothing, we want to do everything.'[12]

He made great play of Article 2 of the Fifa statutes, which at the time spoke of the role of the World Cup in promoting the sport in countries in which it was 'underdeveloped'. Dittborn's other arguments, that Chile had at least entered the two post-war World Cups (which Argentina had not) and that it was politically stable, perhaps carried greater weight. Argentina, after all, had suffered two attempted coups the previous year. In the first, the air force had bombed the Plaza de Mayo, killing more than 300 civilians. The second had toppled Juan Perón, leading to a vicious crackdown on his supporters as part of which the entire executive board of the AFA had been suspended. Not only did that, obviously, place a check on their campaigning but the World Cup bid was an overtly Peronist project.[13]

With Alvear sitting in Santiago pulling the strings, Dittborn forged an unlikely alliance of east and west. To the Soviet bloc, he spoke of the strength of the unions in Chile and emphasised the anti-Communism of the military government in Argentina; to western Europe and the US, he spoke of Chile's modernity and centre-right government while highlighting the undemocratic nature of the new Argentinian regime. The pair proved extremely adept lobbyists[14] and Chile won the vote 32–10.

But on 22 May 1960, Chile suffered the most powerful earthquake ever recorded, its epicentre around 350 miles south of Santiago. Thousands were killed while tens of thousands were left homeless. It's estimated around 40 per cent of buildings in Valdivia, the worst affected city, were destroyed.

Dittborn felt a moral obligation to suggest to the president Jorge Alessandri that Chile should ask to be relieved of hosting responsibilities and the money that had been allocated to the tournament be transferred to the relief effort. But Alessandri refused, saying the people needed the World Cup to give them joy, and wrote to the Fifa president Stanley Rous assuring him that Chile would be able to host.[15] Inevitably, though, plans had to be scaled back with the number of venues reduced from eight to four as Valdivia, Concepción, Talca and Talcahuano withdrew.[16]

Ramshackle and patched together at times, the World Cup went ahead. Dittborn, though, never saw it. A month before the tournament, he suffered a heart attack and died, aged just thirty-eight. Chile wore a black bar below their badge in his memory.

Brazil's preparations for Chile were just as thorough as they had been for Sweden. The squad underwent a lengthy training camp at altitude, even though in Chile they were based in Viña del Mar, at sea level. Recognising that it was pointless to expect the players to curtail their natural desires, Dr Gosling gave every prostitute at the local brothel a health inspection. Alongside the science, there was also superstition. Paulo Machado de Carvalho, still wearing the lucky brown jacket that served him so well in 1958, even had Captain Bugner, the same pilot who had flown Brazil to Sweden four years earlier, take them to Santiago.

The side itself was very similar to that of 1958. With Vicente Feola in poor health, Aymoré Moreira, whose brother Zeze had been in charge in 1954, took over as coach. He was concerned that, as opponents got used to the 4-2-4 formation that had been so important four years earlier, Brazil might be overwhelmed in midfield, so he had the left-winger Mário Zagallo shuttle back to provide an extra body. Zagallo, never much troubled by humility, would proudly tell anybody who would listen that he 'created the modern left winger'.[17]

By 1962, Pelé had become a phenomenon but he suffered a groin injury in a pre-tournament friendly against Portugal, something he blamed on the exhausting schedule of games he was expected to play for both Santos and Brazil.[18] He thought he'd recovered but, in Brazil's second game of the tournament, against Czechoslovakia, he fired a shot against the post and, as he struck the rebound, felt it go again. That kept him out until the semi-final and then, just as he seemed ready to return, he suffered another relapse while practising taking corners. The way was clear for another of the young stars from 1958 to take the limelight.

Garrincha was a very different figure to Pelé. Where Pelé seemed born to stardom, composed and polite in public, careful about his image and keen to capitalise upon it (even if some unwise investments led at one point to near-bankruptcy), Garrincha didn't care for celebrity, had little interest in money and wasn't even really that bothered about football.

The descendant of a group of Fulniôs who had been enslaved by sugar-ranchers, Manuel dos Santos was born in 1933 in the village of Pau Grande, about ten miles south of Petropolis in the state of Rio de Janeiro. His left leg bowed outwards and his right leg inwards so that he swayed rather than walked. Had he been born in a wealthier environment, calipers would have straightened his legs relatively easily, but then perhaps defenders would not have found it so hard to work out which way he was about to run. He was small, and so his sister gave him the nickname 'Garrincha' ('wren').

He had just two years of schooling and, when he was fourteen, started work at the local cotton mill. He was terrible at his job. He often didn't turn up at all and when he did he would spend most of the day asleep. The only reason he wasn't sacked was that the manager wanted him in the factory football team. Garrincha enjoyed playing football, almost as much as he enjoyed drinking and sex, but for him it was just another activity. When everybody else gathered round radios to listen to the final game of the 1950 World Cup, he went fishing and couldn't understand why so many people were so upset by the result.

Garrincha was nobody's idea of an athlete. He started playing for Serrano in Pau Grande but gave up after three months because he couldn't be bothered with the travelling. He went for a trial at Vasco da Gama but didn't take his boots, whether because he was ashamed of the battered old pair he habitually wore, because he believed the club would provide footwear or as an act of self-sabotage is unclear. At São Cristavão they gave him just ten minutes at the end of a session. Fluminense made him wait and, when they asked him to come back the next day, he took the train home. The sense is of a series of coaches unable to believe he had the athletic capacity to be a professional footballer. They weren't alone in doubting his physique: when Garrincha reported for national service, a sergeant pronounced him 'physically handicapped' and discharged him without even bothering to send him to the regimental physician.[19]

Finally, when he was nineteen, Garrincha went for a trial and was given enough of an opportunity to impress. The Botafogo right-back Araty Vianna had seen him when refereeing a game in Pau Grande the previous year and gone away raving about his ability, but it was a fan called Eurico Salgado who made the decisive move, escorting Garrincha to Rio where, after impressing against the youth team, he was thrown into a practice match against Nílton Santos, Brazil's left-back. By the end of the game, Santos was begging the club to sign him.

Garrincha's life was chaotic. His father Amaro had at least twenty-five children and Garrincha was cut from similar cloth: he had at least fourteen children with at least five different women. He drank heavily and seemed always short of money, despite continuing to live in his simple shack in Pau Grande. When baffled journalists visited him at home, they found he lived in squalor, with cash in various currencies and cheques shoved under mattresses, behind the cooker, in fruit bowls and comic books. Some of it was rotting, some of it was no longer legal tender, almost all had been devalued by inflation, yet there was still over £200,000 in today's money.[20]

There was a sense in which Garrincha didn't quite fit into the modern world, that the only place he was truly at home was on the pitch. Although Pelé had been the outstanding star of 1958, the World Cup win in Sweden made Garrincha so popular that when Julinho, having returned from Italy and so become eligible again, replaced Garrincha for a friendly against England in 1959, he was booed by the 127,000 crowd at the Maracanã, at least until he put Brazil ahead after nine minutes.

Garrincha's lifestyle, meanwhile, was beginning to catch up with him. In 1959, catatonic with booze, driving past the factory in Pau Grande, he knocked over his father and ran off, not even realising who it was he had hit. His father, whose health was already in decline, died the following year. Garrincha had married when he was sixteen and, with his wife living in Pau Grande, he maintained a mistress in Rio de Janeiro while having a series of other affairs. In 1961, to boost his chances in a newspaper poll to determine Rio's most popular footballer, Garrincha was introduced to Elza Soares, a remarkable woman who had grown up in poverty and endured a horrific marriage to an abusive husband before becoming one of the greatest singers in Brazilian history. He fell for her in a way he seems never to have fallen for any other woman, but she thought little of him until, with Rio in the grip of a food crisis, he presented her with a 60kg bag of beans. He later killed her mother in another hit-and-run, and she divorced him after he had attacked her in a drunken rage.

A few days before Brazil set off for Chile, the squad attended a reception at the Palacio de Guanabara in Rio. There, Garrincha was very taken by a mynah bird that could bark like a dog, wolf-whistle and speak several sentences. The governor Carlos Lacerda told him he could have it if he came home with the World Cup.

Czechoslovakia had qualified for the World Cup by beating Scotland in a play-off, but few expected much from them in Chile. Their hammering of Argentina in 1958 may have had profound consequences for their opponents, but it was Czechoslovakia's only win in a World Cup match since 1938. They started against Spain, the 'team of a million stars', with Puskás and José Santamaría, who had played for Hungary and Uruguay in 1954, Luis del Sol, Paco Gento and Luis Suárez. Alfredo di Stéfano was also in the squad but he had clashed with Spain's coach Helenio Herrera, and carrying an injury, didn't play a single game. Czechoslovakia were clear underdogs but, with ten minutes remaining, Jozef Štibrányi received the ball in midfield, got away from Jesús Garay and Santamaría and beat the falling goalkeeper Carmelo with a deft chip.

Štibrányi was twenty-two, a third-grade student at the institute of education, and a winger for Spartak Trnava. His emergence had been abrupt. Over Christmas and New Year the previous winter, he'd been called up to Rudi Vytlačil's national squad as they underwent compulsory ski training at Kežmarok Hut in Tatry. At the end of January, he excelled in the national team's physical tests. 'I had unbelievably strong legs and won every discipline,' he said.[21] A sparkling performance in a subsequent friendly win over Uruguay secured his place in the World Cup squad.

Štibrányi maintained the diary throughout the World Cup, offering an insight into the rituals and routines of a squad – and also of just how homely, how *ad hoc*, everything still was in 1962. He details the flights, the meals, the films the squad watched with brief reviews, interspersed with personal reflections: 'What's new at home? *Otek* [Dad] is at work. Mama at home alone crying for sure. What can you do? She's just like that. I've forgotten my toothbrush and toothpaste. I have to buy: socks, Alpa [massage cream], slippers.'[22]

Looking to save money and thinking they would soon be returning home, Czechoslovakia took only nineteen players and neither a kitman nor a masseur, although funds were found for two secret service agents who, despite not speaking Spanish, sought to monitor the Czechoslovak players and their interactions with outsiders. Nor was a great deal spent on accommodation. 'The hotel was an unpleasant surprise for us,' Štibrányi wrote. 'It was cold and dirty and there was only cold water.'[23]

There was, at least, a large fireplace, a billiard table and a gramophone with records by Bill Haley that helped the players pass the time until that opening game. 'Is there anything more prestigious than the World Cup?' Štibrányi asked. 'I don't think so ... I would love to deliver as good a performance as possible ... It will be terrible if they beat us by three goals ... The weather is very bad, drizzling and drizzling since this morning.'[24]

By the time he sat down that night, Štibrányi's tone had changed dramatically: 'Unexpected result! It will be hard to fall asleep tonight! I scored a goal after [Josef] Jelínek´s pass to the centre ... I thought I wouldn't survive. I held my hands up and screamed ... Hugging – they nearly smothered me ... I can never forget this! ... The boss of our hotel bought me and Vilda [the goalkeeper Viliam Schrojf] a big cake.'[25]

Brazil were next up, the game unavoidably overshadowed by Pelé's groin injury. With no substitutes, he was reduced to limping around on the flank and was grateful the Czechoslovak defenders eased back in their tackling, both sides seemingly settling for a 0–0 draw. Had he been fit, Štibrányi reasoned, 'they wouldn't have secured the defence so much; they would have attacked, which would have allowed us to play and manoeuvre in their half better.'[26]

Two goals from Pelé's replacement, the Botafogo striker Amarildo, secured a 2–1 win over Spain and progress for both them and Czechoslovakia, despite a 3–1 defeat to Mexico. The Czechoslovak federation responded by sending out three further players, although by then there seemed little point. Štibrányi noted how all the talk had been of saving money and then they'd blown US$3,000 on what he dismissed as 'an excursion'.[27] None of the three played a single minute.

Garrincha had not played particularly well against either Mexico or Czechoslovakia, but after Elza Soares arrived in Chile to perform at a music festival in Avisa, not far from the Brazil camp at Viña del Mar, he was inspired to perhaps the greatest string of individual performances at a World Cup until Diego Maradona in 1986. First he set up Amarildo's second against Spain. Then, in the quarter-final against England, he put Brazil ahead with a header from Zagallo's corner. Gerry Hitchens levelled, but it was Garrincha's free-kick that led to Vavá nodding Brazil back in front and then his whipped shot from the edge of the box that made it 3–1. During the second half, a stray dog ran onto the pitch, evading capture until Jimmy Greaves got down on all fours and barked at it. As he picked it up, the dog urinated on him. The dog was then raffled off; his luck decisively in, Garrincha won.

Garrincha's team-mates had no doubt that the arrival of Soares had been decisive. 'She was his stimulus,' said Nílton Santos. 'He thought mainly with his you-know-what.'[28]

Brazil's opponents in the semi-final were Chile, who had beaten the USSR 2–1 in the last eight with a pair of long-range strikes that contributed to the scapegoating of the great goalkeeper Lev Yashin when he got back to Moscow. Rival fans jeered him, insults were written in the dust on his car and the windows of his apartment were broken twice. 'There was no TV in Russia at that time and everyone knew about the game against Chile only from a report by the correspondent of APN [the state news agency], who knew much more about politics than about football,' Yashin's widow Valentina explained. 'Because of his reports, everybody decided that Yashin lost the World Cup.'[29]

The semi-final was notable for the number of robust tackles, many of them on Garrincha. He scored the first two goals, a crisp left-foot drive and a header from a corner, as Brazil won 4–2 but, four minutes after Landa was sent off for a foul on Zito, Garrincha reacted to yet another foul by kneeing Eladio Rojas up the backside and was also dismissed.

At the time, there were no mandatory suspensions for players sent off in the World Cup – Bozsik had played in the 1954 semi-final after being sent off against Brazil in the quarter-final – but the other five players sent off in 1962 were all given one-game bans. Brazil were understandably desperate that Garrincha should play in the final, so the president of Peru was prevailed upon to get the country's ambassador to Chile to approach Arturo Yamasaki, the Peruvian who had refereed the semi-final, and persuade him to rescind the sending off.

He said he had been acting on the advice of the Uruguayan linesman Esteban Marino, who had conveniently already left Chile after the Brazilian delegation provided him with a ticket to Montevideo – via Paris.[30] At the same time, the head of the Brazilian delegation, Mozart di Giorgio, insisted to the disciplinary panel that Garrincha had intended the gesture as a joke and that he had never been sent off before; in fact it was his fourth dismissal. The pleas worked and Garrincha was spared a ban.

Czechoslovakia reached the final with a grim 1–0 win over Hungary, followed by a fortuitous 3–1 success against Yugoslavia. 'It's fantastic,' wrote Štibrányi. 'Our style of play isn't very nice, but fortune is always on our side. The opponents don't score from great chances and we often do; nobody knows how.'[31]

But that luck did not hold for the final, even though Garrincha, playing despite a high fever, was unusually quiet. Josef Masopust, the elegant Dukla Prague centre-half who would win the Ballon d'Or later that year, put Czechoslovakia ahead after 14 minutes but Amarildo soon levelled and then, after Djalma Santos had got away with a clear handball in his own box, second-half goals from Zito and Vavá, becoming the first player to score in two finals, sealed a comfortable victory.

Štibrányi returned home and, as the university holidays had begun, went camping with some friends. When he returned, he found his father had already spent his World Cup bonus on parquet flooring for the house; he was still walking on it more than fifty years later.[32] He was given various socialist diplomas, badges and cups, as well as a food mixer and an electric iron. The cooperative workers of Trnava, meanwhile, gave pigs to both Štibrányi and his team-mate Jozef Adamec. 'I got one weighing 15 kilos with a red bow round his neck,' he said. 'I still have a photo of me taking the pig to the Trnava stadium. But the local newspaper printed that picture and that was a problem. When the Communists found out what happened, they got angry. Especially a guy called Karel Bacílek. He had a big head, but a brain like a fingernail – total jerk! He got mad that the co-op workers weren't able to fulfil their quota, yet they gave pigs to footballers. So he ordered us to return the animals. But Joža's mum had already sold the pig and at our home there was chaos.'

Two policemen turned up to collect the pig only to be met by Štibrányi's enraged father, who pointed out that he'd made its sty and that they had no right to take that. 'He opened the sty,' he said, 'the pig ran out with straw and other mess on its body – and the policemen were trying to catch it. Then they put the excited pig directly into the car. Chaos!'[33]

Brazil's chaos was of a different kind. As the third goal in the final had gone in, Lacerda, the governor of Rio, had sent a telegram to Garrincha to tell him the mynah bird was ready for collection. After the players returned to the dressing room following the celebrations on the pitch, Elza Soares walked in. Many were naked and protested, but she walked through to the showers and kissed Garrincha. They agreed to marry.

That Brazil were the best side in the world was beyond dispute, but the overriding sense after the 1962 tournament was that football had changed. *World Soccer*'s review of the tournament spoke of 'thuggery and sadistic brutality'.[34] There had been a tournament-record six sendings off and there should have been more. So many players were injured that the Chilean press took to providing lists of casualties.

Not since 1930 had a World Cup averaged under four goals per game, and the average in 1962 was over a goal per game less than that previous low. In part, that could perhaps be explained by problems with the ball, the first example of what would become a familiar trope. Europeans thought the Chilean balls were light, which they were, although still within Fifa's regulations, but more worrying was that twenty-five of forty-six balls tested by Fifa developed bloated areas causing them to behave erratically in flight and when bouncing.[35]

But there were also tactical issues. After the 6–1 defeat to Czechoslovakia in Helsingborg, Argentina had embraced *anti-fútbol*. It hadn't quite reached the depths of cynicism it would later in the decade when Estudiantes won three successive Copas Libertadores under Osvaldo Zubeldía,[36] but Juan Carlos Lorenzo was not a coach who prioritised beauty.[37]

Argentina may have been an extreme case, but this was not a phenomenon limited to one country. Four weeks before the World Cup began, Béla Guttmann's Benfica beat Real Madrid in the European Cup final. For teams based around the individual ability of players, it was the end. The following year Benfica lost in the final to AC Milan, ushering in the era of *catenaccio*. Under Giovanni Ferrari and Paolo Mazza, Italy's national team was just beginning to explore that approach. Almost every side was capable of negativity. England, for instance, needing a point against Bulgaria to qualify for the quarter-final at Argentina's expense, played out a 0–0 draw that Bobby Charlton described as 'a miserable betrayal of all that I thought English football should stand for'.[38]

Football was entering the era of systematisation. Charlton might not have liked it but, in the unlikely surrounds of Suffolk, a system was beginning to be devised that would end Brazil's reign and win him and England the World Cup.

1966

THREE FACES OF THE LION

The Stampex exhibition was closed on Sundays, but the security men were nonetheless on duty at Westminster Hall, which stands between the Houses of Parliament and Westminster Abbey, less than half a mile from Downing Street, the Home Office and New Scotland Yard. That Sunday, 20 March 1966, a week and a half before the general election, George Franklin, one of the security guards, arrived at 9 a.m., entering through the office where he found his colleague George Hudson doing paperwork. He checked the doors and was satisfied they were 'in order'. Half an hour later, Franklin escorted two maintenance men into the exhibition space for routine cleaning and upkeep. When they left, Franklin insisted he had locked the doors behind them.

Franklin checked the trophy again at 11 a.m., after which he went for a coffee with Hudson. Around twenty-five minutes later, Hudson went into the corridor outside to use the gents'. He saw a man nearby, making a call on the public telephone. He was in his late thirties, 5ft 8in tall, medium build, with slicked-back dark hair; he was wearing a black suit with a light shirt and dark tie and had a long, sallow face with thin lips.[1]

When Hudson returned, the man was still there. He didn't pay particular attention because the doors to the main hall were open to admit the congregation for the Methodist service and Sunday school taking place on the ground floor. At a little before noon, one of the other security guards, McLaren, came upstairs and suggested the pairs should swap over. Hudson agreed. At 12.10, McLaren checked the case again. The Jules Rimet trophy was gone.

McLaren raised the alarm. The rear doors had been opened by the simple expedient of unscrewing the brackets that held the wooden security bar in place. The door from the corridor, though, had not been forced: it had evidently been left open either when the maintenance men left or when Hudson went to the toilet. The padlock on the back of the case had then been removed, and the thieves had presumably made their escape the same way they had come in, using the lifts at the back of the building normally reserved for elderly or infirm visitors.

A woman called Margaret Coombes, who had been attending the Sunday school service with her husband, had seen a man standing outside the toilets at around 11 a.m. and had assumed he was waiting for his wife. The ladies', though, was empty, arousing her suspicions. The man was about forty, 5ft 7in and well-built, with a receding hairline. He was wearing a grey overcoat and scarf. The description is perhaps different enough from that given by Hudson to suggest two suspects, but the appeal put out in *The Times* the following day conflates them into a single man and suggests he may have had a scar (given neither witness mentions this detail, it's probable the word 'scarf' was misheard).[2]

Rewards totalling £5,500 – £3,000 from the FA's insurers, £1,000 from the National Sporting Club, £1,000 from the entertainer Tommy Trinder (but only if it was returned to him at the Latin Quarter club in Soho, where he was resident comic) and £500 from Gillette – were put up for the return of the trophy in an attempt, given its scrap value was only around £3,000, to prevent it being melted down for bullion (that's if, as was widely believed, it was made of solid gold; in fact, it was gold-plated silver and worth far less than that). The FA entered secret negotiations with the silversmith George Bird to supply a replica trophy, apparently seeking to replace it without Fifa's knowledge.[3]

The day after the theft, the FA chairman Joe Mears received an anonymous call and on Wednesday 23 March he received a package at his home, which included the detachable lining from the top of the trophy and a ransom demand for £15,000 from somebody who later identified himself as 'Jackson'. If he agreed to the terms, Mears was to place an advert in the personals column of the *London Evening News* reading, 'Willing to do business. Joe.'

When Jackson called back to confirm details of the drop, he was told Mears had suffered an angina attack – which was true – and that he would have to deal with his assistant, McPhee – in fact an undercover Flying Squad officer, DI Len Buggy. They arranged to make the exchange on Friday 25 March by the gate of Battersea Park opposite the Prince Albert pub.

They met at 3.55 p.m. Jackson checked Buggy's case and believed it contained £15,000 in £5 and £10 notes, although most of the bundles were made up of strips of newspaper. What followed was a fiasco. Jackson got in Buggy's car, telling him the trophy was ten minutes' drive away. As they headed for St Agnes Place in Kennington, he spotted two of the three Flying Squad surveillance vehicles. Spooked, he ran off, but Buggy gave chase, initially in his car and then, after Jackson had cut through a builder's yard, on foot, finally cornering him in a garden. There, Jackson was arrested and soon revealed to be a former soldier called Ted Betchley.

Betchley, who had served six months in 1954 for theft and

receiving stolen goods, claimed he had not been involved in the theft but was merely acting as an intermediary for somebody he knew only as 'the Pole'. Mrs Coombes, though, picked him out of the identity parade as the man she had seen outside the toilets. He subsequently pleaded guilty to charges of being an accessory to the theft and of demanding money with menaces and was jailed for two years.

But as Betchley denied any knowledge of where the Jules Rimet trophy was, it remained missing for a further two days. On Sunday evening, a week after the theft, a twenty-six-year-old Thames lighterman called Dave Corbett left his home in Upper Norwood at around 9 p.m. to use the public telephone. He took with him his dog, a one-year-old black-and-white collie called Pickles, who darted off, sniffing at a package wrapped in newspaper that was propped against the wheel of a car on his neighbour's drive, hidden from view by a hedge. Corbett and the neighbour opened the package and, realising what they had, took it to the police station in Gypsy Hill. 'It doesn't look very World Cuppy,' said an unimpressed desk sergeant.

How the trophy got there remains unclear. Corbett was investigated but exonerated, and police came to the conclusion that 'the Pole' had dumped the trophy, perhaps pressured by underworld figures demonstrating an idiosyncratic patriotism. The FA was hugely grateful. The story of a dog finding the stolen World Cup had transformed a debacle into a conveniently heart-warming story – suspiciously so, some thought. Corbett collected around £6,000 in various rewards and Pickles became a celebrity, being named Dog of the Year in the UK and Germany, starring as himself in a film about the incident and winning several years' supply of free dog food. As a metaphor it was almost too perfect: the dithering bloviators of the English establishment bailed out by a working-class pragmatist from London's penumbra, the grand patriotic quests of

Mussolini or the Brazilians transformed by the irreverence of sixties Britain into suburban comedy.

Yet mysteries remain. The persistent rumours that what Pickles found was the FA's replica are almost certainly false; it would have been almost impossible secretly to reproduce an accurate replica in a week and, besides, the detachable lining sent by Betchley with his ransom note fitted perfectly. Neither Betchley's accomplices nor the identity of the mysterious 'Pole' have ever been established.

But there is an intriguing coincidence. Betchley lived in Camberwell, just a couple of minutes from the crime boss Charlie Richardson who at the time was involved in a gang war with the Krays. To escape extradition to South Africa where he might have faced the death penalty, Richardson had agreed to burgle the African National Congress's London office for the South African Bureau of State Security, who were also keen to discredit the prime minister Harold Wilson.[4] It happens that Richardson carried out his raid on the same weekend the trophy was stolen. Was he trying to embarrass Wilson a few days before the election? Was he hoping for easy cash to fund his war, only to dump the trophy when he realised that it had a scrap value of only £60?[5]

Adding to the sense of unease, as though dark forces had planned the whole thing before removing all potential witnesses, is the fact that so many of the major players in the drama died soon afterwards. Mears never recovered from his angina attack and died on 30 June. Betchley died two years after his release from prison. Even Pickles didn't see his second birthday, hanged from a tree by his own lead as he chased a cat, an oddly grim end to an otherwise charming tale.

When the 1966 World Cup began, with a grimly tedious goalless draw between England and Uruguay, number one in the UK charts was 'Sunny Afternoon' by The Kinks. With its languorous tempo and refrain 'In the summertime', it seems on the surface a straightforward celebration of the lazy summer when Swinging London was at its height. But the lyrics are far more complex than that: this is about a wealthy man who has mistreated his girlfriend, railing against the tax policies of Harold Wilson's government – and the 'big fat mama' of the (almost-)post-imperial state that is 'tryna break' him. As such, it was probably a far truer reflection of the public mood than the myth would allow; the balance of payments deficit had been critical for some time leading to pressure on sterling and, ultimately, devaluation the following year.[6] For Britain, and for English football, 1966 was about recovery.

Any lingering sense of British imperial might had been obliterated by the Suez Crisis of 1956. That led to the widespread view, most famously expressed by the US secretary of state Dean Acheson, that Britain had lost an empire but not yet found a role.[7] But, at least initially, that wasn't true. Rather, by the mid-sixties, Britain had become extraordinarily culturally vibrant; its role had become the arts, and particularly those favoured by youth. The Beatles and the Rolling Stones were in their pomp. Mary Quant was for a time the biggest single influence on global fashion, Jean Shrimpton the most famous model. David Hockney and David Bailey were feted across the world. Between 1964 and 1966, twenty-eight nominations at the Oscars went to British actors, from Julie Andrews to Richard Burton, Julie Christie to Peter O'Toole. James Bond was a phenomenon: *Thunderball*, released in December 1965, was easily the biggest grossing film of 1966, selling 60 million tickets in the US alone.[8]

From Michael Caine to Princess Margaret, British celebrities were recognised and celebrated. What was most striking, perhaps, was the way that so much of that explosion of cultural self-confidence involved playing with ideas of empire, something seen most obviously in the way the Union flag or the RAF roundel became an at least semi-ironic image of pop art and bands such as The Who. Diana Vreeland, the editor of *Vogue*, had described London as 'the most swinging city in the world' in 1965,[9] but it was an edition of *Time* magazine in April 1966 that cemented the notion of Swinging London.

Football's part in that was perhaps best exemplified in the form of World Cup Willie, the tournament's first ever mascot, a lion with a Beatle haircut in a Union flag jersey. Here, overtly, was the imperial lion transformed into something cheeky and welcoming – but it was also a commercial ploy, a mascot whose image could transform anything from T-shirts to tea-towels into a saleable souvenir: imperialism first defanged by an increasingly classless irreverence and then repackaged as commercial tat.

The advent of *Match of the Day* in August 1964, the first regular nationwide screening of league highlights, had begun to increase the cultural heft of football, but it was the World Cup that really brought it into the mainstream. Alf Ramsey may have been a (very) unlikely leader of a youth revolution, but his England, captained by the ineffably cool Bobby Moore, became a central part of that explosion of cultural self-confidence. But English football too had had to recover.

Its Suez had come on 25 November 1953 with the 6–3 home defeat to Hungary, England's first ever defeat at home to non-British or Irish opposition. 'Twilight of the Gods' ran the headline in both the *Telegraph* and the *Mirror* the following day. In truth, it had been decades since English football had been indisputably great and the writing had been on the wall since the late 1920s. But a defeat so comprehensive at Wembley on a foggy Wednesday in November meant the decline could no longer be written off as a consequence of the weather, the pitch or foreign cuisine: English football, England itself, seemed moribund.

It had been only six months earlier that Wembley had staged what stands, in retrospect, as the grand culmination of the old English style, the 1953 FA Cup final, when Stanley Matthews inspired Blackpool to come from 3–1 down to beat Bolton Wanderers 4–3. It was a game watched by a far greater audience than any previous football match in England as many who bought televisions for the Coronation got them a month early.

Matthews was by far the most famous footballer in England and the most old-school of wingers. His glory, winning the first medal of his career at the age of thirty-eight, was regarded as the affirmation of the traditional English game: a W-M with a defensive centre-half, looking to get the ball wide for a winger to cross to a big bustling centre-forward. But like so many of these celebrated moments, it proved not the herald of a golden age but a lament for one just ending.

Suddenly the W-M was no longer sacrosanct. There were experiments with withdrawn centre-forwards, twin centre-forwards and back fours. By the early sixties, the likes of Bill Shankly at Liverpool and Don Revie at Leeds were leading the English game in a radical new direction, away from a focus on the winger and his individual skills and towards a more cohesive, systematic approach. There was, not surprisingly, resistance; it came to a head in the 1965 FA Cup final in which, after a lot of patient 'method' play by both sides, Liverpool beat Leeds. 'I am told that if we are to survive the rigours of the World Cup,' the columnist Peter Wilson wrote, 'we must forget individualism, the brilliant flashes of inspiration which transform a treadmill into a flying machine, the genius which transmutes a muddied oaf into a booted genius.'[10]

Whoever told him was broadly right, but it required a stubborn manager of implacable self-confidence to instil an effective modern style in the face of persistent criticism. Ramsey was repressed, suspicious and bloody-minded, shy in a way that made him seem aloof, riddled with class anxieties and burdened by his sense of responsibility; he was also, at least in footballing terms, a radical. He had played in the 6–3 defeat to Hungary. He knew England had to change and the success he had enjoyed at Tottenham under Arthur Rowe, who evangelised the 'push-and-run' game, showed him the direction it had to take. As a manager he took Ipswich from the Third Division to the First and then, in their first ever season in the top flight, 1961–62, to the league title, largely by dint of having his left-winger, Jimmy Leadbetter, drop deep, confounding opposing full-backs who didn't know what to do when the player they were supposed to be marking wasn't standing where tradition suggested he should.

With England, he slowly edged towards a 4-3-3 similar to that he had used with Ipswich. Then suddenly, in a friendly away to Spain in December 1965, injury offered a glimpse of something else, what would now be recognised as a 4-4-2, or perhaps a 4-1-3-2. Ramsey, instinctively secretive, put the formation away and only brought it out again before England's final pre-World Cup friendly, against Poland in Chorzów. He knew the significance of what he was doing and, as he read out the starting XI to the press, he left a dramatic pause before the final name: Martin Peters. With Alan Ball operating as a shuttler on the right, everybody had expected a bona fide winger. There was uproar, but by then Ramsey was already on his way out of the room.

Peters was twenty-two, a modern, versatile midfielder who offered balance. He was a decent crosser of the ball and a danger making late runs to the back post, but he was also comfortable tucking in and offering defensive cover when Ray Wilson, the left-back, went forward on the overlap. England beat Poland 1–0 and Peters played well in a generally impressive performance. 'A fluid tactical plan,' wrote Geoffrey Green in *The Times*, 'had England flowing back and forth like a red tide in their unfamiliar red shirts.'[11] What thrilled Ramsey, though, was the level of control England had demonstrated. And so he hid his invention away again until it was really needed.

Aged fifteen, Ydnekatchew Tessema had been part of a squad of players from across Addis Ababa put together to take on the crew of a French naval vessel, one of the first notable games of football played in Ethiopia. A year later, he and his family cowered in the home of a Greek friend to avoid a massacre being carried out by Mussolini's invading Italian army in reprisal for a bomb attack. Tessema survived and would go on to become one of the leading figures in the development of African football. Having made fifteen appearances for his country, he was the Ethiopian representative when the Confederation of African Football (CAF) was founded in 1957 and coached them to the Cup of Nations title in 1962.

At the time, Ethiopia was at the forefront of African sport, which rapidly became part of Africa's decolonisation movement. Abebe Bikila's victory in the marathon at the 1960 Olympics could hardly have had greater symbolic resonance. Running barefoot through Rome, he pulled away from his nearest challenger, the Moroccan Rhadi Ben Abdesselam, on the Piazza di Porta Capena as he passed an obelisk Mussolini's troops had looted from the ancient Ethiopian city of Aksum, before crossing the finish line under the arch of Constantine, in the heart of the metropole, to set a new world record and become the first black African Olympic gold medallist. Fourteen African nations sent competitors to the following Olympics.

But as in South America earlier in the century, it was football that became a rare and unifying symbol of national identity.[12] The National Liberation Front team that popularised and raised funds for the Algerian cause represents the most extreme example,[13] while Kwame Nkrumah used football both for nation-building in Ghana and the promotion of pan-Africanism.[14] At a much more basic level, Togo, for instance, celebrated independence from France in 1960 with a friendly against Nigeria.[15] That CAF was based in Cairo was largely because its first president, Abdel Aziz Abdallah Salem, was Egyptian – Tessema had campaigned for it to be in Addis Ababa – but given Gamal Abdel Nasser had led Egypt with such striking success during the Suez Crisis, there were inevitable connotations of resistance to the old colonial powers.

By the Fifa Congress in Tokyo in 1964, the first to have a significant African presence – in part because it coincided with the Olympics, making it easier for delegates from poorer nations to attend – there hadn't been an African side at the World Cup since Egypt in 1934. Indeed, when Ethiopia joined Fifa in 1954, they were only the fourth African member. A desire to protect their own positions while ensuring there was no dilution of quality perhaps isn't necessarily evidence of prejudice on the part of Europe and South America, but where racism is clear is in Fifa's response to the issue of South Africa. The Football Association of South Africa (FASA) had been one of the founder members of CAF, but they had been expelled from the inaugural Cup of Nations in 1957 because of their refusal to send a mixed-race side.[16]

CAF eventually expelled South Africa over the issue of apartheid but FASA were reinstated to Fifa after a tour of the country by Stanley Rous. The Fifa president reported that the 'dissident federations ... would ... be quite unsuitable to represent association football in South Africa', describing 'their attitude' towards their government's policy as 'one of destruction and not construction'.[17] It's not entirely clear exactly how Rous imagined a federation representing black football could be constructive towards an apartheid government, his instinctive support for existing authority highlighting both his paternalistic attitude and the inadequacy of his principle that sport and politics were discrete realms that should be kept separate.

It was the issue of representation at the World Cup that brought matters to a head. One slot had been allocated to Africa and Asia combined for the 1966 World Cup. CAF's general secretary Mourad Fahmy insisted African football was 'paralysed by this grouping'[18] and sought one guaranteed slot. When Fifa refused to amend the allocation, Tessema organised a boycott with Ohene Djan, who had been placed in charge of Ghanaian sport by Nkrumah. All fifteen African sides withdrew from qualifying, with Syria, who were in the European section, also pulling out in sympathy.[19] South Africa had been grouped with Asia following their expulsion from CAF, but they were suspended from Fifa before they could play a qualifier. With South Korea withdrawing for logistical reasons after the qualifying tournament was moved to Cambodia, that left North Korea to beat a shambolic Australia to secure their place at the finals.[20]

North Korea, while posing a major diplomatic problem to Britain, would prove one of the great stories of the tournament, but the longer-term consequence of the boycott was that in 1970, both Africa and Asia/Oceania would be guaranteed a place each. Neither Nkrumah nor Djan were in power to enjoy the fruits of their success, though, the Ghanaian military having seized power in a coup in February 1966.

For the first time since 1934, West Germany went to the World Cup with a manager who wasn't Sepp Herberger. He had retired in 1964 at the age of sixty-seven and been replaced by his assistant, Helmut Schön – although Herberger would have preferred the job to have gone to his perennial favourite, Fritz Walter.

Schön's father had been an art dealer in Dresden. His family was liberal and middle class and, as late as 1939, they were still renting out a flat to a Jewish publisher. His father had not believed the Allies could bomb a city as beautiful as Dresden but on 13 February 1945 came the firestorm. Schön drove through the apocalypse and found his wife in a shelter. Another five days would pass before he found his father, sitting devastated amid the rubble, his faith in the world as shattered as the city around him. For the rest of his life, Schön was haunted by the memories of what he had seen, the corpses everywhere, the charred bodies of women still clutching their children.[21]

Schön had been invalided out of the war because of the knee injuries he had suffered as a player – although he had been able to return to international action even after his second torn cartilage, something which often drew scorn from opposing fans. He eventually fell out of consideration for Germany not because of fitness but because Herberger decided he wasn't tough enough, although there is a suggestion that Herberger, as a working-class autodidact, felt challenged by Schön's bourgeois origins.[22] Schön, whose idol was the Austrian forward Matthias Sindelar, continued to play for Dresden SC and then its successor club in the Communist East, SG Dresden-Friedrichstadt, becoming player-manager.

Increasingly, Schön found himself having difficulties with the Communist authorities. He was reprimanded by the head of the East Berlin sports committee, the future leader of East Germany Erich Honecker, after being asked by a man claiming to be the press officer of the Hamburg club St Pauli to help arrange for the return of the old championship shield to the West. When he then fell out with the sports official Manfred Ewald, who would later become notorious for organising East Germany's state doping programme, Schön knew he had to flee. He contacted Herberger who, whatever his previous misgivings, arranged for Schön to be admitted to a coaching course in Cologne. Then, early one morning in May 1950,

Schön and his wife snuck out of their home in Dresden and made their way north to Berlin, where he had been offered a role as player-manager of Hertha – crucially, it was not based in the Soviet sector.

After only a few months, Schön moved to Wiesbaden and, in 1952, became national manager of the Saarland. He led them in the qualifiers for the 1954 World Cup, in which they beat Norway but lost twice to Herberger's West Germany. When the Saarland was incorporated into West Germany, Schön became Herberger's assistant.

His first task on replacing Herberger was qualification for the 1966 World Cup. It began badly with a 1–1 draw against Sweden in Berlin, placing huge pressure on the return in Stockholm in September 1965. For that game, Schön made two crucial decisions. He picked Uwe Seeler, just four weeks after the centre-forward had returned from a serious Achilles injury, and he handed a full debut to the elegant twenty-year-old midfielder Franz Beckenbauer. He was emphatically vindicated, Beckenbauer making one of his characteristic surges to lay on the winner for Seeler.

West Germany would go to England and, although Schön was so mindful of post-war sensitivities he told his players that what mattered more than anything was that they should behave like gentlemen, the great age of West German achievement had begun.

In October 2002, seven men in red tracksuits visited a housing estate in Middlesbrough. One of them, his side-parted hair streaked with grey, knelt by a small bronze sculpture depicting the imprint of a boot on grass, apparently overwhelmed. It had been on that precise spot, thirty-six years earlier, that he, Pak Doo-Ik, had scored the goal that had beaten Italy in one of the greatest World Cup upsets there has ever been.

The Foreign Office, very obviously, wished North Korea had not qualified. Although the Korean War, to which Britain had committed almost 100,000 troops and its Far East fleet, had ended with an armistice in 1953, the United Kingdom had never formally recognised North Korea, nor had any peace treaty ever been signed. That created three major areas of concern: the anthem, the flag and the terminology to be used. 'North Korea' it was decided was accurate without necessarily conferring statehood; although a North Korean delegation that visited the UK in February 1966 asked for the team to be referred to as the 'Democratic People's Republic of Korea', Rous was able to talk them round.[23] There was a plan to restrict the use of flags but Rous, acting as liaison between Fifa and the Foreign Office, secured government agreement that the flags of all sixteen competing sides could be flown at every game. Anthems, meanwhile, were played before only the opening game and the final, the assumption being that would mean the North Korean anthem would never be heard.[24]

As they lost 3–0 to the USSR and then drew 1–1 against Chile, it seemed North Korea would be going home at the earliest opportunity. Even at that stage, though, they had won friends on Teesside, bewildering other travellers by singing patriotic songs on the train north and then charming locals by presenting the local mayor with an embroidery of a crane (the bird).

Then, three minutes before half-time in their final group game, against Italy at Ayresome Park, Pak ran onto a bouncing ball and, from just inside the box, swept an angled shot just inside the far post. So delighted were Teessiders that 3,000 made the trip to Liverpool for the quarter-final[25] and, even half a century later, cultural exchanges continued between Middlesbrough and North Korea.

Unexpectedly, after all the diplomatic anxiety and manoeuvring, North Korea's visit came as close as anything at a World

Cup ever has to Jules Rimet's vision of promoting a spirit of brotherhood between disparate nations. 'When I scored that goal,' said Pak, 'the people of Middlesbrough took us to their hearts. I learnt that playing football can improve diplomatic relations and promote peace.'[26]

Few doubted that the side to beat were Brazil. 'They may not be what they were,' wrote David Miller in the *Sunday Telegraph*, 'but they still have the capacity for the sudden explosive crescendo.'[27] The double world champions' preparations for 1966 were an odd mixture of complacency and chaos caused largely by the political battle between the president of the CBD, João Havelange (of Rio), and Paulo Machado de Carvalho (of São Paulo), who had been *chef de mission* in both 1958 and 1962. That was a role Havelange wanted for himself, for the first time risking travelling with the team and so being directly associated with their performances.

It was a tour of Europe in 1963, the midfielder Gérson came to believe, that made a third straight victory impossible.[28] In the first game, Brazil lost 1–0 to Portugal in Lisbon, the Belenenses defender Vicente marking Pelé out of the game. There were further defeats, the squad looking stale and demotivated. There were also tactical issues, as European sides, having learned zonal marking in part from the Brazilians, began to develop that into pressing, an innovation that was only partially understood in Brazil. 'As time went by,' Pelé said, 'the European sides ... were physically better prepared and devised knowingly brutal strategies.'[29] Which assuredly was part of it; football did become more cynical as the sixties went on – and not only in Europe. But pressing also meant that it was harder for a player to skip away from an opponent and that, as well as permitting the ball to be won back more efficiently by legitimate means – perhaps by a second or third tackle in quick succession, which would itself be physically gruelling for those on the receiving end – also meant that those intent on cynical hacking were more likely to be close enough to their intended victim to perpetrate a foul.

Havelange responded to Brazil's struggles by bringing back Vicente Feola. But the cardiac problems that had led to Feola being replaced in the first place had not gone away, and he lacked energy. More than that, he was the man of 1958: Moreira had moved Brazil forward as the rest of the world reacted, but Feola wanted to take them back. Machado de Carvalho ended up resigning and was replaced by Carlos Nascimento who may, like Feola, have been Havelange's man but had very different views on personnel. The resulting compromise led to the selection of an unworkably large forty-five-man preliminary squad.

Towns would compete to host the national team's training camps, paying fees to the CBD. Players were feted by their hosts, who would arrange cocktail parties, banquets and other civic events, each trying to outdo the others. If stars were left out of training games, the municipalities would complain, which reinforced the prevailing sense that the champions of 1958 and 1962 should be given another chance, that they had already proved themselves and would inevitably bring home a third world title. Players spoke of a constant sense of pressure.[30] Then, after all the insecurity, Brazil went to England with the oldest squad in the tournament.

Ramsey was distrustful of foreigners in general and South Americans in particular. A 1–0 defeat to Argentina in 1964 had confirmed in his mind that dribbling against South American opposition was essentially pointless given their willingness to commit fouls. What worried him was the possibility of being caught on the break so, in the tournament opener against Uruguay, he refused to overcommit. The result was a cautious game in which England had 16 corners and 15 shots and drew 0–0. A nation howled in boredom. The *Mail*'s headline captured the mood: 'Angry, baffled, goalless England.'[31]

But Ramsey was neither angry nor baffled. He had known what sort of game to expect and had prepared accordingly. He was quite certain about most of his side. All he needed was to find the right attacking blend. England beat both Mexico and France 2–0 to secure their place in the quarter-final, Greaves sustaining a three-inch gash to the shin in that final group game and so allowing Ramsey to complete his machine.

It was in his disdain for ornamentation, for anything beyond the practical, that Ramsey's radicalism lay. This was very much the spirit of the age, particularly in architecture. In the aftermath of the Second World War, there was a need for buildings that could be constructed quickly and inexpensively. There was no time or money for flamboyance or frippery.[32] Elaine Harwood, who led the drive to preserve brutalist buildings as an essential element of Britain's post-war heritage, wrote of brutalism* as prioritising 'pragmatism ... teamwork and [an] emphasis on efficiency'.[33] She could just as well have been speaking of Ramsey's England.

Not that anybody was making such claims at the time. Sportswriters may have been coming round, reluctantly in many cases, to the idea that the game was about organisation and systems as much as the glorious sallies of individuals, but football was a new enough element of popular culture that the idea it should be analysed at all seemed risible to more general columnists.[34]

The debate around Ramsey's functional approach came

* Brutalism was an architectural style established in Britain in the 1950s and associated with the reconstruction projects after the Second World War. Its buildings are minimalist and characterised by exposed, unadorned raw materials, especially concrete. The name derives in part from the French for raw concrete, *béton brut*.

to centre on Greaves, who had notably been absent from the friendly win over Spain in December 1965 when the thought that England might actually win the World Cup first began to be taken seriously. Greaves was a supremely gifted forward, elegant and graceful and a lethal finisher: in 51 internationals before the World Cup, he had scored 43 times. He was as near as English football came to a sacred cow. Which made what happened in Madrid difficult to process. The morning after the game, Peter Lorenzo in the *Sun* was describing 'a thrilling victory, supreme in its tactical brilliance and mastery'[35] but, twenty-four hours later, it was as though the heretical significance of what he had witnessed had dawned on him and he was arguing that 'England Must Recall Luxury Goal Ace' as soon as he regained fitness.[36]

Greaves had played in Poland when, despite the excellence of the performance, he had stood out as the one player slightly remote from the general cohesion. 'Greaves,' Geoffrey Green wrote in *The Times*, 'continues to follow his own infuriating path.'[37] Even Bobby Charlton, who tended to celebrate the individual and to be sceptical of any restrictive tactical schema, had his doubts. 'If Greaves wasn't scoring,' he said, 'his contribution . . . tended to be not much more than the ornamental.'[38] To have dropped Greaves, the darling of the London-based media, would have been an enormous step even for somebody as ruthless and thick-skinned as Ramsey.[39] The injury meant he didn't have to.

Geoff Hurst replaced Greaves but there was one other change for the quarter-final against Argentina and, for the first time since Poland, Ramsey selected both Ball and Peters: the 'Wingless Wonders' were born. 'Well, gentlemen, you know what kind of game you will have on your hands today,'[40] Ramsey said before kick-off. To an extent it was a familiar story of different emphases: South Americans couldn't understand why British sides were so outraged by obstructions and pulls on the shirt, but were appalled by the naked physicality of the northern European game. And, in the aftermath of Helsingborg, this was a particularly cynical period for Argentinian football. But there was a lot else going on as well.

The head of the Argentinian army, Juan Carlos Onganía, had seized power in a coup two weeks before the World Cup began, at which point the squad was already preparing for the tournament in Italy. That, clearly, was a major distraction as players sought news about what was happening at home and the well-being of their families.

Antonio Rattin, the well-respected captain, was appalled by the reappointment of Juan Carlos Lorenzo as coach shortly before they set off for Europe. Argentina had lost only one of thirteen games under José María Minella in 1964 and 1965; this felt like needless disruption and, besides, Rattin hadn't forgiven Lorenzo for, as he saw it, scapegoating him for the defeat to England in 1962. Worse, Lorenzo had spent most of his time since the previous World Cup coaching in Italy and, having seen the effectiveness of *catenaccio*, wanted Argentina to employ a *libero*. But why, the players asked, were they being asked to adopt an entirely new and unfamiliar way of playing on the eve of the tournament?

Organisation was shambolic. Players clashed with delegates, of whom there were a baffling number. Rattin, who suffered so badly from homesickness that whenever he was away he got his wife and children to record messages on tapes that he would play to himself before he went to bed, was thoroughly miserable and so unsettled that he punched the midfielder José Pastoriza. In Turin, the players asked AFA to send a different coach.[41]

They refused and, although the AFA president, Valentín Suárez, flew to Europe, the chaos continued once they'd arrived in England. The Argentina squad was based near Birmingham and, one morning, had a training session arranged at Lilleshall in which they were to go through their secret plan to take on Spain. The bus, though, got lost while trying to evade imagined spies, taking two hours to complete the thirty-mile journey. When they did finally get there, it turned out nobody had packed the kit and the players had to scrounge what they could from a local gym.[42]

After a 2–1 win over Spain, Argentina drew 0–0 against West Germany in a tense, angry game that they finished with ten men after the Yugoslav referee Konstantin Zečević sent off Rafael Albrecht for a dreadful foul on Wolfgang Weber. Even in the permissive climate of the times, nobody could realistically have claimed it was an undeserved dismissal but Argentina were primed to see a European conspiracy and protested long and hard. The Villa Park crowd, seemingly largely amused by Latins fulfilling their hot-headed stereotype, responded with boos. Fifa warned Argentina about their 'unethical' play but why, Lorenzo asked, not entirely unreasonably, had that foul been singled out in a game that was littered with bad tackles?

Further boos followed as Argentina secured their place in the last eight with a 2–0 win over Switzerland. Argentina felt besieged and that sense only intensified after the match officials were allocated for the quarter-finals during a meeting at the Royal Gardens Hotel in Kensington. Argentina's two delegates arrived late and, by the time they got there, it had been decided that a West German, Rudi Kreitlein, would take charge of England v Argentina, while an Englishman, Jim Ramsey, would referee West Germany v Uruguay. The appointments were almost certainly born of bureaucratic blindness to how it would appear rather than any sort of collusion, but minds conditioned by an environment of political paranoia in which a coup was only ever a couple of years away saw conspiracy.

There was, anyway, bewilderment and anger among the South American nations about the degree of physicality tolerated by European referees.[43] 'England can't beat us if there's a good referee,' Marzolini had said after the group stage. 'The public and the conditions don't bother us, but the referee is fundamental.'[44]

The day before the game, Argentina were denied the twenty minutes of practice on the Wembley pitch they were entitled to on the grounds it would interfere with the evening's dog racing. Perhaps they were late again; perhaps they ran into inflexible English jobsworthery; either way, it confirmed to Argentina that everything was stacked against them. They were unfortunate too, although their unpopularity was surely part of it, that their quarter-final was the moment at which the English crowd first seemed truly enthusiastic about Ramsey's England.[45]

The game itself was scrappy and ill-tempered, not helped by the fussiness of Kreitlein. It was effectively decided by an incident ten minutes before half-time. Rattin had been booked a few minutes earlier for clipping Bobby Charlton's heels and the look he shot Kreitlein when he subsequently went through the back of Hurst suggested he knew he was on thin ice. But his dismissal after the ball had gone out for a goal-kick was mystifying. Rattin had complained to Kreitlein persistently but there was no obvious flashpoint; just a punctilious referee losing patience. And perhaps that was enough. Who knows what warnings Kreitlein had given Rattin? They had no language in common, and that was a major part of the problem.

Valentín Suárez had told Rattin he was entitled to an interpreter. Which may sound absurd, but something similar had happened during the Battle of Santiago four years earlier. Marzolini confirmed the story[46] and it does explain Rattin's actions as he refused to leave the pitch for several minutes, pleading, seemingly unable to believe what was happening. 'They wanted me to leave the pitch and I refused,' he said. 'What the fuck did they want? I didn't insult anyone, I didn't kick anyone, so why the fuck should I leave the pitch? Just because I requested a translator to speak to that German *concha*? Because it was arranged, oh yes, a German here and an Englishman there.'[47] At Hillsborough that same afternoon, the English referee he referred to missed an early handball on the line by Karl-Heinz Schnellinger then sent off two Uruguayans as West Germany went through 4–0.

For a time it seemed Lorenzo might take his whole side off and, when he finally departed, Rattin sat for several minutes on the red carpet in front of the royal box before continuing slowly round the pitch, being abused and pelted with missiles. He paused at the corner flag, a Union flag with a World Cup logo at its centre, and held it briefly between thumb and forefinger, an oddly poignant gesture that seemed to ask if this were really what Britain, the supposed home of fair play, had become.

The game eventually carried on in its bad-tempered way. England won it with a header from Hurst thirteen minutes from time, and the ugliness carried on after the final whistle, with the Northern Irish Fifa delegate Harry Cavan spat upon, and damage done to the dressing-room doors. There were those, most notably David Miller in the *Sunday Telegraph*,[48] who criticised Ramsey for not having cut loose against ten men, but that seems to misunderstand Ramsey's insistence on control: he knew his side was extremely fit and had faith that, eventually, the ten men of Argentina would tire and give England an opportunity.

His patience was rewarded, but in his finest hour he committed his gravest mistake. First, he attempted to prevent his players from changing shirts with the Argentinians, which looked petty and churlish, and then he made the comment that would overshadow England's relationship with South American sides for years: 'Our best football,' he said in his post-match interview, 'will come against the right type of opposition – a team who come to play football, and not act as animals.'

*

Pelé was on tour with Santos when, on 31 March 1964, with inflation rampant, João Goulart was ousted in a coup. He returned to find very little had changed.[49] Humberto Castelo Branco, the general who took over the presidency, saw the dictatorship as a temporary intervention to replace the populism of the left with economic discipline. He purged Congress and the civil service and, after the government performed poorly in state elections in 1965, dissolved all political parties, replacing them with a pro-government party and an official opposition. Economic decisions were handed over to technocrats who stabilised inflation. Football was largely irrelevant to the new regime, other than in the matter of unpaid taxes. Didi, Mário Zagallo and Nílton Santos were all pursued by the authorities, while Garrincha's bill was so large that Havelange paid it himself to head off the threat of a prison term that might have caused him to miss the World Cup in 1966.

The values of the dictatorship, inevitably, touched the squad as a whole. For instance, the Beatles offered to play at the Brazilians' hotel in Liverpool only for the directors, reflecting the values of the regime, to refuse, seeing in their 'long hair' and 'decadence', Pelé said, 'a serious threat to the peace and security of the impressionable young men in their charge'.[50] The days of authorised trips to the brothel in Viña del Mar seemed a long time ago.

Brazil began with a 2–0 win over Bulgaria but it was a slow, ill-tempered game. Garrincha had had knee surgery in 1964 and the impact of that and his lifestyle meant he never really achieved any consistency afterwards. Pelé was brutally marked by Dobromir Zhechev. Both scored, but it would be the last of the forty-four games the pair played together, none of them lost.

Feola, worried by the kicking Pelé had taken against Bulgaria, left him out for the second group game, against Hungary. 'That was another mistake,' said Pelé, suggesting the

Brazilian delegation had underestimated Hungary.[51] A decade on from the Uprising, with players such as Flórián Albert, Gyula Rákosi and Ferenc Bene, Hungary were enjoying one last spasm of success, the structures that had made them great not quite exhausted. Hungary won 3–1, their second goal, volleyed in by János Farkas, arguably the goal of the tournament. That left Brazil needing to beat Portugal by three goals in their final game to guarantee progress to the quarter-final. Havelange wrote to Fifa protesting about the appointment of an English official,[52] a measure which bolstered Brazil's subsequent claims of conspiracy, but a three-goal swing was always improbable and, in the event, they were well beaten.

Nascimento took control of the team, recalled Pelé and brought in six players with no previous World Cup experience; faith in the old guard, when it went, went suddenly. Pelé suffered repeated fouls and, with Portugal 2–0 up, a crude lunge by João Morais left him hobbling. Battered and bruised, he was led off the Goodison Park pitch at the final whistle, an overcoat draped over his shoulders, a poignant symbol of the end of Brazil's hopes of a third straight success, and also perhaps of a certain innocence in football. 'The games had been a revelation to me,' Pelé said, 'in their unsportsmanlike conduct and weak refereeing.'[53] Pronouncing himself 'disgusted', he retired from international football.[54]

Portugal may have been physical against Brazil but, more generally, they were regarded as one of the more likeable and watchable teams of that World Cup. It's indicative of the complicated legacy of colonialism that four of their players had been born in what is now Mozambique: Vicente was a robust defender, Hilário a reliable and consistent left-back, Mário Coluna an elegant inside-forward who had been considered the great star of the Benfica side that won the European Cup under Béla Guttmann in 1961. But it was Eusébio, who arrived in Lisbon the following season, who was the true great, explosively quick, technically gifted and blessed with a ferocious shot. He had scored three in the group stage but it was in the quarter-final that he really caught light.

First, though, there came an almighty shock as North Korea raced into a 3–0 lead. Just as the Foreign Office was beginning to panic, Eusébio pulled one back and by half-time he had made it 3–2. He added two more in the second half as Portugal won 5–3 to set up a semi-final against England.

That match came as something of a relief, at last a game that wasn't riddled with violence. Those who declared the whole World Cup a fix claimed the game had been switched from Goodison Park at the last minute to make sure England played every game at Wembley but that simply isn't true; it was always the intention that the semi likely to attract the bigger crowd would be played at Wembley.[55] 'This has been the rehabilitation of football,' said Jean Eskenazi of *Paris Soir.* 'It was everything you like in football when you want football played which is not a street battle.'[56] England won it 2–1 with two goals from Bobby Charlton.

Did it matter that the final was against West Germany, who had beaten the USSR in their semi? As Duncan Hamilton said, of course it did.[57] The war was still fresh in the memory, rebuilding was still going on; it couldn't but colour perceptions. With Bobby Charlton and Franz Beckenbauer each deputed to nullify the other, the game was bitty, England far less composed than in their previous two games. Having gone behind, England led 2–1 when, with a minute remaining, after what might have been a German hand in the box, Wolfgang Weber turned in an equaliser at the back post.

It's a goal that, had West Germany won, would have been remembered as immensely controversial. As it is, because of what followed, it is almost forgotten. Ramsey, before extra time, told his players not to sit down, to give the impression they were still fresh, then delivered a team talk of pithy brilliance: 'You've won it once, now go and win it again.'

They didn't let it slip again, two goals from Hurst sealing the win, although the first almost certainly didn't cross the line after bouncing down off the bar, and there were two overexcited fans encroaching onto the pitch as he thrashed in a late fourth to complete the first hat-trick in a World Cup final. It's Hurst's second that lingers, to the extent that it's mocked up as a crime scene at the German national football museum in Dortmund. 'Too much has been talked about the third goal,' said Weber. 'England entered the annals of football history as worthy world champions.'[58]

The empire may have gone, its legacy seen in the African boycott, but in football terms at least, England had emerged from its conservative past as a proudly modern nation.

1970

BEAUTY AND THE BEASTS

Tostão picks up the loose ball and nudges it back to Wilson Piazza just outside his own box. The ball is moved in a slow triangle through Clodoaldo to Pelé and Gérson and back to Clodoaldo. His touch is slightly heavy, enticing an Italian challenge. Clodoaldo skips round him and then two other tackles. He sidesteps Antonio Juliano and rolls the ball to Rivellino on the left. Rivellino sweeps a 40-yard pass down the line to Jairzinho and the rhythm has suddenly changed.

Jairzinho runs at Giacinto Facchetti and, as he turns inside, Pierluigi Cera advances to close him down. Jairzinho pokes the ball on to Pelé, perhaps 27 or 28 yards out. Tarcisio Burgnich stands between him and the box, but Pelé pauses, turns casually to his right and lays a pass into the path of Carlos Alberto, surging forward from full-back. Just inside the box the ball bobbles so it sits up perfectly. Carlos Alberto doesn't have to break stride as he lashes a shot hard across goal, the force of the strike lifting him high off the ground as the ball flies into the bottom corner. With four minutes of the 1970 World Cup final remaining, Brazil lead 4–1.

For many, it's the greatest goal scored by perhaps the greatest team in the greatest World Cup, a glorious synthesis of team play and individual technical excellence. Yes, it came right at the end of the final and Italy were exhausted by then, accepting their defeat, but it was a goal that encapsulated the joy and virtuosity of that side, that left the world with a shorthand for what the Brazil of 1970 meant. And if by the time it was scored it was almost a goal without an opposition, an exhibition, that felt appropriate too, for Brazil by then had come to feel as though they were about more than games or results, more even than winning the World Cup: they were about an expression of football in its most beautiful form, about pushing the boundaries of human capability.

The impact of Brazil's victory on the global imagination was profound. This felt thrillingly modern. For those who had colour television, who witnessed those vibrant yellow shirts and the shorts of cobalt blue playing with a dash and a verve in iridescent heat on the sun-bleached grass of Mexico, the impact is hard to overstate.[1] The tournament revelled in the sense of progress, naming the official ball, the Telstar, after the satellite that made live global transmission possible. And Brazil, after all, had undergone a Nasa-approved training course before the World Cup. When the *Jornal do Brasil* claimed that 'Brazil's victory with the ball compares with the conquest of the moon by the Americans' the previous year it didn't seem ridiculous.[2]

Just as the moon landing could be regarded as a triumph of human ingenuity, so Brazil's artistry seemed to transcend the tournament, the petty squabble of nation against nation. Much of what posterity has remembered of Pelé in that tournament – the lob from the halfway line against Czechoslovakia, the header that drew the stunning save from Gordon Banks, the dummy on the Uruguay goalkeeper Ladislao Mazurkiewicz in the semi-final – didn't lead to goals, as though this was about more than the bureaucracy of the scoreboard; it was about the greater glory of the game.[3]

Ever since, there has been a sense of football trying to recapture the spirit of 1970, that feeling of rapturous and perhaps impossible excitement. By the time of the 1974 tournament in West Germany, João Havelange had been elected president of Fifa and a new age of commercialism had begun. It's not to present Stanley Rous's tenure as Fifa president as anything other than flawed to suggest that, when a former schoolteacher was replaced by the son of an arms dealer, a certain financial innocence was lost. The 1970 World Cup looks different to every subsequent World Cup because not every surface is covered in advertising. The marketing was not slick, the presentation imperfect, and in that ramshackle aspect there was perhaps a charm: the football, by and large, came first.

And the football in 1970 was thrilling. The contrast to the physicality of the two previous World Cups and England's cautious, mechanistic win in 1966 was obvious and for many those two facets became fused: this tournament was modernity and it had been won by Brazilian artistry, therefore such artistry was modern. But it was not. It had been made possible by the heat and altitude of Mexico that, with the fitness of players as it then was, effectively made pressing impossible. By 1974 in West Germany, pressing was back.

With Japan, Peru and Colombia all withdrawing, Mexico had beaten an Argentinian bid 56 votes to 32 at the Congress in Tokyo in 1964. It had already won the right to host the 1968 Olympic Games, the two events supposed to project an image of Mexico's modernity.[4]

Mexico, said Mario Vargas Llosa, was 'the perfect dictatorship', in that it exhibited all the traits of one while appearing

Popperfoto/Getty Images

The Belgian referee John Langenus (centre) looks on as the respective captains, José Nasazzi of Uruguay (left) and Argentina's Manuel Ferreira (right) shake hands before the 1930 World Cup final in Montevideo.

Associated Press/Alamy Stock Photo

Pablo Dorado (left, standing) puts Uruguay ahead in the 1930 World Cup final despite the efforts of the goalkeeper Juan Botasso and Juan Evaristo.

Keystone/Getty Images

Benito Mussolini presents the Coppa del Duce to the victorious Italy squad after the 1934 World Cup.

Popperfoto/Getty Images

Jules Rimet makes the draw for the 1938 World Cup with the assistance of his six-year-old grandson, Yves Rimet.

STAFF/AFP/Getty Images

The Dutch East Indies line up before their 1938 World Cup match against Hungary. On the far right is the goalkeeper Mo Heng Tan with his lucky doll.

Popperfoto/Getty Images

Juan Schiaffino (left) slams the equaliser past the goalkeeper Moacir Barbosa as Uruguay beat Brazil to win the 1950 World Cup.

Keystone/Getty Images

Max Morlock gets a toe to the ball to divert it past the goalkeeper Gyula Grosics and score West Germany's first against Hungary in the 1954 World Cup final.

Emilio Ronchini/Mondadori/Getty Images

Gilmar (left) and a seventeen-year-old Pelé (right) relax in the garden of Brazil's training base in Hindas during the 1958 World Cup.

The English referee Ken Aston sends off the Italy defender Mario David for punching Chile's Leonel Sánchez (centre, stricken) in the Battle of Santiago.

The Dairy Council uses World Cup Willie, the first Fifa tournament mascot, to welcome visitors to the 1966 World Cup in England.

Daily Express/Hulton Archive/Getty Images

Pelé, injured and frustrated, is helped from the pitch after Brazil's defeat to Portugal at Goodison Park in 1966.

MSI/Mirrorpix/Getty Images

Pelé and Bobby Moore exchange shirts in mutual admiration after Brazil's 1–0 victory over England in Guadalajara in 1970.

Sepia Times/Universal Images Group/Getty Images

The new Fifa president João Havelange and the US national security advisor Henry Kissinger in the crowd at Brazil's 2–0 defeat to the Netherlands in Dortmund in 1974.

STAFF/AFP/Getty Images

Johan Neeskens fires the Netherlands ahead from the penalty spot in the first minute of the 1974 final.

Getty Images

Mario Kempes celebrates his goal against the Netherlands in the 1978 World Cup final.

INTERFOTO/Alamy Stock Photo

Argentina's military leader General Rafael Videla (centre, thumb up) presents the World Cup to his country's captain Daniel Passarella.

to be a democracy.[5] After the turmoil of the early twentieth century, and the revolutions of Pancho Villa and Emiliano Zapata, what was prioritised was stability.[6] The result was the Institutional Revolutionary Party (PRI), which governed Mexico from 1928 to 2000, offering a new leader every six years.* Workers could campaign for their rights through the unions, which were run by the PRI. Peasants could lobby for better conditions through their organisations, which were run by the PRI. The PRI ran everything, and those who objected, zealous labour organisers or journalists, would be bought off, imprisoned or killed.

The one group the PRI did not control was the students, and by the late sixties, thanks to a young population, there were a lot of them. Aware of student demonstrations in the USA and France, and conscious that 78 per cent of disposable income was in the hands of 10 per cent of the population, they protested against the 1968 Olympic Games. Evocations of *les évènements* unfortunately chimed with the paranoid belief of the president, Gustavo Díaz Ordaz, that there was a global conspiracy of French and Cuban radicals to spread disorder,[7] and he ordered a crackdown.

On 2 October 1968, ten days before the Olympics started, an estimated 5,000 students gathered on Plaza de las Tres Culturas in the Mexico City suburb of Tlatelolco, chanting '*no queremos olimpiades, queremos revolución!*' (We don't want the Olympics, we want revolution!) At around 6 p.m., tanks and armoured vehicles closed in, with loudspeakers broadcasting orders to disperse.[8] Special agents in the high-rises around the square opened fire on the crowd and soldiers with automatic weapons responded indiscriminately. Exactly how many were killed remains disputed, but around 400 seems likely.[9] There were no protests against the World Cup as the

* It was known as the National Revolutionary Party until 1934.

massacre drove dissent underground, leading ultimately to the armed rebellions and repressions of the seventies.[10]

It was the first World Cup at which Asia and Africa both had a guaranteed qualifying slot. Israel took Asia's, beating Australia after North Korea had been disqualified for refusing to play them, and although they finished bottom of their group, they drew against Uruguay and Italy. Morocco, the African representative, went ahead against West Germany and forced a draw against Bulgaria, eliminated from the group but having performed creditably.

None of Spain, Yugoslavia, Hungary or France made it through the increasingly challenging European qualifying, but Argentina were the most surprising absentees, their campaign derailed just as it was beginning when Humberto Maschio resigned as coach after Armando Ramos Ruiz had been ousted as head of the AFA by General Onganía. By the time Adolfo Pedernera had taken over, it was too late for Maschio's plan to deal with the altitude in La Paz for a qualifier to be put into effect. The Argentinians lost away to Bolivia and Peru, and despite claims that Argentina had paid off the referee to ensure Bolivia beat Peru,[11] Peru qualified for their first World Cup since 1930. Following a wave of student protests in 1969, Onganía himself was toppled a week into the tournament by a harder-line military faction led by General Alejandro Lanusse.

But the most notorious aspect of the pre-tournament stages was the meeting of El Salvador and Honduras in what were effectively the semi-finals of Concacaf qualifying. What followed became mythologised, largely thanks to Ryszard Kapuściński's book *The Soccer War*. But as with so much of Kapuściński's 'magic journalism' – to use the term coined by the US writer Adam Hochschild[12] – the chapter in that book that deals with the war is thrilling, beautifully written and dotted with fabrication and inexactitude.* Football may have been the final spark, but the kindling had been piling up for years.

For several years it had become common for El Salvadoreans to cross a narrow valley on the border and set up on largely vacant land in Honduras. That alarmed the Honduran government, which gave the 60,000 incomers five years to obtain legal status or get out. Only around 1,000 bothered to do so and that became a major problem when Honduras's military junta, as part of a wider programme of agrarian reform in the areas not owned by US fruit companies, seized farms belonging to Salvadoreans and gave them to relocated Hondurans. The Salvadoreans took up machetes to defend land they'd worked in some cases for several years.

At the end of 1968, Honduras and El Salvador both won their first-phase qualifying round groups, advancing to a play-off, the winner of which would then play in a further play-off against the USA or Haiti for a berth in Mexico. Both sides won the home leg, meaning a decider in Mexico City.

There were around 25,000 fans from each country at the Azteca stadium and widespread violence despite the presence of 7,000 Mexican troops as El Salvador won 3–2 in extra time. Later that day, El Salvador broke off diplomatic relations with Honduras, claiming 11,700 Salvadoreans had been forced to flee Honduras in the previous week and a half. On 14 July, eight Salvadorean P51 Mustangs, the entirety of their air force, bombed targets in Honduras, although as these were repurposed fighters, their role was largely symbolic. At the same time, the Salvadorean army launched incursions along the two main highways into its eastern neighbour. They got to within

* For instance, he tells the story of Amelia Bolaños, an eighteen-year-old Salvadoran woman who killed herself when Honduras scored a last-minute winner in the first of the three play-off games, becoming such a patriotic hero that the national team walked behind her coffin at her funeral. But when the journalists Maria Hawranek, Szymon Oprysze and Rodrigo Arías tried to follow up the story several years later, they could find no evidence she had ever existed.

seventy-five miles of the capital Tegucigalpa before being held up by armed resistance in the jungles and swamps. Fighting with guns and machetes, meanwhile, continued along the border, killing around 3,000 and leaving many more seriously wounded or homeless.[13]

Eight Honduran Corsairs, the entirety of their air force, responded on the morning of 16 July by attacking the Ilopango airbase and oil facilities in the port city of Acajutla. There were numerous clashes between the air forces, the last ever dogfights between piston-engined jets.[14] The Honduran government called on the Organization of American States to intervene and, as it threatened sanctions and the Pope and the UN made disapproving noises, El Salvador reluctantly agreed to a cease-fire. The war had lasted less than four days, although it would be more than a decade before peace terms were finally signed.

El Salvador went on to beat Haiti in the one-legged play-off in Jamaica, Juan Ramón Martínez getting the only goal in extra time. 'The media,' the winger Pipo Rodríguez said, 'charged us with patriotic responsibility ... We were practically soldiers ... heading off to war.'[15]

But there was a big difference between rhetoric and reality. Having failed to win any of their five warm-up games, El Salvador replaced the coach who had seen them through qualifying, Gregorio Bundio, with Hernán Carrasco, who had won four of the previous five Salvadorean league championships. The squad had been promised a bonus of $1,000 each for qualifying and when that failed to arrive, a number of players threatened to strike. The kit, provided by Adidas, went missing so new shirts had to be bought in Mexico and badges stitched on. They lost their three group games by an aggregate of 9–0.

What happened in England in 1966 had stunned Brazilian football, as though the idea they were not automatically the best in the world could not be processed. That perhaps explains why so many figures, Havelange foremost among them – conveniently ignoring, for instance, the annulment of Garrincha's suspension for the 1962 final and the various holidays provided for match officials – continued long after the event to insist Brazil had been the victims of conspiracy in 1966 (they would do so again in 1974 and, with slightly more justification, in 1978).[16] Projection can be a powerful shaper of perception.

In the year after the defeat to Portugal at Goodison Park, Brazil played only three games, all of them draws against Uruguay in Montevideo. Feola was moved aside and replaced by a national selection committee. There was a sense the national team was distrusted. Internal politicking made the committee unworkable and in February 1969 it was disbanded. That Brazil should have a single national coach again made sense: the man Havelange appointed did not.

João Saldanha had briefly coached Botafogo in the fifties, but he was not a former player. Rather, he was an outspoken journalist, a follower of Gilberto Freyre in celebrating Brazil as a great melting-pot, and a Communist. 'I adored him as a person,' said Tostão. 'He was emotional and a humanist. He was a dreamer.'[17] Even if there was some sense that Saldanha would neuter the attacks of an increasingly virulent press, and perhaps dampen their demands for a more physical brand of football, he was a notably odd choice under the military dictatorship.

Saldanha had been born in Rio Grande do Sul in 1917 to a family of wealthy farmers, federalists who wanted independence for the southern states. During the Gaucho Civil War in 1923, the six-year-old Saldanha was involved in the smuggling of arms. When the war was lost, the Saldanhas fled to Uruguay before returning and backing Getúlio Vargas in the 1930 election and subsequent coup.

Saldanha was not a natural follower of Vargas. He joined

the Brazilian Communist Party (PCB), which sent him to Porecatu in Paraná to support peasants in a land dispute. In 1953, he helped organise the 'Strike of the 300,000' as workers in the metal and textile industries demanded improved wages. Saldanha had initially regarded football as an unhelpful opiate but by the late fifties he had come to see it as a vital way of boosting working-class self-esteem. Already a prolific journalist, he became a flamboyant radio pundit.

His backroom staff may have been full of representatives of the regime, but Saldanha had his own romantic image of Brazilian football. He was happy to work with technocrats, realised they could help him, but he still saw football as an art, still believed lionhearted players and their individual skills were worth more than systems.

But fitness mattered. Before Brazil began their World Cup qualifying campaign in August, Saldanha took his squad for a twenty-day training camp at altitude in Bogotá. There, on a single television in a corridor at the Hotel Commendador, players watched the moon landing. They also underwent the Cooper test developed by Nasa to assess aerobic fitness; the message was being sent out that Brazil and its football were part of the space age. Reverting to a 4-2-4, with Pelé and Tostão a pair of mobile centre-forwards, Brazil won six qualifiers out of six, scoring twenty-three and conceding only twice.

General Emílio Médici was named president of Brazil late in 1969. He was, supposedly, a fan of the Atlético Mineiro striker Dadá Maravilha[18] and before a double-header against Argentina in March 1970, Saldanha was asked about Médici's apparent desire to see Dadá in the national shirt. 'I don't pick the ministry and the president doesn't pick the team,' he replied. Video shows a relaxed Saldanha smiling as he made what was clearly a light-hearted comment. But written down, the words could be imagined in a different tone. That was the crack, and the edifice soon collapsed.[19]

Saldanha, never afraid of a provocative opinion, had been much more explicit in criticising the regime to the European press and started writing columns again. When Brazil lost 2–0 to Argentina, he had few friends left to defend him. Saldanha doubled down and made the terrible mistake of questioning Pelé, pointing out he was short-sighted. He wasn't the only one wondering whether Pelé, at twenty-nine, was past his peak – Tostão, for instance, insisted he had been at his best between 1957 and 1964, before Santos exhausted him with their eternal touring,[20] and Pelé had been diagnosed with mild myopia before the 1958 World Cup, but it was almost heretical to suggest it made a difference to his play. As criticism mounted, the Flamengo coach Yustrich insisted Saldanha wasn't qualified for the job. Saldanha responded by racing to Flamengo's training ground with a loaded gun. Yustrich, thankfully, wasn't there but nobody could pretend that was a response that suggested a man ready to lead a team into the high-pressure environment of a World Cup.

When the national side drew 1–1 in a friendly with Bangu, an undistinguished team who that season would finish ninth in the Carioca championship, it was clear something had to be done. On 17 March, Saldanha was sacked. Just how involved Médici or his government were is debatable but most players of the time seem to have believed the military were responsible.[21] It wasn't necessarily that he was removed because of his political beliefs or because he was perceived as a potential embarrassment; rather, he had nothing to sustain him when results went awry. Nonetheless, Saldanha was prevented from flying directly from Brazil to Mexico for the tournament, supposedly for fear he would hijack the plane, and so made his way there via a circuitous route.[22]

The question of the relationship between that side and Médici's government remains fraught but to be overly critical of Brazil's players for their association with the regime is perhaps to fail to appreciate just how pervasive its influence was. Everybody in Brazil at the time ended up having to deal with the military. 'We went to win, but what happened with that win was not our problem,' said Wilson Piazza. 'Maybe our victories reinforced the system the military had been building for years but they helped the Seleçao more than vice versa.'[23] Opinions were mixed. Carlos Alberto and Piazza said they had no real understanding of the nature of the regime. Gérson said the squad 'knew everything that was happening'[24] while Dadá, even half a century later, was adamant that the dictatorship was good for Brazil.[25]

Football had become even more politically important than it had been before. The government needed both economic growth and a sense of the nation striving towards some grand destiny. There was a symbolic as well as a practical significance to the spate of stadium building prompted by the World Cup wins of 1958 and 1962.

In the autumn of 1969, at the Churrascaria Urca at the bottom of Sugarloaf Mountain, Saldanha met the army officers Cláudio Coutinho and Lamartine Da Costa to discuss how Brazil should prepare for the challenge of playing a World Cup at altitude. Da Costa, a specialist in biometeorology, taught at the Pontificia Universidade Católica do Rio de Janeiro. Both had attended the 1968 Olympics, both had made their observations, both had learned, both were determined to employ science to help.

The happy-go-lucky, wandered-off-the-beach samba stereotype was always a myth but, by the late sixties, as the government became increasingly hard-line, everything in Brazil was run by technocrats. Alongside the introduction of Institutional Act No. 5 in 1968, which laid down the legal framework for a crackdown on dissent, Antônio Delfim Netto, an economics professor, was appointed minister of planning. He led a wave of public investment in roads, power plants and the Itaipu Dam, which at the time was the largest in the world, and for a time the economy boomed.

The same spirit had begun to infuse Brazilian football. Saldanha had witnessed the 1966 World Cup and its physicality first-hand as a journalist for *A Ultima Hora*. It was he who had sought out Da Costa, who was no great fan of football and regarded footballers essentially as children.[26] Da Costa was impressed and fifty years later would give Saldanha credit for introducing 'a scientific climate'[27] to football. He proposed a training plan beginning in February 1970 to get the players acclimatised.

Before their departure for Mexico, the players spent 100 days of preparation at army facilities. Everything was monitored in fanatical detail: players' kit was made to measure and the collars designed so they would not accumulate sweat. On the day they left the head of the delegation, Brigadier Major Jerônimo Bastos, wrote to the players, speaking of their 'honourable mission'.[28] Bastos's secretary, Major Roberto Camara Ypiranga dos Guaranys, was the delegation's head of security; he was later revealed to have been one of the regime's torturers.[29]

With Saldanha gone and only ten weeks before the World Cup began, the CBD needed to make a new appointment quickly and plumped for Mário Zagallo, left-winger in the World Cup successes of 1958 and 1962. He had been a success as manager of Botafogo, where his use of a 4-3-3 had earned him a reputation for caution, but at least as importantly, he was measured and reserved and came from a middle-class background, his family having made their money in textiles. He was an establishment figure, everything Saldanha was not.

It was only in the final friendly before departure for Mexico that the team began to come together. Edu, who had done well on the left for Saldanha, was replaced by Rivellino, more usually a central player who was asked to perform the deep-lying winger role Zagallo had in 1962. Clodoaldo came into midfield, with Piazza unexpectedly dropping back to operate at the heart of the defence. 'Zagallo,' said Tostão, 'had this idea for compact football. When we lost the ball, he wanted us to track back; when we had possession he wanted us to advance as one.'[30] Key to that was Gérson, Clodoaldo's partner in the centre of midfield. Nicknamed '*Papagaio*' – 'Parrot' – because of his constant talking, his organisational abilities allied to his reading of the game were crucial in ensuring Brazil's gaggle of number 10s were able to play together. 'It was as if he were a coach on the field,' said Tostão, 'as if he were playing from the stands.'[31]

Brazil beat Austria 1–0 and at full time, Miguel Gustavo's anthem '*Pra Frente, Brasil*' was played at the Maracanã. It had won a competition organised by the TV station Globo to be Brazil's official anthem at the tournament and celebrated national unity and progress, the 90 million 'joining hands' to fight together for the World Cup.[32] The sense of the football team acting as a cipher for the nation was unavoidable.

The technocratic approach succeeded. Almost every country tried to acclimatise to the heat and altitude, some with more success than others. Israel trained in Ethiopia and Colorado. Uruguay went to Quito and Bogotá. England's doctor Neil Phillips took a course on heat, altitude and tropical diseases, then brought in Dr Griffith Pugh, a physiologist who had been on Edmund Hillary's successful mission to climb Everest. Bulgaria trained in the freezing mountains south of Sofia and, even more mystifyingly, restricted their players' access to water to get them used to dehydration. Mexico themselves held a five-month training camp that featured thirteen international friendlies between February and May before a pair of games against Dundee United. But nobody prepared quite so thoroughly as Brazil, who arrived in Mexico City thirty-two days before their opening game against Czechoslovakia. And it worked: twelve of the nineteen goals scored by Brazil in that World Cup came in the second half; they didn't just outplay opponents, they outlasted them.

The preparations of the world champions England, who had been in the same group as Brazil, were at least good in theory. They'd come third in the 1968 European Championship, even if Alan Mullery had become the first player sent off playing for England in the semi-final defeat to Yugoslavia. Later that year, Ramsey had gone to the Olympic Games in Mexico City to assess the impact of altitude, while Dr Neil Phillips, working with Hugh de Wardener from the renal unit at Charing Cross Hospital and the pharmaceutical company Ciba-Geigy, developed a slow-release salt tablet to help players deal with the expected loss of eight to ten pounds of sweat per game.

A tour of Latin America the following year featuring games in Mexico City, Montevideo and Rio de Janeiro was a further sensible step but a crotchety Ramsey managed to offend the Mexicans by complaining about the noise and disorganisation: the damage done by his 'animals' comment three years earlier was compounded. When England decided to import their own bus, food and water for the World Cup itself, the sense of outrage was only magnified further. The Mexican authorities decided the UK was a country stricken by foot-and-mouth; as a result, all the frozen meat was impounded at the docks and burned, leaving England to subsist on Findus fish fingers and ready meals. The boos that greeted their entrance at the opening ceremony made clear just how unpopular they were.

After three weeks of training and acclimatisation in Mexico City, their lifestyle so regimented that Ramsey would stand by the pool, stopwatch in hand, blowing the whistle when it was time for his sunbathing players to turn over, England left for games at altitude against Colombia in Bogotá and against Ecuador in Quito. They arrived at the Tequendama Hotel in Bogotá at around 4 p.m. on 25 May and, as the players hung around the lobby waiting to check in, Bobby Moore, Bobby Charlton and Peter Thompson wandered into a jewellery store called Fuego Verde. A few minutes after they'd left, the alarm was raised. Something had gone missing. There was a weary sigh: shortly before they left Mexico, a jewellery salesman claimed somebody in the squad had stolen a gold Rolex and the players had ended up chipping in to pay him off. This, it seemed, was the same scam.

The shop assistant Clara Padilla insisted she had seen Bobby Moore slip a bracelet into his jacket pocket and, after some confusion, the shop's owner Daniel Rojas decided it was made of gold, studded with diamonds and emeralds and worth £600. Police investigated but, after discovering Moore's hand was too big to fit through the opening in the display case, seemed to have dismissed the accusation.

England beat Colombia 4–0 and Ecuador 2–0. On their way back to Mexico from Quito, there was a stopover in Bogotá. Ramsey had arranged for the players to return to the Tequendama to watch the James Stewart Western *Shenandoah* in the hotel cinema. During the film, Moore was discreetly taken aside and arrested; only when they'd boarded the plane to Mexico City did the rest of the squad learn what had happened to their captain.[33] A hawker of antiques called Alvaro Suárez had come forward, claiming to have seen Moore secrete the bracelet in his blazer, and a magistrate decided Moore had to be detained pending further investigation. He was at least spared jail, placed under house arrest at the home of Alfonso Senior, a director at the Colombian football federation.

The last leg of the flight was turbulent, leading the centre-forward Jeff Astle, a poor flier at the best of times, to drink rather more than he should have. By the time they landed, he was so drunk that he had almost to be carried off the plane. To make matters worse, it emerged that his local brewery in the Midlands, picking up on a comment Astle had made that he would miss his occasional pint while he was away, had sent him twelve dozen cans.[34] 'A team of drunkards and thieves', ran the headline in the Mexican paper *Esto* above a photo of a legless Astle.

In Bogotá a reconstruction was staged. It was farcical, delayed by almost two hours because police initially refused to release Moore to attend. Padilla changed her story to say merely that she had seen Moore put something in his pocket. Suárez, who it later transpired had been paid about £100 by Rojas, insisted he was sure it had been the bracelet.[35]

Moore asked which pocket. The left one, Padilla and Suárez agreed. Moore showed that there was no left pocket in the England team blazer. With diplomatic pressure mounting, he was provisionally released and raced to Guadalajara for England's opening game, although it wouldn't be until December 1975 that the charges were formally dropped. Padilla fled to Los Angeles[36] and the Tequendama refused to renew the lease on the Fuego Verde, citing reputational damage. It transpired this was a common scam and that two Brazilian teams had been the victims of something similar in Colombia in the previous year.[37]

Rumours nevertheless persist that Moore took the fall for somebody else's prank. Padilla initially mentioned a third player in the shop and early reports also describe the presence of a younger squad member, although he soon disappears from accounts. It's been widely assumed that was Thompson, who did visit the shop, but he was twenty-seven by then, only eighteen months younger than Moore. In Jeff Powell's 1976 authorised biography of Moore, it's straightforwardly stated, 'There was no bracelet.'[38] When the book was reissued after Moore's death, that line had vanished. Instead Powell claims that Moore had told him he was covering for a younger squad member.[39] In the book, Powell said he had no idea who that was but, in 2002, he told a BBC documentary that he did know but had vowed never to reveal the culprit's identity.[40] For all the conspiracy theories, though, the most likely explanation is that the incident was a set-up designed to extort money from tourists.

Brazil had begun with a 4–1 victory over Czechoslovakia, a game best remembered for Pelé's attempt to lob the goalkeeper Ivo Viktor from the centre circle. There were claims Pelé had attempted the shot to prove that, despite the myopia Saldanha had highlighted, he was perfectly capable of seeing from at least the halfway line to the goal. His own explanation was more prosaic but revealing in other ways. 'European goalkeepers,' he said, 'had a tendency to stray from their positions in front of the goal whenever play was in the opponent's half . . . Viktor . . . seemed assured that there was no danger so long as the activity was distant.'[41] For him, self-evidently, that tendency to advance represented an opportunity, but what is equally telling is that there is no grasp that a goalkeeper playing in an advanced position might be a deliberate tactic to close the space behind a high offside line. A sweeper-keeper in 1970 was still a very European concept.

That set up the game against England, who had started with a characteristically disciplined 1–0 win over Romania, perfectly. Mexican fans were clearly on Brazil's side, in part because they loved the way they played, and in part because Ramsey's attitude had turned them against England. A large group gathered outside the Hilton on the night before the game, intent on disrupting England's sleep. Some gained access to the corridor where England's rooms were before being chased away by a semi-naked Jack Charlton.

The game itself was a slow-burning classic, played for the most part almost at walking pace because of the 36.6C heat and notable perhaps less for sustained drama than for a constant tension, punctuated by a handful of moments that are ingrained in the collective consciousnesses of both English and Brazilian football: Banks's stunning save from Pelé's header, Bobby Moore's perfectly timed tackle on Jairzinho, Jeff Astle's late miss and the only goal, as Tostão's dribble created space for a cross, Pelé took the ball down and, demonstrating the spatial awareness that was by then probably his greatest gift, rolled the ball outside him for Jairzinho to lash above Banks and into the top corner. Pelé described it as 'the most important game of the tournament'[42] and in the famous image of him and Moore exchanging shirts at the end, it was possible to see both a sportsmanlike recognition of each other's excellence, and the handing on of the baton, England ceding to Brazil. 'If you wanted to become world champions,' said Carlos Alberto, 'you had to beat England.'[43]

Yet while there was clearly a spirit of mutual respect, and no sense of lingering resentment on either side, that was also a physical game, offering plenty of reminders that Brazil, as well as their obvious ability on the ball, were more than capable of looking after themselves. England confirmed their place in the last eight with a nervy 1–0 win over Czechoslovakia, while Brazil took top spot by beating Romania 3–2.

Coached by the former Brazil midfielder Didi, Peru were regarded as plausible outsiders at their first World Cup since 1930. But on the day the tournament began, Peru was struck by a massive earthquake that caused the largest avalanche ever recorded. In total, 70,000 people were killed. Initially the scale of the disaster was hidden from the players but, a day later, as they prepared in the stadium in León for their opening game, against Bulgaria, they were told by fans what had happened.

Bulgaria took a first-half lead but, at half-time, the president of the National Sports Committee José Aramburú Menchaca produced a pot of soil he said came from Huaraz, one of the worst-affected areas. He scattered it on the floor of the changing-room and had the players walk across it before the second half. Although Peru soon conceded again, they came back to win 3–2. That may have been more to do with Bulgaria's idiosyncratic approach to hydration than the mystical power of the scattered earth, but the same trick worked against Morocco too, as a 0–0 half-time scoreline was transformed into a 3–0 win.

Peru played an open and fluid 4-2-4, their three group games yielding seven goals for and five against. There was a sense when they met in the quarter-final that Brazil were playing an earlier version of themselves. Two goals in the first fifteen minutes set Brazil on their way and they were comfortable 4–2 winners. 'Both teams,' Pelé said, 'being South American, refused to play the defensive game preferred by European teams.'[44] It's a curious comment, given Argentina's turn to *anti-fútbol* and the general approach of Uruguay, but it does perhaps underline just how the notion of European football as physical and anti-attacking had penetrated the wider Brazilian consciousness after the embarrassment of 1966.

Uruguay were Brazil's opponents in the semi-final. They had been very defensive through the tournament, conceding once and scoring only three times in their four games. Uruguay took an early lead as Felix, in an echo of 1950, was beaten from a narrow angle by Luis Cubilla, a forward attacking from the right. Clodoaldo and Gérson then switched roles to confound Uruguay's man-marking scheme and Brazil went on to win 3–1.

*

Italy were the European champions, but were without the forward Pietro Anastasi, who had scored in the Euro 68 final replay, after he went down with appendicitis. They topped their group despite scoring only once in the first round to set up a quarter-final against Mexico who, having benefited from some generous refereeing,[45] had been placed second in Group A, behind the USSR, on the toss of a coin.

It was for that quarter-final that Italy's coach Ferruccio Valcareggi devised the '*staffetta*', the 'relay', by which Sandro Mazzola would play in the first half and Gianni Rivera in the second. Although that is often portrayed as an act of tactical diplomacy so he could use both his number 10s, it seems that it was an ad hoc solution to stomach problems suffered by Mazzola, who had played every minute of the group stage while Rivera's only involvement had been as a half-time replacement for Angelo Domenghini in the goalless draw against Israel. Whatever the reasoning, the ploy worked, Rivera's influence helping transform a 1–1 half-time scoreline into a 4–1 win.

Helmut Schön still had eight of the side that had played in the final four years earlier in his West Germany squad, but there were also key additions: Sepp Maier in goal, Jürgen Grabowski and Reinhard Libuda on the flanks and Gerd Müller at centre-forward. They had dropped a single point in qualifying but their preparation had been hampered by a fixture pile-up in the Bundesliga caused by a bad winter.

In the heat of Léon, they found a new way to play, trying to manipulate the ball in such a way they could remain largely in the shade of the main stand at the Estadio Nou Camp. It was from there that the unusual West German style of the seventies developed: although it had a similar focus on maintaining possession and the intermovement of players to Total Football, the revolutionary style that was developing in the Netherlands, there was none of the pressing of the Dutch model. Although they went behind to both Morocco and Bulgaria, they won all three group games, scoring ten goals as Müller got back-to-back hat-tricks against Bulgaria and Peru.

The quarter-final matched them with England, against whom they had recorded a first ever victory, in a friendly in Hanover in 1968. The significance of that game, a warm-up for the Euros, was widely dismissed in England, but it boosted West German self-belief and, in hindsight, can be seen as the second act in the five-game sequence between 1966 and 1972 that transformed the relationship of the two sides.

The orthodox English reading of their loss of a two-goal lead has always been that it changed when Bobby Charlton was withdrawn for Colin Bell with twenty minutes remaining. Charlton himself said he was distracted by seeing the preparations for the substitution, which allowed Franz Beckenbauer to get away from him. Media hindsight has tended to say Ramsey made a mistake in withdrawing him, but he was thirty-two and with the semi-final to come at even greater altitude three days later, it perhaps made sense to rest him. There had, after all, been little indication in the first three-quarters of the game that West Germany could come back.

England had been hampered by poor organisation, failing to arrange accommodation in advance or get clearance to fly into León, meaning they ended up having to make a five-hour bus journey. Bobby Charlton and Keith Newton went down with a stomach bug two days before the game and their room-mate in Guadalajara, Gordon Banks, got it a day later. Charlton and Newton recovered, Banks did not, and was replaced by Peter Bonetti.

Bonetti was a fine goalkeeper and would probably have been first choice for all but five or six sides at the tournament but his international career came to be defined by what had happened after Beckenbauer escaped Charlton. His shot was not cleanly struck but slithered under Bonetti. The assumption is always that Banks would have saved it, and usually he would – but then so too would Bonetti.

Another substitution was probably just as important as Charlton's departure, Grabowski coming on for Libuda after fifty-seven minutes to run at the tiring Terry Cooper. A remarkable back header from Uwe Seeler levelled the scores after eighty-two minutes and Müller got the winner in extra time after Seeler had headed back Grabowski's cross. England had played extremely well against both Brazil and West Germany, arguably better than in any game in 1966, but were out.

West Germany's semi-final against Italy is commemorated by a plaque at the Azteca that describes it as the 'Match of the Century'. It certainly had a dramatic conclusion, although it's notable that when Italy beat Brazil in 1982 and pundits sought another great World Cup fixture to compare it to, they tended to skip back to Hungary's semi-final win over Uruguay in 1954. It was, though, probably the greatest period of extra time in World Cup history, as two exhausted teams hammered away at each other in the afternoon heat, but the ninety minutes of normal time, as Beckenbauer acknowledged, were 'ordinary'.[46]

Boninsegna struck after eight minutes and Italy, again employing the *staffetta* with Rivera replacing Mazzola at half-time, set about defending their lead in the stereotypical manner. They very nearly did so, only for Karl-Heinz Schnellinger to equalise deep into stoppage time. West Germany went ahead in extra time, conceded twice and then equalised again, and all with Beckenbauer playing in a sling having dislocated his shoulder midway through the second half. But within a minute of Müller making it 3–3 with his second of the game, and tenth of the tournament, Boninsegna got away down the left and crossed low for Rivera to sidefoot home.

This was, though, another game of desperately poor

officiating, most of which seemed to go against West Germany. The referee Arturo Yamasaki* denied them two blatant penalties while taking no action to curtail Italian gamesmanship. 'The Italians,' said Seeler, 'lived up to their reputation as time-wasters and stayed on the ground after every duel, kicked the ball up in the stands and argued long and hard about every refereeing decision.'[47] For all the complaints about the refereeing in 1966, it was much worse in 1970. Victory for a glorious attacking side can occlude a multitude of flaws.

As Brazil's team bus made its way through Mexico City to the Azteca for the final, Pelé was struck by the vastness of the occasion. He felt himself beginning to weep so, not wanting to let the other players see him break down, he pretended to drop a rattle he was holding, and crouched down between the seats as though looking for it as the tears dripped from his eyes.

The nation expected victory. After the disappointment of 1966, they demanded it. There was a need to surpass the achievements of Italy and Uruguay, to become the first nation to win the world title three times and so claim the Jules Rimet trophy permanently. Pelé was only twenty-nine, but the end was close, at least in terms of international football. This, he knew even then, would probably be his last World Cup match – and in it he had the perfect opportunity to fulfil the promise he had made his father twenty years earlier to make him forget the pain of the Maracanazo, memories of which had inevitably been stirred by the semi-final against Uruguay.

But there was more even than that. In 1958, Pelé had been seventeen, prodigiously gifted but essentially a kid adding

---

* Yamasaki, who was of Japanese descent, was born in Lima and was a Peruvian when he sent off Garrincha in the 1962 semi-final. He moved to Mexico in 1966.

gloss – a very special gloss it's true – to the efforts of Bellini, Nílton Santos and Didi. In 1962 he had been injured in the second game. But in 1970, fully mature, he was the leader of the side; his third World Cup would be indisputably *his* World Cup. That was true off the pitch as well, as he was the one to lead prayer sessions for the squad – more, he said, to foster a sense of togetherness than for religious reasons.

European champions they may have been, but Italy had no such expectations. Their federation had booked flights home after the group stage and were so keen to make a quick getaway that the players had to pack the night before the final.[48] They probably began the final the better and would have taken the lead but for a couple of fine saves from Felix, who was a far better keeper than his reputation in Europe would allow. But the marking structure with Tarcisio Burgnich on Rivellino and Mario Bertini on Pelé didn't work and Pelé outjumped Giacinto Facchetti to head Brazil into an 18th-minute lead.

A misconstrued backheel by Clodoaldo allowed Boninsegna to level and for a time all the old demons resurfaced in Brazilian minds. Pelé bafflingly claimed that the East German referee Rudi Glöckner had blown for half-time just as he was about to score and feared, as he saw it, that Brazil were about to be cheated again by European refereeing.[49]

Italy, exhausted after their semi-final, held out until the sixty-sixth minute when a long-range Gérson strike gave Brazil the lead. Five minutes later Pelé headed down a Gérson free-kick for Jairzinho to add a third and become the first player since Alcides Ghiggia in 1950 to score in every match in the tournament. Rivera came on only in the eighty-fourth minute, by which point the game was lost. All that remained then was for Carlos Alberto to underline the win with his wondergoal.

That night, the squad had a celebratory meal at which the senior players took a call from General Médici. When they got back home, celebrations were protracted, exhaustingly so.

Médici embraced Carlos Alberto, and said, 'In the name of Brazil, thank you very much. You all showed a lot of vigour and force, how great our country is.'[50] The message was typical of the junta, stressing national unity and, like right-wing governments throughout time, thrusting muscularity. To Pelé, he said, 'You are the great hero, you are the king ... What great luck you were born here.'[51] Of course, there was nothing Carlos Alberto or Pelé could realistically have done other than stand there and accept the congratulations, but equally it's impossible, given Médici's speech, to deny that there was a profound connection between the junta and the national side.

Success at the World Cup combined with the investment in infrastructure projects to create a great moment of Brazilian self-confidence. The players could hardly have been unaware of that but, so pervasive was the military, to boycott the regime would have been effectively to boycott a normal life. Football was both how Brazil advertised itself to the world and, also, a great unifying force, something underlined as a proper national football championship was launched in 1971.

Brazil's World Cup victory in 1970 still has a mythic quality, their performance still used as a shorthand for the best that football can be: it's what gave Pelé's 'beautiful game' cliché currency. That it became fused in the popular imagination with the technology that made it possible to witness the tournament live across the globe is natural: the Telstar was both satellite and ball, ball and satellite, and Brazil's mastery over one was disseminated by the other. Their attacking football was brilliant, but this was a tournament just as tawdry, just as mired in political chicanery, and just as blighted by poor refereeing as any other.

The aptest analogy for the 1970 World Cup from the previous year, then, is perhaps less the moon landings than Woodstock, a festival of love and artistry that has come to embody a moment of lost possibility. Like Woodstock, the future offered by the 1970 World Cup was perhaps always implausible.

It probably was necessary for the growth of the World Cup that it should move into a new commercial era. Certainly Rous had come to seem an anachronism. Pelé himself showed little reluctance about capitalising on his fame – and Pelé was famous, so much so that Andy Warhol, who painted him, commented that for Pelé his formulation about fifteen minutes of fame didn't work; he would have 'fifteen centuries'. 'Never,' Pelé said, 'underestimate the power of a well-known and respected name; and never be afraid to charge an appropriate fee for its use.'[52] As a result, he advertised everything from Puma to Pepsi, from Viagra to diamonds made by heating his own hair under extreme pressure.

Tostão has a theory about the use of nicknames in Brazilian football, that the clamour around players makes it useful for stars to divide themselves into the public figure (the nickname) and the private (the 'real' name). For Pelé, that division ceased to exist: the mask became the man. 'He says that Edson is separate from Pelé, but I don't see it,' Tostão said. 'The only one that exists is the public Pelé ... He passes the impression of never going through depression, anxiety, anguish, sadness as a consequence of loss of identity. He's happy, well adapted. He's always smiling and upbeat. You never see him bad tempered. He loves being Pelé.'[53]

Tactical evolution, driven in part by the physical development of players, was inevitable. There may be a romance to the idea that a portly man doing tricks could be among the best in the world but from 1958 onwards, even Brazil, for all their reputation for off-the-cuff brilliance, had recognised the need for intense preparation.

And, like Woodstock, the romanticised image of the 1970 World Cup was itself largely illusory. The popular conception of Woodstock, great crowds high on the prospect of peace and love, listening to Jimi Hendrix, Creedence Clearwater Revival and a pregnant Joan Baez stems largely from the over-idealised Michael Wadleigh documentary, released three months before the 1970 World Cup. The reality was chaos: several acts performed hours late; a fence was broken down by anarchists leading to potentially dangerous overcrowding; two people were killed, one of them run over by a tractor; and a worn electric cable combined with persistent rain raised the possibility of mass electrocution.

The 1970 World Cup, similarly, once you peer beyond the brilliance of Brazil's football, becomes a much more sinister event. Mexico's governing PRI was repressive and capable of extreme violence. And in Brazil, along with short-term economic growth, victory in Mexico, and its associated modernity, was presented as part of Médici's 'Brazilian miracle'.

The result is that the 1970 World Cup stands amid the darkness as a fragile vision of perfection and possibility, of what football can be, what it could have been. It is, in effect, the equivalent of that epiphanic pause before Pelé lays the ball right in the 86th minute of the final. But where that pass was followed by the explosive fulfilment of Carlos Alberto's shot, football itself went awry. That World Cup is the scene in *Easy Rider*, another cultural touchstone of 1969, in which Wyatt (Peter Fonda) tells Billy (Dennis Hopper) that 'we blew it.'[54]

Like Wyatt and Billy, Fifa took the money and, while much was gained, much also was lost.

1974

COLD WAR BY OTHER MEANS

Perhaps it was inevitable from the moment in 1966 that West Germany was selected as host, that the Cold War would intrude on the 1974 World Cup. What was not expected, though, was that those tensions would be heightened when East Germany qualified for the only World Cup in their history.

Further eastern European representation came in the form of Poland, Yugoslavia and Bulgaria but the Soviets were not there, having refused to play the second leg of a qualifying play-off against Chile at the Estadio Nacional in Santiago. The game was scheduled for 21 November 1973. On 12 September, General Augusto Pinochet had launched his coup against the democratically elected Marxist leader Salvador Allende. In the two months that followed, at least 12,000 and possibly as many as 20,000 prisoners were housed at the stadium. Many were tortured, the Beatles played at top volume to try to block out their screams. Chile's human rights commission confirmed forty-one dead there, although the true figure is almost certainly over 100 and perhaps as high as 300.[1]

In early October, Fifa sent a fact-finding mission. It produced a report of staggering complacency and surely wilful blindness.

'The people in there,' it stated, 'are not prisoners but only detainees whose identity is yet to be established ... the grass on the pitch is in perfect condition.'[2]

On 27 October, the Soviet football federation sent a telegram to Stanley Rous. The 'fascist upheaval', it said, had led to 'bloody terrorism and repressions ... tortures and executions'. It concluded, 'Soviet sportsmen cannot ... play at stadium stained with blood of Chilean patriots.'[3]

But Fifa insisted that they should and so, on 21 November, by which time the detainees had been shifted to a camp in the Atacama, the game kicked off with only one team in front of 15,000 fans. Chile's players walked down the pitch, passing the ball between them, their captain Francisco Valdés scored into an empty net and they were awarded a 2–0 victory.

For Chile, it was barely worth it: they went out of the finals at the group stage after a defeat and a pair of draws. For football, it was a moral outrage. For everybody else there was the sense that not since the 1930s had geopolitics been quite so present at a World Cup as it was in 1974, a time of CIA coups, Communist moles and domestic terrorism.

At the 1972 Olympic Games in Munich, the Palestinian terror organisation Black September had killed eleven members of the Israeli team. They had been aided by German neo-Nazi groups[4] and, after initially taking hostages, had called for the release not only of 234 Palestinian prisoners by Israel but also of Andreas Baader and Ulrike Meinhof, the leaders of the far-left Red Army Faction, who were being held in West German jails.

On 6 October 1973, Yom Kippur, Egyptian and Syrian forces crossed the ceasefire lines drawn up after the Six-Day War in 1967, invading Sinai and the Golan Heights. Israel counter-attacked, driving towards Damascus and Cairo, leading to heightened Cold War tensions as the US and Soviet

Union stepped up their supply of arms to their respective allies in the region. A ceasefire was declared on 25 October but, by then, the Arab members of Opec led by King Faisal of Saudi Arabia had imposed an embargo on Western powers who had supported Israel. By the time it was lifted the following March, prices had quadrupled.

The repercussions were profound. From the end of the Second World War, the West had enjoyed almost unbroken prosperity; almost overnight the fragility of economies dependent on oil was exposed as the global economy suffered its biggest contraction since the Great Depression.[5] Inflation soared across Europe. The UK imposed a three-day working week to save energy. In the Netherlands it became an offence punishable by prison for an individual to exceed their energy ration. Poland, which was still heavily dependent on loans from the West, suffered a tenfold increase in foreign debt; as the economic situation worsened there were mass protests which were met by brutal reprisals. A 1975 report to the US Congress from the Federal Energy Administration estimated that in the US alone the oil spike had cost around 500,000 jobs and wiped between $10bn and $20bn off GNP.[6]

Economic difficulty only intensified existing political tension. Willy Brandt, the social democratic Chancellor of West Germany, had pursued a policy of rapprochement with the Communist bloc but lost his parliamentary majority in elections in 1972. Brandt was then forced to resign in May 1974 after one of his personal assistants, Günter Guillaume, was revealed to have been a spy for East Germany. Brandt was already exhausted, partly by his heavy drinking and repeated scandals about his serial adultery, and partly by the fallout from the oil shock.[7]

By the time of the World Cup, West Germany was an insecure, paranoid place suffering its first economic crisis since before the *Wirtschaftswunder*. At the 1972 Olympics, keen to avoid any resonance of 1936, the security had been deliberately low-key. In 1974, with the threat of both domestic terror and events in the Middle East, it was understandably very visible indeed.

For the first time since they'd first deigned to enter, in 1950, England were not there. Frustration had been mounting with Ramsey since 1970, when the attacking spirit of the triumphant Brazilians stood in obvious contrast to Ramsey's reserve. Those seduced into believing 1970 represented the future demanded more from England. When West Germany beat England 3–1 at Wembley in the first leg of the 1972 European Championship quarter-final with a brilliant display of pass-and-move football, it felt like proof that Ramsey was a conservative holding England back.[8] 'English football has come grinding to the end of an era,' wrote Jeff Powell in the *Mail*. 'Some of the Ramsey doctrine which helped England conquer the world is now as old-fashioned as we made the rest look in 1966.'[9] Powell at least acknowledged that Ramsey had been a radical; for others, this was just an opportunity to give a cussed manager reluctant to play the media game a good kicking. As Hugh McIlvanney wrote in the *Observer*, 'Cautious, joyless football was scarcely bearable even while it was bringing victories. When it brings defeat there can only be one reaction.'[10]

World Cup qualification began to go awry in Chorzów, where a Bobby Moore mistake gifted Poland a decisive second. Age was catching up with him; he had become a symbol of Ramsey's tendency to remain loyal to his World Cup-winners when their form no longer justified it.[11] Still, though, victory over Poland at Wembley would have secured qualification.

Poland were probably better than most in England realised. They'd won the 1972 Olympic football tournament under the relaxed Kazimierz Górski, whose liberal approach to discipline helped forge a tight-knit group. England played well, went behind after mistakes from Norman Hunter and Peter Shilton gifted Jan Domarski a goal, equalised through an Allan Clarke penalty and then missed chance after chance, through a combination of ill-fortune, mounting anxiety and the unorthodox heroics of the Poland goalkeeper Jan Tomaszewski.

But no one wanted to hear about bad luck. Before the game, the tabloid writer Peter Batt had claimed in the *Sun* that it would be better if England failed to win so the English game could be euthanised.[12] Sure enough, Ramsey was sacked after ten years in the job.

There wasn't much football could do about the Cold War other than accommodate itself to it. But the World Cup had to deal with another apparently inexorable force that demanded major adaptation, that of global commercialisation; to an extent at least, that came from within. However thrilling events on the pitch in 1974, however revolutionary the impact of Total Football, however significant West Germany's victory, the moment that had the greatest impact on the game came three days before the start of the tournament, at a conference hall in Frankfurt.

Conmebol, the South American confederation, urged João Havelange to stand against Stanley Rous for the Fifa presidency. He recognised that Europe was unlikely to back him but that votes were available in Africa and Asia, many of whose football federations couldn't afford to travel to Fifa Congresses. Supported by Horst Dassler, the chairman of Adidas,[13] and pushing a post-colonial line, Havelange travelled with Pelé, promising to expand the World Cup, to inaugurate a youth World Cup, to increase African participation and to exclude and isolate apartheid South Africa.

Rous came from a very different world. The son of a grocer,

in the First World War he had served as an NCO in the Royal Field Artillery in France, Palestine, Egypt and Lebanon. When he returned to the UK, he trained as a schoolteacher. He played amateur football before a broken wrist ended his career as a goalkeeper, after which he took up refereeing, overseeing several internationals and the 1934 FA Cup final. He's often portrayed as a conservative, establishment figure but he was never that.[14] Rather he dragged himself up from humble origins, rewriting the Laws of the Game in 1938, developing the diagonal system of control that sought to ensure that a referee and his two linesmen had the fullest possible coverage of the pitch, and establishing the Fifa development programme in 1963. He was knighted for his role organising the 1948 Olympics in London, the austerity games, and raised an estimated £3m for the Red Cross. Nor was he against expansion; as early as 1970 he had talked about a thirty-two-team World Cup, but his efforts were scuppered by Uefa.[15]

He was, though, a product of his time, which was perhaps reflected in his paternalistic attitude to emerging post-colonial nations, and his naive attempts to retain a barrier between sport and politics. He also believed fundamentally in service: he took very little remuneration from the game and saw no reason why football federations should not pay their own way to attend Fifa events.

For Havelange, that was a huge opportunity. If all he had done had been to pay the expenses of delegates from poorer nations, then it would be possible to mount a defence that he was merely trying to ensure that as many Fifa members as possible participated at Congress.[16] But he also offered lavish spending allowances on top of that. One African delegate, for instance, was given CHF300,000* in addition to flights and accommodation.[17] All thirty-seven African delegates turned

* Around £615,000 in 2025 prices.

up at the Congress in Frankfurt, most of them paid for by Havelange. The message was clear: he was not like Rous. He had no racist hang-ups. He, the son of a Belgian arms dealer, was the anti-colonial candidate.

Yet while Rous's stance on South Africa made him easy to portray as a racist, he was not without friends in Africa. Etubom Oyo Orok Oyo, who served twelve years as general secretary of the Nigerian Football Association, for instance, had spent a sabbatical working with Rous at the FA in the fifties. Orok Oyo knew Rous, liked him and trusted him and, in 1971, promised him the vote not only of the NFA but, he thought, of all of English-speaking Africa. By 1974, though, Francophone Africa had come to dominate CAF and Orok Oyo had been ousted in Nigeria. His successor, as Orok Oyo put it, 'swallowed the bait'.[18]

And if the propaganda was insufficient, there was always out-and-out bribery. The Fifa general secretary Helmut Käser said that he saw Havelange's men handing envelopes to delegates before the vote.[19] Venezuela's support reportedly cost $25,000.

Which raised the obvious question of who was paying. Havelange always claimed that his money came from Viaçao Cometa, his bus company, although it was never clear he was the majority shareholder.[20]

Other revenue seemed to come from Orwec, Havelange's waste disposal and chemicals firm, which was widely believed to have operated as a laundry for the hundreds of millions of dollars stolen by the former Portuguese finance minister José Maria Teixeira Pinto and other politicians in flight from the declining years of the Estado Novo after the death of Salazar. By the late sixties Havelange owned 49 per cent and sat on the board. The company had twice been close to bankruptcy but had been saved by injections of cash from a business partner of Havelange, Haddock Lobo. The Portuguese money came as a godsend, and allowed Orwec to buy a number of other companies, including one specialising in the manufacture of bombs which led, among other deals, to a lucrative contract with the Bolivian dictator Hugo Banzer.[21] Between 1974 and 1980 (and possibly later), Orwec maintained a slush fund which seems to have been used in part to evade tax and in part to encourage banks to provide loans. Lobo had no doubt Havelange used Orwec to fund his presidential campaign.[22] Orwec continues to trade as a respectable wholesaler of chemicals.

As losses mounted at the CBD, Ernesto Geisel, who had succeeded Médici in 1974, appointed General Adalberto Nunes to look into the organisation's finances. He found a shortfall of at least US$6.6m from the accounts and clear evidence of embezzlement. To have pursued Havelange through the courts, though, would have been an embarrassment so in 1975 the government had the state-owned bank provide 'technical support' – that is, bail out the stricken federation. Havelange was removed from his position as president of the CBD and succeeded by Nunes's brother Admiral Heleno Nunes.

It wasn't entirely clear how Havelange proposed to pay for the expanded World Cup, the youth tournaments or development programmes, or how he would ensure money didn't drain away into the pockets of officials, but precise costings had never been his way. Rous seemed appalled that anybody should even consider campaigning to be Fifa president, let alone Havelange. 'I treated Havelange as my son and he stabbed me in the back,' he said.[23]

Havelange won 62–56 in the first round of voting, and increased his margin to 68–52 in the second. Football and the World Cup were never the same again.

Mário Zagallo remained as coach, but the defending champions Brazil were not what they had been either in terms of personnel or ethos – certainly not the romantic myth of 1970 but not the more pragmatic reality either. Pelé, Tostão and Gérson had all retired, Carlos Alberto and Clodoaldo were injured and Jairzinho's pace had gone. It was not that they prepared any less diligently than they had four years earlier; if anything the problem was that the preparation, overseen by the army physical training specialist Captain Cláudio Coutinho, was too intense.

Again the squad trained together for weeks before the tournament, first at home and then at a camp in the Black Forest. Security was stiflingly tight, all the more so after a hoax bomb scare and, amid the anxiety, old fissures re-emerged. 'It was *paulistas* against *cariocas*,' said the full-back Zé Maria. 'There was no mutual respect.'[24] Piazza, who had led a media boycott on a European tour the previous year after reports of a liaison with a woman in Sweden, lamented how the players had become stars. 'It was about fashion, bell-bottom jeans, cornrows and the Beatles,' he said, which hinted at tension between traditionalists who had at least some sympathy for the discipline and ideals of the junta and those who sought the freedoms they saw in western Europe and the US.[25]

But most of all, Brazil had failed to keep up with tactical evolution. What they had witnessed in England in 1966 they had largely dismissed as brute physicality permitted by lenient refereeing. If a lesson had been learned beyond paranoia about European officials, it was merely that Brazil had to be fitter and stronger. Zagallo had demanded his side be compact in 1970 and, in the heat and altitude of Mexico, that had been enough.

'The Seleção of 1970 was revolutionary, enchanting the entire world,' Tostão had said, 'but she was the beginning of the fall. The development of the physical and scientific aspects were beginning to be valued in an absurd way with a preference for coaches from the physical education class.'[26] That may have been true in Brazil as the technocrats increasingly took control, but in Europe the physicality was married to tactical evolution.

'It was the Dutch who really took my breath away,' said Arrigo Sacchi. 'It was a mystery to me. The television was too small; I felt like I needed to see the whole pitch fully to understand what they were doing and fully to appreciate it.'[27] At the time, Sacchi was a shoe salesman with ambition; within sixteen years of the Dutch explosion into the popular consciousness, he had won two European Cups and a *scudetto* with AC Milan.

Sergio Markarián had given up his football career when he was eighteen. By the time of the 1974 World Cup he was the manager of a fuel distribution company in Montevideo. As he watched the Dutch destroy Uruguay, Argentina and Brazil, he was both entranced and appalled. He resolved to study for his coaching badges and save South American football. He may not have achieved that, but he did win seven league titles across three countries before taking Peru to third place at the 2011 Copa América.

Terry Venables was inspired by them. So were Arsène Wenger and Francisco Maturana. So were legions of Dutch coaches. Pep Guardiola was such a devotee of the approach that he spoke of Johan Cruyff having built the cathedral and his job being to maintain it. No side has ever had such an influence as the Netherlands of 1974, no post-war coach such a following as Rinus Michels. And yet the Dutch very nearly didn't qualify, and Michels very nearly didn't become their coach. It remains a matter of fevered debate – most things in the Dutch game are – just how planned Total Football was, but wherever on the scale you choose to place it, from organic creation of the players to meticulous blueprint laid out by Michels and/or Cruyff, there was a huge dollop of fortune in the way the style came together in West Germany.

The Netherlands was an unlikely place for a revolution. Albert Camus selected Amsterdam as the setting for *La Chute* in part because it allowed him to riff on the notion of the concentric canals representing the circles of hell, but also because it was a notably boring and staid city, full of 'pipe-smokers ... watching the same rain falling on the same canal'.[28] But the welfare state and the economic boom reduced religious divisions, and television and pop music opened a world of possibilities to the generation born after the Second World War.[29]

In 1963, the reactionary student corps was effectively replaced by a leftist student union. Amsterdam became a city of 'happenings'. In May 1965, an anti-smoking activist and two anarchists launched the Provo movement, which staged a series of pranks designed to provoke the police. When the Provos won a seat on Amsterdam city council, they advocated for progressive causes such as the provision of free bicycles; the reduction of smoke emissions; sex education, free contraception and increased access to abortion; a prohibition on property speculation; and car-sharing.

Their activities, which always retained a sense of the absurd that gave them a very different feel to the *événements* in Paris two years later, reached a height in 1966. In March, they let off smoke-bombs on Raadhuisstraat during the marriage of Princess Beatrix and Claus von Amsberg, a German aristocrat who had served in the Wehrmacht. Police waded in with batons. They had regularly responded with violence before but this time they did it in front of a huge and generally appalled television audience.

Three months later, Communists protesting about pay joined the Provos in street demonstrations. There were further clashes with police, during which a worker suffered a heart attack and died. That led to wild rumours and an intensification of the rioting, which in turn prompted the government to impose a state of emergency.

Once everything had calmed down, the reaction was of embarrassment. Who benefited by the police attacking surrealist peaceniks? In Amsterdam, the mayor and chief of police were deposed and, almost overnight, the attitude became famously easy-going. The British anarchist Charles Radcliffe, writing in 1966, hailed Amsterdam as having become 'almost overnight' the 'capital of youth-rebellion'.[30] There was a reason why John Lennon and Yoko Ono chose the Amsterdam Hilton as the venue for their bed-in in 1969.

At the same time, Dutch football was going through its own transformation. Professionalism was legalised in 1954 but the Dutch didn't even enter a post-war World Cup until 1958. Before the 1970 tournament, the only teams they'd beaten in qualifying were Luxembourg and Albania. But the club game was improving. The former Spurs wing-half Vic Buckingham had given a debut to a young Johan Cruyff and begun the development of what would come to be known as Total Football, but it was after he had been replaced by Michels early in 1965 that Ajax began to emerge as a serious force in the European game.

As a player at Ajax, Michels had been a relaxed practical joker; as a coach he could hardly have been more different. He was, the long-serving Ajax assistant coach Bobby Haarms put it, 'an animal trainer ... a chess master'.[31] He made the club fully professional and did away with the W-M Buckingham had favoured to replace it with a back four. A 5–1 win over Liverpool in a mist-shrouded European Cup tie in 1966 was the first real hint of what was to come. Ajax lost to Milan in the European Cup final in 1969, at which Michels tweaked the 4-2-4 he had favoured to that point, withdrawing a forward to create the 4-3-3 that would remain the default for his devotees for half a century. Feyenoord won the European Cup under the great Austrian coach Ernst Happel in 1970, then Ajax claimed it in each of the following three seasons, although Michels left for Barcelona after the first success. Even in 1965 it would have seemed unthinkable but, by the early seventies, Dutch football was the best in Europe.

At the heart of it all stood Cruyff. He was slight, angular, awkward and brilliant. He saw football like nobody else and was blunt in expressing his views. He was the archetypal boomer, disdainful of the establishment and acutely conscious of his own financial worth. 'Cruyff,' the journalist and historian Hubert Smeets wrote, 'was to the Netherlands in the sixties what the Beatles were to Britain.'[32]

The players themselves tend to reject direct comparison with the Provos or the youth movement. Cruyff himself was no leftist and was often openly scornful of the hippies who had taken over Dam Square.[33] But Ajax shared with them a basic rejection of authority and willingness to question everything, a love of paradox and a sense that play was something to be taken seriously; pressing, defending by running forwards, was characteristically counterintuitive.

As with Alf Ramsey eight years earlier, it is probably through comparison with architecture that the relationship between football and the prevailing cultural mood can best be seen. The term '*totaalvoetbal*' – 'Total Football' – was only coined as a response to how the Dutch played at the World Cup. To an extent that was a reflection of how many more people watched the international tournament than Ajax's European Cup wins and the correspondingly greater impact the World Cup had, but it was also because the prefix '*totaal-*' had only just entered wider Dutch vocabulary, having been coined by architectural theorists.

In *Forum* magazine earlier that year, the structuralist J.B. Bakema had spoken of Total Urbanisation, Total Environment and Total Energy. 'Once,' he said, 'the highest image of interrelationship in society was indicated by the word "God" and man was allowed to use earth and universal space under condition that he should care for what he used. But we have to actualise this kind of care and respect since man came by his awareness nearer the phenomenon of interrelationship called the relation of atoms. Man became aware of his being part of a total energy system.'[34]

Total Football was similarly predicated on players understanding their relationship to other players within the system, and negotiating their own roles accordingly. Whether Bakema is correct that such a worldview was possible only in a country in which faith was waning can be debated, but it is at the very least intriguing that the three countries where pressing emerged – England, the Soviet Union and the Netherlands – were either secular or, at the very least, not Catholic societies, where structures of authority tended to be more top-down.[35]

Some sort of authority, though, was useful. Michels was replaced in 1971 by the affable Romanian Ştefan Kovács. He was far more prepared to allow the players freedom and it was in his two seasons in charge that Ajax probably achieved their greatest heights. But without Michels, Cruyff became increasingly vocal. He was the organiser and he was rarely tactful in explaining what he wanted. Resentment began to build. Velibor Vasović had been captain for Ajax's first European Cup win, in 1971. Piet Keizer was captain in 1972 and Cruyff in 1973. A few weeks after the 1973 final, in which Ajax, after taking a fifth-minute lead against Juventus, had humiliated their opponents, keeping the ball from them and winning by an overwhelming 1–0, Kovács's replacement George Knobel told the players to vote on who should be captain the following season. Cruyff lost to Keizer and, furious, rang his agent to arrange a move to Barcelona, even though it would be several weeks before he was eligible to play.

Cruyff eventually made his Barcelona debut in the eighth league game of the season, at which point they lay fourteenth, having won two of their opening seven fixtures. They didn't lose again until their thirty-second league game, by which point the title, their first in fourteen years, had long since been sealed. Cruyff was named player of the season.

The Netherlands national team struggled to keep up. There had been signs of improvement in the qualifiers for 1970, as they beat Poland in Rotterdam, but they ended up third in the group. Four years later, crushing wins over Norway and Iceland, twice, gave them a goal-difference advantage against Belgium, meaning they needed a point against their neighbours in Amsterdam to qualify. Jan Verheyen seemed to have given Belgium the win with a 90th-minute free-kick, only for the Soviet referee Pavel Kazakov to decide it was offside. He was wrong, but the Dutch got the draw they needed and went to the World Cup.

Dawn was just breaking over West Germany's training camp in Malente, 60 miles north of Hamburg. Their World Cup would begin against Chile five days later, but nobody had gone to bed. Their manager Helmut Schön had packed two suitcases and was insisting that unless all twenty-two players were sent home, he was off. In another room, Franz Beckenbauer was on the phone to the vice-president of the DFB, Hermann Neuberger.

West Germany weren't just the European champions, they were an obviously brilliant side. Their first half-hour at Wembley in that 3–1 win over England in the first leg of the Euros quarter-final had been, as *l'Equipe* put it, 'football from the year 2000'. They were technically gifted and fluent, comfortable with interchanging positions, and had in Beckenbauer arguably the greatest libero the world had ever known and in Müller one of the greatest finishers.

But this was not the atmosphere of Spiez in 1954. It wasn't the modest West Germany of 1966, desperate not to offend.

It wasn't even the camaraderie formed in the heat of León in 1970. The heightened security, the anxiety over external threats seemed to reflect the tension within.

This was a different West Germany, its players more self-assertive, more aware of their own value. Their players had learned that Italy had been promised the equivalent of DM120,000* a head for winning the tournament, while even the Netherlands, who had not so much as qualified for a World Cup before, were on DM100,000. The DFB had offered nothing. The squad suggested DM100,000. The DFB came back with DM30,000. Slowly they had edged towards compromise but, that night, as the players asked for DM75,000, Neuberger insisted he could go no higher than DM70,000.

Beckenbauer put the offer to the players. They were split, eleven votes to accept and eleven to reject. Beckenbauer advised them to accept, which they did. If they had not, Schön may have ended up following through on his threat. The manager struggled to understand the attitude of the players; this was not how Fritz Walter or Uwe Seeler would have behaved. The mood in the camp was dreadful. West Germany did not look like potential world champions. They were poor against Chile, but won 1–0, Breitner getting the goal. Although they then beat Australia 3–0, Beckenbauer was jeered by the crowd in Hamburg after misplacing a pass and responded by spitting in their direction. And then came East Germany.

Three Brazilians stood over the free-kick, perhaps twenty-six yards from goal. The Romanian referee Nicolae Rainea blew his whistle. Rivellino took a pace back, at which the Zaire defender Mwepu Ilunga ran from the wall and belted the ball away. 'What on earth did he do that for . . .?' asked John

* About £180,000 in 2025 terms.

Motson on the BBC commentary, subsequently describing the incident in a voiceover as 'a bizarre moment of African innocence'. The latter comment betrayed the patronising attitude widely taken to African football; the former question opens up a far darker story than anybody was aware of at the time.

After five years of conflict, Mobutu Sese Seko, the head of the army, had taken power in the Democratic Republic of the Congo in a CIA-backed plot in 1965. In the days immediately after independence in 1960, Mobutu had been regarded as the most prudent of the political advisors to Patrice Lumumba, the first prime minister.[36] By the early seventies, though, he had descended into paranoia and megalomania. He rarely left the palace compound for fear of assassination, while daily news bulletins featured an image of Mobutu's face descending from the clouds.

Mobutu explored ways of using sport to consolidate his position, a project that culminated in the Rumble in the Jungle between Muhammad Ali and George Foreman in Kinshasa in 1974. Boxing, though, was an afterthought; football came first. Tout Puissant Englebert from Lubumbashi won the African Champions Cup in 1967 and 1968 and reached the final the following two seasons. The national team won the Cup of Nations in 1968 as well. By the early 1970s Zaire, as Mobutu had renamed the country as part of his programme of decolonisation, were fairly obviously the best team in Africa, reaching the semi-final of the Cup of Nations in 1972 before winning it again in March 1974. Mobutu also banned 'national treasures' from playing abroad, saying that 'Zaire must not become a cradle in Africa for Europe's mercenaries.'[37] As Ilunga pointed out, though, 'what that really meant was that too few of the squad had any real experience of playing non-African sides.'[38]

Zaire had qualified for the World Cup late in 1973, swaggering through the final round of qualifying with a 100 per cent record. In an audience at his palace, Mobutu told a petrified squad how proud he was that Zaire would be the first black African nation at a World Cup. He had helped design their kit, which featured a leopard's head on the chest. The players were promised cars, houses and $20,000 each as a bonus.

They arrived in West Germany on a chartered Boeing 747, were picked up by new Mercedes Benz minibuses and taken to a luxurious hotel, which most of the players seem to have found unsettling. In the dressing-room before their first game, against Scotland, Zaire's Yugoslav coach Blagoje Vidinić read out a telegram from the president: 'Go out and move with the speed and stealth of the leopard. Go out and bring glory to your country. Become heroes. Become legends.'[39] They lost, 2–0.

Which was a reasonable enough result, and they had played well in parts. Dissatisfaction, though, was setting in. The per diems and bonuses they had been promised hadn't arrived – it was never clear whether the money had simply not been sent or whether security staff had stolen it – and so, without cash, they were effectively trapped in the hotel. They trained, and they hung around bored, drinking and smoking. Before the second game, against Yugoslavia, there was a meeting in the room of the goalkeeper, Kazadi Mwamba. As many as eight players were in favour of going on strike. Given Zaire were a few minutes late for the start of the game, the suggestion was negotiations went on until kick-off.

It might have been better if they had. With Zaire unable to handle the tall Yugoslavia centre forward Dušan Bajević, it was 3–0 after eighteen minutes. Vidinić replaced Mwamba with Tubilandu Ndimbi, supposedly a favourite of Mobutu, although none of the goals had been the keeper's fault. The reasons, he later said, had to 'remain a state secret'.[40] By half-time, Yugoslavia were 6–0 up and Ndaye Mulamba had been sent off for kicking the referee, Omar Delgado, in the backside; the aggressor had actually been Ilunga. Although Zaire conceded only another three in the second half, what was seen on television was almost more embarrassing than the scoreline, as players from TP Mazembe (as Englebert had become when the club's links with a Belgian tyre factory were severed) rowed with those from AS Vita from Kinshasa and a couple of substitutes accused Vidinić of having thrown the game to help his home nation.

That night, dinner was eaten in silence, the hotel lobby was cleared of journalists and government officials harangued the players. They accused them of having brought shame on Zaire and said that if they conceded more than three in the final group game against Brazil, they would never see their families again. Brazil, as it happened, knew that a win by three goals would guarantee their qualification.

Jairzinho scored after twelve minutes. Rivellino added a second after sixty-seven. Mwamba then dived over a mishit Valdomiro cross to gift Brazil a third after seventy-eight. It was then that Bwanga Tshimen hacked down Mirandinha to concede the infamous free-kick. 'I panicked,' said Ilunga. 'I thought I could waste some time if I kicked the ball away . . . I felt foolish because the crowd started to laugh and so did the Brazilian players. I bowed to the crowd and shouted, "You bastard!" at them, but it was hard to deny I looked like an idiot . . . We were playing for our lives.'[41]

It finished 3–0. Zaire's players returned home to find the bonuses they had been promised for qualifying had been cancelled, and so, in many cases, had their club contracts. Zaire didn't win a game at the 1976 Cup of Nations and withdrew from 1978 World Cup qualifying when funding dried up. Mobutu had abandoned football.

Distance tends to elide the success of Ajax with the Netherlands' performance in 1974; that's not unreasonable, but the links were not perhaps as direct as is often thought. It was Feyenoord who won the league in 1973–74 – with Ajax third – and they also lifted the Uefa Cup. In a way that probably helped; it was very hard for Ajax's players to maintain any resentment towards Cruyff when they had been so much poorer after his departure. Michels was only appointed as national coach three months before the tournament, replacing the Czechoslovak František Fadrhonc, who stepped down to work as his assistant. Cruyff, who had come to feel Fadrhonc didn't fully trust him, was relieved; he and Michels had a similar vision and Michels was strong enough to hold the squad together.

The PSV goalkeeper Jan van Beveren, who often clashed with Cruyff, was injured. The obvious choice to replace him was Piet Schrijvers, but Cruyff insisted Michels should turn to Jan Jongbloed of FC Amsterdam, who had only ever played for the national side once before – and that in a 4–1 defeat to Denmark in 1962. He was not a notably brilliant goalkeeper by orthodox measures but he was very good with his feet, meaning he could sweep up behind a high defensive line and operate effectively as a very deep-lying playmaker.

The tough Feyenoord centre-back Rinus Israël was unavailable early on following the death of his father which, with Barry Hulshoff injured, left a hole at the centre of defence. Ajax had prospered with the Yugoslav Velibor Vasović and then the German Horst Blankenburg as libero; with candidates limited, Cruyff suggested the Ajax midfielder Arie Haan should step back.[42] The Feyenoord right-back Wim Rijsbergen was moved infield alongside him, with the Ajax duo of Wim Suurbier and Ruud Krol as attacking full-backs. Gerrie Mühren's son was ill, so Wim van Hanegem came into midfield, with the clever Anderlecht forward Rob Rensenbrink generally preferred on the left to Keizer, who had always had a difficult relationship with Michels and was, anyway, thirty-four. There was nothing inevitable about any of this; plenty of patching and tweaking and developing was needed to get from the great Ajax to the Netherlands of 1974.

In West Germany, the Dutch were brilliant from the off. In the first-phase group they beat Uruguay 2–0 and Bulgaria 4–1, and drew 0–0 with Sweden, the game in which Cruyff beat the defender Jan Olsson with the turn that now bears his name. In the second group phase, they thrashed Argentina 4–0 and beat East Germany 2–0 to set up a decider against Brazil for a place in the final.

It turned out to be the game of the tournament, physical and frequently brutal but also packed with moments of great skill. Marinho Peres laid out Johan Neeskens in response to a high challenge and also clattered Wim Jansen with his shoulder. Rivellino raised a knee into Johnny Rep and received an elbow to the face in reply. The West German referee Kurt Tschenscher was a curiously detached figure, which helped facilitate subsequent Brazilian claims of a fix, although the truth is that they came determined to get their retaliation in first and found the Dutch more than willing to match their aggression. Only in the 84th minute did Tschenscher finally take decisive action, dismissing Luis Pereira for a two-footed waist-high lunge on Neeskens. By then, though, it was far too late to bring the game under control, and the Dutch were already two up. Cruyff set up the first with a cross from the right for Neeskens to sweep in a deft first-time shot and then scored the second with a flying volley. For him, that was 'the moment you could point to and say that was Total Football'.[43]

The Dutch had qualified for the final, winning all three second-phase games by an 8–0 aggregate. But the seeds of their destruction had already been sown.

When the eleven-year-old West Berlin choirboy Detlef Lange had drawn East Germany in the same group as West Germany, the head of East German sport Manfred Ewald, the same official whose disagreement with Helmut Schön in Dresden in 1949 had prompted the coach to defect, reacted in the way he tended to react to most difficulties: he screamed at an underling. Why, he demanded of the secretary general of the East German football federation, Günter Schneider, had he not fixed the draw? When Schneider pointed out the impossibility of doing so, Ewald asked whether East Germany could withdraw. Schneider gently explained that the financial penalties would cripple East German football and the upheaval would make it even harder than it already was to arrange fixtures against those from outside the Soviet sphere of influence. If the game could not be avoided, Ewald told Schneider to make sure they didn't lose.

Most, at least in the West, assumed the East would be defeated. On the day of the game, for instance, Uwe Seeler appeared in an advert for a chocolate company in which he said, 'There's no need to be afraid because we have much better players.'[44] But East German football was on a high. Magdeburg had beaten AC Milan in the Cup Winners' Cup final the previous month, while Dynamo Dresden had pushed Bayern extremely close in the European Cup that season.

It wasn't just the East who were uneasy about the game. Schön, of course, had his own reasons for wanting to prove himself against his former home. Beyond that, West Germany didn't officially recognise East Germany as a nation and its constitution insisted on the goal of reunification. But one of the results of Willy Brandt's *Ostpolitik** had been an agreement in 1972 for an exchange of de facto ambassadors – although for appearances' sake, they had to be referred to as 'permanent representatives'. Michael Kohl, a forty-four-year-old doctor of law, was inaugurated as East Germany's

* His policy of normalisation of relations with East Germany.

first representative to West Germany on 20 June 1974; his first official engagement came two days later at Hamburg's Volksparkstadion.

Both sides knew they were already through but that a draw would leave West Germany top, which perhaps influenced how the West Germans played. Breitner, Hoeneß and Grabowski were notably diffident, drawing angry criticism from the usually calm Schön at half-time. Beckenbauer told the side that if it was still level at 70 minutes they should drop off and accept the draw. Perhaps it was with that in mind that, on 68 minutes, Schön withdrew Georg Schwarzenbeck for the veteran Hans-Dieter Höttges. The central defender had had a difficult evening, repeatedly drawn out of position by the wily Magdeburg forward Jürgen Sparwasser, who kept dropping deep. Höttges was an uncompromising player, as his nickname of '*Eisenfuß*' (Iron Foot) suggested. But as it also implied, he wasn't quick. With 12 minutes remaining, Höttges was drawn out of position by a decoy run and couldn't recover to prevent Sparwasser dinking the winner over Sepp Maier before celebrating with a euphoric forward roll.

In the moment, it felt like a great victory for the East and great embarrassment for the West; in the event, the aftermath was far less clear cut. But why had West Germany lost? Amid all the theories, it was Breitner who surely offered the best explanation. 'What happened,' he said, 'was nothing more and nothing less than that we picked up where we had left off. If we had played the first or the second game against the GDR instead of the third, we would have lost the first or the second game instead of the third.'[45]

Two days later, the East Germany forward Hansi Kreische found himself seated on a flight next to West Germany's minister of finance Hans Apel. They got talking, and Kreische told Apel that what had happened in the European Cup tie between Bayern and Dynamo Dresden persuaded him West Germany would win the World Cup. Maier, Beckenbauer, Hoeneß and Müller just had too much quality and, more importantly, too much competitive will not to. Apel said that if he was right he would send Kreische five bottles of Scotch.

He was as good as his word. For Apel, it was a matter of honouring a promise; for Kreische, the gesture had serious consequences. Even by talking to Kreische he had consorted with the enemy, and that led to him being omitted from East Germany's squad for the 1976 Olympics despite being top scorer in the Oberliga in 1975–76.

Sparwasser didn't benefit from his heroics either. He faced hostility in East Germany from those who were jealous of the rewards they wrongly assumed he must have received, from those who had hoped the Communist system would be embarrassed by a heavy defeat and, because he refused to make public appearances ascribing the win to socialism, from the authorities. Eventually, in January 1988, in Saarbrucken with Magdeburg's veterans side, as the rest of the squad went for pre-game walk, he slipped out of a back door and into a getaway car. Almost two years before the Wall came down, the greatest hero of East German football defected.

The West German players returned to Malente, got drunk and smoked cigars. Outraged and mortified, Schön arranged training for 10 a.m., after which the squad was to move on to Kaiserau near Dortmund, their base for the second phase, then locked himself in his room, refusing to come down for breakfast. The DFB, fearing Schön was suffering some sort of breakdown, considered promoting Jupp Derwall, his assistant, to share some of the burden.

In the end, it was Beckenbauer who oversaw the transfer to Kaiserau, and it was Beckenbauer who took centre stage at the subsequent press conference. Schön, having initially confined himself to his room, picking at food that had been mashed to make it easier to consume, sat awkwardly alongside him. It would be an exaggeration to say he had completely taken over, but it was clear that control lay with Beckenbauer.

Yugoslavia had impressed in the group stage. As well as thrashing Zaire, they had arguably had the better of a 0–0 draw with Brazil in which Brane Oblak headed against the woodwork, and had ensured Scotland's elimination on goal difference by drawing with them, 1–1. But during the tournament Pero Korobar took over as president of the football federation and decided he had no need to honour the bonus agreement made by his predecessor. 'There was resignation and anger in the camp,' said the midfielder Jovan Aćimović. 'Everything was negative.'[46] At the same time, Miljan Miljanić, the head of the national team's coaching commission, flew to Spain to negotiate his contract to become manager of Real Madrid. Although the visit of Tito resolved the bonus issue, the damage was done.[47]

With Tito in the stand, Yugoslavia lost 2–0 to West Germany, and went on to lose to Poland and Sweden as well. West Germany's 4–2 victory over Sweden in a classic in Düsseldorf set up a straight shoot-out between the hosts and Poland for qualification. It rained a lot in West Germany that month, but nowhere more than in Frankfurt on the day of the game. As firefighters pumped water from the pitch, which already had large bare patches after the opening ceremony, kick-off was delayed by forty-five minutes.

The Poland captain Kazimierz Deyna won the toss and, not realising that the relief efforts had been focused at one end, opted to kick off. Beckenbauer promptly chose to defend the end that was still extremely wet. In the legend of what became known as *Die Wasserschlacht* (the Water-battle), that was crucial. Poland's great strength was the pace of their wingers Grzegorz Lato and Robert Gadocha, but they were negated in the quagmire and exhausted by the time they got onto the firmer ground in the second half. 'I don't know whether we would have won on a dry field,' said the coach Kazimierz Górski, 'but we would have stood a better chance.'[48] Maier was exceptional and, after Tomaszewski had saved a Hoeneß penalty, Müller got the only goal of the game with fourteen minutes remaining.

A couple of days before the final, *Bild* published allegations that, in the build-up to their win over Brazil, a number of Netherlands players had been involved in a 'naked party' with German women in the pool at the Wald Hotel.[49] The Dutch initially denied the story, and the photographs *Bild* claimed to have never surfaced, but there had been a party. There was a performance by the Cats, a rock group from Rotterdam whose music players listened to before games. Some players drank *sekt* and smoked cigars with locals, among them an undercover reporter called Guido Frick, and, at some point in the early hours, they did end up swimming naked in the pool.[50] It was seemingly all fairly innocent – and it certainly didn't have a negative impact on their performance against Brazil – but it caused enormous disquiet, especially with Cruyff.

In his autobiography Cruyff denied anything untoward had taken place, and insisted that stories he had spent most of the day after the breaking of the story on the phone to his wife Danny were untrue; she had been in their holiday home in the Pyrenees, he said, which had no telephone.[51] But other members of the squad remember Cruyff spending hours on the public phone in the lobby of the hotel, trying to persuade Danny that nothing significant had happened. Neighbours, meanwhile, recalled her going to the telephone exchange in a nearby village[52] before returning to her father's house in Amsterdam because it was easier to phone from there. Cruyff, who roomed alone, sat up smoking and did later admit that by the time of the final he was 'mentally exhausted'.[53]

Yet the Netherlands began the final well enough. No West German player had touched the ball when Neeskens smashed home a penalty after Cruyff had been fouled by Hoeneß. 'You are an Englishman,' Beckenbauer said to the referee Jack Taylor, a butcher from Wolverhampton. Was that on Taylor's mind when Jansen challenged Bernd Hölzenbein after 25 minutes? Hölzenbein probably did go down easily but, as Taylor said, 'It was a trip or an attempted trip and the laws of the game are that's a penalty.'[54] Breitner converted. The Dutch seemed bewildered. Two minutes before half-time, Rainer Bonhof crossed low for Müller. His first touch took him away from goal but also away from his marker and into the arc of his right foot so he could swivel and drag a shot across goal and past Jongbloed.

In the second half, the Dutch were more like their usual selves. Maier made a fine save from a Neeskens volley and Rep hit the post. What then had gone wrong for the Dutch before half-time? Perhaps they had tried to do what Ajax had done against Juventus in 1973 and humiliate West Germany by keeping the ball away from them: 'We forgot to score the second goal,' Rep said.[55] Perhaps it was the decision to play Rensenbrink, although he was carrying a thigh injury that meant he had to be replaced at half-time by René van der Kerkhof. Perhaps it was, as Michels admitted, that Cruyff was not 'mentally in optimal condition'; perhaps the affair of the pool had taken its toll.[56] Perhaps it was that the tape by the Cats that the Dutch had played before every other game at that tournament had gone missing so they ended up playing 'Sorrow' by David Bowie. 'Sometimes,' Cruyff said, 'you can lose a game in your head.'[57] Or perhaps it was, as Kreische had told Apel, that having lost to East Germany, Beckenbauer, Maier and Müller knew that the only way they could make amends was to win the tournament.

'*Zijn we er toch nog ingetuind,*' said the Dutch commentator Herman Kuiphof at the final whistle – 'we've fallen for it again.' He subsequently denied he had been talking about 1940 when, right up until the moment the Luftwaffe started bombing Rotterdam, the Netherlands had been unable really to believe Germany would attack a major trading partner.[58] But that was how many interpreted it.

The Dutch returned to a huge party on the Leidseplein. From one perspective, reaching the final of the first tournament for which you'd qualified, playing a style of football that delighted and inspired the world, was an achievement worth celebrating. But they had lost, and the hurt lingered. For most of the West, the oil shock can be seen as marking the end of the optimism of the sixties, perhaps the moment when the impact of globalisation was first felt.[59] For the Netherlands, there was a much more specific moment at which it became clear that beauty and good intentions were not enough; the moment at which Müller turned and hooked in his shot two minutes before half-time in the World Cup final.

But there was little euphoria among West Germany's players. Some sense of team spirit had returned in the second group stage but there was still a widespread distrust of the DFB. When it turned out wives had not been invited to the celebratory banquet, the majority of players walked out.

West German football had been on the same journey as Maria Braun. The days of modesty, humility and patriotic service were over, replaced by a world in which cost was prized over value. Disillusioned, Schön wanted to step down, only to be persuaded by Neuberger to stay on for Argentina in 1978. *Die Ehe der Maria Braun* was released in 1979; it's easy to see why, when Fassbinder was making it with West Germany as world champions, the contrast with the champions of twenty years earlier would seem so stark, why Zimmermann's commentary from the 1954 final would seem such a fitting soundtrack to the climactic destruction of Maria and her world.

1978

GLORY IN A TIME OF TERROR

Graciela Daleo was a member of the Montoneros, a revolutionary Peronist movement, opposed to the military junta that had seized power in Argentina in 1976. She was arrested on 18 October 1977 and taken to the Esma (the Navy School of Mechanics), and there, beyond the manicured lawns, the whitewashed walls and the four proud columns of the entrance, she was tortured.

By the time the World Cup began, eight months after her arrest, Daleo had been set to work in *la Pecera* (the Fishbowl), a basement area where she performed secretarial tasks, typing, précising news articles and generating misinformation. From foreign newspapers, she learned that the Montoneros had decided to reduce their activities for the duration of the tournament, although they issued press releases that ended with the phrase, 'Argentina champions, Videla [the leader of the junta] to the wall'.

Officers would take prisoners out in a car with them so they could point out their fellow dissidents; during the tournament, with more and more people taking to the street in celebration the number of 'rides' increased. Those in *la Pecera* were able to watch matches on a small black-and-white television. There were whispered discussions as to whether to support Argentina was to support the regime. Those in the cells could hear games played at El Monumental, a mile and a half to the south-east. Nobody at the Esma was in any doubt that Argentina had won the final. At the final whistle, Captain Jorge 'el Tigre' Acosta, one of the most notorious of the torturers, came in, shouting euphorically, 'We won, we won!'

'If they won,' Daleo reflected, 'we lost.' And yet, despite not really caring about football, she also felt a surge of exhilaration.

A number of the prisoners were taken to witness the celebrations. Daleo went out in a green Peugeot 504 with the prefect Héctor Febres and a petty officer called Mendoza. They allowed her to poke her head through the sunroof. 'If I start screaming that I'm a disappeared nobody will give a shit,' she thought and began to weep. They went to a *parilla* on Avenida Maipú and sat at a table together, torturers and tortured. Daleo never knew whether the intention was a perverse act of humanity, allowing the prisoners to share the celebrations, or whether they were demonstrating that the mass of the people had no interest in their protest.[1] For Argentina, the legacy of 1978 remains complex and contested.

The coup against Isabelita Perón, the president of Argentina, that had been expected, had perhaps been inevitable since the death of her husband Juan in 1974, came around 12.45 a.m. on the morning of 24 March 1976. Juan Perón's Justicialist Party was an awkward coalition of wildly opposed views and without his charisma there was nothing to hold them together. Even on the day of his return from exile in Spain in 1973, right-wing death squads had shot at leftists in the crowd that welcomed him back at Ezeiza. By March 1976, inflation was running at over 560 per cent and the violence between the radical wings of the party was out of control: a bomb went off in Buenos Aires on average every three hours and there was a political assassination every five hours as leftist guerrillas clashed with paramilitary groups tacitly sanctioned by the state. In Córdoba alone, there were thirty-two kidnappings in the first two months of that year. With the country seemingly ungovernable, a military takeover came to seem inevitable.

General Jorge Videla, who would become president after the coup, preferred to wait until the government invited him to take over but on 15 March, he narrowly escaped a bomb attack in the car park of a military base in Buenos Aires that killed one person and injured a further twenty-nine. He decided he could wait no longer. The junta instituted the Proceso de Reorganización Nacional, defining Argentina as a Christian country fighting Communism. Every state institution, even the national oil company, developed its own private army: over the seven years that followed, they were responsible for the deaths of an estimated 30,000 people, while thousands more were kidnapped, imprisoned and tortured. And in the middle of it all, Argentina hosted the World Cup.

Argentina had won the right to host the 1978 World Cup under its previous military government, that of Juan Carlos Onganía, in July 1966 – although as he had taken power only a month earlier, it was really a legacy of the civil government of Arturo Illia. At that moment, for all its proud footballing tradition, Argentina was simply not equipped to host a tournament. It wasn't until Perón had returned from exile in 1973 that the first organising committee was set up. 'We are so behind in the organisation of our World Cup,' *El Gráfico* reported in January 1974, 'that we doubt that we will be able to do things in dignity in the time remaining that such an important event for our country deserves.'[2]

The Fifa president Stanley Rous was worried enough that he sounded out Montevideo and Porto Alegre about offering support and considered moving the tournament to Spain. Havelange, having blamed the economic turmoil on 'internal disturbances',[3] confirmed in February 1975 that Argentina would indeed host the tournament;[4] his power base in the developing world demanded that it go ahead as planned and not be shifted to Europe.

However general the desire to end its status as the only Latin American footballing power not to have hosted the tournament, though, the truth was that Argentina could not afford to host the World Cup. The 1976 Argentinian Grand Prix, for instance, was abandoned for want of the $500,000 needed to organise it.[5] 'The 1978 World Cup,' the Argentinian journalist Dante Panzeri wrote, 'should not take place for the same reasons that somebody who doesn't have enough cash to put petrol into a Model T Ford shouldn't buy himself a Torino. If he does that, it's because he's stealing from somebody.'[6]

For the junta, the World Cup was both a burden and a tremendous opportunity. A tournament beset by bomb attacks and kidnappings was clearly unthinkable, but equally the World Cup could demonstrate that the coup had brought stability, while on-field success could stimulate the sort of patriotic fervour that might validate military rule – just as it had in Brazil in 1970.

General Omar Actis, who had played for River Plate's third team in the 1940s, was placed in charge of the local organising committee (EAM). He envisaged an 'austerity World Cup'[7] but the navy – notably Admiral Carlos Alberto Lacoste, the personal delegate to Admiral Emilio Massera, the naval representative on the junta – argued for something far grander that would project Argentina's self-confidence. On the morning of 19 August, Actis called a press conference to announce his plans. He was killed by a car bomb later that day.

The attack was blamed on guerrillas but the widespread suspicion, articulated by Eugenio Menéndez in his book

Almirante Lacoste ¿quién mató al general Actis? was that his murder had been planned by Lacoste, who effectively replaced him (although General Antonio Merlo was appointed as the notional head of the EAM) and, it's alleged, embezzled millions from the World Cup budget.

Initial estimates for the cost of the tournament were between US$70m and US$100m, but even official figures placed it at US$521.5m.[8] The secretary of the treasury Juan Alemann, though, admitted the true figure was over US$700m.[9] (To put that in context, Spain's total expenditure for the 1982 World Cup was US$150m.) Some of the money was spent on infrastructure projects with benefits beyond football – airports, roads, a press centre and facilities for colour television transmission – but much went on renovating the stadiums of River Plate, Vélez Sarsfield and Rosario Central and building new grounds in Córdoba, Mar del Plata and Mendoza. Talk of making up at least some of the shortfall through the arrival of 50,000–60,000 tourists from abroad proved overly optimistic; in the event only around 7,000 turned up.[10]

A further US$5.5m, between 1976 and 1980, went to the US public relations company Burson-Marsteller to try to improve Argentina's international image, while a concrete wall was built alongside the motorway that led from Ezeiza into the centre of Buenos Aires to hide the *villas miserias* from view.[11]

Not everything, though, could be controlled. The tournament logo, designed in 1974, comprised a pair of blue-and-white lines sweeping vertically upwards before parting to embrace a football, an obvious evocation of Perón's characteristic arms-aloft gesture. The EAM was very aware of the symbolism, but decided a redesign and a recall of any merchandising already released would be overly expensive while drawing attention to the issue.

Then there was the matter of foreign journalists, of whom around 2,400 were accredited.[12] The local press had been cowed, but Amnesty International urged those from abroad to probe beneath the junta's propaganda and report what they discovered. Some were more willing to do so than others. The night before the draw, the Italy manager Enzo Bearzot, the former Argentinian greats Omar Sívori and Néstor Rossi and the editor of *Tuttosport* Gian Paolo Ormezzano went out for an ice-cream and were threatened by gun-toting officers in an unmarked green Falcon, the preferred car of the secret police. Their only offence had been to park near the house of Leopoldo Galtieri, a senior general who would become president in 1981. To his regret, Ormezzano never wrote the story. That was, perhaps, an isolated incident, but there were clear links between the junta and the Italian media via the P2 masonic lodge that meant a tendency to soft-pedal on stories about the dictatorship.[13]

The duo from *Vrij Nederland*, Frits Barend and Henk van Dorp, present an obvious contrast. They agreed that Van Dorp should cover the football and Barend look into everything else. As West Germany drew with Poland in the tournament's opening game, Van Dorp was at El Monumental, while Barend was in the Plaza de Mayo to watch the weekly gathering of mothers of the disappeared, the Madres, three of whose original leaders were themselves subsequently disappeared.

Van Dorp was questioned by police about the empty seat next to him and Barend's photograph was later shown on television with a warning he should be avoided. They began sharing a room for security. Nevertheless, Barend spent the rest of the tournament interviewing dissidents, speaking to the disaffected in the *villas miserias* and exposing illicit meetings between Dutch ambassadorial staff and the regime. Using the Dutch defender Wim Rijsbergen's ID, Barend even gained access to the post-tournament banquet and managed to ask Videla directly about the disappeared. The general mumbled a response about the food and Barend left, only to endure an agonising three days before being able to depart for Chile because his photographer Bert Nienhuis had left behind his jacket, with his passport in the pocket, as they rushed away from the banquet.[14]

The domestic press, meanwhile, particularly the publications owned by Editorial Atlántida, run by the Vigil family and aimed at conservative middle-class Argentina, the most ardent backers of the coup, robustly defended the regime and its tournament. The women's glossy *Para Tí*, for instance, produced a series of postcards for readers to send to human rights bodies and relatives abroad, urging them to recognise 'the truth of a country that lives in peace'.[15] The children's magazine *Billiken* told its young readers to encourage their parents to send the postcards: 'Help to show the true Argentina.'[16] The national daily *Clarín* even argued that anything less than full support was somehow unpatriotic. 'When a World Cup is played,' it said, 'and is situated in our own country, it makes it difficult to understand the attitude of those that remain voluntarily marginalised from the popular fervour . . . This World Cup has cost our country a lot of effort and sacrifice.'[17]

Although the Madres were celebrated by the foreign media as dignified leaders of dissent, at home their poignant circuits of the Pirámide, holding aloft photographs of their missing children, made very little impact. Nor, in truth, at least in the short term, did the work of foreign journalists.

To combat their message, Videla launched a slogan, '*Los argentinos somos derechos y humanos*' ('We Argentinians are honest and humane'), that was plastered on the wall of the airport at Ezeiza, on shops, in offices and on taxis.[18] At that stage, though, many Argentinians simply couldn't believe that their government could wage such a war on its own people. According to the Argentinian Commission for Human Rights, forty-eight people were disappeared during the World Cup.[19]

But World Cups are complicated symbols. While the 1978

tournament clearly became a propaganda tool for the regime, it was also a month of great release for a population who had suffered a quarter of a century of political and economic turmoil. The Montoneros' commitment not to disrupt the World Cup as it was the 'Festival of the People' was a recognition of that.[20] That said, they did manage to intercept Channel 10's transmission in Mar del Plata of Argentina's second-phase win over Poland and insert a propaganda message amid the half-time adverts.

For many of those involved, players, coaches and fans, that contradiction between the football on the one hand and what it represented, what it meant, who benefited, was never reconciled.

César Luis Menotti had been a tall and angular centre-forward for Rosario Central and Boca Juniors, good enough to win eleven caps. Plagued by fitness concerns, he quit at the age of thirty and returned to Rosario, where he set up a used-car dealership. At Central, he had been team-mates with Miguel Antonio Juárez, who in 1970 became coach of Central's great rivals, Newell's Old Boys. Menotti began to attend training sessions, initially as an observer, but then he would regale the players with tales of his playing days and his theories. Juárez suffered a long-term lung condition as a result of his heavy smoking and when illness prevented him taking charge of a friendly tournament in Rosario, Menotti stepped in. Newell's won, and from then on they were joint managers.

Menotti and Juárez both rebelled against the *anti-fútbol* that had become the default after 1958, and a joint trip to Mexico for the 1970 World Cup only confirmed their view that skill could trump defensiveness. Menotti liked to hark back to the golden era of *la nuestra* and to claim he was reinvoking the traditional spirit of the Argentinian game – and, to an extent, he was. But he had also realised the benefits of a compact team, which meant fitness, something that would have been anathema to the wine-drinking, casserole-eating legends of the thirties and forties. 'Most of the players needed to be close to each other,' said the Newell's playmaker Mario Zanabria. 'Everyone was involved and a potential recipient of a short pass, and those little coalitions were one of the secrets of our success.'[21]

The pair left Newell's for the modest Buenos Aires club Huracán in 1971. Huracán had never won the Argentinian title and had nothing like the resources of the *grandes*. But then, at one of the bigger clubs, with greater pressure for immediate results, Menotti might not have been able to put his revolution into effect. He would later be hailed as the great adversary of *anti-fútbol*, and by the eighties he was playing up to his image as the louche, heavy-smoking philosopher-prince of Argentinian football, but his approach was never quixotic. 'I play to win,' he said, 'but I don't give in to tactical reasoning as the only way to win, rather I believe that efficacy is not divorced from beauty.'[22]

He was proved right: playing football of startling beauty and attacking intent, in 1973 Huracán won the Metropolitano for the only time in their history. Menotti was appointed national coach after Argentina's disappointing showing at the 1974 World Cup and immediately set about imposing his principles. He appointed Juárez as his assistant and was clear about how he believed football should be played: he wanted to 'overwhelm our opponents footballistically'.[23]

Menotti was scathing of how AFA had previously prepared for major tournaments and insisted on a long-term plan, to begin in 1975; bohemian he may have been, but he believed in rigorous preparation just as surely as the coach with whom he would always be contrasted, Carlos Bilardo.

Although Menotti in one of his more self-consciously

romantic moments would insist he had no style of his own but was restoring the people's love for 'the inner nature of the Argentinian football player: his creativity',[24] in a 1975 interview with *El Gráfico*, he set out six core principles: talent and technical ability were to take precedence over physicality and power; there was to be a 'dialectical articulation' between physical and mental speed – no running without thinking or thinking without running; the team would use a flexible system of zonal and man-to-man marking; going forward, Argentina would look to use two wingers and one centre-forward as the best way of outflanking the 4-4-2 that had become increasingly prevalent elsewhere after 1966; possession was to be regained as soon as possible after the ball was lost; and players were to be made aware of belonging to a football tradition with a canon of heroes.[25]

But, as a committed leftist who had once volunteered as an election observer for the Communist Party,[26] he was also aware of the ideological position he had taken up and what it could mean in the political context of the time. 'If we could win the World Cup the way I would like us to,' he said, 'it would inspire others to reassess the way we play the game – our basic philosophy. Perhaps it would also stop us relying so much on violence and cynicism, which are the tools of fear.'[27]

In March 1976, he took his players on a tour of eastern Europe as much for the bonding experience as for the football. Those games, and a further seven friendlies against European opposition the following year, convinced him that the shift to *anti-fútbol* after 1958 was based on a misconception, one that had haunted South American football in general since 1966. 'We had to get rid of the idea that in order to win, we had to play as the Europeans did,' Menotti said.[28]

That October he got the junta to forbid the sale of players to clubs outside Argentina until after the World Cup, although Mario Kempes had already moved to Valencia from

Rosario Central. But while he was quite prepared to use the government's power when it suited him, he was uneasy about the identification of the national team with the government, claiming always that his side represented the people rather than the country. 'Playing we did not defend our borders, the Motherland, the flag,' he insisted in 1977. 'With the national team nothing essentially patriotic dies or is saved.'[29]

The distinction between the Argentina national team and the junta, though, was extremely hard to sustain. Videla had little interest in football, but recognised an opportunity. The players, he said, 'were obliged to demonstrate the quality of the Argentinian man'.[30]

Menotti had evolved since leaving Huracán. 'He was the same when it came to his philosophy and ball possession,' said the midfielder Omar Larrosa, who played for him with both club and country, 'but a completely new Menotti in terms of fitness, diets and training.'[31] Whereas at Huracán, players reacted to losing possession by dropping behind the line of the ball, with Argentina Menotti had them press. He may have scorned the Dutch and Total Football in public, but he had learned their lessons.

Never has a British nation gone to an overseas World Cup with such a sense of optimism as Scotland in 1978; rarely have hopes been quite so abruptly punctured. Ally MacLeod had won promotion with Ayr United and taken Aberdeen to success in the League Cup when he succeeded Willie Ormond as national manager in 1977. 'My name is Ally MacLeod and I am a winner,' he said confidently at his first press conference.[32] And for a time he seemed as good as his word. An elegant team featuring Bruce Rioch and Don Masson in midfield beat England 2–1 at Wembley, prompting a celebratory pitch invasion in which a goalframe collapsed under the weight of delirious fans. Later that year they outplayed the European champions Czechoslovakia at Hampden and sealed qualification with victory over Wales – although only after a penalty awarded for handball against the Wales centre-back Dave Jones, when the guilty arm had belonged to the Scotland striker Joe Jordan.

Still, given the doubts over all the familiar favourites and the obvious talent in the Scotland squad, the expectation wasn't a merely local phenomenon: bookmakers had Scotland as fourth favourites behind Brazil, Argentina and West Germany.[33]

By the time they set off for Argentina, Rioch and Masson had lost form, the experienced full-back Danny McGrain was injured, and Scotland had failed to win any of their three games in the Home Internationals, but MacLeod remained relentlessly positive. 'You can mark down 25 June 1978 as the day Scottish football conquers the world,' he said. Scots, he said, should prepare for 'a national holiday: a national Ally-day'.[34]

MacLeod's bullishness was part of a more general wave of Scottish self-confidence.[35] The discovery of North Sea oil had given a major boost to the Scottish economy, which in turn had elevated the Scottish National Party. In 1975 they had polled more than Labour and the Conservatives for the first time and they made significant gains in local elections in 1977. The *Daily Mail* suggested that if Scotland actually fulfilled MacLeod's boast and won the World Cup, patriotic pride 'would be like distilled firewater. Hooched up on that, the nationalists could rampage to victory up there in any general election that followed.'[36]

Around 20,000 turned up at Hampden Park to see Scotland off, and the roads to the airport were lined with well-wishers. Endorsements had pulled in around £5m, from Chrysler, to Esso, to the Valentine greetings card company, which paid £25,000 for the exclusive rights to the Scotland team photo. 'Ally's Tartan Army', the song the squad had produced with the comedian Andy Cameron, reached number six in the charts. It was all going remarkably well – until they got to Argentina.

The team hotel in Alto Gracia was dilapidated. The swimming pool was dry, there was no net on the tennis court and the plaster on the ceilings of the bedrooms was peeling. By the side of the road to their training base near Córdoba lay two dead horses. Scotland began against Peru, who had failed to qualify in 1974. Two stunning Teófilo Cubillas goals meant the march to glory began with a 3–1 defeat. 'The myth of beer as a form of athletic preparation is beginning to come apart,' sniffed *El Gráfico*,[37] whose coverage blended tub-thumping for the regime with a grand disdain for Argentina's competitors – the Dutch, for instance, were explicitly linked with drugs, homosexuality and excess.

Worse followed. Willie Johnston tested positive for the mild stimulant Reactivan and was sent home. After a 1–1 draw against Iran, Scotland left the field to boos as their fans flicked V-signs at them. 'MacLeod ought to be ashamed of himself,' one outraged fan, wearing kilt, cape and tam o'shanter, hissed at a television camera.[38]

Chrysler pulled their advertising. A record shop in Dundee slashed the price of 'Ally's Tartan Army' from 65p to 1p, urging customers to buy copies and smash them on the counter with a hammer. The press weighed in with gusto. The parallels with nationalist populism did not go unnoticed. MacLeod, *The Times* noted, arrived in Argentina 'more as a cheerleader than as team manager . . . [yet] . . . his attitude of "let the opposition worry about us" was typical of a certain school of thinking that has too many followers in Britain.'[39]

The anecdote about MacLeod being approached at a press conference by a stray dog and bending down to pat it, commenting that at least somebody still loved him, only for it to bite his finger, seems sadly not to be true[40] but it captures perfectly the odd mix of farce and desolation that hung over the Scotland camp. And then, Scotland almost pulled off the greatest result in their history.

They had to beat the Netherlands by three goals to progress and fell behind to a Rensenbrink penalty. But Kenny Dalglish levelled a minute before the break and an Archie Gemmill penalty gave them the lead a minute after. When Gemmill then picked his way between four Dutch defenders before casually lifting his finish over Jongbloed, the impossible suddenly became thinkable. It remained so for only four minutes as Johnny Rep thrashed a 25-yard drive into the top corner, but they were four minutes of rare and stirring hope. Eventually, as Dominic Sandbrook said, 'Scotland's 3–2 victory became famous as a magnificent failure, a kind of sporting Culloden',[41] but at the time it did little to quell the frustration that came with dashed expectation. Even the baggage handlers at Glasgow Airport jeered the squad on their return.

It may have been despite himself, but Menotti clearly helped the junta. The question though is the extent to which the junta helped him. Argentina did not play well in the group stage. They beat Hungary 2–1 with a late goal after falling behind and then beat France by the same scoreline thanks in part to a contentious penalty, two games characterised by tactical fouling. Hungary became so frustrated they had two men sent off.

Abraham Klein, the Israeli who refereed Argentina's third group game, against Italy, was in no doubt that the referees for Argentina's first two games, António Garrido of Portugal and Jean Dubach of Switzerland, had allowed themselves to be influenced by the crowd.[42] Klein turned down two Argentina penalty appeals in the first half and was subjected to vicious abuse from the stands as he left the pitch at half-time. But he remained implacable and Italy won 1–0 to top the group. That meant Argentina would play their second-phase games, against Poland, Brazil and Peru, in Rosario.

With Leopoldo Luque, whose brother had been killed in a car crash on the day of the Italy game, missing with an elbow injury, Kempes was shuffled further forward against Poland. Finally, they played with a degree of fluency, Kempes scoring twice in a 2–0 win. Argentina then drew 0–0 against Brazil, a brutal slog which meant they went into their match against Peru, thanks to the fact that final group games did not kick off simultaneously, knowing they needed victory by at least three goals while scoring a minimum of four to finish above Brazil in the group and make the final. They achieved that and more, winning 6–0 – but that is far from the full story.

There is a lot of circumstantial evidence that something untoward was going on. Before kick-off, Videla and Henry Kissinger, whose eight-year term as US secretary of state had ended in January the previous year, visited Peru in their dressing-room. 'It seemed like they were there just to greet and welcome us,' said the captain Héctor Chumpitaz. 'They also said that they hoped it would be a good game because there was a great deal of anticipation among the Argentinian public. He wished us luck, and that was it. We started looking at each other and wondering: shouldn't they have gone to the Argentina room, not our room? What's going on? I mean, they wished us luck? Why? It left us wondering . . .'[43]

In 2012, a former Peruvian senator, Genaro Ledesma, gave evidence to a Buenos Aires judge that the game had been thrown as part of Operation Condor, a grim agreement between a number of South America's dictatorships in the seventies to help each other deal with dissidents. According to Ledesma, Videla agreed with Peru's military leader, Francisco Morales Bermúdez, that Argentina would hold and torture thirteen dissidents, so long as they got the result they required.[44]

On the day Argentina met England in the World Cup

quarter-final in Mexico City, the *Sunday Times*, citing an anonymous civil servant, claimed that the Argentinian government shipped 35,000 tons of grain – and possibly some arms – to Peru and that the Argentinian central bank released $50m of frozen Peruvian assets in exchange for victory.[45]

'Were we pressured? Yes, we were pressured,' the midfielder José Velásquez said. 'What kind of pressure? Pressure from the government. From the government to the managers of the team, from the managers of the team to the coaches ... Something happened. Our team was changed. I was replaced in the tenth minute of the second half – when we were already losing by two goals. There was no reason to change me. I was always an important piece in our team. So what can one think?'[46]

Which sounds damning, particularly as Velásquez had had a very good tournament. Except, by the time he went off in the 52nd minute, Peru were actually 4–0 down. If taking him out of the game was part of some grand plot, that was an odd time to do it. His memory, and perhaps others', have been skewed by time and the widespread global scepticism.

Brazilians point out that Peru's goalkeeper, Ramón Quiroga, had been born in Argentina, but he made a string of outstanding saves. If he were part of some skulduggery, nobody has ever disguised it so well. Juan Muñante hit the post for Peru early on; again, that is not proof of anything – how better, after all, to disguise a fix than for the team that is destined to lose to take the lead? – but it adds to the wider impression that Peru, with nothing to play for, collapsed amid the ferocious atmosphere of the Arroyito. Larrosa maintained that the game had changed when he and Gallego switched positions, which allowed him to support Jorge Olguín in shutting down Cubillas.[47]

During the game – it's said at the very moment the vital fourth goal went in – a bomb went off at the house of the minister of the interior, Juan Alemann, one of those who had questioned the expenditure on the tournament. But for most, the win brought euphoria. It's estimated 60 per cent of the population of Buenos Aires went out onto the streets in celebration. This was exactly the patriotic fervour the junta sought to harness.

Havelange received a welcome endorsement for his plan to expand the World Cup in the performances of Tunisia. Zaire in 1974 had been something of an embarrassment to Fifa; it would have been hard to justify handing another qualifying slot to Africa had Tunisia also lost all three games by a combined score of 14–0. So there must have been a sense of anxiety when, three months before the tournament, Tunisia stormed off the pitch during their Africa Cup of Nations third-place play-off when a penalty was awarded against them, leading to a two-year ban from African football.

But in Argentina, Tunisia impressed. Although they fell behind to a 45th-minute penalty against Mexico in their first group game, Tunisia retained their composure, kept playing counter-attacking football and, inspired by the 1977 African footballer of the year Tarek Dhiab, won 3–1, the first victory by an African side at the World Cup. A 1–0 defeat to Poland meant they needed to beat West Germany to progress to the second phase, and they might have done so had Manny Kalz been penalised, as he surely should have been, for tripping Mohamed Ben Rehaiem in the box. But no penalty was given and, when Ben Rehaiem was denied by a brilliant late save from Sepp Maier, West Germany had the goalless draw they needed to progress.

It said much for how well Tunisia had played that their coach Abdelmajid Chetali ended up frustrated, accusing his players of being 'happy to have achieved a draw against the world champions' and not really going for it in the final 10 minutes.[48]

African football was to be taken seriously – as West Germany would learn four years later.

Carlos González was forty-six. He had just split with his wife, who was from Rotterdam, and after losing his job, he took to driving aimlessly round Spain in a camper van, smoking weed. He was frustrated by Johan Cruyff who, after recovering slowly from surgery on his calf, had then gone down with flu. His absences, he felt, were undermining Barcelona. Then he read that Cruyff was facing a huge tax bill and seems to have reasoned that meant he must have piles of cash lying around at home. So, pretending to be a courier and armed with a sawn-off shotgun and a knife, he knocked on the door of Cruyff's apartment in Barcelona. Cruyff's wife Danny answered. He made her lie on the floor, then began tying Cruyff's feet to the legs of the sofa. Their six-year-old daughter Chantal came to find out what the commotion was, creating enough of a distraction for Danny to rush to the door and raise the alarm.[49] González, who was jailed for seven years, appears to have been a pothead acting alone but the incident unnerved Cruyff, and despite some fine performances from the Netherlands in 1977, he decided he couldn't leave his family to go to Argentina.[50]

The Dutch of 1978, under Ernst Happel, were not the Dutch of four years earlier, although in the second phase they became a little more like the Netherlands people remembered. They demolished Austria 5–1, twice came from behind to draw with West Germany and secured their place in the final as Arie Haan's 35-yard drive saw off Italy.

It had been the defeat to the Netherlands in 1974 that had led to the rejection of *anti-fútbol* and the appointment of Menotti with his promise to restore the values of *la nuestra*, so it was fitting that it should be against the Netherlands that Menotti would achieve his greatest victory. However romantic his vision, though, there was little romance about Argentina's success.

In the build-up to the final, the propaganda campaign behind the hosts intensified. An article in *El Gráfico* attacked 'the insidious and malicious journalists who for months pursued a campaign of lies about Argentina',[51] while there was a clumsy attempt to pretend the Netherlands defender Ruud Krol had written a letter celebrating the harmoniousness of life under the junta. Many had expected Klein to be named as the referee for the final but he was overlooked for the Italian Sergio Gonella, supposedly on the casting vote of the Italian chairman of the refereeing committee, Artemio Franchi. The Welsh referee Clive Thomas, who had also officiated at the finals, called the decision 'an utter disgrace'.[52]

On the day of the final, the Netherlands were taken to El Monumental via a circuitous route, allowing fans to hammer on the side of their bus, a deliberate act of intimidation. Argentina came out late from the tunnel for kick-off, leaving the Dutch to stand exposed to the fury of the crowd. When they did emerge, it was to protest about the cast René van der Kerkhof was wearing on his wrist, something he had done without complaint throughout the tournament.

Yet for all the chicanery, it was Argentina who seemed the more nervous. 'The emotions as we stepped on the pitch were incredible,' said Larrosa. 'We couldn't even see the aisles, the stairs, because the stadium was so full that people couldn't move.'[53]

They would have fallen behind to Johnny Rep but for a startling tip-over from Fillol, 'the best save of my life' as he described it.[54] Kempes, slipped through by Osvaldo Ardiles, put Argentina ahead seven minutes before half-time. Klein might have cracked down on the spoiling and timewasting of the Argentinians; Gonella did not. But with eight minutes remaining, the Dutch substitute Dirk Nanninga headed an equaliser. The Dutch almost won it in injury time as Rensenbrink stretched to reach a long free-kick and poked the ball past Fillol. It bounced once, hit the post and bobbled back into play. Two inches to the right and it was probably a goal. 'The silence was like a cemetery after that,' said Larrosa. 'But that made us react. If that didn't go in, this was our World Cup.'[55] Goals from Kempes and Daniel Bertoni completed a 3–1 win.

'The final against the Netherlands was the greatest example of what I wanted from the team,' said Menotti.[56] Videla and the junta were just as delighted. Havelange, never one to miss the opportunity to praise a right-wing dictator, offered a post-tournament vote of thanks to Argentina in general and Admiral Lacoste in particular. When Lacoste, who served as interim president of Argentina for eleven days in December 1981 before Galtieri was confirmed as the successor to Roberto Viola, was later accused of murder and embezzlement after democracy had returned to Argentina, Havelange backed him to the extent of claiming he had loaned him the US$500,000 with which he had bought land in Punta del Este in Uruguay. 'Now the world has seen the true face of Argentina,' Havelange said.[57]

Others were less convinced. Brian Glanville spoke for many when he wrote of a tournament 'disfigured by negative football, ill temper, dreadful refereeing, spiteful players and the wanton surrender of Peru'.[58]

The day after the final, *Clarín* claimed 'the victory covers all the moments of darkness ... the achievement of Menotti is great. His style won. His convictions won. It is possible to be world champions with technical and attacking players.'[59] Even in context, it's not clear what is meant by 'moments of darkness'. Perhaps it refers simply to the defeat to the Netherlands in 1974 and the failure to qualify for the World Cup four years before that; perhaps it's the years of *anti-fútbol* as a whole, *Clarín* recanting the Argentinian game's deviation from the one true path. Or perhaps there was some subtle, possibly even subconscious, reference to the junta and its crimes?

That's certainly how Menotti would have liked to have regarded his success, something he made explicit in the dressing-room before kick-off. 'We are the people,' he said. 'We come from the victimised classes and we represent the only thing that is legitimate in this country – football. We are not playing for the expensive seats full of military officers. We represent freedom, not the dictatorship.'

He was appointed to the job before the junta had taken power. What should he then have done, he asked: 'coach teams that played badly ... that betrayed the feelings of the people? No, of course not.'[60]

Yet it is impossible to look at the footage of a grinning Videla, neatly parted hair gleaming in the floodlights, handing the trophy to Daniel Passarella without a sense of nausea. The unease has meant a sense among players from the 1978 squad that their achievement is not celebrated like that of 1986. 'Critics aligned us to the dictatorship and we did not have anything to do with it,' said the defender Rubén Pagnanini. 'I believe that the journalists never gave our team the credit we deserved.'[61]

Many who vehemently opposed the junta still supported Argentina at that World Cup, a point made by Claudio Tamburrini, a goalkeeper for the lower-league club Almagro who was imprisoned as a political activist (which he was not) before escaping in March 1978. 'What is the fascination of sport that makes it possible for torturers and tortured to embrace each other after the goals scored by the national team?' he asked. 'During the 1978 World Cup, the Argentinians – including myself – replaced critical political judgement with sporting euphoria ... Given the imperfectability of life and history, it is perhaps rational to celebrate football triumphs alongside a society's concrete political context.'[62]

The players, like most Argentinians, had little idea what was going on. Most players like most people got on with their lives as best they could. 'To many,' said Fillol, 'the World Cup in 1978 means 30,000 disappeared. But none of us tortured or killed anyone. We just helped our country to have a bit of joy and we defended the Argentinian colours with bravery. I cannot be ashamed of that.'[63]

1982

ECTOPLASMIC REDEMPTION

With four minutes remaining, Carlo Ancelotti scored to put Roma 4–0 up against Perugia. Soon afterwards, police cars pulled up on the running track at the Stadio Olimpico and then, at the final whistle, officers crossed the pitch and made for the tunnel to arrest Mauro Della Martira and Luciano Zecchini. Paolo Rossi, the great young hope of Italian goalscoring, was handed a notice inviting him to appear before a magistrate. At the same time, similar scenes happened across Italy. In total that day, thirteen players and the AC Milan president Felice Colombo were arrested, while a further fourteen received notices similar to that given to Rossi.

Betting on football was illegal in Italy, other than the *toto-calcio*, a state-run pool in which punters tried to predict the result of thirteen matches, which made it very hard to fix. Anybody wishing to bet on the result of an individual game had to turn to an illegal bookmaker – *totonero*, which was the name eventually given to the affair – which tended to be run by criminal gangs.

In 1979 a Roman restaurateur, Alvaro Trinca, and the

grocer who supplied much of his produce, Massimo Cruciani, had begun to attempt to fix games by paying off players. They proved remarkably bad at it and were soon losing huge amounts of money. Eventually, panicking, Trinca and Cruciani involved lawyers, seemingly planning to blackmail players, clubs or the league into covering their debt. Eventually the story broke in the press, prosecutors were forced to act and Cruciani told police everything he knew – and perhaps a bit more.

Rossi had been playing bingo with other members of the Perugia squad during a training camp on the Amalfi coast when Della Martira approached him and asked him to come outside and speak to two friends: Cruciani and a market porter called Cesare Bartolucci. Cruciani suggested that Perugia might draw against Avellino that coming Sunday and that Rossi might score twice, at which point Rossi apparently walked away.[1] The game finished 2–2, Rossi getting both Perugia goals. And that was enough to earn Rossi a three-year ban.

It's very hard to know how the evidence was ever taken seriously; even if it were possible for Rossi to try to arrange a draw, how could he possibly promise to score two goals? It was only ever Cruciani's word against Rossi's; although Bartolucci initially backed up his friend, in court he retracted his evidence, claiming to have been provoked by Rossi's lawyer.[2] There was no documentary evidence, no suggestion Rossi had been paid. He was acquitted of the criminal charges. No player (or Colombo), in fact, was convicted, largely because match-fixing had never been criminalised.

The sporting sanction against Rossi remained, although the ban was reduced to two years on appeal. Artemio Franchi resigned as head of the FIGC but the suspicion was that certain players had been sacrificed for the sake of covering up just how deep the scandal ran. It was an open secret that significant numbers of matches in Italy were fixed for 'sporting reasons' – the attitude seems to have been that if a draw suited both sides, then why not draw? – and that players would then bet on those games.[3]

Throughout the hearings, Rossi remained pale and silent, as though not quite able to believe something so apparently trivial had taken such a serious turn. He was a player whose career had already been characterised by miserable fortune. He had joined Juventus as a fifteen-year-old in 1972 but by the time he was sent out on loan to Como in 1975–76 he had had as many operations on his knees as he had made appearances for the first team: three.

When he joined Vicenza on loan in 1976–77, he was regarded because of his pace and his slight physique as a wide forward. But the striker Alessandro Vitali then fell out with the management, and the coach Giovan Battista Fabbri, having few options, moved him to centre-forward. Rossi turned out to have a natural capacity to find space and a calm head in front of goal. He scored 21 that season to be the top scorer in Serie B. The following year he finished top scorer in Serie A as Vicenza, to widespread disbelief, finished second.

Enzo Bearzot took Rossi to the World Cup in Argentina, where he excelled, scoring three goals and setting up four others as Italy finished fourth. Vicenza broke the world transfer record to sign him outright that summer, but injuries struck again and Vicenza were relegated. He was loaned to Perugia for 1979–80 to give him Serie A football.

The ban would expire on 29 April 1982, forty-six days before the start of the World Cup. It seemed impossible that he would be ready, implausible that Bearzot would want a player who hadn't played for two years. But before Italy's penultimate qualifier, they trained at the Campo Combi in Turin. On a neighbouring pitch, Juventus, including Rossi, were training with their youth team. Bearzot wandered over. He put his hands on Rossi's hips. 'They're like those of a Norman broodmare,' he said. Rossi promised to get the excess weight off; he understood Bearzot wanted him for the World Cup.[4] It would prove one of the most inspired decisions any manager has ever made.

Spain had been selected as host of the 1982 World Cup as early as 1964, when it was still ruled by Franco. By the time the World Cup came round, though, the generalissimo had been dead for six years, Juan Carlos I had been sworn in as head of state, a new constitution had been ratified by a referendum and, despite an attempted military coup in February 1981, parliamentary democracy had been established. Even after £100m was spent on upgrading stadiums and organisational costs, there were concerns about Spain's capacity to cope with the expanded tournament after undergoing such political upheaval.

The democratisation of sport meant decentralisation, which led to problems with funding as the economy worsened and unemployment hit 14 per cent. Then there was the threat of domestic terrorism: the Basque separatist group ETA killed ninety-seven people in 1980 and thirty-two before the World Cup began on 14 June 1982.[5] Even on that opening day, an officer in the Guardia Civil was murdered in Pasajes. As Raimundo Saporta, the president of the organising committee, observed, 'It would have been better ten years ago or in ten years, with autocracy or with democracy already established.'[6]

The doubts were not allayed by the draw, in which a revolving drum jammed, one of the plastic balls containing the name of a team split open, a Fifa official could be heard berating the Spanish orphans taking the balls from the drums and the procedures to keep South American sides apart confused those making the draw into initially grouping Scotland with

Argentina before backtracking and admitting they should have been in with Brazil.

That Scotland had avoided the world champions came to seem fortuitous when the Argentinian junta invaded the Falklands on 2 April. The UK investigated the possibility of having Argentina banned, but that proved impossible because of Spain's refusal, owing to its policy on Gibraltar, to back a UN resolution declaring Argentina the aggressor. There was then talk of a UK boycott, but the prime minister Margaret Thatcher ended that by saying that nothing would improve the morale of troops more than good performances by the home nations in Spain. What would happen if one of the home nations actually had to play Argentina nobody dared contemplate.

As it turned out, fears about the Spanish reaction to England as the Falklands War drew to an end proved unfounded – as Peter Corrigan pointed out in the *Observer*, Bilbao was less the 'city of hate' that had been envisaged by some than a 'city of hake'.[7] England's high came early as Bryan Robson's goal after 27 seconds set them on their way to a 3–1 win over France, but they went out with a pair of goalless draws in the second group phase. Northern Ireland exceeded expectations to reach the same stage before running into a France side just hitting form, while Scotland, for the third tournament in a row, went out on goal difference in the first phase.

For the junta, by then under the control of General Leopoldo Galtieri, the war was a desperate attempt to bring the country together with a grand patriotic gesture as they faced mounting financial problems and rising dissent. They had assumed that Britain, itself in dismal economic health, would not bother to defend a few rocks several thousands of miles across the sea; it came as a terrible shock when Thatcher dispatched a task force to reclaim the islands.

For Argentina, football and the war were inextricably

linked, and not just because Osvaldo Ardiles's cousin José Leónidas Ardiles, a twenty-eight-year-old captain in the 6th Air Brigade, was shot down and killed. One state television channel showed heavily propagandised news from the war, using footage from other battles to suggest that Argentina was winning, while the other broadcast re-runs of the 1978 World Cup, linking the two events as great patriotic ventures. Even at the time, though, there was unease. 'The progressive disintegration of Argentinian optimism,' a piece published in *La Nacion* ten days before the tournament noted, 'is causing a real national neurosis observable in certain social phenomena, such as compulsive attention to the 1978 World Cup, at which the triumph ... gave an ersatz consolation for wounds to the national soul.'[8]

Nevertheless, before they set off for Spain, the Argentina squad posed with a banner proclaiming '*Las Malvinas son Argentinas*', while Menotti drew an overt parallel between the World Cup campaign and the war. 'Each man has a part in the struggle,' he said. 'In these moments there is national unity against British colonialism and imperialism. We feel immense pain for our brothers in the battle fleet, but we have been assigned a sports mission and we will try to fulfil it with dignity.'[9]

It was not a role every player accepted willingly. The centre-forward Jorge Valdano was at Real Zaragoza at the time and had a far better idea of what was really happening in the Falklands than his team-mates based at home. 'Somehow,' Valdano said, 'we were the sporting ambassadors of a country at war ... personally, I was not for the war.'[10]

When the rest of the squad reached Spain and started reading local newspapers, they soon realised that the merry optimism of the media at home was a lie, that Argentina's poorly equipped army of under-trained conscripts was doomed. 'We were convinced we were winning the war and like any patriot my allegiance was to the national flag,' said Diego Maradona. 'It was a huge blow to everyone on the team.'[11]

The result was an insipid performance and defeat to Belgium in the opening game of the tournament. The following day, Port Stanley fell and Argentina surrendered. The junta soon collapsed, and democratic elections were held the following year. Argentina did make it out of the group, but reports of ill-discipline were rife. Menotti's lifestyle could not accommodate early mornings, so training was pushed back into the heat of the afternoon. He was often seen with a German model, while the full-back Alberto Tarantini was widely reported to have had a row with his wife on the beach, culminating with her threatening to sleep with another man in revenge.[12] Maradona, meanwhile, struggled to live up to the his billing as the greatest player in the world and was sent off for thrusting his studs into the midriff of Juan Barbas as a 3–1 defeat to Brazil confirmed their second-phase elimination.

The concerns about Spain's capacity to host the tournament were well-founded. Ticketing was chaotic while Mundiespaña, the company set up to handle logistics, took advantage of its monopoly position to sell match tickets only with accompanying accommodation, usually at grossly inflated prices and with needlessly extended minimum stays.[13] Also cheated were the designers who came up with the World Cup mascot Naranjito, a cheery anthropomorphised orange. They were never paid, while organisers, overestimating the average spend on merchandise by a factor of twenty, were left at the end of the tournament with warehouses full of Naranjito-branded tat.

Spain themselves performed poorly, despite extremely generous refereeing. Debatable penalties helped them to a draw against Honduras and then a win over Yugoslavia, but even the extremely soft red card shown to Mal Donaghy with 27 minutes remining couldn't save them from defeat against Northern Ireland. Defeat to West Germany and a draw against England put the hosts out in the second phase.

After the Second World War, there had been no real purge of the fascists in Italy, no reckoning for the crimes of Mussolini's regime.[14] No Italian soldier or politician was ever prosecuted for war crimes committed during the thirties or the Second World War.[15] The monarchy was abolished following a referendum in 1946 and a new constitution established, the preferred system of proportional representation leading to a world of constant coalitions, negotiations and collapses of government. The economy nonetheless boomed amid rapid social liberalisation and urbanisation, with a willing supply of cheap labour and a ready market for consumer goods.[16]

But there was also a constant sense of instability, particularly after *l'Espresso* reported in 1967 that, three years earlier, two members of the Quirinale, the office of the president, had plotted a coup. Then, on the afternoon of 12 December 1969, three bombs exploded in Rome and two in Milan, the beginning of what became known as the Years of Lead. At the Agricultural Bank on Piazza Fontana in Milan, sixteen people were killed and ninety injured. Who actually carried out the attacks has never been established.[17]

As extremists on both sides adopted terrorist tactics, the instability intensified. Hundreds were killed in bomb attacks, the majority of them apparently carried out by the secret service and far right and aimed at discrediting the left and establishing a more authoritarian, less democratic regime.[18] A coup had been feared since the military seized power in Greece in 1967. Finally, in 1970, one was attempted, led by Junio Valerio Borghese, who had been an officer under Mussolini, although it rapidly fizzled out and it was four months before most people knew anything about it.[19]

The same year, demonstrations in Reggio Calabria after it was overlooked for a new university escalated into a full-scale revolt. In 1977, as dramatised in Dario Fo's play *Non Si Paga! Non Si Paga!* (*Can't Pay! Won't Pay!*), people refused to pay utility bills. There were protests and clashes with police. Then, in March 1978, the former Christian Democrat prime minister Aldo Moro was kidnapped, one of the most high-profile acts of the left-wing terror group the Brigate Rosse (Red Brigades). He was held for fifty-five days then, after being sentenced to death by a 'people's court', he was shot and dumped in the boot of a Renault 4. The Years of Lead culminated on 2 August 1980 when an explosion at Bologna train station killed eighty people and wounded two hundred.

Although attacks continued, by the time of the 1982 World Cup, the worst was over and Italy was in need of an event to unify the nation. Football was perhaps the only pursuit that could offer that. As Umberto Eco had asked during the previous World Cup, 'is it possible to have a revolution on a football Sunday?'[20]

After Italy's group stage exit in 1974, the head of the FIGC Artemio Franchi had realised there was need for major change. It wasn't just the coach Ferruccio Valcareggi who needed replacing, but the squad needed rejuvenating while the Total Football of the Netherlands suggested to him that *il giocco all'italiano* (the Italian game), into which *catenaccio* had evolved, was finished. To lead the revolution, he turned to Fulvio Bernardini.

Bernardini was already sixty-eight, a hugely respected figure who had led both Fiorentina and Bologna to the scudetto as a manager. He had been a clever, elegant midfielder for Lazio,

Inter and Roma, but had been omitted from Pozzo's World Cup squads in 1934 and 1938 because he was not a good tactical fit. By 1974, he believed Italian football needed to undergo 'a programme of renewal'[21] and that probably meant the likes of Sandro Mazzola, Gianni Rivera and Gigi Riva had had their day. Franchi told Bernardini to speak to his two assistants, Azeglio Vicini and Enzo Bearzot, and decide which of them he wanted to work with most closely. Bernardini's wife preferred the gregarious Vicini; Bernardini himself went for Bearzot. 'He's a closed and shady Friulian,' he said, 'but he knows about football.'[22]

By 1975, Bearzot had effectively taken charge and by 1977 he was the sole national manager. He had attracted the nickname '*Vecio*' – old man – towards the end of his playing days, and it stuck because it seemed so apt. He liked jazz and smoked a pipe, and was phlegmatic and meticulous. He felt the Dutch model was too open for the Italian temperament and so decided he would base his national team on Poland. On 4 June 1976, Italy beat Romania 4–2 at San Siro. The Milanese crowd booed, furious at the absence of Rivera and Mazzola, but that was the beginning of the new Italy.

They finished fourth at the 1978 World Cup and won many admirers. Notably more progressive than previous Italy sides, they were the only team to beat Argentina in the tournament and at half-time in their final group game, against the Netherlands, they led 1–0 and were set for the final. But two long-range strikes – Ernie Brandts from 20 yards and Arie Haan from almost 40 – turned the game. Italy then lost 2–1 to Brazil in the third-place play-off, and again both goals were shots from outside the box, the first of them Nelinho's famous swerving shot from the right wing with the outside of his right foot. 'Zoff condemns us',[23] read the headline in *Gazzetto dello Sport* above a piece questioning the logic of playing a thirty-six-year-old goalkeeper. Bearzot didn't care; he kept picking his fellow Friulian.

Italy missed out on the final of the Euros in 1980, finishing behind Belgium in their group on goals scored, and as their form faltered towards the end of World Cup qualifying, Bearzot began to be criticised. Had he been right to change the style? And why was he so intent on waiting for Rossi? In the eighteen months after beating Greece in December 1980, Italy won just twice: against Bulgaria and Luxembourg.

On 2 May 1982, Rossi returned to action, scoring in Juventus's 5–1 win at Udinese. He played in their final two league games of the season as they wrapped up the title on the final day with a highly contentious 1–0 win at Catanzaro. On the basis of those three matches, he was called up to the World Cup squad. Roberto Bettega, who had combined well with Rossi in 1978, was injured, while Bruno Giordano, who had emerged as an effective partner for Rossi after the World Cup, had also been banned as part of the *totonero* fallout. It seemed Bearzot had to turn to the prolific Roma striker Roberto Pruzzo, who had played at the Euros. But he left him out, reasoning that Rossi would be unable to relax if he had an obvious replacement breathing down his neck.

It was an astute and astonishingly bold piece of man-management, but one that contributed to the fractious atmosphere that surrounded the Italy squad before they departed. A Roma fan spat on Bearzot and he slapped a twenty-two-year-old Inter fan called Anna Ceci when she called him a 'bastard ape' for leaving out her favourite, Evaristo Beccalossi.[24] When he then apologised and explained his reasoning, she burst into tears and accepted he was right. They hugged, exchanged addresses and became such good friends that Bearzot attended her wedding.

The expansion from sixteen teams to twenty-four meant representation from Asia/Oceania, Africa and Concacaf doubled from one side each to two, which led to concerns about a dilution of quality.

El Salvador, preparations complicated by conflict between the US-backed right-wing government and guerrillas supported by Cuba and the USSR, lost all three matches, which included a record 10–1 defeat to Hungary.[25]

Kuwait, having forced a creditable draw with Czechoslovakia, disgraced themselves in defeat to France. The score was 3–1 with six minutes remaining when, apparently hearing a whistle from the crowd, Kuwait's defence stopped, allowing Alain Giresse to score, at which the head of their delegation, Sheikh Fahd Al-Sabah, came down from the stands to remonstrate with the Soviet referee Miroslav Stupar, who cravenly disallowed the goal. Maxime Bossis ensured it did finish 4–1.

New Zealand failed to pick up a point in a tough group but Honduras performed creditably, drawing two of their three games. Cameroon went one better and drew all of theirs, denied a place in the second phase only on goals scored.

But the positive impression of north African football left by Tunisia in 1978 was maintained by Algeria, backed by 3,000 fans who made the short hop across the Mediterranean to Spain. The West Germany goalkeeper Harald Schumacher predicted his side would score somewhere between four and eight goals against them,[26] while the coach Jupp Derwall admitted that he hadn't bothered to pass on warnings from his assistants Erich Ribbeck and Berti Vogts, after two scouting trips, because he'd known his players wouldn't listen.[27]

Schumacher would end that World Cup as the villain, but he had begun the tournament appalled by the conduct of his teammates. Derwall had become national coach when Schön retired after the 1978 World Cup. He had led West Germany to the European Championship in 1980 and they went into the 1982 World Cup as favourites. On 2 June 1982, the squad gathered at a hotel near Schluchsee – later nicknamed *Schlucksee* (Lake

Swig) – for their pre-tournament camp. That first evening, Schumacher revealed in his 1987 autobiography, some players gambled to excess while others 'would live it up until the early hours and turn up for training on their knees'. He was so disturbed by what he'd seen that he called his agent and asked how he could get away from the camp.[28]

Algeria had a number of technically gifted players and, if the midfield creator Mustapha Dahleb, who held Paris Saint-Germain's league goalscoring record before Zlatan Ibrahimović, was the only one playing at a high level in Europe, that was more to do with restrictions on players leaving Algeria than a reflection of their quality. They took the lead through Rabah Madjer and although Karl-Heinz Rummenigge levelled, Lakhdar Belloumi converted Salah Assad's low cross to give Algeria the win after a performance of style and technical excellence.

They lost 2–0 to Austria, amid arguments over bonuses and the regulation that said players couldn't move abroad until after their twenty-eighth birthday, but rallied and, with Assad scoring twice, surged into a three-goal lead against Chile within 34 minutes. A second-half wobble brought the score back to 3–2, which proved crucial.

After the defeat to Algeria, West Germany's players had returned to their hotel and been woken at 4 a.m. by fans chanting 'Derwall out!' but a Rummenigge hat-trick in a 4–1 win over Chile offered hope. Algeria's win over Chile was played a day before Austria faced West Germany, which meant everybody knew a West Germany victory by two or fewer goals would see both sides through.

In the build-up, much of the talk was of Austria's 3–2 win in Cordoba in the previous World Cup, their first victory over either Germany for forty-seven years. It made Hans Krankl, who scored twice, a star, and ensured that for the first time since 1962 West Germany did not finish in the top four of a World

Cup. West Germany began as though determined to avenge that defeat and went ahead through Horst Hrubesch. In the first 20 minutes, they had six corners. And then ... nothing. 'There were agreements between Austrian and German players during the break,' claimed the Austria centre-forward Walter Schachner.[29] Breitner denied it, arguing all games are managed to an extent, but it was the midfielder who Krankl said had made the suggestion to him of leaving it at 1–0.[30]

Whoever initiated it, both teams just stopped playing. The Spanish in the crowd jeered and the Algerians waved banknotes. 'What's happening here,' said Eberhard Stanjek, the ARD commentator, 'is disgraceful and has nothing to do with football ... You can say what you want but not every end justifies every means.'[31] In the end, he just stopped talking. In Austria, the ÖRF commentator Robert Seeger told viewers to switch off. The headline in *Bild* the next day read, 'Shame on You'.[32]

Nobody involved seemed to grasp what the problem was. 'Of course, today's game was tactical,' said Hans Tschak, the head of the Austrian delegation, before launching into a rant that made clear that just because the World Cup had expanded, it didn't mean racist attitudes towards football's emerging powers had disappeared. 'If 10,000 sons of the desert want to start a scandal in the stadium because of it, that just shows that they don't have enough schools. A sheikh comes from an oasis, gets to sniff World Cup atmosphere for the first time in 300 years and thinks he can now open his mouth.'[33]

Back at their hotel that evening, the West Germany squad was pelted with tomatoes and eggs by their own fans. At least two players responded by hurling water bombs down from their balconies onto the furious mass of spectators below. One fan tearfully pointed out he had used his holiday, travelled 1,500 miles across Europe and spent a fortune to watch a non-event.

The players regarded the outcry with contempt. 'I can't worry about the prestige of German football,' said the midfielder Wolfgang Dremmler. 'I'm a professional.'[34]

'What do I care if Aunt Frieda is making a fuss at home?' asked the forward Uwe Reinders.[35]

'We've gone through,' said Lothar Matthäus. 'That's all that counts.'[36]

Even in 1974, Schön had sensed the players moving into a new sphere, one remote from those who supported them, in which a sense of patriotic duty had been replaced by a brattish individualism; a similar journey to that undergone by Maria Braun. Richard Gaulke was the closest thing West Germany had to a celebrity fan. He had been going to national team matches since two days before his eleventh birthday, initially by bike and then, as he became better known, travelling with the players. Between 1965 and 1978 he didn't miss a single fixture. But by 1982, even he had become disillusioned, complaining about the way modern players chewed gum during the anthem and scribbled their autographs contemptuously. Nonetheless, he travelled to Spain and stayed in the same hotel as the squad. He celebrated his sixty-seventh birthday eating with the players a few hours before the win over Chile.

Gaulke hated what had happened against Austria. He kept telling people how 'upset' he was. But it was worse than that; it seemed to have made him ill. The next day, during dinner with some journalists, he suffered a heart attack and died.[37] Rainer Werner Fassbinder had died in the week before the tournament, aged thirty-seven. In the space of a fortnight, West German football had lost its biggest fan; a director who served as a (flawed) conscience for the nation; and its sense that the game might be about more than just winning. 'Never before,' as *Süddeutsche Zeitung* put it, 'have German football fans been told with such insolent directness that they shouldn't really count on being offered matches worth seeing.'[38]

Remarkably, West Germany's reputation would sink even lower before the tournament was done.

For French football, the 1982 World Cup represented a long-overdue reawakening, as they could celebrate a dashing side led by a majestic playmaker in Michel Platini. Whatever promise there had been in the performances of Reims in the European Cup in the late fifties, or in the performance of the national team in 1958, quickly evaporated.

France failed to qualify for the 1962, 1970 and 1974 World Cups and took a solitary point in going out in the group stage in 1966, while no French side reached a European final again until Saint-Étienne in 1976. The success in 1958 dulled the fervour of those who would have taken French football down a more utilitarian route but, as standards slipped, the clamour began again, echoing the economic language of the time to demand organisation, effort and productivity. That led, in 1969, to the appointment of Georges Boulogne as national coach. He spoke of '*football labeur*' and insisted that football had to stop being '*une activité ludique*'.[39] The appointment of the Romanian Ștefan Kovács, who had led Ajax to their second and third European Cups, after the failure to qualify for the 1974 World Cup was a step away from Gaullist authoritarianism but it was when Michel Hidalgo took over a year later that France once again had a manager who could speak of '*le plaisir de jouer*'.

His France side went out in the group stage in 1978, but there was no disgrace in defeats to Argentina or Italy. They narrowly missed out on qualifying for the 1980 Euros behind Czechoslovakia but by 1982 France were a swashbuckling, attractive side, based around the *carré magique* (magic square) midfield of Platini, Alain Giresse, Jean Tigana and Bernard Genghini, all of them playmakers. Or at least that is the myth. In fact, that quartet played together only twice in that tournament.

The tournament had begun with some stereotypically French shenanigans as the midfielder Jean-François Larios, *France Football*'s player of the year for 1980, was sent home after the defeat to England amid rumours he was having an affair with Platini's wife.[40] A 4–1 win over Kuwait was enough to secure qualification behind England and, the *carré magique* in place, another 4–1 win, this time over Northern Ireland, saw them into a semi-final against West Germany.

On a sweltering night in Seville, a Platini penalty cancelled out Pierre Littbarski's opener. Early in the second half, with France taking control, Platini flighted a through-pass to the substitute Patrick Battiston. When he got to the ball about a yard outside the box, Schumacher had only just passed the penalty spot. Battiston jabbed at the bouncing ball and sent it just wide of the right-hand post. The goalkeeper carried on his run, half-turned, and clattered Battiston hip-first.

It was a clear penalty and, even by the lax standards of the day, at least a yellow card, possibly a red. The Dutch referee Charles Corver gave a goal-kick. Battiston was knocked unconscious, lost three teeth, damaged vertebrae and slipped into a coma. Platini said he feared Battiston was dead as medical assistance was delayed by inexplicable bureaucracy. Oxygen was eventually administered on the pitch. As Battiston lay stricken, team-mates gathered round in horror, Schumacher leaned against his post chewing gum. He later admitted he was guilty of 'cowardice', fearing both the reaction of the French players and seeing the consequence of his recklessness.[41] 'The image of the ugly German,' the journalist Dietrich Schulze-Marmeling wrote, 'came back to life.'[42]

Manuel Amoros hit the bar with a long-range effort in the final minute, and the game went to extra time. Marius Trésor and Giresse had France 3–1 up by the 98th minute. France kept attacking but, perhaps because the loss of Battiston, who had been on the pitch only four minutes when he was knocked unconscious, effectively cost them a substitute, they slowly wilted. Rummenigge flicked in a cross and then, with 12 minutes remaining, Klaus Fischer levelled with a trademark overhead. From then on, the outcome was inevitable. West Germany won on penalties and French hearts were broken.

That was how it had to be. Germany were the strutting winners, apparently unconcerned by the means by which they achieved their ends, while France were the gallant losers. In the 1960s, the French public had always preferred the cyclist Raymond Poulidor, an aggressive and attacking climber, to his great rival Jacques Anquetil, who controlled races in the mountains and dominated the time trials. Anquetil won five Tours de France; Poulidor didn't win any, yet his appeal was so striking that *l'Équipe* wrote that 'no rider had ever incited so many sociological investigations, so many university theses, seeking to find the cause of his prodigious popularity'.[43] *La complexe Poulidor* came to be seen as characteristically French, seen in the national fervour generated by Saint-Étienne in the 1970s by their near-misses in the European Cup.[44]

Seville fitted the pattern perfectly. As the philosopher Raymond Aron had put it, the French seemed to prefer to be right or to do things properly even if the cost was defeat.[45] By 1985, the condition had morphed into *le complexe d'Astérix*, as defined by the sociologist Alain Duhamel: France as the last village holding out gloriously against inevitable defeat.[46]

Italy had set off for Spain amid acrimony and the mood didn't improve much once the tournament began as they drew 0–0 against Poland and 1–1 against Peru. In that second game, Rossi was withdrawn at half-time, looking, as the journalist Gianni Brera had it, like 'an ectoplasm of himself'.[47] As the players came out for the second half, Rossi was bent over the bench, one boot on, one off, certain his World Cup was over. Bearzot told him to prepare for the next game; he had staked his whole campaign on Rossi. The Italian press was merciless. As well as criticism of Bearzot for having invested so much in a player just returned from a two-year ban, there were baseless rumours about the players' personal lives and the bonuses they were supposed to be on. The players imposed a media blackout.

A controversial 1–1 draw against Cameroon took Italy through,[48] but did little to silence the criticism, especially when their opponents in the second-phase group became apparent: Brazil and Argentina.

But Italy, slowly beginning to find their form, beat Argentina 2–1 as Claudio Gentile, by fair means and foul, marked Maradona out of the game. Brazil then beat Argentina 3–1, which meant they needed just a draw against Italy to go through. It would be played, thanks to the complication of seeding caused by Argentina and Italy both coming second in their group, not at the Camp Nou in the evening but at the other stadium in Barcelona, the ramshackle Sarrià, in the heat of the afternoon.

It would prove one of the greatest of all World Cup matches.

Brazil too were in a process of transformation. The obsession with the idea that Europeans were physically fitter meant the physical trainer Cláudio Coutinho took on a more central role alongside Mário Zagallo in 1974. Coutinho then took over as coach in 1978. He spoke of 'polyvalence' as a sort of South American variant of Total Football and condemned 'the dribble, our speciality, as a waste of time and proof of our weakness'.[49] The result was a functional and unadventurous side that didn't lose a game, but thrilled no one.

Coutinho, apparently regarded as conveniently pliable by Admiral Nunes, stayed on until the 1979 Copa América, but a semi-final defeat to Paraguay brought his dismissal. He moved to the US where he coached the LA Aztecs and, aged forty-two, was killed in a diving accident on a holiday back in Rio in 1981.

It was indicative of the loosening grip of the military, the general process of liberalisation after João Figueiredo had replaced Geisel as national president that when, in 1979, football devolved from the CBD to have its own governing body, the CBF, Nunes was replaced by a civilian businessman, Giulite Coutinho. There was a desire for football to break free of technocracy and return to more traditional Brazilian values, and so he appointed Telê Santana, a coach who preached a style of football based on fluidity and intermovement. 'Those who need a team with fixed tips and position specialists,' he said, 'are already dead and don't know it.'[50]

Santana's captain was Sócrates, tall, elegant, bearded and extremely conscious of football's place in society. He was at the heart of a movement at Corinthians by which the players not only voted on key aspects of club policy but also sought to nurture the nascent democracy by, for instance, encouraging fans to vote. 'We'd been living under a dictatorship since 1964,' said the Corinthians forward Walter Casagrande, 'and all the country's companies, schools and clubs were run along military lines: someone at the top gave the orders and you just did what you were told. We had to invent democracy by doing democracy.'[51]

Brazil arrived at the World Cup in fine form, with only a couple of questions about personnel. Would there be a place in midfield for Falcão, who played for Roma and had linked up with the squad late? And with Careca injured and Reinaldo out of favour, would the lumbering Serginho, top scorer in the domestic league the previous season, be able to lead the line ahead of the array of gifted creators? To which the answers were yes and not really.

Although Valeriy Lobanovskyi's high-class USSR took a first-half lead against them, stunning goals from Sócrates and Éder in the final fifteen minutes gave Brazil a 2–1 win. Victories over Scotland, New Zealand and even Argentina were more straightforward. The general sense was that Brazil were back. Zico insisted that their 4-2-2-2, with Éder on the left and a square in midfield of Sócrates and himself backed up by Falcão and Toninho Cerezo, was 'the football of the future'. By contrast, 'Italy . . . still use man-to-man marking, sad football from the past. In this century, it's ridiculous.'[52] There were just two notes of concern: that Zico struggled at times to cover the right flank, and that the previous time Brazil had faced man-to-man marking, against Uruguay eighteen months earlier, was the last time they had lost.

But Italy under Bearzot had developed. They no longer played a pure man-to-man game, even if that remained the basis. Gentile was deployed to pick up Zico, Fulvio Collovati on Serginho and Gabriele Oriali on Éder. But Oriali was told to push into midfield when he could to back up Bruno Conti on the wing, while Antonio Cabrini was encouraged to surge from left-back into the space Zico often vacated on that flank. Behind them all, plugging any gaps that might emerge, was Gaetano Scirea, the unflappable *libero*.

Three times in the opening minutes, Rossi was knocked to the ground. Then it happened again after he had found space in the box to meet a Marco Tardelli cross only to miskick badly. There was little to suggest those who felt he was not physically ready for a World Cup were wrong. But the next time he touched the ball, before it had even gone out of play again, everything changed. A Brazil attack broke down. Italy advanced on their right flank. Conti abruptly cut infield past Éder, before sending a pass out to the left flank with the outside of his left foot. Cabrini had advanced into that space behind Zico. He had time to measure his cross. The Brazil defence shuffled over, but in doing so they left Rossi unmarked. He arrived at the back post and headed past Waldir Peres. It had been three years since his previous goal for his country.

Sócrates levelled from a clever pass from Zico, but then a loose Toninho Cerezo backpass set Rossi through. Having remembered again how to score, he drilled a shot from the edge of the box past Waldir Peres. There were still only 25 minutes played. Collovati turned his ankle and had to be replaced by the eighteen-year-old Giuseppe Bergomi. Brazil kept probing. Italy kept resisting. Zico had his shirt ripped by Gentile. Finally, midway through the second half, Falcão levelled.

A draw was enough for Brazil but the game by then had a momentum of its own. 'We lacked humility,' said Luizinho. 'There was no leadership on the field; someone out there on the pitch should have said, "Leandro, Júnior, stay back. Let's tighten up in midfield, let's make sure of the draw."'[53]

Nine minutes later, Italy won their first corner of the match. It was cleared to the edge of the box. Tardelli hooked the ball goalwards. Six yards out, it passed between Graziani and Rossi. Both swung at it, Graziani with his left foot, Rossi with his right. Waldir Peres, initially frozen, had to make a guess. He plunged to his right, where the ball would probably have gone had Graziani kicked it. But it was Rossi who made contact, diverting the ball to the goalkeeper's left to complete an implausible hat-trick.

Giancarlo Antognoni had a goal wrongly ruled out for a tight offside and then came the final chance: an Éder free-kick from the left, Oscar rising at the far post and meeting it with a firm downward header, and Zoff, defying the critics with a stretching save down to his left, grasping the ball on the goal line. Italy had won; Brazil were out.

It was, as Zico said, the day that football, or at least a certain idea of football, died.[54] Although Santana stayed on for the following World Cup, the consequences for Brazilian football were profound. The sense was that the return to the old ways had failed. Brazil's football may have been beautiful, but they had come up short. 'From that moment on the emphasis changed to focus even more on results,' Sócrates said. 'Brazilian football would never be the same.'[55]

Once the euphoria had subsided, even the Italians seem to have felt a sense of loss. How could anything ever be that good again?[56] Poland, who had come through their second-phase group thanks largely to Zbigniew Boniek's hat-trick against Belgium, were beaten 2–0 in the semi-final, Rossi getting both goals with finishes inside the six-yard box. Even Derwall's West Germany couldn't upset this dream. Cabrini missed a first-half penalty but second-half goals from Rossi, Tardelli and the substitute Alessandro Altobelli gave them a comfortable 3–1 win. Italy were world champions for the third time and Rossi won both the Golden Boot for top-scorer and Golden Ball for best player.

Sandro Pertini had fought in the First World War and in the Second had been a leader of the anti-Fascist resistance. He had become president of Italy in 1978, at the age of eighty-one. He was a unifying figure, respected for his humility – he lived in an ordinary flat rather than the Quirinale Palace and drove a Fiat 500 – and for his humanity – he attended the funerals of as many victims of the Years of Lead as he could.

As the political violence waned, the eighties became a time of relief and reconciliation in Italy. For a country often riven by regionalism and factionalism, the World Cup offered a rare period of unity. As Italy progressed through the competition, their matches enjoyed a 95 per cent audience share, while there were huge parties, not only in Italy itself but among the global diaspora.[57] 'There have never been so many flags in the streets,' wrote Luciano Curino in *La Stampa*, going on to note that many still bore the Savoy crest, which had been removed in 1946, suggesting they'd lain around in cupboards for four decades, just waiting for the moment when they could be unfurled again.[58]

Pertini understood the symbolism, and understood the association with his fellow pipe-smoker, Bearzot; both were old, one by chronology and one by temperament. He flew to Spain for the final and, in reacting to the third goal, raised his hands in a way that mirrored Altobelli. He flew back with the squad, playing cards with the players as the World Cup sat on a table alongside them. When they arrived back in Rome, Pertini got off the plane first, but Bearzot was just behind him. The pair, plus Zoff, travelled in the presidential car to the Quirinale, with the rest of the squad in convoy behind them. The association of the World Cup with Pertini was universal, as was made clear by Matteo Renzi in his first speech after becoming president in 2014.[59]

In the end, the image that summed up their triumph was that of Tardelli after firing in from the edge of the box in the final, fists clenched, arms out to the side, head shaking, sweat-soaked hair clinging to his face as he yelled his own name and ran towards the bench, his entire being a scream of ecstasy. This wasn't just victory but redemption: for Rossi, who had been banned on the flimsiest of evidence; for a squad that had been doubted and abused; for football, as the cynicism of that West Germany was overcome; and perhaps even for a nation that had suffered so much.

1986

THE REVENGE OF THE GAUCHO

On 20 October 1960 at the Policlinico Evita in Lanús on the outskirts of Buenos Aires, Dalma Salvadora Franco gave birth to a son. The boy was short and squat, had a mischievous grin and a habit of getting into trouble. He grew up in Villa Fiorito, a shanty so rough police would be bussed out each evening. When he was a toddler, he fell into an open cesspit and nearly drowned, saved only by his Uncle Cirilo, who shouted at him to 'keep his head above the shit', a tale that in adulthood would take on obvious allegorical significance.[1]

Everything in the boy's early life came to take on a symbolic importance. On his third birthday he was given a football and took it to bed. It soon became apparent he was a player of exceptional talent and, at the age of eight, he joined the youth ranks of Argentinos Juniors. By sixteen he had made his professional debut. He was not just a footballer; even at that early age he was something else, something profoundly Argentinian.

In 1928, the editor of *El Gráfico*, Borocotó, had proposed raising a statue to the inventor of dribbling as the person who had defined the soul of Argentinian football. It should, he said, depict 'a *pibe* [urchin] with a dirty face, a mane of hair rebelling against the comb; with intelligent, roving, trickster and persuasive eyes and a sparkling gaze that seem to hint at a picaresque laugh that does not quite manage to form on his mouth, full of small teeth that might be worn down through eating yesterday's bread'.[2]

He could have been describing the boy. Even now, it comes as something of a jolt to realise he was not drawing a picture of Diego Maradona, that he wrote those words thirty-two years before Maradona was born, forty-nine years before he made his international debut. Maradona arrived with the force of prophecy. There had been *pibes* before, others even who had had a similar blend of indigenous and Italian blood to identify as the *cabecitas negras* – the 'little blackheads' – that Evita described as the heart of the nation. But none had quite the talent, quite the charisma. They had been *pibes*; Maradona was *el pibe de oro*.

Pibes mattered. They were central to the self-mythology of Argentina and of Argentinian football in particular. In the early twentieth century as the British retreated – although Argentina had never been part of the Empire, it was firmly within the informal Empire as Britain controlled the banking system and the export of beef, wool and hide – Argentina was left as a relatively new country with very little sense of itself, comprising an awkward mix of very different people with very different ideas about society and how it should be structured.[3] What did it mean to be Argentinian?

Adding urgency to that question were the profound social changes as, in the forty years after the civil wars finally came to an end in 1876, Argentina shifted rapidly from a rural agrarian to an urban industrial economy. Allied to mass immigration from Europe, that brought political pressure which led to the introduction of universal male suffrage for the 1912 general election and ended the hegemony of the conservative land-owning elites. The sense, from all the major parties, was that there was a need for a patriotic project to create a unifying sense of national identity and temper the threat of the far left.

But of what did that consist? In the years immediately before the First World War, it was a matter of regular debate in newspapers and at political rallies. In 1913, Leopoldo Lugones, the pre-eminent poet of the era, gave a series of lectures at the Odeón Theatre in Buenos Aires, attended by the president Roque Sáenz Peña, asking *¿Qué es argentinidad?* – what is Argentinianness? The answer, he said, was to be found in the pampas, the great grasslands that stretched across Patagonia, roamed by the enormous herds of cattle from which Argentina's wealth was derived, and specifically in the figure of the *gaucho*.[4]

That made a certain amount of sense. The hero of José Hernández's national epic, *Martín Fierro*, published in two parts in the 1870s, is a *gaucho* – although the poem is far more equivocal about *gaucho* culture than many seemed to realise – and the figure of the cowboy, aloof, solitary, capable of great technical virtuosity but also able to look after himself, has an obvious cross-cultural appeal.

But only a certain amount. The *gaucho* was a hero for the old days when Argentina was a largely rural society. His significance as a political force had been diminished by the importation of wire fencing by the Englishman Richard Newton in 1844; suddenly cattle could be corralled without recourse to a cowboy while selective breeding could be practised far more easily. The introduction of barbed wire in the 1870s accelerated the process and for a time selective breeding became a media obsession, to the point that an English prize bull called Tarquin was transformed into a celebrity.[5]

Where anyway could that spirit be found in an urban environment? For a time, *gaucho* clubs were popular in Buenos Aires, their members dressing in idealised versions of *gaucho* costume and attending *asados*, which remain a key aspect of

Argentinian social life. Jorge Luis Borges derided the *gaucho* clubs but was intrigued enough by the myth to found, with other intellectuals, a magazine named after Fierro. Other legends of the pampas caught the public imagination. There was Don Segundo Sombra, the eponymous hero of a hugely popular 1926 novel by Ricardo Güiraldes, and the (mythologised) real-life examples of Santos Vega, a *payador* (an itinerant *gaucho* troubadour) who was undefeated in song-contests, it was said, until the devil himself took him on, and Juan Moreira, a teetotal, guitar-playing outlaw who was supremely gifted at knife-fighting.*

So was there anywhere in the 1920s that the *gaucho* spirit could still be found? For the writers of *El Gráfico*, it could be discovered in the *pibe*. In 1928, Borocotó set out his theory that the *pibe*, playing on the *potreros*, the vacant lots of the burgeoning city, on small uneven pitches, had to learn both tight technical skill and a sense of cunning or streetwiseness to look after himself, had to demonstrate that same blend of virtuosity and self-reliance that characterised the *gaucho*.[6] And, like the *gaucho*, there was a sense the *pibe* existed in opposition to the British; the game of the *pibe* was far removed from the running game based in stamina that was practised on the great grassy pitches of the British schools; on the *potreros* there was no teacher with a whistle waiting to intervene if matters got out of hand.

For Chantecler, another writer for *El Gráfico*, dribbling

---

* The anthropologist Eduardo Archetti, whose work on the centrality of tango and football to Argentinian national identity has been so influential, has demonstrated how Argentinian culture, especially tango, the origins of which are urban, underwent a process of '*gaucho*-isation' in the early part of the twentieth century. ('Gaucho, Tango, Primitivism and Power in the Shaping of Argentine National Identity'). 'Buenos Aires, in spite of being packed with two million individual destinies, will remain deserted and without a voice until a symbol will inhabit her,' Borges wrote. 'The province is people: there are Santos Vega and the gaucho, Cruz and Martín Fierro, possibilities of gods. The city is still awaiting poeticisation.' (*El idioma de los argentinos*, p126)

was expressive of the 'wily and crafty *criollo*',[7] an idea he later expanded into a broader theory of '*viveza criollo*' which incorporated not only skill, imagination and cleverness but also 'disreputable cunning'.[8] Although he was specifically writing of football, Chantecler's ideas were part of a wider movement that celebrated Argentina's *criollo* identity. For Lugones, the *gaucho* was explicitly a character of mixed blood. Domingo Faustino Sarmiento, president from 1868 to 1874, had feared the 'corruption' of European blood in South America[9] but by the early twentieth century, as with Gilberto Freyre's theories in Brazil, 'hybridisation' was perceived as being precisely what would equip Argentina to thrive. Just so long, that is, as it didn't involve Britain; *criollo* is a loose term, meaning somebody of European heritage born in South America, but it was never used of anybody of British parentage.

It didn't take a huge amount of retrofitting to see Argentinian football as having had two births.[10] The game had been introduced by the British community in the 1860s and the league had been established by the Scottish schoolteacher Alexander Watson Hutton in 1893. It was dominated by Anglo clubs until 1913 when Racing became the first Argentinian champions, football serving as a convenient indicator of the British retreat.

In the debates around nationhood, football was recognised as being of great significance. What, after all, connected communities from the jungles of Tucumán in the north to the blasted tundra of Tierra del Fuego in the south, from the Atlantic littoral to the heights of the Andes? The only activity they all really had in common was listening to the radio, and what they were listening to was broadcasts from the tango halls and football stadiums. Support for the national team was one of the very few things that connected all Argentinians, no matter what their background. And while the idea of national character can to an extent be dismissed as unhelpful essentialism, it is relevant when related to football because it was so self-conscious: how the national team played was regarded *at the time* as a direct expression of national character. 'Show me how you play,' as Galeano said, 'and I will tell you who you are.'[11]

The framing of football in contradistinction to the British was of a piece with a more general shift in the feeling towards Britain. Where Sarmiento had seen the British as a civilising force and British capital had been regarded as encouraging liberalism and progress, by the early part of the twentieth century the British came to be considered an obstacle to nationhood and autonomy. For much of the twentieth century, football remained the stage for the meetings of England and Argentina, that oppositional relationship underlying the spikiness of various games, culminating in the notorious quarter-final of 1966. By the 1986 World Cup, in the aftermath of the ill-conceived invasion of the Falklands, the idea of Argentina and England as irreconcilable rivals had been given a whole new impetus. With a sense of inevitability, they met in the quarter-final.

The 1986 tournament had been given to Colombia before Havelange's accession, a decision that was probably doomed from the start. Even before the earthquake that hit the north Andean city of Tumaco in December 1979, claiming six hundred lives, there were concerns that Colombia's preparations were lagging behind. Julio César Turbay, who was elected president in 1978, had neither time nor resources to devote to the World Cup as he fought a left-wing guerrilla insurgency.

Moving the World Cup was probably necessary but, for Havelange, it was also an opportunity; bidding wars meant money sloshing around the system. Only a cynic would see significance in the fact that, after the 1982 final, Havelange boarded a private jet belonging to Emilio Azcarraga, the head of Televisa Mexicana, and flew to Mexico City.[12] After a Fifa inspection found multiple faults, Colombia's new president Belisario Betancur admitted defeat in January 1983. Four countries declared themselves as candidates to take over: Brazil, Canada, Mexico and the US.

Wouldn't Havelange, patriotic Olympian that he was, a leader who insisted his country only ever failed to win World Cups because of conspiracies against them, have backed Brazil? Perhaps at another time he would, but Havelange was trying to install his son-in-law Ricardo Teixeira as head of the CBF; the incumbent, Giulite Coutinho, could not be allowed a propaganda coup.

The decision was taken at the Fifa Congress in Stockholm in May 1983. Mexico's presentation lasted a desultory eight minutes. For the US, Henry Kissinger gave a detailed and coherent speech that was entering its second hour when he realised the Mexicans were already celebrating downstairs. For Kissinger this was a personal humiliation: 'it made me nostalgic for the Middle East,' he said.[13]

For US football, already ailing, it was devastating. Perhaps a World Cup could have kept investors interested and perhaps a boom would have followed the tournament but, by 1983, the North American Soccer League was in trouble. The league president Howard J. Samuels described it as 'a major league operating with a minor league income',[14] a situation that was very hard to change with the unemployment rate and interest rate both in double figures. To make matters worse, Warner, one of the league's major backers, was struggling, with one of its subsidiaries, Atari, losing $1m a day. Rosters were cut and a salary cap introduced, which mitigated debts, but by 1984, only nine franchises remained. In 1985, just Minnesota and Toronto were left and the NASL was over.

Mexico had a budget deficit of over US$80bn. Inflation was running at almost 100 per cent. The peso had lost two-thirds of its value over the previous year. Havelange had used the state of its economy to warn off Brazil, but Mexico's was far worse. There were major issues with drug gangs and walls were built to hide the slums. Then on 19 September 1985, a devastating earthquake hit Mexico City, killing over 7,000 people and leaving more than 30,000 homeless.

But Mexico pressed on regardless.

There was still scepticism about the expansion of the World Cup, and the case of Iraq did little to convince the doubters. They had shown flashes of quality at the 1984 Olympics and, leading Yugoslavia 2–0 at half-time in their final group game, they were on course for the quarter-final. After a second-half collapse and a 4–2 defeat, though, the coach Ammo Baba was sacked and replaced by Akram Salman; he immediately recalled the combative midfielder Basil Gorgis and the forward Ahmed Radhi, who had fallen out with Baba in a dispute over the intensity of training.

Radhi was one of a number of players signed later that year by Al Rasheed, a new club founded the previous year in the affluent Baghdad suburb of Mansour by Uday Hussein, the son of the dictator Saddam. They won promotion in their first season and then embarked on a spree, signing a raft of internationals. Al-Rasheed were fourteen points clear at the top of the table when the 1984–85 season was suspended after seventeen games to allow the national team to prepare for the World Cup qualifiers, and the B side to compete in the Arab Cup and the Pan-Arab Games. The B team won both competitions, their winner in the final of the Pan-Arab Games scored by Gorgis. Not long after, his family was told that his sister, who had been arrested at the College of Agriculture five years earlier, had been executed for her activities with the Iraqi Communist Party. On hearing the news, his father suffered a stroke and died.

Uday was not only club president but soon became president of the Iraq football association, after the other candidates in the election mysteriously stepped down. Even as Iraq progressed through the qualifiers – despite war with Iran meaning they had to play home games in Saudi Arabia – he kept sacking coaches; the former Brazil manager Evaristo, who led them into the World Cup, was the fifth of the campaign. Sceptical of Iraq's chances and focusing on hard runners who might at least keep the score down, Evaristo left the thirty-five-year-old creator Falah Hassan out of his squad for Mexico – although Hassan always claimed it was because Uday was jealous of his popularity;[15] after the first Gulf War in 1991, he was forced to go into exile and his name was erased from the record books.

Adidas had offered to provide Iraq with kit. They usually wore white or green or occasionally red but, supposedly because the IFA wanted a kit distinct from that worn by other countries at the tournament, they went for a yellow first kit (only Brazil of the other qualifiers in 1986 wore yellow) and pale blue away kit. Yellow and pale blue happened to be the colours of Uday's club, Al Rasheed. 'We felt alienated,' a player said.[16]

They began against Paraguay, fell behind but seemed to have levelled just before half-time through Radhi; the referee, Edwin Picon-Ackong of Mauritius, though, had blown before the ball crossed the line. Iraq lost 1–0. They lost their discipline in defeat to Belgium and had Gorgis dismissed – although it had actually been Ghanim Oraibi who had stamped on Enzo Scifo.

Uday was not yet in the habit of imprisoning and torturing the national team after performances he deemed substandard,[17] but his interventions clearly undermined the team.

By the mid-eighties, Constitution Day wasn't taken as seriously in Denmark as it once had been, but still most people took the afternoon off work. In 1985, almost everybody did because Denmark were playing the USSR in the biggest World Cup qualifier they had ever been involved in.

Denmark had never qualified for a World Cup. Professionals had only been allowed to play for the national team from 1971 and a professional league had only been established in 1977. Even then, the sense was that the national team was more about the drinking afterwards than the matches themselves.[18] But in 1979, Carlsberg took over sponsorship and targeted World Cup qualification for their investment. Kurt Nielsen was sacked and replaced by Sepp Piontek, who had been born in Breslau in 1940, three years after Denmark's 8–0 defeat there to Herberger's Germany.

As a manager at Werder Bremen and Fortuna Düsseldorf, Piontek had gained a reputation as a martinet but he was mellowed to an extent by stints with Haiti and St Pauli. Denmark saw him as being German but not too German; somebody who could instil discipline without being totally out of sync with the more relaxed Danish footballing culture.

His time in charge of Denmark didn't start auspiciously with defeats in his first five competitive games, but after Piontek changed the team base from the luxurious Marina Hotel in Vedbæk to the Idrættens Hus in Brøndby, a grim concrete block with no phones or televisions in the rooms, performances picked up. The players, Piontek had decided, had to understand that failure had consequences. It was in the qualifiers for Euro 84 that everything came together.

Denmark trailed 2–1 at home to England in the final minute when Jesper Olsen, a wisp of a player, picked up the ball in the inside-left channel and set off goalwards, gliding through two challenges before slipping the equaliser under Peter Shilton. A 1–0 win over England at Wembley later in qualifying ensured they topped the group. They were unlike any side in Europe at the time, playing a direct, attacking, hard-pressing and extremely fluid 3-5-2 with an eclectic mix of players. Some were based at Europe's elite clubs, others were semi-pros; after Piontek had fallen out with Club Brugge's Birger Jensen, his choice in goal for the Euros came down to Ole Qvist, a Copenhagen traffic policeman, and Ole Kjær, who worked in a sports shop in Esbjerg. Denmark played hard and drank hard, a disconcerting blend of furious intensity on the pitch and relaxed indifference off it.

Denmark lost their opening game in France 1–0 to the hosts, but worse than the result was the loss of Allan Simonsen, their Ballon d'Or winner, to a broken leg. They rallied to thrash Yugoslavia 5–0, the first game in which the two forwards Michael Laudrup and Preben Elkjær played together, and then came from 2–0 down in a brilliant, brutal game to beat Belgium and set up a semi-final against Spain.

Between claiming the Euros in 1964 and 2008, Spain only ever won four knockout games in major tournaments. Two of them were against Denmark, and this was the first. It went to penalties, Elkjær missing the decisive kick with his backside showing through his shorts, which had been ripped by a challenge from the Spain goalkeeper Luis Arconada.

If you could reach the last four of the Euros, it stood to reason you could qualify for the World Cup. The qualifying group was not an easy one, featuring not just the Soviets who, after failing to qualify for Euro 84, had temporarily binned the scientific football of Valeriy Lobanovskyi for the 'sincerity' and individualistic attacking of Eduard Malofeev, but also Switzerland and Ireland. Although Denmark lost away to Switzerland, there was enough enthusiasm after wins over Norway and Ireland that when tickets went on sale for the game against the USSR in February, one shopkeeper in the suburb of Valby turned up to find six hundred people had queued overnight to buy his allocation.[19]

By the time the game came round, though, there was a

shadow. A week earlier, thirty-nine fans, mostly Italian supporters of Juventus, had been killed at the European Cup final as a charge by Liverpool fans led to a wall collapsing. That had nothing to do with either the Danes or the Soviets but all of football felt the shock of Heysel, a doubt as to whether football had any future.

A strike at the Carlsberg factory meant that until the day before the game, when a deal was done with the Belgian brewers Palm, there was a danger it might not be possible to serve beer at Parken. The game alone would have been enough to intoxicate the packed crowd. Elkjær and Laudrup were both brilliant and both scored twice, but the Soviets were superb as well. 'The tempo was crazy,' said the defender Søren Busk. 'My tongue was hanging out of my mouth all the time.'[20] It finished 4–2 to Denmark but there was a sense that the spectacle had been vital. 'One week before football died,' the commentator Svend Gehrs said. 'The week after it stood up from the grave.'[21] It was that night that the Danish newspaper coined the term '*roligans*' – from '*rolig*', the Danish for calm – to describe Denmark's drunk but benign fans.

As it turned out, both sides qualified, but by the time the World Cup began, Lobanovskyi had returned after the USSR lost four friendlies in a row. 'Malofeev became very nervous, and there was no clear pattern to our football,' the Dynamo Minsk midfielder Sergei Aleinikov said. The final straw came in May with 'a colourless 0–0 draw' against Finland at Luzhniki.[22] At the same time, Lobanovskyi's Dynamo Kyiv were playing awe-inspiring football, the apotheosis of his vision, on their way to the Cup Winners' Cup.

Malofeev was called away from the training camp at Novogorsk and didn't return. Instead, back came Lobanovskyi. 'Lobanovskyi made us train harder,' said Aleinikov. 'To say it was difficult would be an understatement. In the evening I was just looking to get to bed as soon as possible. For Lobanovskyi the game was about the result, not about fun. Football had to be rational. For him, 1–0 was better than 5–4.'[23]

But his methods worked, at least at first. Hungary were much fancied, but the USSR hammered them 6–0 as they finished top of their group to set up a last-sixteen tie against Belgium. Aleinikov was the only outfielder in the Soviet line-up not at Dynamo Kyiv. They dominated for long periods but, undone by individual errors and poor refereeing, lost 4–3 after extra time.

Denmark's campaign in Mexico took on a doomed beauty. An acclimatisation trip to Bogotá was ill-omened from the start. The manager of the Hilton where they stayed gleefully told the players they were a prime target for kidnap. A rep for the manufacturer of their striking red and white kit, Hummel, was mugged on the steps of the hotel. After a car accident outside the hotel, a corpse was left in full view for several hours. And training was hard, perhaps too hard. Players sensed that the German side of Piontek's personality had kicked in again. 'Sepp was trying to win the World Cup,' said Ivan Nielsen. 'We just wanted a beer!'[24]

But the preparations seemed to have paid off. Scotland, under the management of Alex Ferguson after Jock Stein had collapsed on the touchline at the end of their crucial qualifier away to Wales, dying soon after, were a difficult, canny side, but Denmark beat them 1–0. Although adorned with the talent of Enzo Francescoli, Uruguay – whose manager Omar Borrás had coined the term '*Grupo de la Muerte*' after the draw – were brutal. Elkjær scored a hat-trick as they were beaten 6–1, Uruguay fortunate to have only one man sent off.

Against Scotland, José Batista then set a record for the earliest red card in a World Cup game, dismissed after 56 seconds for a lunge on Gordon Strachan. At the same time, Denmark met West Germany, a strange game in which the winners knew they would face Spain in the last sixteen, while the losers would have an ostensibly easier tie against Morocco. Much was made in the build-up of the clash between the Verona duo of Elkjær and the former decathlete Hans-Peter Briegel, Danish flair against German discipline; flair won 2–0, but it came at a cost.

A couple of days before the game, Frank Arnesen's wife Kate had fallen ill. At first, it was thought she had sunstroke, but as she lost the ability to speak, it became apparent she had meningitis. Arnesen spent forty-eight hours sitting by her bedside but insisted on playing.[25] Already booked for diving when he had been fouled by Ditmar Jakobs, Arnesen was fouled late on by Lothar Matthäus, flicked out his heel in response and was sent off for retaliation. After the game restarted, it carried on for just 35 seconds before the final whistle blew.

And so was set in train the chain of events that would lead to Denmark's elimination. Piontek already thought he had detected a shift in the mood after the group stage, a sense the players felt they had proved their point, that homesickness was beginning to kick in.[26]

The night before the last-sixteen game against Spain, John Sivebæk went down with a stomach problem. That meant Olsen switching to the other flank as Henrik Andersen came in. He put Denmark ahead with a penalty but then, just before half-time, Tómas Reñones skewed a cross out for a goal-kick. Had the cross been better, it would not have been a goal-kick. Had Sivebæk not been ill, Olsen would have been on the other flank. Had Arnesen not been suspended – had he been subbed off as he often was, had he not been exhausted from his bedside vigil, had Matthäus not kept playing when most of his team-mates had given up – Olsen would not have been on the pitch. For the want of a nail, the kingdom was lost.

Lars Høgh, the goalkeeper, took the goal-kick short to Olsen who shimmied past Julio Salinas with a deft stepover. He could have played it down the line. Høgh assumed he would. But Olsen expected Høgh to move square to receive a return and passed the ball blind across the top of his own box, where Emilio Butragueño, the arch-poacher, was waiting: 1–1. 'Jesper, Jesper, Jesper,' Gehrs said on commentary, 'That one is lethal.'

Butragueño, unmarked, headed in a corner 12 minutes into the second half and Denmark, chasing the game, fell apart. Spain won 5–1, Butragueño getting four of them. It could have been a repeat of Denmark against the USSR in the quarter-final; instead, Belgium beat Spain on penalties.

The Danish Dynamite era, which had begun with Jesper Olsen's solo goal against England, had ended with Jesper Olsen's misplaced pass.

Democracy had returned to Brazil in 1985 with the election of Tancredo Neves, who died before he was able to take office, having refused to seek treatment for what turned out to be cancer for fear of giving the generals an excuse to cancel elections.[27] José Sarney, who had been a member of the pro-dictatorship party until a year earlier, stepped in. But democracy proved not to be a panacea, and for Sócrates at least, the mood approaching the World Cup was of disillusionment.

With Sócrates playing for Fiorentina in Italy, Corinthian Democracy had come to an end on 1 April 1985 with the election as club president of the octogenarian conservative Roberto Paschoa, the democratic project defeated at the ballot box.[28] Sócrates returned to Brazil with Flamengo and found the temptations of Rio de Janeiro hard to resist. As his marriage fell apart, he began drinking increasingly heavily, and there was scandal when he judged carnival floats while obviously inebriated.[29]

As Brazil cycled through coaches, before ending up back with Telê Santana, Sócrates drifted in and out of the national side. He was included in Santana's pre-World Cup training camp in Belo Horizonte, using the same facilities they'd used in preparing for Spain, but he was frustrated. He'd struggled for weeks with a persistent thigh niggle and he hated camps like these. Corinthian Democracy had managed to replace them, yet with actual democracy, it felt nothing had changed. They were in the same camp, run by the same officials as four years earlier. One of them, José Maria Marin, head of the CBF when Brazil hosted the World Cup in 2014, was clearly implicated in the apparatus of state control that had resulted in thousands of instances of torture and death under the dictatorship.[30] 'Nobody,' Sócrates said, 'has the guts to change anything.'[31]

At the same time, the CBF was short of cash. There was little clarity on bonuses or, for a long time, on where Brazil would base themselves in Mexico. Although the source of Sócrates's thigh problem was determined in time for him to be fully fit for the start of the tournament, Zico kept aggravating a twisted knee. Then on the eve of the World Cup, the right-back Leandro withdrew from the squad – he said because of his knee, although he was unhappy at being asked to play at full-back rather than in the centre where he played for Flamengo; others wondered whether his decision was related to the omission of his close friend Renato Gaúcho.

Compared to the meticulous preparation of previous World Cups, it all felt shambolic. But Brazil progressed through the group smoothly enough. The absence of Leandro unleashed Josimar, who followed up a long-ranger against Northern Ireland with an even better goal in a 4–0 win over Poland in the last sixteen. Brazil, it seemed, had found their rhythm. Their quarter-final opponents were France, the other loser from the 1982 tournament's pair of epic games.

For Brazil, 1982 marked an ending; for France it was another stage in their development under Michel Hidalgo. Platini had signed for Juventus six weeks before the World Cup; by the time he played a league game for them, six of his team-mates were world champions. He brought a winning mentality back to the France squad, made them more professional.[32] The *carré magique* was reconfigured, with Luis Fernandez, a more naturally deep-lying figure, replacing Genghini. The result was an extravagantly brilliant triumph on home soil at Euro 84, Platini scoring nine goals in five games.

Hidalgo quit at the top and was replaced by Henri Michel, who had led France to gold at the 1984 Olympics. In a tough group, they drew with the USSR before sealing progress with a 3–0 win over Hungary. A pair of cleverly worked counter-attacks took them past the ageing world champions Italy in the last sixteen.

And then the classic against Brazil. Careca swept Brazil into an early lead, but Platini, on his thirty-first birthday, rolled in a deflected Dominique Rocheteau cross to level just before half-time. Careca headed against the bar and Zico, having come off the bench, had a penalty saved in an end-to-end second half. And then, five minutes from the end of extra time, came a reminder of traumas past as Bruno Bellone, running on to Platini's through-ball, nudged the ball past the goalkeeper Carlos, who grabbed at him just outside the box. Bellone stayed up, but he had been forced wide and cover got back. As Brazil broke, Sócrates somehow failed to turn a Careca cross into an open net at the other end. It wasn't as violent as Schumacher's assault on Battiston, but Carlos had been just as cynical. 'In those days it wasn't a red card,' the keeper said, 'so you did what you did.'[33]

This time, though, France were not to be cheated. Joël Bats saved from Sócrates and, although Platini skied his effort, Júlio César thumped his kick against the post. Crucially, Bellone's penalty had hit the post, bounced back onto Carlos and gone in; in a shoot-out, it shouldn't have counted, but this time the refereeing error favoured France.

After the disappointment of the 1982 World Cup, Menotti had been replaced as Argentina manager by Carlos Bilardo. Any pretence Argentina were reinvoking the days of *la nuestra* vanished. Bilardo, a qualified gynaecologist, had been part of Osvaldo Zubeldía's aggressive and cynical Estudiantes, a remarkable figure who combined running his parents' furniture store with being one of the most feared midfielders of his generation, somebody so desperate to win that he would supposedly take pins onto the pitch with him to stab opponents.[34]

Menotti was soon sniping at Bilardo, and Bilardo wasn't slow to respond. 'Football is played to win,' he said. 'Shows are for the cinema, for the theatre ... Football is something else.'[35] Everything about them seemed opposed. 'Menotti,' said the central defender Juan Simón, who played for both, 'is laid-back, relaxed, always measured, his speech full of metaphors. Bilardo, on the other hand, was pure vertigo, talking quickly and with a bunch of ideas that you had to process. You could only understand half of the things he said, but you could recognise his knowledge and wisdom. He knew what he wanted, he knew how to achieve it. Menotti left more for individuals to resolve, trusting in an absolute conviction in his ideas and how to impose them, while Bilardo relied more on his tactical wisdom and studying the opposition; he depended less on individuals and more on the team as a whole.'[36]

There was an irony here, a reminder that football teams should never be considered a direct representation of the state whose name they bear. Under the junta, Argentina's coach had been, at least notionally, a leftist romantic trying to recreate the glorious freedoms and self-expression of half a century earlier; as democracy returned in 1983, the national team was placed in the hands of a ruthless pragmatist, a coach for whom the ends justified the means.

For a long time, it seemed not to be working. Argentina won just four of their first twelve games under Bilardo and, not helped by a tough draw, didn't make the semi-finals of the 1983 Copa América. After Bilardo's house had twice been attacked, he would have his wife put up a 'Sold' sign before key games to deter would-be vandals.

Part of the problem was Maradona. After his red card at the 1982 World Cup, he didn't play again for Argentina for almost three years. He'd moved to Barcelona soon after that World Cup, but never settled. He suffered from homesickness and loneliness, and then from hepatitis, fell out with club officials, developed a cocaine habit and suffered a horrific broken ankle after a disgraceful foul by the Athletic defender Andoni Goikoetxea. When Athletic then beat Barça in an ill-tempered Copa del Rey final, Maradona reacted by kicking the substitute Miguel Ángel Sola in the head as he knelt in celebration, knocking him unconscious and sparking a mass brawl. He was banned for three months and, with a degree of relief, Barça accepted a world record $13m offer for him from Napoli in the summer of 1984.

Bilardo had gone to see Maradona in January 1983 as he recovered from hepatitis on the Costa Brava. As they jogged along the beach together, Bilardo made clear that Maradona was central to his thinking and offered him the captaincy, although he wouldn't actually play again for the national side until a friendly against Paraguay in May 1985.

Without Maradona, Bilardo was able to experiment and on a tour of Europe in September 1984, he made the tactical tweak that would ultimately lead to World Cup glory. Realising that hardly anybody played with wingers any more, he decided to do away with the full-back, using his midfielders to cover the entire flank in a 3-5-2. Others, notably Sepp Piontek with Denmark and Ćiro Blažević with Dinamo Zagreb, did something similar at around the same time, but there's no reason to doubt Bilardo's claim that he came up with the idea independently. On that tour, Argentina played Switzerland, Belgium and West Germany and, with their new system, won each game by two goals. At which Bilardo, much like Ramsey in 1966, hid away his big idea so that no rival should get wind of what he was doing.

Argentina wouldn't even have qualified for the World Cup had Daniel Passarella not cleared a shot off the line with nine minutes remaining of the final qualifier, against Peru. But Bilardo's football was all about peaking at the right time. A 7–2 win over Israel in their final friendly before Mexico was their first win in seven games. Passarella then left the squad after clashing with Maradona, who had replaced him as captain. Nobody expected much from Argentina and, as Maradona put it, fans watched the opening group game, a 3–1 win over South Korea, 'with their eyes half-closed'.[37]

A draw against Italy and a 2–0 win over Bulgaria meant Argentina topped the group and set up a last-sixteen tie against Uruguay. Weakened by suspensions, Uruguay scrapped hard against their neighbours, but a Pedro Pasculli goal just before half-time carried Argentina through.

When Antonio Macedo's late header eliminated West Germany from Euro 84, the reaction across Europe was one of relief. 'German football, this brute animal, deserved to be drowned in its own urine,' observed the French newspaper *Libération*.[38] Jupp Derwall may have led them to the European title in 1980 and the World Cup final two years later, but he was asked to stand aside.

Hermann Neuberger, the head of the DFB, saw Franz Beckenbauer as the sort of clean-cut figure who could inaugurate a new era, but Beckenbauer had made clear that he had no interest in coaching. Neuberger's second choice was Helmut Benthaus, a composed and intelligent forty-nine-year-old who had just led Stuttgart to the Bundesliga title. But Benthaus was unsure about the national job and would, anyway, have found it difficult to escape his contract.

Neuberger was at a loss, but two days after the defeat to Spain came unexpected salvation as the tabloid *Bild* ran the headline, 'Franz: I'm ready.'[39] It was a story confected by the sports editor and Beckenbauer's agent, but it had the desired effect. As public pressure mounted, Beckenbauer, feeling 'a moral obligation', agreed to speak with Neuberger and was persuaded to take the job until Benthaus could be sprung from his contract.[40] As it turned out, Stuttgart had a poor season in 1984–85 and Benthaus returned to Basel, his candidacy for the national job forgotten.

Because of his lack of qualifications, Beckenbauer was officially described as '*Teamchef*' – team boss – rather than coach. He was scathing of his side, which featured Rudi Völler, an ageing Rummenigge and not a lot else. He did manage to persuade the Hamburg playmaker Felix Magath to return to the national set-up after falling out with Derwall, but Bernd Schuster, the most gifted West German player of his generation, remained beyond him. Beckenbauer had telephoned him at his home in Barcelona but got his wife, Gaby, who said Schuster would only consider coming back for DM1m.[41] Beckenbauer may have been the leader of Germany's first commercially minded generation, but even for him that was too much.

There were, Beckenbauer said, 'no artists; just reliable men, most of them blind'.[42] But that could still take a team a long way, provided they still demonstrated what Beckenbauer referred to as the 'proverbial German values: fighting spirit and solid defending'.[43] Other characteristics remained: players broke curfew, insulted the manager and threatened to fly home.

Uli Stein, frustrated at being reserve goalkeeper behind Harald Schumacher, who described him as 'a poisonous presence', was at the heart of much of the discontent.[44] When it transpired he was calling Beckenbauer '*Suppenkasper*' behind his back – a reference to the Knorr adverts Beckenbauer had done in the sixties and to a character from a German children's book – he was sent home, against Beckenbauer's wishes. Stein denied this in his memoir and claimed he was only second choice because of pressure from Adidas.[45] Matters got so bad that Beckenbauer offered to quit; Neuberger rejected his resignation and Beckenbauer, realising he quite enjoyed coaching, stayed on.[46]

Despite going behind in all three group games, West Germany clawed their way through in second, then beat Morocco with an 88th-minute Lothar Matthäus winner before two saves from Schumacher saw them through a penalty shoot-out against Mexico. That set up a semi-final against France and this time few protested about the result, even if it did seem slightly cruel that it should be Battiston who gave away the free-kick from which Andreas Brehme put West Germany ahead. Völler made it 2–0 in the 89th minute.

Argentina proved too good in the final, but even being there seemed incredible. 'Can you believe,' Beckenbauer once asked, bursting into laughter during a newspaper interview, 'that we reached the World Cup final with those players?'[47]

Solid rather than spectacular, Bobby Robson's England, having failed to qualify for Euro 84, had cruised unbeaten through qualifying, conceding just twice in their eight games. But in what would become a feature of his side at major tournaments, they began the group stage badly. After losing 1–0 to an unfancied Portugal, they drew 0–0 with Morocco, a game in which, in a five-minute spell just before half-time, they lost their captain Bryan Robson to a dislocated shoulder and his fellow midfielder Ray Wilkins to a red card for throwing the ball at the referee. Robson switched shape and his reward was a hat-trick for Lineker against Poland and two more as Paraguay were dismissed 3–0 in the last sixteen. That set up a quarter-final against Argentina.

'Before the match, we said that football had nothing to do with the Malvinas War,' said Maradona, 'but we knew a lot of Argentinian kids had died there.'[48] England would subsequently claim the moral high ground because of the nature of Maradona's first goal but Terry Fenwick, who had been set to man-mark him, could easily have been sent off for fouls on Maradona before half-time. Maradona's two goals, scored after 51 and 55 minutes, captured the twin faces of the *pibe*. First, as he nudged Steve Hodge's sliced clearance past Peter Shilton with his hand, there was the cunning, the ethical code that says right is whatever you can get away with. Then came the virtuosity, spinning in his own half and slaloming through England defenders to score 'the goal you dream of as a kid ... in the *potrero*'.[49]

As John Barnes came on and began to exploit the space behind the right wing-back, Lineker pulled one back, but England had adopted the proactive approach too late. And besides, by then this was Maradona's tournament, his destiny. He scored two fine goals in the semi-final against Belgium and, while he was more subdued in the final against West Germany, he and Matthäus effectively cancelling each other out, he ultimately had a decisive impact. Goals from José Luis Brown and Jorge Valdano had Argentina two up after 55 minutes, but Rummenigge and Völler struck in the space of six minutes to level. At which, for the first time, Maradona found a space on halfway, jabbing a first-time through-ball for Jorge Burruchaga to run on and score the winner.

As with Italy at the previous World Cup, though, the sense was that the big game had come two matches before the final.

England in 86 were not at the level of Brazil in 82, but that was the game that had to be won, that engendered belief and that is remembered most fondly by the eventual champions. The *gaucho* had had his revenge on England.

1990

WIND OF CHANGE

Ivo Knoflíček was Czechoslovakia's striker and had a distinct sense he had outgrown Slavia Prague. He had scored fine goals on the break in both Euro 88 qualifiers against Wales, and that had attracted the attention of Derby County, whose owner Robert Maxwell had been born in Czechoslovakia. But Knoflíček was twenty-six and the regulations said that Czechoslovak players couldn't move abroad until they were thirty-one. So he decided to defect.

In November 1988, Slavia went on a winter training camp to Hanover in West Germany. An hour before the Slavia bus set off back to Prague, Knoflíček slipped away, leaving his wife and family in the capital. But he did take his room-mate, the twenty-four-year-old Slavia full-back Luboš Kubík. They had to leave their passports behind, but managed to get into Belgium, where they were threatened by a member of the Czechoslovak secret police,[1] and then moved to Spain, living in a former monastery owned by the Guinness family, which had recently made a major loan to Maxwell. There, Bolivian passports were secured for them, which allowed them to travel via Gibraltar to Derby. All the while, Maxwell was sending money to their families.

The players were installed in a flat above an Italian

restaurant and impressed in training, as negotiations went on to try to secure their transfer. Eventually Kubík, frustrated by the lack of football and worried for his family, decided to return to Prague.[2]

Derby had regarded them as a pair, so Knoflíček went to Italy, where he trained with Juventus and Foggia. It became apparent that he would be allowed to play after an eighteen-month break, and St Pauli agreed to sign him on those terms.

The collapse of the Communist regimes of eastern Europe came gradually, then all at once. Mikhail Gorbachev had initiated reforms in 1985 in response to severe economic problems, which affected the USSR's relationship with its satellite states,[3] leading in July 1989 to the formal abandonment of the Brezhnev Doctrine that proclaimed that any threat to socialist rule in any of the Warsaw Pact countries was a threat to them all, justifying intervention.[4] At the same time, East Germany was in trouble, its debt to the West growing rapidly. There was an awareness that it could no longer afford its welfare programme – and if that disappeared, so too did the whole ideological justification for state socialism.[5]

Hungary and Poland had already begun to institute democratic reforms and, in May 1989, barbed wire began to be removed from the border between Hungary and Austria. On 10 September, the border was officially opened for East German citizens; at a stroke, the Berlin Wall was rendered meaningless. Tens of thousands of East German citizens travelled south-east through Czechoslovakia to Hungary and round through Austria into West Germany. Initially, East Germany responded by closing the border to Czechoslovakia. But that was clearly untenable. On 1 November, travel between Czechoslovakia and West Germany was legalised and then, via a series of confused and contradictory statements, directly between East and West Germany although, ultimately, it was the weight of crowds that led to the euphoric scenes on the night of 9 November as thousands crossed from East Berlin into the West.[6]

One by one the dominoes fell. Communist government came to an end in Poland in August. Hungary and Bulgaria soon followed. In December, street protests overthrew the Ceauşescu regime in Romania; he and his wife were shot dead on Christmas Day. Four days after that, Václav Havel was appointed the first post-Communist president of Czechoslovakia as the culmination of the Velvet Revolution. Suddenly all Czechoslovak players were free. Knoflíček could start playing in the Bundesliga and Kubík joined Fiorentina.

Kubík was reselected for the national side almost immediately, and scored twice in a crucial qualifying win against Portugal in October 1989. Knoflíček had to wait, with a widespread feeling that those who had got Czechoslovakia to the World Cup deserved to play in it. But he was recalled in April 1990 for a 4–2 friendly defeat against England at Wembley, the match that secured Paul Gascoigne his trip to the tournament. The coach Jozef Vengloš had to switch from 4-4-2 to 3-5-2 to accommodate him, but it seemed to work as Knoflíček set up the first for Tomáš Skuhravý and Kubík got the second. Both attempted defectors earned their place in Italy, where Czechoslovakia, in their final tournament before the Velvet Divorce, reached the quarter-final.

The redrawing of the map of eastern Europe meant it was the last tournament not only for Czechoslovakia, but also the USSR, Yugoslavia and West Germany, but this was a time of great upheaval elsewhere. Everywhere, there were narratives and twists and unbearable drama. That the football was largely dreadful, perhaps the worst of any World Cup finals, was almost an irrelevance. Soundtracked by Pavarotti, Italia 90 was the most emotionally fraught, the most melodramatic World Cup there has ever been.

On the opening day of the World Cup, Thomas N'Kono's wife went shopping in Milan. She did not expect her husband to play against Argentina that evening. As a result, she missed him keeping a clean sheet in one of the greatest shocks in World Cup history. The disorganisation that caused her to miss the game was entirely characteristic. Cameroon's players were brilliant and changed perceptions of African football around the world, but they did so in spite of leaders who could be blamed indirectly for their eventual exit.

Everything was chaotic. The Russian Valery Nepomnyashchy, whose previous frontline coaching experience comprised a single season in charge of the Turkmen side Kolhozchi Ashkabat, had travelled to Cameroon in 1988 believing he would be working in youth development, only to be asked to fill the vacancy left by Claude Le Roy, the French manager who had led Cameroon to success in the Cup of Nations earlier that year but had been unable to agree a new contract.

Nepomnyashchy was invited to stay with Joseph Fofe, the minister of youth and sports, just as soon as renovations on his villa in Yaounde were completed. After a few weeks he was told he could move in and left his hotel, only to discover neither the water nor the electricity had been reconnected. He returned to the hotel, leaving most of his belongings, which were then stolen.[7]

Cameroon went out of the 1990 Cup of Nations at the group stage, although Nepomnyashchy maintained that he had sacrificed that tournament so as to peak at the World Cup three months later. As they moved from a preliminary training camp in Bordeaux to Yugoslavia, there was little sign of that as they had to borrow balls and kit from their hosts while Grégoire

M'Bida, who had scored Cameroon's only goal in the 1982 World Cup, was sent home for missing a bus. And then Roger Milla turned up.

Milla was widely regarded as the greatest player in Cameroon's history, but he was thirty-eight and had quit Montpellier the previous year and moved to Réunion in the Indian Ocean. With preparation going badly, though, there were public calls for Milla to be selected. Nepomnyashchy was told that the president Paul Biya wanted him to call up Milla 'to prevent massive unrest in the country'.[8]

'It was brave, but if I had not been up to standard,' said Milla, 'the president would have taken some of the blame.'[9] He arrived at the camp two days before the squad was submitted to Fifa. 'With his very first touch,' Nepomnyashchy said, 'he left the pair of centre-backs, [Benjamin] Massing and [Emmanuel] Kundé, behind, and scored a brilliant goal.'[10] Milla was included.

The goalkeepers Joseph-Antoine Bell and Thomas N'Kono were automatic selections but Bell, significantly, was given the number 1 shirt. They are two of the greatest African keepers of all time, born just fifteen miles and two years apart on opposite sides of Lac Ossa. While each would acknowledge they were inspired to greater heights by the other, their rivalry became problematic. They were not just very different personalities – N'Kono placid, reserved and humble; Bell loquacious, ebullient and self-confident – but very different types of goalkeepers. N'Kono was a great shot-stopper who liked to stay on his line, reacting to the opposition; Bell was far more proactive, preferring to leave his box to sweep up. N'Kono needed the defensive line to play deep; Bell needed it to push up. Every time one replaced the other, it meant a major change for the team as a whole.[11]

N'Kono had been first choice at the 1982 World Cup, but Bell played as Cameroon won the 1984 Cup of Nations.

N'Kono returned as Cameroon lost on penalties in the final of the 1986 Cup of Nations, but Bell was back for the success at the Cup of Nations in 1988, before N'Kono took over again for the poor showing at 1990 Cup of Nations. But when N'Kono got to Yugoslavia, he was told he would be back-up to Bell at the World Cup: 'The coach said he wanted to change the system and play with a keeper like a libero.'[12]

Every warm-up match was lost, although Milla offered some hope by coming off the bench to score twice in a 3–2 defeat to Hajduk Split. Senior players told Nepomnyashchy that they had to be more defensive, so N'Kono played in the final warm-up, which was won 1–0. 'Bell's style didn't always suit the team,' said Nepomnyashchy. His problem was that his two experienced central defenders, Kundé and Massing, were slow, while his two quick central defenders, Victor N'Dip and Jules Onana, were inexperienced. 'That's why it was more logical to choose N'Kono in goal – he was comfortable with his defenders playing deeper.'[13]

But that sounds like post hoc rationalisation. Everybody thought Bell would play against Argentina – until Bell told *France Football* that preparations had been terrible and that a 3–0 defeat against Argentina would be a good result. 'When I saw that magazine, I was appalled,' said Nepomnyashchy. 'He was right, of course, but you can't say things like that in the press.'[14]

On the morning of the game, hours before kick-off, came the order – nobody quite knows from whom – that Bell had to be dropped. 'We have been used through politics to understand that if somebody stands up and says this is not right, then he is a dangerous man,' Bell said.[15]

N'Kono was back in the team: 'I asked, "Five hours before the first game of the World Cup? How can I play?" So I was trying to reach my wife to tell her things had changed. She'd gone shopping with the wives of the other players and this was before mobile phones. I said no way. I had no confidence in the coach. The federation, the minister of sports, seven or eight people were telling me I had to play and I was saying I didn't feel ready.'[16] But eventually, N'Kono was persuaded.

What followed was confirmation of the rise of African football over the previous decade. Maradona, playing with pads over both his shins and his calves, and with a reinforced boot to protect an in-growing toenail, was booed throughout by Milan fans who resented him for his achievements with Napoli. André Kana-Biyik received a very harsh red card just after the hour and Benjamin Massing a very obvious one as he whacked an already tumbling Claudio Caniggia in the final minute; in between François Omam-Biyik, André's brother, scored the winner with a header that squirmed under Nery Pumpido. Cameroon had not just beaten the world champions but had become the first sub-Saharan African side to win a game at the World Cup.

After that, it became about Milla. He scored two after coming off the bench against Romania, celebrating with a loose-hipped wiggle by the corner flag that became his trademark. He got another two against Colombia in the last sixteen, the second after dispossessing the Colombia keeper René Higuita twenty yards outside his box. That set up a quarter-final against England, for whom the World Cup proved even more transformative.

Stretching, Paul Gascoigne gathered the ball in the centre circle ahead of Olaf Thon and bustled forwards. Stefan Reuter closed in and, although Gascoigne shrugged him off, he was forced to turn left, towards Lothar Matthäus. As he sidestepped the West Germany captain, the ball ran away from him a fraction. It wasn't much, but it was enough. Thomas Berthold nipped in, Gascoigne over-reached, lunged and caught him on the ankle. Gascoigne, realising the likely consequence, rushed to the stricken player, arms flapping apologetically. He bent over Berthold, apparently solicitous, and then shoved a hand in his mouth as though he could silence his howls and, by so doing, head off what was coming. He could not. The Brazilian referee José Roberto Wright brandished a yellow card and Gascoigne was out of the final, if England got there.

Gascoigne swallowed, looked to the heavens and set his jaw, but it was too late; the tears were already rolling down his sweat-soaked cheeks. With them, it would come to seem that he washed away the sins of English football.

On 11 May 1985, fifty-six people were killed in a fire at Valley Parade as they watched Bradford City play Lincoln in the Third Division,* prompting the notorious *Sunday Times* editorial that described football as 'a slum sport played in slum stadiums increasingly watched by slum people'; although the language was less than sympathetic, it made the reasonable point that minimum safety and security standards needed to be imposed. Rejecting the notion of subsidy, it went on to argue that if the cost was that some clubs went to the wall, a more streamlined game might be 'leaner, healthier, safer, more prosperous and more fun ... football, like any other professional entertainment, is nothing if it does not draw crowds on its own merits.'[17]

Ten days later came Heysel. Few quibbled when English clubs were banned from European competition.

On 15 April 1989, ninety-seven Liverpool fans were killed

---

* Differing views of the fire are presented by Paul Firth in *Four Minutes to Hell* and Martin Fletcher in *56*. The official inquiry determined it had been caused by a discarded cigarette igniting rubbish that had accumulated under the stand over the course of decades. The fire had then spread rapidly through the wooden stand, escalating when the flammable bituminous roof-felting caught light. There were no extinguishers and many of the doors at the back of the stand were locked. Nobody disputes the safety measures in place were inadequate, but Fletcher makes serious allegations of institutional neglect and more.

by a crush at Hillsborough at the FA Cup semi-final against Nottingham Forest. A second coroner's hearing returned a verdict of 'unlawful killing', blaming 'errors or omissions' by senior police officers, Sheffield Wednesday (whose ground it was), the ambulance service and the certification of the stadium.[18]

The three tragedies, all with different causes, although linked by inadequate and unsafe stadiums, have come to sum up the darkest period of English football. It wasn't just football that was in decline, so too were the industrial heartlands that had dominated the game's professional era. By summer 1985, manufacturing was in retreat, the miners' strike was lost and with it coal as an industry, and steel and shipbuilding were following. In the six years from October 1981, the UK unemployment rate never fell below 10 per cent.[19] The inner cities erupted into riots in Handsworth, Brixton and Tottenham. Yet despite the poverty and misery and anger, a Labour Party riven by in-fighting seemed unable to present meaningful opposition to Thatcherite economic policy.

Every aspect of working-class life, it felt, was being stripped away, including football. Hooliganism had been an issue for a couple of decades but there was an escalation in the spring of 1985 as Millwall fans tore Kenilworth Road apart and Chelsea fans rioted during their Milk Cup semi-final against Sunderland. On the day of the Bradford fire, Ian Hambridge, a fifteen-year-old Leeds fan, was killed when a wall fell on him during trouble in a game at Birmingham. Two and a half weeks later came the Heysel disaster, after which English clubs were banned from Europe. Thatcher demanded something be done, linking terrace violence to clashes on the picket line and the Troubles in Northern Ireland, and calling for an ID card scheme for fans.[20]

What began the recovery, though, was less any government initiative than a change from within. A new sort of fan emerged, making themselves heard through fanzines, which mushroomed over the second half of the decade. Although the quality varied enormously, they shared a general self-deprecatory irony that was difficult to square with violence. The birth of acid house and the widespread use of hallucinogens perhaps contributed to a mellower atmosphere.[21] The decline of industry meant fewer industrial disputes and so fewer clashes on the picket lines; if you weren't fighting police, or seeing others fighting police on the news, why fight them on the terraces? Although the First Division average crowd of 22,681 in the season after the World Cup was the highest for a decade, it was the fifth successive year in which attendances had gone up.

Hillsborough came as a terrible shock. As the fences which had trapped fans came down, so encroaching onto the pitch became taboo. Lord Justice Taylor's report into the disaster, published in January 1990, completed the process, dismissing the ID card scheme but mandating all-seater stadiums for the top two divisions of English football. That in turn suited the newer, more gentrified audience drawn by Italia 90 with its opera, classical backdrop and emotion, and then by the glamour of the Premier League, which launched in 1992. It was a demographic deliberately courted by the FA, as is made clear by their 1991 *Blueprint for the Future of Football*, which encouraged the game 'to move upmarket so as to follow the affluent middle-class consumer'.[22]

Gascoigne was catnip to those middle-class consumers. In the *London Review of Books*, Karl Miller wrote a diary that included a passage, both effusive and prescient, in which he described Gascoigne as 'fierce and comic, formidable and vulnerable, urchin-like and waif-like, a strong head and torso with comparatively frail-looking, breakable legs, strange-eyed, pink-faced, tense and upright, a priapic monolith in the Mediterranean sun'.[23] The poet Ian Hamilton, in a lengthy meditation on Gascoigne in the literary magazine *Granta*, pointed out that 'the warrior's tears were felt as patriotic tears, our tears'.[24] Stuart Pearce, no less working-class and a far less likely blubber, was also sobbing by the end, but that somehow seemed less important. He did not have Gascoigne's childlike energy.

From an England point of view, it was Gascoigne's World Cup and yet, until two months before the tournament, there was no guarantee he would be involved. He was gifted enough that in 1988 Tottenham signed him, aged twenty-one, from Newcastle for a British-record fee of £2.2m, but for all his talent, he remained unreliable, unable to settle off the pitch and ill-disciplined on it. 'He was fat and played only twenty minutes in each half,' as Bobby Robson put it.[25] Gascoigne had made only one start for England when he was given his opportunity in a friendly against Czechoslovakia. By the time the final whistle blew on a 4–2 win, having scored one, set up two and had a hand in the other, Gascoigne was a certain starter.

Yet England did not go to Italy with optimism. Having qualified well, they had lost every game at Euro 88 and, although they were the only side to make it to Italy without conceding a goal in qualifying, they did so as best runner-up. Robson had been hammered on all sides by a vicious media but when he decided not to renew his contract and agreed a deal to take over at PSV Eindhoven after Italia 90, it was treated as treachery. Some of the attacks were startlingly personal. In the end the players declared a media boycott after stories of 'hi-jinks' with a 'stunning' hostess at their hotel.[26]

There were fears too over fans. Moves to press for post-Heysel readmission to European competition had been abandoned in 1988 after violence during the Euros in Düsseldorf, although it was subsequently accepted that was at least in part caused by Dutch and German hooligans. Italia 90 was seen as a test case and, while there were clashes involving

England fans, it was clear that at times they had been the victims of Italians seeking revenge for Heysel and over-aggressive and indiscriminate policing.

And then there were the issues with the captain Bryan Robson, who compounded ongoing problems with his shoulder and heel when he dropped a bed on his toe while drunkenly trying to tip Gascoigne out of it. He was eventually ruled out of the tournament after being substituted in the second game.

By then, though, the glimmers of renaissance had become visible. The miserable draw against Ireland, coupled by memories of how Marco van Basten had destroyed England at Euro 88, led Robson to abandon precedent and switch to a back five against the Netherlands. It worked remarkably well as England had the better of a 0–0 draw. With the back four in place again, a grim 1–0 win over Egypt secured progress.

The sweeper returned against Belgium, the game settled in the final minute of extra time as David Platt volleyed in Gascoigne's free-kick. England weren't playing particularly well, but by then it had ceased to matter.

They probably should have lost the quarter-final; 'We were,' as Terry Butcher put it, 'so, so lucky.'[27] With eight minutes remaining, Cameroon led 2–1, Milla having been fouled by Gascoigne for the penalty that brought the first before laying on the second for Eugène Ekéké. 'We should have closed out the game, but kept going forward, while the defence played too high,' said Nepomnyashchy. 'That's how we got caught twice and were punished with two penalties.'[28] Lineker was brought down for both and converted both. England's winner stemmed from a Gascoigne through-ball behind a high defensive line. With Bell there to mop up outside his box, might the chance have been stifled before Lineker could latch onto it? He certainly thought so: 'We lost against England because of that.'[29]

There were, inevitably, thoughts in Cameroon of what might have been, but they were the first African side to reach a World

Cup quarter-final, an achievement that prompted Fifa to award CAF a third qualifying slot for the 1994 World Cup.

For Ireland, Italia 90 was transformative in even more profound ways. Five months afterwards, Mary Robinson became the first woman to be elected president, promising to tap into the 'vitality and energy that was there in Italy during the World Cup'.[30] Jack Charlton didn't make Ireland a liberal country, but his team was integral to the process of modernisation, such a vital symbol of the mood of change that it felt entirely natural for Robinson to appeal to his example.

Ireland had never qualified for a major tournament; Charlton took them to three. And yet his appointment, in February 1986, was the result of a characteristic Football Association of Ireland fiasco of committee-room politicking. Charlton was effectively appointed Ireland manager by mistake after a misguided attempt to use him to smoke out anti-English feeling before naming the former Liverpool manager Bob Paisley.[31] Charlton had quit as manager of Newcastle United the previous summer disillusioned with modern football[32] and fitted in his interview with the FAI while filming a fishing documentary. At least in popular myth, by the time he was finally appointed, he had forgotten he was ever in the running.[33]

Football in Ireland had been improving for a while, despite the hostility of the Gaelic Athletic Association which, promoting hurling and Gaelic football, dismissed it as the 'garrison game', one of the reasons why the appointment of an Englishman made so many so uneasy.

Charlton went to Mexico, and was unimpressed. Nearly every team, he said, played the same way, building slowly through a playmaker. His team would not do that. 'Ours is basically a hustling game,' Charlton explained. 'We play the ball in behind people, aiming to turn them all the time.'[34]

It wasn't to everybody's taste, but it was effective. Finally enjoying the luck they had never previously enjoyed in qualifying, Ireland made it to Euro 88, where they beat England and drew with the USSR. A first World Cup qualification was sealed with a run of five straight wins. As at the Euros, Ireland faced England first. It was a dire game, Kevin Sheedy cancelling out Gary Lineker's bundled opener. 'No football please, we're British,' read the headline in the following day's *Gazzetta dello Sport*. The 0–0 draw against Egypt that followed was even worse; Ireland always struggled when there was no space to hit behind the full-backs. 'Anybody who sends out a team to play like that should be ashamed of themselves,' said the reliably uninhibited Eamon Dunphy on RTÉ.[35]

But few others in Ireland cared: they were revelling in being part of a tournament; in the sense of patriotic unity, both in Italy and back home, in the stadiums and the bars; in that feeling of life suddenly being rearranged around the schedule of matches. Football offered a sense of participation in a global event other sports could not; the Gaelic Athletic Association seemed parochial by comparison.

There was a symbolic potency to that. The Church supported the GAA to the extent that it would not allow football to be played on any of its property, and that the Ireland internationals Ray Treacy and Eoin Hand had been beaten for playing the game by the Christian Brothers who ran their schools.[36] The Church had come to be seen as a repressive power holding Ireland back, sequestering it from the wider world; playing football at the World Cup, by definition, was engagement with that wider world. As the author Declan Lynch had it, what Jack Charlton achieved with Ireland represented a liberation 'from all that bullshit of ours about the great poets and the great patriots and the great saints'.[37] In his enormously successful 2005 book *The Pope's Children*, the economist David McWilliams argued that in the 1980s Irish society was divided between the Hibernian – Catholicism, nationalism and the GAA – and the Cosmopolitan – liberalism, metropolitanism and Europe.[38] Football, or rather success in football, drew the two together.

Ireland needed a draw against the Netherlands from their final group game to go through. They fell behind to Ruud Gullit but, with 19 minutes remaining, Berry van Aerle, in attempting to deal with a monstrous kick from Packie Bonner, skewed the ball towards his own goal. It squirmed out of the grasp of the goalkeeper Hans van Breukelen and Niall Quinn forced the loose ball over the line. 'I was glad I was Irish,' wrote the novelist Roddy Doyle. 'I'd never felt that way before.'[39]

And it got better. Ireland beat Romania on penalties in the last sixteen – the Taoiseach Charles Haughey suspended a press conference following a summit of European leaders to watch – before losing narrowly to Italy in the quarter-final. A quarter of a million people, 5 per cent of the entire country, turned out in Dublin to welcome the squad home. It had been an extraordinary, hallucinatory three weeks. So focused was everybody on the World Cup that Dublin Bus stopped running services during games while Mick Jagger and Prince both had concerts at Lansdowne Road cancelled. On match days and the day after there was mass absenteeism and nobody seemed to care. As the journalist Con Houlihan's famous quip had it, 'I missed the World Cup. I was in Italy at the time.'

Over the course of the tournament, it's estimated as many as 30,000 fans made their way to Italy, often having to take out loans to do so. That became a social phenomenon in itself, a point made by the feminist writer Nell McCafferty. For many, this was their first experience of abroad, at least beyond a package holiday; dealing with everyday logistics, booking travel and accommodation, inevitably offered new perspectives and weakened ties to the old Ireland.[40]

Charlton himself had done that, in part simply by offering

a different version of Englishness to the cliché of the cruel landowner or the duplicitous civil servant. Blunt and uncomplicated, fond of fishing and a drink, as Lynch put it, 'this was the sort of Englishman we *could* take orders from'.[41] His policy of seeking Ireland-qualified players from the diaspora, the likes of Mick McCarthy, Ray Houghton and John Aldridge, meanwhile forced a reassessment of the complications of Irish identity: 'You've always exported people,' Charlton said. 'And it's nice of them to come back and help you out now and again.'[42]

Of all the countries that played their last tournament in 1990, none left with such a sense of regret as Yugoslavia.* 'Maybe I am an optimist,' Ivica Osim, Yugoslavia's coach in 1990, said almost twenty years later, 'but in my private dreams I wonder what would have happened if Yugoslavia had played in the semi-final or the final ... maybe there would have been no war if we'd won the World Cup.'[43] But Yugoslavia did not get that far and, as even Osim acknowledges, by the summer of 1990 war was almost certainly inevitable. It may have been since the death of Tito in 1980.

The second round of Croatia's first democratic elections since 1938 were held in May 1990. The Croatian Democratic Union (HDZ), led by Franjo Tuđman, were overwhelming winners. Tuđman had fought with Tito's partisans during the Second World War and then worked as a historian until he was jailed in 1972 after campaigning for greater freedoms for Croatia as part of the Croatian Spring. As the regime in Belgrade creaked under the strain of a collapsing economy, Tuđman invited back several emigré Croats, many of whom had been accused of war crimes, and courted comparison with the Ustaše, the Croatian fascists who had collaborated with Nazi Germany, partly in his

* They did compete as Yugoslavia again in 1998, but by then only Serbia and Montenegro remained in the union.

use of the *šahovnica*, the red-and-white chequerboard emblem that had been their symbol, but also more directly. 'Thank God,' he had said six weeks before the vote, 'my wife is not a Jew or a Serb.'[44]

A week after Tuđman's elections, as Zagreb simmered with nationalist sentiment, a league game at the Maksimir Stadium between Dinamo Zagreb and Crvena Zvezda* of Belgrade was abandoned amid running battles between nationalist ultras on both sides, Dinamo's Bad Blue Boys (BBB) and the Delije of Zvezda. The Delije at the time were led by Željko Ražnatović – better known as Arkan – who was on Interpol's most wanted list throughout the seventies and eighties. His Tigers, many of them drawn from the Delije, perpetrated numerous atrocities during the war. Arkan had been indicted by the International Criminal Tribunal for crimes against humanity when he was gunned down in the lobby of the Belgrade Intercontinental in 2000.

As fights rolled along the terraces and onto the pitch, Dinamo's twenty-one-year-old captain Zvonimir Boban, a key member of the Yugoslavia side that had won the Under-20 World Cup in Chile three years earlier, launched a flying kick at a police officer who was laying into a Dinamo fan with a baton, becoming a reluctant hero of the BBB. Zvezda's captain, Dragan Stojković, remembers his side locking themselves in the dressing-room as chaos raged outside.[45] In total, there were 132 arrests, while seventy-nine police and fifty-nine fans were injured in what some like to portray as the first battle of the war.

Three weeks later, Osim's Yugoslavia played their final warm-up game for the World Cup at the Maksimir, against the Netherlands. Local fans turned their backs at the national anthem and chanted for the Dutch, who won 2–0. The

---

* Red Star.

experienced sweeper Faruk Hadžibegić, a Bosnian Muslim, was picked up by a TV microphone saying, 'There are eleven of us and 22,000 Croatians.'

The history of Yugoslav football to that point was of narrow failure and near misses. There were always rumours that when pressure was on they were undermined by tension between different ethnicities, talk even of a 'key' that stipulated how many players from each republic should be selected.

Hadžibegić, though, insisted that in 1990, there was no such ill-feeling. The reaction of the crowd at the Maksimir came as 'a very bad surprise. It really unsettled us.'[46] There was a far greater surprise coming. When the psychologist at his club FK Sarajevo, an award-winning poet, was jailed for fraud after using government funding meant for agriculture to build a house in the ski resort of Pale,[47] Hadžibegić had visited him in prison, taking him cigarettes.[48] By 1989, the poet-psychologist had co-founded a pro-Serb party in Bosnia and by 1992 he had been elected president of the Republika Srpska, the Bosnia Serb administration. In 2016, Radovan Karadžić was convicted of genocide, war crimes and crimes against humanity in the Hague and sentenced to forty years' imprisonment.

In Italy, Yugoslavia had the misfortune to start by running into one of West Germany's great World Cup performances, losing 4–1. A nervy 1–0 win over Colombia followed by a 4–1 victory over UAE took them through to a last-sixteen tie against Spain. The Yugoslav media, though, was unconvinced. A photograph of empty bottles that had been found outside the hotel restaurant was used as supposed evidence that Osim was clandestinely a heavy drinker.

But a 2–1 extra-time win over Spain silenced a lot of the abuse. Stojković scored both goals, feigning to smash a volley before casually stepping round a defender and dinking the first and then whipping in a free-kick. He made a point of running to Osim in his celebration; the players at least were behind their coach.

Before the quarter-final against Argentina, there came a problem – at least according to Osim. Srečko Katanec insists he was merely injured, but Osim claimed that the midfielder, who had been born in Slovenia to Croatian parents, received death threats. 'How could he play?' Osim asked.[49]

The key figure turned out to be Refik Šabanadžović. Set to man-mark Maradona, he was booked early for encroaching at a free-kick, and then sent off on the half-hour after collecting a second yellow card for a foul on the Argentinian. Even then, Yugoslavia had the better of it, but the game went to penalties. Stojković, who had only previously missed one penalty in his career, fired over. Maradona also missed, as did Pedro Troglio and Dragoljub Brnović. That meant that Hadžibegić had to score to keep Yugoslavia in the competition. Sergio Goycochea saved.

The following season, Zvezda, with a starting XI that featured four Serbs, two Montenegrins, two Macedonians, a Croatian, a Bosnian Muslim and a Romanian of Serb descent, won the European Cup, one final glorious celebration of the Yugoslav ideal. Between the two legs of the epic semi-final win over Bayern, though, the first ordnance of the war had been fired. Four weeks after the final, a year less a day after the victory over Spain, Slovenia and Croatia declared independence. Yugoslavia still qualified for the finals of Euro 92, but four days after they had beaten Austria in their final qualifier, the eastern Croatian town of Vukovar fell to the Yugoslav army following a three-month siege. As the UN imposed sanctions, Yugoslavia were expelled from Euro 92, which was won by Denmark, the team who had replaced them.

Stojković rejects any notion the game against Argentina was anything other than a football match, but Hadžibegić, like Osim, remains haunted by his miss. 'We can,' he said, 'all imagine the scenario whether it's true or not. It was a very talented generation, a great generation. You can imagine the euphoria if we'd been world champions.'[50]

By the time of that quarter-final, Argentina were not really playing football. The defeat to Cameroon had tipped them into a trance in which the usual rules didn't apply and all they were able to do was keep on advancing by whatever means they could. Maradona, half-fit, was a shadow of what he had been four years earlier, and yet still had the capacity to produce moments that won matches.

After the 1986 World Cup, Argentina had relapsed into the sort of miserable form that had characterised them before. Maradona inspired Napoli to the first *scudetto* in their history in 1986–87, the culmination of a year of golden form. He celebrated that success at a party with Camorra bosses and was never quite the same again. He clashed with team-mates and coaches and struggled constantly with injuries. In 1988–89, Napoli won the Uefa Cup but finished eleven points behind the champions Inter, and Maradona was jeered when he limped out of a late-season game against Pisa. Many blamed his hectic socialising, which was common knowledge despite a convention that the press did not report it.

Railing at his critics, Maradona insisted he was the victim of a conspiracy – and while that was probably a reflection of his paranoia, it was true that his sister's flat and his car had been damaged, and that there had been a break-in at his own apartment during which nothing was taken but objects were moved around. Could that have been the Camorra offering a warning?

Unsure he wanted to return to Italy, Maradona married in Buenos Aires Cathedral, an ostentatiously opulent affair at which it was rumoured that cocaine and prostitutes had been provided to guests. Against the backdrop of economic crisis, it was a public relations disaster, the first time his public image in Argentina had begun to suffer. Several kilograms overweight,[51] Maradona eventually went back to Napoli after photographs of him in the company of the Giuliano crime family were published in *Il Mattino*.[52] Was that the Camorra pulling Maradona back in to line?

He was palpably unfit and, that November, an hour before a Uefa Cup tie against the Swiss side Wettingen, he was suspended by the club. The World Cup was only eight months away but with that to aim for, Maradona set himself to regaining fitness. Napoli had done well without him and as he returned they accelerated, going top on the penultimate weekend of the season before claiming the second title in their history. It would be thirty-four years before they won another.

Argentina needed a good World Cup. The currency was collapsing and inflation raging, street demonstrations had become commonplace and the military kept threatening to mutiny in response to attempts to prosecute the perpetrators of human rights abuses under the junta. When leftist radicals attempted to occupy a garrison at La Tablada in 1989, leading to at least forty-three deaths and the torture of the alleged attackers,[53] there seemed a genuine danger the cycle of violence might be starting again.

Carlos Menem, a political chameleon who deliberately cultivated the image of a *gaucho*, growing his hair, sporting bushy sideburns and affecting a poncho, defeated Raúl Alfonsín in elections and succeeded him in July 1989, the first time since 1916 that an Argentinian incumbent had peacefully surrendered power to a civilian. Having become president, Menem centralised power in the executive and embarked on a series of quasi-Thatcherite economic reforms. Alfonsín had sought to transform Argentina by working with the old institutions but they proved resistant to change. Menem was far more radical but that meant he needed the support of conservatives and the military, leading in 1990 to his decision to pardon Videla, Massera, Galtieri and others convicted in the Trial of the Junta. But still he needed popular support so, as well as making vague noises about claiming Las Malvinas, Menem cultivated Maradona, making him 'Ambassador for Sport' at a press conference in Milan shortly before the World Cup and granting him a diplomatic passport. Menem had no qualms about linking his popularity to the national team.

But Argentina's form heading into the World Cup was terrible, leading to the embarrassment against Cameroon. Bilardo called it 'the worst moment of my sporting career'.[54] According to Maradona, 'We were all dead, dead of shame.'[55]

The players sat in silence on the bus journey to the airport and then throughout a two-hour delay. Finally, on the flight back to their training base near Rome, Bilardo decided to refocus minds. 'Either we reach the final,' he said, 'or let's hope the plane carrying us back to Argentina falls out of the sky.'[56]

They made it out of the group as a best third-place side, beating the USSR after Maradona got away with handling an Oleg Kuznetsov flick off the line, and then drawing with Romania. 'Without the individual brilliance of 1986,' said Juan Simón, 'our tactics became a measure we took to survive.'[57] And yet what followed was one of the most memorable games in Argentinian history, a last-sixteen tie against Brazil.

After World Cup exits to Italy and France in the previous two tournaments, the response in Brazil had been much as it was after the exit in 1966; what was needed, it was decided, was greater physicality, as though being outmuscled was the only way Brazil could possibly lose to a European side. That led in 1987 to the appointment of Sebastião Lazaroni, another coach whose origins lay in the physical education department of the military. He sought to implement a *libero*, something which at the time was entirely alien to Brazilian football. Players used to freedom and earning vast salaries reacted badly to the attempt to impose military discipline, leading to a stream of media stories about rows and unpaid drinks bills.

Although Brazil won all three group games, they scored only four goals in doing so, and nobody was especially impressed. 'This team,' Pelé wrote (in a syndicated column sponsored by Seiko; by this stage almost everything he did was endorsed by some company or other), 'has nothing to do with the Brazilian team you know . . .'[58]

Against Argentina in the last sixteen, Brazil dominated. Dunga headed against the post. Careca and Müller both put good chances over. Goycochea made an astonishing recovery after pushing a cross against the woodwork to divert a follow-up from Alemão against the angle of post and bar. Goycochea hadn't played for seven months because he was contracted to the Bogotá club Millonarios and the Colombian league had been suspended following the murder of a referee; he was only in the side because the first-choice Nery Pumpido had broken his leg against the USSR. Against all logic, Argentina hung on. Maradona, struggling with his toe and his ankle and with Brazil's brutal marking, was barely involved.

And then, with nine minutes remaining, came a goal that Argentinian fans were still celebrating three decades later. Maradona gathered the ball in the centre circle and started to run left, then turned abruptly towards goal. He went past the outstretched leg of Alemão. He brushed off Dunga. There were still four defenders and the goalkeeper between Maradona and goal, plus Claudio Caniggia. Brazil panicked. All four yellow shirts converged on Maradona, who squirted a pass through to Caniggia. As Ricardo Rocha and Ricardo Gomes ran into each other, the forward had time to sidestep Taffarel and clip a shot into the empty net. 'The Brazil game,' said Simón, 'lifted us up again and made us feel that we couldn't lose. We were revitalised.'[59]

On the face of it, Argentina's win was a classic smash and grab, but there have since been rumours of something far more sinister. The Brazil forward Bebeto claimed several years later that the Argentina physio Miguel di Lorenzo had admitted that at a break in play he'd thrown a bottle of spiked water to Branco, Brazil's left-back, who later said he'd felt dizzy after drinking from it. Asked directly about the allegation in 2005, Bilardo said only, 'I'm not saying it didn't happen.'[60]

Having squeaked by Yugoslavia, Argentina faced Italy in Naples. In this most operatic of World Cups, that semi-final was perhaps the most operatic occasion of all.

Italy in 1990 held an almost mythical position in football's consciousness. Serie A was, by some distance, the best league in the world, rich, glamorous and dotted with foreign stars, offering a glimpse of the globalised future. Arrigo Sacchi's AC Milan, built around their Dutch trio of Frank Rijkaard, Ruud Gullit and Marco van Basten, had just retained the European Cup, while Napoli with (an admittedly diminished) Maradona, Careca and Alemão had just taken the title from Inter, who boasted three West Germans: Andreas Brehme, Lothar Matthäus and Jürgen Klinsmann.

To those used to the grimy terraces of English football, its stadiums also seemed impossibly grand and futuristic, although delays and strikes drove up costs so the infrastructure came in 84 per cent over budget, and it would turn out over the following years that many had been poorly constructed. The third tier at San Siro, for instance, took the capacity to 80,000 but meant the pitch no longer received adequate sunshine. The Stadio Delle Alpi replaced the crumbling Communale in Turin, but the running track that was included at the insistence of Primo Nebiolo, the Italian president of the

IAAF who had been a close ally of Horst Dassler and thus Havelange, meant the stadium lacked atmosphere; disliked by players and fans, it was pulled down in 2008. And then there was the 58,000-capacity Renzo Piano-designed Stadio San Nicola in Bari. It looked beautiful, and hosted the 1991 European Cup final, but did Bari, at best a yoyo club, really need the third-biggest stadium in the country? Their president Vincenzo Matarrese, coincidentally, was the brother of the president of the FIGC.[61]

Enzo Bearzot had been replaced by Fulvio Bernardini's other assistant, Azeglio Vicini. He had taken Italy to the semi-finals of Euro 88 and there was significant expectation. Italy began slowly and struggled to break down a dogged Austria in their first game. But then, with a quarter of an hour remaining, Vicini withdrew Andrea Carnevale for Salvatore Schillaci.

Schillaci was small, quick and mobile. He may not have had the technical ability or looked as elegant as some of his team-mates, but he had a tremendous capacity to be in the right place at the right time. He had only made his international debut at the end of March and, although twenty-five, had spent just one season in Serie A. But that campaign had brought fifteen goals after his move from Messina to Juventus. He was the form man. Schillaci hadn't even expected to be named on the bench but, granted an opportunity, he seized it. 'The train,' he said, 'only leaves the station once.'[62] With his first touch, he headed in a Gianluca Vialli cross, and Italy had a 1–0 win.

They beat the USA 1–0 as well and, although Schillaci didn't score after coming on, the reaction of Carnevale to being taken off ensured he would start the third group game, against Czechoslovakia. Roberto Baggio's brilliant second, beating four players as he swooped in from the left, is the overriding memory of that match, but it had been Schillaci who had put Italy ahead with an opportunistic header. He scored against Uruguay in the last sixteen and against Ireland in the quarter-final as well. 'It was like a fairy-tale but I was the hero of the story,' Schillaci said. 'Everything I touched turned to gold.'[63]

Then came Argentina at the San Paolo, playing Maradona in front of his own fans. 'The choice of Naples was very good,' said Luca Cordero di Montezemolo, the Piedmont aristocrat and chairman of Ferrari who served as general manager of the tournament. He had secured a geographical spread of the major games: the final in Rome, the opening match in Milan, the third-place play-off in Bari, the semis in Turin and Naples. 'The problem was the goalkeeper made a mistake and Caniggia scored.'[64]

Maradona appealed to locals, who had definitely been on the side of Argentina in their games against the USSR and Romania. 'For 364 days of the year,' he said, 'you are considered to be foreigners by your own country; today you must do what they want by supporting the Italian team. By contrast, I am a Neapolitan for 365 days of the year.'[65] Perhaps a couple of years earlier, his appeal would have cut through but, even if Neapolitans were sceptical about Italy, the San Paolo was not a hotbed of Argentinian support. '*Maradona*,' read one banner, '*Napoli ti ama ma l'Italia è la nostra patria*.' (Maradona, Naples loves you but Italy is our country.) There are contradictory accounts of the degree to which the San Paolo crowd sided with Argentina, but the sense was that the atmosphere wasn't as fervently supportive as it might have been elsewhere. 'The fans in Rome had treated us in a very different way,' said Vicini,[66] but perhaps that was natural given how the game went.

Argentina were leaden and aggressive. Schillaci put Italy ahead. Everything seemed to be going right for the hosts but for one thing. The goal had come after seventeen minutes, and this was the seventeenth international played in Naples.

For superstitious Italians, seventeen is an unlucky number.* Gradually, Italy dropped deeper. Anxiety set in. Bilardo had pointed out to his side that Italy's wide midfielders, Luigi De Agostini and Roberto Donadoni, often failed to track back after possession was lost. 'When we recover the ball,' he told his team, 'we'll always have a two-to-one advantage on each side.'[67] He was right. Midway through the second half, Caniggia glanced Olarticoechea's cross past a dithering Walter Zenga to equalise, the first goal Italy had conceded in the tournament. Ricardo Giusti was sent off with 11 minutes of extra time remaining but Italy's nerve had gone and they could not take advantage. Both sides scored their first three penalties, then Donadoni, Italy's number 17, stepped up. Goycochea kept it out.

When Maradona scored, that meant the substitute Aldo Serena had to score. He felt a pressure unlike anything he had ever felt before. He tried breathing exercises without success. 'Nothing,' he said, 'was working as normal – my legs had gone. I was struggling to actually feel the ground.'[68] Goycochea saved his effort as well, meaning in two shoot-outs he had saved four penalties; the Argentinian post office rewarded him with his own postcode: 0004.

Argentina had somehow scrapped and spoiled their way to the final. 'I've never seen anything unify the nation like that,' said Bilardo. 'Not politics or music or anything.'[69]

Between Argentina and a second successive World Cup stood the side they had beaten in the final four years earlier, but this was a very different West Germany. Beckenbauer

---

* Written in Roman numerals, XVII, the number could be rearranged to read VIXI – I have lived – which, by analogy with Cicero's announcement of the execution of the Catiline conspirators, '*vixerunt*', could be taken to mean 'my life is over'.

had stayed on as *Teamchef* and had grown into the role. A younger core had emerged and they had been a little unfortunate to lose to the Netherlands in the semi-final of Euro 88. And the prospect of reunification had changed the mood. A number of players, including Klinsmann and Pierre Littbarski, had relatives in the East, but there was a more nebulous feeling that the coming down of the Wall, the most visible symbol of the post-war settlement, meant that it was permissible to be proud of being German again. Klinsmann spoke of never having seen so many German flags before as he did in Italy.[70]

Yet a year before the tournament, there was no guarantee that West Germany would qualify. Beckenbauer's position remained unclear, complicated by his fraught personal life. West Germany needed to beat Wales in Cologne in their final qualifier, in November 1989, to secure their place in Italy, the first game they had played since the Wall came down. They came from behind to lead early in the second half, but Littbarski missed a penalty and, with two minutes remaining, Mark Aizlewood was gifted a free header eight yards out. Had he scored, Denmark would have gone to the World Cup in West Germany's place. Aizlewood headed over.

Ten days later, Beckenbauer confirmed that he would stand down after the World Cup. He had dabbled unconvincingly with a back four and zonal marking, before returning to man-marking for the tournament. The result was a group stage negotiated with a crushing lack of jeopardy, nine goals scored in their first two games. Their reward was another game against the Netherlands.

Although the Netherlands had finished above West Germany in qualifying, they were ill at ease. Thijs Libregts had replaced Michels after the Euros but he lost a vote of no confidence from the players. They wanted Cruyff, who at the time was just beginning his revolution at Barcelona,[71] but Michels, heading the committee to find a new coach, turned instead to Leo Beenhakker, who had done the job without great success in 1985–86. As he was managing Ajax, he couldn't take over until the domestic season finished in May.

Gullit had been plagued by injury for two years and Van Basten was struggling with the ankle problems that would end his career. When the Netherlands began with a drab 1–1 draw against Egypt, Gullit described it as 'the result of two years of bad work, bad football and bad coaching'.[72] Two further draws got the Netherlands through with an identical record to Ireland. They drew lots to determine which side was second and which third; the Dutch lost.

For West Germany, that was the game that gave them belief. Twenty minutes in, Rijkaard and Völler were sent off after squaring up to each other twice in quick succession; it seemed unfair on the West German, who was spat on twice. A deft finish from Klinsmann and Andreas Brehme's curler gave West Germany a 2–1 win.

A Klinsmann collapse in the box and Matthäus's consequent penalty saw West Germany through their quarter-final against Czechoslovakia. And so to Turin, and the night that changed English football for ever.[73] It was by some margin the best game of the tournament, Brehme's free-kick looping off Parker and over a flat-footed Peter Shilton before Lineker scrambled a late equaliser. Both teams had chances, Platt had a goal wrongly ruled out for offside and Gascoigne wept – but it was decided in West Germany's favour by penalties.

Afterwards, Robson made for Gascoigne and hooked an arm around his shoulders in consolation. 'You've been absolutely magnificent, haven't you, yeah?' he told him. 'You've got your whole life ahead of you. This is your first.'[74]

But Gascoigne, a martyr to his injuries and his demons, never played in the World Cup again.

*

Argentina's preparation for the final was typically chaotic. Two days after the semi-final, Maradona's brother Lalo was arrested for speeding in Maradona's Ferrari. He didn't have his ID on him, so police drove back with him to Argentina's training base. When they arrived, a brawl broke out, in which Maradona's brother-in-law, Gabriel Esposito, played a leading role. The following morning, the players woke to find the Argentinian flag at the base had been torn down. A hoax bomb call was made to the Argentinian embassy in Rome. It doesn't mean there was a conspiracy, as Maradona would subsequently claim, but nobody in Italy wanted Argentina to win.

The crowd for the final in Roma was more hostile even than in the opener against Cameroon. Bilardo was so worried he considered cutting the anthem short to reduce the amount of time his players would be exposed to concentrated booing and jeering. Argentina were without four players through suspension but, in the end, what undid them was a combination of their own ill-discipline and the excitability of the Mexican referee Edgardo Codesal.[75]

Argentina committed a series of bad fouls and sought to put pressure on the officials at every opportunity. In the end, Codesal snapped at Pedro Monzón's 65th-minute foul on Klinsmann. It was a bad challenge, studs clattering into shin, but there seemed little reason for Klinsmann to pivot up, writhing, onto his neck in response. It brought the first red card in a World Cup final, and Codesal delivered it with great ceremony, arching his back and thrusting his arm up with a theatrical flourish.

The penalty from which West Germany scored the only goal was debatable, Néstor Lorenzo seeming to take the ball before his hip sent Völler tumbling, but then an obvious earlier foul in the box on Augenthaler had gone unpunished. Matthäus was the designated penalty-taker but he had been forced to change his boots at half-time and felt uncomfortable, so passed the responsibility on to Brehme. At the previous World Cup, Brehme had taken a penalty against Mexico with his left foot; he took this one with his right, and scored.

At that, all dignity left Argentina. Troglio could have been sent off for barging the referee and Gustavo Dezotti was sent off for grabbing Köhler round the neck. Codesal could have sent off at least two or three more as he was surrounded after that decision, but restricted himself to booking Maradona.

Argentina returned home with a familiar sense of outrage, blaming Italy, Fifa and the world in general. They were moral champions again.

In the real world, West Germany were the champions for the third time. Beckenbauer strolled alone around the pitch after the presentation, hands in pockets, apparently deep in thought. Saying he had already won more than enough, he handed his medal to the press officer Wolfgang Niersbach, who hung it above the fireplace in his home; a quarter of a century later, another transaction involving the pair would become the subject of a major scandal.

Beckenbauer had followed Mário Zagallo in winning the World Cup as both a player and a coach. But this was about more than that. Just as winning the World Cup in 1954 had been about West Germany stepping back onto the world stage, so 1990 was about introducing a new Germany. 'The bad image of Germany turned from that moment,' said the goalkeeper Bodo Illgner. 'The World Cup in 2006 completed this development.'[76]

By no footballing measure was 1990 a good World Cup. Goals per game were at a historic low of 2.21 per game. In only two matches did teams come from behind to win. Twenty-nine per cent of all games finished 1–0. Fifa had already begun the process of improving the game as a spectacle, instructing referees to send off players for fouls that denied a clear goalscoring opportunity. Offside was tweaked so that a forward level with the penultimate defender was considered onside, and from 1992 the back pass was outlawed. Additionally, the practice of having referees run the line was abandoned, in part because linesman was a specialist job, and in part because there was an implicit sense of competition between those on the line and those who had been granted the prime job in the middle. From 1994, referees were grouped into teams with a pair of linesmen.

But the average attendance of 48,368 was the highest for any World Cup since 1970 and the global TV audience doubled from Mexico to 26.6bn. And the sense of spectacle was unsurpassed. The tweaks to the laws that Fifa made were right and necessary but 1990 proved that, sometimes, narrative drama is enough.

1994

LIFE CAN BE BRIGHT

'The United States was chosen,' the columnist George Vecsey wrote in the *New York Times*, 'because of all the money to be made here, not because of any soccer prowess. Our country has been rented as a giant stadium and hotel and television studio.'[1] Nobody could seriously doubt that. The USA had played in only two World Cups since the Second World War and hadn't had a national professional league for a decade. And that meant there was a great deal of scepticism from outsiders, even after Fifa had made clear there would be no wacky law changes to try to appeal to the domestic audience: would anybody actually turn up to watch?

But there was also hostility in the US. A piece in *USA Today* on the day of the draw told Americans they were right not to care about the World Cup of what it sneeringly described as the biggest sport in 'Cameroon, Uruguay and Madagascar'. 'Hating soccer,' wrote the columnist Tom Weir, 'is more American than mom's apple pie, driving a pickup or spending Saturday afternoon channel surfing with the remote control.'[2]

Behind both, perhaps, lay the same thought. What if the World Cup turned out to be the stimulus the US needed to embrace football? Foreign sceptics perhaps feared too much growth in the US and possible domination of the global game;

American sceptics worried what a football boom might mean for the four major US sports. Fifa just hoped there was money to be made.

What nobody doubted was that the US would bring glitz, glamour and razzmatazz. The draw was held in Las Vegas and starred such luminaries as Bill Clinton, Faye Dunaway, Jeff Bridges and Jessica Lange. The opening ceremony, staged at Soldier Field in Chicago before the defending champions Germany, playing at a World Cup as a unified nation for the first time since 1938, faced Bolivia, was a lavish, sun-drenched affair presented by Oprah Winfrey and featuring turns by Diana Ross, Daryl Hall and the B-52s. But the omens were terrible. Winfrey fell off the stage and twisted her ankle. Ross dragged a shot wide of an open goal from three yards. Germany won a desultory opening game 1–0. And the whole thing was overshadowed by the LAPD's televised pursuit through Los Angeles earlier in the day of the American football star turned murder suspect, O.J. Simpson.

The US had been awarded hosting rights, appropriately enough, on 4 July 1988. Chile had withdrawn from the race and Brazil had still not installed Havelange's son-in-law Ricardo Teixeira as CBF president, which effectively left a straight fight between the US – whose campaign was again fronted by Kissinger – and Morocco. It was a close-run thing, the US winning out by ten votes to Morocco's seven, with Brazil on two. It was the third tournament awarded by the Havelange regime and already the process was drowning in paranoia and suspicion. Had the ban Mexico received from the 1990 World Cup for fielding over-age players in a youth tournament been an attempt to smooth the USA's passage to 1994 by giving them tournament experience?[3]

The USA's qualification for 1990 did little to assuage fears about hosting the tournament in the US. The crowd for their final home qualifier, a 0–0 draw against El Salvador in St Louis, was only 8,500. That left them having to beat Trinidad & Tobago in Port of Spain to pip them to a place in Italy. They achieved that with a Paul Caligiuri volley but more notable was the crowd. Jack Warner, the head of the Trinidad & Tobago football association, sold at least 15,000 more tickets than there were spaces in the 28,000-capacity National Stadium, leading to serious overcrowding and safety concerns.[4] Quite apart from the fact that people's lives had been put at risk to make additional profit, the fact that the US administrator Chuck Blazer, who would be named Concacaf general secretary when Warner won the presidency the following year, visited him the following day led to rumours that the overcrowding was not just about maximising revenue but a tactic to ensure the result of the game could be overturned had the US failed to win.[5] Warner has always dismissed the allegation. In Italy, the USA derived some credit from hard-fought defeats to the hosts and Austria, but the tone had been set by their opening 5–1 defeat to Czechoslovakia.

Havelange was certain the US was a market ripe for exploitation but while Fifa talked boldly of hosting the World Cup as a way of stimulating interest in the game,[6] there were plenty of doubters. Would it be possible to lay grass over the artificial surfaces at the Pontiac Silverdome in Michigan and the Giants Stadium in New Jersey? What would the impact be of staging the tournament over such a vast geographical area? And how would players cope in the heat and humidity, particularly with games kicking off at noon and in mid-afternoon to accommodate European TV markets?

More broadly, what did prioritising potential commercial markets over traditional football countries suggest about the way the game was going? The Italian president of Uefa, Artemio Franchi, had been clear he could 'never agree to a World Cup for multinationals'[7] and he wasn't the only one who disliked the overtly commercial route football was taking under Havelange. He was killed in a car crash in 1983 and there were enough unexplained details about his death to prompt an investigation by the journalist Alberto Ballarin, who identified two untraced foreign motorcyclists as potential suspects in a possible murder. Among the wilder theories about what happened on the road to Siena that night is the claim that elements at Fifa who had seen the USA miss out on hosting 1986 and 1990 took out a key obstacle to the success of their third bid.[8]

Plotting definitely was going on in Brazil, where Teixeira finally became president of the CBF in 1989. Pelé, who had done so much to help Havelange win the 1974 Fifa election, accused the CBF of seeking a $1m bribe from a TV company for which he worked for rights to the tournament. Teixeira sued and Pelé, the NASL's great star, was banned from the draw. Allegations of bribery and money-laundering would dog Teixeira throughout his career. He was eventually banned for life by Fifa in 2019.

By 1994, Havelange was also mired in crisis, after a raid on the home of the Rio mafia boss Castor de Andrade revealed how close Havelange's relationship with illegal gambling was. At the same time he clashed with Werner Fricker, the head of the US Soccer Federation, over the sale of broadcast rights for the tournament.

Two weeks before the USSF's presidential election in 1990, Havelange persuaded the Los Angeles lawyer Alan Rothenberg, who had been involved with two franchises in the NASL and had overseen football at the 1984 Olympic Games in Los Angeles, to stand against Fricker. With Fifa's backing, he won. As Rothenberg saw it, given how far preparations had fallen behind schedule under Fricker, he saved the World Cup. He refused to take a salary for his work – although he did subsequently claim a $3m bonus and $4m in 'deferred compensation',[9] while his own law firm, Latham & Watkins, handled

$2.7m's worth of World Cup business and roles were found for both his son and his wife.[10]

Carlos Valderrama was a player who represented much of what Argentinians thought great about their own game. He was a classic *enganche*, nicknamed *el Pibe*, a languid playmaker with an instantly identifiable mane of gingery hair who could control the tempo of games through the precision of his passing and his capacity to find space. When he orchestrated Colombia's 5–0 win in Buenos Aires in World Cup qualifying in September 1993, three days after his thirty-second birthday, he didn't just inflict on Argentina its worst defeat since Helsingborg in 1958, but did so in a way that demonstrated that it was possible to update the classic Argentinian style for the modern age.

Argentina had missed out on automatic qualification. The domestic reaction was furious and disbelieving. 'Disgrace!' screamed the front page of *El Gráfico*, which was otherwise blacked out as though in mourning for Argentinian football.[11] Largely because of a fifteen-month ban for failing a drugs test in 1991, Maradona had played only two games for Argentina since the 1990 World Cup. He was thirty-three and out of shape. But he was the designated messiah, and so Argentina recalled him for their two-legged play-off against Australia, a decision that would have profound consequences.

But the consequences in Colombia would be even more profound – and, to an extent, they were foreseen even amid the euphoria at El Monumental. An estimated eighty people died amid the celebrations in Bogotá that night. As the fourth goal went in, the assistant coach Hernán Dario Gómez turned to the manager, Francisco Maturana. 'Now we're fucked,' he said.[12]

*

In Europe, the qualifying campaign was no less tumultuous. Graham Taylor, the likeable former Watford and Aston Villa manager, carried the blame for England's failure to qualify and was savaged by the press. The fly-on-the-wall documentary he authorised, without the FA's knowledge, was at the time regarded as making him look ridiculous with a number of lines, delivered with eccentric syntax, entering the wider consciousness: 'Do I not like that!'; 'Can we not knock it?'; 'I'm just saying to your colleague, the referee has got me the sack. Thank him ever so much for that, won't you?'[13]

More recent interpretation has been kinder: Taylor comes across as a decent man struggling desperately with the pressure, waking drenched in sweat, helped neither by the vicious tabloid circulations wars nor the shortcomings of a generation of players bequeathed him by the misguided coaching theories instilled by its technical director Charles Hughes. Taylor himself was regarded as the acceptable face of that philosophy, although he had been aware of the limitations of its application since at least 1982.[14]

And, however awful a lot of the football was, at Euro 92 in particular, Taylor was unlucky. By World Cup qualifying, a toe injury had effectively curtailed Lineker's career, while Gascoigne, who arguably never fully recovered from the torn knee ligaments he sustained in the 1991 FA Cup final, was wrestling with what Taylor euphemistically referred to as his 'refuelling' issues. The draw grouped England not just with the Netherlands, but also with a rapidly improving Norway – who, as if to rub Taylor's nose in it, practised under Egil Olsen a variant of the direct football for which he was so condemned.[15] England played well in the home games against both the Netherlands and Norway, only to draw both, thanks to brilliant goals against the run of play. Then, in Rotterdam, Ronald Koeman should have been sent off for hauling down David Platt with the score at 0–0; shown only a yellow, he flicked in a free-kick seven minutes later, setting the Dutch on their way to a 2-0 win.

The epitaph for Taylor came in the final qualifier in Bologna as Davide Gualtieri seized on a short Stuart Pearce back pass to put San Marino ahead. England ended up winning 7–1, and it didn't matter anyway as the Dutch won in Poland, but the humiliation of that moment summed up an era.

France's failure to qualify was altogether more ridiculous. They had won six of their first eight qualifiers and were highly fancied under Gérard Houllier. With two home games remaining they led Bulgaria by five points. But they then contrived to lose having been 2–1 up with seven minutes to go against Israel. Against Bulgaria in the final qualifier they had the 1–1 scoreline they needed and a free-kick deep in opposition territory. It was pushed to David Ginola, who could have taken it to the corner and run the clock down. Instead, he crossed. Houllier never forgave him. His ball in was too deep. Bulgaria worked a counter and Emil Kostadinov powered a shot in off the underside of the bar. Unthinkably, Bulgaria had qualified and France were out.

It turned out Kostadinov, who had also scored Bulgaria's first, shouldn't even have been in the country. He and Lyuboslav Penev had both had problems with their visas and had been driven into France at an understaffed border-post known to the midfielder Georgi Georgiev, who played for nearby Mulhouse.[16]

For any side to beat Argentina 5–0 in Buenos Aires would have been a major shock; for Colombia to do it felt apocalyptic because Colombia had never been a footballing power. When Maturana was appointed national coach in 1987, they had never won the Copa América and their only appearance at the World Cup had come in 1962, when they'd failed to win a game and conceded eleven goals in three matches. Maturana was an unlikely visionary. Although he had won two league titles and six international caps, he had also worked as a dentist throughout his playing career. In 1982, along with teaching odontology at the Universidad de Antioquia and running his dental surgery, he began learning to be a coach, reading books, going to Uruguay to study and working with the youth set-up at Atlético Nacional.

In 1986, Maturana was named coach of Once Caldas. A year later he led the national team to third place in the Copa América. Two years after that, his Atlético Nacional side became the first Colombian winners of the Copa Libertadores and Colombia beat Israel in a play-off to qualify for the World Cup. In Italy, they beat the UAE and drew with West Germany to reach the last sixteen, where they were beaten by Cameroon.

Maturana had played under Osvaldo Zubeldía and Carlos Bilardo, two managers notorious for the defensiveness and cynicism of their approach, but at least as big an influence was José Ricardo De Léon, a Uruguayan who was also accused of '*anti-fútbol*' in Colombia. The term, though, is so loose as to be meaningless beyond very precise contexts: *anti-fútbol* is often in the eye of the beholder. De Léon had been inspired by Rinus Michels and practised a version of the Dutch pressing game; for all that Europeans delighted in the patterns of Total Football, there were many in South America who saw it as diminishing the role of individual artistry, another variant of the organised physicality they had feared for years.

Maturana never made any secret of the Dutch influence on his thinking, but he tempered that for the local market. 'We used a style of play to express what Colombia the country was all about,' he said, 'people who are known for being happy, people who are dreamers, people who are easily inspired, but within that idea we also implemented some order.' What that meant was that players had to run less. 'Tactical intensity is all about concentration,' Maturana explained. 'The more players you have involved in a move, the less players have to move.'[17]

His changes weren't just tactical; they were also psychological. He insisted his players should stay only in five-star hotels and that they should wear suits when travelling because he believed it 'boosted their self-esteem'.[18] He would hand out books of poetry, particularly the works of the Uruguayan Mario Benedetti.

There was, though, another force lifting Colombian football in the eighties: the drugs cartels. 'There was a lot of anguish,' said Maturana, 'there was insecurity and we were at war with ourselves. When people thought about Colombia they immediately identified the country with drugs and Pablo Escobar, so football ensured Colombia appeared in the news for the right reasons. It helped our own people when we were really struggling.'[19]

The identification was reasonable enough. Atlético Nacional were funded by Escobar, who had been two years below Maturana at the same Medellín high school. 'As a criminal, who should worry about him: me, or the authorities?' Maturana asked. 'It wasn't my business to stand in the way of him or do anything else.' Probed on whether, when they met, they talked only about football, Maturana replied only that they weren't going to talk about dentistry.[20]

One of Maturana's key players for Atlético and then for Colombia was René Higuita. In Europe, he was regarded almost as a figure of fun, '*el Loco*', the crazy goalkeeper with the long curly hair who went on reckless dribbles outside his box and performed the scorpion kick at Wembley in 1995. But his habit of leaving the box, although it could go wrong, as it did against Cameroon in 1990, was part of a conscious strategy. 'We had eleven players instead of ten able to generate play,' Maturana explained.[21]

In 1993, Marcela Molina, the eleven-year-old daughter

of the narco-baron Luis Carlos Molina, was kidnapped in Medellín on the orders of Escobar. Escobar had escaped prison in 1992 but, unable to access his bank accounts, he needed money and, when his former associates proved reluctant to supply him with loans, he turned to ransom. Molina, an investor in Atlético Nacional, called Higuita and asked for his help, giving him US$300,000 and telling him to wait for Escobar's people to contact him. Higuita had twice met Escobar before – most famous footballers in Medellín had – and, having little option, agreed. Eventually, he was told to take the money to a particular street corner and the exchange was done. As he sees it, all he did was save a young girl.[22] But Molina pressed $64,000 on him to say thank you, which some interpreted as profiting from a kidnapping.

Higuita was jailed for seven months without ever being charged and released only after going on hunger strike. Officially he had been unable to regain fitness before the World Cup, although Miguel Silva Pinzón, the chief of staff to President César Gaviria Trujillo, openly admitted he feared what the reputational damage might be if Higuita, whom he described as 'an apologist for Escobar', went to the World Cup: Colombia would just be 'the narco team'.[23] Either way, Higuita did not go to the US. But then he had also missed the 5–0 win over Argentina; Higuita's absence was not the reason for what happened at the World Cup when, as it turned out, for the most tragic reasons, Colombia's reputation as 'the narco team' would be cemented.

Colombia played well enough against Romania in their first group game, had plenty of chances but went down 3–1, in part because of a majestic floated chip – or mishit cross? – from Gheorghe Hagi. In 1990, when they'd lost to Yugoslavia, Maturana had been able to get the squad together and sort out the issues. In the Fullerton Marriott, where a lot of journalists and fans as well as the squad were staying, players were more inclined to stay in their rooms and so problems festered.

A little over five hours before kick-off in their second game, against the USA in Pasadena, a message was left with the hotel threatening the life of the midfielder Gabriel Jaime Gómez and his family if he played, and that of Maturana if he picked him. Gómez, younger brother of Maturana's assistant Hernán Dario Gómez, immediately returned home to be with his wife and children. An own goal from Andrés Escobar set the US on the way to a 2–1 win. Colombia, having been many people's pre-tournament favourites, were the first team eliminated.

There were various wild theories as to what had gone wrong, ranging, Maturana said, 'from the mafia ... [to] some act of witchcraft'. Before the World Cup, at least some of the squad had been taken blindfolded by bus to a luxury *finca* in the mountains where they discussed bonuses with members of the Cali cartel. Did that bring extra pressure? Had the rival cartels been betting either on or against Colombia? For Maturana, the explanation lay in football. 'If the World Cup had been two months after that Argentina game, we'd have won it,' he said. 'But a lot happened after that game. Lots of players fell out of form, others weren't playing regularly, there were a few injuries and we didn't know how to deal with it.'[24]

Whatever the causes, the consequences were tragic. Escobar was popular and well-respected. He had a column in *El Tiempo*. He had once told the journalist Gonzalo Medina that 'in football, unlike bullfighting, there is no death'.[25] It was that line that his sister repeated to her young son Felipe when he responded to the own-goal by expressing the fear that somebody was going to kill his uncle. But Felipe was right.

In the early hours of 2 July 1994, ten days after defeat to the USA, Escobar left a restaurant at a stadium to the east of Medellín. At the bar, he had been hassled by a group who blamed him for Colombia's exit. As he crossed the car park, he was approached by Humbert Muñoz, a bodyguard and chauffeur for two brothers, Juan Santiago and Pedro David Gallón Henao, ranchers and narco-traffickers. One of the brothers got into Escobar's car and turned the radio up to full volume. As Escobar got out, Muñoz shot him six times with a .38 calibre revolver.

That year, Gabriel García Márquez agreed with the proposition that only three important things had happened in Colombia throughout the whole of the twentieth century: the assassination of the opposition leader Jorge Eliécer Gaitán in 1948, which led to riots in Bogotá (and, indirectly, to the establishment of the rebel Colombian league as a government ruse to head off the threat of civil war[26]); the publication of *One Hundred Years of Solitude* in 1967; and the 5–0 win at El Monumental.[27] But nine months after that win, the idea of football as national salvation was over. Colombia's greatest chance at World Cup glory, their greatest team, came to an end in the most grimly stereotypical way: murder on the streets.

Like Colombia, Italy played with a back four and zonal marking, adapting the tenets of Total Football for their own market. And like Colombia, they had a brilliant and radical coach whose rise had been vertiginous. Arrigo Sacchi had been a shoe salesman for his father's factory when, in 1979, aged thirty-three, he had quit to devote himself full-time to coaching. His big break came in the 1986–87 Coppa Italia when his Parma side, then in Serie B, beat AC Milan, who had just been acquired by Silvio Berlusconi. Berlusconi saw in Sacchi something of himself, a disruptor unbound by convention.

Appointing him was an extraordinary risk but it was rapidly justified as AC Milan won the league in Sacchi's first season and followed it up with a pair of European Cups. After the first of them, in 1989, Milan faced Atlético Nacional in the Intercontinental Cup. They won 1–0 and Sacchi and Maturana, realising how much they had in common, began to speak regularly.

Like many who plan meticulously, Sacchi was extremely superstitious. He hated people wishing him luck; to say 'good luck' to Sacchi was to lay a curse upon him. The night before Italy began their World Cup campaign against Ireland the president Oscar Luigi Scalfaro rang to wish the Italy squad good luck. What followed was, to Sacchi's mind, typical: a classic Jack Charlton victory.

In one way, Ireland were shambolic. Having misread Fifa's protocols, they turned up in white shirts and had hastily to change into green on finding that Italy were, correctly, wearing their change kit of white. It was all so last-minute that Terry Phelan missed the team photograph. But in the important details, they were supremely well-organised, taking the lead through a Ray Houghton chip and then defending superbly, Paul McGrath having perhaps the greatest of his many great games for his country. But then, having secured a 1–0 win, arguably the best result in their history, the plane they'd chartered to fly them back to Florida didn't turn up, leaving the squad sat for hours on a bus round the back of Newark airport. More seriously, the forward Tommy Coyne was taken ill, having apparently flooded his kidneys with the amount of fluid he'd drunk to try to provide a urine sample after being called for the post-match drugs test. It was negative.

Sacchi, meanwhile, faced savage criticism. 'Bankrupt Italy, what a disaster, Sacchi!' screamed *La Gazzetta dello Sport.*[28] As he knew, there were many in Italian football waiting to see him fail. Since the late fifties the orthodoxy in Italian football, set out most eloquently by Gianni Brera, was that Italians had to play defensive football because they were physically weak; it was the story of a people who had been subject throughout history to invasion.[29]

Selling shoes, Sacchi had travelled widely and had realised that Italians were no smaller or weaker than anybody else in Europe. Between 1950 and 1980 the height of the average Italian man went up by 5cm.[30] Why, then, shouldn't they play the sort of progressive football played in northern Europe? His hard-pressing approach brought him success but it also made him 'a heretic ... a subversive ... an adversary who, if it was possible, had to be beaten down because it created a crisis in their pre-eminence and their role as possessors of an old, old knowledge'.[31] Although there was a paranoid streak to Sacchi, the tactical argument was ferocious, with Gianni Mura in *La Repubblica* writing of 'almost a religious war' between advocates of Sacchi's pressing and zonal marking on the one hand, and the more traditional Italian man-marking game on the other.[32]

Berlusconi had used the popularity his success with Milan brought him to establish a political party, Forza Italia – it even drew its name from a football chant – and had been elected prime minister early in 1994. The squad had visited Berlusconi before setting off for the US. As a consequence, many saw Sacchi as Berlusconi's man and that also set certain newspapers against him.

Exhausted, Sacchi had left Milan in 1991, intending to take a year off with an eye to possibly replacing Vicini after the Euros in 1992. But when Italy failed to qualify, Vicini departed and Sacchi was pressed into immediate service. At Milan, his success had come from remorseless repetition, shape and style made automatic by drill after drill. That was never going to be possible with Italy given the limited amount of time national managers spend with their squads, although Sacchi didn't help himself by calling up ninety-six players over his five years in charge, scrabbling to find those capable of taking his instructions on board. It was, he said, 'like filling a cistern drop by drop' and left him feeling 'like a eunuch in a harem of beautiful women'.[33]

After losing to Ireland, the pressure before the second group game, against Norway, was immense. They started well, but after 21 minutes, the Parma left-back Antonio Benarrivo did not step up with Franco Baresi and Alessandro Costacurta, two of Sacchi's Milan stalwarts. The offside trap failed, and an exposed Pagliuca committed a foul that drew a red card. Sacchi had to make a decision: who should he take off to bring on his reserve goalkeeper Luca Marchegiani? The option he took, he said, was 'the most tactically correct, the most unpopular at the time, the most foolish, the one that would cause a scandal'. He withdrew the fans' favourite, the great creator Roberto Baggio, who raised a finger to his temple as he slouched off, as though to signify insanity. So controversial was the switch that it's often forgotten that it worked. Dino Baggio headed the only goal after 69 minutes. A scrappy draw against Mexico took Italy through as one of the best third-place teams from a group in which all four sides finished on four points.

Sacchi knew that his side were struggling to perform as he wanted them to, something he blamed on 'an impossible climate ... contrary to my football, speed and high tempo'.[34] In the last sixteen, they faced Nigeria at noon in the terrible heat and humidity of Foxborough. One-nil down and reduced to ten men by the harsh dismissal of Gianfranco Zola, Italy looked to be on the way out. Struggling with a knee injury, Roberto Baggio asked to be taken off. Sacchi told him to keep going. With two minutes remaining, Baggio levelled and then, in extra time, it was his clever scooped pass that led to Benarrivo being hauled down for a penalty that Baggio converted. Somehow the friction had produced the spark that took Italy to the quarter-final.

Finally, against Spain, Italy produced the sort of performance Sacchi had envisaged. Again Robert Baggio was decisive, scoring the winner in a 2–1 victory with two minutes remaining, although Mauro Tassotti elbowed Luis Enrique in the face after that, breaking his nose. It wasn't seen by the Hungarian referee Sándor Puhl and so, although Tassotti was subsequently banned for two games, Spain were denied the penalty they should have been awarded.

Argentina's coach Alfio Basile called the 5–0 home defeat to Colombia 'a crime against nature' and spoke of wanting to a dig a hole in the ground and bury himself in it.[35] Argentina had won the Copa América in 1991 and 1993. How could it have gone so wrong?

In crisis, Argentina turned to Maradona. After the 1990 World Cup, his form and fitness had been a source of increasing concern. Criticism became increasingly intense and, as the Camorra faced a government crackdown, they had less appetite to protect their star. Police began to investigate Maradona for alleged possession and distribution of cocaine and then, in March 1991, he failed a random drugs test, his old trick of filling a rubber bladder with somebody else's urine and squirting it through a fake penis having failed him.*

Suspended, Maradona returned to Buenos Aires. He was arrested in April 1991 for possession of cocaine and then in August, when police raided his chauffeur's apartment, they found Maradona passed out after a day of cocaine-fuelled drinking. At last, he accepted he needed help, undertook a radical detox programme and began jogging in a park. He attended therapy sessions at which the image that kept recurring was his childhood fall into the cess-pit and his uncle telling him to keep his head above the shit.

He began playing again, joining Bilardo at Sevilla. But he remained unfit and controversial. He was arrested for driving at 200km/h, involved in a brawl outside a nightclub sparked

* A Buenos Aires museum bought the fake penis but it went missing during a nationwide tour in December 2003 and has never been recovered.

when he was denied access for wearing trainers and then blamed for a squad trip to a brothel. When Bilardo substituted him after he'd had a painkilling injection in his knee to enable him to start, Maradona reacted furiously and called his coach a '*hijo de puta*'. He never played for Sevilla again.

Without a club and the structure of training, Maradona fell back into bad habits. When his daughter Djamla caught him snorting a line in the bathroom one morning, he broke down, and returned to stay with his parents in Esquina, the village on the Paraná River where they had lived before moving to Buenos Aires. When he was ready to start playing again, he joined Newell's Old Boys. And yet as the Colombian goals flew in, it was Maradona's name that the crowd chanted. Basile had no choice but to recall him.

Against Australia, he did enough, setting up the only goal in the away leg of the play-off. A 1–1 draw at home secured Argentina's qualification. A redemptive arc seemed possible. That was November 1993. But within two months, Maradona had fallen out with the new coach at Newell's, Jorge Castelli, who he said had restricted his 'freedoms'.[36] He quit the club on 1 February and, when journalists gathered outside his house to find out what was going on, he shot at them with an air rifle, injuring four.

By the time the World Cup began, Maradona looked back in shape. Argentina started well enough with a 4–0 win over Greece, Gabriel Batistuta scoring a hat-trick and Maradona getting the other, sweeping the ball home from the edge of the box after a couple of slick one-twos. He ran to a touchline camera, screaming with manic abandon.

Argentina came from behind to beat Nigeria 2–1 in their second game. As the players celebrated on the pitch, a nurse called Sue Ellen Carpenter, dressed in white with a green cross on her back, her hair held in a ponytail by a green bow, approached Maradona. He had been selected for a random drugs test. They walked off together, hand in hand, Maradona smiling and waving to the crowd.

He tested positive for ephedrine. Perhaps it was true that, as he claimed, the US version of a supplement that he had been using legally in Argentina contained the stimulant. Perhaps he had been unlucky, but given he had spent a decade dodging the testers – for cocaine, if not for performance-enhancing drugs – global sympathy was patchy. In Argentina, there was a mood akin to public mourning; that confirmation of his offence with a positive result from the B sample came on the twentieth anniversary of Perón's death seemed almost too apposite. And even in Argentina there were those who acknowledged this might be the result of broader cultural issues rather than a plot, as many claimed, to ensure Brazil won the World Cup, or the result of the weakness of one man.

'We Argentines break the rules,' said the journalist Bernardo Neustadt. 'Ours is ... a country that violated its own constitution every time it felt like it, a country that breached its international commitments ... Argentina paid with Maradona [for] a way of life, of not heeding the law.'[37] And if you venerate the *pibe*, insist on the urchin ideal, can it really be a surprise when those *pibes* fail to grow up, fail to take responsibility, believe above all else in the value of mischief?

Maradona never played for Argentina again.

Todor Zhivkov resigned as prime minister of Bulgaria in November 1989 as protests swept the country. Although the Communists were returned to power in elections the following year, the mood had changed. As state subsidies to football clubs came to an end, the only way for them to survive was to sell players. Previously players had had to stay in Bulgaria until they were twenty-eight; suddenly, there was an exodus. CSKA sold Emil Kostadinov to Porto, Lyuboslav Penev to Valencia and Hristo Stoichkov to Barcelona. Levski sold Nasko Sirakov to Real Zaragoza and Nikolai Iliev to Bologna. Only nine of Bulgaria's twenty-two-man squad that went to the USA in 1994 were based at home.

Briefly, Bulgarian football enjoyed a golden age, as players developed in state-funded academies enjoyed the advantages of playing high-level football abroad. It was a similar story in Romania, whose players acknowledged in 1990 that they had been distracted by the constant visits of agents to their base, making almost unbelievable offers. Florin Răducioiu, for instance, went from earning US$1,000 a year at Dinamo Bucharest in 1989–90, to $400,000 a year at Bari in 1990–91. Eight of their 1994 squad was based abroad.

In the long run, the decline of the academies and the morass of financial crisis, corruption and match-fixing into which football in both countries descended would have a dismal impact but 1994 came as a glorious pinnacle for a generation who had enjoyed the best of both worlds.

Although they lost 4–1 to Switzerland, wins over Colombia and the USA saw Romania top their group, and they took advantage of an Argentina mourning the loss of Maradona with a brilliant counter-attacking 3–2 win in the last sixteen. Sweden put them out in the quarter-final in a penalty shoot-out.

Bulgaria went one better. They had qualified for four previous World Cups without winning a game and, when they lost their opener 3–0 to Nigeria, it looked like being more of the same. But an early Stoichkov penalty set them on their way to a 4–0 win against a weak Greece and they beat a demoralised Argentina despite the sending-off of Tzanko Tzvetanov. A penalty shoot-out success against Mexico in a game ruined by abysmal refereeing saw them to the last eight and a meeting with Germany that Bulgaria's manager Dimitar Penev described as 'the finest day in the history of Bulgarian football'.[38]

After West Germany had won the World Cup in 1990, Beckenbauer, never a natural diplomat, had said, 'I feel sorry for the other countries, but now we can incorporate all the great players from the East, the German team will be unbeatable for a long time to come.'[39] But as the 1938 World Cup had shown, it's not easy to graft one team onto another.

It perhaps didn't help that Beckenbauer was succeeded by Berti Vogts. Like Derwall, he believed in giving the players freedom and like Derwall, the result was ill-discipline. And, like Derwall, he struggled with the public relations side of the job, often appearing thin-skinned in his dealings with the media. Germany scratched their way to the final of the Euros in 1992 but lost to Denmark and never really got going in the USA. Having overcome Belgium 3–2 in the last sixteen, Germany seemed on course to beat Bulgaria and reach the last four for the seventh time in eight World Cups when Matthäus put them ahead with a cheap penalty, but a Stoichkov free-kick and a plunging Yordan Letchkov header put Bulgaria through. The old German sense of indomitability has never quite been recovered.

Carlos Alberto Parreira graduated from the Escola Nacional de Educação Física e Desportos in Rio de Janeiro in 1966, his approach conditioned by the technocratic ethos that dominated Brazilian life. His was an unusual career. At the age of twenty-four he set off to work in Ghana and he had managed Kuwait and the UAE at World Cups when, in 1991, he was appointed manager of Brazil, succeeding Falcão. The former midfielder had come in after the misery of the 1990 World Cup with the hope he could restore some of the Santana sparkle but in the 1991 Copa América, as at the 1982 World Cup, he was undone by a 3–2 defeat, this time to Argentina. As Santana celebrated his greatest achievements, winning the Copa Libertadores in

1992 and 1993 with São Paulo, Brazil were back in the hands of a bureaucrat obsessed by process, who insisted 'the goal is just a detail'.[40]

Parreira instilled a shape not dissimilar to that used by Santana in 1982, but the style was very different. Rather than the elegance of Falcão and Toninho Cerezo at the back of midfield, he employed the grim enforcers Dunga and Mauro Silva. The captain Raí had shown for São Paulo that, while he may not have been quite the player his brother Sócrates was, he could perform a passable impression, but he was never quite at home in the national team, while nobody ever confused Zinho for Zico. Parreira's Brazil were a functional team elevated only by the excellence of their two forwards, Romário and Bebeto.

Still, they were good enough to top their group. A last-sixteen tie against the USA on 4 July in San Francisco had obvious potential for embarrassment, which was only narrowly avoided thanks to a 73rd-minute Bebeto goal after Leonardo had fractured Tab Ramos's skull with a swinging elbow.

On the one hand, that promoted mass celebrations back home; so all-consuming was the fascination with the World Cup that electricity consumption fell by a third during games as schools, factories and shopping malls closed. But, on the other, the Brazilian press and many fans in the stadiums were furiously critical. Parreira was booed whenever he appeared on the big screens, Pelé wrote an excoriating column in *USA Today* and both the president of the republic Itamar Franco and Parreira's mother publicly criticised team selection.[41] Parreira defended his caution by speaking of the 'unbearable, almost inhuman pressure' of managing Brazil.

The quarter-final against the Netherlands was probably the best game of the tournament. Brazil went 2–0 up, the Dutch pulled it back to 2–2 and then Branco belted in the winner from a free-kick, all five goals coming in the space of 29 second-half minutes.

One semi-final was played in New Jersey and one in California, which, with the final to be played in Pasadena, was a problem. At the Giants Stadium, two early goals from Roberto Baggio effectively secured Italy's win against Bulgaria. But the 2,500-mile journey cost Italy a day of preparation which Sacchi thought decisive. In the second semi-final, Thomas Ravelli had already made a couple of fine saves before Sweden's captain Jonas Thern was sent off for a studs-up jab on Dunga's ankle. Romário headed the winner with 10 minutes remaining.

Determined to avoid the misfortune of a good luck message, Sacchi instructed reception in the team's hotel in Los Angeles not to put through any calls to him. But at 4 a.m. on the morning of the final, his phone rang. It was 'a girl from Bologna'. He had no idea who she was but she uttered the fateful words: 'Good luck.' Sacchi knew that the game was up.[42]

Baresi made a miraculous recovery from his knee injury to start,[43] but it wasn't enough. Although Sacchi said that 'in the defensive phase, we played very well' he thought they were 'mediocre' going forward, for which he blamed fatigue.[44] The game was anxious and drab, ignited only after Viola had come on for Zinho with 14 minutes of extra time remaining. It finished 0–0 and so, for the first time, a World Cup was settled on penalties.

Roberto Baggio didn't want to go first, so Baresi took responsibility, and put his kick over the bar. Marcio Santos and Daniele Massaro both had their efforts saved, which meant that when Baggio stepped up to take Italy's fifth kick, he had to score. He too shot over and Brazil had their fourth World Cup.

In Brazil, the day after the final was declared a national holiday, but the players did not return to the adulation which had greeted previous World Cup-winning squads. When customs officials at the airport in Recife tried to get them to pay import tax on goods they'd bought in the US, the result was a five-hour stand-off that was ended only when the finance minister waved them through. A subsequent poll, though, showed that 70 per cent of Brazilians thought they should have paid the duty; players were not the national heroes they had once been.[45]

It had been a desperate final after a World Cup that, at least by comparison with 1990, felt anti-climactic. But, generally, Fifa felt vindicated. Goals per game climbed to 2.71 from 2.21 in Italy, while a total of 3.6 million attended games, an average of 68,991 per match, more than 30 per cent more than at any other World Cup before or since. The tournament turned a profit of $60m, more than double expectations. As a team, the USA had not embarrassed themselves, drawing with Switzerland and beating Colombia to get out of the group before the narrow defeat to Brazil.

There were other signs of development beyond the traditional power centres, with South Korea showing promise and Saudi Arabia making it to the last sixteen, thanks in part to a mesmerising goal against Belgium from Saeed Al-Owairan. Nigeria maintained the positive impression of African football generated by Cameroon four years earlier. Although neither of the other two African qualifiers, Cameroon and Morocco, won a game, the decision to grant CAF a third slot at the World Cup seemed vindicated when Nigeria went on to win Olympic gold in Atlanta two years later.

And a national professional league was established in the US, with Major League Soccer kicking off in 1996. By 2024 it was ranked the tenth biggest sports league in the world by revenue. MLS, a private company headed by Alan Rothenberg, received $500,000 from World Cup USA, chaired by Alan Rothenberg, to present its business plan to the US soccer federation, whose president was Alan Rothenberg. USSF, whose president was Alan Rothenberg, then opted for MLS, headed by Alan Rothenberg, for which it received $3.5m from World Cup USA, chaired by Alan Rothenberg.[46]

But to question that is simply to misunderstand how Fifa works.

1998

A NEW KIND OF GLORY

The Brazil squad wait in an airport. They are bored, listless. Romário makes a call at a payphone. When their flight is delayed, Ronaldo takes a ball from his bag, performs a couple of keepie-ups and chips it up for a team-mate to nod on. Soon the game spreads, along a travelator, through an X-ray machine, around planes and along a baggage carousel as '*Mas Que Nada*' plays in the background: the mythical golden age of Brazilian football, repackaged to sell sportswear. It's probably the most famous footballing advert of all time: Brazil's players are young and lithe, athletic but also playful, defying authority for the sheer joy of the game. More than anything else, that Nike ad created the image of *jogo bonita* in the popular imagination. It is very much of its time: three years later, after 9/11, provoking airport security would seem far less like innocent fun.

And what is often forgotten is that, in the final scene, Ronaldo bears down on the goal Roberto Carlos has created by unclipping a Tensabarrier and, as a crowd of fellow travellers looks on expectantly, sidefoots his shot against the post. After the thrill of the build-up, Ronaldo fails at the last.

*

Ultimately, the beneficiaries of Ronaldo's fallibility were the hosts France, whose road to glory in Paris had begun in Tokyo in 1960. France won just five medals at those Olympic Games, none of them gold, an embarrassment that prompted De Gaulle's government to appoint a *Directeur Technique National* (DTN) for each major sport. Implementation, though, took time.

The directors of the FFF stayed on in England after elimination and drew a very simple conclusion: France had been left behind physically by the likes of England and West Germany. That was the biggest issue Georges Boulogne had to address on becoming the first DTN for football in 1970. Two years later, he established the Institut National de Football (INF) in Vichy to coach the best teenagers from across the country, and in 1973 he mandated all professional clubs to set up their own youth academies.

By the eighties, there was a sense that the INF was failing in two ways: the clubs retained the very best young talent, and there was too great an emphasis on fitness rather than technique. When Gérard Houllier became DTN in 1988, he moved the centre to Clairefontaine, about 35 miles south-west of Paris, established twelve further centres across the country, and began training children from the age of twelve. The results began to be seen in 1996 as a France side featuring Thierry Henry, Nicolas Anelka and William Gallas and managed by Houllier won the European Under-18 championship.

At the same time, inspired by the success of Euro 84, France put together a plan to host the 1998 World Cup. As commercial revenues grew, the squabble over hosting rights was reaching new levels of tawdriness, the situation complicated by the expansion of the tournament to thirty-two teams, the cost of which had to be covered by sponsors.[1] The US delegate Chuck Blazer later admitted taking a bribe from the Morocco bid[2] but, after Switzerland withdrew, France won by twelve votes to seven.

The outcome was greeted with anxiety. France was a country whose relationship with football had always been ambivalent. For much of the twentieth century, it drew significant crowds only in the north, the south-east and Paris,[3] seemingly because of the patchy nature of industrialisation in France.[4] Without enclosure of land effectively driving people into cities, as happened in the UK, the population remained a lot more rural with the result that it took much longer for football, a predominantly urban phenomenon, to take off[5] as it had in, say, Budapest, Vienna, Montevideo or Buenos Aires in the 1920s.[6] By the time France did finally urbanise in the 1960s[7] the range of potential leisure options had multiplied.[8] In addition, the fact that it took until 1936 for a five-and-a-half-day week to become standard (it had been made law in the UK by the Factory Act of 1850), and the French Communist Party's opposition to watching football, regarding it as alienating,[9] meant the routine of large crowds gathering to watch matches on a Saturday afternoon never developed. Not until the 1999–2000 season did the average attendance in Ligue 1 exceed 20,000.[10]

Even in 1998, shortly before the final, the former rugby player turned columnist Olivier Villepreux was writing of France as a nation of fans more comfortable in bars and cafés than in the stadium, of critics with a tendency to intellectualise who expected the national team to play with an 'emotive perfection'.[11] Perhaps he was expressing the views of the educated middle-class readership of his employers *Libération*, but the widespread doubts expressed before the tournament about whether France was really 'a football country'[12] indicate just how different France seemed to its European neighbours.[13]

The Euros France had won as hosts in 1984 had been a huge success, but back then they had had a brilliant team who had been transformed into martyrs by Harald Schumacher's assault in Seville. Nobody was certain whether the World Cup would capture the public imagination, but an early indication came as the president, Jacques Chirac, latched on to Aimé Jacquet's side, demanding regular meetings with the squad and briefings from the manager. Chirac was no football fan – before the final he could be seen on camera awkwardly mouthing the names of French players as they were announced to the stadium, lacking the confidence to say them aloud – but with his popularity tanking after calling early legislative elections to try to gain a mandate for his programme of neoliberal reform, he saw associating himself with a successful national team as a means of reconnecting with the country. Perhaps that was only logical: from the time of Vichy onwards, the French state had sponsored sport, and the government subsidised the 1998 World Cup with a grant of £190m.[14] And Chirac, who had a France shirt with the number 23 on the back draped over his shoulders for the celebrations, did seemingly enjoy a bounce in popularity for his association with the team.[15]

Despite an abortive coup by Sepp Blatter, Havelange was re-elected in 1994. 'I can talk to any president and they'll be talking to a president too,' he said three years later. 'They've got their power and I've got mine: the power of football, which is the greatest power there is.'[16] But by then his own power was diminishing. In November 1995 he had made a critical mistake, having tea with Sani Abacha, the military leader of Nigeria, two days before the hanging of the novelist Ken Saro-Wiwa and eight other activists. The Ogoni Nine, as they were known, had accused Shell of waging ecological war in the Niger delta and had been convicted of the murder of four other Ogoni leaders in a deeply flawed trial – Shell later settled without admitting liability.[17] Nelson Mandela condemned the executions and called for sanctions against Nigeria, who then withdrew from the 1996 Cup of Nations, to be hosted in South Africa, and were banned from the 1998 tournament as a consequence. When it came to Mandela against Abacha, for most of Africa there was no debate. Havelange reaped the backlash, not just from those appalled by his willingness to deal with Abacha, but also from those who looked at that incident and began to wonder whether his judgement was going.

With Uefa outraged by the way Havelange had rejigged various committees, effectively creating sinecures designed to funnel money to delegates in return for their favour, its shambling Swedish president Lennart Johansson emerged as a contender for the Fifa presidency. He signed the Meridian Convention in 1997 to promote greater cooperation between European and African football and agreed a deal whereby, if the CAF president Issa Hayatou backed him in 1998, he would stand down after one term and back Hayatou for election in 2002.

It might have worked but in November 1996 Johansson was recorded making racist remarks about African delegates. At the CAF Congress in Ouagadougou in 1998, Hayatou pledged his support for Johansson, but he no longer brought another fifty CAF members with him. By then, though, Johansson's opponent was not Havelange but Blatter. At the age of eighty, perhaps realising that with his power base in Africa fractured he was vulnerable, Havelange had announced that he would not seek a seventh term as president.

Blatter, his disloyalty forgotten, became Havelange's nominated successor, announcing Michel Platini as his running mate. Like Havelange, he travelled the world in a private jet drumming up support; as with Havelange it was never entirely clear who was funding him. Havelange had secured support for Blatter in Concacaf, where Chuck Blazer had emerged as a major player, and in the Gulf, and it had become clear that Blatter had made inroads in east and central Africa. The president of council of East and Central African football associations, the Somalian Farah Addo, revealed that he had been offered US$100,000 by a former Somalian diplomat, calling on behalf of 'a Gulf country'. He was certain at least eighteen African countries had sold their votes.[18] England, meanwhile, cravenly pursuing their ambition to host the 2006 World Cup, were one of fifteen Uefa nations who had abandoned Johansson.

Yet the night before the vote, Havelange believed Johansson had a majority. That evening, a number of delegates reported being approached in their rooms at the Hotel Meridien in Montparnasse by smartly dressed men speaking Arabic and offering briefcases containing $50,000 in cash if they pledged their support for Blatter.[19] Hayatou had no doubt how what on the evening of 7 June looked like victory had been transformed into defeat by the morning of 8 June.[20]

In the end, it wasn't even close. Blatter took 111 of the 191 available votes, at which he announced that in addition to their already lavish expenses, ExCo members would receive a $50,000 salary, the clientelism of the Havelange years enhanced for a new era.

With 15 minutes remaining of the second leg of their World Cup qualification play-off in front of a full house at the Melbourne Cricket Ground, Australia led Iran 2–0, and 3–1 on aggregate. Soon after their second goal, Peter Hore, a local irritant with a track record of disrupting sporting events and celebrity funerals, ran onto the pitch and cut a hole in the Iranian net. That delayed the game and offered Iran a lifeline, allowing them to regain their composure.

Karim Bagheri pulled one back, although Khodadad Azizi had been obviously offside in the build-up. Four minutes later, Ali Daei played a clever defence-splitting pass for Azizi to roll in the equaliser. Iran went through on away goals and Australia, unthinkable as it had seemed for the majority of the tie, were out. As Johnny Warren, captain in 1974 when Australia had qualified, wept on national TV, their manager Terry Venables spoke of 'one of the saddest sporting moments of my life'.[21]

In Iran, the celebrations were extraordinary. An estimated 3 million in Tehran, perhaps 6 million across Iran as a whole, took to the streets in celebration. Weight of numbers offers a degree of immunity: soon there were chants against the regime and the Basij, the paramilitary militia established by Ayatollah Khomeini. Men and women mixed freely, loud music was played, women took off their headscarves. When a mob converged on the French embassy, those inside feared the worst, but the crowd wanted merely to hand over bouquets.

The regime panicked. They delayed the return of the team for two days before organising a celebration at the Azadi Stadium. Women were told not to attend, but it's estimated between 3,000 and 5,000 did turn up. Under the Shah, crowds at games had been roughly 20 per cent female, but in 1987 a fatwa was declared against women attending football.

Iran had been one of the early powers of Asian football, winning three successive Asian Cups before reaching the 1978 World Cup at which they drew with Scotland. After the revolution in 1979, though, football clubs were disbanded and football discouraged because, as a government decree put it, 'Players have a tendency to behave aggressively when they play the sport. In the aftermath of games, supporters can also, under influences which aren't good for them, behave in an unbecoming manner.'[22] The league was suspended, and didn't return as a national professional championship until 1991–92. Ayatollah Khomeini had died in 1989 and his successor, Ali Khamenei, was more open to sport.

They weren't far off qualifying for the 1994 World Cup, which would have been a source of great political awkwardness for the hosts, but needing an emphatic win in their final qualifier against Saudi Arabia, Iran lost, 4–3. A meeting with the Americans, though, was coming.

For the USA to be drawn with the Federal Republic of Yugoslavia three years after the Dayton Peace Accord and a year before the Nato bombing of Belgrade would have been politically sensitive enough, but the meeting with Iran was on a different level. There had been no formal diplomatic relations since 1980 and in 1995 the US president Bill Clinton had imposed a complete embargo on Iran. The election of the reformer Mohammad Khatami as president of Iran had led to a thaw in relations before the World Cup although, as it turned out, that amounted to little more than easing travel between the countries and a lifting of the US ban on Iranian pistachios and carpets.

Both teams lost their opening games which, coupled with Germany's draw with Yugoslavia earlier in the afternoon, meant defeat in their meeting at Lyon's Stade Gerland would mean elimination. The diplomatic situation remained tense. Fifa protocol dictated that Iran, as Team B, should walk towards the US for the pre-match handshake but Khamenei instructed them not to. Eventually, the US players were persuaded they should approach the Iranians, who gave them white roses.[23] At the toss, the Iran captain Ahmad Reza Abedzadeh presented the USA captain Thomas Dooley with an enormous silver shield; a sheepish Dooley handed over a small pennant in return.

Of far greater concern was the fact that 7,000 members of Mujahedin Khalq, an Iraq-based group funded by Saddam Hussein with the aim of destabilising the Iranian regime, had managed to buy tickets for the game. They smuggled in banners in small pieces, fastening them together with Velcro, but

TV cameramen were largely able to avoid showing them. Riot police were deployed to head off a potential pitch invasion. The game itself, with everybody on their best behaviour, was oddly anticlimactic, Iran winning 2–1. It was the only win for any of the four Asian nations at the World Cup. Between them, the twelve AFC, CAF and Concacaf sides managed a total of three wins against European and South American sides. It was not a ringing endorsement of expansion.

'Tonight, again,' Khamenei said on television, 'the strong and arrogant opponents felt the bitter taste of defeat at your hands. Be happy that you have made the Iranian nation happy.'[24] Again there were huge celebrations on the streets, and again they led to anti-government protests, a pattern that would become common. Iran were eliminated when they lost their final group game, against Germany.

Eighteen months later, looking to build on the goodwill generated in Lyon, the USA played Iran in a friendly in Pasadena. But then came the 9/11 attacks and George Bush's designation of Iran alongside North Korea and Iraq as part of an 'Axis of Evil'.[25] Whatever diplomatic progress football had hinted towards was lost.

'In preparation I draw diagrams,' said Ćiro Blažević, 'and in the diagrams I always win.'

The Croatia coach's diagrams focused on the Germany striker Oliver Bierhoff. Blažević knew none of his central defenders could beat Bierhoff in the air, so he decided his priority had to be stopping crosses into the box. But what was the best way of getting that message across to his players? 'I was thinking about telling the players about Rommel and Montgomery,' he said. 'Rommel was much, much better at strategy, but he didn't have fuel so the tanks couldn't move and Montgomery won.'

But on the morning of that World Cup quarter-final, Blažević took a call from the president of Croatia, Franjo Tuđman, who said, 'Ćiro, you have to win.' Suddenly he felt pressure. As he walked into the dressing-room he caught sight of himself in a mirror. 'I was a kind of green colour,' he said. 'So I thought, "Oh my God, am I going to die?"' When he looked at the players, he realised they had also turned green with the pressure and he knew that it would be pointless to issue lengthy tactical instructions. He crumpled up his pages of notes. 'Fuck the theory,' he said. 'No Rommel, no Montgomery, no Bierhoff, nothing. I just said, "You have to go outside and die today for the Croatian flag and all the people who have given their lives."

'You have to understand the psychology of the players. 3-5-2? 4-4-2? This is bullshit: what is most important is if they decided to win or not. Are they willing to die on the pitch or not?'[26]

That, at least, is Blažević's version of what happened, although it should be stressed he was a gregarious master of exaggeration and confabulation. That was part of his genius. 'At team meetings he'd be talking about Estonia as though they were fucking Brazil,' said the central defender Slaven Bilić. 'You'd know he was lying, you'd know it wasn't true, but you say, "Fuck, yeah, it's going to be hard." And he'd be talking about their players, and he'd be writing their names on a board, and you'd know it was wrong; he'd be saying, like, this guy, he's so quick, he's so good, and you'd know that he'd never seen him in his fucking life.'

But the converse was also true. When Croatia played Argentina in the World Cup, Bilić was the player called to the pre-match press conference alongside Blažević. 'I know even the twenty-second player in their squad plays for Inter, and everybody else is at AC Milan, Real Madrid, Barcelona ... all at the best teams, and we have Boban at Milan, but he doesn't play, and Šuker at Real Madrid, and he doesn't play,' said Bilić.

'The rest of us were playing in great leagues but not for great teams. So he says to the press, "Argentina, not a bad team, not a bad team, but none of their players play for the best teams in Europe." So I looked at him, and said, "What the fuck are you talking about?" But that's what he was like. It was all nonsense, but it was great nonsense . . . He was everybody's father, a great motivator.'[27]

Blažević had been appointed in 1994 and proved adept at harnessing the patriotic mood in the aftermath of the war. He was voluble and charismatic, always on the look-out for a gimmick. When he had led Dinamo Zagreb to the Yugoslav title in 1981–82 – the season when, as he tells it, he invented the back three ('Bilardo? What does that prick know?') – he started wearing a lucky white silk scarf. He was still wearing it in 1998, when the story got about that it had been blessed by the Pope, leading a factory in Varteks to manufacture 30,000 to sell to fans.[28] During the World Cup he also started wearing the cap belonging to a gendarme who had been beaten to death by German hooligans, simultaneously an affecting tribute and a useful means of securing local support.

As early as October 1990, eight months before the declaration of independence, a Croatia team wearing the red-and-white *šahovnica* kit beat USA in a friendly. They joined Fifa in July 1992, just too late to enter for the 1994 World Cup. After finishing above Italy in qualifying, Croatia reached the quarter-final of Euro 96, and victory over Ukraine in a play-off secured their place at the 1998 World Cup.

In the second leg of that tie, played in Kyiv, one of the hoardings reserved for Croatian use carried not an advert but the slogan '*U boy, u boy, za narod svoy*' (To battle, to battle for your nation). It's a common chant among fans, but also suggests the extent to which the war shaped the mentality. 'We knew we were the first generation to play for the new Croatia,' said Bilić, whose father had been a leading Croatian dissident.

'We knew we had a bloody war behind us. Tuđman said to us that we were like ambassadors for the country.' Although he insisted there was no 'extreme nationalism' he acknowledged that, particularly during Euro 96, he felt 'extra motivation' on hearing the anthem.[29]

A side based on the Croatian-dominated Yugoslavia team that had won the Under-20 World Cup in Chile in 1987 beat Jamaica and Japan to qualify for the last sixteen, in which a Šuker penalty was enough to see off Romania, setting up the clash with Germany. As Blažević had feared, Bierhoff did have a good headed chance, after 31 minutes, but Dražen Ladić saved low to his left, before hooking the ball way as Klinsmann closed in. The game turned on the 41st-minute dismissal of Christian Wörns for a cynical foul on Davor Šuker. Robert Jarni put Croatia ahead soon after and second-half goals from Goran Vlaović and Šuker completed a 3–0 win, Germany's heaviest World Cup defeat since 1954.

After the dismay of the failure to qualify in 1994, England had enjoyed a resurgence under Terry Venables at Euro 96, a tournament that, at the time at least, seemed an expression of a friendlier, more emotionally open country. Thanks to Britpop and Danny Boyle, Damien Hirst and the return of James Bond after a six-year hiatus, Britain seemed culturally relevant in a way it hadn't been since 1966. Gone was the direct football of Graham Taylor and in its place was something much more sophisticated: the 4–1 group-stage win over the Netherlands was England's best tournament performance since 1966 and suggested they could beat the Dutch at their own game.

The Euros ended for England in penalty disappointment and Venables didn't have his contract renewed, in part because he was embroiled in legal wrangles over his business activities that led to him being suspended as a company director, and in part because he overplayed his hand in demanding a new deal before the Euros.

Still, it seemed his legacy was being continued by Glenn Hoddle, under whom England qualified impressively for the World Cup, sealing their place in France with a tactically astute 0–0 draw away to Italy and progressing to the last sixteen where they met Argentina.

Under the management of Daniel Passarella, Argentina had finished top of South American qualifying and were a formidable side, even if Fernando Redondo was left out for refusing to cut his hair. The game against England was a classic. Gabriel Batistuta and Alan Shearer exchanged penalties in the first ten minutes, before Michael Owen, at just eighteen, surged through to score a stunning goal. Javier Zanetti levelled from a cleverly worked free-kick before the break. Two minutes after half-time, David Beckham, having been barged over by Diego Simeone, flicked a petulant foot at him and was sent off, at which England mounted one of the great rearguard actions, defending superbly and having a header from Sol Campbell ruled out for Alan Shearer's challenge on Carlos Roa. But, as at Italia 90, as at Euro 96, as so often in the future, England were undone by penalties.

Argentina's quarter-final against the Netherlands was arguably an even better game. With the score at 1–1, Argentina seemed to have the advantage when Arthur Numan was sent off with 14 minutes of normal time remaining. But Ariel Ortega then headbutted Edwin van der Sar on the underside of the chin and was sent off before, in the final minute, a leaping Dennis Bergkamp took down a long pass from Ronald de Boer, turned inside Ayala and shot past Roa; three touches of glorious precision to score a beautiful winner.

Chirac's faith in Jacquet placed him in a tiny minority. Performances and results in friendlies were poor and by the start of the World Cup, Jacquet was being openly ridiculed. What he had achieved, though, was to forge a robust team spirit, something that was far from a given in France squads.

There was little on-field evidence of his meticulous preparations having a positive effect. France failed to win a game in le Tournoi, a four-team tournament staged in 1997 as a World Cup warm-up. They lost to South Africa in October 1997, and were booed off after beating Scotland in Saint-Étienne a month later. They won only two of their last six games before the finals, what Jacquet saw as useful rotation being regarded by the media as indecisiveness. *L'Équipe* was particularly scathing. After France had beaten Finland 1–0 in their final pre-tournament friendly, the sports paper described France attempting to win the World Cup being like 'trying to climb Everest in espadrilles'.[30] Hurt by the persistent and personal criticism, Jacquet restricted media access to Clairefontaine; a siege mentality developed.

The big doubt remained over who should play at centre-forward. Stéphane Guivarc'h started against South Africa but was forced off because of injury after 26 minutes. He was replaced by Christophe Dugarry who was greeted by boos from the stands; he had not scored for his country in two years and it was widely rumoured that he owed his place in the team to his friendship with Zinedine Zidane. He had been on the pitch eight minutes when he headed home Zidane's inswinging corner, and celebrated by sticking his tongue out at the press box. It was the first indicator of the powerful sense numerous France players have described since that this was somehow meant to be.

France won that game 3–0 and followed it up with a 4–0 win over Saudi Arabia. But with the score at 2–0, Zidane stamped on the Saudi captain Fuad Anwar and was sent off. It meant a three-game ban and was notable at the time chiefly for its senselessness. France were winning the game comfortably: why get involved? With hindsight, it became a precursor, Zidane bookending his World Cup career with a pair of red cards.

Denmark were beaten in the final group game to set up a last-sixteen tie against Paraguay. It was a scratchy, edgy game, settled by the first golden goal in World Cup history, Blanc finishing calmly after Trezeguet had nodded down a Robert Pirès cross. Blanc's mother Yvonne missed it, so overwhelmed by nerves she had retreated to the stadium toilets.

Whatever the anxiety, though, morale remained good. Jacquet's tactical legacy is contested, but nobody can question the spirit that ran through the squad. When Alain Boghossian got stuck in the middle of a *rondo*, for instance, Vincent Candela started singing 'I will Survive' in good-natured mockery. For France it became the anthem of the tournament.

France beat Italy on penalties in the quarter-final as Zidane returned. Given seven of the France squad played in Serie A, which was still the best league in the world at the time, it felt like an enormous psychological barrier had been scaled. Croatia in the semi-final must have seemed almost anticlimactic in comparison, which perhaps explains France's slightly flat performance. They fell behind to Šuker in the first minute of the second half, Lilian Thuram caught deep and playing him onside, but the full-back made amends within a minute, winning the ball deep in Croatian territory, exchanging passes with Djorkaeff and sidefooting home. That was his first goal for his country. His second came 22 minutes later. Again he regained possession before, from the edge of the box, whipping a low shot just inside the post. Although he would amass 142 caps, Thuram never scored another international goal. 'I've tried to find that person who scored two goals in a World Cup semi-final,' he said, 'but he's never surfaced again.'[31]

There was, though, a shadow: the sending-off of Laurent Blanc after an innocuous clash with Bilić, who was widely criticised for the way he collapsed after slight contact with his face. Bilić explained that, terrified of receiving a booking that would have ruled him out of a potential final, he had panicked and thrown himself down to try to ensure the referee didn't just show a yellow card to both players. 'I swear,' he said, 'that if I could change it so he could play in the final, I would ... but the bottom line is he made a mistake.'[32]

But he could not change it, and so Blanc, France's great leader, missed the final.

Mário Zagallo had been on Carlos Alberto Parreira's staff and succeeded him after victory in the 1994 World Cup. What followed might not have been a return to the style of 1970 but under him, Brazil played far more progressive football and won the 1997 Copa América in some style, scoring twenty-two goals in their six games. By 1998, Brazil had a pair of exciting attacking full-backs in Cafu and Roberto Carlos, Rivaldo had added flair and Bebeto was partnered by Ronaldo, a centre-forward of extraordinary gifts. He'd been included in the 1994 squad when he was just seventeen; at twenty one he was a phenomenon. He had explosive pace, tremendous power and remarkable technical ability. And he could finish. His one season at Barcelona had brought thirty-four league goals and, after joining Inter for a world record £19.5m in 1997, he'd scored twenty-five in Serie A. At the time, before the injuries struck, it was reasonable to ask whether he might be the greatest pure striker in history.

Romário, by then thirty-two and back in Brazil with Flamengo, was omitted. He did not take the decision well, attacking Zagallo and his staff as 'sons of bitches, liars, bastards, traitors and backstabbers'.[33] That ramped up the pressure on Ronaldo, who was already struggling with a knee problem. Although he scored four goals in the tournament and produced occasional moments of genius, the award of the Golden Ball to him was, frankly, baffling, as though the pre-written narrative were being followed. One in three of his touches led to the ball being lost. Pelé said Ronaldo was the worst player on the pitch in the opener against Scotland.[34]

The tournament never quite caught light for Brazil. They topped their group, despite needing a Tommy Boyd own-goal to beat Scotland and losing to Norway. They thrashed Chile in the last sixteen, which raised the prospect of a meeting with Nigeria, who had beaten them 4–3 in the Olympic semi-final two years earlier. It's widely believed that Bora Milutinović was about to be replaced as Nigeria's coach shortly before the tournament, only to be reprieved when the dictator Sani Abacha suffered a heart attack and died. Milutinović's players never seemed entirely comfortable under his management, but Nigeria produced one of the performances of the group stage to beat Spain 3–2. But after conceding early against Denmark in the last sixteen, they lost discipline and were beaten 4–1.

Denmark threatened to upset Brazil in the quarter-final, taking the lead and levelling the game at 2–2 before Rivaldo's second of the match secured a 3–2 win. That set up another meeting with the Netherlands in the semi-final. But just as Argentina in the quarter-final seemed wearied by the exertions of beating England, so the Dutch in the semi-final perhaps felt the effects of their win over Argentina. Patrick Kluivert cancelled out Ronaldo's opener, but Brazil won on penalties.

After lunch on the day of the final, Ronaldo went to bed. When he woke up, he was surrounded by team-mates and the team doctor, Lidio Toledo. Roberto Carlos remembered Ronaldo lying on his side, shaking. He had no idea what the problem was but feared his room-mate was having some sort of seizure and summoned help.[35] Ronaldo went back to sleep and, later in the afternoon, was taken for a walk in the hotel grounds by the midfielder Leonardo, who explained what had happened and told Ronaldo he would not be risked that evening. Ronaldo protested and underwent a series of tests with Dr Toledo. He passed them all and raced to the stadium.

When Zagallo had submitted the team-sheet 72 minutes before kick-off, Ronaldo's name was not on it. Instead, Edmundo was to partner Bebeto. But then he saw Ronaldo, who handed him the test results and insisted, 'I'm fine. I'm not feeling anything ... I want to play.'[36] So 30 minutes after Zagallo had put in a first team-sheet, he presented a revised version: Ronaldo was back and Edmundo was on the bench. But Ronaldo clearly wasn't right. He touched the ball only twenty times in the game, fewer than Edmundo, who only played the final 17 minutes.

For France, all that had been lacking in the tournament was a contribution from Zidane. He had neither scored nor recorded an assist at the Euros, and his only positive involvement at the World Cup had been his corner for Dugarry's opener against South Africa. Tall, powerful and elegant, he was the image of the modern street player, having learned the game on the Place Tartane in the suburb of Marseille where he grew up. When he joined Cannes as a seventeen-year-old, his coaches were startled to see how he ducked away from balls in the air. 'In the *banlieues*,' he said, 'we don't give a fuck about headers. You play with your feet.'[37] But 27 minutes into the World Cup final, he rose at the near post to meet a right-wing corner with a neat downward header. In first-half injury time, he did it again from a corner from the opposite side.

When he was a child, Emanuel Petit had dreamed of a World Cup final in which France beat Brazil 2–0. It seemed to be coming true, despite the 68th-minute dismissal of Desailly. In the end, it was Petit who undid his own premonition, running clear in injury time to make it 3–0. The French were no longer the gallant losers; Poulidor and Asterix had been consigned to the past. They were winners and if their football had been a little functional, if they'd ridden their luck at times, what was the problem with that? 'There's not only one way to win,' said Petit. 'Personally, the duel between the romantics and pragmatists, I don't get involved in that. History only remembers the winner.'[38]

The Hungary of 1954, the Netherlands of 1974 and the Brazil – and France – of 1982 would beg to differ, but it turned out France did like a winner. They conceded only two goals in seven games at that World Cup, instilling a defensive outlook that, carried on most successfully by Jacquet's captain in the final, Didier Deschamps, would underlie French football for decades. But if nostalgists wondered whether the concept of *la gloire* had to be sacrificed quite so absolutely, nobody in Paris cared that night. It perhaps helped the national embrace of football that the Festina doping scandal had undermined the Tour de France that summer, but a record 26 million French people watched the final on television with well over a million taking to the Champs-Elysées in celebration, the biggest crowds seen in Paris since liberation.

Brazil, meanwhile, struggled to deal with the reality of defeat. What had happened to Ronaldo and why had he played? Edmundo was one of many who wondered if Nike had influenced Zagallo, pressurising him to field their biggest star,[39] although a subsequent Brazilian Senate inquiry found no evidence that the sportswear giants had any influence over selection. There were theories that Ronaldo had suffered an allergic reaction to a painkilling injection in his knee, or that he was suffering from depression, possibly related to complications in his private life. The most likely explanation appears that believed by Ronaldo himself, which is that he suffered some sort of fit brought on by stress and then played because it's very difficult for any coach to leave out the most expensive player in history.[40] The Senate inquiry may not have unearthed fault on Nike's part but it did expose widespread corruption and nepotism in Brazilian football as a whole, expose how the game had been hijacked by financial concerns. Of the seventeen individuals the report highlighted, though, none were ever charged.[41]

As an image of Zidane's head was projected onto the Arc de Triomphe, it was apparent that for France this was about more than just winning a football tournament. This, said Thuram, was a victory for 'the real France, not the banal idea that people have about French people, but the heterogenous France.'[42] It was a victory over the right-wing attitudes expressed by Jean-Marie Le Pen's attack on the 'artificiality' of an ethnically diverse France squad. It was a victory, to use the term coined on the fifty-day March for Equality and Against Racism that was everywhere in 1998, of the *black-blanc-beur*,* overseen by Jacquet, who had been transformed over the course of the tournament from dull bumpkin into an avatar of *la France profonde*, characterised by solidarity, work, honesty and professionalism.[43] 'What better example,' asked the prime minister Lionel Jospin, 'of our unity and diversity than this magnificent team?'[44] But then football in France had always been an immigrant game.

'French people, all French people,' *l'Éxpress* claimed, 'were able to identify with this team because it was a multi-racial team.'[45] And, while the same issue also carried a report on the popularity of the Front National among disaffected and unskilled young workers, for at least a brief time, it did seem to make a difference. 'Young women in the street [were] in love with Zidane, Karembeu, Desailly and all the other "*blacks et beurs*",' said Olivier Poivre d'Arvor, the director of the Institut

* '*Beur*' in this context comes from slang French known as *verlan*, in which syllables are inverted. A corruption of '*arabe*', it's used to refer to people born in France whose parents are from the Maghreb.

Français in the UK.[46] Romance was a recurring theme. 'All of us Arabs were now handsome,' said the French-Moroccan comedian Jamel Debbouze. 'They'd abolished racism.'[47]

But at best, that was temporary. 'A football match,' Jean-Marie Colombani, the editor-in-chief of *Le Monde*, wrote the following day, 'cannot eradicate the sum of other ills . . . [but] . . . there is this overriding sense, amid the euphoria sweeping the country, that something has changed, or that something can change.'[48]

The caveat was well-judged. Symbols matter, and to have an ideal as an aspiration may be helpful – in his editorial in *Libération*, Laurent Joffrin described the sense of racial harmony as an '*illusion utile*'[49] – but harmonious better worlds glimpsed in moments of triumph rarely add up to much. France had won a World Cup and, while that did change French football, it did not change France.

2002

THE GLOBAL GAME

'Globalisation,' the South Korean president Kim Young-sam said in January 1995, 'is the short-cut which will lead us to building a first-class country in the 21st century. This is why ... the government has concentrated all its energy in forging ahead with ... realising globalisation in all sectors – politics, foreign affairs, economy, society, education, culture and sport.'[1] Hosting the World Cup was a key part of that, particularly given that '*segyehwa*', the Korean concept of globalisation, explicitly embraced the political, cultural and social as well as the economic.

The 2002 World Cup was a festival of globalisation. Not only did Fifa expand into new territories and stage the tournament outside Europe and the Americas for the first time but, almost everywhere, it felt, the complexities of nationhood in the twenty-first century were on display. When Senegal beat France in the tournament's opening game, their starting XI were all based in France, while only one of the France side was. Ten of the Brazil squad that won the tournament played outside the country, while Germany (although they reached the final) blamed their poor form on the influx of non-Germans to their league. Only six of the thirty-two competing nations did not have a player who played in the Premier League. Japan and Tunisia had players who were born in Brazil (Alex and José Clayton), Poland a centre-forward who was born in Nigeria (Emmanuel Olisadebe), and Nigeria came very close to selecting a centre-forward who had been born in Uzbekistan (Peter Odemwingie). Even England had a foreign manager.

Broader issues, such as fears about security, were cast in a globalised framework following 9/11,[2] while few doubted that the various economic crises gripping South American economies were related to their struggles to be competitive within the global financial system.

Both South Korea and Japan were relatively late adopters of football. It was under Major General Chun Doo-hwan, who had become the leader of South Korea after a coup in 1979, that Seoul successfully bid to host the 1988 Olympics but, by the time the Games took place, mass opposition to military rule had led to democratic elections. The Games both raised South Korea's international profile and became a symbol of its opening up to the rest of the world.[3]

A sports ministry had only been established in 1982, a division of the state intelligence agency, which perhaps gives some idea of how central its propaganda mission was seen to be. After the Korean War, the presence of US forces helped popularise baseball in South Korea and, although the national team qualified for the 1954 World Cup, football remained the preserve of the schools, universities and amateur sides attached to the big corporations.

After the success of the Seoul Olympics of 1988, sport was given a greater priority. The baseball league was professionalised in 1982 and a small, eccentric football league established a year later, comprising teams of various degrees of professionalism representing the corporations and banks, plus Hallelujah, a side run by evangelical Christians. Only with the establishment of the K League in 1996 did South Korea have a truly national professional league. By that time, they'd already been qualifying for World Cups regularly for a decade.

In the late twentieth century, Japan was a more democratic country than South Korea and baseball more deeply entrenched, which made transitioning to football much harder. As in so many other areas, Japan looked overseas and successfully imported best practice. The J.League, which began in 1992 in part as a way of catching up with South Korea,[4] was a remarkable feat of reverse engineering as clubs dropped their corporate branding and tried to develop local followings.[5] It also became the focus for something else, a breakaway from the workaholic Japan of the economic miracle and the embrace of something foreign, ostentatiously so in the way that fan culture deliberately aped Europe and South America.[6]

Where the 1964 Tokyo Olympics had been about demonstrating to the rest of the world that the post-war recovery was nearing completion, the attitude in 2002 was far more about enjoyment, offering a boost to football and, if possible, a fillip to a stagnating economy.[7] Japanese football had improved through the nineties. Only a last-minute equaliser from Iraq's Jaffar Omran in the 'tragedy of Doha' denied them a place at the 1994 World Cup,[8] but they did qualify in 1998. They may have lost every game in France, but just being there meant a lot. The Japanese writer Shinobu Yamanaka wrote movingly of his delight at celebrating in a London pub as a former schoolmate, Masashi Nakayama, scored Japan's first World Cup goal. They had already been eliminated and were 2–0 down to Jamaica at the time, but that didn't really matter: 'I felt Japan had finally become a small part of the football world.'[9]

The bidding for 2002 soon came down to a battle between the two Asian nations, both of which were so determined not to lose face against a historical rival that, in the build-up to the vote, lavish gifts were sent to delegates on a daily basis.

Uefa and the AFC suggested joint-hosting. Even forty-eight hours before the vote, Havelange, who had backed Japan, maintained his opposition to a joint bid but then, apparently fearing defeat, he came round. In the end, Korea–Japan was chosen by acclamation.

There followed an arms race as both nations sought to equip themselves with the best stadiums, each determined not to be outdone by the other. And then there was the shadow of Japan's occupation of Korea between 1910 and 1945, described by the Fifa vice-president Chung Jung-moon as the 'most barbarous' in human history.[10] As Choi Sang-young, a former South Korean ambassador to Japan, put it, the countries had had plenty of experience of exchanges but very few of working together.[11] Whether in the end they did actually work together or ran parallel tournaments simultaneously is debatable; the lavish opening ceremony in Seoul managed to avoid a single reference to Japan. But a poll conducted shortly after the World Cup by the Korean newspaper *Chosun Ilbo* and the Japanese newspaper *Mainchi Shunbun* showed that 42 per cent of Koreans felt friendlier to Japanese people and 77 per cent of Japanese people felt friendlier to Koreans than they had before the tournament.[12]

Both ended up turning to foreign coaches after group-stage exits in 1998 under domestic coaches. In the immediate aftermath of that tournament, Japan appointed the Frenchman Philippe Troussier, who had worked with Ivory Coast, Nigeria and Burkina Faso before leading South Africa at the World Cup. He took Japan's Under-20 side to second at the World Youth Championship in 1999 and, recognising that the Under-23 side he was preparing for the 2000 Olympics was of a higher technical level than the senior team, began to promote younger players, something that would have been much harder for a Japanese manager to do given social conventions.[13]

Victory at the Asian Cup in 2000 suggested preparations

were going well, but there were still times when Troussier was clearly infuriated by the culture. Ivica Osim, who took over in 2006, spoke of how 'there is no risk ... no improvisation in Japan, and football can't exist without that. And also players were so afraid of the coaches that they didn't want to do anything on their own initiative.'[14] Troussier similarly spoke of the lack of the 'killer' instinct he had found when working in Africa. One day at the Asian Cup in 2000, to try to encourage players to use their initiative, he had closed the restaurant at the Beirut hotel where Japan were staying and put a notice on the door telling them to find their own lunch; that evening he discovered that many had not eaten.[15]

South Korea looked overseas after a poor performance in the Concacaf Gold Cup (at which they were an invitee) in 2000, making the former PSV and Netherlands manager Guus Hiddink their second foreign manager. He rejected suggestions that the Brazilian Suwon Samsung forward Sandoro should be naturalised, but did manage to persuade the Korean authorities to suspend the league for three months before the World Cup so he could lead a dedicated training camp, at which he instilled in his players a flexible, hard-running style and made them prodigiously fit. The dividends were enormous.

In football, perhaps the most striking example of globalisation is how the club game has come to be dominated by a small handful of giants who are based in western Europe but whose players, coaches, owners and fans are drawn from across the world. It does not now seem strange that an American should own a club in, say, west London and employ an Italian coach to oversee a squad comprising players from France, Ukraine, Senegal and Ecuador, nor that that club should be followed passionately in India, Australia and west Africa. But those trends were in their infancy at the turn of the millennium; the

2002 World Cup was probably the first seriously to be affected by the demands of the club game.

To avoid the rainy season, the tournament kicked off on 31 May, a couple of weeks earlier than had become usual, and that meant the western European season either having to be compressed or to begin earlier, reducing the break from the previous season. Some leagues have always had to accommodate themselves to World Cups but this was the first time that western Europe had had to do so at a time when the vast majority of the best players in the world played there. Misfortune played its part, but it was hard not to see the schedule as a contributory factor as a string of high-level players went down with injuries and others complained of fatigue. The result was a tournament of many shocks, leading to claims that the rest of the world had caught up with the traditional powers;[16] subsequent World Cups, though, would suggest the case was overstated.

Still, there was no doubting the magnitude of the shock that began the tournament, as the world champions France lost to Senegal, who were playing in their first World Cup. It hadn't taken long for the *black-blanc-beur* idyll to be exposed as the transient and superficial artifice it so inevitably was. A friendly between France and Algeria at the Stade de France in October 2001 had to be abandoned after a pitch invasion by youths of North African descent. A World Cup could not suddenly mend the social divisions of the *banlieues*. In presidential elections the following year, Jean-Marie Le Pen, leader of the far-right Front National, was the second-most popular candidate, although he polled only 18 per cent in a run-off against the centre-right Jacques Chirac.

The national team, though, seemed imperious. Roger Lemerre had replaced Jacquet after the World Cup and led France to success at Euro 2000 where they were widely regarded to have been rather more impressive than they had in winning the World Cup, as the young talent of Henry, Trezeguet and Patrick Vieira added zest to the existing structures. It seemed entirely plausible that they could become the first team to retain the World Cup since Brazil forty years earlier.

But after Pirès was ruled out of the tournament with a knee injury, Zidane pulled up in the final warm-up game with a tear in his quadriceps. Should he really have been risked just eleven days after scoring a brilliant winner in the Champions League final? Perhaps not, but the sponsor demanded it – France had fifty-four official partners by this point, making their demands a persistent drain – and the timing of the World Cup meant a certain strain was unavoidable. 'We were knackered,' said Youri Djorkaeff.[17]

The defending champions facing an African team in the opening game of the World Cup? What could possibly go wrong? But Senegal, for so long the great underachievers of west African football, had offered far more reason in the months leading up to the tournament to suggest they might be a threat than Cameroon had in 1990. Under their long-haired French coach Bruno Metsu, an unusually gifted generation had developed into a formidable unit. 'You have to really understand the African mentality, and the difference between a European environment and an African environment,' the midfielder Salif Diao explained. 'It's very delicate. Africa is a free spirit. Players express themselves. You cannot just come in and start instigating rules: you have to do this or that. Metsu would say it does not matter what we do, how we prepare, but when the referee whistles, he wanted to see lions ready to eat whatever is in front of them.'[18]

They qualified from a tough group that also included Morocco, Egypt and Algeria and, in February 2002, were denied a first ever Cup of Nations success only by a penalty shoot-out defeat in the final against Cameroon. In Seoul, Senegal made France look old and ponderous. Perhaps they rode their luck to an extent, France twice hitting the woodwork, but Khalilou Fadiga also hit the post and, vitally, on the half-hour, Papa Bouba Diop scrambled in an El Hadji Diouf cross for the only goal. From a global perspective, it was almost certainly the most famous moment in Senegalese history.

'We lacked humility,' Thuram admitted,[19] but for France the tournament would only get worse. Henry, who was struggling with a knee injury, had been heavily criticised after the opener and, against Uruguay, he lost his head, lunged in with studs raised on Marcelo Romero and was sent off. It finished 0–0. Zidane returned against Denmark but France lost 2–0. The France squad included the top scorers from the previous season in France (Djibril Cissé), Italy (Trezeguet) and England (Henry), but they went home without scoring a goal. In France, the reaction was a collective shrug; there was none of the anguish that greeted, for instance, Italy's far less humiliating exit. This, perhaps, was evidence that the French fan remained a '*supporteur de circonstance*', as Jean-Michel Normand put it in *Le Monde*.[20]

Among those who did care, there were plenty of theories as to what had gone wrong. There was an over-reliance on Zidane. All the starting defenders were over thirty. Desailly and Blanc had retired. Marcel Desailly had taken over the captaincy but he was not an on-field leader in the same way.[21] But perhaps the biggest issue had simply been the environment. A huge delegation led to a culture of excess such that the president of the French football federation Claude Simonet, later a convicted fraudster, responded to the defeat to Senegal by ordering a €4,800 bottle of Romanée-Conti with his dinner in the Seoul Sheraton. For certain players, meanwhile, if reports in the French press are to be believed, the top-floor casino and the dancers who frequented its bar proved an irresistible temptation, the lack of professionalism from those who indulged generating disillusionment in those who did not.[22]

Yet results are the great validators. There may have been disquiet at France's apparent lack of focus but Senegal's camp, at least at first, was notably relaxed. As Metsu had told his players before that opening game, they needed to beat France to stop people talking about the incident five days before the tournament in which Fadiga, as a prank, had stolen an eighteen-carat heart-shaped necklace from a jewellery store.[23]

And there was, of course, an unavoidable symbolic resonance. Of Senegal's twenty-three-man squad, twenty-one were based in France, of which it had been a colony for around 100 years. 'It was,' said Diao, 'an occasion for Africa, or Senegal, to say yes we can beat the colonial power.'[24]

Two Henri Camara goals saw Senegal past Sweden in the last sixteen, making them the first African side since Cameroon in 1990 to reach the quarter-final. They were Africa's sole representatives at that stage, although South Africa and Cameroon had at least each won a game before their elimination. By that point, Senegalese politicians had started to take an interest. The president of Senegal, Abdoulaye Wade, sent an envoy, who was bewildered by the atmosphere at the team hotel, where players sat around, playing the drums, having fun. He insisted on a far more structured, less open environment, and as a result the squad spent their time in their rooms, staring at the ceiling and fretting about the forthcoming match. That left them 'psychologically wrung out', as Fadiga put it.[25]

Turkey beat them 1–0 in extra time.

For the majority of Argentinians, Carlos Menem's neoliberal reforms had disastrous consequences. In 1974, the richest 10 per cent of society held 28.2 per cent of GNP; by 1999 that figure was 37.3 per cent. Over the course of the nineties, the official unemployment rate rose from 5 per cent to 16 per cent.[26] And that had profound, if complex, consequences for football.

There has always been a nostalgic streak to Argentinian culture that runs in parallel to its utopianism – think of the country we could have been[27] – but that tendency reached a peak in the late 1990s. 'This,' the cultural critic Beatriz Sarlo wrote in *Perfil* shortly before the 1998 World Cup, 'was the country of abundance in which people ate like no other country on Earth. Compared to the rest of Latin America, this was the country of an industrialised working class, of an educated middle class: the country with the highest consumption of newspapers and books, a country of total literacy and no unemployment.'

Whether that was ever more than a comforting myth is debatable, but by the mid-sixties it could no longer be sustained. Development in local infrastructure had stalled, Brazil was emerging as a greater industrial power, the series of coups had undermined confidence in the institutions of government and exposure to the global market had revealed just how inefficient Argentinian industry had become. 'Very little is left of what Argentina was as a nation,' Sarlo went on, before coming to the sort of conclusion *El Gráfico* had drawn seventy years earlier. 'In the explosion of identities that some call post-modernism, football is an adhesive: it is easy, universal and televised.'[28]

Menem's second term as president came to an end in December 1999. His legacy was dismal. The economic situation was impossible. In March 2001 alone, Argentina burned through three ministers of finance. Public sector pay cuts led to a general strike in July 2001 and then, claiming £35m in unpaid wages, footballers went on strike until AFA provided clubs with a short-term loan to get the season moving again. That November, as inflation neared 40 per cent, fears of devaluation led to a run on the banks. The government responded by limiting withdrawals to US$250 a week. Thousands took to the streets in protest, and there were attacks on property belonging to banks and major European and US companies. The IMF, citing Argentina's failure to meet targets for the reduction of the budget deficit, refused to release a US$1.3bn loan, demanding cuts of 10 per cent to the federal budget. The president Fernando de la Rúa declared a state of emergency. The league was placed on hold.

On 20 December, thousands of demonstrators gathered on the Plaza de Mayo. For two days, they fought running battles with police who deployed tear gas, water cannon and rubber bullets before eventually firing live rounds, resulting in five fatalities. In total thirty-nine people were killed in protests across Argentina. De la Rúa, who always insisted he had never authorised the use of such force, was left impotent, watching cartoons in the Casa Rosada* as his government collapsed and violence raged in the square outside. Eventually, he fled by helicopter and resigned. On 23 December, Argentina defaulted on a debt of US$132bn.

There was chaos, as a succession of governments battled to solve the crisis. The peso was unpegged from the dollar and lost three-quarters of its value in a year. Given Argentina's reliance on imports, that drove up prices. In April 2002, there were further mass protests and the banking system was frozen again. In 1998 the poverty rate had been around 15 per cent; by 2002 it was over 40 per cent.

What Sarlo had said about the national football team in 1998 was even more true four years later; it was essentially the only entity capable of engendering a sense of national pride.[29] The iconoclastic Marcelo Bielsa had been appointed coach in 1998 and, while some Boca Juniors fans couldn't forgive him his refusal to pick Juan Román Riquelme, whose thoughtful approach had no place amid the intense pressing and incessant verticality he demanded, results were undeniable. Argentina

* The iconic building on the Plaza de Mayo that houses office of the president.

finished comfortably top of South American qualifying, losing only one of their eighteen games.

Bielsa hadn't been paid in eight months, but they went to Japan unbeaten in almost two years. Like many major teams, though, Argentina were blighted by injury. None of Roberto Ayala, Juan Sebastián Verón, Claudio Caniggia, Gabriel Batistuta and Matías Almeyda were fully fit and as a team they never quite got going. When a Batistuta header gave them a 1–0 win over Nigeria, the government used the celebrations as cover to announce plans to convert all remaining savings into government bonds. Riots ensued. Defeat to England and a draw against Sweden followed. Argentina had more shots and won more corners than anybody else in the group stage, but they were eliminated.

'We are sad,' said the journalist Fernando Niembro on the cable TV channel TyC, 'but this doesn't change our lives. People in Argentina have the same problems as yesterday and continue to worry about getting a job and avoiding being mugged on street corners.'[30] Faith in the national team had waned just as it had in every other institution of state. The national team had once seemed to offer an answer to the question of '*que es argentinidad?*' By 2002 the sense was that it was just another thing you couldn't trust, which is perhaps why so many had come to identify more with their clubs, impoverished and ridden with violence as many were, than with the national team.[31]

Globalisation, paradoxically, had led to a turn inwards.

When Ireland arrived at their training base on the Pacific island of Saipan, they discovered their training gear hadn't turned up. There were no balls and no medical supplies. The pitch was hard and littered with stones and hadn't been watered because nobody had told the local authorities to expect them. When the squad came back the following day, a twenty-yard strip was flooded while the rest remained like concrete.

Roy Keane was not impressed by what training was possible and saw little point in the game with which they ended, played with full-size goals but no goalkeepers; they were, he was told when he questioned the purpose of the exercise, tired after a hard session. He rowed with the keeper Alan Kelly which, for many, was the first public sign anything was amiss.

For Keane, this was just another example of Ireland's 'happy camper' approach.[32] He approached the manager, Mick McCarthy, and told him he wanted to go home. McCarthy agreed, seemingly with a certain amount of relief, having realised that Keane was on edge and that an eruption was possible at any time.

But after a conversation with the experienced physio Mick Byrne, Keane decided to stick it out until the end of the tournament. McCarthy did not react to the news as warmly as he'd have liked, concerned about other players having to 'walk on eggshells' around Keane.[33] So Keane decided to leave. That night he rang his club manager Alex Ferguson, who persuaded him to stay. Keane did an interview with the *Irish Times* in which he laid out many of his frustrations. 'I've basically had enough of certain things,' he said. 'If I feel we're not all wanting the same things, there's no point.'[34]

That evening, after the players' dinner, as the band played 'Stand By Me', McCarthy approached Keane and criticised him for the interview.[35] According to Keane, McCarthy then claimed Keane had feigned injury to miss the second leg of the qualifying play-off against Iran. According to the centre-forward Niall Quinn, the issue of Keane's absence from that game came up only later, as McCarthy scrabbled around for a weapon to hit back.[36] Keane felt McCarthy was trying to provoke him into a reaction. He got one.

The tell-tale vein stood out on Keane's temple, his voice went up a couple of octaves and he delivered a ten-minute evisceration of his manager. 'All the fuck-ups and bullshit I and every other Irish player had put up with for ten years flashed through my mind,' Keane explained. His frustration came spewing out. 'Mick, you're a liar ... I didn't rate you as a player, I don't rate you as a manager, and I don't rate you as a person. You're a fucking wanker and you can stick your World Cup up your arse. The only reason I have any dealings with you is that somehow you are the manager of my country. You can stick it up your bollocks.'[37]

At a chaotic press conference conducted in a small Chinese restaurant near the hotel, McCarthy announced that Keane had been expelled from the squad.

What happened in Saipan was the culmination of a number of issues. Keane and McCarthy hadn't got on since Keane had first been selected for Ireland on a tour of the US in 1992, when McCarthy was captain. When Keane turned up late for the bus to the airport, McCarthy reportedly reprimanded him, asking 'You call that professionalism?' To which Keane replied, 'You call that a first touch?'

Tension had been evident during the World Cup campaign. The day before Ireland's first game, away against the Netherlands, Keane was appalled that no pasta, fruit or cereals were available. 'Do you think [the Dutch forward] Jimmy Floyd Hasselbaink is eating fucking cheese sandwiches?'[38] he raged. Ireland led 2–0 with 20 minutes remaining but drew 2–2; Keane was outraged how delighted everybody seemed. They did beat the Dutch 1–0 at home, despite having Gary Kelly sent off. Keane barely acknowledged McCarthy afterwards. He declined an invitation to Quinn's testimonial, the proceeds of which went to fund a children's ward at Sunderland Royal Hospital, because of a persistent knee injury, and then refused to contribute a written endorsement when he learned parts of the programme had been put together by a journalist close to

McCarthy who had criticised Keane for supposedly picking and choosing his games.[39]

As Keane saw it, subsequent media coverage unfairly portrayed him as having snubbed sick kids.[40] There was a sense he was nearing breaking point even before setting off for the World Cup. When players then had to lug their own gear through a crowded airport, he realised how different his expectations were to those of the FAI. Watching the Michael Mann film *Ali* on the flight confirmed in his mind the sense that he should not compromise on his principles. 'The world loved us,' he said. 'Weren't we the cabaret act, there to get the party going before leaving when the tournament got serious?'[41]

The broader resonance is clear, as Quinn pointed out. He too was frustrated by the FAI's haplessness but, at the same time, he lamented the loss of the 'old excited innocence' between his first World Cup in 1990 and his last in 2002, putting it down to 'the economic boom' and Ireland being 'more confident as a nation'.[42] Keane was only five years younger than Quinn, but it doesn't take too much extrapolation to see him speaking up for a new, more aggressive and assertive – more global – Ireland against a culture of complacency and insularity.[43]

Without Keane, Ireland drew with Cameroon before a late Robbie Keane equaliser earned a point against Germany. A 3–0 win over Saudi Arabia took them through to a last-sixteen tie with Spain. Again Robbie Keane equalised late, this time from the penalty spot, but Spain won on penalties. Ireland had come very close to emulating the achievement of 1990.

Wanting a grand finale for the old Wembley before it was demolished and rebuilt, the Football Association had arranged that they would play Germany in their first qualifier for the 2002 World Cup. On a gloomy, wet afternoon, England were dreadful against an uninspired Germany and lost 1–0, unable to create chances having fallen behind when a 40-yard Didi Hamann free-kick scudded past a flat-footed David Seaman – as it turned out, a moment of foreshadowing. Kevin Keegan resigned as manager in the toilets.[44]

Keegan had been appointed on an interim basis in February 1999 following the resignation of Glenn Hoddle. The 1998 World Cup had done little to affect his reputation; David Beckham was the designated scapegoat and the sense was that England remained on the progressive path they had been set upon by Terry Venables. But Hoddle was not a great man-manager and the publication of his tournament diary was regarded by players as a breach of confidence.

That unease undermined performances but what did for him was an interview in the *Times*. 'You and I,' he said, 'have been given two hands and two legs and half-decent brains. Some people have not been born like that for a reason. The karma is working from another lifetime.'[45] He had said similar things before – and it would have been interesting had he tried to brazen it out, defending a belief that is, after all, a central tenet of a number of major faiths. But the mood of the public – and the prime minister Tony Blair, who leapt on the bandwagon when put on the spot on daytime TV – had turned against him and he was sacked.

Keegan vowed he would get everybody singing the national anthem[46] but his emphasis on motivation and passion soon ate away at the tactical advances England had made under Venables and Hoddle. At Euro 2000, they looked sluggish and old-fashioned and went out in the group stage despite beating an even more old-fashioned and sluggish Germany.

There was a dearth of English candidates, so the FA, led by a Scot in its CEO Adam Crozier, took the unprecedented step of appointing a foreigner, the urbane and mild-mannered Swede Sven-Göran Eriksson. While there were legitimate concerns as to whether it was really in the spirit of international football for one of the game's major nations to appoint a foreign coach, there was also rank xenophobia. In the *Daily Mail*, Jeff Powell wrote of 'sell[ing] our birthright down the fjord to a nation of seven million skiers and hammer throwers who spend half their year living in total darkness'.[47]

But initially, Eriksson, with his rimless glasses, well-tailored suits and unflappability, his belief in consensus and consultation, seemed very grown-up after the end of Hoddle's reign and Keegan's overwrought tenure. Successive wins over Finland, Albania and Greece meant that England were on course for at least a play-off spot for qualification when they went to Munich to face Germany, who had only lost one of their previous sixty qualifiers. What followed was an inconceivable 5–1 win as Michael Owen, again and again, got in behind Germany's leaden-footed defensive line. In the aftermath, Crozier coined the term 'Golden Generation', which would haunt the side while encapsulating the spirit of entitlement that seemed to undermine it.[48]

It still took an extraordinary performance from David Beckham, culminating in an injury-time free-kick, to secure the draw against Greece that sealed qualification, but it mattered little: Eriksson was cast as the iceman who could cure English football's woes, with Beckham an inspirational on-pitch presence. English football had always loved a messiah more than the effort of constructing a team.

There were, though, two problems. First, Beckham kept trying to replicate his performance against Greece and the result, as he deserted his position to go looking for the ball, was incoherence. And second, six weeks before the World Cup began, Beckham fractured a metatarsal. England's build-up suddenly became focused on his race to be fit.

Beckham did recover sufficiently to start in the World Cup, enjoyed his moment of redemption by scoring the penalty that beat Argentina and was one of the faces of the tournament, if only because of the ubiquity of his adverts for Police sunglasses and the way he was followed everywhere by screaming female fans.[49] This was something new: celebrity footballers with a global appeal that had very little to do with their footballing ability. And Beckham was the perfect focus: at ease in the spotlight and unfailingly gracious and polite.

But a fully fit Beckham might have been more decisive in making a challenge in the move that led to Rivaldo's equaliser for Brazil in the quarter-final. A Ronaldinho free-kick, arced over a flat-footed Seaman, gave Brazil the win despite Ronaldinho being sent off with 33 minutes remaining. In that final half-hour, England seemed dreadfully flat. Suddenly Eriksson's calmness didn't look such a virtue. 'We needed Churchill,' said Gareth Southgate, 'and we got Iain Duncan Smith.'[50]

Germany came through their play-off against Ukraine, but all was not well. Erich Ribbeck had succeeded Berti Vogts and the squad he selected for Euro 2000 was old, with only Sebastian Deisler under the age of twenty-three. That in part reflected the conservatism of German football, but it also suggested just how few young players were emerging in a Bundesliga that was increasingly populated by foreign players. The Bosman ruling of 1995 which, as well as determining a player could move on a free transfer once his contract had expired, effectively abolished restrictions on foreigners, led to a great influx of players to Europe's wealthier leagues. In 1993–94, 17 per cent of players in the Bundesliga were foreign; a decade later, that figure was 49 per cent.[51]

Beckenbauer had claimed that reunification would lead to endless German domination; instead, a decade later, the sense was that German football was tactically retrograde, its players capable of stifling opponents and little more. When Germany went out of Euro 2000 without winning a game, Beckenbauer coined the term '*Rumpelfußball*' – literally 'rumble football', robust but slow and unimaginative.[52]

But in Korea/Japan that was enough. Rudi Völler had taken over as manager after the Euros, and the 5–1 defeat in Munich had taught a valuable lesson in the dangers of leaving space behind the defensive line. Inspired by their hulking goalkeeper Oliver Kahn, Germany hammered Saudi Arabia 8–0 in the group and then relied on not making mistakes, which brought them to the semi-final thanks to 1–0 wins over Paraguay and the USA. There, they met South Korea, who had enjoyed a remarkable run.

The four Asian representatives enjoyed mixed fortunes. The affable Serbian Bora Milutinović became the first manager to lead five different countries at the World Cup as he inspired China to their first qualification, but at the finals they lost all three group games without scoring a goal, finishing with a goal difference of minus 9. Saudi Arabia fared even worse, ending with no goals scored and twelve conceded.

Japan met their pre-tournament target of reaching the knockouts thanks to wins over Russia and Tunisia, before losing to Turkey in the last sixteen. But South Korea exceeded all expectations. With Portugal missing Figo and Poland, as so often, failing to meet pre-tournament expectations, South Korea finished top of their group to set up a last-sixteen meeting with an underwhelming Italy.

What followed was simultaneously glorious and at least slightly suspicious. Gianluigi Buffon saved a contentious penalty from Ahn Jung-Hwan, Christian Vieri headed Italy in front and Seol Ki-Hyeon levelled with two minutes remaining. Francesco Totti, booked for a flailing arm in the first half, then collected a second yellow for diving and was sent off. Damiano

Tommasi, set clean through for what might have been a golden goal, was called back incorrectly for offside and, with nine minutes to go, Ahn headed a golden-goal winner. For South Korea, this was achievement beyond any realistic expectation; for Italy it was evidence of a disgraceful fix by the Ecuadorean referee Byron Moreno.

At least initially, few in the rest of the world had much sympathy. Totti's first yellow was undisputable; his second harsh but not wrong. The offside against Tommasi was incorrect but it was an understandable mistake. The response of the BBC commentator Barry Davies was typical as, frustrated by Italy's caution having taken the lead, he announced that 'the Italians are out, because they will not learn!' In Italy, though, the blame fell on the president of the FIGC, Franco Carraro, for failing to amass sufficient political capital at Fifa to ensure referees favoured Italy. The accusations, as so often, seemed to say more about those making them than about the incident itself.[53]

Italian claims, though, did begin to gain credence later that year when Moreno, while seeking election to Quito city council, was suspended for twenty matches after time-keeping errors in two league games. He lasted three matches after his return before being suspended again for sending off three Deportivo Quito players in a draw away to Deportivo Cuenca. He retired from refereeing in June 2003 and was subsequently jailed for two and a half years after attempting to smuggle 6kg of heroin in his underwear through John F. Kennedy Airport in New York.[54]

And then there was what happened in the quarter-final against Spain, who had two goals ruled out as they drew 0–0 and lost on penalties. The first, bundled in off Rubén Baraja and Kim Tae-young, was correctly disallowed – actually a very good spot by the Egyptian referee Gamal Al-Ghandour as the Spain midfielder grabbed his marker's shirt. The second, though, in extra time, was a dreadful decision by the

Trinidadian linesman Michael Ragoonath, a goal-kick given even though the ball had barely so much as touched the line when Joaquín crossed for Fernando Morientes to score what would have been a golden-goal winner.

South Korea's luck, though, could not survive the blunt reality of a semi-final with Germany, who may have been in a period of unfamiliar soul-searching, but remained a great *Turniermannschaft* (tournament team). Michael Ballack got the only goal on the break with 15 minutes remaining.

To claim the tournament was fixed, as many did, was probably to overstate the case but South Korea did get the benefit of a number of key decisions and that, inevitably, tarnished their achievement.[55] Within South Korea, though, joy was unconfined. An estimated 4 million took to the streets for the game against Italy, with 7 million out for the game against Germany. 'Hiddink Syndrome' became a popular phrase, used both as an attack on cronyism within Korea[56] and to argue for a more open economy.[57]

It had been a tournament characterised by underdog successes. Five confederations were represented in the quarter-finals. As well as South Korea and Senegal, the USA got to the last eight and Turkey, in their first World Cup since 1954, to the last four. Turkey beat South Korea 3–2 in the third-place play-off, their opener, the earliest goal in World Cup history, scored after 11 seconds by Hakan Şükür, who was forced to flee Turkey in 2016 after being accused of involvement in an attempted coup against the president, Recep Tayyip Erdoğan. As he invested in a bakery in Palo Alto and set up home in the US, Şükür's name was erased from Turkish record books.[58]

Given how the traditional powers hit back at subsequent tournaments, the widespread claims of fatigue were evidently more than mere excuses. And it may be that the success of the minnows was a part of the first phase of globalisation in football: in those first years after the Bosman ruling, nations from outside the European elite – not just the likes of Turkey and Senegal, but also Greece, who won Euro 2004 – were advantaged by having their best players playing at the highest level before the impact of the loss of quality in their domestic leagues was felt. Certainly by 2018 the sense would be that western European powers, having effectively industrialised youth production, were reaping the dividends of the players they produced having relatively easy access to the highest-level leagues in the world.[59]

Besides which, after all the novelty and unpredictability, the final ended up being a meeting between two of the three most successful sides in World Cup history, Brazil and Germany – and not even especially notable iterations. Brazil had been dismal in qualifying as Vanderlei Luxemburgo was sacked after suspicious land transactions were unearthed, and the outspoken former goalkeeper Émerson Leão won just four of eleven games before being replaced by Luiz Felipe Scolari.

Scolari was uncompromising, frequently boorish, and successful. Despite defeat to Honduras in the quarter-final of the Copa América, he rescued the qualifying campaign, building a platform for the extremely talented attacking trio of Ronaldinho, Ronaldo and Rivaldo. Turkey, China and Costa Rica represented a straightforward group and there were few scares against a lacklustre Belgium in the last sixteen. After beating England in the quarter-final, Ronaldo's clever toe-poke early in the second half saw off Turkey in the semi-final. That was his sixth goal of the tournament and his redemption after the 1998 final was completed as he scored both goals in a 2–0 win over Germany in the final. It was Brazil's fifth World Cup, but never before had they won after facing so few challenges, a triumph lubricated by a benevolent draw and the failings of others.

For all the shocks, for all the progress of supposed minnows, the overriding impression was of a tournament in which very few of the best had played anywhere near their best. Amid all the bold talk of the globalised nature of the modern game, a lot of the actual football was mediocre.

2006

THE HEADBUTT AND THE FAIRY TALE

In October 2013, a huge statue was unveiled on the Corniche in Doha. Around sixteen feet high and cast in bronze by the French-Algerian artist Adel Abdessemed, it depicted two men. Looking at it from the west, facing the sea, to the left was the France forward Zinedine Zidane, his back to the Sheraton and the cluster of skyscrapers alongside it, head bowed, in a posture that, were he alone, would appear humble, perhaps supplicant. But he is not alone. To the right, falling backwards, mouth open in shock, is the Italy defender Marco Materazzi, having been headbutted in the chest by Zidane in the 2006 World Cup final.

Four weeks later, the statue was removed for promoting 'idolatry'.[1] The specific issue was Islamic prohibitions on the representation of people, but there was a secular resonance as well. *Coup de tête*, to give the work its correct title, was, after all, strikingly odd. When it was unveiled at the Centre Pompidou in Paris in 2012 it was described by the exhibition organiser Alain Michaud as 'an ode to defeat'.[2] Zidane, in his final professional match, was sent off ten minutes from the end of extra time with the score at 1–1. He had put France ahead

Bob Thomas Sports Photography/Getty Images

Paolo Rossi, the top scorer at the 1982 World Cup, celebrates his goal in the 1982 World Cup final.

Archivo El Grafico/Getty Images

Diego Maradona, having beaten Peter Shilton, finishes off his brilliant second against England in the 1986 World Cup final, despite the lunge of Terry Butcher.

Eric RENNARD/Corbis/Getty Images

Roger Milla, having dispossessed René Higuita, runs on to score Cameroon's second against Colombia in 1990.

Tony Quinn/Alamy Stock Photo

Diana Ross, minutes before missing an open goal from three yards, performing at the opening ceremony in 1994.

Michael Kunkel/Bongarts/Getty Images

A nurse called Sue Carpenter leads Diego Maradona away for a routine drugs test after Argentina's victory over Nigeria at Foxborough in 1994.

Antonio Scorza/AFP/Getty Images

Ronaldo in despair after Brazil's defeat to France in the 1998 World Cup final.

Paul Popper/Popperfoto/Getty Images

Zinedine Zidane (left), Marcel Desailly (centre) and Laurent Blanc (right) lift the trophy after France's victory in the 1998 World Cup.

Chung Sung-Jun/Stringer/Getty Images

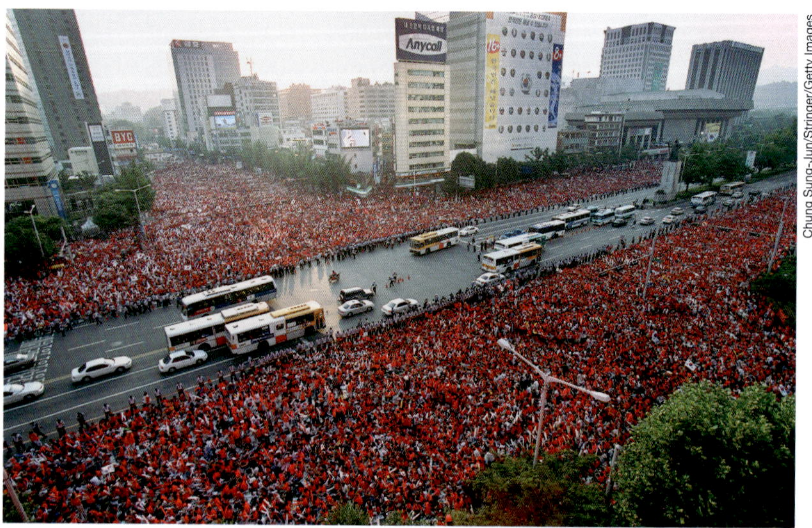

Thousands of red-clad South Korea fans flood the streets of Seoul before their decisive group game against Italy in 2002.

Simon Bruty/Anychance/Getty Images

Zinedine Zidane awaits his fate after headbutting Marco Materazzi in the 2006 final.

Clive Mason/Getty Images

A South Africa fan at Soccer City, Johannesburg, blows a vuvuzela before the opening game of the 2010 World Cup.

FRANCK FIFE/AFP/Getty Images

France's captain Patrice Evra explains to his manager Raymond Domenech that the players are going on strike at their training base in Knysna 2010.

Reinaldo Coddou H/Getty Images

The enormously expensive 43,000-capacity Arena da Amazônia during Italy's win over England in the group stage of the 2014 World Cup.

FAYEZ NURELDINE/AFP/Getty Images

The seats of power: a screen in a Saudi fan tent shows (left-to-right) Mohammed bin Salman, Gianni Infantino and Vladimir Putin watching the opening game of the 2018 World Cup, in which Russia beat Saudi Arabia 5–0.

Simon Stacpoole/Offside/Getty Images

The president of Russia Vladimir Putin (front, second from left) gets the umbrella at the presentation ceremony for the 2018 Word Cup in Moscow. The president of Fifa Gianni Infantino (front row, left), the president of France Emmanuel Macron (front row, third from left) and the president of Croatia Kolinda Grabar-Kitarović (front row, fourth from left, in red and white shirt, hugging Croatia's manager Zlatko Dalić) do not.

Dan Mullan/Getty Images

Lionel Messi skips by Joško Gvardiol to set up Argentina's third goal against Croatia in the 2022 World Cup semi-final.

Julian Finney/Getty Images

Lionel Messi, wearing a *bisht*, lifts the World Cup in the Lusail Stadum just outside Doha.

from an early penalty and Materazzi had equalised, but Zidane was not there for the penalty shoot-out, which France lost.

The statue didn't just capture a moment of defeat, but one of self-immolation. There are countless theories as to why Zidane acted as he did. It was the fourteenth red card of his career, twelve of them for retaliating after provocation. 'My passion, temper and blood made me react,' Zidane said.[3] Quite what Materazzi said to Zidane has never been settled but it seems probable he made a crude insinuation about his sister. Materazzi himself published a book listing 249 variations of what he might have said.[4]

Some saw deeper symbolism in Zidane's act. The cricketer turned columnist Ed Smith suggested that what had undone Zidane was the spectacular save Gianluigi Buffon had made from his 104th-minute header, and the realisation, which manifested initially in a scream at the sky, that, at the last, the fates were deserting him, that this was not, as so many other major occasions had been, to be his day.*[5]

But it was also, of course, a selfish act, the fleeting catharsis of individual retribution elevated above the needs of the team and the nation. Germany 2006 was a tournament of egos, from Zidane's red card to the nonsense of Baden-Baden to the cussedness of Scolari to the dispute between Emmanuel Adebayor and Stephen Keshi that led to the coach being replaced before the tournament by Otto Pfister. There was also the first emergence at the World Cup of Cristiano Ronaldo and Lionel Messi.

---

* In *The Denial of Death*, the cultural anthropologist Ernest Becker argued that the ego, unable to accept the essentially random determinants of its own coming-into-being, created a 'heroism' – religious devotion, romantic love, physical courage, the accumulation of wealth, success in a given sphere – to give meaning to life and to offer the possibility of validation. For Becker, the ultimate expression of that would be suicide or *de facto* suicide in pursuit of the heroism: what was Zidane's act but a symbolic variant of this, taking control of the dissolution of the ego, occluding the randomness of its coming-into-being, by pursuing to the ultimate the ideals by which he had conducted himself throughout his career, never letting an insult or slight go unpunished?

The globalisation of 2002 had led to stars having genuinely global status and that, inevitably, changed the dynamic.

Zidane's headbutt was the most memorable moment of a tournament born amid scandal and dominated by celebrity, yet won by the side seeking redemption for scandal that best sublimated its stars into the team unit. And it was salvaged by its hosts and their *Sommermärchen*, the final redemption of the unified Germany coinciding with the rebirth of their football.

By the turn of the millennium, German excitement about reunification had dimmed. It wasn't just in football that the expected benefits had failed to materialise. Germany was suffering *Reformstau* (reform blockage) as industry complained of high taxes and business of excessive bureaucracy. Unemployment pushed through 4 million, more than 10 per cent of the total workforce.[6] The early years of the new century were marked by a series of investigations into the stagnation,[7] but by 2005, unemployment had hit 5 million. Gerhard Schröder's Social Democratic government had undertaken a controversial overhaul of the pension and social security system in 2004, which was in part responsible for the election of the Christian Democrat Angela Merkel the following year. There was a sense that the German economy, Germany itself, needed a shot in the arm.

Looking back to the early fifties, when the *Wirtschaftswunder* created the stereotype of Germans as disciplined hard-workers, the seminal cultural event, the great symbolic moment of (West) Germany's re-emergence had come at the 1954 World Cup. Around the fiftieth anniversary, *das Wunder von Bern* became fetishised, most obviously in Sönke Wortmann's sentimental film but also in at least fifteen books and television documentaries. Very few had much to do with lived reality at the time, but rather offered a welcoming fiction for the birth of the federal republic.[8] There was a sense that, as Markus Brauck wrote in the *Frankfurter Rundschau*, Germany needed another Bern, another moment of 'national therapy'.[9] The decision to bid to host the World Cup, the need to host it, the delight in hosting it, can only be understood through that lens.

Charles Dempsey wasn't there, and that was vital.

Had the affable seventy-nine-year-old Scot, the president of the Oceanian Football Confederation and the head of the New Zealand Football Association, remained in Zurich for the third round of voting to determine who should host the 2006 World Cup, it was widely expected he would have voted for South Africa. That would have left the Fifa Executive Committee equally split between South Africa and Germany, giving the president, Sepp Blatter, the casting vote. He had always been open about his dream of taking the World Cup to Africa for the first time; that had been part of his pitch to the African voters who had elected him. After the 2002 World Cup had been granted to Asia, though, sponsors were keen for Germany to prevail, which has led to speculation that Blatter might have been backing South Africa in public while hoping for a German victory: why not bank the money and then go to South Africa four years later? The problem with a casting vote was that everybody would know who he had backed.

But as it turned out, Blatter wasn't called on for a casting vote. Germany won the vote 12–11 because Dempsey had left Zurich and was headed to Singapore to play golf. Nelson Mandela had rung him in his hotel room. A letter was slipped under his door telling him to call a number in Berlin. Was it a bribe? Entrapment? In a panic, Dempsey rang the general secretary of the OFC, his daughter Josephine King. She advised him to abstain so as to protect his reputation. And so he fled. Or at least that was his story.[10] At a press conference soon after the vote, he claimed he had been warned by 'influential European interests' of 'adverse consequences' for Oceania if he backed South Africa.[11]

But Theo Zwanziger, the former president of the DFB, believed Dempsey was the mysterious 'E16' who had received a US$250,000 payment from the Swiss sports marketing company International Sport and Leisure (ISL) a day before the vote.[12] In the fallout, Dempsey was forced to resign the OFC presidency, but he was soon made honorary president for life and invited by Blatter to serve on Fifa's disciplinary committee. Once Blatter had won a second term as president in 2002, Dempsey was also made an honorary life president of Fifa, which guaranteed him free first-class travel to any future Fifa event.

The bid for 2006 had come down to four nations, although nobody took Morocco's especially seriously and they were eliminated in the first round of voting. England's bid was a moral disgrace and a practical shambles. The Football Association was just as prepared to dabble in the shadier aspects of lobbying as everybody else; they just weren't very good at it. It was to support the bid that the FA backed Blatter over Johansson in the 1998 Fifa presidential election, that they forced the holders Manchester United to withdraw from the 1999–2000 FA Cup to compete instead in the first vainglorious stab at a Club World Cup, and that they clumsily attempted to replace the Scot David Will as Great Britain & Northern Ireland's representative on the Fifa Executive Committee with the FA chairman Keith Wiseman. Wales agreed to support the FA for a £3.2m loan but Northern Ireland refused to go along with it. When the payment was exposed, Wiseman and the FA CEO Graham Kelly resigned.[13]

In return for German backing for England's bid to host Euro 96, the Football Association had agreed to support a German bid to host the 2006 World Cup. The FA for a long time denied the existence of this 'gentleman's agreement', but unhelpfully for them it is referenced in the minutes of a meeting of the FA's International Committee in August 1991.

Not that Germany could take the moral high ground.[14] Shortly before the vote, a shipment of rocket-propelled grenades was delivered to Saudi Arabia,[15] Daimler put together a €100m package to aid Hyundai, Bayer invested in Thailand and Volkswagen in South Korea.[16] Saudi Arabia and Thailand both had delegates on the ExCo, while Hyundai was the family firm of the South Korean Fifa vice-president Chung Jung-moon. Kirch, the media company backing the German bid, had Bayern play friendlies against Thailand, Malta, Trinidad & Tobago and a club from Tunisia, in each case paying the local federation US$300,000 for the privilege.[17] Thailand, Malta, Trinidad & Tobago and Tunisia all had votes.

In addition, the CEO of Adidas, Robert Louis-Dreyfus, had loaned the DFB €6.7m which was then used to help secure the four Asian votes, the payment coming to light when Louis-Dreyfus was repaid via a Fifa account in 2005, supposedly for work on a World Cup opening ceremony that never happened.[18] The CEO of the DFB, Wolfgang Niersbach, the press officer to whom Beckenbauer had given his medal after the 1990 World Cup, denied the allegations, insisting the payment had been agreed between Beckenbauer and Blatter as part of separate financial arrangements for the tournament. On the same day, though, Fifa contradicted his claims.[19] Niersbach later resigned over the issue[20] and he was charged with tax evasion relating to the World Cup. The case was discontinued in August 2024 although the presiding judge in Frankfurt ruled it was not an acquittal.[21]

Swiss prosecutors, considering possible charges of breach of trust and money-laundering against Beckenbauer, uncovered a payment of at least €1.7m that same year to an account he held in Gibraltar, apparently for his work as a consultant to the South African Football Association as it took a loan from

Fifa to cover pressing financial difficulties.[22] Also receiving payments were two confidants of Beckenbauer, Fedor Radmann and Andreas Abold. Radmann, who had worked for Kirch and had connections with Adidas, used Abold's company to design the widely derided logo for the 2006 World Cup; he resigned from his work on the World Cup after the sports minister Otto Schily demanded an explanation of various apparent conflicts of interest.[23]

By the time the dubious payments to Beckenbauer were revealed, there was a sense that nobody could come close to a World Cup bid without contamination.

Everything around Fifa at that time seemed tainted: the early years of Blatter's presidency were mired in scandal, much of it inherited from Havelange. The problems began when Horst Dassler died in 1987, aged fifty-one, leading to major problems for both Adidas and ISL, which had been set up by Dassler and handled Fifa's media rights deals. Two key figures, Klaus Hempel and Jürgen Lenz, quit ISL and set up Television Event and Media Marketing (TEAM), which won the rights for the Champions League when it launched in 1992. When ISL then lost the rights to the Olympics in December 1995, there was huge pressure not to lose international football as well and, seeking secure revenues, it came up with a plan to bid for two World Cups at once.

Blatter gave competing bidders very little warning and, as Kirch agreed to support ISL in return for the German rights, their bid for the 2002 and 2006 World Cups was accepted in July 1996. A little over two years later, a CHF1m payment from ISL arrived in Fifa's account, a bribe intended not for them but for a member of the executive committee. Fifa knew exactly what it was and forwarded it but, crucially, there was a paper trail and it could be traced.[24]

In July 1998, the Brazilian media company Globo paid ISL US$60m for World Cup rights. Of that amount, $22m should have gone to Fifa but it never arrived. The ambitious young general-secretary Michel Zen-Ruffinen, who had only taken the role a month earlier when Blatter had ascended to the presidency, was furious, beginning the process of his disillusionment.

Meanwhile, the tennis side of ISL's business was struggling. The banks were beginning to talk about calling in loans. Blatter was under pressure as well, having gifted each of Fifa's members $250,000 for development – and if that encouraged them to vote for Blatter, that was their business. Fifa was forced to take out a loan of CHF300m from Credit Suisse. ISL had no such route to easy credit and were forced to ask Blatter for help.

In April 2001, a Swiss court ordered ISMM, the parent company behind ISL, to begin bankruptcy proceedings. By that point ISL's losses stood at US$1.2bn. ISMM collapsed the following month. Blatter claimed the losses to Fifa were only around $30m; a truer figure might have been around ten times that.[25] When Kirch then went bankrupt in April 2002, Fifa had to take out a resecuritisation deal with Credit Suisse for $420m.

In May 2001, a flurry of stories began to appear in the Swiss and German press investigating the relationship between Blatter, Fifa and ISL. The Swiss business magazine *Bilanz* revealed that ISL had run a slush fund from Liechtenstein.[26] The liquidator Thomas Bauer confirmed that it had been used for paying off sports officials.[27] The missing Globo money became public knowledge. Forced to take action, Fifa discovered it was appalled by the shortfall and accused ISL executives of fraud and embezzlement.

The process of Swiss justice is slow and complicated. Finally, in a court in Zug in 2008, Jean-Marie Weber, the former head of ISL, was found to have taken a CHF90,000 bribe, although few believe he was the ultimate beneficiary.[28] In the same hearing, it was established that ISL had made a total of 175 payments worth more than CHF122m between 1989 and 1999, including the one that inadvertently ended up in Fifa's accounts.[29] Such payments were not against Swiss law at the time.

Uefa called for a vote of confidence in Blatter. He survived by acclamation. Issa Hayatou, with Johansson by his side, announced his intention to run in the 2002 presidential election. By then, Zen-Ruffinen had lost all faith in Fifa and Blatter. He spoke out against what he described as the 'general mismanagement, dysfunctions in the structure and financial irregularities' at Fifa. He accused Blatter specifically of working against Fifa's statutes, 'manipulating the whole network through the material and administrative power he gained to the benefit of third persons and his personal interests. Fifa today is run like a dictatorship . . .'[30] In May 2002, eleven members of the executive committee, those from Uefa, CAF and the South Korean Chung Jung-moon, raised thirteen specific charges of questionable payments by Blatter in the Swiss courts.

But Blatter was ready. He had learned from Havelange, the master, promoting policies that, on the face of it, looked benevolent but which could be used to establish a culture of clientelism.[31] On succeeding Havelange, Blatter had established the Goal Project, described by its own rubric as 'a tailor-made development and assistance programme designed to realise projects based on the specific needs of national associations'.

In terms of how it was used, the first initiative it funded is instructive. In November 1999, Blatter went to Monrovia, Liberia, to celebrate the scheme's inauguration. He shook hands with Liberia's president Charles Taylor and gave US$50,000 to the president of the Liberian Football Association, Taylor's son-in-law Edwin Snowe, to study sports management in the US.

The LFA at the time was so poor that when they unexpectedly qualified for the Cup of Nations in Mali in 2002, their kit and team bus were paid for by their centre-forward, George Weah.[32] Snowe remained as president of the LFA, drawing his salary throughout his period of study. When he returned to Liberia after graduating, he quit football and became managing director of the Liberia Petroleum Refining Company.[33] Taylor, by that point, had been indicted by a UN special court on charges of murder, mass rape, amputation and mutilation, taking slaves, forcing children to act as soldiers, attacking humanitarian workers and the theft of an estimated $100m from his own country.

Blatter, like his mentor, knew Africa was the real battleground for votes, even if he was standing against an African. He spent the first half of 2002 travelling the continent, promising funding from the Goal Project and insisting that South Africa, having missed out so cruelly in 2006, should host the 2010 World Cup.

The Seoul Congress in 2002 was a farce. Only two of Fifa's vice-presidents remained loyal to Blatter but the only opponent of Blatter called upon to speak was the Norwegian delegate Karen Esplund.[34] Blatter made great play of the fact that Fifa had turned a profit, but that was only because future marketing deals for 2006 had been securitised. Without that, as David Will pointed out, there would have been a loss of CHF536m. Had Fifa been a company rather than an association, it would have been compelled to declare itself bankrupt under Swiss law. Yet Blatter beat Hayatou 139 votes to 56.

After breaking ranks, Zen-Ruffinen couldn't be allowed to stay on as general secretary, so Blatter turned to his chief financial officer Urs Linsi to replace him while retaining his previous role. That seemed to be a breach of the basic principle of separation of administrative and financial arms, so Blatter established an independent audit commission to ensure everything remained above board. And who better to serve as its secretary than Urs Linsi?

Any pretence that Fifa might at some level be a benign institution protecting the good of the game was long since gone.

Australia shouldn't even have been in Lourenço Marques. It was November 1969. They had finished top of a three-team group with South Korea and Japan, and then faced a play-off against Rhodesia – clumsily inserted into Asian/Oceanian qualifying because no African side would play the apartheid state – for the right to play Israel, who had beaten New Zealand in what effectively became a play-off after North Korea withdrew. Rhodesia's status as a pariah made finding a venue extremely difficult, until the capital of Mozambique stepped in.

The first leg was frustrating. Australia were the better side but the game was drawn 1–1.[35] In the second leg, with the captain Johnny Warren sidelined by food-poisoning, Australia missed a raft of chances and the game finished goalless. That meant a third game.

Australia's team doctor Brian Corrigan and travel consultant Tommy Patrick were sitting in a bar lamenting their side's misfortune when a local journalist suggested visiting a *nyunga* to guarantee victory. Corrigan and Patrick agreed and, in a meeting in his office at a local brothel, it was arranged that the *nyunga* would bury bones under one of the goals at the stadium while casting a spell that would sap Rhodesia's powers. The keeper was notably shaky and ended up being stretchered off after a collision with the Australia forward Ray Baartz. The returning Warren scored in a 3–1 win but when the *nyunga* came to the team hotel demanding his $1,000 fee he was turned away. In response, he cursed Australian football.

An outbreak of political violence in Angola delayed

Australia's flight to Israel, with the result that the trip took thirty-six hours and two players were so travel sick they couldn't play. A deflected free-kick gave Israel a 1–0 win. Australia were then denied what they felt was a clear penalty in the second leg and drew 1–1 to miss out on qualification for the 1970 World Cup.

They did qualify four years later, but lost every game – and Warren played only the first after turning his ankle, after which their story was of near-misses and play-off mishaps. 'As the disasters and freak occurrences that have befallen Australian teams since 1970 pile up,' Warren said, 'my belief in the curse has only strengthened.'[36]

Warren explained his theory about the curse to the comedian John Safran and in 2004, Safran set off for Mozambique to track down the *nyunga* and pay him what he was due. The *nyunga* had died, but another *nyunga* promised he could perform the necessary ritual if Safran met him in the stadium where the bones had been buried. 'That involved us sitting in the middle of the pitch and he killed a chicken and splattered the blood all over me,' said Safran. He and Warren then had to go to the Telstra Stadium in Sydney and smear themselves in clay the *nyunga* gave him.[37] That November, Warren died. A year later, Australia faced Uruguay in a World Cup qualifying play-off. Having lost 1–0 in Montevideo, they won 1–0 at Telstra before winning on penalties. The curse had been lifted.

Australia impressed in Germany. They came from behind to beat Japan 3–1 and, despite defeat to Brazil, they progressed to the last sixteen with a 2–2 draw against Croatia, secured when Harry Kewell's offside equaliser was allowed to stand in the game in which the English referee Graham Poll showed the Croatia defender Josip Šimunić three yellow cards before eventually sending him off.

*

First along the path by the canal came Carly Zucker, the fitness instructor girlfriend of the forward Joe Cole, leading a gaggle of players' wives and girlfriends – WAGs, as they'd recently been dubbed – on a jog through the park in Baden-Baden. Then came a security detail and behind them British paparazzi, and behind them foreign paparazzi gleefully recording the whole circus.

The summer of 2006 was when the celebrity culture around the England team, hinted at in Japan, reached its hysterical peak. The squad itself was billeted in the luxurious Schlosshotel Bühlerhöhe in the Black Forest about ten miles away, while the WAGs stayed in the Brenners Park in the town itself. The lawns usually sweep down to the canal, but for that month they were interrupted by a series of screens preventing photographers getting snaps of the WAGs as they sunbathed. Every night, a bar or restaurant would be taken over, there'd be drinking, wild behaviour, dancing on tables. The bar at the Brenners Park became a journalistic goldmine. It was gossipy, bitchy, enthralling and exhausting – and totally unsuitable for the business of winning a major football tournament.

England had had an impressive if flawed Euros in 2004. Inspired by the eighteen-year-old Wayne Rooney, they'd played well enough in beating Switzerland 3–0 and Croatia 4–2 to look like potential champions, but a warning had come in their opening group game, against France, when Beckham had missed a penalty with England 1–0 up and they'd ended up conceding two late goals to lose 2–1. The midfield four of Beckham, Steven Gerrard, Frank Lampard and Paul Scholes was full of talent, but lacked balance, an issue that would continue to undermine the Golden Generation. There was a lack of width on the left and Scholes disliked playing there, while Gerrard and Lampard never worked out how to play together. To use both probably meant bringing in a holding player but that would have meant a switch from 4-4-2 to 4-3-3 and leaving out Beckham, and Eriksson was never going to do that. But still, England reached the quarter-final and were 1–0 up against the hosts Portugal when Jorge Andrade trod on Rooney's foot, fracturing his metatarsal. England drew 2–2 and lost on penalties.

The euphoria of the 5–1 win in Munich in 2001 had faded long before England returned to Germany in the World Cup. There were high-profile flings with the TV personality Ulrika Jonsson and the FA secretary Faria Alam while a *News of the World* fake sheikh sting revealed the shock news that, if offered lots of money, Eriksson would be prepared to manage Aston Villa. In themselves the stories didn't amount to much, but taken together alongside Eriksson's apparent willingness to endorse absolutely any product, the result was an atmosphere of tawdriness. At the same time, Scholes had retired from international football, his place on the left taken by Joe Cole. He was, at least, a player used to operating on that side, but the basic issue in the centre was never addressed, Eriksson seemingly unwilling to leave out any of his three big-name midfielders, the potential of the Golden Generation sacrificed on the altar of celebrity. Eriksson's enlightened age of consensus became in Baden-Baden a culture of complacency and excess.

England were uninspired. Again, their campaign was blighted by a metatarsal injury, with Rooney fracturing a bone in his foot a month before the tournament. He returned for the third group game against Sweden, having announced his arrival in Baden-Baden following treatment with the words 'the big man is back in town'.[38]

Belatedly, Eriksson moved away from his preferred 4-4-2 in the knockouts, using Rooney as a lone striker with first Owen Hargreaves and then Michael Carrick deployed at the back of midfield but, after scraping past Ecuador in the last sixteen, England suffered another penalty shoot-out defeat to Portugal in the quarter-final, after Rooney had been sent off for stamping on Ricardo Carvalho. There had, at least, in their exit been signs of resilience but the overriding feeling was of talent indulged and ultimately wasted.

Eriksson had become the first manager since Alf Ramsey to take England to the quarter-finals or beyond of three successive tournaments but he resigned after the World Cup. What followed was far worse.

After Jacques Santini's France had reached the quarter-final of Euro 2004, Raymond Domenech was the slightly surprising choice to take over as national manager. He had led Lyon to the second division title in 1988–89 but for the previous eleven years he had been manager of the national Under-21 side, in which role his results were mixed. He did, though, represent continuity, having been Jacquet's captain at Lyon and also played under him at Bordeaux, while his role in the youth set-up meant he was already well acquainted with the many Clairefontaine graduates who were beginning to break into the senior squad. One of his first acts as national coach was to visit Zidane; a week later, at the age of thirty-two, Zidane quit football.

From the start, Domenech's reign seemed ill-starred. He tried to impose discipline: squad breakfast at 8.30 a.m., punctuality, no mobile phones during physio and massage sessions, shinpads to be worn during training. Certain players resisted. Patrick Vieira liked his lie-ins, and that apparently trivial issue underlay what became known as *le problème Arsenal* as evidence of a broader tension emerged between the manager and Pirès, who was supported by Henry. When Pirès was taken off at half-time in a 2–0 win on Cyprus in October 2004 he, according to Domenech, spent the second half sitting in the car park[39] and never played for his country again.

The Barcelona winger Ludovic Giuly was also frozen

out – the coincidence that both he and Pirès knew Domenech's girlfriend, the television presenter Estelle Denis, was noted by those concerned. Domenech was allowing his personal life to interfere with team selection. And then, in August 2005, Zidane recanted of his retirement.[40] Claude Makélélé and Thuram also returned. All three played in a friendly against Ivory Coast in Montpellier and, almost immediately, France found a fluency, Zidane getting the second in a 3–0 win. The popular narrative has it that that was the beginning of a Zidane-inspired surge that carried France to the World Cup final, but there is an alternative view. Perhaps not surprisingly, it is expressed most eloquently by Vikash Dhorasoo, the Paris Saint-Germain playmaker whose chances of making the World Cup squad were effectively ended by Zidane's return. For him, Zidane interrupted the process of regeneration. The consequences of that, the uneasiness of the transition that followed, perhaps, would be seen in South Africa four years later.

It's also true that there was no sudden uptick in form.[41] Qualifying remained a slog and, had Ireland's Shay Given not denied Switzerland's Alexander Frei in a one-on-one on the final night of qualifying, France would have been consigned to the play-offs. They were hardly more impressive in the group, drawing with Switzerland and South Korea before limping through with a 2–0 win over Togo.

Before the last-sixteen tie against Spain, *Marca*, foolishly provocative, declared on their front page that Spain were going to 'retire Zidane'.[42] As it turned out, it was a Zidane free-kick that led to Vieira bundling in the goal that put France ahead before he rounded off a 3–1 win in injury time, gliding past Carles Puyol before beating Iker Casillas.

Still, though, there was no hint of what was to come. Zidane, indeed, was a doubt for the quarter-final against Brazil with a thigh injury. Within two minutes, though, he had performed a double dragback that took him away from three Brazil players and laid the ball off. From that moment, Domenech said, he knew something special was happening. Zidane was masterful, controlling the game and setting up the only goal for Henry – remarkably the only time the two ever combined for a goal despite fifty-eight internationals together.

As at Euro 2000, a Zidane penalty saw off Portugal in the semi-final to set up a final against Italy.

Investigating doping allegations against Juventus, prosecutors tapped the phone of the Juventus general manager Luciano Moggi and discovered instead that he, and other clubs, had been involved in trying to ensure referees supposedly favourable to their cause were appointed to their games. As the scandal, dubbed *Calciopoli*, escalated, numerous other clubs were implicated, although many were protected from prosecution by the statute of limitations. Juventus ended up being stripped of two league titles and forcibly relegated while Fiorentina, Lazio, Milan and Reggina were all docked points. Although economic factors were already turning against Italy, it's arguable that its football has never recovered from the reputational damage.

The scandal was only part of a picture of broader misery. The government had introduced an austerity package. Taxi drivers were on a go-slow protest. In the middle of the tournament, the former Italy international Gianluca Pessotto, a former team-mate of many in the squad, recently appointed sporting director of Juventus, fell from a fourth-storey window at the club's headquarters; although he survived, he suffered serious injuries. He had a rosary in his hand, but his wife insisted it was not a suicide attempt but that he had simply blacked out.[43]

Three days later it was announced that the Italian cyclist Ivan Basso would not be riding in the Tour de France because of suspicion of blood doping.[44] When Beckenbauer suggested that the chaotic background meant Italy would be quickly eliminated, the great former Italy striker Gigi Riva called him 'childish' and promised to bring him some toys.[45]

Calciopoli broke less than a month before the World Cup began and inevitably came to involve many in the Italy squad: thirteen of their twenty-three-man squad played for a club that would eventually be sanctioned (so did three of the France squad) while the captain Fabio Cannavaro spoke in defence of Moggi.[46] At the same time the coach Marcello Lippi's son Davide, an agent, was initially implicated although he was eventually cleared.

As in 1982, though, the backdrop of scandal proved galvanising. Lippi was a master of making the most of his resources. All twenty outfield players played at least some part, while he happily changed formation between 4-3-1-2 and 4-2-3-1. The group stage was negotiated without drama, then Francesco Totti's injury-time penalty took them past Australia after Materazzi had been sent off. Ukraine were comfortably dispatched in the quarter-final to set up a semi against the hosts.

For Germany, Euro 2004 had confirmed that their progress to the final of the 2002 World Cup had been something of a freak as, for the second Euros in a row, they were eliminated without winning a game. Völler resigned as coach. Ottmar Hitzfeld turned the job down. So did Otto Rehhagel, who had led Greece to the Euro 2004 title. There was an element of desperation about the DFB's hunt for a successor.

It seemed an invidious job. As Klinsmann had put it on the day of the Euros final, there was no vision, no great forward, no attacking plan and only Philipp Lahm was capable of playing at high tempo.[47] Klinsmann had retired from playing in 1998 and moved to California, where he worked for a sports marketing company. Nobody saw him as a potential manager, but he had his coaching licence. Vogts happened to be outside San Diego, where Klinsmann lived, on his way to Las Vegas for a holiday with his son. He called Klinsmann and they met. Vogts asked Klinsmann if he could imagine being national coach. He said he could, but only if he had the freedom to do things his way. The next day, the DFB called and set up a meeting in New York. Klinsmann arrived with a dossier entitled 'Project World Cup 2006'.[48] He was appointed at the end of July 2004. Beckenbauer wanted his former assistant Holger Osieck appointed to work alongside Klinsmann, but Klinsmann opted for Jogi Löw, who had been a fellow student when he'd done his coaching badge and had been able to explain, with greater clarity than anybody else, how a back four should move across the pitch.

Klinsmann changed the culture around the Germany national side. He made squad get-togethers more like corporate team-building exercises, with motivational talks and activities such as go-karting, archery and watchmaking. He brought in a psychologist and US fitness and conditioning coaches, both huge steps for a national side historically convinced its players were mentally tougher and could run harder than opponents, although perhaps not as big a step as the decision he made over his goalkeeper, leaving out an outraged Oliver Kahn for the more mobile Jens Lehmann. Germany began to press in a focused way and to focus on transitions. It was all very alien to their traditional way of playing and that, inevitably, led to tension.

Once the tournament began, though, everything rapidly fell into place. Costa Rica were beaten 4–2 which was almost the perfect start in that it got casual fans excited while also highlighting to the players the need to close spaces down quicker. A scratchy 1–0 victory over Poland led to a great eruption of emotion. A 3–0 win over Ecuador completed the process. 'The fear of failure,' the midfielder Thomas Hitzlsperger said, 'was gone. It became a big party ... Germany discovered itself as a welcoming country, a fun place.'[49]

This was what the sports minister Otto Schily had dreamed of as he planned the World Cup, although he seemed to think the best way to generate the impression of a 'welcoming, open-minded and lively' country was for Germans to pretend to be Austrian, as he encouraged taxi drivers, policemen and those in the hospitality industry to adopt a 'Viennese, southern touch'.[50] It worked. The fan parks, based to an extent on the public viewing areas that had drawn millions onto the streets of South Korea, proved an enormous success. No tournament is ever entirely without incident but in Germany in 2006, the mood was notably upbeat. Amid the relaxed atmosphere, in the first major sporting event staged in a united Germany since the 1936 Olympics, the *Schwarz-Rot-Gold* flag began to be seen in large numbers, far more even than in 1990. 'Patriotism,' Hitzlsperger said, 'was suddenly okay, cool even.'[51]

Two early Lukas Podolski goals saw off Sweden to set up Germany's first World Cup meeting with Argentina since the 1990 final. Bielsa had left after winning Olympic gold, to be replaced by José Pékerman, who had enjoyed remarkable success with the youth sides. His team, built around Juan Román Riquelme, swept through the group, Esteban Cambiasso scoring one of the all-time great team goals in a 6–0 demolition of Serbia-Montenegro. A stunning Maxi Rodríguez volley in extra time had got them past Mexico in the last sixteen.

Roberto Ayala's header gave Argentina the lead just after half-time in the quarter-final but the game turned on the substitutions. Argentina were forced to replace their goalkeeper Roberto Abbondanzieri, which reduced their options, but took off Riquelme for Cambiasso after 72 minutes. For many, that was a moment of cowardice, of Pékerman losing faith in the game plan and retreating. But Pékerman had worked with Riquelme at youth level; he saw he was exhausted. More than that, he was troubled by Germany's increasing aerial dominance, which is why he brought on Julio Cruz when Hernán Crespo was withdrawn. Subsequent accounts have often focused on the fact he left Messi on the bench, but Messi at the time was nineteen, only just returning from injury and would not have helped the issue of height – which as it turned out was what undid Argentina, the German substitute Tim Borowski nodding on for Miroslav Klose to head in with five minutes to go. Pékerman had correctly identified the problem; it's just his solution was insufficient.[52]

The game went to penalties before which Kahn made a point of shaking hands with Lehmann and wishing him good luck. Love was breaking out in even the most unlikely places. That morning, Lehmann had taken a sheet of hotel notepaper and scribbled down how seven Argentinian players liked to take their penalties. He made great play of taking the note, which is now housed in the German football museum in Dortmund, from his sock and consulting it before each kick, even though only two of the players who actually took penalties were on it. It didn't matter. Doubt was sown, Ayala and Cambiasso missed and, as Argentina lost control and a mass brawl broke out, Germany were in the semi-final.

Their meeting with Italy was probably the game of the tournament, catching light in extra time as Italy decided to gamble rather than face penalties. Alberto Gilardino and Gianluca Zambrotta both hit the woodwork before, in the 119th minute, the Palermo left-back Fabio Grosso swept in Andrea Pirlo's smart pass and celebrated with a pastiche of Marco Tardelli's scream in the 1982 final. A minute later, Gilardino teed up Alessandro Del Piero for a second on the break. 'If we had won,' said Klinsmann, 'it might have been a little much for other nations to stomach.'[53] By bowing out in the semi-final, Germany proved themselves perfect hosts.

And so to the final. Italy had conceded only one goal in getting there but fell behind to a Zidane penalty after seven minutes, before Materazzi, who had conceded the penalty by clipping Florent Malouda, equalised with a powerful header. Luca Toni hit the bar but everything was prelude to Zidane's headbutt.

The referee Horacio Elizondo had been following play at the other end of the field. It was only after whistling for a handball that he realised Materazzi was down. He began to walk towards him, speaking to his two linesmen through his headset. Neither had seen anything. But the fourth official Luis Medina Cantalejo had: 'a really violent headbutt,' he said. Elizondo asked if he were aware of any provocation first. Cantalejo said he'd seen nothing. By that point, Elizondo had reached Materazzi and knew he was going send Zidane off.

'It didn't seem very correct to me,' Elizondo said, 'to just *BANG!* take a red card out like that, as if from nowhere, with the crowd and players all having seen that I'd been in the other half and hadn't seen anything. So, since the headsets were only new ... I went over to Darío Garcia [the linesman], but I knew Darío didn't know anything. So, why? Well, because that *is* understandable. Everyone understands if you go over to the assistant that it's because the assistant is going to tell you something to help you make a decision ... I turn around and go to Zidane and take out the red card.'[54]

Nobody could dispute that the decision was correct, but there was some controversy when Raymond Domenech suggested Cantalejo had seen the incident on a television monitor; at the time, officials were not supposed to use video assistance. Elizondo, though, pointed out the monitor was part-way down the tunnel, several feet behind the fourth official, who had remained near the touchline throughout.

Zidane walked, David Trezeguet hit the bar with his penalty and Italy, for the fourth time, were world champions.

2010

FALSE DAWN

John Paintsil swung in the free-kick. Kevin-Prince Boateng flicked on and, as the Uruguay goalkeeper Fernando Muslera challenged with John Mensah, the ball dropped for Stephen Appiah. His shot on the turn from four yards out hit Jorge Fucile on the line and bounced away. Mensah started to go for the loose ball, but Dominic Adiyiah, coming from further out, had more momentum and got there first, heading the ball goalwards. His effort flew past the despairing flail of Fucile but Luis Suárez, diving back and to his right, clawed the ball away. It was a penalty and a red card but, in the final minute of extra time, preventing a goal probably made the punishment seem worth it.

Still, Asamoah Gyan had a penalty to give Ghana a 2–1 win over Uruguay and make them, at the first World Cup hosted in Africa, the first African side ever to reach a World Cup semi-final. Gyan's kick, though, struck the top of the bar. He did score in the shoot-out that followed, but Uruguay prevailed.

For those determined to see it – and in the African World Cup there was a need for an African story to celebrate – Ghana's performances represented a great leap forward for African football. Another handball that was just as significant, however, was talked about far less. Late on in Serbia's 2–1 defeat to Australia in their final group game, Tim Cahill handled a Nemanja Vidić header but no penalty was awarded. Had it been given and converted, Serbia would have gone through at Ghana's expense and none of the six African representatives would have made it out of the group.

And that, for Africa's World Cup, would have been disastrous.

After South Africa had lost out in the bidding for 2006, Blatter's determination that Africa should host the tournament led Fifa to introduce a policy under which the World Cup would rotate between confederations: 2010 was Africa's turn. Its job done, the policy was discontinued in 2007.[1] South Africa beat Morocco 14–10 to the prize with Egypt failing to secure a single vote. Nelson Mandela, having retired from public life, was dragged out for one last trip, visiting Trinidad to secure the backing of Jack Warner and the three votes he controlled,[2] but it later transpired that South Africa had won through corruption[3] – although in terms of the total of the bribes paid, it was one of the less tainted bidding processes of the twenty-first century.[4]

South Africa was the first of a new era of tournaments in which the World Cup landed in a country, contributed very little and left again a few weeks later having made itself a fortune, leaving the hosts to pick up the bill. The South African president when the bid was won, Thabo Mbeki, had spoken of transforming the country into 'a diverse and tolerant society' with an economy 'surging ahead like an express train'[5] but the reality was very different. Previously, Fifa had always shared the broadcast, sponsorship, licensing and ticketing revenues with the host; from the 2010 World Cup onwards, though, Fifa has taken 100 per cent of those revenues[6] while, at the same time, demanding tax breaks. Essentially the World Cup can function in the form it took from 2010 only with what is, in effect, an enormous subsidy from the host nation.[7] Some are better able to afford that than others.

Perhaps staging an enormous event – a party for the nation, a vast soft-power jamboree – is in itself desirable, and Johannesburg did briefly become a place of celebration and carnival,[8] but the costs are rarely made explicit. That may be because individual politicians see only their personal gain – whether to prestige or bank balance – or because they are naively optimistic, but it is a recurring pattern.[9] Talk of legacy tends to be hokum. A month after the World Cup, the South African president Jacob Zuma admitted it had cost ten times more than expected and delivered ten times less benefit.[10] It was probably worse even than that as costs spiralled to $2.1bn, an estimated $765m of which was the result of price-fixing and corruption within the construction industry.[11]

There were also decisions that seemed to ignore local realities. In Cape Town, the plan had initially been to develop the Athlone Stadum on Cape Flats but Fifa pressured local authorities to build a new facility at Greenpoint, a spectacular location between Table Mountain and the ocean.[12] The views were great, but a golf course was destroyed and the stadium was situated away from the traditional football fanbase, while the cost was enormous (US$610m), with upkeep costs spiralling to $60m a year.[13] The Moses Mabhida Stadium in Durban is a magnificent arena and remained in regular use, but was it really necessary with the vast Kings Park rugby stadium standing just over the road? By the time the Mbombela Stadium, built at a cost of $170m despite the assassination of a major critic of the project,[14] was used at the Cup of Nations three years later, neglect had led to the pitch being ruined by a fungal infection. That waste had specific implications for the local area as the Mbombela municipality struggled to finance much-needed development in electricity, sanitation and roads, even to pay the salaries of officials.[15]

But it wasn't just the financial cost. The South African authorities used the World Cup as an excuse for clearing informal housing, with little thought given to how those displaced would be rehoused. Around 20,000 people, for instance, were shifted from Joe Slovo in Cape Town; 250 families, meanwhile, were forcibly evicted from Umlazi township as part of the refurbishment of the King Zwelithini Stadium, a training base near Durban. They were initially housed in a temporary settlement, away from their jobs and schools, and despite promises new homes would be provided within six months, remained there for fourteen years.[16] Claims the tournament had been used as cover for the authorities to push through unpopular measures would become increasingly common.

White elephant stadiums had been a theme in South Korea and Japan but it got worse in South Africa and then, four years later, in Brazil. Paradoxically, as Fifa sought desperately to expand the game, preparedness to actually host a tournament became a reason why a country should not host it; less construction means fewer kickbacks, and who benefited from that?

There is nobody Spain could have been less eager to face in the quarter-final of Euro 2008 than Italy. It wasn't just that they hadn't beaten them in a competitive game since the 1920 Olympics, it was that Italy seemed to represent a wholly different mentality. It was during Spain's run to Olympic silver in 1920 that the '*furia roja*' (red fury) ideal had been established; thereafter, Italy had always seemed calmer, more clinical, tougher. They'd beaten them in the 1934 World Cup quarter-final, in the group at Euro 88 and then in the quarter-final at the 1994 World Cup when Mauro Tassotti had broken Luis Enrique's nose. In Spain, Luis Enrique called for vengeance; in Austria, that was the last thing Luis Aragones wanted.

Aragones, bad-tempered and abrasive, was a very unlikely

leader of the progressive revolution. César Luis Menotti had said that Spanish football would never improve until it decided it was better to be the bullfighter than the bull;[17] Aragones was the man who made that happen. When they faced Italy in Vienna, Spain still represented a different idea of football to Italy but, by then, they were the cold ones, the side with the unflappable temperament. Italy remained tactically excellent and held a physical advantage, but Spain's development of a possession game based around the short pass had outflanked them.

The transition was difficult. Aragones was a gifted forward who, after coming through at Real Madrid, became a legend at Atlético; in that regard he was the inverse of Raúl who, at the time of his retirement, was Spain's all-time leading scorer. That difference would become extremely relevant. Aragones managed Atlético six times and Barcelona, winning a league and four Copas del Rey. He struggled with depression, which in part explains an itinerant coaching career. He turned down the Real Madrid job in 1996 and, two years later, said no to Spain. He was already sixty and it seemed unlikely he would be offered the national role again. At that point, he was firmly committed to *la furia*. 'The best thing we can do,' he said, 'is respect our own idiosyncrasies. Every country has its own way of living football and that is the way to act.'[18]

But after Spain had gone out of Euro 2004 at the group stage, they turned to Aragones again. That time he said yes, but by then he was undergoing a remarkable transformation, seeing the possibility offered by technical players such as Xavi, Cesc Fàbregas and David Villa. It was a slow process. At the 2006 World Cup, the team was still based around the great Real Madrid forward Raúl, but discontent was growing. Aragones wanted to switch to a 4-3-3 and play a more possession-based style, but how did Raúl fit into that? Then there was an incident when a group of players arrived back at the team base after curfew: Raúl reportedly notified Aragones, seemingly because one of those who was late was his direct rival for a place, David Villa.[19] As it turned out, the players had warned coaching staff in advance they'd been delayed and Aragones was irritated by what he saw as interference. The sense of a squad divided was confirmed when Raúl equalised with 19 minutes remaining against Tunisia and celebrated only with his Madrid team-mates.

Spain took the lead against France in the last sixteen but conceded two late goals to lose 3–1. The sense of anti-climax was familiar; Spain's best finish in a World Cup at that stage was fourth in 1950. After a 3–2 defeat to Northern Ireland in a European Championship qualifier in September 2006, Aragones did the unthinkable and dropped Raúl. When they then lost 2–0 to Sweden, three hundred Spain fans in Stockholm abused players and called for Aragones to resign. Even in March 2008, before a friendly against France in Málaga, by which point Spain had secured qualification for the Euros and were unbeaten in twelve, fans ambushed the squad at the railway station and chanted for Raúl, brandishing replica shirts with his name on the back. Aragones had already decided he would quit after the Euros.

As Spain soared through the group in Austria, team spirit was notably good. When Villa's late winner against Sweden was celebrated by the whole squad together, including substitutes, the contrast with the Tunisia game two years earlier was clear. Italy, though, still represented a psychological challenge.

Spain produced their worst performance of the tournament and drew 0–0, but won the shoot-out. With it came a tremendous sense of vindication and relief. Victories over Russia and Germany brought Spain's first major tournament victory since 1964 and ensured the revolution against *la furia* would go on.

*

The team bus pulled up at the training ground in Knysna, about two-thirds of the way from Cape Town to Port Elizabeth on the Garden Route. The France team got out and signed autographs for the two hundred or so local fans who had turned up to watch their practice. But something was wrong. The players were wearing trainers, not boots. Domenech and the captain Patrice Evra disappeared behind the bus for a private chat. When they emerged and began walking across the pitch, both looked tense. The fitness coach Robert Duverne joined them and suddenly began wagging his finger furiously at Evra, who looked on impassively, hands in pockets. Domenech stepped between them and the pair separated, Evra joining his team-mates and Duverne storming away, pausing only to hurl his stopwatch to the ground. After a quick conversation with the rest of the squad, Evra took a folded sheet of A4 from his pocket and handed it to the press officer François Manardo. Then the players got back onto the bus.[20]

For forty minutes there was a stand-off. The players refused to train and Domenech refused to let the driver take them back to their hotel. Nobody wanted to read out the statement Evra had given the press officer, so in the end Domenech did it himself. The players had gone on strike in protest at the FFF's decision the previous day to expel Nicolas Anelka from the squad. But in truth, that was merely the trigger. This had been building for years.

Domenech was not a popular leader. Although he seemed unfailingly charming to foreign journalists, with the French he was often brusque or sarcastic. He had flippantly said that he would not pick Mikaël Silvestre because he distrusted Leos; it was printed as fact. He was secretive to the point of paranoia and poor at communicating with the clubs. After France had been eliminated from Euro 2008 in the group stage, he responded by proposing to his girlfriend Estelle Denis live on television. He became a figure of ridicule, being duped by a prank caller claiming to be Jacques Chirac, who was ill in hospital, asking for the France side to sing the anthem with their hands over their hearts to speed his recovery with their patriotism.

By 2010, discipline was long gone. Before Euro 2008, Domenech had gathered a thirty-man provisional squad at Tignes. Towards the end of the camp, he told the players to go to their rooms and stay there while he went round informing the seven who had to be cut before the final twenty-three-man squad for the tournament was submitted. Samir Nasri went round knocking on doors, impersonating his coach; Domenech said if he had known he would have dropped him.

But that was only the start. A younger player sat in Thierry Henry's seat on the bus and refused to move – a seemingly trivial incident but one that suggested both how seriously Henry took himself (although he is not alone in that, in either football or France) and the lack of respect the rising generation had for their elders.[21] After a grim 0–0 against Romania, most of the squad preferred to play cards on the train back to their hotel rather than watch a re-run of the game. They went out with sulky defeats to the Netherlands and Italy.

As France struggled in World Cup qualifying, there were regular flare-ups. When Domenech cancelled a day off following a defeat to Austria, he claims players threatened to then deliberately underperform in their next game, against Serbia.[22] In September 2009, *Le Parisien* reported that Henry had stopped a training session to complain, saying the players were bored and that the team lacked shape and identity.[23] France secured their place in South Africa only thanks to William Gallas's extra-time goal against Ireland, headed in after a blatant handball by Henry. And then, just before the squad was announced, the general unease took on a far darker tone as Franck Ribéry, Karim Benzema and Sidney Govou were accused of having sex with an underage escort. They were finally acquitted almost four years later, but it didn't help a growing public perception of footballers as 'a generation of trash', as the essayist and provocateur Alain Finkielkraut put it.[24]

Domenech had visited Henry in Barcelona, seemingly to tell him he would not be selected, only to be talked around by the thirty-two-year-old. Then there were the more usual gripes within the squad as players squabbled over roles within the side. The staff sent to South Africa was inexperienced, and the players had no faith in them. Govou spoke of how they seemed to spend most of their time on safari and claimed one asked him to sign a hat for him and to write his name underneath as he didn't know who he was.[25]

In the final training session before France began their campaign against Uruguay, Malouda, apparently frustrated that, as he saw it, Ribéry was receiving preferential treatment, clattered into Mathieu Valbuena and Abou Diaby, his two rivals for a starting place.[26] Meanwhile Anelka kept ignoring instructions and dropping deep, then complaining that he wasn't getting the right passes.

It was obvious even in the warm-up that something was amiss. Gallas was in a huff because he wanted to be captain, while Yoann Gourcuff wandered around alone. An elegant playmaker, he was unpopular with the rest of the squad, apparently because he was middle class and well-educated, although he didn't help himself with some overly frank media appearances. On one occasion, Ribéry had reportedly wrenched a book from his hand when he began reading it on the bus; Domenech said he treated him with 'jealousy tainted with hatred'.[27] In the first half, Anelka and Ribéry seemed deliberately not to be passing to him. On the morning of the strike, Ribéry had wandered onto the set of *Téléfoot*, a TF1 show broadcast live from the team hotel, and tearfully denied reports he was bullying Gourcuff.

The first game finished goalless. Malouda replaced Gourcuff

for the second game, against Mexico. At half-time, with the score at 0–0 and with France having been no more effective than in their opener, Domenech replaced Anelka, who had continued to drop deep. 'Go fuck yourself, you dirty son of a whore,' Anelka replied.[28] France went on to lose 2–0 and, when Anelka refused to apologise to his manager, he was kicked out of the squad.

The president Nicolas Sarkozy told the minister for health and sports, Roselyne Bachelot, who was in South Africa, to 'go and see the players and shout at them'.[29] It did little good. France lost their final game 2–1 to South Africa. Back in the Assemblée Nationale, Bachelot laid into 'the disaster of a France team' in which 'immature bullies command frightened kids' unconstrained by 'a helpless coach who has no authority and a federation in disarray'.[30] The term she used for 'bullies' was '*caïds*', which has a specific usage in relation to gang culture; as such, she seemed to be drawing a deliberate correlation between what had gone wrong in the national team and the problems of the *banlieues*. Nobody needed reminding that when minister of the interior, Sarkozy had responded to rioting in 2005 by vowing to 'clean out' the '*racaille*' (scum) from the *banlieues*[31] – a term that, for many, carried a racial charge.

The champions of 1998 criticised their successors. Thuram, who had earlier fretted about the growing individualism of the new generation, said that Evra should never play for France again. A clear divide was drawn between immigrants regarded as happy by-products of *les Trente Glorieuses*, the thirty-year period of post-war growth in France, and the more recent generation spawned by the *banlieues*. Anelka had always, for some, been a troublesome figure. His quality as a footballer was obvious, and he had style and swagger, but he was an oddly ungracious figure, often surly, while his brother, his agent, reportedly repeatedly engineered transfers for him, racking up signing-on fees.[32] Perhaps that was an issue of

Clairefontaine: he had no loyalty to any one club. Or perhaps it was an issue of the *banlieues*: just how loyal to France, it was asked, were these players from a variety of ethnic backgrounds, who didn't sing the anthem? 'When France fail to win,' Anelka said, 'people start talking straight away about the players' skin colour and religious beliefs.'[33] The *black-blanc-beur* vision had come to seem impossibly idealistic.

France did it most spectacularly, but they weren't the only former champions to collapse in South Africa. Marcello Lippi had left Italy after winning the World Cup in 2006 but returned when Roberto Donadoni was sacked following a disappointing Euros. He could not, though, elevate an ageing squad short on attacking talent. After failing to beat Paraguay and New Zealand, who ended up going home unbeaten after three straight draws, they were eliminated following a 3–2 defeat to Slovakia.

England had missed out on Euro 2008 after a qualifying campaign of numerous pratfalls and three memorable defeats, outplayed in Moscow and Zagreb, where Gary Neville's back pass hopped over Paul Robinson's foot for a comical own goal, and then eliminated in a rain-sodden 3–2 defeat at Wembley against Croatia. Steve McClaren, who had dropped David Beckham and then been forced to recall him, was sacked as manager after what was, at the time, the shortest ever tenure of any permanent England manager.

The FA sought to reignite England by turning again to a foreign manager, appointing Fabio Capello, who had been consistently successful at club level across the previous two decades. In qualifying it seemed to have worked. He rebalanced the midfield by bringing in Gareth Barry and moving Steven Gerrard to the left, and secured 4–1 and 5–1 wins over Croatia. But in South Africa, England were dreadful, their campaign enlivened only by John Terry's abortive mutiny as England players rebelled against the strictures of their camp in Rustenburg. Against Germany in the last sixteen, they went 2–0 down but then seemed to have pulled level with two goals in two minutes only for Frank Lampard's effort, which bounced down off the bar a couple of feet behind the line, not to be given. Had it counted, Germany might have crumbled, but Germany were much the better side for 85 of the 90 minutes.

Argentina, meanwhile, were undone by a crisis almost entirely of their own making. Pékerman had resigned after the 2006 World Cup and been replaced by Alfio Basile, who had led them to their previous two trophies, the Copas América of 1991 and 1993. He got them to the final of the 2007 Copa as well, playing some stunning football as they scored sixteen goals in five games. The final, though, was lost 3–0 to Brazil, and the sense of momentum never really returned. When they went down 1–0 to Marcelo Bielsa's Chile in October 2008, they had sixteen points from ten qualifiers and were set for South Africa. But they had won only one of their previous six, and that was only their sixth defeat to their western neighbour. Amid the outcry that followed, Basile resigned.

With even a vaguely orthodox appointment, Argentina would have qualified with ease, but they did what they always did in times of crisis and turned to Maradona. At that point he had had two stints as a manager, totalling twenty-three games, only three of them won. Appointing him was an act of blind faith.

His first game brought a 4–0 Messi-inspired home win over Venezuela. His second was against Bolivia in La Paz. His solution to the issue of altitude was to fly in on the day of the game, having dosed his players with Viagra.[34] They lost 6–1, Argentina's joint-record defeat alongside the humiliation of Helsingborg.

With two games remaining, there were five teams within

three points of each other, all chasing one automatic and one play-off spot. Argentina faced Peru amid torrential rain in el Monumental, Martín Palermo sliding through the standing water in injury time to prod a winner. A 1–0 win in Uruguay, secured through Mario Bolatti's 84th-minute winner, confirmed qualification. On the touchline, Maradona, swaddled in a vast tracksuit and with a red bib flapping behind him, bounced up and down then fell over. He had used fifty-five players in thirteen games and had won just four of eight qualifiers, but he told his critics in the press to 'suck it and keep on sucking'.[35]

Maradona selected a bizarre squad that, with Javier Zanetti inexplicably omitted, lacked a high-class right-back, a position taken first by the midfielder Jonás Gutiérrez and then by the central defender Nicolás Otamendi. Without ever finding any great fluency, they won all three group games and then beat Mexico in the last sixteen to set up a quarter-final against the team perhaps best equipped to exploit their sluggish rearguard: Germany.

Thomas Müller touched in an early free-kick and then, as Argentina chased the game, Germany picked them off, winning 4–0. By the end, Argentina were a heavy-footed shambles, with six attacking players on the pitch, Maradona's limitations as a manager horribly exposed. In the dressing room after the final whistle, Messi slumped between two benches, sobbing. 'The players,' said the report in *Clarín*, 'discovered Father Christmas doesn't exist – Maradona isn't what they thought he was.'[36]

That came as a terrible realisation, too terrible for many who, unable to give up the old gods, preferred to blame the new messiah. As the novelist Eduardo Sacheri noted, 'It isn't Messi's fault that we Argentinians are incapable of ending our mourning for Diego.'[37]

*

In the summer of 2008, as Spain won the Euros, Pep Guardiola took over as manager of Barcelona and football as a whole moved decisively into its new age. The time of attrition, of José Mourinho, Rafa Benítez and Greece's success at Euro 2004, was over and the pass dominated all. Pitch and kit technology had reached a point whereby players could trust their first touch, and so could focus far earlier on the next passes in the sequence rather than having to worry about a bobble that could cost them possession. At the same time, changes to the offside law had increased the effective playing area while a crackdown on intimidatory tackling had made it harder for technically accomplished players to be bullied out of the game. Football was ripe for the coming of *juego de posición*, a form of the game in which possession was taken almost as a given and an emphasis placed on strategy, on the manipulation of space and the creation of overloads; Guardiola was the great leader of that movement, the genius who saw the possibilities of Total Football in the new world, and took its principles to previously unimaginable levels.

The revolution was in one way distinctively Spanish (or at least Catalan) and yet at the same time it was about Spain's integration into the wider world after the days of dictatorship. The historian Michael Richards compared Spain under Franco to 'an isolation ward', distancing itself from the 'toxin' of liberalism;[38] with the coming of democracy there was a slow and not always easy process of opening up. The movement of players abroad,[39] the rejection of *la furia roja* and the adoption of a philosophy that was Dutch in origin can be seen as belatedly analogous – and it's no coincidence that that style, building on the foundations laid by Rinus Michels and Johan Cruyff in the 1970s, developed in Barcelona, in a region that self-consciously sets itself in opposition to the orthodoxies of Spain's establishment.

The irony then is that the manager who took them to the

World Cup was somebody inextricably associated with the club of the Spanish establishment, Real Madrid – Vicente Del Bosque. Loan deals aside, Del Bosque the player was a one-club man, making 445 league appearances for Madrid and winning five league titles. He worked his way up as a coach at the club, twice having short-term stints as manager before taking the job on a permanent basis in November 1999. Between then and the summer of 2003, he led Madrid to two league titles and two Champions Leagues.

Yet Del Bosque was never the stereotypical Madridista – a stereotype that, anyway, is at best lacking in nuance and at worst, highly misleading.[40] During the civil war his republican father had spent three years in a prison camp for storing pro-democracy leaflets. He himself had been a union organiser. His politics were entirely opposed to those of the club's president Florentino Pérez and the ethos behind the *galácticos* project on which Madrid had embarked. There was a sense that made Pérez uncomfortable, but Del Bosque's on-field success made it impossible to sack him. But then at the end of the 2002–03 season, the players expressed frustration at the club's acquiescence with Madrid council's decision to deny them permission to follow tradition by hanging a scarf from the Cibeles fountain while insisting they should turn up for functions at the cathedral and city hall. The dispute offered an excuse to get rid of Del Bosque as well as the captain Fernando Hierro.

To be dumped like that after thirty-five years hurt Del Bosque, but the bond he had forged with Hierro proved significant. Hierro was made national sporting director in September 2007. When Aragones stood down, he turned to Del Bosque, out of work after an indifferent spell at Beşiktaş, to replace him.

To an extent, Del Bosque's job with Spain was just to keep everything ticking over. He played Aragones football but more so. The 2009 Confederations Cup was the spur for change. Spain beat South Africa to claim a record fifteenth straight victory and match Brazil's record of thirty-five games unbeaten. But in the semi-final against the USA they lost, beaten 2–0 despite having had twenty-nine shots and won seventeen corners. Late on, as they chased the game, they went long and put more and more crosses into the box. That, Del Bosque concluded, had been a mistake. By the time the World Cup began, he had switched from a midfield diamond with David Villa and Fernando Torres as twin forwards to a 4-2-3-1, in which Sergio Busquets and Xabi Alonso functioned as double-pivots and Xavi played as the central creator, in a more advanced role than he occupied for Barcelona. With those three in the middle and Andrés Iniesta on the left, Spain had four of the smartest passers in world football; if they wanted to hold possession, there were very few teams good enough to get the ball off them.

But the World Cup began in much the same way as their Confederations Cup hopes had ended. Spain had twenty-four chances against Switzerland and won twelve corners, but lost 1–0. Was this the familiar old Spain? It was not. They beat Honduras and Chile to top the group, then beat Portugal in the last sixteen before an edgy 1–0 victory over Paraguay in the quarter-final, a game in which both sides missed a penalty before Villa's 83rd-minute winner. That set up a repeat of the Euro 2008 final in the semi: Germany.

Klinsmann had stood down as Germany coach after the World Cup, but the revolution was carried on by his former assistant, Jogi Löw. He was obsessed by speeding up the German game, in which he was successful, but he struggled always to balance attack and defence. After an unconvincing group stage at Euro 2008, he switched from 4-4-2 to 4-2-3-1, but subsequent wins over Portugal in the quarter-final and Turkey in the semi were both by 3–2, which suggested a lack of control even before the comprehensive 1–0 defeat to Spain in the final. A 3–3 draw against Finland in the second game of World Cup qualifying highlighted the issue, after which Löw adopted a more counter-attacking approach. In their eight remaining games they conceded just twice and were hugely impressive in a Mesut Özil-inspired 1–0 win away to Russia.

The approach was effective, if limited. In South Africa, Germany's games fell into two distinct categories. If they scored first, as they did against Australia, England and Argentina, Germany's forwards, Özil, Thomas Müller, Lukas Podolski and Miroslav Klose, were ruthless in countering against opponents who were forced to attack against them, scoring four in each of those games. But when they did not score early, they struggled, losing to Serbia and only narrowly beating Ghana.

The semi-final followed a predictable pattern. Spain controlled possession and the game and, eventually, the attrition told on Germany as Carles Puyol powered home a header from Xavi's corner. 'It is,' Löw said, 'extremely difficult to get the ball back if you lose it to Spain.'[41] Between Spain and their first World Cup stood only the country whose style they had appropriated and developed.

For the Netherlands, everything changed with the defeat away to Ireland in September 2001 that cost them a place in Korea/Japan. As Simon Kuper has argued, that was the end of the second phase of Dutch football.[42] Until the early seventies, the Netherlands national team was largely hopeless. Then came Rinus Michels, Johan Cruyff and Total Football, and defeats in the World Cup finals of 1974 and 1978. Glorious failure came to be celebrated; winning mattered less than style. Defeats on the pitch could still be regarded as moral victories, a convenient consolation that played into the notion of 'Netherlands, guide land', a phrase that dominated Dutch political discourse from the 1960s onwards. The Netherlands, the theory ran, might not be powerful, but in its democracy and tolerance, it could be an inspiration to bigger nations.[43]

It was one thing to lose beautifully in big games against major nations, quite another to be eliminated from the World Cup by Mick McCarthy's Ireland. People began to wonder whether winning might possibly be more important than following commandments laid down three decades before. Slowly, the emphasis changed. Ten days after the defeat in Dublin, the planes crashed into the World Trade Center in New York, and the Netherlands began to reconsider its approach to immigration. How could a liberal approach to immigration be squared with the fact that many immigrants were not themselves liberal? Perhaps this was an inevitable paradox of globalisation: that as Dutch society became more diverse, so the Netherlands lost its sense of itself as a beacon to the world and became more inward-looking and parochial.[44]

After an unimpressive showing under Dick Advocaat at Euro 2004 – the Netherlands reached the semi-final but won only one of five games – Marco van Basten was appointed as national manager to restore the classic Dutch style.[45] In May 2005, the assistant manager John van 't Schip was boldly insisting, 'our way of playing is more important than the result',[46] but there was little sign of that at the 2006 World Cup, where the Netherlands were eliminated in the last sixteen by Portugal in the 'Battle of Nuremberg' which featured a record four red and sixteen yellow cards. 'This,' the commentator Hugo Camps said, 'is not our football.'[47]

Did that matter? When the Netherlands won all three group games at Euro 2008, hammering both Italy and France playing a game based in transition, it seemed a validation of the new approach. Even when they lost to Russia in the quarter-final, a memorable game that fitted the pattern of glorious defeats, it seemed significant that their opponents were managed by Guus Hiddink, who had called for a more pragmatic interpretation of the old principles and whose side seemed a living embodiment of what Dutch football could look like in the modern age.

But by 2010, the tone had changed. A Nike advert released just before the tournament summed up the new mood. It showed players sweating and looking determined with captions such as 'Tears of joy are made of sweat' and 'Destroy egos, starting with your own'. Then the players march along a corridor, studs clacking menacingly. 'Football is not total without victory,' says one slogan. 'A beautiful defeat is still a defeat,' says another. This is a rejection of the past, a call not for aesthetic expression but for stiffened sinews, the portrayal of football not as art but as war.

In South Africa, Bert van Marwijk's side was extremely physical. They ground their way through the group and past Slovakia in the last sixteen, with a double pivot of Mark van Bommel and Nigel De Jong, with Johnny Heitinga whacking the ball aimlessly clear, and with Khalid Boulahrouz a lumbering, clumsy full-back. The Netherlands came from behind to beat Brazil in the quarter-final, their first goal the result of an overhit cross that glanced in off Felipe Melo, the second coming from a near-post flick at a corner. It was a hard-fought win in a fractious game, and there was merit in that, but it was far removed from the flowing football of Dutch legend. A 3–2 win over Uruguay in the semi was more comfortable than the scoreline perhaps suggested but even then the second goal was both deflected and manifestly offside.

There was a fear in the Netherlands that liberalism had led to erasure, that by being open to the world, everything characteristically Dutch had been swept away on the tide of globalisation. In major companies, and some universities, English was used rather than Dutch. And as the Dutch embraced a more pragmatic model, variants of the traditional Dutch style had been adopted elsewhere: by Russia, by Germany but most of all by Spain.

For Andrés Iniesta the previous year had been dreadful. In the summer of 2009, his close friend Dani Jarque had collapsed during pre-season training with Espanyol and died. As Iniesta struggled with his grief, he battled a thigh injury all season and then, on 13 April, a week before the first leg of Inter's Champions League semi-final victory over Barcelona, arguably the last great victory of the old risk-averse style over the new, the muscle tore again. Between then and the end of the season, he played only five minutes. Del Bosque initially used Iniesta sparingly, regularly withdrawing him during the second half of games and resting him entirely against Honduras. But from the Chile game onwards, Iniesta played every minute and in the knockout stages he was Spain's most decisive player.

The final was brutal. Heitinga was eventually sent off for collecting a second yellow but at least two others could have been shown a straight red, most notoriously De Jong for planting his studs into the chest of Xabi Alonso. In total, the referee Howard Webb showed fourteen yellow cards and it could have been more. One of them went to Iniesta for removing his shirt to reveal a T-shirt bearing a tribute to Jarque after he had scored a 116th-minute winner, firing in Fàbregas's diagonal pass after a missed clearance by Rafael van der Vaart, who probably wouldn't have been in the position had it not been for the dismissal of Heitinga.

Johan Cruyff was devastated, less by the Netherlands' third defeat in a World Cup final than by how the team had played. 'I thought my country would never dare to play like this and would never give up its own way of playing,' he said, dismissing

Van Marwijk's approach as 'nasty, vulgar, hard, closed ... barely football anymore'.[48] The influential literary football magazine *Hard Gras* printed a photograph of De Jong's foul on Xabi Alonso on its cover with the headline, '*Hollandse School*' and called for Van Marwijk to resign.[49] But perhaps that is the nature of revolutions: the young rise up and the old resist. Around 600,000 orange-clad fans turned out in Amsterdam to welcome the Netherlands home. Maybe this *was* the Netherlands; maybe it *did* exist and it was only the canal-belt intellectuals who felt uneasy – betrayed, even – by the shift in style.

The political parallel was unavoidable. After September 2001, the Netherlands experienced the rise of an anti-Islamic far right, first under Pim Fortuyn with his tell-it-like-it-is bluntness and then, after his assassination in 2002, under Geert Wilders, who called for the Qur'an to be banned. Elections in October 2010 led to a centre-right government that required Wilders's support. The far right had come into the mainstream and 'Netherlands, guide land' had vanished just as surely in politics as it had in football.

For Spain, the World Cup success was the high point of a glorious hat-trick of titles that would be completed at the Euros in Poland and Ukraine two years later, by which point they had stopped bothering with a centre-forward at all.[50] No other side has ever won three successive major tournaments. Their excellence was never doubted and yet they were not much loved outside of Spain. They were, perhaps, *too* good, at least at controlling games. Across the three tournaments, they did not concede a single goal in the knockout phase; in 2010, they won all four 1–0. Perhaps Xavi was right when he said that ultra-defensive opponents forced Spain to play sterile controlling football, but there were plenty who considered their style boring.[51]

That contributed to a slightly unsatisfactory feeling around the tournament, to which the obvious inadequacy of the ball was a major contributory factor. There had been various innovations in technology before, usually with the questionable aim of making the ball 'rounder', and complaints from players, especially goalkeepers, at each of the previous two tournaments. But they reached a peak with the Jabulani in 2010, both because goalkeepers found the ball wobbling unpredictably in the air and because players more generally couldn't control it. The ball was, effectively, too round, without the rough elements that allowed it to generate the air resistance necessary to stabilise it in the air.[52] It's possible that the generally high altitude in South Africa exacerbated the problem, but the Jabulani also misbehaved earlier that year at the Cup of Nations in Angola. The ball had an undoubted negative impact on the quality of the play and it's no coincidence that the one team who thrived were Spain, whose entire philosophy was based on rapid flurries of just the sort of short low passes that would not be affected by a ball that couldn't be trusted in flight.

But perhaps most disappointing was the sense that this was not, really, an African World Cup, for all the branding and platitudinous speeches; around 250,000 seats went unsold across the tournament.[53] Although 3 per cent of tickets were made available to South Africans, they cost ZAR140, about 10 per cent of the average monthly wage for black workers, and they were accessible only to those with credit cards and internet access, or in person at certain banks. Most black fans who did go were given tickets by employers and many expressed frustration at the unfamiliarity of the experience, the sense of the World Cup as a non-space, a sterilised Fifa zone into which local quirks could not intrude.[54]

At the same time, Fifa's corporate model meant local traders were banished far from stadiums. The tournament didn't look African or feel African: the official song, 'Waka Waka', may have borne some resemblance to a Cameroonian march but it was sung by Shakira, a Colombian. Fonts, colours and design all fitted a stylised Western ideal of Africa.[55]

When the tournament sounded African, thanks to the droning of vuvuzelas, the plastic horns familiar in South African football, many found that irksome,[56] leading to a flurry of analysis. While some linked them to ancient rites and saw the vuvuzela as a modern interpretation of the kudu horn,[57] others pointed out they were a nineties fad and were manufactured in China.[58] Certain television networks were so concerned by the complaints that they dampened the sound for fear viewers might turn off,[59] a fitting encapsulation of the preoccupations and priorities of modern football.

There perhaps was symbolic significance in South Africa hosting a tournament and doing so largely successfully,[60] but the idea that this was an African World Cup rather than a sterile, globalised vehicle that happened to park itself in Africa for a time existed only in the stereotypes of propaganda and mindless reportage. There was no upturn in the performances of African teams, no upturn in domestic league attendances,[61] and South Africa was left with a series of stadiums and other infrastructure projects that not only didn't make a profit but, it subsequently transpired, had themselves often been a conduit for corruption[62] and required vast annual outlay to maintain them. The world, once again, had come to Africa, left an array of problems and made off with the loot.

2014

THE MOST EXPENSIVE BUS STATION IN THE WORLD

On 7 January 1897, the Teatro Amazonas in Manaus, 900 miles up the Amazon, opened with a performance of Amilcare Ponchielli's *La Gioconda* in front of an audience of 1,600, who were dressed in the finest silks and diamonds. This was the peak of its *belle époque* rubber boom; automobiles demanded rubber tyres and Manaus effectively had a global monopoly. In a couple of decades it had grown from a ramshackle village built around the ruins of a sixteenth-century Portuguese fort into a grand town with tree-lined avenues 100 feet wide, a racecourse, parks and an array of up-market shops. It had more cinemas than Rio and more theatres than Lisbon.[1]

Even in that context, the opera house was an extraordinary spectacle, with electric lighting, intricate murals of great composers and a stage curtain that featured an ornate etching of the nearby confluence of the Rio Negro and Solimões to form the Amazon.[2] It had taken fifteen years to build and cost US$2m[3] as almost everything had to be imported: the iron framework came from Glasgow, the marble from Verona, crystal from

Venice and cedar from Lebanon. Only the floor was Brazilian, but even the 12,000 pieces of oak, brazilwood and jacaranda it comprised were transported across the Atlantic to be worked by Portuguese craftsmen before being brought back again.[4]

There was a sense of the opera house as a magnificent folly; certainly that is how it appears in the 1982 Werner Herzog film *Fitzcarraldo*, but at the same time there was something grotesque about it.[5] The rubber boom and the sudden expansion of Manaus were based on the brutal exploitation of the indigenous people of the area, many of whom were pressed into service; at one point there was a 'stud farm' of around six hundred local women used for 'breeding purposes'.[6]

From the start, the opera house was ill-starred. Three months before opening night, the asphyxiophiliac local governor Eduardo Ribeiro who had overseen its construction died 'in a fit of erotic mania'.[7] His ghost is said to haunt the Teatro Amazonas along with those of sixteen members of an Italian opera company who died of yellow fever.[8]

Even before a member of the local House of Representatives had the bright idea of building an opera house in 1881, the destruction of the Brazilian rubber boom was sprouting in Kew Gardens. Henry Wickham, a British adventurer, had smuggled 70,000 rubber seeds out of Brazil in 1876 and, after cultivation in London, they became the origin of plantations in Malaya and Sumatra which, free of parasitic insects and fungi, were able to produce rubber far more cheaply than Manaus.[9]

The Brazilian market crashed. The opera house fell on hard times and was closed in 1924. An attempt to reopen it in 1990 was abandoned after local protests about the cost. Only in 1997 did operas begin regularly to be staged there again, but the opera house remains an ambiguous symbol, a warning for those who arrive from the outside with grand plans and a callous attitude. Yet Manaus bid to stage games at the 2014 World Cup, building a 43,000-capacity stadium at enormous cost, a project of similar ambition to the opera house but far less long-term benefit. Over its first four years it's estimated the stadium cost $150,000 per spectator; by 2019 it lay largely abandoned, hosting only local games for which attendances rarely crept above 1,000.[10]

The 2014 World Cup was the second and last for which hosting rights were awarded under Fifa's policy of rotation between the continents. After Africa came South America, for the first time since Argentina in 1978. Despite the obvious problem that Brazil did not have a single stadium up to Fifa standards,[11] it was the only bidder and was confirmed as host in July 2007.

The result, inevitably, was a grotesque overspend. In total, the cost was around $14bn, of which only around 15 per cent came from private sources.[12] That placed an enormous strain on an already stretched government for very little obvious return. It wasn't just Manaus where the outlay came to look absurd. Within a year of the World Cup, the Estadio Mané Garrincha in Brasilia, the second-most expensive stadium in history when it was built at a cost of $900m, was being used as a bus depot.[13] Quite aside from the direct cost, many of the stadiums involved people being forcibly displaced from their homes and businesses being uprooted. By 2014, the trend for white elephants that had begun in 2002 had become a scandalous stampede.

And as in South Africa, the World Cup became a justification for manifest abuses of human rights. At least 18,000 households were forcibly evicted to make way for World Cup projects[14] (some estimates have the figure at 1.5m people[15]) while a month before the tournament a counter-terrorism bill was introduced that was criticised by the United Nations for a vagueness which 'carried the potential for deliberate misuse'.[16] Public protests against the expenditure on the tournament were met with brutality: on the day of the Confederations Cup final, rubber bullets were fired into crowds and demonstrators beaten indiscriminately.[17]

Jogi Löw went for another run along the beach. The whole German reboot felt at crisis point. They'd beaten Portugal 4–0 in their first game in Brazil, but had Jordan Ayew squared for Asamoah Gyan rather than shooting wildly when Ghana led 2–1, they might have lost their second game which would have put them under enormous pressure. As it was, a 2–2 draw followed by a mutually beneficial 1–0 win over the USA took them through. But a 2–1 extra-time win over Algeria in the last sixteen was edgier than most Germans had hoped.[18]

Could Löw really keep picking Philipp Lahm in midfield? Lahm, because of his importance to Guardiola's Bayern, had become emblematic of the new ways, a full-back redeployed on the basis of his football intelligence. But given the dearth of full-backs, the use of Lahm in midfield meant Germany lining up with four central defenders, and that made them both clunky in possession and vulnerable to pace. *Bild* took to referring to them as '*der Ochsenspieß*' (the skewer of ox-meat). On the beach, Löw reached a decision. He would go back to basics. Lahm would return to right-back, with Sami Khedira coming into midfield and Miroslav Klose restored as an orthodox centre-forward with Müller dropping deeper and Mario Götze left out.

As though in symbolic acknowledgement that a Rubicon had been crossed, Löw turned up for his pre-match press conference before the quarter-final against France dressed not in his usual black shirt but in a casual white T-shirt. For those looking for symbols, this was evidence that appearance didn't matter any more: this was all about getting the job done.[19]

Germany did get the job done, Mats Hummels heading in an

early Toni Kroos free-kick in a game of few clear-cut chances. *Das Reboot* was nearing completion.[20]

The 2014 World Cup would be defined by an almost unthinkable thrashing in its third-last game, but for a long time it looked like being defined by an almost unthinkable thrashing in its third. For most of the first half of the repeat of the 2010 final, it looked like just another tournament game for Spain. They had a method and a style that worked. They'd lost just two of their previous thirty-seven games. When Xabi Alonso put them ahead from the penalty spot, it seemed like business as usual. But then, just before half-time, Robin van Persie met Daley Blind's raking cross behind the Spanish line with an extraordinary header, hurling himself forward as he shaped his finish over Iker Casillas from the edge of the box. In the second half, Spain fell apart. Arjen Robben, in an unusual central role, got in behind them again and again and, even though van Persie hit the bar and Casillas made two remarkable saves, the Dutch won 5–1.

It was one of the most stunning results in the history of the World Cup: Spain, the country whose national team and clubs had dominated and redefined football over the previous six years, were devastated. They couldn't pick themselves up for the game against Jorge Sampaoli's Chile, lost 2–0 and were eliminated.

There had, perhaps, been warning signs at club level. In Guardiola's final season at Barcelona, 2011–12, they had lost in the Champions League semi-final to Chelsea, unable to break down a deep-lying defence and caught on the break. In the following season's semi-final, Barcelona, by then under Tito Vilanova, had been hammered 7–0 over two legs by Bayern, undone on the counter and by set plays. In the months before the World Cup, Barcelona had lost in the Champions League quarter-final to a deep-lying Atlético, while Guardiola's Bayern had lost 5–0 on aggregate in the semi-final to a counter-attacking Madrid. To suggest that possession football was over, that the Guardiola method was outmoded, was to stretch the point, but it was perhaps true that opponents had become more comfortable with the idea of being without the ball for long periods of the game.

And nothing is ever only about tactics. Success, Xabi Alonso acknowledged, had cost Spain their edge. They lacked 'ambition and hunger'. Del Bosque spoke of 'a nervousness, a timidity'.[21] Either way, Spain, the serial winners, were on their way home, their era of dominance over.

The great irony was that the manager who had inflicted the great defeat on Spain was one of the architects of the modern Spanish game, Louis van Gaal.

Van Gaal, after leading Ajax to the Champions League in 1995, had two stints in charge of Barcelona. Although he twice won the league, he was not a natural fit for Catalonia and his time at Camp Nou was at best uneasy and often rancorous. But he did make an impact. Both Xavi and Guardiola are clear about Van Gaal's influence in refining the Barcelona model and thus the Spanish style.[22]

Cussed and dogmatic as he could be, Van Gaal turned out to be far less fundamentalist than many of the other Dutch coaches who came in the wake of Cruyff. After the defeat in Dublin in 2001, he too discovered a previously unanticipated pragmatism.[23] Having been a coach who had always insisted on dominating possession while at Ajax and Barça, he led AZ Alkmaar to a shock league title playing counter-attacking football. Although he in some ways laid the foundations for Guardiola at Bayern, his approach there was flexible. Taking over the reins from Van Marwijk in 2012 after the stylistic controversy had come to a head with three defeats in the group at the Euros in Ukraine, there was an expectation Van Gaal would return the Netherlands to something closer to the classical Dutch model.

For a time he did. In World Cup qualifying they played a 4-2-3-1/4-3-3 hybrid, the wingers stayed wide and, playing attacking football, the Dutch took twenty-eight points from ten games while racking up a goal difference of +29, the best in the Uefa section. But Van Gaal was not convinced. Putting four past Romania or eight past Hungary, he knew, had little to do with the winning of major tournaments and he was concerned by the way his defenders struggled in individual duels. When Kevin Strootman, who would have been a playmaking deep-lying midfielder, was ruled out of the finals with a serious knee injury, Van Gaal decided he had to rethink his approach.

Van Gaal was no great ally of Ronald Koeman, but he was intrigued by the way Koeman had set up his Feyenoord team, playing with a back three that was often a back five, content to sit deep and pick opponents off on the break. He took Van Persie to watch Feyenoord beat PSV 2–0, outlining how he envisaged the Netherlands playing. Three of Koeman's back five – Daryl Janmaat, Bruno Martins Indi and Stefan de Vrij – were also in Van Gaal's thinking for Brazil. Against Spain, the shape was a 5-3-2, with Nigel De Jong deep in midfield and Van Persie and Robben as mobile central forwards. In part, Van Gaal said, that was 'because of the quality and the profile of my defenders' and in part 'to provoke the space behind the defenders of our opponents'.

There were those in the Netherlands who thought anything but 4-3-3 was a betrayal of the grand old tradition, but Van Gaal insisted he had not changed his stylistic principles. 'The cover over the pitch is fantastic,' he said. 'You have always triangles . . . always occupation of the width.'[24]

It wasn't classic Total Football and it wasn't idealistic, but it wasn't so opposed to the Dutch tradition as Van Marwijk's side had been four years earlier. And while they didn't go quite so far as that team, the Netherlands did reach the semi-final.

Argentinian fans travelled to Brazil en masse. Many parked nose-to-tail along the Copacabana beachfront, cars, minibuses, camper vans, heating water on Primus stoves for their *mate*. The Fifa FanFest, with £8 face-painting and bottles of official wine at £126, stood at one end of the beach, but this felt the true heart of the World Cup, a throwback to less corporate times. But for Brazilians, Argentina carried a sense of menace; the thought of them potentially winning the World Cup at the Maracanã was horrifying. And everywhere Argentinian fans went came their inevitable song, '*Brasil, decime qué se siente*' ('Brazil, tell me how it feels ...') sung to the tune of 'Bad Moon Rising' and celebrating Maradona's dribble and pass for Caniggia's winner against them in the 1990 World Cup.

There seemed something very Argentinian about commemorating a victory that was, at best, fortuitous and quite possibly the result of serious skulduggery, not in the tournament they had won four years earlier, but in the World Cup in which they scrapped and brawled their way to the final. As it turned out, for Messi at least, this was a World Cup with far more similarities to 1990 than 1986.

The problem with being the appointed Messiah is that when things go wrong, there will be calls for crucifixion. From the moment Argentina lost to Brazil in the final of the 2007 Copa América, there were those in Argentina who doubted Messi. Just how committed was he, really, to Argentina? After all, he had left the country at the age of thirteen and had never played for an Argentinian club. The answer was remarkably obvious: Messi remained incredibly Argentinian. Despite having spent most of his life in Spain, he spoke with an Argentinian accent, his favourite films, music and food were all Argentinian, he married his Argentinian childhood sweetheart, he risked irritating Barcelona by insisting on playing for Argentina at the 2008 Olympics and, unlike Maradona, with whom he was constantly being compared, he never skipped friendlies, qualifiers or Copa América matches.

But the grumbling went on. Why didn't he sing the anthem more passionately? Why didn't he celebrate goals more enthusiastically? Psychoanalysts were dredged up to claim Messi felt a latent resentment towards his homeland. When Argentina hosted the Copa América in 2011, the question was asked whether Messi and Carlos Tévez could play together in the same team (although they had done so extremely well in 2007), and if one were to be dropped who it should be. Many, remarkably, preferred Tévez, although that would change by the end of the tournament.

Before the game against Colombia in Santa Fé, Messi's home province, when the stadium announcer read out the teams, he referred to Messi as 'the best player in the world', generating polite applause; when he then described Tévez as 'the player of the people', there were raucous cheers. And that, perhaps, hinted at one of the issues. While his family was far from rich, Messi had not grown up in desperate poverty, nor was he squat with the requisite mass of unruly curls. He may have had the skillset of a *pibe* but, unlike Tévez, he did not fit the template.

The 2014 tournament had been marked out as Messi's World Cup, the one he was supposed to dominate as Maradona had dominated 1986. In the autumn of 2005 when, aged eighteen, Messi had negotiated his first contract as an adult with Barcelona, the club had wanted him to sign until 2014, but his father had insisted the deal should run only until 2013; if he suffered injury or fell out with a coach, he wanted his son to have the freedom to find a club that would give him a run-up to the World Cup.

At first the focus on 2014 looked astute. Alejandro Sabella seemed a resolute coach capable of distancing himself from the noise and choosing between Argentina's great array of attacking talent. They qualified impressively, scoring thirty-five goals in eighteen games and losing only twice. Injuries to Fernando Gago and Sergio Agüero, though, disrupted preparations and disrupted the balance Sabella had achieved.

The result was an oddly disjointed and bitty tournament for Argentina, in which Messi played only in isolated spurts. Capitalising on Higuaín's movement to create space, he scored the second as they began with a 2–1 win over Bosnia-Herzegovina and then hit a long-range late winner against Iran after a team performance so poor that Maradona had already stormed out of the stadium in disgust. Two goals in a 3–2 victory over Nigeria meant Argentina had won all their group games without having played well, largely thanks to the brilliance of Messi who had been, at best, fitful.

'We know he is our main player, our captain, the best player in the world,' said Zabaleta. 'Every time we recover the ball we try to pass to him.'[25] That seemed a very old-fashioned view of football, the focus on an individual playmaker Jack Charlton had sneered at in 1986.[26] Messi was the creative hub at Barcelona but there he would receive the ball, lay it off and move into space to receive another pass. With Argentina, he would get the ball and then look around to see everybody waiting for him to do something.

In the last sixteen, Switzerland tried to keep three or four players around Messi at all times. It largely worked. Argentina struggled. At full time it was 0–0. The two teams gathered in loose huddles. Messi, as captain, might have been expected to speak – as Maradona in 1986 assuredly would have done. Instead he lingered at the back of the group, tipping a bottle of water over his head. Sabella spoke. Javier Mascherano spoke. But Messi remained silent. His style of leadership was strangely detached.

Part of Messi's genius had always lain in his minimalism, his capacity to select the least-difficult option to achieve his goal in any given circumstance. But at that World Cup there was a new feature: an astonishing lack of movement. Against Switzerland, he ran just 10.7km in the 120 minutes, 3km less than Neymar in the same round against Colombia. Messi performed thirty-one sprints as opposed to Neymar's fifty-seven.[27] And yet Messi still decided the game, finding space at last from a 117th-minute throw-in. As panicking defenders converged on him, in a moment reminiscent of Maradona's celebrated pass for Caniggia's winner against Brazil in 1990, he slipped the ball through for Ángel Di María to score the winner.

Perhaps still there was a chance for Messi to fulfil the destiny his father had mapped out for him; twenty-eight years earlier, Maradona had only really come alive in the quarter-final. But he was quiet against Belgium, even if Higuaín's header did carry Argentina through to the semi-finals.

Few revolutions ever have a clearly defined start or finish. When did Germany's *Reboot* begin? Some would date it from the failure to progress from the group at Euro 2000, the great shock of a tournament in which Germany not merely failed to win a game but even suffered the embarrassment of losing to England. But it had been a couple of months before the tournament that the DFB had mandated all eighteen Bundesliga clubs to establish academies that met national criteria. Some clubs, such as Werder Bremen, argued that they had a social function and that it was not their remit to be selective while others quibbled on the grounds of cost but, after Euro 2000, it was hard to make the case that German football was not in need of a major overhaul.[28]

Bundesliga clubs were then brought on board, while there was a concerted drive to increase the number of coaches in

Germany: by 2015 there were four times as many as there had been in 2000. According to the former Darmstadt defender Ulf Schott, who helped design the new system, it wasn't so much that more modern football was being taught, as that more coaching led to more talented players and that led naturally to more modern football.[29]

At the same time, German football enjoyed two strokes of fortune that were beyond its control. In 2000, a new citizenship law allowed anybody who had lived in Germany for eight years to claim citizenship, whereas previously they had had to have a German relative. The likes of Yıldıray Baştürk, İlhan Mansız and Ümit Davala, all of whom were born in Germany but played for the Turkey side that got to the semi-final of the 2002 World Cup, would have been eligible for Germany under the new regulation. Then in 2002, Kirsch Media collapsed. Although that caused financial difficulty for a number of German clubs as broadcast deals disappeared, it effectively forced them to give opportunities to the players who were beginning to emerge from the new academies, accelerating their development. A study in 2011 showed that, a decade after the academies had been established, 52 per cent of players in the Bundesliga had come through the clubs' own youth structures. Of the twenty-three-man squad that won the World Cup in 2014, twenty-one were products of the academy system. The two who predated the academies were the reserve goalkeeper Roman Weidenfeller and the striker Miroslav Klose, which was testament both to his fitness and to the fact that academies often seem to struggle to produce strikers, an issue that would dog German football in the years that followed.[30]

The first real evidence of an upturn came in 2009, when Germany won the European Under-21 championship. It said much for the sides' respective fortunes that while six of that team would go on to win the World Cup with the senior side in 2014 (with others going on to play for Iran, Poland and the

USA), seven of the England squad they beat 4–0 in the final would go on to play for Sunderland.

With that sense of something building came pressure. The sense of liberation that had begun in 2006 continued to 2008 and 2010; winning seemed less important than the new, progressive form of football. But in 2012, there were the beginnings of frustration. This was a great generation of players: was it being wasted by Löw? Qualifying only added to the unease, as Germany won nine and drew one of ten matches, scoring thirty-six goals but conceding seven in their two games against Sweden. The fear was that, for all their attacking talent, they were frivolous.

Three wins and three draws in their friendlies between qualification and the World Cup convinced nobody. Germany's general manager Oliver Bierhoff admitted he was troubled by the team's lack of efficiency. 'They get carried away with their own beautiful football from time to time,' he said.[31]

There was a feeling that Löw didn't help matters with his reluctance to pick a striker: for him, Spain were the model,[32] and by Euro 2012 they were using Fàbregas as a false nine. In November that year, for a friendly against the Netherlands, Löw selected the first ever Germany national team not to feature a centre-forward, with Müller deployed as the false nine. It finished in a drab 0–0 draw. With Mario Gómez and Klose regularly injured, though, Löw continued the experiment, regularly playing Özil as his false nine. To the extent that he scored eight goals in qualifying, it worked, but everybody knew that the step up to a tournament was huge.

The immediate build-up could hardly have gone worse. A drunk Kevin Großkreutz urinated in the lobby of a Berlin hotel after Borussia Dortmund had been defeated in the Cup final,[33] Löw had his driving licence removed after being caught speeding and using his mobile while driving[34] and, worst of all, a steward and a passer-by were seriously injured during a

PR stunt for Mercedes-Benz involving Benedikt Höwedes and Julian Draxler.[35] But there were football concerns as well. Löw had said he would not take players to a tournament who were not fully fit, but he adapted his principles for Manuel Neuer, Philipp Lahm, Bastian Schweinsteiger and Sami Khedira, all of whom were carrying problems. It got worse as Lars Bender was ruled out and Marco Reus suffered an injury in the final warm-up game.

Klose, who turned thirty-six just before the World Cup began, was the only striker in the squad, so the false nine remained for the group stage. Although Müller got a hat-trick against Portugal, it was otherwise unconvincing. Then, after 70 minutes of the last-sixteen win over Algeria, Shkodran Mustafi, who had been playing at right-back, suffered a muscle tear and was forced off. Sami Khedira came on and Lahm returned to full-back. Almost immediately, Germany found a balance and scored twice in extra time. In that, lay the basis of the decision Löw made on his famous run along the beach.

For Brazil, hosting the World Cup inevitably awoke memories of the Maracanazo, and the great trauma of 1950. After the defeat to Uruguay that had cost them that World Cup, Brazil hadn't even played another game until April 1952 and they didn't play again at the Maracanã for twenty-one months. Everything was filtered through the shock of that result. There was a desperate need for affirmation. Jacques de Ryswick, the football editor at *L'Équipe*, was at the Maracanã as Brazil sealed qualification for the 1954 tournament with victory over Paraguay. 'Thousands of shirts were torn off, set alight and waved about like triumphal torches,' he wrote. 'For me, the game . . . was only a pretext . . . a sort of safety valve invented to allow the superabundant life of the people, their exuberance and need for excitement.'[36]

That emotion was powerful. The growth of organised fan groups, the *torcidas*, through the fifties and sixties, encouraged by initiatives such as the *Jornal dos Sports* awarding points for displays and maintaining a league table, was an attempt to harness it, but there was a recognition that the intensity of feeling was dangerous. In her 1974 short story '*A procura de uma dignidade*' ('In Search of Dignity'), Clarice Lispector depicts a woman having a breakdown on the concourse at the Maracanã which invoked the psychological collapse of the Maracanazo.[37] The jingoistic hysteria that had undone Brazil in 1950 would do so again in 2014.

Even at the Confederations Cup the year before, there had been a strange intensity to the atmosphere in the stadiums and in the media. As Brazil swept to victory in that tournament, beating Spain 3–0 in the final, there was a sense that no side had ever been quite so invested in winning a competition that was generally regarded as a series of glorified friendlies.

It was a dangerous win, one that perhaps created a false sense of expectation. There were warning signs throughout. Brazil came through the group stage with seven points but seemed over-reliant on Neymar. They needed penalties to beat Chile in the last sixteen and then faced Colombia in the quarter-final.

Colombia had impressed under José Pékerman, winning all three group games and then thrilling as they beat a Uruguay shorn of Luis Suárez, suspended for biting Italy's Giorgio Chiellini. Both goals had come from their inspirational playmaker, James Rodríguez, the first of them a chest, turn and dipping volley in off the underside of the bar from 25 yards. They were a team based on the speed of their wide men and individual technique; there had been no sense of them as an overtly physical side. The game against Brazil, though, was ferocious. Brazil won it 2–1, David Luiz scoring a stunning free-kick, but Colombia had a goal ruled out for a mystifying offside and the Brazil goalkeeper Júlio César could easily have been sent off in conceding the penalty that gave Rodríguez his sixth goal of the tournament, earning him the Golden Boot.

The key moment came with four minutes remaining when, as Brazil cleared a corner and the ball dropped about 10 yards outside their box, the Colombia defender Juan Camilo Zúñiga kneed Neymar in the back, fracturing a vertebra and putting him out of the rest of the tournament. The Brazilian federation called for retrospective action against Zúñiga,[38] and social media campaigns were mounted against him. Zúñiga expressed sorrow that Neymar had been injured, sending him a letter insisting 'there was no intent to injure, malice nor negligence'[39] and in truth there probably wasn't: perhaps Zúñiga was a little clumsy or over-enthusiastic as Colombia scrambled to regain possession but at the time it appeared an ordinary collision; the Spanish referee Carlos Velasco Carballo allowed play to continue as Oscar broke.

There was talk of concerted physicality from Colombia – even though Brazil committed thirty-one fouls to Colombia's twenty-three, and after the quarter-final had committed more fouls than any other side at the tournament. Had they targeted Neymar? The injury that damaged his spine came from the fifth foul on him in the game, which given how he invited fouls, played for them even, didn't seem excessive. And besides, if you're looking to put a player out of the game, you don't wait till you're 2–1 down with four minutes remaining to do it. Brazil, by contrast, fouled Rodríguez six times in the first 49 minutes of the game. There was a sense of perspective being lost, of a nation intoxicated by the prospect of victory, whipped up by the need for victory, unable to handle adversity on their path to that victory. As it turned out, the more significant absence from the semi-final may have been the central defender Thiago Silva, suspended after picking up a second yellow card of the competition.

Hubris had often underlain Brazilian football. Just as there had been those who had proclaimed Brazil champions before the game against Uruguay in 1950, just as there had been celebratory parades before the squad set off for England in 1966, so there was a distinct sense in 2014 that Brazilian victory was inevitable, the other thirty-one teams merely supporting cast. There was, at times, an unpleasant edge to the atmosphere at Brazil games, as though an element of the local support couldn't tolerate the idea of an opposition that was actually trying to win.

But perhaps that attitude is compensation for insecurity, for a fear that victory will not arrive. After Neymar was injured against Colombia, Brazil fell into a state akin to mourning. There was a hush about the streets; newspapers were printed with black borders. As the semi-final against Germany approached, the nationalistic fervour intensified. Brazil had been engaging in *a capella* renditions of the national anthem since the Confederations Cup success the previous year, and there was something impressive about the passion that seemed to unleash. But at that semi-final, as David Luiz brandished Neymar's shirt, the emotions tipped into hysteria.

That transmitted itself to Brazil's play. Germany won their first corner after 11 minutes. Toni Kroos took it from the right. Brazil's defence, inexplicably, moved en masse to the near post, leaving Müller alone to volley in. Most of all, it was a goal about scrambled Brazil minds, but it was also about a tweak Germany had made. In the four tournaments between 2006 and 2012, Germany scored fifty-three goals, of which five came from non-penalty set plays. It was as though Löw felt them beneath him, not quite part of the bold new progressive football he was supposed to be instilling. His assistant Hansi Flick suggested it was an area in which they could improve. Lars Voßler was brought in from Freiburg as a specialist set-play coach. Müller's goal was the fifth Germany had scored from non-penalty set plays in the tournament.

Having fallen behind, Brazil lost all discipline. Germany repeatedly sliced through them, scoring four times in an incomprehensible 6 minutes and 41 seconds. By the half-hour, it was 5–0, and the fevered pre-match mood had turned to shock. There were tears, one fan was pictured apparently eating his shirt and, in response to isolated incidents of violence, the military police sent twelve officers to the stadium.[40] Mostly, though, there was stunned silence. Germany won 7–1. Belo Horizonte was remarkably quiet that night, just as Rio de Janeiro had been after the Maracanazo sixty-four years earlier.

After the phantasmagoria of the first semi-final, the second was far quieter. The mood was notably sombre following the death the night before the game of the Argentinian journalist Jorge López, killed when the taxi he was travelling in was hit by a stolen car being chased by police. Players were, anyway, wearing black armbands for Alfredo Di Stéfano, who had died the previous week. It finished 0–0, thanks largely to a startling surge and slide from Javier Mascherano to deny Arjen Robben which, as the midfielder put it, 'tore my anus'.[41] Argentina won the penalty shoot-out after which Messi, who had been close to him, dedicated the victory to López.

It was a repeat of the 1986 and 1990 World Cup finals: Argentina against Germany, Messi against the reset of an entire system. Had Messi sparkled in the final at the Maracanã, perhaps it might still have been seen as his tournament. His four goals in the group stage and his assist for Di María in the last sixteen, plus the desire to see him crowned, were, after all, enough for him to be named player of the tournament, an award he accepted grim-faced. Yet even in the days leading up to the final, quotes attributed to his father, although quickly denied, suggested he felt his legs 'weighed 100kg each'.[42] He had developed a habit of vomiting on the pitch: were the two connected? As Messi's form returned with Barcelona the following season, he did acknowledge that he had not physically been at his best during the World Cup.

Even without Messi at his peak, Argentina might have won the final. Higuaín missed a number of chances and had a goal – correctly – ruled out for a tight offside, while Manuel Neuer probably should have been sent off and conceded a penalty for a wild challenge on the forward early in the second half. Germany lost Khedira to a calf injury in the warm-up and his replacement Christoph Kramer was then forced off with concussion after 32 minutes, which perhaps explained their struggle for rhythm.

They won it with seven minutes of extra time remaining as André Schürrle, a substitute, crossed for another substitute, Mario Götze, to volley in. Bastian Schweinsteiger, battling on bloodied after being caught by a stray arm from Agüero, was the hero, but the victory really was a triumph for *das Reboot*, a triumph fourteen years in the making.

2018

A NEW LEAF

The bald man on the right spread his hands and looked across at his two companions. The bald man in the middle, tie loosened, copied the gesture, widening his eyes and turning down his lips as he turned to the third man. The third man, wearing a red-and-white keffiyeh, raised his hands, palms open, and smiled in reluctant acceptance. When the bald man on the right reached across and offered his hand, the man in the keffiyeh shook it and the bald man on the right patted his wrist. No words appeared to be exchanged, but they didn't need to be. This was excruciating VIP banter: the mock-apologetic expression of the sentiment, 'ah, football, what can you do?' What makes the scene disturbing is that this was the opening game of the 2018 World Cup, Russia had just taken the lead against Saudi Arabia and these men were, from right to left, Vladimir Putin, Gianni Infantino and Mohammed bin Salman.

Putin had been leader of Russia since 2000. Even before he hosted the World Cup, he had ordered the invasion of Crimea and eastern Ukraine, sent Russian troops into Georgia and reportedly had the dissident Alexander Litvinenko murdered in London. Three months before the World Cup, the double agent Sergei Skripal and his daughter Yulia were poisoned in Salisbury with Novichok;[1] the British government believed

Putin responsible – the investigative website Bellingcat later identified two suspects as agents of the GRU, the Russian secret police[2] – and so sent no ministerial or royal delegation to any World Cup match.[3]

Bin Salman had become Saudi defence minister in January 2015. Within two months a Saudi-led coalition had begun a bloody campaign in Yemen against Houthi insurgents who had seized the capital, Sanaa.[4] He became crown prince in June 2017, a month after launching a purge against competing business interests and political elites. Around two hundred were detained at the Ritz Carlton where they were tortured to reveal assets held abroad;[5] at least forty princes and ministers were subsequently charged with corruption.[6]

Infantino, the former secretary general of Uefa, was elected Fifa president in 2016, defeating Sheikh Salman bin Ebrahim Al Khalifa of Bahrain, who had been accused of complicity in the use of torture and mass incarceration against the country's pro-democracy movement.[7] Salman denied the allegations: 'The question is, do you have proof that the Bahrain FA, under my presidency, took part in non-football activities?'[8] Replacing Sepp Blatter, who had been forced to resign amid a welter of corruption allegations linked in part to the vote that gave the 2018 World Cup to Russia and the 2022 World Cup to Qatar, Infantino had promised to reform the organisation. Blatter himself has never been convicted of corruption.

The sight of Infantino hobnobbing with autocratic leaders would become increasingly common over the years that followed.

France won their second World Cup in Moscow, but the origin of their victory lay in the second leg of their qualifying play-off for 2014. They had lost the first leg 2–0 in Ukraine. Coming second in their group, behind the world champions Spain, was no disgrace, but they had not played well. In Kyiv, they had been terrible. After the disgrace of Knysna, there was a real fear that France might not even make it to Brazil. What made it worse was that 2014 was when the celebrated *Génération 87*, which had won the Under-17 Euros in 2004 with a squad that included Samir Nasri, Hatem Ben Arfa, Jérémy Ménez and Karim Benzema, should have been coming to its peak.

Didier Deschamps made five changes for the return leg. Nasri complained at being dropped and was never selected again. Amid various appeals to posterity and patriotism, Deschamps showed the squad Nabil Ben Yadir's recently released film *La Marche*, which told the story of the peace march from Marseille to Paris thirty years earlier that had led to the coining of the phrase '*black-blanc-beur*'. In the four days between the two legs, something in the general mood changed.

France players had often been critical of the atmosphere at the Stade de France.[9] The crowd was routinely dismissed as comprising '*Footix*' – those who were attracted by the euphoria of 1998, more concerned by the spectacle than an understanding of or love for football, the term derived from that tournament's grinning cockerel mascot. But that night the atmosphere was fervent and supportive and France beat Ukraine 3–0 thanks to two goals from Mamadou Sakho and one from Benzema, both players Deschamps had recalled. France had qualified for the 2014 World Cup and the journey to the triumph of 2018 had begun.

Any thought of winning a second World Cup seemed a very long way off when Deschamps was appointed in 2012. Domenech had been replaced by Laurent Blanc, who had led Bordeaux to the title in his second season as a coach and, as the captain from 1998, seemed to have the authority and broad-based appeal to restore a sense of togetherness to the national side. He spoke of the need for 'rigour and discipline',[10] prohibited the use of phones at dinner, banned players from wearing headphones as they arrived at games and circulated the words of '*la Marseillaise*'.

France ground their way through qualifying for Euro 2012, but that hardly mattered alongside a scandal that broke in April 2011 when the Mediapart website revealed it had a recording of an FFF meeting at which the imposition of an unofficial racial quota system was discussed. That would have been controversial enough, but Blanc also spoke of, as he saw it, the impossibility of introducing Spain-style possession football in France. 'You get the impression,' he said, 'that we produce the same kind of players: big, strong, powerful ones. And who are the big strong powerful ones? The blacks.'[11] Blanc insisted he had been taken out of context, no quota was imposed and he kept his job. But the damage had been done.

The indiscipline continued at the Euros as Nasri and Alou Diarra rowed in the dressing-room, Ben Arfa answered his phone during a post-match briefing and Nasri became involved in an expletive-littered argument with a reporter in the mixed zone. France went out in the quarter-final to Spain; that was an improvement on South Africa, but only because nothing could have been worse. Blanc stood down at the end of the tournament.

Sepp Blatter's obsession with winning the Nobel Peace Prize had led him to run the bids for the 2018 and 2022 World Cups simultaneously; his dream was for Russia to host in 2018 and the USA in 2022 with the two local organising committees working harmoniously together.[12] But two votes meant enormous potential for horse-trading.

The whole process was corrupt from the start, and every candidate was guilty to some extent, as was outlined in the 434-page report produced for Fifa by the US lawyer Michael Garcia and his Swiss assistant Cornel Borbély. They spoke of 'a culture of expectation and entitlement', with members of the Fifa Executive Committee regarding perks and sweetheart business deals as simply part of their job.[13] US Justice explicitly referenced bribes.[14] England tried to get involved, distributing handbags for delegates' wives[15] and arranging a friendly away against Trinidad & Tobago to try to appeal to Jack Warner,[16] but they weren't thinking anywhere near big enough. The Paraguayan ExCo member Nicolás Leoz demanded a knighthood, an invitation to the wedding of Prince William and Kate Middleton[17] and that the FA Cup be named after him.[18]

The idea that bids were being assessed on their merits is almost laughable: every bid was ranked as 'low-risk' by Fifa's own evaluation apart from two: Russia (medium-risk) and Qatar (high-risk).[19] Yet it was Russia and Qatar, the two least democratic countries bidding, who prevailed. As Bonita Mersiades, who worked on the Australia bid for 2022 before turning whistleblower, put it, the decisions had nothing to do with facilities, legacy or cost but on 'what goes on behind closed doors'.[20]

Despite commissioning the report, Fifa obfuscated the obvious flaws in the bidding process. The Garcia Report was delivered in 2014 but all that was published was a 42-page summary by the chairman of Fifa's Adjudicatory Committee, Hans Joachim Eckert, that Garcia regarded as so misleading he resigned.[21] Only in 2017 was the report published in full and then only because the German tabloid *Bild* had accessed a copy.

It began with Sam Allardyce drinking a pint of wine. Except he didn't really; he drank a pint of lager, it just looked oddly like wine in the murky recording offered by the secret camera and that was a better story, one that seemed to capture the emotional mood. In truth the *Telegraph*'s sting operation didn't reveal very much at all,[22] merely that Allardyce was interested in making an enormous amount of money from speaking engagements abroad – which can have surprised nobody – and that, having been the West Ham manager when they had signed Carlos Tévez and Javier Mascherano, he was prepared to act as a consultant for other clubs looking to sign players with third-party contracts to ensure they complied with Premier League regulations.[23] But the FA, spooked by the prospect of further revelations, persuaded Allardyce to resign over what the FA's CEO Martin Glenn described as 'entrapment',[24] meaning his England reign had lasted just sixty-seven days and one game, a 1–0 win away to Slovakia.

Whatever the specifics of the allegations – a police inquiry found Allardyce had committed no offence – English football was in the mire. After the dismal World Cup in 2014, they performed even worse at the Euros in 2016, losing to Iceland in the last sixteen. Allardyce had replaced Roy Hodgson and, to no great enthusiasm, was himself then replaced by the Under-21 coach Gareth Southgate, whose managerial career at that point amounted to an unremarkable three seasons in charge of Middlesbrough, culminating in relegation. As Under-21 coach, though, Southgate had helped with the implementation of the England DNA programme, the second stage, after the Elite Player Performance Plan which redrew the regulations around academies, of the great reset that followed the failure to qualify for Euro 2008. He had played a key role in shaping how future English footballers should be developed.[25]

Southgate was initially appointed as an interim and didn't appear especially keen to take the job permanently. But then neither did anybody else. England at that point seemed a dead end. An odd narrative would develop, perhaps because of how good he was at the ambassadorial side of the job, that Southgate was inherently conservative and lacked the steel to leave out big names, but his squad for Russia was radical, with both Wayne Rooney and Joe Hart omitted. It was just that expectations were so low that there was no furore or even discussion.

England were lucky with the draw, but then they had often in the past made hard work of beating unexceptional opposition. An injury-time Harry Kane winner saw off a dogged Tunisia and he then got a hat-trick in a 6–1 demolition of Panama. Defeat to Belgium with both sides already qualified didn't much matter – indeed, it made England's potential route to the final somewhat easier.

Colombia in the last sixteen was perhaps the defining game. England played well, and took the lead from a Kane penalty after a foul committed as Colombia struggled to defend a corner. England's set pieces, their practice of lining up four players who would then break, caused chaos. It was, essentially, the weaponisation of queueing, but it also demonstrated a strength of Southgate, who had identified set pieces as a sphere in which a relatively small amount of practice on the training ground could have a significant impact on the pitch.

Another area Southgate had focused on was penalties. England shouldn't have needed them, conceding a last-minute equaliser after needlessly dropping deep to protect their lead, but the game went to a shoot-out and, for the first time at a major tournament after six failures, they won. In his Marks & Spencer waistcoat, Southgate, who had missed the decisive penalty in the semi-final of Euro 96, consoled Carlos Bacca, who had missed for Colombia, an image of statesmanlike decency that offered a reminder of a distant vision of Englishness, far removed from the grubby self-interest and tawdry squabbling that characterised Westminster as Brexit was forced through Parliament. Meanwhile, as beer was hurled into the air at box parks and beer gardens, people danced on bus shelters and sales of waistcoats went through the roof,[26] there was a sense of the country, for the first time since Italia 90, really rallying behind the England national team at an overseas tournament.

The outcome was much the same: disappointment in the semi-final and a sense the mood had been rather better than the actual achievement. England beat Sweden comfortably enough in the quarter-final and led and had chances against Croatia in the semi but as the game began to turn against them, Southgate was slow to give Jordan Henderson help in midfield and Croatia won 2–1 in extra time.

The result mattered less than the vibe. Southgate had made England care about the national team again, but his reach stretched further even than that.[27] Amid the post-Brexit culture wars, Southgate wrote an open letter, '*Dear England*', in which he set out his vision of 'a tolerant and understanding society'.[28] James Graham took the title for a play about Southgate's reign that examined issues of nationalism and the male psyche. The contrast with 1966, when columnists had lamented the expenditure of any intellectual effort on football, was striking.

Yet as England began to rise on the back of their reset, the country whose example they had most tried to follow faltered. Germany had won the Confederations Cup the previous summer with a young squad, but Jogi Löw struggled to integrate that with his world champions. There was talk of splits in the camp, with the 'Bling-Bling Gang' of Özil, Sami Khedira, Jérôme Boateng and Julian Draxler on one side and the 'Bavarians' – Manuel Neuer, Mats Hummels, Thomas Müller and Toni Kroos – on the other.[29] As the right-wing *Alternative für Deutschland* weighed in, making predictable points about immigration, Özil, who had been heavily criticised for posing for a photograph with Recep Tayyip Erdoğan, the president of Turkey, said he had the sense that, 'I am German when we win but I am an immigrant when we lose.'[30]

The racial issues were not as stark as those that had undermined France in South Africa but they were there. From a more overtly footballing point of view, Germany went out because they had no centre-forward to replace Klose; they weren't the only country to discover that academies tend to produce technically gifted creators but few ruthless goalscorers.[31]

Putin got involved with the bid only very late, when it looked like Russia might not win. He summoned the oligarchs and hatched a plan. Dossiers were drawn up on each of the ExCo members providing detailed psychological portraits and asking which might be susceptible to bribery.[32] The Belgian ExCo member Michel d'Hooghe, who claimed to have voted for the Belgium/Netherlands bid, at least in the first round, admitted he had accepted 'a small painting' from Russia's state collection.[33]

There was very obvious collusion between Russia and Qatar. Eight months before the vote, Russian officials visited Qatar to discuss a huge gas deal that British intelligence believed was linked to the World Cup bid.[34] A month before the vote, the emir Sheikh Hamad bin Khalifa Al Thani met Putin to discuss general co-operation[35] and, on the eve of the 2022 tournament, Hamad's successor as emir, Sheikh Tamim bin Hamad Al Thani, thanked Russia for its support.[36]

The process was Blatter's, but he had never wanted Qatar to win. And perhaps even as, with glassy eyes and a rictus smile, he announced Qatar was to host 2022, he saw the danger to his own presidency. Blatter believed that the USA only went after Fifa because of Bill Clinton's anger in Zurich that the vote had gone against him and, while the FBI had been looking into Fifa for several months before the vote, the sense of outrage perhaps spurred the investigation.[37]

Events moved slowly. First the Qatari Mohammed bin Hammam stood against Blatter for the presidency in 2011, but his campaign was undermined when it was revealed that envelopes containing US$40,000 were being distributed to members of the Caribbean Football Union to secure their votes.[38] After Blatter hinted that the vote for 2022 could be rerun,[39] Bin Hammam was persuaded to stand down[40] and Blatter was elected unopposed. But the stench of corruption was unmistakable.

Chuck Blazer was the larger-than-life US ExCo member who had two apartments in Trump Tower, one for himself and one for his cats. He claimed to have made his fortune with the smiley face; in fact, he had defrauded the Spain brothers, who owned the rights to it, selling smiley-branded products in breach of their contract.[41] His blog showed he loved dressing up – Santa Claus, Obi Wan Kenobi, anybody with a beard.[42] When Putin suggested he looked like Karl Marx, he high-fived him.[43] He was the cheery face of Fifa corruption, who was flipped and wore a wire after being accused of tax evasion and racketeering.

It was partly thanks to Blazer's evidence that Swiss police, acting under the direction of the FBI, raided the Baur au Lac hotel in Zurich in May 2015 and arrested seven Fifa officials. Blatter defeated Prince Ali bin Al Hussein of Jordan in presidential elections a month later. But the drip of revelations continued and, in May 2016, he resigned at an extraordinary congress.

Like Blanc, Didier Deschamps sought to impose discipline; unlike Blanc, he largely succeeded. There were the usual selection issues. When, for instance, the midfielder Adrien Rabiot played poorly in a World Cup qualifier against Bulgaria and sought to excuse his performance by saying he'd been worried about injuring himself in the cold, Deschamps dropped him for Steven Nzonzi. Nobody thought Nzonzi was anywhere near as talented, but he was more reliable and more committed to the collective, a point Rabiot underlined by ranting about his omission on Instagram.

Most notoriously, there was '*l'affaire de la sextape*' in which Benzema was implicated in a plot to blackmail his international team-mate Mathieu Valbuena. Arrested in 2015, he was eventually convicted and given a one-year suspended sentence in November 2021, having seemingly agreed to act as an intermediary for a friend from Bron-Terraillon, a *banlieue* of Lyon. Benzema was banned from the national team between December 2015 and May 2021 and attacked Deschamps for having 'bowed to pressure from a racist part of France'.[44] While omitting a player accused of such an egregious breach of trust may seem entirely reasonable, the word '*raciste*' was daubed on Deschamps's house in Brittany. Deschamps remained implacable.

In Brazil in 2014, France had been unremarkable, topping their group and squeezing by Nigeria in the last sixteen before defeat to Germany in the quarter-final. Euro 2016, played on home soil, took on additional significance after the terror attacks in Paris on 13 November 2015. As concertgoers were shot at the Bataclan theatre, three suicide bombs were detonated around the Stade de France during a friendly against Germany. There were 130 fatalities that night; had any of the bombers gained entrance to the stadium, the death toll would have been far, far higher. France were probably the best team at the tournament, and raucously enjoyed their semi-final victory over Germany in Marseille, but they struggled to break Portugal down in the final, even after Cristiano Ronaldo had been forced off through injury, and succumbed to an extra-time winner from Eder.

That 1–0 defeat led to the first real doubts about Deschamps. Although he had grown up under Jean-Claude Suaudeau at Nantes, he had none of his swagger. As a player he had been hard-working and disciplined, mocked by Eric Cantona as a 'water-carrier', and he took that attitude into management. This was the lesson of 1998: no matter how many gifted creators might be available, what won tournaments was solidity. It wasn't just Deschamps: this was French football.

In 2004, Deschamps had led his well-organised Monaco to the Champions League final where they were beaten by José Mourinho's equally unyielding Porto. French football, though, took the general astringency to extremes and, in 2005–06, goals per game in Ligue 1 dropped below 2.00.

Other than the calls for efficiency and an approach that followed the utilitarian ideals of the early days of the Fifth Republic, there had always been a belief that France should play '*football-champagne*'.[45] Attempts to define that beyond a basic improvisational quality are never particularly convincing[46] but the sparkle of France under Michel Hidalgo between 1976 and 1984 was undeniable. This was what made the Poulidor or Asterix Complex bearable: they might be losers, but they were gallant losers. After 1998 that was no longer true. France, thanks to Clairefontaine and the academy system, was producing high-level players in greater numbers than perhaps anywhere else, certainly in Europe, yet the football of its national team was often uninspiring. The stylish underachievers had become remorseless and largely unloved. Somehow, France had transformed themselves into West Germany.

This was Jacquet's legacy and when Houllier replaced him as technical director of the FFF in 2007, he sought to remove the emphasis on physique and refocus youth coaching on technical development. Even a decade later, though, Ligue 1 habitually yielded fewer goals per game than other major European leagues and that, understandably, conditioned how France approached tournaments. 'We tried to play,' the defender Samuel Umtiti said of the 2018 World Cup, 'but we realised that it wasn't us. We had to play to our strengths ... having a low block and knowing that in attack we'd have chances.'[47]

Three goals in three games were enough to yield seven points and top spot in the group, which set up a last-sixteen tie against Argentina that would, simultaneously, confirm the extraordinary talent of Kylian Mbappé, and, given the drama and the scoreline, create an entirely unrepresentative impression of how France played.

Argentina reached the final of the 2015 Copa América, drew 0–0 against Chile and lost on penalties. They reached the final of the 2016 Copa América Centenario, drew 0–0 against Chile and lost on penalties. Messi, the second time, was one of those who missed in the shoot-out. In the dressing-room, he wept. This was unbearable. Why could the side that had won the Under-20 World Cup in 2005 and 2007 and retained Olympic gold in 2008 not win a senior trophy? Why was it so often let down by a sclerotic federation, by team-mates who missed big chances in big games and by the fates? And why did everybody always blame him? Two days after his twenty-ninth birthday, he retired from international football.

Retirement was the making of Messi, at least at international level. Overnight, the attitude of the Argentinian public was transformed; all the doubts evaporated. Suddenly he ceased to be the relentless winner who couldn't do it at international level and became a beautifully flawed genius. His sobs made clear how much he cared; nobody was bothered any more by his habit of mumbling the anthem. At last he had his flaw; all he needed to do was to overcome it.

Argentina united to get Messi back. Political programmes on television were devoted to the topic. Messages on the departure boards on the Subte in Buenos Aires begged him to stay. Edgardo Bauza had succeeded Gerardo Martino as coach and, eventually, after he had made a personal appeal, Messi agreed to return. Bauza, though, lasted just nine months before, with World Cup qualification in doubt, he was sacked and replaced by Jorge Sampaoli, a Bielsa disciple who had led Chile to the 2015 Copa América. A Messi hat-trick away to Ecuador in the final qualifier secured Argentina's place in Russia.

Sampaoli's game was based around a ferocious high press, entirely unsuited to the slow defenders available to him with Argentina. A 1–1 draw against Iceland followed by an embarrassing 3–0 defeat to Croatia meant Argentina had to beat Nigeria to qualify. A moment of Messi brilliance and an improbable late Marcos Rojo volley brought an unconvincing 2–1 win and progress as group runners-up. While the group winners Croatia had only to beat Denmark, Russia and England to reach the final, Argentina faced a brutal challenge in the last sixteen.

It began with the sort of exhilarating burst that would soon become characteristic of Mbappé as he surged from inside his own half before being dragged down by a panicked Rojo. Antoine Griezmann converted the penalty. There were 13 minutes played and at that stage the game seemed to be following a predictable script. But just before half-time, Ángel Di María whipped in a 30-yard drive, and just after half-time a Messi shot deflected in off Gabriel Mercado. From nowhere, Argentina had the lead. At World Cups, Messi had carried with him always a sense that he was merely the agent of much greater forces: was this his destiny at work at last?

It was not. Within nine minutes France were level, Benjamin Pavard meeting a bouncing ball on the edge of the box with a slice into the top corner, before two goals in four minutes from Mbappé. Agüero pulled one back in injury time but the truth is that it was never as tight as 4–3 made it sound. The game may have been widely described as a seven-goal thriller, but there were only ever around 10 minutes when it seemed conceivable France might not win.

After winning the World Cup bid, Russia took an increasingly authoritarian turn. In 2012, the Kremlin launched what Human Rights Watch described as 'the worst political crackdown in Russia's post-Soviet history', with major restrictions on civil society and journalism.[48] A year later the 'promotion of homosexuality among minors' became an offence.[49] Foreign policy became increasingly aggressive.

Internal restrictions made an assessment far harder to make than in South Africa or Brazil but, by May 2017, the official cost had hit $11.4bn, while it was clear that contracts were being given to Putin allies[50] and the Yabloko Anti-Corruption Policy Centre reported widespread price-gouging.[51] At the same time, there were mounting concerns about labour practices, prompting Fifa in September 2016 to set up a programme to monitor conditions at World Cup sites.[52] Six months later the Norwegian investigative journalist Håvard Melnæs discovered more than a hundred North Korean workers building the stadium in St Petersburg, living in shipping containers surrounded by barbed wire.[53] As they were forced to send the majority of any hard currency they earned back to North Korea, they fell under the UN designation of forced labour.[54] Others reported wages being paid late or not at all, workers toiling in dangerously cold conditions and employers failing to provide contracts and appropriate documentation.[55] In April 2017, between two and three hundred central Asian workers went on strike in Rostov to protest at having gone unpaid for five months, while Builders and Woodworkers International reported at least twenty-one deaths on stadium sites, which it blamed on negligence or poor health and safety practices.[56]

And, of course, Russia used measures introduced for the World Cup as a tool of oppression. There had been concerns before the tournament that the Fan ID apps required on phones to access stadiums gave Russia's communications ministry access to a raft of personal information.[57] Sure enough, the app was required after the World Cup for Russian league games and was used to target civil society activists.[58]

Kazan, pretending to be closer to Moscow than it actually is, is in the wrong time zone, which means that dawn breaks at around 2.30 in the morning. The first glimmers were beginning to lighten the sky as Brazil left the Kazan Arena after their quarter-final defeat to Belgium. As the other players approached the team bus, Neymar stood alone, silhouetted against the dawn and the vast LED display that fronts the stadium, head bowed, the terrible burden of carrying the hopes and expectations of Brazil clear. In a different context, perhaps his career would have been very different, but Neymar was unfortunate enough to emerge just at the time Brazil needed an answer to Lionel Messi. And because he could never live up to the impossible standard of Messi, Neymar was doomed always to remain a prisoner of his potential.

In June 2011, when he was nineteen, Neymar scored the opening goal in the second leg of the final as Santos won the Copa Libertadores for the first time since 1963, when they had been inspired by Pelé. Neymar seemed to have been anointed. But there had been warning signs. When he was eighteen, Santos won the Copa do Brasil even though Neymar missed a penalty in the final. Soon after, Neymar was brought down in the box in a league game and when his coach, Dorival Júnior, instructed somebody else to take the penalty, a furious Neymar had to be placated by a linesman, turned his back on the penalty and engaged in a public row with his captain. When Dorival called for him to be suspended for two weeks, the board sacked him. From a very early age, Neymar was indulged.

It wasn't just Santos; it was institutional. Referees in Brazil had a tendency to protect him, even if only subconsciously: he was the great young hope. The consequences of that when he had to deal with the outside world were soon apparent. Within a month of winning the Libertadores, Neymar faced Venezuela in Brazil's first game of the Copa América. Roberto Rosales, an unremarkable right-back, marked Neymar out of the game, his play physical but not excessively so. It finished 0–0. It was a similar story in the quarter-final as Paraguay's Darío Verón, an aggressive central defender deployed on the right, who had already played well against Neymar in the group, neutralised him to the extent he was taken off after 80 minutes. 'It's always me, me, me with him,' said the former forward Walter Casagrande on *O Globo*'s coverage. 'He's forgotten or maybe he never knew that football is a collective activity.'

Neymar left Brazil for Barcelona when he was twenty-one, for a fee initially reported as €57.1m although by the following January, investigations from the Spanish tax authorities had revealed the actual figure was €86.2m with €45m going directly to Neymar's parents. The scandal led to the resignation of the Barcelona president Sandro Rosell[59] and his replacement by Josep Maria Bartomeu, whose reign proved disastrous for Barcelona.[60] Neymar took time to adapt, scoring only nine goals in his first season as he struggled with the physicality of the European game. That first season, 2013–14, Barcelona won nothing.

Then came the World Cup on home soil. He was targeted as great players always are, and there was enormous pressure on him, particularly after his uninspired first season in Spain. Although there was widespread sympathy when he fractured a vertebra in the quarter-final, his simulation and petulance irritated many.

The following season, after Luis Suárez had arrived at Barcelona to form the MSN – Messi, Suárez, Neymar – forward line, was the best of Neymar's career, and he rounded off the scoring in the Champions League final as Barcelona won the treble. Within a couple of weeks of that final, though,

Neymar faced Colombia again in the group stage of the Copa América in Chile and was sent off for a backward headbutt. He continued to remonstrate with the referee, and wound up with a four-game ban.

Neymar didn't even play at the Copa América Centenario in the USA the following year because of Brazil's obsession with the Olympics. They had never previously won gold in the men's football and were determined to do so at the Games they were hosting. Neymar scored in every knockout round and then converted the decisive kick in the shoot-out as Brazil beat Germany in the final. While he and Brazil celebrated, the rest of the world wondered why such focus was being given to a glorified youth tournament. It was his only success with his national side.

As Barcelona drifted, the midfield often left defenceless against high-level opponents by the reluctance of their forward line to press, Neymar moved, joining PSG for an unthinkable €222m, more than doubling the previous world transfer record. Having secured the rights to host the 2022 World Cup, Qatar had then invested in PSG. For them the deal made sense on a number of levels: they were getting a very talented player; they were making a show of their economic might against the pre-existing elite; and they were inflating the market, pushing up prices to a level it was very difficult for clubs without enormously wealthy state backers to match.

And there was also perhaps significance in the fact that, two months earlier, Qatar had been blockaded by the Arab League, led by Saudi Arabia and the UAE. What better way for Qatar to signal its defiance to the Saudis and its status as a major player in the world game than by smashing the world transfer record?

Neymar favoured the move, partly because it earned him an enormous pay rise, and partly because he believed that, by escaping the shadow of Messi, his chances of winning the

Ballon d'Or were enhanced. He was wrong. Domestic achievements stacked up, but Neymar never won the Champions League, his time in Paris ultimately characterised by injuries and revelations about his partying.

In 2018, there was still a belief his move to PSG might work out, a sense he had unfinished business from 2014. His tournament was like his career, occasionally brilliant but often frustrating. In the quarter-final, Belgium called Neymar's bluff, Roberto Martínez fielding the centre-forward Romelu Lukaku wide on the right in a 4-3-3. As Belgium's right-back Thomas Meunier tore past Neymar again and again, Belgium dominated that flank and won 2–1. While it would be unfair to blame Neymar entirely for their exit, Brazil's dependency on him and his lack of defensive work exposed them to just the sort of assault to which they succumbed.

As he stared at the ground in the car park at dawn in Kazan, Neymar perhaps knew the World Cup would never be his.

After the excitement of the Argentina win, France reverted to type in the quarter-final against Uruguay and the semi-final against Belgium: a conservative approach, defensive solidity and wins based on clean sheets. 'I would prefer to lose with this Belgium than to win with this France,' said Eden Hazard after his side had lost to Umtiti's header from a corner.[61]

That had become the Belgian way. Like so many other golden generations, Belgium's never quite achieved what it might have. The squad that went to the 2014 tournament was packed with talent but never gelled under Marc Wilmots and they were eliminated by Argentina in the last eight. Wales put them out of Euro 2016 at the same stage. Under Roberto Martínez they showed more life and imagination, but in the semi-final it felt as though they were undone by their inferiority complex against their neighbours.

So France went on to meet an experienced and seemingly indefatigable Croatia, inspired by Luka Modrić, in the final. The 4–2 scoreline was just as misleading as the 4–3 against Argentina. France took the lead from another set play as Griezmann's free-kick glanced in off Mandžukić. Ivan Perišić levelled, before the game turned on one of the absurd handball decisions that had begun to afflict football after the adoption of VAR. The ball skimmed off Blaise Matuidi's back and struck the hand of Perišić who was no more than a yard behind him and unsighted with his arm by his side. Griezmann converted the penalty. Fine finishes from Paul Pogba and Mbappé took France 4–1 clear before Mandžukić pulled one back. By then, though, the game was long since done and France were world champions for the second time. Deschamps followed Mario Zagallo and Franz Beckenbauer in having won the World Cup as captain and manager, while Olivier Giroud followed Stéphane Guivarc'h in winning the competition as a centre-forward without scoring a single goal in the finals.

Nobody this time, at least not in France, was naive enough to think a World Cup win could usher in an era of racial harmony. 'This is what France is,' shrugged Pogba, while Benjamin Mendy responded to a social media post that showed the twenty-three members of the squad with flags denoting their families' origins with a photograph of the squad and twenty-three *tricolores*. But as the historian Yvan Gastaut pointed out, the fact that such a racially diverse team promoted such a relative lack of reaction in France was perhaps a positive sign in terms of integration and mutual assimilation.[62]

That said, many of the more optimistic depictions of the players as happy beacons of a new France were soon made to look naive. Reports surfaced that threats had been made against the agent of N'Golo Kanté,[63] while Pogba was held to ransom by an armed gang.[64] It was very difficult, it seemed, for anybody to escape the problems of the *banlieues*.

Shortly after the final whistle, the rain began to teem down. It fell on Moscow and on St Petersburg, it fell on the great Pannonian plain, it fell on Bucharest and on Kyiv, on Kazan and the Urals beyond. It fell on the celebrating France players and on the dejected Croatians. It fell on the hordes of photographers who had swarmed onto the pitch, and it fell on the temporary stage erected for the presentation of the medals. It fell on Gianni Infantino, and it fell on Emmanuel Macron. But it did not fall on Vladimir Putin, because a lackey held an umbrella over him. There was only one umbrella on the pitch and there was no doubting the power of the man it protected.

Russia in 2018 felt a welcoming, prosperous place. There were coffee shops and boutiques, a thriving middle class who, with their foreign holidays and smart restaurants, had never had it so good. Russia felt then like a place that was ready to do business, out of sync with a leader who had seized Crimea and the Donbas, maintained Bashar al-Assad in Syria and ordered the murder of dissidents abroad, a paradox explicable only when the time lag of World Cups is remembered. Russia was awarded the World Cup in 2009 when Putin had stepped back from being president to be prime minister, as though trying to persuade other world powers that he believed in constitutions and such petty details as term limits. Russia joined the World Trade Organisation, hosted a meeting of the G8 and played an active role in the United Nations as though determined to prove itself a law-abiding member of the global community. Hosting the Winter Olympics and World Cup were seemingly conceived as elements of that same programme of normalisation.[65]

But after resuming the presidency in 2012, Putin became increasingly aggressive. Other than the Mexican president

Miguel de la Madrid, whose nation had only been awarded the 1986 tournament in 1983, Putin was the first post-Second World War leader to be in charge for both the bid and the tournament itself. A state-run doping programme led to Russia winning more medals than any other country at the Winter Olympics.[66] Crimea was taken in March 2014. From 2015 there was direct military involvement in Syria. Over the years that followed, the number of assassinations and attempts to manipulate elections increased. From late 2018, the Wagner Group, a Russian private military company, was given increasing freedom to act in Africa.

And a little over three and a half years after the World Cup final, Russia launched its full invasion of Ukraine.

2022

DESERT GOLD

There were two World Cups in Qatar in 2022. There was the World Cup of Lionel Messi and Argentina, and there was the World Cup of Abdullah Ibhais and all the others jailed or abused in the name of the tournament. Some of the football in Qatar was spectacular, the final was thrilling and the core narrative of Messi's success, after so many failures, was one of the greatest in sporting history, but the cost was incalculable: countless deaths, thousands forced to work in inhumane conditions and routinely mistreated, the normalisation of prejudice in direct contravention of Fifa's own statutes.

And presiding over it all was Gianni Infantino, who the day before the tournament began proudly told the world that 'Today I feel Qatari. Today I feel Arabic. Today I feel African. Today I feel gay. Today I feel disabled. Today I feel [like] a migrant worker.'[1] And what of those who had detailed the terrible conditions in which migrant workers toiled, the confiscation of their passports, the non-payment of wages, the intimidation to which those who protested were subject?[2] What of those who pointed out that homosexuality is not only illegal in Qatar, but the subject of a police entrapment campaign, with rape and torture a common outcome?[3] 'We have been told many, many lessons from some Europeans, from the

Western world,' Infantino said. 'I think for what we Europeans have been doing the last 3,000 years we should be apologising for the next 3,000 years before starting to give moral lessons to people.'[4]

But of course. This was the same tactic used by the defenders of Abu Dhabi ownership of Manchester City. As such, the Qatar World Cup stands as the perfect image of the new colonialism in a globalised world. When Havelange became Fifa president in 1974, it signalled the end of the domination of football by the traditional European powers. But the opening up of the game to the rest of the world has led merely to football being seized first by commercial interests and then increasingly by petro-states, who run football for their own ends, ruthlessly exploiting the poor and oppressed of the world, the migrant labourers of south Asia and west Africa. Any criticism of those abuses is immediately combated by accusations of racism, the sins of the colonial past weaponised to justify a colonial present.

Death was everywhere in Doha, death and destiny.

It was there in the infrastructure. Every building, every apartment block, every hotel, every mall, every stadium was a monument to human suffering.

It was there very directly for journalists in the death of Grant Wahl, the long-time *Sports Illustrated* writer who collapsed in the press box at Lusail and, despite rapid medical attention, never regained consciousness. He had tweeted about Wout Weghorst's injury-time equaliser for the Netherlands but was dead by the time Argentina won on penalties. As it turned out, it was an aortic aneurysm that killed him, but he also had the flu that, incubated and disseminated by the stadium air conditioning, afflicted many journalists at the tournament. With the memory of Covid so fresh, there could have been very few in the hours and days after Wahl's passing who did not feel more acutely their own mortality. That same night, a twenty-four-year-old Kenyan security guard, John Njau Kibue, fell from the eighth floor of the stadium and was killed.

It was there in the knowledge that Qatar could afford all this because of its natural gas reserves, which had made it rich beyond measure, and also that it *had* to afford this because of its natural gas reserves, which had made it rich beyond measure. Qatar is tiny. It gained independence only in 1972. It is ruled by the Al Thani family which for years married into Saudi royalty. But then came Hamad who, in 1995, seized power from his father Khalifa, who had been installed by Saudi relatives after they had deposed his cousin Ahmad in 1972. Hamad was notably assertive against the Saudis and, even after abdicating for his son Tamim in 2013, was widely believed to have been pulling the strings – which was one of the reasons for the Saudi blockade of Qatar in 2017. It's certainly a primary motivation for Qatar establishing a joint squadron with the RAF, why 11,000 US and coalition troops are based at the Al Udeid air base in Qatar and why Qatar has been such an enthusiastic customer of the US, British, French and Italian arms industries.[5] There are many ways to ward off attacks by acquisitive and hostile local powers. You can have lots of Western weaponry. You can have lots of Western troops. And you can also make sure everybody in the West has heard of you, is aware of your status as an independent state, by hosting major sporting events.

But the ironies stack up. Qatar is rich because of a product that causes climate change. An awareness of that has led it and neighbouring economies to seek to diversify, to establish themselves as global players before the gas and oil runs out or yields to more environmentally friendly energy. To build the necessary infrastructure, it imported thousands of workers, largely from poorer countries already beginning to be affected by the climate crisis. The construction itself spewed tonnes of carbon into the atmosphere. Qatar is heating as quickly as any place on earth. In 2018, the World Bank ranked Qatar the highest emitter of CO_2 per capita in the world, largely because it is so hot already that everything has to be air-conditioned.[6] That includes the football stadiums, which were cooled by vast pipes belting out chill air. Some reports suggest Qatar could be uninhabitable by 2070.[7] The sense of futility was impossible to avoid; the death cycle goes on. Qatar claimed it would be the most environmentally friendly World Cup in history, that it would be carbon neutral. Those claims would prove inaccurate.[8]

And a sense of mortality was there too in the figure of Messi. Here was football, this phenomenon we absorb week after week, month after month, year after year, in which we have invested so much emotional and intellectual energy, and he was the best anybody too young to have seen Maradona in his prime had seen at that phenomenon, and this was his final appearance on the biggest stage. His brilliance, his imagination, his technical excellence, was what we held up in the face of the void, in him somehow was bound a sense of the extremes of human excellence. Yes, death is inevitable. Yes, there may be no greater meaning or purpose. Yes, there may be a terrible randomness both to the formation of every ego and to its dissolution. But at least as a species we are capable of artistic creation like that.

Yet in Doha, as death pressed in on all sides, there seemed an appalling fragility to Messi's genius.

On 23 November 2010, ten days before the vote, Michel Platini had lunch at the Élysée Palace with the French president Nicolas Sarkozy; the crown prince of Qatar, Sheikh Tamim bin Hamad Al Thani; the Qatari prime minister Sheikh Hamad bin

Jassim Al Thani;* and Sébastien Bazim of Colony Capital, the US fund that owned 98 per cent of struggling PSG.[9] After the lunch, Sarkozy apparently advised Platini to vote for Qatar.[10] Platini had previously said that a World Cup in Qatar would be disastrous[11] but changed his mind, Blatter later alleged, having been placed under great pressure.[12] It's a claim Platini rejects.[13]

Seven months after he had cast his vote, Qatar Sports Investment bought a majority stake in PSG. Five months after that, beIN SPORTS was launched by Al Jazeera, challenging Canal+, which was disliked by Sarkozy.[14] By 2018, Qatar had ordered thirty-six Rafale fighter jets from France at a cost of around $10bn.[15] Although everybody who was there denies there was any relationship between the lunch and Platini's vote,[16] the relationship between France and Qatar was mutually beneficial and extremely lucrative.

In the immediate aftermath of the vote, the tendency was to focus on individuals and the bribes they may have received but, although an indictment from the US justice department did refer to 'bribe payments in exchange' for votes,[17] and the whistle-blower Phaedra Al-Majid described how development money would be offered in exchange for votes,[18] football had moved on from the days of Havelange and ISL. This was a country with extraordinary resources able to use gas deals and air routes to secure support, to pay the likes of Zinedine Zidane, Pep Guardiola and David Beckham to be ambassadors or, for instance, to sponsor a CAF conference.[19]

Then there was the £1bn Aspire academy, which was launched in 2005. Trials were held across the country, but also, in a reality show broadcast on Al Jazeera, across Africa to try to unearth young talent that could be naturalised to give Qatar a more competitive side[20] – the Football Dreams project.

* He would later be linked with a bid to buy Manchester United when the Glazer family ended up selling a stake in the club to the British businessman Jim Ratcliffe.

As Aspire were not a professional club, Fifa's regulations on moving juveniles across national borders did not apply.[21] When Fifa changed its regulations so that a player could only switch nationality once he had lived in a country for five years after the age of eighteen, Qatar insisted naturalisation had never been the point of the academy.[22] As it turned out, only one player in their 2022 squad was not born in Qatar, the Sudan-born Almoez Ali.

But Aspire wasn't only about talent production. Of the fifteen Aspire projects launched around the world, five – in Cameroon, Guatemala, Nigeria, Paraguay and Thailand – were in the countries of members of the Fifa Executive Committee; it didn't take a cynic to wonder if this was just a country learning the lessons of Fifa's Goal Project.[23] And that's before you get to details in the Garcia Report such as the former Barcelona president Sandro Rosell, who ran Football Dreams in its early days, making a £2m payment to an account in the name of the ten-year-old daughter of the disgraced Brazilian ExCo member Ricardo Teixeira,[24] who had been best man at his wedding; nothing to do with the World Cup, those involved insisted.[25]

Qatar spent an estimated £200bn on staging the World Cup, and who knows what on winning the vote. Money can buy a lot in modern football, but it can't buy a functioning team, not even after a six-month training camp. Although they were the reigning Asian champions Qatar started badly, going 2–0 down to Ecuador inside 31 minutes in the opening game and never recovered. They were eliminated after three straight defeats, by far the worst record of any host.

Nor can money buy a football culture. By half-time in that opener, the stadium was silent but for the yellow splash of Ecuador fans behind one goal and the maroon swathe of Qatar fans, most of them shipped in from Lebanon,[26] behind the other. The second half was played out in front of thousands of empty seats. By the end, probably more than half the stadium was empty. It was not an auspicious start.

That game had been moved forward twenty-four hours, seemingly on a whim, just in time to ruin the '100 days to go' advertising blitz – apparently so it could stand alone rather being one of four matches on the first day of the tournament. On the Friday before the World Cup began, there was an abrupt announcement that there would be no beer sales in the stadiums. Which, of course, is absolutely a host's right; it's entirely understandable that in a Muslim country the presence of alcohol would make a lot of people very uncomfortable. It just seemed strange that an issue that had been obvious from the moment the bid had been won given Budweiser's status as an official sponsor was resolved not by negotiation or amendments to the contract but by fiat. That, perhaps, is simply how things are done in dealing with absolute monarchies.

The other great cultural issue of the early days of the tournament was the outlawing of the 'One Love' armbands seven European nations had planned to have their captains wear in support of LGBTQ+ rights. It always seemed a meek gesture but became rather more than that once Fifa threatened to book players, or more, for wearing them, doing the bidding of its Qatari masters. The federations backed down. Wales fans had rainbow bucket hats confiscated, Belgium were banned from bearing the message 'Love' on the collars of their away shirts and Grant Wahl was detained for around half an hour for wearing a T-shirt bearing the rainbow symbol.

There was a notable protest, though, as Iran's players refused to sing the national anthem before their first game, against England, apparently in support of those at home demonstrating about the death of the twenty-two-year-old Mahsa Amini after she was arrested by the morality police for not wearing her hijab in accordance with government standards. After warnings from government officials, the players did sing before the game against Wales, while Qatari authorities confronted Iran fans wearing shirts with Amini's name on the back, or carrying flags bearing the slogan, 'Women, Life. Freedom.'[27]

Messi's triumph seemed almost predestined, a narrative that was too powerful for even football in all its capriciousness to resist. Flip the perspective, look back from the vanishing point and a series of disparate contingencies necessarily look as though they're all pointing towards an inevitable outcome. But even within that context, Argentina's path from the disappointment of 2018 to the glory of 2022 was peculiarly winding. Nobody inspecting the wreckage after defeat to France in Kazan would have planned the route they ended up taking – although, given the chaos that pervades AFA, it's likely nobody would have planned any route, or at least not in any realistic expectation of it being followed.

Where to begin? Perhaps with Lionel Scaloni. If Jorge Sampaoli hadn't failed so badly, the AFA wouldn't have needed to pay him off. If he hadn't been so expensive, they might have been able to appoint a proven coach rather than turning to his assistant, Scaloni. The former Deportivo La Coruña and West Ham full-back – most famous in England for his aimless punt forward in the final minute of the 2006 FA Cup final that cost West Ham possession and led to Steven Gerrard's equaliser – had been assistant to Sampaoli at Sevilla and the national team, but had no frontline managerial experience. Nobody would have willingly appointed him to one of the biggest jobs in international football. But he turned out to be perfect for it, largely because he had so little ego and because there were so few expectations.

Scaloni was a welcome and necessary calm voice, repeating his mantra, after every win, after the defeat to Saudi Arabia,

'The sun will come up tomorrow.' Almost alone among Argentinians, he kept insisting football just isn't that important, not worth ruining your life over. Perspective is one thing, a necessary thing, but nobody should be in any doubt what this meant to him. The footage of Scaloni, this restrained and dignified man, standing calmly amid the mayhem of his technical area during the penalty shoot-out in the final and then, in the moment of victory, retreating to his bench to sit alone for a moment, his face slowly crumpling as the magnitude of his achievement sank in, was profoundly moving.

Or perhaps the best place to begin is at the Amex Stadium in June 2020, 36 minutes into Brighton's win over Arsenal, as Neal Maupay jumped into Bernd Leno, causing the Arsenal goalkeeper to land awkwardly, damaging his knee. Emi Martínez, the unheralded back-up keeper, neither restrained nor dignified, was called from the bench for his first Premier League game in over three years. He was twenty-seven and, at that point, he had started just sixty-one league games across a career that had taken him on loan to Oxford, Sheffield Wednesday, Rotherham, Wolves, Getafe and Reading. He played eight further games that season, doing enough to earn a move to Aston Villa. A little over two years later he was holding a golden Marigold to his crotch and thrusting gleefully after being named Goalkeeper of the Tournament in Doha.

Or perhaps the real beginning was at a press conference in May 2022, when Kylian Mbappé said that 'in South America, football is not as advanced as in Europe, that's why when you look at the last World Cups it's always Europeans who win.' If he had been making a point about the financial inequalities in the game, it might have been possible to sympathise with his view. But he was not, as his next sentence proved. 'The advantage we have here in Europe is that we always play matches at a high level,' he said[28] – and that was far more debatable, for all the impact of the Uefa Nations League in making (semi-)

competitive matches between Europe's elite more common. As a result, his words fired the *bronca* within Argentina, who are always at their best when they have the perception of an arrogant outsider to rail against.

Even the opening defeat to Saudi Arabia probably helped. Argentina came into the tournament unbeaten in thirty-six games, having ended their twenty-eight-year trophy drought by lifting the Copa América – beating Brazil in the final in the Maracanã – and followed that up by winning the Finalissima against the Euro 2020 winners, Italy. Yet that, paradoxically, brought expectation and generated a pressure not to change the team. The only doubt was that, Italy aside – and Italy hadn't even qualified, beaten in a play-off by North Macedonia – they hadn't faced a European team other than Estonia in three years.

Given how Europe had dominated the previous four World Cups, providing thirteen of the sixteen semi-finalists, that was a major concern. Western Europe had, effectively, industrialised youth production and, because its leagues were the richest in the world, they provided ready pathways for development for young talent that did not require relocation across the Atlantic as a teenager. The major leagues of western Europe, the Premier League in particular, had also become great exchanges of knowledge and ideas, modes where the best players and coaches, whatever their nationality, tested themselves against each other; inevitably those playing regularly in that environment had an advantage.

Not that anybody saw much hope for Argentina in that first game. Although Messi put Argentina ahead with a first-half penalty, goals in the first ten minutes of the second half from Saleh Al-Shehri and Salem Al-Dawsari transformed Argentina into the side they had been at the previous World Cup, toiling with neither imagination nor conviction and desperately looking to Messi for inspiration. It wasn't until the second half of their second game, against Mexico, that he provided it, drifting into space just outside the box and drilling in a ferocious low shot but, once he'd started, he never stopped. Argentina beat both Mexico and Poland 2–0 to top the group but just as significant was the fact that Scaloni, liberated to make changes by the defeat, brought in Enzo Fernández, Julián Alvarez and Alexis Mac Allister, aged twenty-one, twenty-two and twenty-three respectively. All three would have decisive roles to play.

In December 2010, fifteen days after Qatar won the vote to host the 2022 World Cup, a Tunisian street vendor called Mohamed Bouazizi, frustrated by the confiscation of his wares by a municipal official, set himself on fire, an act of defiant despair that sparked the Tunisian Revolution and then the Arab Spring. While the majority of Arab governments were hostile to the movement, Qatar was willing to accommodate political Islam, which emerged as the most coherent strand of a disparate protest movement, even giving it a voice on Al Jazeera.

Since Sheikh Hamad had taken power in 1995, Qatar had always been slightly more willing to countenance heterodox thought than its neighbours, which was one of the reasons Saudi Arabia and the UAE backed the counter-coup a year later.[29] The issue came to a head during the Arab Spring as Saudi Arabia and the UAE backed the Egyptian leader Hosni Mubarak against the Muslim Brotherhood, which was able to state its case on Al Jazeera.[30] The crown prince of the UAE, Mohamed bin Zayed, even jokingly asked the US to bomb Al Jazeera's offices.[31] Saudi Arabia and the UAE accused Qatar of supporting 'terrorism'[32] and, in June 2017, blockaded the country.

After three weeks, the Saudi- and UAE-led coalition issued thirteen demands, which included shutting down Al Jazeera, breaking ties with Iran and paying reparations for supporting the Muslim Brotherhood.[33] Qatar was essentially told to abandon an independent foreign policy. But there was another issue, acknowledged by Hassan Al Thawadi, the secretary general of the Qatar 2022 Supreme Committee, which was that other Arab countries were jealous of Qatar for having won the right to host the World Cup.[34] Leaked emails from Yousef Al Otaiba, UAE's ambassador to the US, suggested a deliberate policy of raising concerns about human rights to try to force Qatar to share the tournament.[35] At the same time, Infantino talked about expanding the tournament so that more countries in the region could host games.[36]

Doha ran out of goods and for a time there seemed a serious threat of invasion. Iran and Turkey flew in 4,000 cows to help.[37] Donald Trump had met both Mohammed bin Salman, the Crown Prince of Saudi Arabia, and the president of UAE, Mohamed bin Zayed two weeks before the blockade began, apparently offering support[38] as he tweeted disapprovingly of 'radical ideology' in Qatar,[39] but it appeared his position was at odds with that of the Pentagon and the State Department as the US – and the UK – agreed deals to supply Qatar with fighter jets.[40] Joe Biden's victory over Trump in the US presidential election in November 2020 led to a softening of Saudi Arabia's stance and the blockade was lifted in January 2021.

When Qatar submitted its bid to host the 2022 World Cup, it didn't have a single stadium that met Fifa's requirements and insisted it would stage the tournament in summer when temperatures average 41C. To meet Fifa regulations, it claimed it had seven host cities, which may have been true in some technical administrative sense but none were more than 35 miles from the centre of Doha. Before long, the usual stipulations melted away and the tournament was switched from the June–July dates everybody else thought they'd been bidding for to the cooler temperatures of November–December.

The amount of construction required was astonishing. Immediately red flags were raised about the conditions in which labourers would have to work, but the only reference to Qatar's labour laws in Fifa's evaluation report was the confirmation that existing legislation would be suspended for building work related to the World Cup.[41] From the moment Qatar was confirmed as host, the reports of abuse began. In 2012, for instance, 102 of the 174 Nepalese nationals who died in Qatar did so from 'cardiac issues' – a further 23 were listed as 'misc'.[42] Subsequent research published in the *Cardiology Journal* proved the link between working in extreme heat and cardiac death.[43] In 2022, the Nepalese government suggested almost 200 of its citizens had taken their own life in Qatar in the previous decade.[44] Exactly how many migrant workers died on the construction sites is unknown, but in February 2021, it was reported that at least 6,500 migrant workers from India, Bangladesh, Pakistan, Sri Lanka and Nepal had died in Qatar since it was awarded the World Cup.[45] Not all of those died specifically on World Cup projects, but the number gives some sense of the scale of the issue, particularly given how many workers came from Africa and the Philippines.

Foreign workers in Qatar were employed under the *kafala* system, under which they required a sponsor and were bound to their contracts for a specific time period, meaning they were unable to change jobs. Often that meant their passports would be confiscated, their contract effectively tying them to exploitative employers.[46] In 2013, Aidan McQuade of Anti-Slavery International spoke of 'clear proof of the use of systematic forced labour.'[47]

The 2017 blockade led to a concerted effort to improve Qatar's image abroad and a range of labour reforms were announced. Any actual impact, though, was extremely limited.[48] As Vani Saraswathi of Migrant Rights put it, 'Qatar can do the dance with Western critics, knowing well that it doesn't have to change anything on the ground.'[49]

Stories of abuse were legion: workers who finished at 2 a.m.

and had to be on a 5 a.m. bus back to the construction site, breakdowns, salaries unpaid, pay docked arbitrarily, dismissals without cause, cramped and unsanitary living conditions.[50] 'In the end,' said one security guard, 'this is just a big prison where you can work.'[51]

When Abdullah Ibhais, a Jordanian media manager for the Supreme Committee for Delivery and Legacy, responded to a strike by workers at the al-Shahaniya labour camp who had no drinking water and had not been paid for four months by sending a senior official a WhatsApp urging him to admit the workers were active on two stadiums, he was arrested and accused of bribery. He was jailed for three years, despite the UN Working Group on Arbitrary Detention concluding that there was no legal basis to hold him and that there were multiple violations of his right to a fair trial.[52] During the World Cup, his family reported that he had been beaten in jail for contributing to the ITV documentary *Qatar: State of Fear* and then subjected to four days of solitary confinement in, according to a letter released by his family, 'a cell of two by one metres with a hole in the ground as a bathroom and with temperatures near freezing. I was already suffering from several bruises after the prison guards' assault and I was shivering all the time, as the cold air directed to me never stopped.'[53]

As Argentina rose through the tournament, others fell away. Germany, the problems of 2018 still unresolved, went out in the group stage for the second successive tournament. England played well but ran into France in the quarter-final, Harry Kane's missed 82nd-minute penalty denying them extra-time. Croatia, endlessly dogged, eliminated a weary Belgium in the group, then put out Japan and Brazil on penalties.

Spain suffered their familiar issues of struggling to turn possession into chances and lost on penalties to Morocco, who became the first African side to reach the semi-final by beating Portugal 1-0 in the quarter-final. Fernando Santos, the Portugal coach, had taken the bold step of dropping Cristiano Ronaldo in the previous round and had been rewarded when the forward he picked in his place, Gonçalo Ramos, scored a hat-trick in a 6-1 win over Switzerland; a significant proportion of the crowd chanted for Ronaldo anyway, an indication, perhaps, of how celebrity and tourism have come to shape football.

In the last eight, though, Portugal toiled against Walid Regragui's disciplined Morocco, missed a handful of chances and lost to Youssef En-Nesyri's fine header. As Mbappé's defensive shortcomings were laid bare by the forward surges of Achraf Hakimi from right wing-back, Morocco might have won the semi-final with better finishing and better decision-making; as it was, the introduction of Marcus Thuram on the left, with Mbappé moving into the middle, rebalanced the game and France won 2-0 to reach their fourth final in seven World Cups.

Modern football, even for national teams, isn't supposed to be about individuals any more, but this was. Just as it wasn't quite fair to say that 1986 was about Maradona and ten others, so it would be unfair to overlook the parts played in Qatar by Fernández, Álvarez, Mac Allister, Di María, Rodrigo De Paul, Leandro Paredes and, perhaps most especially, Emí Martínez. But it was still really all about Messi.

He would walk through games, involving himself only intermittently, but when he did it would be decisive. Argentina were struggling to impose themselves on Australia in the last sixteen when Papu Gómez's mishit pass out to Messi lured Riley McGree into a challenge. But the awkward spin made no difference to Messi, who cut infield, exchanged passes with Mac Allister and fired into the bottom corner. Then he set up the opener for Nahuel Molina against the Netherlands in an ill-tempered quarter-final, sending a through-ball on an apparently impossible path through a thicket of defenders. He added a second with a penalty and, although Weghorst struck twice to equalise, scored the first penalty in the shoot-out as Argentina rallied to win. '*Qué mirá, bobo*?' ['What are you looking at, fool?'] Messi, breaking off from a TV interview, said to Weghorst afterwards, a phrase of such curious lack of menace it immediately captured the imagination, becoming Argentina's catchphrase for the tournament.[54]

It had been against Croatia four years earlier that Argentina had reached a nadir, a 3-0 humbling that might not have been a defeat of the same magnitude as the disgrace of Helsingborg, but was probably as low as Argentinian football had felt since. This time, Argentina controlled the game from the off and won 3-0. Messi scored a penalty and then, in setting up Álvarez's second goal, so confounded Joško Gvardiol with a pause and change of pace that the defender, one of the players of the tournament, toppled like a falling oak.

So what had changed between the two games? In Russia, Argentina played a 3-4-2-1 with Mascherano and Enzo Pérez holding behind Messi, Maxi Meza and Agüero, but Pérez went off for Paulo Dybala midway through the second half with the score at 1-0 as Argentina chased the game. In 2022, the shape was more of a 4-4-2 with Messi behind Álvarez playing on a platform of De Paul, Paredes, Fernández and Mac Allister. 'For me that was key,' said Matías Manna, Argentina's head of video analysis. 'Have an extra man in the midfield. Argentina respected its sources, its history, the short pass and the ball and did not get carried away by a direct, physical game. Argentina played a Latin American-style game.'[55]

Scaloni watched the second semi-final in his office with his children and his team of analysts. It wasn't clear whether Di María, who had been struggling with a muscular problem in his foot, was going to be fit to play in the final. Argentina had been training with the back three they had used against the Netherlands in the quarter-final but as they saw Jules Koundé, France's right-back, struggle against the direct running of Sofiane Boufal, Scaloni realised that if Di María played it had to be not on the right where he had started every group game, but on the left, against Koundé. That may sound obvious, but it meant a complete rejig and leaving out Leandro Paredes, who had been consistently excellent for Scaloni's Argentina. 'It was,' said Manna, 'the most important decision in the history of Argentinian football.'[56]

Di María ran the final before being replaced after 64 minutes. It was Di María who was brought down by Ousmane Dembélé for the penalty from which Messi put Argentina ahead, and then Di María who rounded off a crisp break to make it 2-0 just before half-time. When he went off, the game seemed safe. France, who had been afflicted by the flu virus that had hung around Doha throughout the tournament, looked desperately flat, Deschamps forced into a double change four minutes before the break so he could switch Mbappé into the middle, where his inability to track opponents would be less damaging. That did stabilise matters but still there was little sign of France getting back into the game before Nicolás Otamendi, always a great man for a pratfall, tripped Randal Kolo Muani in the box with 10 minutes remaining. Mbappé converted from the spot; it was France's first attempt at goal. 97 seconds later, he volleyed a brilliant equaliser after a move that had begun with Messi being dispossessed.

At that moment it seemed he might be denied again, that, of all the blows the World Cup had dealt Messi this might be the most grievous. Argentina might have collapsed but, as in the quarter-final, they rallied. Both sides had chances and Lloris made a remarkable save from Messi, but it went to extra-time. Twice Lautaro Martínez wasted one on ones but when Lloris denied him again after 108 minutes, Messi was on hand to force it over the line. Was that his moment of redemption, to score the goal that, at last, won the World Cup? It was not. With two minutes remaining, an Mbappé shot struck Molina's arm and he completed his hat-trick from the resulting penalty.

Even then France might have won it, but Martínez made a final save in the third minute of injury-time from Kolo Muani. Although it was, of course, Messi's tournament, it turned out to be Martínez who won it, his shoot-out histrionics generating enough doubt for him to save from Kingsley Coman before Tchouameni put his effort wide. Messi had completed his grand quest.

As the Turkish restaurateur Salt Bae was inexplicably permitted to join the players on the pitch for the trophy presentation, a *bisht*, a traditional local cloak, was draped over Lionel Messi by the Emir, Sheikh Tamim bin Hamad al-Thani, before Infantino handed over the trophy. Perhaps it was meant as a token of respect, but no other nation had ever done this, no other host had ever draped the winning captain in local garb, covered his national team colours, for the presentation.

And so the final image from Lusail was of football tradition occluded by Qatari custom, the World Cup shrouded in uneasy geopolitical compromise.

EPILOGUE

For Jules Rimet, the World Cup was about using football to foster understanding among nations. Even he didn't think it was purely about sport; his idealism, in fact, saw from the beginning that the football was a means to an end, even if that end was rather more wholesome than the goals of the present incarnation of Fifa.

The brave new world supposedly ushered in by the arrests at the Baur au Lac hotel in 2015 has all worked out rather neatly. As Michel Platini became mired in allegations of corruption, all of which were denied and none of which came to anything, Gianni Infantino became president of Fifa.[1] The USA will co-host the 2026 World Cup with Mexico and Canada. Loretta Lynch, the US attorney general who effectively toppled Blatter, praised their new 'transparency and accountability' in a lucrative speaking gig with Fifa.[2] Others are less convinced by Infantino's amendments to the ethical superstructure[3] and the way he has managed to bypass the Fifa Council.[4]

The 2026 World Cup will be the first to feature forty-eight teams, an expansion that appeals to Infantino's base but so ill-conceived that the format initially proposed in 2017 was scrapped, apparently by presidential fiat, in 2022.[5] In 2030, the centenary of the first tournament will be marked by three games in South America before the tournament moves to

Spain, Portugal and Morocco, a compromise that is not merely environmentally questionable but was apparently designed to smooth the path for Saudi Arabia to host in 2034, a decision that instantly raised concerns about human rights abuses and the treatment of migrant labourers.[6] The cynicism and lack of accountability are enough to make the days of necklaces, handbags and larger-than-life shysters who enjoy dressing as Obi Wan Kenobi seem quaintly appealing.

And yet the World Cup retains an extraordinary appeal. Fifa claims 1.5bn people watched the 2022 final;[7] even if the precise figure can be questioned, it is the most-watched event in the world. It's easy to hark back to an illusory past – almost everybody's first World Cup is their personal favourite, a time when horizons open up and there is a realisation of the vastness and diversity of the world, and how everybody in it obsesses over this one game, a curious sense both of profound difference and profound community – but whatever else is happening, however corrupted and exploited the institution of the World Cup may become, that magic goes on.

It survived Mussolini and the Argentinian junta, it survived British indifference and João Havelange, it survived the scandals of Russia and Qatar and it will survive also Mohammed bin Salman and Gianni Infantino. Countries have always used the World Cup to promote themselves, to fight proxy wars, to project an image of unity and strength, to negotiate their position in the world, but some small spark of Rimet's vision still remains.

ACKNOWLEDGEMENTS

No book is ever the work of one person, and I owe debts of gratitude to vast numbers of people who have helped, directly and indirectly, on the road from watching my first World Cup in 1982 to this. Without my parents, I doubt I would ever have had such a love of football and books, and I owe them a huge amount, far more than I realised or articulated while they were alive. Although I still don't really understand why we had to go for a walk round Fort William rather than watch England v Czechoslovakia.

At the Fifa Library in Zurich, Michael Schmalholz could not have been more helpful or accommodating. I owe a debt of thanks also to the staff of the British Library at St Pancras, particularly for their work as they restored the service after the cyber-attack.

At Brigham Young University in Utah my thanks to Rex Nielson for his advice on Brazilian art and culture (and for taking me to an excellent Mexican restaurant), to Mac Wilson for his thoughts on Argentina and, especially, to Jeffrey Shumway for being such an excellent host and reliable source of information and suggestions.

The Authors Cricket Club WhatsApp group proved, as ever, a robust source of gossip, mirth, distraction and occasionally useful advice. My thanks in particular to Peter Frankopan,

David Owen, Adam Rutherford and Michael Taylor for their practical help.

For suggesting avenues of enquiry, recommending books and articles, sharing contacts, clarifying details and generally offering feedback, my thanks to Araceli Alemán, Philippe Auclair, John Brewin, Hendrik Buchheister, Martin da Cruz, Hajni Déak, Miguel Delaney, Jonathan Freedland, Alison Gamble, Paul Gamble, Cassiano Gobbet, Karel Häring, Henrik Hedegűs, Uli Hesse, Jesper Högström, Dan Jackson, Elis James, Egor Kretsan, Sam Kunti, Cecilia Lagos, Richard Lapper, Martín Mazur, Maher Mezahi, Paul Myers, Willy Niba, Oluwashina Okeleji, Johan Orrenius, Gunnar Persson, Kat Petersen, Jack Pitt-Brooke, Jakob Rosenberg, Emi Rosu, Gábor Sisak, Daniel Storey, Péter Szegedi, Colin Udoh, Tim Vickery, Matt Watson-Broughton and Shinobu Yamanaka. The malevolent balloon salesman Barry Glendenning did nothing at all but likes to be mentioned, while Max Rushden offered unstinting backing for a good eight seconds.

At Little, Brown, my thanks to Richard Beswick, Zoe Carroll, Steve Gove, Tom Feltham and Caroline Eley.

Thanks as ever to my agent David Luxton, without whom very little would actually happen.

But most of all thanks to Nicola, a source of constant love, support and inspiration. Sorry about the messy desk.

ENDNOTES

The Dreamers

1. Simon Burnton, 'World Cup stunning moments: the Conte Verde's trip to Uruguay in 1930', *Guardian*, 10 May 2018
2. Folke Havekost and Volker Stahl, *Fußballweltmeisterschaft 1930 Uruguay*, p42
3. Jon Spurling, *Death or Glory*, p5
4. Philippe Aziz, *Tu Trahiras Sans Vergogne*
5. Marie-Cécile de Taillac, *Marga, Comtesse de Palmyre*
6. Philippe Auclair, 'The Collaborator', *Blizzard*, 1 (2011)
7. Havekost and Stahl, *Fußballweltmeisterschaft 1930 Uruguay*, p43
8. Fifa, *One Hundred Years of Football*, p59
9. David Goldblatt, *The Ball is Round*, p228
10. David Winner, *Those Feet*, pp6–40; Goldblatt, *The Ball is Round*, pp160–1
11. Michael Duggan, 'The Catholic visionary who founded the World Cup', *Catholic Herald*, 14 June 2018
12. Pope Leo XIII, *De rerum novarum*, §3: https://www.vatican.va/content/leo-xiii/en/encyclicals/documents/hf_l-xiii_enc_15051891_rerum-novarum.html
13. Renaud Leblond and Yves Rimet, *Jules Rimet, le père du Mondial*
14. John Lichfield, 'Jules Rimet: the man who kicked off the World Cup', *Independent*, 5 June 2006
15. Goldblatt, *The Ball is Round*, p244
16. Soledad Mocchi-Radichi and Rodrigo Viqueira, 'Between Offside and Orsaí', p117

17. Andreas Campomar, *Golazo,* p104
18. Martin da Cruz, *From Beauty to Duty,* p10
19. Da Cruz, *From Beauty to Duty,* pp18–19
20. For more on how Muscular Christianity shaped the development of football in the English public schools, see Jonathan Wilson, *Inverting the Pyramid*, pp13–19
21. Aldo Mazzucchelli, *Del Ferrocarril al Tango*, p49
22. Da Cruz, *From Beauty to Duty,* p59
23. Da Cruz, *From Beauty to Duty,* p38
24. Da Cruz, *From Beauty to Duty,* p49
25. Da Cruz, *From Beauty to Duty,* p202
26. George Reid Andrews, *Blackness in the White Nation*, pp85–111
27. Mazzucchelli, *Del Ferrocarril al Tango*, p273
28. Campomar, p98
29. *Le Figaro*, 2 June 1924
30. Henri de Montherlant, *Revue de l'Amerique Latine*, 2 July 1924
31. Mazzucchelli, *Del Ferrocarril al Tango*, p17
32. Mazzucchelli, *Del Ferrocarril al Tango*, p31
33. Mazzucchelli, *Del Ferrocarril al Tango*, p367
34. *Le Miroir des Sports*, 12 June 1924
35. Mazzucchelli, *Del Ferrocarril al Tango*, p348
36. Brian Oliver, 'The First Superstar', *Blizzard*, 29 (2018)
37. Hans Ulrich Gumbrecht, *In Praise of Athletic Beauty*, p249
38. George Reid Andrews, 'Rhythm Nation', *ReVista – Harvard Review of Latin America* (Winter 2003)
39. *Le Matin*, 2 June 1924
40. *L'Auto*, June 1924
41. Mocchi-Radichi and Viqueira, 'Between Offside and Orsaí', pp122–3. An exhibition at the Orangerie in Paris in 2023 showed the influence of the collector Paul Guillaume, who had been trained by Apollinaire, in establishing the fashion. He not only exhibited Picasso and Matisse, but promoted Modigliani, Soutine, Laurencin and Dérain.
42. Sieglinde Lemke, *Primitivist Modernism*
43. Brian Oliver, 'Before Pelé there was Andrade', *Observer*, 24 May 2014
44. *Le Miroir des Sports*, 12 June 1924
45. Luis Prats, *Crónica celeste*, p55
46. Mazzucchelli, *Del Ferrocarril al Tango*, pp362–3

47. *Mundo Uruguayo*, 19 June 1924
48. Alejandro Mejías-López, *The Inverted Conquest*, p9 (although he, of course, is referencing Harold Bloom, *The Anxiety of Influence*)
49. Jonathan Wilson, *The Names Heard Long Ago*, pp55–159
50. Tony Mason, *Passion of the People?*, p36
51. Gianni Brera, *Storia critica del calcio italiano*, p98
52. Mazzucchelli, *Del Ferrocarril al Tango*, pp518–20, 653ff
53. Julio Bayce, '1928 Amsterdam', *100 años de fútbol*, 11, 12 February 1970
54. https://www.youtube.com/watch?v=3gELBavbzWQ
55. R. Keifu (ed.), *1. Fußballweltmeisterschaft 1930 in Uruguay*, p118
56. *Fifa Bulletin*, 16 April 1929, p4
57. IOC, Official Report of the 1928 Olympic Games, pp81–3
58. Mazzucchelli, *Del Ferrocarril al Tango*, pp534ff
59. *Negociaciones Internacionales: la organización de la Coupe du Monde*, March 1932, pp125–9
60. Dario Ronzulli, *Vittorio Pozzo*, p72
61. *El Día*, 14 July 1930
62. Jawad, *Four Weeks in Montevideo*, p94
63. Ioan Chirilă, *Finala se joacă azi*, p43
64. Chirilă, *Finala se joacă azi*, p44
65. John Langenus, *Fluitend door de wereld*. However, the official report submitted by the USA manager Wilfred Cummings says the bottle was knocked out of his hand by an Argentinian player. (Colin José, 'The true story of Jock Coll and the 1930 World Cup chloroform incident', Soccer History USA, https://soccerhistoryusa.org/asha/colin.html)
66. Varallo, fifa.com, 5 February 2010
67. *El Gráfico*, 2 August 1930
68. Varallo, fifa.com, 5 February 2010
69. Varallo, fifa.com, 5 February 2010
70. *La Prensa*, 31 July 1930
71. Alfredo Rossi, *El Gráfico*, 2 August 1930
72. Mazzucchelli, *Del Ferrocarril al Tango*, p637
73. *El Gráfico*, 2 August 1930

The Triumph of Fascism

1. 'Two men in a boat', *TIME*, 28 August 1933
2. Patrizia Gogliani, *Il fascismo degli italiani*, p200

3. Nino Macellari, *Sport e Potenza*, p34
4. D'Ascanio, *La Vittoria del 1934*, pp20–23
5. *Il Littorale*, 25 May 1928
6. Wilson, *Inverting the Pyramid*, pp53–73
7. Dario Ronzulli, *Vittorio Pozzo*, p49
8. For a thorough summary of the various theories around Carcano, see John Irving, 'Peculiar Personal Inclinations', *Blizzard*, 38 (September 2020)
9. Wilson, *The Names Heard Long Ago*, pp124–39
10. Jo Araf, *Generazione Wunderteam*, p51
11. Ronzulli, *Vittorio Pozzo*, p81
12. Ronzulli, *Vittorio Pozzo*, p105
13. *Sport-Tagblatt*, 10 April 1933
14. Araf, *Generazione Wunderteam*, p62
15. Alessandro D'Ascanio, *La Vittoria del 1934*, p23
16. Peter Beck, *Scoring for Britain*, p151
17. Jesper Högström, '*Svensk-VM domare på den anklagades bänk*', *Offside*, 4, 2013, pp132–3
18. *All Sport*, 3, 1949
19. Ronzulli, *Vittorio Pozzo*, p131
20. Araf, *Generazione Wunderteam*, p218
21. Uli Hesse, *Tor!*, p91
22. Hesse, *Tor!*, p101
23. Karl-Heinz Huba, *Fussball Weltgeschichte*, p151
24. Brian Glanville, *The Story of the World Cup*, p25
25. Matthew Taylor, *The Association Game*, p163
26. Frederick Wall, *Fifty Years of Football*, p236
27. Jonathan Wilson, *The Anatomy of England*, pp13–38
28. Mark Donnelly, 'The remarkable tale of when Sunderland AFC beat the Spanish national team – and changed the trajectory of football', *Sunderland Echo*, 19 July 2020; David Hewitt, 'When Sunderland AFC gave Spain a lesson in football it sparked national introspection', *The Conversation*, 14 June 2018
29. *La Gazzetta dello Sport*, 13 June 1934
30. *Il Bargello*, 17 June 1934

The Last Waltz

1. Ronzulli, *Vittorio Pozzo*, p196
2. Giles MacDonogh, *1938: Hitler's Gamble*, p35

3. Ian Pickup, 'French football from its origins to Euro 84', in Dauncey and Hare (eds.), *France and the 1998 World Cup*, p27
4. Wilson, *The Names Heard Long Ago*, pp208–11
5. Hesse, *Tor!*, pp98–9
6. Hesse, *Tor!*, p115
7. Hesse, *Tor!*, p102
8. *Pariser Tageszeitung*, 25 January 1939
9. David Förster, '*Das Versöhnungsspiel*' in Förster, Rosenberg and Spitaler (eds.), *Fußball unterm Hakenkreuz in der 'Ostmark'*, p257
10. *Völkischer Beobachter*, 4 April 1938
11. *Neue Wiener Tagblatt*, 4 April 1938
12. *Völkischer Beobachter*, 11 April 1938
13. Hesse, *Tor!*, p105
14. Roman Horak and Wolfgang Moderthaner, 'A Culture of Urban Cosmopolitanism,' in Richard Holt, J. A. Mangan and Pierre Lanfranchi (eds.), *European Heroes* p153; David Förster, 'Cafe Sindelar Revisited: *Verlauf und Folgen der Sildelar-Debatte*', in Förster, Rosenberg and Spitaler (eds.), *Fußball unterm Hakenkreuz in der 'Ostmark'*, p315
15. Hesse, *Tor!*, p104
16. Araf, *Generazione Wunderteam*, p253
17. Hesse, *Tor!*, p109
18. For far more on this, see the first part of my book *The Names Heard Long Ago*.
19. Emilio de Martino, *Campioni del Mondo*, p5
20. Ronzulli, *Vittorio Pozzo*, p206
21. Ronzulli, *Vittorio Pozzo*, p228
22. *Nemzeti Sport*, 20 June 1938
23. Interview with Zsolt Zsengellér
24. Géza Toldi, *Fodboldnavn paa flygtningepas*
25. Péter Szegedi and Tamá Dénes, *Az 1938-as magyar vb-ezüst*
26. Interview with Péter Szegedi

Hubris and the Salami Salesman

1. Sam Kunti, *Brazil 1970*, p106
2. Alex Bellos, *Futebol*, p46
3. *Diário Carioca*, 15 July 1950
4. The story appears in slightly different forms in Alejandro Giménez Rodríguez, *La pasión laica*, p136; and in Andreas Cantor, *Goooal*, p68

5. Glanville, *The Story of the World Cup*, p55
6. See, for instance, Franklin Morales, *Maracanã*, p406; Bellos, *Futebol*, p51; Paulo Perdigão, *Anatomia de una derrota*, p176
7. Jorge Iwanczuk, *Historia del Fútbol Amateur en la Argentina*, p206
8. Perdigão, *Anatomia de una derrota*, p27
9. Roberto Muylaert, *Barbosa*, pp20–2
10. In '*O drama das sete copas*' (June 1966) in *A Pátria em Chuteiras: Nocas Crônicas de Futebol*, pp112–19
11. Josh Lacey, *God is Brazilian*
12. Mário de Andrade, *Macunaíma*, p42
13. The full story of Kürschner's remarkable life is told in my book *The Names Heard Long Ago*, while the tactical significance of his move to Brazil is explained in more detail in *Inverting the Pyramid*.
14. Gilberto Freyre, *Correio da Manhã*, 15 June 1938
15. Amurabi Oliveira, 'Thirty Years Later: The Actuality of Gilberto Freyre to Think Brazil'
16. *Revista del CESLA*, no. 20, 2017, pp341–352; David Lehmann, 'Gilberto Freye: the Reassessment Continues,' *Latin American Research Review*, Vol 3, 1, 2008, pp208–18
17. Goldblatt, *Futebol Nation*, p85
18. R. Levine, 'Sport and society: the case of Brazilian *futebol*', *Luso-Brazilian Review* 17, 2 (1980)
19. Goldblatt, *Futebol Nation*, p89
20. Roberto Thoeni, *L'ultimo urlo per il grande Torino*
21. *La Mañana*, 9 July 1950
22. Wilson, *The Names Heard Long Ago*, pp106–11
23. Hámori, *Régi gólok, edzősorsok*, p55
24. *La Cancha*, 28 September 1933
25. Rory Smith, *Mister!*, p163
26. Campomar, *Golazo!*, p202
27. Atilio Garrido and Joselo González, *El gol del siglo* (El País & Tenfield, 2000), pp112
28. Atilio Garrido, *Maracaná: La historia secreta* (Atilio Garrido, 2014)
29. Pedro Escartín, *Lo de Brasil fue así*, p54
30. *El Bien Público*, 19 July 1950
31. *Nemzeti Sport*, 31 October 2014
32. Perdigão, *Anatomia de una derrota*, p12

33. Aldyr García Schlee, *Cuentos de Fútbol*, p78
34. Bellos, *Futebol*, pp73–5
35. Goldblatt, *Futebol Nation*, pp94–95
36. Alex Bellos, 'For Fifty Years One Moment has Haunted Brazil. Why?', *Guardian*, 15 July 2000
37. Alex Bellos, 'Obituary: Moacir Barbosa', *Guardian*, 13 April 2000
38. Roberto DaMatta, '*Ópio do povo x drama de justiça social*', *Novos Estudos* 1, 4 (November 1982), p57

'Call Me Crazy'

1. Friedrich Christian Delius, *Der Sonntag, an dem ich Weltmeister wurde*, p109
2. Günter Grass, *Mein Jahrhundert*, p138
3. Delius, *Der Sonntag, an dem ich Weltmeister wurde*, p124
4. *Süddeutsche Zeitung*, 6 July 1954
5. Wilson, *The Names Heard Long Ago*
6. Ferenc Török, *Mandula*, pp83–87
7. Wilson, *The Anatomy of England*, pp65–106
8. Or Hungarian Working People's Party as it was renamed in 1948.
9. 'The Transformation of the Hungarian Economy', prepared by the Institute for the History of the Hungary Revolution (2003)
10. Sándor Bognár, Iván Pető and Sándor Szakács, *A hazai gazdaság négy évtizedének története 1945–1985*
11. Interview with Grosics
12. Wilson, *The Names Heard Long Ago*, pp267–8
13. Hesse, *Tor!*, p149
14. Fritz Walter, *3-2: Die Spiele zur Weltmesiterschaft*, p47
15. *Der Spiegel*, 23 June 1954
16. Ferenc Puskás, *Captain of Hungary*, p159
17. Nándor Hidegkuti, *Óbudától Firenzéig*, p115
18. Hesse, *Tor!*, p156
19. Graham McColl, *'78*, p46
20. Guy Hodgson, 'Ellis a knockout during Battle of Berne', *Independent*, 9 June 1998
21. Wilson, *Inverting the Pyramid*, pp111–52
22. Guzstáv Sebes, *Örömök és csalódások*, p249
23. Ruy Castro, *Garrincha*, pp61–2
24. David Yallop, *How They Stole the Game*, p35

25. Goldblatt, *Futebol Nation*, p95
26. Jonathan Wilson, 'Hungary 4 Uruguay 2', *Blizzard*, 13 (June 2014)
27. Mervyn Griffiths, *The Man in the Middle*, p77
28. Franz-Josef Brüggemeier, *Zurück auf dem Platz*, pp174–81
29. *Der Spiegel*, 7 July 1954
30. Lothar Mikos, '*Freunde furs Leben. Kulturelle Aspekte von Fußball, Fernsehen und Fernsehfußball*', in Schwier (ed.), *Mediensport*, p29
31. Brüggemeier, *Zurück auf dem Platz*, pp144–54
32. Cited in Hesse, *Tor!*, p129
33. Lothar Mikos and Harry Nutt, *Als der Ball noch rund war*, p27
34. Ferenc Puskás, *Puskás on Puskás*, p126
35. Hesse, *Tor!*, p167
36. '*Doping in Deutschland von 1950 bis heute aus historisch-soziologischer Sicht im Kontext ethischer Legitimation*', report by Humboldt University, Berlin, and the University of Münster, 2013. More detail is given in an interview with the leader of that study, Erik Eggers, here: https://correctiv.org/aktuelles/fussballdoping/2012/05/23/was-in-bern-passiert-ist-war-verboten/
37. Puskás, *Puskás on Puskás*, p126
38. Interview with Grosics
39. Interview with Grosics
40. Wilson, *The Names Heard Long Ago*, pp343–61
41. Wolfram Pyta, 'German Football: A Cultural History', in Tomlinson and Young (eds.), *German Football*, p8
42. Paul Cooke and Christopher Young, 'German football in literature and film', in Tomlinson and Young (eds.), *German Football*, p188
43. Arthur Heinrich, '*Eine saubere Geschichte*', *Die Zeit*, 16 March 2006
44. Brüggemeier, *Zurück auf dem Platz*, p177
45. *Westdeutsche Allgemeine Zeitung*, 5 July 1954
46. Thomas Raithel, *Fußballweltmeisterschaft 1954*, p153
47. Habbo Knoch, '*Gemeinschaft auf Zeit. Fußball und die Transformation des Nationalen in Deutschland und England*', in Peter Lösche, Undine Ruge and Klaus Scholz (eds.), *Fußballwelten*, pp117–53

48. Raithel, *Fußballweltmeisterschaft 1954*, p162
49. Arthur Heinrich, *Tor, Tor, Tor: Vierzig Jahre 3:2*; Joachim Fest, '*Fußball ist niemals nur ein Spiel*', *Frankfurter Allgemeine Zeitung*, 4 July 2004
50. Florian Breitmeier, '*Ein wunder, wie es im Drehbuch steht: Die WM 1954 – ein deutscher Erinnerungsfilm*', in Pyta (ed.), *Die lange Weg zur Bundesliga*; Erik Eggers, '*Der Mythos*', in Dernhardt (ed.), *Das Wunder von Bern*, pp172–7.
51. Norbert Seitz, '*Was symbolisiert das "Wunder von Bern"?*' in *Aus Politik und Zeitgeschichte*, 21 June 2004, p3

Prodigy

1. Pelé, *Pelé, the Autobiography*, p47
2. Hunt, *World Cup Stories*, p85
3. John Camkin, *World Cup 1958*, pp42–3
4. Yallop, *How They Stole the Game*, p28
5. '*O plano*', *Jornal da Tarde*, 29 June 2008
6. Wilson, *Inverting the Pyramid*, pp143–6, 175
7. Yallop, *How They Stole the Game*, p36
8. Piero Trellini, *The Match*, p62
9. Pelé, *My Life and the Beautiful Game*, p41
10. Castro, *Garrincha*, p126
11. Ariel Scher and Héctor Palomino, *Fútbol: pasión de multitudes y de elites*, p85
12. Daniel Szabon, '*El fútbol argentino en los años cincuenta: tensiones entre tradición y modernidad en la prensa deportiva*', *Historia y problemas del siglo XX* 16, year 13 (Jan–Jul 2022), pp78–9
13. Wilson, *Angels with Dirty Faces*, pp32–54
14. *El Gráfico*, 1 May 1967
15. Neil Franklin, *Football at Home and Abroad*, p89
16. Interview with Maschio
17. Brian Glanville, *The Sunday Times History of the World Cup*, p73
18. Interview with Ramos Delgado
19. Dante Panzeri, *El Gráfico*, 4 July 1958
20. Interview with Maschio
21. Wilson, *Angels with Dirty Faces*, pp10–12
22. V.S. Naipaul, *The Return of Eva Perón*, pp106–9

23. Enrico Udenio, *La hipocresía Argentina*, p35; he consciously here echoes Segundo Moreno's 1937 work *La Argentina, futura gran potencia mundial*
24. Interview with Ramos Delgado
25. Patrick Mignon, 'New supporter cultures and identity in France', in Giulianotti and Williams (eds.), *Game without Frontiers*, p277
26. Jacques Ferran, '*Ne pas confondre: l'Equipe de France et le football français*', *France Football*, 8 July 1958
27. Pierre Lanfranchi and Alfred Wahl, 'The immigrant as hero: Kopa, Mekloufi and French football', in Holt, Mangan and Lanfranchi (eds.), *European Heroes* p116
28. Stéphane Beaud and Gérard Noiriel, '*L'immigration dans le football*', *Vingtième siècle*, Apr–Jun 1990, p95
29. Gabriel Hanot, '*La France exprimera la valeur veritable de son football si chaque selection a la volonté de faire plus qu'il ne peut faire*', *France Football*, 4 February 1958
30. Alfred Wahl, '*Raymond Kopa: une vedette du football, un mythe*', *Sport Histoire*, 2 (1988), p87
31. Gabriel Hanot, '*Le talent Argentina, la méthode anglaise, la fierté suédoise, la sûreté yugoslave*', *France Football*, 3 June 1958
32. Benoît Hopquin, '*Just Fontaine, le héros parmi le héros de 1958*', *Le Monde*, 19 June 1998
33. Wahl, 'Raymond Kopa', p91
34. Hopquin, '*Just Fontaine, le héros parmi le héros de 1958*'
35. Interview with Simonyan
36. Interview with Simonyan
37. For a fuller investigation, see Jonathan Wilson, *Behind the Curtain*, pp267–79, or for a fictionalised consideration of the issues, see my novel, *Streltsov*.
38. Aleksandr Nilin, *Streltsov*, p76
39. *Sovetsky Sport*, 'Это не герой матча', 12 April 1957
40. *Sovetsky Sport*, 15 April 1957
41. Axel Vartanyan, 'Летопись 1957 год. Часть первая', *Sport-Express*, 29 October 2010
42. Semyon Narignani, 'Звездная болезнь', *Komsomolskaya Pravda*, 2 February 1958
43. Interview with Simonyan
44. Interview with Simonyan

45. John Charles, *King John*, p147
46. Gabriel Lorince, 'How Imre Nagy Died', *New Statesman*, 4 February 1966
47. Trevor Ford, *I Lead the Attack*, pp13–23
48. Mario Risoli, *When Pelé Broke Our Hearts*, p40
49. Risoli, *When Pelé Broke Our Hearts*, pp120–1
50. Castro, *Garrincha*, pp197–8
51. Castro, *Garrincha*, pp132–4
52. Pelé, *Autobiography*, p96
53. Pelé, *My Life and the Beautiful Game*, p51
54. Pelé, *Autobiography*, p97
55. Nelson Rodrigues, '*Complexo de vira-lata*' in *À sombra das chuteiras imortais: crônicas de futebol*, p51
56. Kunti, *Brazil 1970*, p27
57. Nelson Rodrigues, *A Pátria em Chuteiras*, pp186–7
58. DaMatta, *Explorações: Ensaios de Sociologia Interperativa*, p130

A Pig, a Dog and a Mynah Bird

1. Cecilia Lagos, 'Chile v Italy', *The Squall*, 2 (2020)
2. Lagos, 'Chile v Italy'
3. BBC, *World Cup 1962*, 5 June 1962
4. Lagos, 'Chile v Italy'
5. José Lizana, *Ceacheí – Palabra de Campeón*, p78
6. Interview with Maschio
7. Lagos, 'Chile v Italy'
8. BBC, *World Cup 1962*
9. Brenda Elsey, *Citizens and Sportsmen*, pp194–205
10. Ricardo Ruiz de Viñaspre Puig (ed.), *Libro Nuestro Mundial*, p14
11. Elsey, *Citizens and Sportsmen*, pp194–205
12. Javier Zamorano, '*Porque no tenemos nada . . .': la icónica respuesta a Argentina que pasó a la historia*', BioBioChile, 31 May 2022
13. Lucie Hémeury, 'Narrow Miss: the failure of Argentina's bid for the 1962 World Cup (1954–56)', *Soccer and Society*, 21, 8, pp932–45
14. Ruiz de Viñaspre Puig (ed.), *Libro Nuestro Mundial*, p24
15. Puig (ed.), *Libro Nuestro Mundial*, p38
16. Lagos, 'Chile v Italy'
17. Kunti, p83
18. Pelé, *Autobiography*, p123

19. Castro, *Garrincha*, p29
20. Castro, *Garrincha*, pp206–7
21. Kaliba, 'Jozef Štibrányi's Diary', *Blizzard*, 25 (2017)
22. Jozef Štibrányi's diary, 11 May 1962
23. Jozef Štibrányi's diary, 22 May 1962
24. Jozef Štibrányi's diary, 31 May 1962
25. Jozef Štibrányi's diary, 31 May–1 June 1962
26. Jozef Štibrányi's diary, 2 June 1962
27. Jozef Štibrányi's diary, 6 June 1962
28. Hunt, *World Cup Stories*, p110
29. Igor Rabiner, 'The Jersey that wasn't Black', *Blizzard*, 9 (June 2013)
30. Ruy Castro, *Garrincha*, p195
31. Jozef Štibrányi's diary, 13 June 1962
32. Kaliba, 'Jozef Štibrányi's Diary'
33. Kaliba, 'Jozef Štibrányi's Diary'
34. Roger Macdonald, *World Soccer*, August 1962
35. 'Ball paradox', *Der Spiegel*, 5 June 1962
36. Wilson, *Angels with Dirty Faces*, pp197–225
37. Interview with Rattin
38. Bobby Charlton, *The Autobiography, My England Years*, p135

Three Faces of the Lion

1. Martin Atherton, *The Theft of the Jules Rimet Trophy*, pp51–2
2. *Times*, 21 March 1966
3. Atherton, *The Theft of the Jules Rimet Trophy*, p55
4. Charlie Richardson, *The Last Gangster*, pp41–9
5. *The Sound of Football*, episode 249
6. Alain Naef, *An Exchange Rate History of the United Kingdom 1945–92*, pp127–47
7. 'Britain's role in the world', *The Guardian*, 6 December 1962
8. Dominic Sandbrook, *White Heat*, p288
9. John Crosby, *Weekend Telegraph*, 16 April 1965
10. Peter Wilson, 'This method madness made me sad for soccer', *Daily Mirror*, 3 May 1965
11. 'Ramsey's Case Rests on Sound Evidence', *Times*, 6 July 1966
12. Ossie Stuart, 'The Lions Stir: Football in African Society', in Steven Wagg, *Giving the Game Away: Football, Politics and Culture on Five Continents*, pp 24–51

13. Ian Hawkey, *Feet of the Chameleon*, pp101–22
14. Paul Darby, '"Let Us Rally Round the Flag": Football, Nation-building and pan-Africanism in Kwame Nkrumah's Ghana', *Journal of African History*, 54, 2 (July 2013), pp221–46; Jonny Coffey, 'Real Republikans', *Blizzard*, 53 (2024)
15. Peter Alegi, *African Soccerscapes*, p54
16. Alegi, *African Soccerscapes*, p67
17. John Sugden and Alan Tomlinson, *Badfellas*, p136
18. Letter from Mourad Fahmy to Fifa, 15 August 1964
19. Paul Darby, 'Politics, resistance and patronage: the African boycott of the 1966 World Cup and its ramifications', *Soccer and Society*, 20, 7–8 (2019), pp941–2
20. Duncan Mackay, *They Came from a Land Down Under*, pp17–34
21. Duncan Hamilton, *Answered Prayers*, pp 241–2
22. Jürgen Leinemann, *Sepp Herberger*, p206
23. J. Simon Rofe and Alan Tomlinson, 'The Untold Story of Diplomacy and the 1966 World Cup: North Korea, Africa and Sir Stanley Rous', in *International History Review*, 42, 3, p517
24. Martin Polley, 'The Diplomatic Background to the 1966 World Cup', *The Sports Historian*, 18, 2 (1998), pp1–8
25. Quoted in Louise Taylor, 'How little stars from North Korea were taken to Middlesbrough's heart', *Guardian*, 8 June 2010
26. Quoted in Scott Wilson, 'Fifty years on, the memories of North Korea's Middlesbrough miracle refuse to fade', *Northern Echo*, 16 July 2016
27. David Miller, 'The Managers' Game of Chess', 10 July 1966
28. Kunti, *Brazil 1970*, p14
29. Pelé, *Autobiography*, p138
30. Pelé, *My Life and the Beautiful Game*, pp143–4
31. Brian James, 'Angry, baffled, goalless England', *Daily Mail*, 12 July 1966
32. Barnabas Calder, *Raw Concrete*, p 10
33. Elaine Harwood, *Space, Hope and Brutalism*, pp v–xix
34. J.L. Manning, 'What is fascinating the senior gnats?', *Daily Mail*, 15 July 1965
35. Peter Lorenzo, 'England Wonders Crush Spain', *Sun*, 9 December 1965
36. Peter Lorenzo, 'England Must Recall Luxury Goal Ace', *Sun*, 10 December 1965

37. 'Ramsey's Case Rests on Sound Evidence', *Times*, 6 July 1966
38. Bobby Charlton, *My England Years*, p236
39. Dave Bowler, *Winning isn't Everything*, p208
40. Bowler, *Winning isn't Everything*, p209
41. Interview with Rattin
42. Interview with Marzolini and Rattin
43. Neil Clack, *Animals!*, p86
44. Quoted in Clack, *Animals!*, p89
45. This is a point made both by Martin Peters, *The Ghost of 66*, p211, and by the writer David Downing who was in the crowd that day, *England v Argentina*, p102
46. Interview with Marzolini, March 2014
47. Interview with Rattin, March 2014
48. David Miller, 'The butchers of Buenos Aires make football a farce', *Sunday Telegraph*, 24 July 1966
49. Goldblatt, *Futebol Nation*, p121
50. Pelé, *My Life and the Beautiful Game*, pp9–10
51. Pelé, *My Life and the Beautiful Game*, pp144
52. Yallop, *How They Stole the Game*, pp79–80
53. Pelé, *My Life and the Beautiful Game*, p151
54. Pelé, *My Life and the Beautiful Game*, p146
55. Fifa moved to clarify misinformation as early as January 1966: 'In order to rectify statements that appeared in the football press we would like to recall herewith that according to Article 26, para 5, "the semi-finalists shall be assigned to the venues previously selected as soon as the semi-finalists are known."' *Fifa News* 32, Jan 1966, p5
56. Roy Peskett, 'World's Press agree: Super soccer', *Daily Mail*, 27 July 1966
57. Hamilton, *Answered Prayers*, pp xv–xix
58. Hesse, *Tor!*, p230

Beauty and the Beasts

1. Goldblatt, *The Ball is Round*, p392
2. *Jornal do Brasil*, 22 June 1970
3. Hugh McIlvanney, *McIlvanney on Football*, p194
4. 'The Rank Outsider: Mexico City's Bid for the 1968 Olympic Games', *International Journal of the History of Sport*, 26 (6), 2009, pp748–63

5. Mario Vargas Llosa, '*México es la dictadura* perfecta,' *El Pais*, 31 August 1990
6. Mark Kurlansky, *1968*, pp325–6
7. Kurlansky, *1968*, p333
8. John Rodda, 'Trapped at gunpoint in the middle of fighting', *Guardian*, 3 October 1968
9. Gilbert M. Joseph and Jürgen Buchenau, *Mexico's Once and Future Revolution*, p140
10. Joseph and Buchenau, *Mexico's Once and Future Revolution*, p165; Oscar Lopez, 'Search for lost brother reveals dark secret of Mexico's death flights', *Guardian*, 19 December 2024
11. Miguel Garcia, '*Perú vs. Bolivia en 1969: la historia de Chechelev, el árbitro que le ganó a la Blanquirroja en La Paz*', *El Comercio*, 17 November 2023
12. Adam Hochschild, 'Magic Journalism', *New York Review of Books*, 3 November 1994
13. Thomas P. Anderson, *The War of the Dispossessed*
14. Preston Lerner, 'The Last Piston-Engine Dogfights', *Air and Space Magazine*, September 2015
15. Quoted in Downie, *The Greatest Show on Earth*, p17
16. Alan Travis, 'Papers reveal outrage at World Cup "fix",' *Guardian*, 1 December 2000; '1966 & 1974 World Cups Were Fixed – Former Fifa President', goal.com, 26 June 2008
17. Kunti, *Brazil 1970*, p58
18. Sam Kunti, 'The Salesman', *Blizzard*, 47 (2022)
19. Kunti, *Brazil 1970*, p74
20. Kunti, *Brazil 1970*, pp127–8
21. Kunti, *Brazil 1970*, pp77–8
22. Dawson, *Back Home*, pp63–5
23. Kunti, *Brazil 1970*, p78
24. Kunti, 'The Salesman'
25. Kunti, 'The Salesman'
26. Kunti, *Brazil 1970*, p46
27. Kunti, *Brazil 1970*, p57
28. Kunti, *Brazil 1970*, p80
29. Daniel Mundim, '*De jogador preso a torturadora, quandy ditadura e futebol se misturaram*', *O Globo*, 31 March 2014
30. Kunti, *Brazil 1970*, p88
31. Kunti, *Brazil 1970*, p116

32. Luisa Prochnik, 'O *Futebol na Telinha: A Relação Entre o Esporte Mais Popular do Brasil e a Mídia*', paper delivered at the XVth Congresso de Ciências da Comunicação na Região Sudeste (2010), available at: http://www.intercom.org.br/papers/regionais/sudeste2010/resumos/R19-1397-1.pdf
33. Matt Dickinson, *Bobby Moore*, p167
34. Dawson, *Back Home*, p98
35. Matt Dickinson, *Bobby Moore*, p193
36. Matt Dickinson, *Bobby Moore*, p192
37. Matt Dickinson, *Bobby Moore*, p192
38. Jeff Powell, *Bobby Moore* (1976), p107
39. Jeff Powell, *Bobby Moore* (1993), p133
40. *Mooro*, BBC, 2002
41. Downie, *The Greatest Show on Earth*, p73
42. Downie, *The Greatest Show on Earth*, p91
43. Kunti, *Brazil 1970*, p11
44. Downie, *The Greatest Show on Earth*, p126
45. Yallop, *How They Stole the Game*, pp97, 104–5
46. *The Greatest Game in World Cup History?* (Fifa TV), https://www.youtube.com/watch?v=L9EZQgK6dZQ
47. Downie, *The Greatest Show on Earth*, p165
48. Downie, *The Greatest Show on Earth*, p187
49. Downie, *The Greatest Show on Earth*, p190
50. Kunti, *Brazil 1970*, p121
51. Kunti, *Brazil 1970*, p121
52. Pelé, *My Life and the Beautiful Game*, p155
53. Tim Vickery, 'Mario Zagallo and Tostão', *Blizzard*, 3 (2011)
54. For an explanation of the meaning of the line and the chaotic context of the film, see Peter Biskind, *Easy Riders, Raging Bulls* (Bloomsbury, 1998).

Cold War by Other Means

1. Ezequiel Fernández Moores, '*Chile 1973: El estadio nacional del dolor*', *La Nación*, 13 September 2023
2. Sugden and Tomlinson, *Badfellas*, p72
3. Football Federation of the Soviet Union telegram to Fifa, 27 October 1973
4. Gunther Latsch and Klaus Wierefe, 'Files Reveal Neo-Nazis Helped Palestinian Terrorists', *Der Spiegel*, 18 June 2012

5. Robert Lacey, *The Kingdom*, pp414–15
6. Benjamin Shwadran, *Middle East Oil Crises Since 1973*, p58
7. Gregor Schöllgen, '*Der Kanzler und sein Spion*', *Die Zeit*, 25 September 2003
8. Wilson, *The Anatomy of England*, pp168–81
9. Jeff Powell, *Daily Mail*, 1 May 1972
10. Hugh McIlvanney, ''Why Sir Alf should end this field warfare', *The Observer*, 7 May 1972
11. Dickinson, *Bobby Moore*, p222
12. Peter Batt, 'I honestly hope we go out', *The Sun*, 16 October 1973
13. For more on Dassler's role and influence, see Andrew Jennings, *Foul!* pp19–31; David Conn, *The Fall of the House of Fifa*, pp44–51
14. Luiz Guilherme Burlamaqui, *The Making of a Global Fifa*, pp28–30
15. Conn, *The Fall of the House of Fifa*, p36
16. Luiz Guilherme Burlamaqui, *A dança das cadeiras*
17. Yallop, *How They Stole the Game*, p118
18. Sugden and Tomlinson, *Badfellas*, p58
19. Yallop, *How They Stole the Game*, p196
20. Yallop, *How They Stole the Game*, pp125–6
21. Yallop, *How They Stole the Game*, pp125–8
22. '*Em carta ao sócio, cita a existência de caixa dois na sua empresa*', *Folhe de São Paulo*, 8 June 1998
23. Jennings, *Foul!*, p18
24. Kunti, p139
25. Kunti, p140
26. Kunti, pp141–2
27. Interview with Sacchi, February 2008
28. Albert Camus, *La Chute*
29. This is covered in far more detail in David Winner, *Brilliant Orange*
30. Charles Radcliffe, 'Daytripper! A Visit to Amsterdam', *Heatwave*, 1 (July 1966)
31. Winner, *Brilliant Orange*, p16
32. Hubert Smeets, '*Johan Cruijff gaf Nederland vorm*,' *Hard Gras*, April 1997
33. Auke Kok, *Johan Cruyff*, p161
34. J.B. Bakema, *Thoughts about Architecture*, p138

35. Wilson, *Inverting the Pyramid*, pp331–2
36. Brian Urquhart, 'Character Sketches: Mobutu and Tshombe', *UN News*, 13 February 2019
37. Jonathan Barker, 'Zaire 1974', *When Saturday Comes*, 252 (2008)
38. Jon Spurling, *Death or Glory*, p19
39. Spurling, *Death or Glory*, p26
40. Spurling, *Death or Glory*, p27
41. Spurling, *Death or Glory*, pp29–30
42. Kok, *Johan Cruyff*, p264
43. Johan Cruyff, *My Turn*, p29
44. Uli Hesse, 'Never the Twain', *Blizzard*, 13 (June 2014)
45. Hesse, 'Never the Twain'
46. Interview with Jovan Ačimović
47. Interview with Brane Oblak
48. Ryan Hubbard, *From Partition to Solidarity*, p211
49. Guido Frick, '*Cruyff, Sekt, nachte Mädchen und ein kühles Bad*', *Bild*, 4 July 1974
50. Kok, *Johan Cruyff*, p273
51. Cruyff, *My Turn*, pp61–2
52. Kok, *Johan Cruyff*, p277
53. Kok, *Johan Cruyff*, p278
54. Neil Aitcheson, 'World Cup final changed my life', BBC, 6 July 2006
55. Winner, *Brilliant Orange*, p96
56. Kok, *Johan Cruyff*, p282
57. Cruyff, *My Turn*, p56
58. Winner, *Brilliant Orange*, p98
59. Dominic Sandbrook, *State of Emergency*, pp518–19

Glory in a Time of Terror

1. Graciela Daleo, 'When a Win is not a Victory', papelitos.com.ar
2. *El Gráfico*, 15 January 1974
3. *World Soccer*, October 1972
4. Paul Dietschy, 'Making Football Global? FIFA, Europe and the Non-European football world, 1912–1974', *Journal of Global History* 8, 2 (2013), p297
5. Mark Orton, '*La Nuestra*: Football and Identity in Argentina 1913–78' (PhD thesis, De Montfort University, 2020)

6. Ariel Scher and Héctor Palomino, *Fútbol: pasión de multitudes y de elites*, p157
7. Pablo Alabarces, 'Football and *Patria*: Sport, National Narratives and Identities in Argentina 1920–98' (PhD thesis, Brighton University, 2001)
8. Mabel Veneziani, '*El Mundial*', *Todo es Historia*, 229 (1986)
9. *Guardian*, 16 February 1977
10. Veneziani, '*El Mundial*'
11. Matias Bauso, *78: Historia Oral del Mundial*, pp250–2
12. Veneziani, '*El Mundial*'
13. *Elenco degli iscritti alla Loggia P2*, seized on 17 March 1981 from Licio Gelli and distributed by the Presidency of the Council on 21 May 1981; Susana Viau and Eduardo Tagliaferro, '*En el mismo barco*', *Pagina* 12, 14 December 1998; Tina Anselmi, *Commissione Parlamentare d'Inchiesta sulla Loggia Masonica P2* (Rome, 1984)
14. Adam Bushby, 'Truth to Power', *Blizzard*, 39 (2020)
15. Jorge Lanata, *Argentinos*, pp589–94
16. *Billiken*, August 1978
17. *Clarín*, 23 June 1978. These last three examples of regime propaganda are collated in Orton, '*La Nuestra*: Football and Identity in Argentina 1913-78'.
18. Marguerite Feitlowitz, *A Lexicon of Terror*, p36
19. *Guardian*, 7 July 1978
20. Maurice Biriotti Del Burgo, 'Don't Stop the Carnival: Football in the Societies of Latin America' in Wagg (ed.), *Giving the Game Away*, pp61–3
21. Interview with Mario Zanabria
22. César Luis Menotti, *El Fútbol sin Trampas*, pp28-9
23. Menotti, *El Fútbol sin Trampas*, p31
24. Menotti, *El Fútbol sin Trampas*, p102
25. César Luis Menotti, *El Gráfico*, 1 August 1975
26. *Noticias*, XIX, 19 October 1996
27. Menotti, *El Fútbol sin Trampas*, p117
28. César Luis Menotti, '*Como Ganamos la Copa del Mundo*', *El Gráfico* (1978)
29. César Luis Menotti, *El Gráfico*, 19 April 1977
30. *Suplemento Clarin Mundial,* May 27, 1978, pp6–7
31. Interview, November 2014
32. McColl, *'78*, p27
33. McColl, *'78*, pp57–8

34. *Daily Express*, 12 May 1978
35. Sandbrook, *Seasons in the Sun*, pp518–24
36. *Daily Mail*, 16 January 1978
37. *El Gráfico*, 6 June 1978
38. Dominic Sandbrook, 'My Name is Ally MacLeod and I am a Winner', *Blizzard*, 5 (2012)
39. Norman Fox, *Times*, 13 June 1978
40. McColl, *'78*, pp127-8
41. Sandbrook, 'My Name is Ally MacLeod and I am a Winner'
42. Rob Smyth, 'The Forgotten Story of ... Abraham Klein, the "master of the whistle"', *Guardian*, 22 March 2012
43. Channel 4 News, 4 April 2012
44. Matt Roper, 'We fixed it! Peru senator claims 1978 World Cup game was fixed', *Daily Mail*, 9 February 2012
45. 'Argentina bribed Peru in World Cup scandal,' *Sunday Times*, 22 June 1986
46. Channel 4 News, 4 April 2012
47. Interview, with Larrosa
48. Ian Hawkey, *Feet of the Chameleon*, pp128–9
49. Kok, *Johan Cruyff*, pp311–14
50. Cruyff, *My Turn*, pp63–4
51. '*Gracias al fútbol*,' *El Gráfico*, 6 June 1978
52. Smyth, 'The Forgotten Story of ... Abraham Klein, the "master of the whistle"'
53. Interview, with Larrosa
54. Interview with Fillol
55. Interview with Larrosa
56. Menotti, *Como Ganamos la Copa del Mundo*', *El Gráfico*, 1978
57. Yallop, *How They Stole the Game*, p190
58. Glanville, *The Sunday Times History of the World Cup*, p178
59. *Clarín*, 26 June 1978
60. Menotti, *El Fútbol sin Trampas*, p27
61. 'World Cup 78: Cursed generation,' *Ha'aretz*, 2003
62. Claudio Tamburrini, *Perfil*, 12 June 1998
63. Interview with Fillol

Ectoplasmic Redemption

1. Paolo Rossi, *Ho fatto piangere il Brasile*, pp69–104
2. Trellini, *The Match*, p148

3. Trellini, *The Match*, pp134–41
4. Trellini, *The Match*, p155
5. Juan Antonio Simón, *España 82*, pp40–8
6. Raimundo Saporta, ABC, 8 March 1981
7. Peter Corrigan, 'Why England are the blue-eyed boys of the Basques', *Observer*, 13 June 1982
8. *La Nacion*, 3 June 1982
9. Alberto Ciria, 'From soccer to war in Argentina: preliminary notes on sports-as-politics under a military regime 1976–1982' in Archibald R.M. Ritter, *Latin America and the Caribbean: geopolitics, development and culture. Proceedings of the 1983 Conference of the Canadian Association for Latin American and Caribbean Studies* (Ottawa, 1984), pp80–95
10. Hunt, *World Cup Stories*, p196
11. Burns, *The Hand of God*, p94
12. Wilson, *Angels with Dirty Faces*, p327
13. Juan Antonio Simón, *España 82*, pp119–29
14. Michele Battini, *The Missing Italian Nuremberg*
15. John Foot, *The Archipelago*, p34
16. Emanuele Scarpelli, *Material Nation*, p229
17. Foot, *The Archipelago*, p193
18. Paul Ginsberg, *A History of Contemporary Italy*, p334
19. Jack Greene and Alessandro Massignani, *Il Principe Nero*
20. Umberto Eco, 'The World Cup and its Pomps', in *Faith and Fakes*, p172
21. Trellini, *The Match*, p106
22. Trellini, *The Match*, p102
23. '*Zoff ci condonna*', *Gazzetta dello Sport*, 25 June 1978
24. Trellini, *The Match*, p24
25. Martin Mazur, 'Two Men Down', *Blizzard*, 13 (2014)
26. Hawkey, *Feet of the Chameleon*, p130
27. Uli Hesse, 'The Great Disgrace', *Blizzard*, 29 (June 2018)
28. Harald Schumacher, *Blowing the Whistle*, pp41–2
29. '*Vor 25 Jahren: Die Schmach von Gijon*', *Bild*, 21 June 2007
30. Hesse, 'The Great Disgrace'
31. Hesse, *Tor!*, p311
32. '*Schäm dich*!', *Bild*, 26 June 1982
33. Marc Zeilhofer, '*Die Schmach von Gijon*', *Stern*, 23 June 2014
34. Hesse, *Tor!*, p311

35. Zeilhofer, '*Die Schmach von Gijon*', *Stern*, 23 June 2014
36. Hesse, *Tor!*, p311
37. Hesse, 'The Great Disgrace'
38. Hesse, *Tor!*, p311
39. Hugh Dauncey and Geoff Hare, 'The Impact of France 98' in Dauncey and Hare (eds.), *France and the 1998 World Cup*, pp209–10
40. https://www.leparisien.fr/sports/football/jean-francois-larios-je-suis-un-clochard-de-luxe-16-11-2017-7395492.php
41. Schumacher, *Blowing the Whistle*, p36
42. Hesse, *Tor!*, p314
43. '*L'indemodable*', *L'Équipe*, 27 June 2003
44. James Horncastle, 'Saint-Étienne 0 Dynamo Kyiv 3', *Blizzard*, 2 (2011)
45. Raymond Aron, *Le siècle du intellectuals*, programme 4, *De Sartre á Foucault 1958–90* (Desfons and Winock, France 3, 1999)
46. Alain Duhamel, *Le Complexe d'Astérix*
47. Trellini, *The Match*, p24
48. Claims the game was fixed are explored in Oliviero Beha and Roberto Chiodi, *Mundialgate*
49. Goldblatt, *Futebol Nation*, p145
50. Trellini, *The Match*, p204
51. Moara Passoni, 'Corinthian Democracy', *Blizzard*, 38 (2020)
52. Trellini, *The Match*, p233
53. Andrew Downie, *Doctor Sócrates*, p176
54. Downie, *Doctor Sócrates*, p4
55. Sócrates's unpublished memoir, in Downie, *Doctor Sócrates*, p4
56. Trellini, *The Match*, p493
57. John Foot, 'How Italian Football Creates Italians: The 1982 World Cup, the "Patriotic Myth" and Italian National Identity', *International Journal of the History of Sport*, 33, 3, pp341–5
58. Luciano Curino, '*La lunga notte in tricolore*', *La Stampa*, 13 July 1982
59. Foot, *The Archipelago*, p250

The Revenge of the Gaucho

1. Jimmy Burns, *Hand of God*, p10
2. Borocotó, *El Gráfico*, 7 July 1928

3. Eduardo Archetti, *Masculinities*
4. The lectures were collected and published as *El Payador*
5. Alistair Hennessy, 'Argentines, Anglo-Argentines and Others,' in *The Land that England Lost*, p15
6. Borocotó, *El Gráfico*, 15 September 1928
7. Chantecler, *El Gráfico*, 16 June 1928
8. Chantecler, *El Gráfico*, 9 and 16 June 1932
9. Sarmiento, *Facundo: Civilización y Barbarie* (1845)
10. Eduardo Archetti, *Masculinities*, pp57ff
11. Eduardo Galeano, *Football in Sun and Shadow*, p209
12. Yallop, *How they Stole the Game*, p222
13. Sugden and Tomlinson, *Badfellas*, p68
14. Gavin Newsham, *Once in a Lifetime*, p216
15. Hassanin Mubarak, 'The Yellow Shirts of Doom', *Blizzard*, 35 (2019)
16. Mubarak, 'The Yellow Shirts of Doom'
17. James Montague, *When Friday Comes*, pp139–40
18. Rob Smyth, Lars Eriksen, Mike Gibbons, *Danish Dynamite*, pp15–16
19. Smyth, Eriksen, Gibbons, *Danish Dynamite*, p116
20. Smyth, Eriksen, Gibbons, *Danish Dynamite*, p125
21. Smyth, Eriksen, Gibbons, *Danish Dynamite*, p120
22. Sergei Aleinikov, 'И жизнь, и слёзы, и футбол . . .', pp94–5
23. Aleinikov, 'И жизнь, и слёзы, и футбол . . .', p96
24. Smyth, Eriksen, Gibbons, *Danish Dynamite*, pp151–2
25. https://www.theguardian.com/football/blog/2009/oct/13/forgotten-story-denmark-1980s
26. Smyth, Eriksen, Gibbons, *Danish Dynamite*, p183
27. Barbosa Lima Sobrinho, '*Entrevista de Tancredo Neves*', *Acervo*, 13 March 1985
28. Passoni, 'Corinthian Democracy', *Blizzard*, 38 (2020)
29. Downie, *Doctor Sócrates*, pp267–9
30. Marius Lien, 'A Troubled History', *Blizzard*, 13 (2014)
31. *Folha de São Paulo*, 8 March 1986
32. Williams, *Va-Va Voom*, pp12–16
33. Interview with Carlos
34. https://adage.com/creativity/work/tie/25655
35. Jonathan Wilson, 'Maradona the coach can learn from Maradona the player,' *Sports Illustrated*, 27 June 2010

36. Interview, July 2013
37. Maradona, *El Diego*, p121
38. *'Le football allemand, cet animal brut, a mérité de se noyer dans sa propre urine'*, *Libération*, 21 June 1984
39. *'Franz: Ich bin bereit'*, *Bild*, 22 June 1984
40. Hesse, *Tor!*, p318
41. Hesse, *Three Lives of the Kaiser*, pp207–8
42. Hesse, *Tor!*, p319
43. Hesse, *Tor!*, p319
44. Schumacher, *Blowing the Whistle*, p82
45. Stein, Uli, *Halbzeit. Eine Bilanz ohne Deckung*
46. Hesse, *Three Lives of the Kaiser*, p210
47. Hesse, *Tor!*, p319
48. Maradona, *El Diego*, p127
49. Maradona, *El Diego*, p128

Wind of Change

1. Graham Barnes, 'Czech spy revealed', *Mirror*, 8 August 1988
2. Jaromír Novák, *'Jak byl Ivo Knoflíček nějaký čas Bolivijcem'*, *iDNES*, 24 July 2007
3. Mikhail Gorbachev, *Memoirs*, pp187
4. Thomas Blanton, 'When did the Cold War end?' *CWIHP Bulletin* 10 (March 1998), pp184–7
5. Sigrid Meuschel, *Legitimation und Parteiherrschaft in der DDR*
6. Hans-Hermann Hertle, 'The Fall of the Wall: The Unintended Self-Dissolution of East Germany's Ruling Regime', *Cold War International History Project Bulletin*, 12/13, pp135–9
7. Michael Yokhin, 'The Indomitability of Lions,' *Blizzard*, 13 (2014)
8. Yokhin, 'The Indomitability of Lions'
9. Oliver Pickup, 'Milla's Time', *Blizzard*, 13 (2014)
10. Yokhin, 'The Indomitability of Lions'
11. For more on their rivalry, see Jonathan Wilson, *The Outsider*, pp222–48
12. Interview with N'Kono
13. Yokhin, 'The Indomitability of Lions'
14. Yokhin, 'The Indomitability of Lions'
15. Interview with Bell
16. Interview with N'Kono

17. 'Putting the boot in', *Sunday Times*, 19 May 1985
18. 'Hillsborough – Statement', *Hansard*, 27 April 2016, vol 608, col 1433
19. https://www.statista.com/statistics/279898/unemployment-rate-in-the-united-kingdom-uk/
20. 'European Cup final – Brussels', *Hansard*, 3 June 1985, vol 80, col 33
21. James Corbett, *England Expects*, p380
22. Football Association, *Blueprint for the Future of Football* (1991), p9
23. Karl Miller, 'On the 1990 World Cup', *London Review of Books*, 12, 14, 26 July 1990
24. Ian Hamilton, 'Gazza Agonistes', *Granta*, 45, p31
25. Simon Hart, *World in Motion*, p323
26. Ramsay Smith and John Jackson, 'Beauty Booted Out of England Camp', *Mirror*, 14 June 1990
27. Hart, *World in Motion*, p244
28. Yokhin, 'The Indomitability of Lions'
29. Interview with Bell
30. *Wogan*, BBC, 28 November 1990
31. Paul Rowan, *The Team that Jack Built*, pp65–92
32. Jonathan Wilson, *Two Brothers*, pp274–6
33. Jack Charlton, *The Autobiography*, p197
34. Hugh McIlvanney, 'Ireland's Honest Hustler', *Observer*, 25 February 1990
35. Eamon Dunphy, *Ireland v Egypt*, RTÉ, 17 June 1990
36. Rowan, *The Team that Jack Built*, p149; https://www.oireachtas.ie/en/debates/debate/dail/2023-07-12/10/
37. Declan Lynch, *Days of Heaven*, pp131–2
38. David McWilliams, *The Pope's Children*
39. Roddy Doyle, 'Republic is a beautiful word', *My Favourite Year*, pp9–28
40. Rowan, *The Team that Jack Built*, pp136–44
41. Lynch, *Days of Heaven*, p43
42. In *Finding Jack Charlton*, dir. Gabriel Clarke, 2021
43. Interview with Osim
44. Tom Gallagher, *Outcast Europe*, p266
45. *Italia 90: Four Weeks that Changed the World* (Sky Original, 2022)

46. Hart, *World in Motion*, p272
47. Chuck Sudetic, *Blood and Vengeance*
48. Hart, *World in Motion*, p273 (an interview with Hadžibegić)
49. Interview with Osim
50. Hart, *Italia 90*, p272
51. Hart, *World in Motion*, p18
52. Jimmy Burns, *Hand of God*, pp176–78
53. Felipe Celesia and Pablo Waisberg, *La Tablada. A vencer o morir. La última batalla de la guerrilla argentina*
54. Simon Burnton, 'Cameroon shock Argentina in 1990', *Guardian*, 13 March 2018
55. Maradona, p155
56. Burnton, 'Cameroon shock Argentina in 1990', *Guardian*, 13 March 2018
57. Interview with Juan Simón
58. Hart, *World in Motion*, p199
59. Interview with Juan Simón
60. Alex Bellos, 'Brazil revive drug row after 15 years', *The Guardian*, 21 January 2005
61. James Horncastle, 'If you build it, they will come: Serie A's stadium problem', *Athletic*, 27 November 2021
62. *Italia 90: Four Weeks that Changed the World*
63. *Italia 90: Four Weeks that Changed the World*
64. Hart, *World in Motion*, p294
65. *Gazzetta dello Sport*, 2 July 1990
66. John Foot, 'Even the Thieves are Watching TV', *Blizzard*, 44 (2022)
67. Interview with Juan Simón
68. Hart, *World in Motion*, pp294–5
69. Burnton, 'Cameroon shock Argentina in 1990', *Guardian*, 13 March 2018
70. *Italia 90: Four Weeks that Changed the World*
71. Jonathan Wilson, *The Barcelona Legacy*, pp20–7
72. Hart, *World in Motion*, p215
73. Wilson, *The Anatomy of England*, pp215–58
74. Lipreading from *One Night in Turin*
75. Ben Lyttleton, 'Argentina vs. Germany final referee controversy echoes, 24 years later', si.com, 11 July 2014
76. Hart, *World in Motion*, p206

Life Can Be Bright

1. George Vecsey, *New York Times*, 12 June 1994
2. Tom Weir, *USA Today*, 17 December 1993
3. Sugden and Tomlinson, *Badfellas*, p98
4. Jennings, *Foul*, pp136–8
5. Hart, *World in Motion*, pp126–7
6. Michael Lewis, 'How USA was chosen to host World Cup 94: the inside story of a historic day', *Guardian*, 4 July 2015
7. Trellini, *The Match*, p473
8. Trellini, *The Match*, p475
9. Sugden and Tomlinson, *Badfellas*, p103
10. Sugden and Tomlinson, *Badfellas*, p106
11. *El Gráfico*, 7 September 1993
12. Worswick, 'The Dentist and Colombian Rebirth', *Blizzard*, 22 (2016)
13. 'The Impossible Job', *Cutting Edge*, Series 5 Episode 1, Chrysalis 1994
14. Wilson, *Inverting the Pyramid*, pp322–3
15. Wilson, *Inverting the Pyramid*, pp326–30
16. Interview with Borislav Mihailov, November 2003
17. Worswick, 'The Dentist and Colombian Rebirth'
18. Worswick, 'The Dentist and Colombian Rebirth'
19. Worswick, 'The Dentist and Colombian Rebirth'
20. Worswick, 'The Dentist and Colombian Rebirth'
21. Worswick, 'The Dentist and Colombian Rebirth'
22. James Reston Jr, 'The Goalie and the Drug Lord', *Esquire*, June 1994
23. Reston Jr, 'The Goalie and the Drug Lord'
24. Worswick, 'The Dentist and Colombian Rebirth'
25. *La Semana*, 2 July 2009
26. Worswick, 'The Ball and the Gun', *Blizzard*, 7 (2012)
27. Erna Von Der Walde, '*De Garcia Márquez y otros demonios en Colombia*', *Nueva Sociedad*, 150 (1997), cited in Campomar, p422
28. '*Italia in bancarotta. che disastro sacchi!*', *La Gazzetta dello Sport*, 20 June 1994
29. Gianni Brera, *Storia critica del calcio Italiano*
30. Francesca Tosi, Francesco Scalone, Rosella Rettaroli, 'Variations in male height during the epidemiological transition in Italy:

A cointegration approach', *Demographic Research*, 48 (15 Feb 2023), pp189–202
31. Sacchi, *Calcio totale*, p101
32. Gianni Mura, '*L'Italia s'arrende e Vicini dice addio*', *La Repubblica*, 13 October 1991
33. Sacchi, *Calcio totale*, p206
34. Interview with Sacchi
35. Arnau Segura, '*Trágico o inolvidable: el 0-5 de Colombia a Argentina*', *Panenka*, 5 September 2023
36. Maradona, *El Diego*, p199
37. *LA Times*, 2 July 1994
38. Brian Glanville, 'Berbatov maintains the tradition of great Bulgarian centre-forwards', *World Soccer*, 27 February 2013
39. Hesse, *Tor!*, p322
40. Cleber Castro, '*O gol é apenas um detalhe*', *Administradores*, 17 April 2019
41. Mason, *Passion of the People?*, p148
42. Sacchi, *Calcio totale*, p239
43. Sheridan Bird, 'Franco Baresi', *Blizzard*, 8 (March 2013)
44. Sacchi, *Calcio totale*, p240
45. Noll Scott, 'Strange cargo puts sting in World Cup tale', *Guardian*, 30 July 1994
46. Sugden and Tomlinson, *Badfellas*, p104

A New Kind of Glory

1. Sugden and Tomlinson, *Badfellas*, p268
2. Owen Gibson and Paul Lewis, 'Fifa informant Chuck Blazer: I took bribes over 1998 and 2010 World Cups', *Guardian*, 3 June 2015; Tarik El Barakah, 'US Judge Claims that Morocco Bribed FIFA to Host 1998 World Cup', *Morocco World News*, 28 May 2015
3. Pierre Lanfranchi and Alfred Wahl, '*La professionalisation du football en France (1920–39)*', in Dauncey and Hare (eds.), *France and the 1998 World Cup*, p98
4. Jacques Marseille, '*Une histoire économique du football en France est-elle possible?*', *Vingtième siècle*, April–June 1990, pp67–72
5. Patrick Mignon, 'Fans and Heroes', in Dauncey and Hare (eds.), *France and the 1998 World Cup*, p82
6. For the Hungarian and Argentinian cases see, respectively,

Wilson, *The Names Heard Long Ago*, pp9–68, and *Angels with Dirty Faces*, pp45–54

7. Philip N. Jones, 'Urban Population Changes in France 1962–75', *Erdkunde*, Bd 32, H3, Sep 1978, pp198–212
8. Gérard Noiriel, *Les Ouvriers dans La Société Française*
9. Patrick Mignon, 'New Supporter Cultures and Identity in France: the Case of Paris Saint-Germain', in Giulianotti and Williams (eds.), *Games Without Frontiers*, pp277–8
10. Dominique Rocheteau and Denis Chaumier, *Le guide du football 2001*, p309
11. Olivier Villepreux, '*En France, le foot se vit plus. Au bar qu'au stade*', *Libération*, 9 July 1998
12. Joachim Barbier, *Ce pays qui n'aime pas le foot*
13. Dauncey and Hare, 'The Impact of France 98', p205
14. Geoff Hare, *Football in France*, pp29–31
15. Dauncey and Hare, 'The Impact of France 98'
16. Yallop, *How They Stole the Game*, p8
17. Ed Pilkington, 'Shell pays out $15.5m over Saro-Wiwa killing', *Guardian*, 9 June 2009
18. Jennings, *Foul!*, p82
19. Sugden and Tomlinson, *Badfellas*, pp159–61
20. Interview with Hayatou
21. *The Mourning After*, SBS, 2000
22. Spurling, *Death or Glory*, p98
23. Neil Billingham, 'USA vs Iran at France '98: the most politically charged game in World Cup history', *FourFourTwo*, 1 April 2022
24. Montague, *When Friday Comes*, p41
25. David Frum, *The Right Man*
26. Interview with Blažević
27. Interview with Bilić
28. Interview with Blažević
29. Interview with Bilić
30. Williams, *Va-Va Voom*, p198
31. Matt Spiro, *Sacré Bleu*, p30
32. Interview with Bilić
33. Stuart James, 'Revisiting Ronaldo's traumatic 1998 World Cup final — 20 touches on a night to forget', *Athletic*, 16 December 2022

34. James, 'Revisiting Ronaldo's traumatic 1998 World Cup final — 20 touches on a night to forget'
35. *The Phenomenon*, dir. Duncan McMath, 2022
36. Celso de Campos jnr, 'What REALLY happened to Ronaldo before the 1998 World Cup Final – in his own words,' *FourFourTwo*, 20 March 2020
37. Williams, *Va-Va Voom*, p205
38. Williams, *Va-Va Voom*, p208
39. Celso de Campos jnr, 'What REALLY happened to Ronaldo before the 1998 World Cup Final – in his own words'
40. *The Phenomenon*, dir. Duncan McMath, 2022
41. Goldblatt, *Futebol Nation*, p168
42. Williams, *Va-Va Voom*, p207
43. Hare, *Football in France*, p2
44. Jacques Buob, '"*La France voit la vie en bleu*",' *Le Mondial*, 11 July 1998
45. *L'Éxpress*, 13 July 1998
46. Dauncey and Hare (eds.), *France and the 1998 World Cup*, p x
47. In *12 Juillet 1998, le jour parfait* (Black Dynamite, France 2 Cinéma, 2018)
48. Jean-Marie Colombani, *Le Monde*, 13 July 1998
49. Laurent Joffrin, '*Illusion utile*', *Libération*, 10 July 1998

The Global Game

1. Samuel S. Kim, 'Korea and Globalisation (*Segyehwa*)', in Samuel S. Kim (ed.), *Korea's Globalisation*, p1
2. Mikkel Vedby Rasmussen, '"A Parallel Globalisation of Terror": 9-11 Security and Globalisation', *Cooperation and Confict*, 37 (3), pp323–49; https://www.imf.org/external/pubs/ft/fandd/2002/03/aninat.htm
3. Lee Hyun-hee, Park Sung-soo and Yoon Nae-hyun, *New History of Korea*, pp605–8
4. Sebastian Moffett, *Japanese Rules*, pp17–18
5. Goldblatt, *The Ball is Round*, pp837–42
6. Moffett, *Japanese Rules*, pp3–4
7. Hiroyuhi Morita, 'Nippon's Blue Heaven', p147
8. Moffett, *Japanese Rules*, p64
9. Shinobu Yamanaka, 'At Home', *Blizzard*, 29 (2018)
10. Sugden and Tomlinson, *Badfellas*, p121

11. Morita, 'Nippon's Blue Heaven', p154
12. Kwon Yong-Seok, 'Korea, Red Devils and the Hiddink factor', p164
13. Morita, 'Nippon's Blue Heaven', p150
14. Interview with Ivica Osim
15. Interview with Philippe Troussier
16. Martin Jacques, 'Playing the Global Game', *Going Oriental*, pp41–8
17. Philippe Auclair, *Thierry Henry*, p193
18. Jack Pitt-Brooke, '"All the gods were with us": Salif Diao tells the inside story of Senegal's historic campaign at the 2002 World Cup', *Independent*, 19 June 2018
19. Spiro, *Sacré Bleu*, p99
20. Jean-Michel Normand, '*Y a pas péno. Supporteur de circonstance*', *Le Monde supplement Mondial*, 27 June 2002
21. Hare, *Football in France*, p178
22. Auclair, *Thierry Henry*, p193
23. Interview with Kalilou Fadiga
24. Pitt-Brooke, '"All the gods were with us"'
25. Interview with Kalilou Fadiga
26. Javier Auyero, *Poor People's Politics*, pp29–45
27. Wilson, *Angels with Dirty Faces*, pp9–13
28. Beatriz Sarlo, '*Una comunidad llamada Nación*', *Perfil*, 8 June 1998
29. Alabarces, 'Football and *patria*', pp198–217
30. Campomar, *Golazo!*, p454
31. Alabarces, 'Football and *patria*', pp170–97
32. Roy Keane, *Keane*, pp256–8
33. Keane, *Keane*, p261
34. Tom Humphries, 'People were not happy but life goes on. Nobody died', *Irish Times*, 23 May 2002
35. Keane, *Keane*, p261
36. Niall Quinn, *Niall Quinn*, p100
37. Keane, *Keane*, p267
38. Keane, *Keane*, p251
39. Keane, *Keane*, p247–8
40. Keane, *Keane*, p255
41. Keane, *Keane*, p258
42. Quinn, *Niall Quinn*, p16
43. Mike Cronin, *Sport and Nationalism in Ireland*

44. David Davies, *FA Confidential*, p144
45. Matt Dickinson, *Times*, 30 January 1999
46. Mark McGuinness, 'Faith Healer', *Daily Mirror*, 19 February 1999
47. Jeff Powell, 'We've sold our birthright down the fjord to a nation of seven million skiers and hammer throwers who spend half their lives in darkness', *Daily Mail*, 1 November 2000
48. Richard Williams, 'Golden generation passes on after 12 frustrating years', *Guardian*, 27 June 2010
49. Jim White, 'At our Becks and Cool', p172
50. Sarah Winterburn, 'Quote unquote: Southgate's Churchill/Duncan-Smith', *Football365*, 6 October 2016
51. Raphael Honigstein, *Das Reboot*, p16
52. Franz Beckenbauer, '*Jetz spielt die EM Traumfußball … Da hätten wir eh' nur gestört*,' *Bild*, 27 June 2000
53. Foot, *Calcio*, p49
54. Washington Paspuel, '*Byron Moreno enfrenta otra indagación*', *Diario El Comercio*, 4 December 2012
55. Paul Hayward, 'Korean miracle spoilt by refereeing farce', *Telegraph*, 23 June 2002
56. Herschel I. Grossman, 'World Cup heralds a new Korea', *Op-ed*, 24 June 2002
57. Kwon, 'Korea, Red Devils and the Hiddink factor', p160
58. Nick Miller, 'Hakan Şükür and his exile in US: "I'm like a good version of Voldemort – he who shall not be named",' *Athletic*, 5 September 2024
59. Miguel Delaney, 'How the likes of Andres Iniesta and Thomas Müller helped industrialise youth coaching', *Independent*, 13 June 2018

The Headbutt and the Fairy Tale

1. 'Qatar removes Zidane statue after outcry', Hassan Al Thawadi, 31 October 2013
2. 'Zinedine Zidane headbutt statue unveiled in Paris', *France 24*, 26 September 2012
3. Matt Pomroy, 'Zinedine Zidane', *Esquire*, 6 July 2014
4. Marco Materazzi, *Che cosa ho detto veramente a Zidane*
5. Ed Smith, *What Sport Tells Us About Life*, p31
6. https://www.destatis.de/EN/Themes/Labour/Labour-Market/Unemployment/Tables/lrarb001.html#242346

7. For example, Gabor Steingart, *Deutschland – Der Abstieg eines Superstars* (2004), or Hans Werner Sinn, *Ist Deutschland noch zu retten?* (2005)
8. Erik Eggers, 'All around the Globus', p226
9. Heinz Peter Kreuzer and Herbert Fischer-Solms, '*Es muss ein Bern durch Deutshcland gehen*', Deutshclandfunk, 2 July 2004
10. Sugden and Tomlinson, *Badfellas*, pp225–39
11. 'Dempsey: "I was threatened",' BBC, 10 July 2000
12. 'Charlie Dempsey took US$250,000 bribe on eve of World Cup vote, claims former German football boss', *New Zealand Herald*, 27 October 2015; Conn, *The Fall of the House of Fifa*, p265; Jennings, *The Dirty Game*, p86
13. 'Wiseman resigns as FA chairman', *Guardian*, 4 January 1999
14. Thomas Kistner, '*Perfekt Timing des Deutschland AG*', *Süddeutsche Zeitung*, 15 July 2000
15. Oliver Fritsch, '*Die verkauften WM-Turniere*', *Die Zeit*, 4 June 2015
16. Adam Shergold, 'German armoury to win World Cup bid included RPGs', *Saturday Star*, 6 June 2015
17. Jennings, *Foul!*, p269
18. 'Germany appears to have bought right to host 2006 tournament', *Spiegel*, 16 October 2015
19. '*FIFA widerspricht DFB-Präsident Niersbach*', *Tagesschau*, 22 October 2015
20. Dan Palmer, 'Niersbach resigns as DFB President amid World Cup vote buying allegations', *InsidetheGames*, 9 November 2015
21. 'Tax evasion trial against ex-DFB chief Niersbach to be discontinued', DPA International, 26 August 2024
22. Peter Rossberg and Marc Schmidt, '*Ex-Fifa-Finanzchef spricht von bisher unbekannten Zahlungen*', *Bild*, 19 February 2017
23. Peter Penders, '*Schily sieht Klaerungsbedarf – Partner Abld's Keine Bevorzugung*', *Frankfurter Allgemeine Zeitung*, 28 March 2003
24. Jennings, *Foul!*, pp1–4
25. Sugden and Tomlinson, *Badfellas*, p18
26. '*Solange die Vermarktungsfirma ISL florierte, lobbyierte Fifa-Präsident Sepp Blatter fleissig für sie – beileibe nicht uneigennützig. Der ISL-Konkurs gefährdet nun auch Blatters Position im Verband*', *Bilanz*, 31 May 2002

27. Jennings, *Foul!*, p183
28. Andrew Jennings, *The Dirty Game*, p184
29. Jens Weinreich, '*Die geheime Liste der Bestechung im Weltsport*', *Der Speigel*, 28 April 2013. More detail is given here: https://www.playthegame.org/media/qh2jof52/jens_weinreich_-_the_isl_bribery_system.pdf
30. *Le Temps*, 18 April 2002
31. Miguel Delaney, *States of Play*, pp268ff
32. Interview with George Weah, January 2002
33. Jennings, *Foul!*, pp200–1
34. Jennings, *Foul!*, pp225
35. Johnny Warren, *Sheilas, Wogs and Poofters*, p101
36. Warren, *Sheilas, Wogs and Poofters*, p103
37. David Sygall, 'Safran helps lift curse of the Socceroos', *The Age*, 20 November 2005
38. Jeremy Armstrong, 'The Big Man is Back in Town', *Mirror*, 8 June 2006
39. Domenech, *Tout Seul*, p117
40. '*Der Mönch als Schurke*', p155
41. Spiro, *Sacré Bleu*, pp131–2
42. *Marca*, 27 June 2006
43. '*Pessotto wilde niet dood*', *Trouw*, 11 October 2006
44. Gregor Brown, 'Basso: "It was only attempted doping",' cyclingnews.com, 8 May 2007; 'Basso handed two-year doping ban', BBC, 15 June 2007
45. Birgit Schönau, '*Rache für Bär Bruno!*', *Süddeutsche Zeitung*, 19 May 2010
46. Foot, *The Archipelago*, p369
47. Honigstein, *Das Reboot*, p42
48. Ludger Schulze, '*Im Namen des Vaters*', pp20–1
49. Honigstein, *Das Reboot*, p83
50. Esther Kogelboom, '*Schilys Schäh: Wie der Sportminister die Deutschen zir WM-Freundlichkeit motiviert*', *Der Tagesspiegel*, 22 September 2004
51. Honigstein, *Das Reboot*, p87
52. Interview with Hugo Tocalli (Pékerman's assistant)
53. Honigstein, *Das Reboot*, p89
54. Sam Kelly, 'The Final Whistler', *Blizzard*, 11 (2013)

False Dawn

1. Mark Ledsom, 'Fifa end World Cup rotation policy', *Mail & Guardian*, 29 October 2007
2. Ray Hartley, *The Big Fix*, p41
3. Owen Gibson and Paul Lewis, 'Fifa informant Chuck Blazer: I took bribes over 1998 and 2010 World Cups,' 3 June 2015
4. Will Pavia, 'South Africa "paid $10m bribe" to host tournament in 2010', *Times*, 29 May 2015
5. Thomas Peeters, Victor Matthews and Stefan Szymanski, 'Tourism and the 2010 World Cup', *Journal of African Studies*, May 2014
6. Andrew Zimbalist, *Circus Maximus*, p86
7. Martin Müller, David Gogishvili and Sven Daniel Wolfe, 'The structural deficit of the Olympics and the World Cup: Comparing costs against revenues over time', *Environmental and Planning A: Economy and Space*, 54 (6), May 2022
8. Marc Fletcher, 'Integration, Marginalisation and Exclusion in World Cup Johannesburg', in Peter Alegi and Chris Bolsmann (eds.), *Africa's World Cup*, p33
9. Zimbalist, *Circus Maximus*, pp38–42
10. Government of South Africa, 'Address by President Jacob Zuma to the Joint Sitting of Parliament on the occasion of the debate on 2010 Fifa Soccer World Tournament', 18 August 2010
11. 'World Cup stadium construction cartel gets its comeuppance', *Mail & Guardian*, 3 December 2015; FairSquare, *Substitute*, p81
12. Karen Schoonbee and Stefaans Brümmer, 'Public loss, Fifa's gain: How Cape Town got its "white elephant",' in 'Player and Referee: Conflicting Interests and the 2010 Fifa World Cup', *Institute of Security Studies* (2010), pp133–67
13. Alex Duval Smith, 'The Empty Stadiums: South Africa's White Elephants', *Monocle*, 21 October 2010
14. Riot Hlatshwayo, 'Who Killed Jimmy Mohlala?' *Sowetan*, 1 February 2012
15. FairSquare, *Substitute*, p82
16. FairSquare, *Substitute*, pp93–6
17. Luis Martín, '*El fútbol se lo robaron a la gente*', *El País*, 11 July 2011
18. Graham Hunter, *Spain*, p93
19. Diego Torres, *El País*, 19 June 2006

20. Williams, *Va-Va Voom*, p132
21. Spiro, *Sacré Bleu*, p140, quoting William Gallas's autobiography
22. Domenech, *Tout Seul*, p134
23. *Le Parisien*, 5 September 2009
24. Williams, *Va-Va Voom*, p239
25. Williams, *Va-Va Voom*, p239
26. Spiro, *Sacré Bleu*, p151, quoting Domenech's autobiography
27. Domenech, *Tout Seul*, p141
28. *L'Équipe*, 19 June 2010
29. Spiro, *Sacré Bleu*, p158
30. Williams, *Va-Va Voom*, p236
31. 'Suburban unrest spreads in France', *New York Times*, 2 November 2005
32. https://www.independent.co.uk/sport/football/scottish/from-real-to-raith-how-the-other-anelka-changed-his-life-555019.html
33. Williams, *Va-Va Voom*, p244
34. '*Los jugadores argentinos tomarán Viagra para combatir el mal de altura en Bolivia*', *La Vanguardia*, 28 March 2017
35. '*Diego Armando Maradona: "Que la chupen y la sigan chupando"*', *20 Minutos*, 15 October 2009
36. *Clarín*, 4 July 2010
37. Eduardo Sacheri, *El Gráfico*
38. Michael Richards, *A Time of Silence*
39. Hunter, *Spain*, pp116–18
40. Sid Lowe, *Fear and Loathing in la Liga*
41. Press conference, Durban, 7 July 2010
42. Simon Kuper, 'The Dutch Style and the Dutch Nation', *Blizzard*, Issue 0 (2010)
43. Auke Kok, *1974: Wij Waren die Besen*, pp321–9
44. Frank J. Lechner, *The Netherlands: Globalization and National Identity*, pp xiii–xv
45. Auke Kok, *Onze Jongens*, p166
46. John van't Schip, *Nummer 14* (May 2005)
47. Hugo Camps, NOS Studio Sportzomer, 17 June 2016
48. Johan Cruyff, *El Periodico*, 12 July 2010
49. *Hard Gras*, Number 73, August 2010
50. Michael Cox, *Zonal Marking*, pp269–90
51. Rob Smyth, 'Euro 2012: where does this Spain side stand in the pantheon?' *Guardian*, 2 July 2012

52. Sophie Eiley, 'The Jabulani: Why Footballs Can be Too Round', STEMPowerment, 24 June 2022
53. Alistair Grant, 'Over a million 2010 World Cup tickets went unsold but FIFA stay quiet', *Mail Online*, 17 July 2010
54. Fletcher, 'Integration, Marginalisation and Exclusion in World Cup Johannesburg', pp35–7
55. Jennifer Doyle, 'World Cup music and football noise', in Peter Alegi and Chris Bolsmann (eds.), *Africa's World Cup*, pp61–2
56. Trevor Cox, 'What makes the sound of the vuvuzela so annoying?', *New Scientist*, 15 June 2010
57. Solomon Waliaula, 'The Vuvuzela as Paradox of Leisure and Noise: A Sociological Perspective', in Alegi and Bolsmann (eds.), *Africa's World Cup*; Jeffrey W. Kassing, 'Noisemaker or Cultural Symbol: the Vuvuzela Controversy and Expressions of Football Fandom', in Tendai Chari and Nhamo A. Mhiripiri, *African Football, Identity Politics and Global Media Narratives*
58. Albert Grundlingh and John Nauright, 'Worlds Apart?' in Alegi and Bolsmann (eds.), *Africa's World Cup*, p196
59. R. Ottosen, N. Hyde-Clarke and T. Miller, 'Framing the football fan as consumer', in R. Krøvel and T. Roksvold (eds.), *We Love to Hate Each Other*, p121
60. Owen Gibson, 'World Cup 2010: South Africa leaves a World Cup legacy to remember', *Guardian*, 12 July 2010
61. Quinton Fortune, 'South Africa spent £2.4bn to host the 2010 World Cup. What happened next?' *Guardian*, 23 September 2014
62. 'World Cup stadium construction cartel gets its comeuppance', *Mail & Guardian*, 3 December 2015

The Most Expensive Bus Station in the World

1. Greg Grandin, *Fordlandia*, p27
2. Drew Reed, 'Manaus's opulent Amazon Theatre – a history of cities in 50 buildings, day 15', *Guardian*, 14 April 2015
3. Roughly US$750m in 2025
4. Sy Montgomery, *Journey of the Pink Dolphins*, p21
5. Barbara Weinstein, *The Amazon Rubber Boom, 1850–1920*, p193
6. Richard Collier, *The River that God Forgot*, pp11–68
7. Collier, *The River that God Forgot*, p20
8. Montgomery, *Journey of the Pink Dolphins*, p37

9. 'What Brazil's 19th-century rubber crash could teach today's oil drillers', *Economist*, 20 December 2022
10. Gene Kim and Clancy Morgan, '$300m World Cup stadium is nearly abandoned', *Business Insider*, 8 July 2019
11. 'Brazil in position to host 2014 World Cup: Fifa' AP, 28 September 2006
12. Chris Herman, '$13.5 billion later, did the World Cup help or hurt Brazil?', *Diplomatic Courier*, 11 August 2014; https://www.statista.com/statistics/296493/total-costs-fifa-world-cup-2014-brazil/; 'The Tale of Two Tournaments: A Football Story', *Berkeley Economic Review*, 20 November 2023
13. 'Brazil's World Cup Problem and How to Future-Proof Modern Stadiums', RMJM, https://rmjm.com/brazils-world-cup-problem-and-how-to-future-proof-modern-stadiums/
14. FairSquare, *Substitute*, pp97–100
15. Dave Zirin, *Brazil's Dance with the Devil*, p180
16. United Nations Office of the High Commissioner of Human Rights, 'Brazil anti-terrorism law too broad, UN experts warn', UNHCHR press release, 4 November 2015
17. FairSquare, *Substitute*, p102
18. Alfred Draxler, '*Verschluckt sich Löw am „Ochsenspieß"?*', *Bild*, 3 July 2014
19. Claudio Catuogno, '*Ohne ästhetischen Ballast*', *Süddeutsche Zeitung*, 5 July 2014
20. Raphael Honigstein, 'Joachim Löw must fulfil the promise of Germany's golden generation', *Guardian*, 7 July 2014
21. Sid Lowe, 'Spain are here but they are not here. The World Cup, and the joy, has gone', *Guardian*, 22 June 2014
22. Wilson, *The Barcelona Legacy*, pp52–3
23. Interview with Van Gaal
24. Interview with Van Gaal
25. Mixed zone, São Paulo, 1 July 2014
26. Wilson, *Two Brothers*, pp290–91
27. Ken Early, 'Walking to Stay One Step Ahead', slate.com, 2 July 2014
28. Honigstein, *Das Reboot*, p112
29. Honigstein, *Das Reboot*, p135
30. Miguel Delaney, 'Arsène Wenger reveals his blueprint for the future of football', *Independent*, 6 September 2023

31. Honigstein, *Das Reboot*, p27
32. Honigstein, *Das Reboot*, p29
33. John Payne, 'German World Cup star Kevin Grosskreutz pees in hotel lobby', *Metro*, 25 May 2014
34. David Kent, 'Joachim Low banned from driving just before World Cup . . . and admits: "I know I've got to slow myself down a bit here"', *Daily Mail*, 27 May 2014
35. Phil Duncan, 'German World Cup hopefuls Julian Draxler and Benedikt Howedes (along with Nico Rosberg) involved in car accident during Mercedes film shoot', *Daily Mail*, 27 May 2014
36. Jacques de Ryswick, *100,000 Heures du Football*, pp244–5
37. In *Onde estivestes de noite*
38. Andrew Das, 'Brazil lobbies for punishment of the Colombian player who injured Neymar', *New York Times*, 6 July 2014
39. 'World Cup 2014: Juan Zuniga apologises for Neymar injury', BBC, 5 July 2014
40. http://copadomundo.uol.com.br/noticias/redacao/2014/07/08/alemao-leva-soco-ao-comemorar-gol-no-mineirao-e-perde-audicao.htm
41. James Orr, 'Javier Mascherano reveals he "tore his anus" in heroic match-saving tackle on Arjen Robben', *Independent*, 11 July 2014
42. 'Messi is tired, says father', *Today*, 12 July 2014

A New Leaf

1. Guy Faulconbridge and Michael Holden, 'Russia was behind Litvinenko assassination, European court finds', Reuters, 21 September 2021
2. https://www.bellingcat.com/news/uk-and-europe/2018/10/09/full-report-skripal-poisoning-suspect-dr-alexander-mishkin-hero-russia/
3. 'World Cup 2018: Ministers & Royal Family will not go to Russia', BBC, 14 March 2018
4. https://www.cfr.org/global-conflict-tracker/conflict/war-yemen
5. Martin Chulov, '"Night of the Beating": Details emerge of Riyadh Ritz-Carlton purge', *Guardian*, 19 November 2020
6. 'Alwaleed bin Talal, two other billionaires tycoons among Saudi arrests', *Daily Sabah*, 5 November 2017
7. Owen Gibson, 'Fifa candidate Sheikh Salman al Khalifa is linked to Bahrain crackdown', *Guardian*, 16 October 2015

8. https://www.bbc.co.uk/sport/football/34556364
9. Villepreux, '*En France, le foot se vit plus. Au bar qu'au stade*', *Libération*, 9 July 1998
10. Williams, *Va-Va Voom*, p241
11. Fabrice Arfi, Michaël Hajdenberg and Mathilde Mathieu, 'French football chiefs' secret plan to whiten "*les Bleus*"', mediapart.fr, 28 April 2011
12. Delaney, *States of Play*, p102
13. Michael J. Garcia and Cornel Borbély, 'Report on the Inquiry into the 2018/2022 Fifa World Cup bidding processes', p331.
14. Tariq Panja and Kevin Draper, 'US Says Fifa Officials were bribed to Award World Cups to Russia and Qatar', *New York Times*, 6 April 2020
15. Matt Scott, 'Handbag gifts come back to haunt England's 2018 World Cup bid', *Guardian*, 4 November 2009
16. Paul Kelso, 'Trinidad trip the ultimate political football', *Guardian*, 30 May 2008
17. Martyn Ziegler, 'Fifa Royal Wedding bribe claim denied', *Independent*, 5 May 2011
18. Barney Ronay, 'Fifa's World Cup debacle isn't just about money – there's horror and death too', *Guardian*, 17 November 2017
19. Fifa, 'Evaluation reports on the bids for the 2018 and 2022 World Cups', November 2010
20. Bonita Mersiades, *Whatever It Takes*, p112
21. Graham Dunbar, 'Fifa prosecutor Michael Garcia resigns, slams leadership, loses faith in Eckert', AP, 17 December 2014
22. 'Exclusive: How Sam Allardyce tried to make as much money as possible as England manager – before his first match', *Telegraph*, 26 September 2016
23. 'The governance of football', parliament.uk, 17 October 2016
24. Owen Gibson, 'FA's Martin Glenn: Why does the shirt weigh so heavy?', *Guardian*, 22 October 2016
25. Jonathan Northcroft and Rob Draper, *Dear England*, pp211–38
26. Cam Wolf, 'England Manager Gareth Southgate Has Everybody Buying Waistcoat', *GQ*, 11 July 2018
27. Northcroft and Draper, *Dear England*, pp131–2
28. Gareth Southgate, '*Dear England*', *The Players Tribune*, 8 June 2021

29. David Hytner, 'Germany in crisis as Mesut Özil's "Bling-bling gang" take on Bavarians', *Guardian*, 22 June 2018
30. Mesut Özil, Twitter post, 22 July 2018; https://x.com/M10/status/1020984884431638528?ref_src=twsrc%5Etfw%7Ctwcamp%5Etweetembed%7Ctwterm%5E1020984884431638528%7Ctwgr%5E8645bb83ae364c13e6bad93541b267d8d3c1fed1%7Ctwcon%5Es1_&ref_url=https%3A%2F%2Fwww.itv.com%2Fnews%2F2018-07-22%2Fmesut-ozil-statement-quits-german-national-team
31. Amy Lawrence, 'Arsenal's Arsène Wenger: Europe doesn't produce strikers any more', *Guardian*, 11 September 2015
32. James Corbett, 'Inside Russia's plot to buy the World Cup – big consequences for England', *OffthePitch*, 6 November 2019
33. 'Fifa's Michel d'Hooghe says he is being treated "like a murderer"', *Guardian*, 2 December 2014
34. Blake and Calvert, *The Ugly Game*, pp188ff
35. Sputnik Mediabank #794606: sputnikmediabank.com/media/794606.html?context=list&list_sid=list_65673
36. Ali Walker, 'Qatar's emir praises Vladimir Putin for World cup support', *Politico*, 13 October 2022
37. Conn, *The Fall of the House of Fifa*, p79–80
38. Bensinger, *Red Card*, pp65–74
39. Martyn Ziegler, 'Rerun of 2022 World Cup vote a possibility, says Sepp Blatter', *Independent*, 19 May 2011
40. Blake and Calvert, *The Ugly Game*, pp25–6
41. Mary Papenfuss and Teri Thompson, *American Huckster*; Conn, *The Fall of the House of Fifa* pp20–2
42. https://chuckblazer.blogspot.com/
43. Bensinger, *Red Card*, pp367
44. Pablo Polo, '*Benzema: "Deschamps se pliega a la presión de una parte racista de Francia"*', *Marca*, 1 June 2016
45. Pierre Nusslé, '*Jouons "à la français"*', in Bureau and Chancel (eds.), *L'amour foot*, p33
46. John Marks, 'The National Team and French National Identity', in Dauncey and Hare (eds.), *France and the 1998 World Cup*, p47
47. Williams, *Va-Va Voom*, p247
48. HRW, 'Russia's Worst Crackdown Since Soviet Era', 31 January 2013

49. Amnesty International, 'Russia's anti-gay "propaganda law" assault on freedom of expression', 25 January 2013
50. *Building Workers International*, 'Another death at the 2018 World Cup stadium in St Petersburg', 25 October 2016
51. Alexey Karnaukhov and Alexey Chumakov, 'World Cup gold: Report on inflated costs of the main arenas of the 2018 World Cup', YACPC, 2018
52. FairSquare, *Substitute*, p106
53. Håvard Melnæs, 'The Slaves of St Petersburg', *Josimar*, 28 March 2017
54. Minky Worden, 'Russia's Bloody World Cup', *Politico*, 13 July 2018
55. HRW, 'Red Card: Exploitation of Construction Workers at World Cup Sites in Russia', 14 June 2017
56. *Building and Woodworkers International*, 'Foul Play: Fifa's failures at the 2018 World Cup', 2018: https://www.bwint.org/web/content/cms.media/1145/datas/WCRussia-Report.pdf
57. Tariq Panja, 'The World Cup's Hot New Accessory Comes With a Few Questions', *New York Times*, 3 July 2018
58. FairSquare, *Substitute*, p109
59. Luis F. Rojo, 'The Taxman Cometh', *Marca*, 23 January 2014
60. Sid Lowe, 'Barcelona president Laporta blames Bartomeu for "worrying" €1.35bn debt', *Guardian*, 16 August 2021
61. Mixed Zone, 11 July 2018
62. Spiro, *Sacré Bleu*, pp320–1
63. Yann Filipino and Matthieu Suc, '*N'Golo Kanté: le magot, les menaces et le «calibre»*', *Mediapart*, 27 November 2019
64. Eric Collier and Rémi Dupré, '*L'affaire Paul Pogba, un scenario digne d'un filme de gangsters*', *Le Monde*, 21 October 2022
65. Oliver Bullough, 'Putin wanted the World Cup 2018 and got it whatever the cost', 30 May 2018
66. Rebecca Ruiz, 'Russians No Longer Dispute Olympic Doping Allegation', *New York Times*, 31 December 2016

Desert Gold

1. Sean Ingle, '"I feel gay, disabled . . . like a woman too!": Infantino makes bizarre attack on critics', *Guardian*, 19 November 2022
2. *Josimar*, International Edition: Fifa World Cup 2022
3. Patrick Strudwick, '"Qatari officials gang raped me for being

gay": The truth about how the World Cup hosts treat LGBT people', *I*, 2 November 2022

4. Ingle, '"I feel gay, disabled ... like a woman too!"'
5. Barney Ronay, 'Forget "sportswashing": Qatar 2022 is about military might and hard sports power', *Guardian*, 14 October 2022
6. John McManus, 'Taking the Heat: Can Qatar survive climate change', geographical.co.uk, 28 June 2022
7. Christopher Schär, 'The Worst Heat Waves to Come', *Nature Climate Change*, 6, 26 October 2015, pp128–9
8. Paul MacInnes, 'Fifa misled fans over "carbon-neutral Qatar World Cup", regulator finds,' *Guardian*, 7 June 2023; Philippe Auclair, 'Smoke and Mirrors', *Blizzard*, 54 (2024)
9. Tariq Panja and Rory Smith, 'The World Cup that Changed Everything', *New York Times*, 19 November 2022
10. Martyn Ziegler, 'What does Michel Platini's detention mean for the Qatar World Cup?', *Times*, 18 June 2019
11. Panja and Smith, 'The World Cup that Changed Everything'
12. Conn, *The Fall of the House of Fifa*, pp302–3
13. James Montague, *When Friday Comes*, pp278–9
14. Martyn Ziegler, 'Michel Platini held over Qatar World Cup bid', *Times*, 19 June 2019
15. 'Qatar takes delivery of first French-built Rafale jet fighter', Al Jazeera, 6 February 2019
16. Jack Pitt-Brooke, Adam Crafton, Dominic Fifield and James Horncastle, 'No final glory but PSG are now part of Europe's elite – and they're here to stay', *Athletic*, 24 August 2020
17. Martyn Ziegler, 'Qataris get dream World Cup final – for $200bn', *Times*, 17 December 2022
18. Conn, *The Fall of the House of Fifa*, p96
19. Blake and Calvert, *The Ugly Game*, pp114–26
20. Sebastian, *The Away Game*, pp74–6; David Goldblatt, *The Age of Football*, pp153–4
21. Richard Gillis, Brian Oliver and Nick Briggs, 'Spoil Sport', *Observer*, 11 November 2007
22. Abbot, *The Away Game*, pp122–4
23. Barney Ronay, 'Was Aspire Project a vehicle to deliver votes to Qatar's World Cup bid?' *Guardian*, 3 December 2012
24. Michael J. Garcia and Cornel Borbély, 'Report on the Inquiry into the 2018/2022 Fifa World Cup Bidding process', p188

25. Ronay, 'Was Aspire Project a vehicle to deliver votes to Qatar's World Cup bid?'
26. James Montague, 'The Fans Screamed for Qatar. Their Passion hid a Secret,' *New York Times*, 28 November 2022
27. Patrick Wintour, 'Iran players end silent protest at World Cup amid threats of reprisals', 25 November 2022
28. Pascual Ruiz, 'Argentina have a score to settle with Mbappé after his disrespectful comments on South American football', *Marca*, 15 December 2022
29. Randeep Ramesh, 'The long-running family rivalries behind the Qatar crisis', *Guardian*, 21 July 2017
30. Miller, *Desert Kingdoms to Global Power*, p248
31. Caroline Matthews, 'UAE Crown Prince asked the US to bomb Al Jazeera during the War on Terror', *Independent*, 29 June 2017
32. Montague, *When Friday Comes*, p345
33. Patrick Wintour, 'Qatar given 10 days to meet 13 sweeping demands by Saudi Arabia', *Guardian*, 23 June 2017
34. Martyn Ziegler, 'Just five years to solve issues plaguing the Qatar World Cup', *Times*, 20 November 2017
35. Rayn Grim and Ben Walsh, 'Leaked Documents Expose Stunning Plan To Wage Financial War On Qatar – And Steal The World Cup', *Intercept*, 9 November 2017
36. Martyn Ziegler, 'Fifa president Gianni Infantino wants 48-team World Cup in Qatar 2022, not 2026', *Times*, 31 October 2018; Tariq Panja, 'Fifa considering Oman and Kuwait to Host Some 2022 World Cup Games', *New York Times*, 6 March 2019
37. Bradley Hope and Juston Scheck, *Blood and Oil*, p182
38. David Smith, Sabrina Siddiqui and Peter Beaumont, 'Gulf crisis: Trump escalates row by accusing Qatar of sponsoring terror', *Guardian*, 9 June 2017
39. Patrick Wintour, 'Donald Trump tweets support for blockade imposed on Qatar', *Guardian*, 6 June 2017
40. David Wearing, *Anglo-Arabia*, pp183–4
41. Fifa, '2022 Fifa World Cup Bid Evaluation Report: Qatar', 2010, p29
42. Amnesty International, 'The Dark Side of Migration: Spotlight in Qatar's construction sector ahead of the World Cup', 18 November 2013, p36

43. Annie Kelly, Niamh McIntryre and Pete Pattisson, 'Revealed: hundreds of migrant workers dying of heat stress in Qatar each year', *Guardian*, 2 October 2019
44. Tariq Panja and Bhadra Sharma, 'The World Cup's Forgotten Team', *New York Times*, 16 November 2022
45. Pete Pattisson, Niamh McIntyre, Imran Mukhtar, Nikhil Eapen, Imran Mukhtar, Md Owasim, Uddin Bhuyan, Udwab Bhattarai, Aanya Piyari, 'Revealed: 6,500 migrant workers have died in Qatar since World Cup awarded', *Guardian*, 23 February 2021
46. Christina Bouri, 'The Kafala System Is Facilitating Labor Abuses in the Middle East', *Lawfare*, 17 September 2023
47. Pete Pattisson, 'Revealed: Qatar's World Cup "Slaves"', *Guardian*, 25 September 2013
48. FairSquare, *Substitute*, p118
49. Vani Saraswathi, 'Workers in Qatar remain voiceless and invisible, despite reforms and international furore', migrant-rights.org, 2 November 2022
50. James Corbett, 'The building Legacy', *Blizzard*, 45 (May 2022)
51. Nick Ames, 'Qatar's forgotten migrant workers stuck in a "prison where you can work"', *Guardian*, 21 December 2022
52. Amnesty International, 'Qatar: jailed official who blew whistle on World Cup labour abuses should be freed', 24 July 2024
53. Sean Ingle, 'Qatar World Cup whistleblower was tortured, claims family', *Guardian*, 7 December 2022
54. '*"Andá pa' allá bobo": a dos años de la frase histórica de Lionel Messi que revolucionó al mundo del fútbol,*' *La Nación*, 10 December 2024
55. Interview with Matías Manna
56. Interview with Matías Manna

Epilogue

1. 'How Fifa's president failed to clean up football', *Der Spiegel*, 2 November 2018
2. 'Fifa President Gianni Infantino and former US Attorney General Loretta Lynch open 3rd FIFA Compliance Summit', Inside Fifa, 12 October 2020
3. 'Fifa's Weakened Code of Ethics – President Infantino Intervened Personally', *Der Spiegel*, 2 November 2018

4. Les Murray, 'Fifa reforms dead and buried', SBS Sport, 22 May 2017
5. 'Fifa to reconsider format of 2026 World Cup after "best ever" tournament', BBC 16 December 2022
6. Amnesty International, 'Confirmation of Saudi Arabia as 2034 FIFA World Cup host puts many lives at risk', 11 December 2024
7. https://inside.fifa.com/fifa-world-cup-qatar-2022-in-number

BIBLIOGRAPHY

Abbot, Sebastian, *The Away Game* (W.W. Norton, 2019)

Alabarces, Pablo, 'Football and *Patria*: Sport, National Narratives and Identities in Argentina 1920–98' (PhD thesis, Brighton University, 2001)

Alegi, Peter, *African Soccerscapes* (Ohio University Press, 2010)

Alegi, Peter and Chris Bolsmann (eds.), *Africa's World Cup* (University of Michigan Press, 2019)

Aleinikov, Sergei, 'И жизнь, и слёзы, и футбол …' (Polimya, 1992)

Anderson, Thomas P., *The War of the Dispossessed* (University of Nebraska Press, 1981)

Andrews, George Reid, *Blackness in the White Nation* (University of North Carolina Press, 2010)

'Rhythm Nation'. *ReVista – Harvard Review of Latin America* (Winter 2003)

Araf, Jo, *Generazione Wunderteam* (Pitch 2021)

Aron, Raymond, *Le siècle du intellectuals*, programme 4, *De Sartre á Foucault 1958–90* (Desfons and Winock, France 3, 1999)

Atherton, Martin, *The Theft of the Jules Rimet Trophy* (Meyer & Meyer, 2008)

Auclair, Philippe, *Thierry Henry* (Macmillan, 2012)

'The Collaborator', *Blizzard*, 1 (2011)

Auyero, Javier, *Poor People's Politics* (Duke University Press, 2000)

Aziz, Philippe, *Tu Trahiras Sans Vergogne* (Fayard, 1969)

Bakema, J.B., *Thoughts about Architecture* (St Martin's, 1982)

Barbier, Joachim, *Ce pays qui n'aime pas le foot* (Hugo Sport, 2012)

Battini, Michele, *The Missing Italian Nuremberg* (Palgrave Macmillan, 2007)

Bauso, Matias, *78: Historia Oral del Mundial*

Beaud, Stéphane and Gérard Noiriel, '*L'immigration dans le football*', *Vingtième siècle*, Apr–Jun 1990

Beck, Peter, *Scoring for Britain* (Routledge, 1999)

Beha, Oliviero and Roberto Chiodi, *Mundialgate* (Tullio Peronti, 1984)

Bellos, Alex, *Futebol* (Bloomsbury, 2002)

Bensinger, Ken, *Red Card* (Profile, 2018)

Bird, Sheridan, 'Franco Baresi', *Blizzard*, 8 (March 2013)

Biriotti Del Burgo, Maurice, 'Don't Stop the Carnival: Football in the Societies of Latin America' in S. Wagg (ed.), *Giving the Game Away*

Biskind, Peter, *Easy Riders, Raging Bulls* (Bloomsbury, 1998)

Blake, Heidi and Jonathan Calvert, *The Ugly Game* (Simon & Schuster, 2015)

Blanton, Thomas, 'When did the Cold War end?' *CWIHP Bulletin* 10 (March 1998)

Bognár, Sándor, Iván Pető and Sándor Szakács, *A hazai gazdaság négy évtizedének története 1945–1985* (Közdazdasági és Jogi Könyvkiadó, 1985)

Bowler, Dave, *Winning isn't Everything* (Gollancz, 1998)

Breitmeier, Florian, '*Ein wunder, wie es im Drehbuch steht: Die WM 1954 – ein deutscher Erinnerungsfilm*', in Pyta (ed.), *Die lange Weg zur Bundesliga*

Brera, Gianni, *Storia critica del calcio Italiano* (Bompiani, 1975)

Brüggemeier, Franz-Josef, *Zurück auf dem Platz* (DVA, 2004)

Burlamaqui, Luiz Guilherme, *A dança das cadeiras* (Intermeios, 2021)
The Making of a Global Fifa (De Gruyter Oldenbourg, 2020)
Burns, Jimmy, *Hand of God* (Bloomsbury, 2002)
Bushby, Adam, 'Truth to Power', *Blizzard*, 39 (2020)
Calder, Barnabas, *Raw Concrete* (William Heinemann, 2016)
Camkin, John, *World Cup 1958* (Sportsman's Book Club, 1959)
Campomar, Andreas, *Golazo!* (Riverrun, 2014)
Cantor, Andreas, *Goooal* (Touchstone, 1997)
Castro, Ruy, *Garrincha* (Yellow Jersey, 2013)
Celesia, Felipe, and Pablo Waisberg, *La Tablada. A vencer o morir. La última batalla de la guerrilla Argentina* (Aguilar, 2024)
Chari, Tendai and Nhamo A. Mhiripiri (eds.), *African Football, Identity Politics and Global Media Narratives* (Palgrave Macmillan, 2014)
Charles, John, *King John* (Headline, 2003)
Charlton, Bobby, *The Autobiography, My England Years* (Headline, 2008)
Charlton, Jack, *The Autobiography* (Partridge, 1996)
Chirilă, Ioan, *Finala se joacă azi* (Uniunii, 1966)
Ciria, Alberto, 'From soccer to war in Argentina: preliminary notes on sports-as-politics under a military regime 1976-1982' in Archibald R.M. Ritter, *Latin America and the Caribbean: geopolitics, development and culture. Proceedings of the 1983 Conference of the Canadian Association for Latin American and Caribbean Studies* (Ottawa, 1984)
Clack, Neil, *Animals!* (Know the Score, 2010)
Coffey, Jonny, 'Real Republikans', *Blizzard*, 53 (2024)
Collier, Richard, *The River that God Forgot* (Collins, 1968)
Conn, David, *The Fall of the House of Fifa* (Yellow Jersey, 2017)

Cooke, Paul and Christopher Young, 'German football in literature and film', in Tomlinson and Young (eds.), *German Football*

Corbett, James, *England Expects* (De Coubertin, 2010)

'The building Legacy', *Blizzard*, 45 (May 2022)

Cox, Michael, *Zonal Marking* (HarperCollins, 2019)

Cox, Trevor, 'What makes the sound of the vuvuzela so annoying?', *New Scientist*, 15 June 2010

Cronin, Mike, *Sport and Nationalism in Ireland* (Four Courts, 1999)

Cruyff, Johan, *My Turn* (Macmillan, 2016)

Da Cruz, Martin, *From Beauty to Duty* (Pitch, 2022)

DaMatta, Roberto, *Explorações: Ensaios de Sociologia Interperativa* (Rocco, 2012)

'*Ópio do povo x drama de justiça social*,' *Novos Estudos*, v1, 4, November 1982

Darby, Paul, '"Let Us Rally Round the Flag": Football, Nation-building and pan-Africanism in Kwame Nkrumah's Ghana', *Journal of African History*, 54, 2 (July 2013)

'Politics, resistance and patronage: the African boycott of the 1966 World Cup and its ramifications', *Soccer and Society*, 20, 7–8 (2019)

D'Ascanio, Alessandro, *La Vittoria del 1934* (Solfanelli, 2010)

Dauncey, Hugh and Geoff Hare (eds.), *France and the 1998 World Cup* (Frank Cass, 1999)

'The Impact of France 98' in Dauncey and Hare (eds.), *France and the 1998 World Cup*

Davies, David, *FA Confidential* (Simon & Schuster, 2008)

Dawson, Jeff, *Back Home* (Orion, 2001)

De Andrade, Mário, *Macunaíma* (Cupolo, 1928)

De Martino, Emiliano, *Tre Volte Campioni del Mondo* (Milano, 1937)

De Ryswick, Jacques, *100,000 Heures du Football* (La Table Ronde, 1962)

De Taillac, Marie-Cécile, *Marga, Comtesse de Palmyre* (Feryane, 2000)

Delaney, Miguel, *States of Play* (Seven Dials, 2024)

Del Burgo, Maurice Biriotti, 'Don't Stop the Carnival: Football in the Societies of Latin America' in Wagg (ed.), *Giving the Game Away*

Delius, Friedrich Christian, *Der Sonntag, an dem ich Weltmeister wurde* (Rowohlt, 1996)

Dickinson, Matt, *Bobby Moore* (Yellow Jersey, 2014)

Dietschy, Paul, 'Making Football Global? FIFA, Europe and the non-European football world, 1912–1974', *Journal of Global History* 8, 2 (2013), p297

Domenech, Raymond, *Tout Seul* (Flammarion, 2012)

Doyle, Jennifer, 'World Cup music and football noise', in Peter Alegi and Chris Bolsmann (eds.), *Africa's World Cup*

Downie, Andrew, *Doctor Sócrates* (Simon & Schuster, 2017)

The Greatest Show on Earth (Arena, 2021)

Downing, David, *England v Argentina* (Portrait, 2003)

Doyle, Roddy, 'Republic is a Beautiful Word', in Nick Hornby (ed.) *My Favourite Year*

Duhamel, Alain, *Le Complexe d'Astérix* (Gallimard, 1985)

Duval Smith, Alex, 'The Empty Stadiums: South Africa's White Elephants', *Monocle*, 21 October 2010

Eco, Umberto, *Faith in Fakes* (Vintage, 1995)

Eggers, Erik, 'All around the Globus' in Alan Tomlinson and Christopher Young (eds.), *German Football*

'Der Mythos', in Dernhardt (ed.), *Das Wunder von Bern*

Elsey, Brenda, *Citizens and Sportsmen* (University of Texas Press, 2011)

Escartín, Pedro, *Lo de Brasil fue así* (Pueyo, 1951)

Fletcher, Marc, 'Integration, Marginalisation and Exclusion in World Cup Johannesburg' in Alegi and Bolsmann (eds.), *Africa's World Cup*

Foot, John, *The Archipelago* (Bloomsbury, 2018)

Calcio (Harper, 2007)

'Even the Thieves are Watching TV', *Blizzard*, 44 (2022)

'How Italian Football Creates Italians: The 1982 World Cup, the "Patriotic Myth" and Italian National Identity', *International Journal of the History of Sport*, 33, 3

Ford, Trevor, *I Lead the Attack* (Stanley Paul, 1957)

Förster, David, 'Cafe Sindelar Revisited: *Verlauf und Folgen der Sildelar-Debatte*', in Förster, Rosenberg and Spitaler (eds.), *Fußball unterm Hakenkreuz in der 'Ostmark'*

'*Das Versöhnungsspiel*' in Förster, Rosenberg and Spitaler (eds.), *Fußball unterm Hakenkreuz in der 'Ostmark'*

Förster, David, Jakob Rosenberg & Georg Spitaler (eds.), *Fußball unterm Hakenkreuz in der 'Ostmark'* (Die Werkstatt, 2014)

Franklin, Neil, *Football at Home and Abroad* (Stanley Paul, 1956)

Frum, David, *The Right Man* (Weidenfeld & Nicolson, 2003)

Galeano, Eduardo, *Football in Sun and Shadow* (Fourth Estate, 2003)

Gallagher, Tom, *Outcast Europe* (Routledge, 2005)

Garrido, Atilio, *Maracaná: La historia secreta* (Atilio Garrido, 2014)

Garrido, Atilio & Joselo González, *El gol del siglo* (El País & Tenfield, 2000)

Giménez Rodríguez, Alejandro, *La pasión laica* (Rumbo, 2007)

Ginsberg, Paul, *A History of Contemporary Italy* (Penguin, 1991)

Giulianotti, Richard and John Williams (eds.), *Game Without Frontiers* (Routledge, 1994)

Glanville, Brian, *The Story of the World Cup* (Faber, 2001)

Gogliani, Patrizia, *Il fascismo degli italiani* (UTET, 2104)

Goldblatt, David, *The Ball is Round* (Penguin, 2007)

Futebol Nation (Penguin, 2014)

Gorbachev, Mikhail, *Memoirs* (Doubleday, 1995)

Grandin, Greg, *Fordlandia* (Icon, 2010)

Grass, Günter, *Mein Jahrhundert* (MBH, 2001)

Greene, Jack and Alessandro Massignani, *Il Principe Nero* (Mondadori, 2017)

Griffiths, Mervyn, *The Man in the Middle* (Stanley Paul, 1958)

Grundlingh, Albert and John Nauright, 'Worlds Apart?' in Alegi and Bolsmann (eds.), *Africa's World Cup*

Gumbrecht, Hans Ulrich, *In Praise of Athletic Beauty* (Harvard University Press, 2006)

Hamilton, Duncan, *Answered Prayers* (Riverrun, 2023)

Hamilton, Ian, 'Gazza Agonistes', *Granta*, 45

Hámori, Tibor, *Régi gólok, edzősorsok* (Lapkiadó Vállalat, 1984)

Hare, Geoff, *Football in France* (Berg, 2004)

Hart, Simon, *World in Motion* (De Coubertin, 2018)

Hartley, Ray, *The Big Fix* (Jonathan Ball, 2016)

Harwood, Elaine, *Space, Hope and Brutalism* (Yale University Press, 2015)

Havekost, Folke and Volker Stahl, *Fußballweltmeisterschaft 1930 Uruguay* (Agon Sportverlag, 2005)

Hawkey, Ian, *Feet of the Chameleon* (Portico, 2009)

Heinrich, Arthur, *Tooor, Toor, Tor: Vierzig Jahre 3:2* (Rotbuch, 1994)

Hémeury, Lucie, 'Narrow Miss: the failure of Argentina's bid for the 1962 World Cup (1954–56)', *Soccer and Society*, 21, 8

Hennessy, Alistair and John King (eds.), *The Land that England Lost* (British Academic Press, 1992)

Hennessy, Alistair, 'Argentines, Anglo-Argentines and Others,' in Alistair Hennessy and John King (eds.), *The Land that England Lost*

Hertle, Hans-Hermann, 'The Fall of the Wall: The Unintended Self-Dissolution of East Germany's Ruling Regime', *Cold War International History Project Bulletin*, 12/13

Hesse, Uli, *Three Lives of the Kaiser* (Simon & Schuster, 2023)
Tor! (WSC, 2013)

'The Great Disgrace', *Blizzard*, 29 (June 2018)

'Never the Twain', *Blizzard,* 13 (June 2014)

Hidegkuti, Nándor, *Óbudától Firenzéig* (Sport, 1961)

Holt, Richard, J.A. Mangan and Pierre Lanfranchi (eds.), *European Heroes* (Frank Cass, 1996)

Honigstein, Raphael, *Das Reboot* (Yellow Jersey, 2016)

Hope, Bradley and Justin Scheck, *Blood and Oil* (John Murray, 2020)

Horak, Roman and Wolfgang Moderthaner, 'A Culture of Urban Cosmopolitanism,' in Richard Holt, J. A. Mangan and Pierre Lanfranchi (eds.), *European Heroes*

Hornby, Nick (ed.), *My Favourite Year* (Gollancz, 1994)

Horncastle, James, 'Saint-Étienne 0 Dynamo Kyiv 3', *Blizzard,* 2 (2011)

Huba, Karl-Heinz, *Fussball Weltgeschichte* (Copress, 1973)

Hubbard, Ryan, *From Partition to Solidarity* (RAH, 2019)

Hunter, Graham, *Spain* (BackPage, 2013)

Irving, John, 'Peculiar Personal Inclinations', *Blizzard*, 38 (2020)

Iwanczuk, Jorge, *Historia del Fútbol Amateur en la Argentina* (Autores, 1992)

Jacques, Martin, 'Playing the Global Game', in Mark Perryman (ed.), *Going Oriental*

Jawad, Hyder, *Four Weeks in Montevideo* (Seventeen, 2009)

Jennings, Andrew, *The Dirty Game* (Century, 2015)

Jones, Philip N., 'Urban Population Changes in France 1962–75', *Erdkunde*, Bd 32, H3, Sep 1978

Joseph, Gilbert M. and Jürgen Buchenau, *Mexico's Once and Future Revolution* (Duke University Press, 2013)

Kaliba, Jan, 'Jozef Štibrányi's Diary', *Blizzard*, 25 (2017)

Kassing, Jeffrey W., 'Noisemaker or Cultural Symbol: the Vuvuzela Controversy and Expressions of Football Fandom', in Chari and Mhiripiri, *African Football, Identity Politics and Global Media Narratives*

Keane, Roy, *Keane* (Michael Joseph, 2002)

Keifu, R. (ed.), *1. Fußballweltmeisterschaft 1930 in Uruguay* (Agon, 1993)

Kim, Gene and Clancy Morgan, '$300m World Cup stadium is nearly abandoned', *Business Insider*, 8 July 2019

Kim, Samuel S., 'Korea and Globalisation (*Segyehwa*)', in Samuel S. Kim (ed.), *Korea's Globalisation*

Kim, Samuel S. (ed.), *Korea's Globalisation* (Cambridge University Press, 2000)

Knoch, Habbo, '*Gemeinschaft auf Zeit. Fußball und die Transformation des Nationalen in Deutschland und England*', in Peter Lösche, Undine Ruge and Klaus Scholz (eds.), *Fußballwelten*

Kok, Auke, *1974: Wij Waren die Besen* (Rainbow, 2019)

Johan Cruyff (Simon & Schuster, 2023)

Onze Jongens (Thomas Rap, 2006)

Krøvel, R. and T. Roksvold (eds.), *We Love to Hate Each Other* (Nordicom, 2012)

Kunti, Sam, *Brazil 1970* (Pitch, 2022)

Kuper, Simon, 'The Dutch Style and the Dutch Nation', *Blizzard*, Issue 0 (2010)

Kurlansky, Mark, *1968* (Jonathan Cape, 2004)

Kwon Yong-Seok, 'Korea, Red Devils and the Hiddink factor', in Mark Perryman (ed.), *Going Oriental*

Lacey, Josh, *God is Brazilian* (The History Press, 2007)

Lacey, Robert, *The Kingdom* (Hutchinson, 1981)

Lagos, Cecilia, 'Chile v Italy', *The Squall*, 2 (2020)

Lanata, Jorge, *Argentinos* (Ediciones B, 2002)

Lanfranchi, Pierre, Christiane Eisenberg, Alfred Wahl and Tony Mas (eds.), *100 Years of Football* (Weidenfeld & Nicholson, 2004)

Lanfranchi, Pierre and Alfred Wahl, 'The immigrant as hero: Kopa, Mekloufi and French football', in Holt, Mangan and Lanfranchi (eds.), *European Heroes*

'La professionalisation du football en France (1920–39)', in Dauncey and Hare (eds.), *France and the 1998 World Cup*

Langenus, John, *Fluitend door de wereld* (Snoeck Ducaju en Zoon, 1942)

Leblond, Renaud and Yves Rimet, *Jules Rimet, le père du Mondial* (Librinova, 2018)

Lechner, Frank J., *The Netherlands: Globalization and National Identity* (Routledge, 2007)

Lee Hyun-hee, Park Sung-soo and Yoon Nae-hyun, *New History of Korea* (Jimoondang, 2005)

Lehmann, David, 'Gilberto Freye: the Reassessment Continues', *Latin American Research Review*, Vol 3, 1, 2008

Leinemann, Jürgen, *Sepp Herberger* (Rowohlt, 1997)

Lemke, Sieglinde, *Primitivist Modernism: Black Culture and the Origins of Transatlantic Modernism* (Oxford University Press, 1998)

Levine, R., 'Sport and society: the case of Brazilian *futebol*', *Luso-Brazilian Review* 17, 2 (1980)

Lien, Marius, 'A Troubled History', *Blizzard*, 13 (2014)

Lizana, José, *Ceacheí – Palabra de Campeón* (Ceachéi, 2008)

Lösche, Peter, Undine Ruge and Klaus Scholz (eds.), *Fußballwelten* (VS Verlag für Sozialwissenschaften, 2014)

Lowe, Sid, *Fear and Loathing in la Liga* (Yellow Jersey, 2014)

Lynch, Declan, *Days of Heaven* (Gill & Macmillan, 2010)

MacDonogh, Giles, *1938: Hitler's Gamble* (Constable, 2010)

Macellari, Nino, *Sport e Potenza* (Aldo Chica, 1940)

Mackay, Duncan, *They Came from a Land Down Under* (Choir, 2024)

Maradona, Diego, *El Diego* (Yellow Jersey, 2004)

Marks, John, 'The National Team and French National Identity', in Dauncey and Hare (eds.), *France and the 1998 World Cup*

Marseille, Jacques, '*Une histoire économique du football en France est-elle possible?*', *Vingtième siècle*, April–June 1990

Mason, Tony, *Passion of the People* (Verso, 1995)
Materazzi, Marco, *Che cosa ho detto veramente a Zidane* (Mondadori, 2006)
Mazur, Martin, 'Two Men Down', *Blizzard*, 13 (2014)
Mazzucchelli, Aldo, *Del Ferrocarril al Tango* (Taurus, 2019)
McColl, Graham, *'78* (Headline, 2008)
McWilliams, David, *The Pope's Children* (Gill & Macmillan, 2005)
Mejías-López, Alejandro, *The Inverted Conquest: The Myth of Modernity and the Transatlantic Onset of Modernism* (Vanderbilt University Press, 2009)
Menotti, César Luis, *El Fútbol sin Trampas* (Perfil, 1986)
Meuschel, Sigrid, *Legitimation und Parteiherrschaft in der DDR* (Suhrkamp, 1991)
Mignon, Patrick, 'Fans and Heroes', in Dauncey and Hare (eds.), *France and the 1998 World Cup*
'New supporter cultures and identity in France', in Giulianotti and Williams (eds.), *Game without Frontiers*
Mikos, Lothar, '*Freunde furs Leben. Kulturelle Aspekte von Fußball, Fernsehen und Fernsehfußball*', in Schwier (ed.), *Mediensport*
Mikos, Lothar, and Harry Nutt, *Als der Ball noch rund war* (Campus, 1997)
Miller, Karl, 'On the 1990 World Cup', *London Review of Books*, 12, 14, 26 July 1990
Miller, Rory, *Desert Kingdoms to Global Power* (Yale University Press, 2016)
Mocchi-Radichi, Soledad and Rodrigo Viqueira, 'Between Offside and Orsaí: Uruguayan Soccer: a (Trans) National Sport' in Pedro Cameselle-Pesce and Debbie Sharnak (eds.) *Uruguay in Transnational Perspective* (Routledge, 2023)
Moffett, Sebastian, *Japanese Rules* (Yellow Jersey, 2002)
Montague, James, *When Friday Comes* (Penguin, 2022)

Montgomery, Sy, *Journey of the Pink Dolphins* (Chelsea Green, 2009)

Morales, Franklin, *Maracanã* (Aguilar, 2000)

Moreno, Segundo, *La Argentina, futura gran potencia mundial* (self-published, 1937)

Morita, Hiroyuhi, 'Nippon's Blue Heaven' in Mark Perryman (ed.) *Going Oriental*

Mubarak, Hassanin, 'The Yellow Shirts of Doom', *Blizzard*, 35 (2019)

Müller, Martin, David Gogishvili and Sven Daniel Wolfe, 'The structural deficit of the Olympics and the World Cup: Comparing costs against revenues over time', *Environmental and Planning A: Economy and Space*, 54 (6), May 2022

Muylaert, Roberto, *Barbosa* (RMC, 2000)

Naef, Alain, *An Exchange Rate History of the United Kingdom 1945–92* (Cambridge University Press, 2023)

Naipaul, V.S., *The Return of Eva Perón* (Penguin, 1981)

Newsham, Gavin, *Once in a Lifetime* (Atlantic, 2006)

Nilin, Aleksandr, *Streltsov* (Molodaia Gvardiia, 2002)

Noiriel, Gérard, *Les Ouvriers dans La Société Française* (Points, 2002)

Northcroft, Jonathan and Rob Draper, *Dear England* (Blink, 2024)

Oliveira, Amurabi, 'Thirty Years Later: The Actuality of Gilberto Freyre to Think Brazil,' *Revista del CESLA*, no. 20, 2017

Oliver, Brian, 'The First Superstar', *Blizzard*, 29 (2018)

Orton, Mark, '*La Nuestra*: Football and Identity in Argentina 1913–78' (PhD thesis, De Montfort University, 2020)

Ottosen, R., N. Hyde-Clarke and T. Miller, 'Framing the football fan as consumer', in R. Krøvel and T. Roksvold (eds.), *We Love to Hate Each Other*

Papenfuss, Mary and Teri Thompson, *American Huckster* (Harper, 2016)

Passoni, Moara, 'Corinthian Democracy', *Blizzard*, 38 (2020)

Peeters, Thomas, Victor Matthews and Stefan Szymanski, 'Tourism and the 2010 World Cup', *Journal of African Studies*, May 2014

Pelé, *My Life and the Beautiful Game* (New England Library, 1978)

Pelé, the Autobiography (Simon & Schuster, 2007)

Perdigão, Paulo, *Anatomia de una derrota* (L&PM, 2014)

Perryman, Mark (ed.), *Going Oriental* (Mainstream, 2022)

Peters, Martin, *The Ghost of 66* (Orion, 2006)

Pickup, Ian, 'French football from its origins to Euro 84', in Dauncey and Hare (eds.), *France and the 1998 World Cup*

Pickup, Oliver, 'Milla's Time', *Blizzard*, 13 (2014)

Polley, Martin, 'The Diplomatic Background to the 1966 World Cup', *The Sports Historian*, 18, 2 (1998)

Powell, Jeff, *Bobby Moore* (Alpine, 1976 and Robson, 1993)

Prats, Luis, *La crónica celeste: Historia dela Selección Uruguaya de Fútbol: triunfos, derrotas, mitos y polémicas* (Fin de Siglo, 2000)

Puskás, Ferenc, *Captain of Hungary* (History Press, 2007)

Puskás on Puskás (Robson, 1998)

Pyta, Wolfram (ed.), *Die lange Weg zur Bundesliga* (Lit Verlag, 2004)

'German Football: A Cultural History', in Tomlinson and Young (eds.), *German Football*

Quinn, Niall, *Niall Quinn* (Headline, 2002)

Rabiner, Igor, 'The Jersey that wasn't Black', *Blizzard*, 9 (June 2013)

Radcliffe, Charles, 'Daytripper! A Visit to Amsterdam', *Heatwave*, 1 (July 1966)

Raithel, Thomas, *Fußballweltmeisterschaft 1954* (Bayerische Landeszentrale für politische Bildungsarbeit, 2004)

Rasmussen, Mikkel Vedby, '"A Parallel Globalisation of

Terror": 9-11 Security and Globalisation', *Cooperation and Confict*, 37 (3)

Richards, Michael, *A Time of Silence* (Cambridge University Press, 1998)

Richardson, Charlie, *The Last Gangster* (Arrow, 2014)

Risoli, Mario, *When Pelé Broke Our Hearts* (St David's, 2001)

Ritter, Archibald R.M., *Latin America and the Caribbean: geopolitics, development and culture. Proceedings of the 1983 Conference of the Canadian Association for Latin American and Caribbean Studies* (Ottawa, 1984)

Rocheteau, Dominique and Denis Chaumier (eds.), *Le guide du football 2001* (Lucarne, 2000)

Rodrigues, Nelson, *A Pátria em Chuteiras: Nocas Crônicas de Futebol* (Companhia des Letras, 2013)

'*Complexo de vira-lata*' in *À sombra das chuteiras imortais: crônicas de futebol* (Companhia das Letras, 1993)

Rofe, J. Simon, and Alan Tomlinson, 'The Untold Story of Diplomacy and the 1966 World Cup: North Korea, Africa and Sir Stanley Rous', in *International History Review*, 42, 3

Ronzulli, Dario, *Vittorio Pozzo* (Minerva, 2022)

Rossi, Paolo, *Ho fatto piangere il Brasile* (Limina, 2002)

Rowan, Paul, *The Team that Jack Built* (Mainstream, 1994)

Ruiz de Viñaspre Puig, Ricardo (ed.), *Libro Nuestro Mundial* (Artistas de Acero, 2012)

Sacchi, Arrigo, *Calcio totale* (Mondadori, 2015)

Sandbrook, Dominic, *Seasons in the Sun* (Penguin, 2013)

State of Emergency (Allen Lane, 2010)

White Heat (Little, Brown, 2006)

'My Name is Ally MacLeod and I am a Winner', *Blizzard*, 5 (2012)

Scarpelli, Emanuele, *Material Nation* (Oxford University Press, 2011)

Scher, Ariel & Héctor Palomino, *Fútbol: pasión de multitudes y de elites* (Centro de Investigaciones Sociales sobre el Estado y la Administración, 1988)

Schlee, Aldyr García, *Cuentos de Fútbol* (Mercado, 1997)

Schoonbee, Karen, and Stefaans Brümmer, 'Public loss, Fifa's gain: How Cape Town got its "white elephant",' in 'Player and Referee: Conflicting Interests and the 2010 Fifa World Cup', *Institute of Security Studies* (2010)

Schumacher, Harald, *Blowing the Whistle* (W.H. Allen / Virgin, 1987)

Schwier, Jürgen (ed.), *Mediensport* (Brill, 2009)

Sebes, Guzstáv, *Örömök és csalódások* (Gondolat, 1981)

Segura, Arnau, '*Trágico o inolvidable: el 0-5 de Colombia a Argentina*', *Panenka*, 5 September 2023

Seitz, Norbert, 'Was symbolisiert das "Wunder von Bern"?' in *Aus Politik und Zeitgeschichte*, 21 June 2004

Shwadran, Benjamin, *Middle East Oil Crises Since 1973* (Routledge, 1986)

Simón, Juan Antonio, *España 82* (T&B, 2006)

Sinn, Hans Werner, *Ist Deutschland noch zu retten?* (Econ, 2005)

Smeets, Hubert, 'Johan Cruijff gaf Nederland vorm,' *Hard Gras*, April 1997

Smith, Ed, *What Sport Tells Us About Life* (Viking, 2008)

Smith, Rory, *Mister!* (Simon & Schuster, 2016)

Smyth, Rob, Lars Eriksen, Mike Gibbons, *Danish Dynamite* (Bloomsbury, 2015)

Spiro, Matt, *Sacré Bleu* (Biteback, 2020)

Spurling, Jon, *Death or Glory* (Vision, 2010)

Steingart, Gabor, *Deutschland – Der Abstieg eines Superstars* (Piper, 2004)

Stuart, Ossie, 'The Lions Stir: Football in African Society', in Steven Wagg (ed.), *Giving the Game Away: Football, Politics and Culture on Five Continents*

Sudetic, Chuck, *Blood and Vengeance* (Penguin, 1999)

Sugden, John and Alan Tomlinson, *Badfellas* (Routledge, 2003)

Szabon, Daniel, '*El fútbol argentino en los años cincuenta: tensiones entre tradición y modernidad en la prensa deportiva*', *Historia y problemas del siglo XX* 16, year 13 (Jan–Jul 2022)

Szegedi, Péter and Tamá Dénes, *Az 1938-as magyar vb-ezüst* (Akadémiai, 2018)

Taylor, Matthew, *The Association Game* (Routledge, 2007)

Thöni, Roberto, *L'ultimo urlo per il grande Torino* (GET, 2023)

Toldi, Géza with Axel Hansen, *Fodboldnavn paa flygtningepas* (Martin, 1962)

Tomlinson, Alan and Chirstopher Young (eds.), *German Football* (Routledge, 2005)

Török, Ferenc, *Mandula* (Nyik-Ki, 1999)

Tosi, Francesca, Francesco Scalone, Rosella Rettaroli, 'Variations in male height during the epidemiological transition in Italy: A cointegration approach', *Demographic Research*, 48 (15 Feb 2023)

Trellini, Piero, *The Match* (Pitch, 2023)

Udenio, Enrico, *La hipocresía Argentina* (Libros en Red, 2008)

Veneziani, Mabel, 'El Mundial', *Todo es Historia*, 229 (1986)

Vickery, Tim, 'Mario Zagallo and Tostão', *Blizzard*, 3 (2011)

Wagg Steven (ed.), *Giving the Game Away: Football, Politics and Culture on Five Continents* (Leicester University Press, 1995)

Wahl, Alfred, 'Raymond Kopa: une vedette du football, un mythe', *Sport Histoire*, 2 (1988)

Waliaula, Solomon, 'The Vuvuzela as Paradox of Leisure and Noise: A Sociological Perspective', in Alegi and Bolsmann (eds.), *Africa's World Cup*

Wall, Frederick, *Fifty Years of Football* (Cassell, 1935)

Walter, Fritz, *3-2: Die Spiele zur Weltmesiterschaft* (Copress, 1954)
Warren, Johnny, *Sheilas, Wogs and Poofters* (Random House, 2003)
Weinstein, Barbara, *The Amazon Rubber Boom, 1850–1920* (Stanford University Press, 1983)
Williams, Tom, *Va-Va Voom* (Bloomsbury, 2024)
Wilson, Jonathan, *The Anatomy of England* (Orion, 2010)
Angels With Dirty Faces (Orion, 2014)
The Barcelona Legacy (Blink, 2018)
Behind the Curtain (Orion, 2006)
Inverting the Pyramid (Orion, 2008)
The Names Heard Long Ago (Blink, 2019)
The Outsider (Orion, 2012)
Streltsov (Blizzard Media, 2022)
Two Brothers (Little, Brown, 2022)
'Hungary 4 Uruguay 2', *Blizzard*, 13 (June 2014)
Winner, David, *Brilliant Orange* (Bloomsbury, 2000)
Those Feet (Bloomsbury, 2006)
Worswick, Carl, 'The Ball and the Gun', *Blizzard*, 7 (2012)
'The Dentist and Colombian Rebirth', *Blizzard*, 22 (2016)
Yallop, David, *How They Stole the Game* (Constable, 2011)
Yamanaka, Shinobu, 'At Home', *Blizzard*, 29 (2018)
Yokhin, Michael, 'The Indomitability of Lions,' *Blizzard*, 13 (2014)
Zimbalist, Andrew, *Circus Maximus* (Brookings Institution Press, 2016)
Zirin, Dave, *Brazil's Dance with the Devil* (Haymarket, 2016)

INDEX